Milnthorpe

THE CHRONICLES OF MILNTHORPE

THE CHRONICLES OF MILNTHORPE

by

ROGER K. BINGHAM

CICERONE PRESS
MILNTHORPE, CUMBRIA, ENGLAND

ISBN 0902363 98 0

By the same author

Our Village – A Pictorial Record of Milnthorpe from 1860

The Church at Heversham –
A History of Westmorland's Oldest Recorded Church

For John Fawcett, son of Peter and great-great grandson of 'Happy Jack'
and
Nicholas Miles, son of Hugh and grandson of Richard Miles DFC

Acknowledgements

I began writing this book on the 21st April, 1986 and finished it on the 21st April, 1987, but preparation and research started thirty years earlier when as a schoolboy historian I first made enquiries about the origins and development of my native village. Consequently I regret that I am unable to recall all who helped and inspired me – some, however readily spring to mind. They include Mrs Christine Strickland, Local History Librarian and the staff of Kendal Public Library; Miss Shiela MacPherson, Deputy County Archivist and the staff at the Cumbria Record Office, Kendal, especially Mr Richard Hall and Mr Jim Grisenthwaite; the Vicar, Churchwardens and PCC of St Peter's Church, Heversham and of St Thomas's Church, Milnthorpe; the owners of the archives of Dallam Tower and of Leven's Hall and to Mr John Mashiter who generously loaned me many papers, including valuable notes by Neddy Stones.

Many others provided additional material such as photographs documents and above all, anecdotes, which have often illuminated the essentially documentary basis of this study. They include Miss Alice Ashburner, the late Mr Henry M. Atkinson, the late Mrs V. Mary Audland, Sir Christopher Audland, Mr John A. Balmer, Mr J. Berry, Dr Keith Bland, Mr Ken Blenkharn, Mrs Elsie Bragg, Mrs Kathleen M. Byrne, the late Professor Patrick S. Byrne, the late Mr Joseph T. Cookson, the late Mrs Winnie Craig, Mrs Margaret Dobson, Mrs Muriel Don, Dr William Douthwaite, the late Mr Harold Fawcett, Mr John Fawcett (No. 4), Mrs Elizabeth Forman, the late Mr John Garnett, Mr Wilson Garnett, Mrs Nelly Garth, Mrs Phyllis Hall, Mrs Sylvia Ham, Mr Joseph Hardman, Mrs Betty Harrower, the late Mr Larry Ion, Mrs Mary Jackson, Mrs Elsie Ladell, Mr W. John Ladell, the Rev. Cyril Lee, Mr James Melling, Mrs D. Margaret Miles, Mrs Addie Pickthall, Mr Eric Proctor, the late Mr and Mrs Geoffrey Scott, the late Mrs Mary I. Sheldon, Mr Mike Singleton, Mr Arnold Tauber, Mr Reg Taylor, Mrs Jean Taylor, Brigadier C. E. Tryon-Wilson, the late Mrs Fanny Walker, Mr Len Walling, Mr Jack Whitfield.

I am particularly grateful to Mr Brian Ormerod and Mr John Phillips for help with illustrations, to Mr Ken Blenkharn and Mr Ian Robinson who drew the maps and to Mrs Annie Johnstone, Mrs Hilary Bentley, Mrs Judith Ashford and Mrs Gwyn Weston who deciphered and typed the manuscript.

The responsibility for interpretations, errors and omissions remains mine. Without the help of so many people there would have been many more faults. Their assistance has made my work a labour of love.

Roger Bingham
The Smithy
Ackenthwaite
Milnthorpe
1987

Contents

1

Milnthorpe:
The Setting and Origins

Milnthorpe is an in-between place. North to South it lies at the mid-point along the diagonal route across Britain. Lands End is 416 miles away and John of Groats 420. East to West it is on the western edge of the narrow waist of England, being less than a mile from the eastern extremity of the Irish sea which here terminates in the Kent and Bela estuaries of Morecambe Bay. Three miles to the east the Pennine foothills begin to rise at Farleton Knott. Between these higher hills and the bay the bumpy South Westmorland plain is crossed by several main roads, a motorway, a link road, a canal, the main railway line, three aqueducts, two pipe lines and the major arteries of the national grid and tele-communications. To the North is the Lake District National Park, to the East that of the Yorkshire Dales.

Set astride the A6, 15 miles from Lancaster and 7 from Kendal, Milnthorpe from the dawn of the motor age to the opening of the M6 was a traffic black spot,[1] associated with some of the nation's worst traffic jams, especially at holiday time. Few of the motorists snarled up at the notorious traffic lights could have guessed that the surrounding scenery is often as lovely as that of the more famous tourist traps for which they were heading.

Man was partly to blame. Insensitive road-widening in the 1920's created an ugly focal point for Milnthorpe at the cross roads of the A6 and the B6385.[2]

Nature has also conspired to hide the prettier truth for Milnthorpe nestles in a shallow valley formed by boulder clay drumlins deposited on the limestone bed-rock as the final glaciers of the ice-age melted some 10,000 years ago. Milnthorpe's highest drumlin, St Anthony's Hill, is crowned by a folly tower known as the Summer House, built to commemorate the Reform Bill of 1832.[3] From here the outer mountainous rim can be seen in full circle. To the south beyond the smokey grey village "the clump," or wooded top of Dallam Park points to Warton Crag, to Clougha and the Bowland Fells of Lancashire. Round to the east the naked screes of Farleton Knott bulge out from the green of the plain. To the north the triangular slopes of the Howgills and Tebay fells carry the eye over Heversham Head, close at hand, towards the crenellated backcloth of the Lakeland massif. This tumbles to the flatter land of the Lyth valley at Whitbarrow Scar, four miles away. Like Farleton to the south east Whitbarrow's almost tree-less bulwark to the north west contrasts with the darker stretches of Cartmel Fell. This fell closes the western skyline opposite Milnthorpe and seemingly touches the nobbled mass of Arnside Knott on the south western chord of the mountainous rim. The rim is not complete, for between Arnside Knott and Cartmel Fell the waters of Morecambe Bay snake in and then swell out in the channels and sands that press up against the drained mosses of Milnthorpe Marsh. These lie between the mouths of the Kent and Milnthorpe's own smaller river, the Bela.

Yet not even on the flattest of the mosses can the hills be ignored. Milnthorpe is very much part of the "Westmoringa land,"[4] the land of the western moors – Westmorland.

The old County disappeared administratively with local Government re-organisation in 1974 and Milnthorpe became part of the county Cumbria and the District of South Lakeland. Even so, most Milnthorpians, whether descended from the Westmoringas[5] or not, are still proud to call themselves Westmerians.

If Milnthorpe's location makes it an "in-between" place so, in a metaphorical sense, does its character-for Milnthorpe is not quite a village nor yet a town. Milnthorpe's population at the 1981 census was 1,971[6] – smaller than that of the "village" of Arnside which had 2,084. On the other hand with its straggling village greens and lack of tall urban buildings it is less like a town than Kirkby Lonsdale whose population was only 1,557.

Historically Milnthorpe was always regarded as a town. Its population in 1841 was 1,599,[7] a figure it did not exceed until 1961, and in size and general importance it far out-weighed all other places in South Westmorland except Kendal. In the decades around the Great War its population fell to below 1,000 and it was at that time that the term "village" became current. In the late twentieth century Milnthorpe has retained many of the best features of village life. Unlike many neighbouring communities it is neither a retirement place nor a residential dormitory. Socially well balanced, with many young people and excellent schools, village societies and organisations of all kinds proliferate. Most people

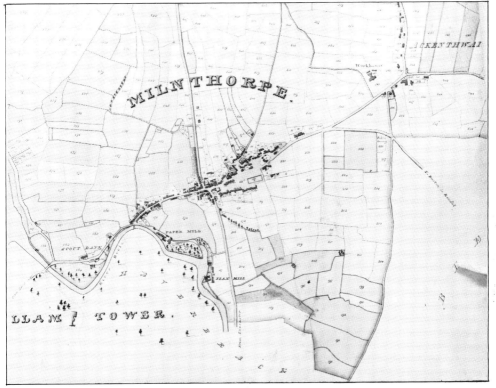

Blount's Map 1826.

seem to know most of the others.

Economically Milnthorpe is a town. Its shops, services and market (of medieval origin[8] but revived only in 1966) serve a wide area. It has retained and developed industries such as canning, comb making, coach building, computers, printing, publishing and a variety of transport concerns. Many people, therefore, can still work in the place in which they live. In this sense Milnthorpe is still the "Mylna porp"[9] – the village around the mill.

Above all the land remains. The rolling hillsides are still a multi-hedgerowed patchwork of many cornered meadows and though mechanisation has meant that few are directly employed on the land, Milnthorpe continues to regard itself as a rural place, attached to the land and subject to the elements and seasons which have forever shaped it.

A local gibe is that Milnthorpe's climate can be summed up as "no snow in winter; no sun in summer." Victorian Sunday-school children used to sing "it mizzles and drizzles and it donks it does and it comes down with a great clash."[10] Pointing south-westwards, the estuary and the bay receive the direct force of the wet and windy Gulf Stream giving the district a typically maritime climate.[11] The average rainfall is about 36 inches, twice that of south-east Britain but half the figure for parts of upper Lakeland only thirty miles away. August often rivals February and October for the distinction of being the wettest month; but compensating for damp and cloudy summers are the winters whose mean temperature is around 39°F. Often mild autumn weather stretches beyond the "seasonal norms" of other northern places and beasts may be seen in the fields almost up to Christmas.

Wet or fine, country people have always liked to know what the weather will do next. Camden in the sixteenth century and Nicolson and Burn in the eighteenth recorded a method of weather forecasting based on sounds made by Beetham waterfall and Force Falls in Levens Park:

"The water at these places falls with a mighty noise which to the neighbouring inhabitants is a prognostication of the weather. When that which is north from them sounds more loud and clear, they look for fair weather; when that on the south side doth the same, they expect rain. The philosophy of which is no more than this; that the south west winds blowing from the sea, bring the vapours along with them, and generally produce rain; consequently blowing from the north or north-east, they have the contrary effect."[12]

In more modern times if trains on the main line a mile to the east of Milnthorpe can be heard clearly it means cold clear weather.

With a milder climate than neighbouring areas the Morecambe Bay coast-lands must have been attractive to early man. Long before the low whale-backed drumlins had been cleared and cultivated, primitive hunters and collectors could have been lured to Milnthorpe's borders by the wild-life of the mosses and shallow waters. Flint blades fashioned by Stone Age gatherers, around 8,000 B.C.[13] have been found on Walney Island at the entrance to the Bay. Several millenia later their New Stone Age descendants operated the stone axe "factories" in the Langdales and exported their products down Coniston and Windermere to the Bay and the wider world. Others at about the same time could have made their way along the banks of the Bela from the coast towards the settlements on Ingleborough and the higher eastern fells, some 20 miles inland.

Another thousand years or so later the Bay was ideally suited to receive the earliest verifiable wave of immigrants – the Celts who probably came from Iberia at the start of the Bronze Age, c.1900 B.C.[14] They were the first people to leave a firm imprint on the landscape by clearing hill tops and erecting impressive stone circles as at Orton and Shap. A minor earthwork at Castlesteads, Natland, might date from this period; otherwise no Bronze Age remains exist near Milnthorpe.

During the Iron Age, which bridged the last centuries before Christ with the Romano – British period, the north west begins to enter recorded history. A tough and adaptable race inhabited the region. Called the Brigantes (or Brigands) by the Romans, and the Cumbraes[15] (Cumbrians) by the Angles, they were said to be as "wild and uncultivated as their native hills. . . subsisting principally by hunting the spontaneous fruits of the earth, wearing for their clothing the skins of animals, dwelling in habitations formed of the pillars of the forest rooted in the earth enclosed by branches or in caves in the earth."[16] Yet it was these people who systematically cleared the hill tops where the forests were less dense, drainage better and from where watch could be kept for enemies, both human and animal. Over-looking Milnthorpe the earthwork now capped by the "Clump" in Dallam Park could have been constructed by Cumbraes. With the Bela and a boulder clay cliff to the east and long clear slopes of excellent ground (which was ploughed until c.1800) on the other sides the site was ideal for a fortified farmstead, if not a larger fort. The circular ramparts are over thirty feet in diameter and up to five feet high. They resemble smaller works in Levens Park generally held to belong, at the latest, to the Romano-British period. On the other hand the Royal Commission on Historical Monuments[17] believes the remains to be of medieval date, yet they neither resemble a Norman Motte nor the foundations of a shell keep or a Pele tower. (The Dallam Pele was close to the site of the eighteenth century mansion, either at the top of the garden to the south west, or on the eastern lawn where in drought, marks of foundations can still be seen.)

Even more speculative are remains behind Wray Cottage on Haverbrack, half a mile to the west. Here are the ruins of a series of stone galleries, of which a six and a half feet stretch has survived intact. Being about two and a half feet high by two feet broad the R.C.H.M. concludes that they were probably kilns. No date is suggested.[18] Nearby are several massive drystone walls up to five feet thick and six feet high. These resemble in part a similar structure of c.200 A.D. on Heaves Fell but may be much later, and could perhaps be post-medieval deer fences.

The Milnthorpe district's main archaelogical site is the Fairy or Dog Hole on Haverbrack. The hole itself is probably just a pothole, a fairly common feature in water-worn limestone. When first excavated in 1912 its upper layers yielded a sixteenth century potsherd and many bones including those of sheep, pigs, goats, deer, horses, five wolves and no less than 50 dogs.[19] The wolf remains confirm the tradition that wolves were numerous in the area which is also contained in the legend that England's last wolf was killed on Humphrey Head on the other side of Morecambe Bay. The name of the adjacent village of Heversham, which might be derived from the Anglian "eofor"[20] meaning wild boar, could also suggest that swine were a common local species.

In 1956 a chance discovery of a lower cavern by Milnthorpe Boy Scouts led to further investigations. By a happy co-incidence two of the scouts, Don Benson and Keith Bland were preparing to go to University to read respectively archaeology and zoology. As a result what started as a freelance amateurish dig became a controlled and documented excavation. Eventually material was removed from two zig-zag positioned caverns going down some thirty feet. The quantity of bones discovered was remarkable and included remains of 20 sheep, 18 oxen, 17 dogs, 3 pigs, 3 wolves, 2 horses, 2 red deer, 2 roe deer, 2 voles, 2 cats, 2 moles and single fox, badger, and rabbit. Most important of all, the skeletal remains of 23 individual humans were the largest collection from any archaeological site in Cumberland, Westmorland and Lancashire North of the Sands.[21] Few of the bones were complete, having been smashed by debris, but further research indicated that three skeletons were aged 6 to 7 years on death, eleven were 12 to 15 years, four were 25 to 50 years and three over 50 years. Adult heights ranged from 4 feet 8 inches to 5 feet 5 inches with a mean height of 5 feet 1 inch.

Either within the cavern or in sieved material from the spoil heap were found the remains of five bronze bracelets, one bronze armlet, 2 bronze finger rings, an Iron Penannular Brooch, several iron studs, some glass beads variously coloured blue and yellow, jet (presumed to have come from Whitby) and three types of pottery respectively coloured blue, grey, soft brown and pink. Expert opinion ascribed the brooch to between 1st century B.C. and second century A.D.; the bracelet to second or third century A.D. and the beads to fifth to ninth century A.D.

No occupation levels were discovered and it was presumed by Benson and Bland that the mixed up deposits had been washed from the site of a nearby settlement into the hole which is "a focal point of a local catchment area." Subsequently the cave was used as a den by wild (or ferral) dogs and wolves. Later still, cast antlers were dumped in the same cave.

An alternative theory about the lower levels could be that the deposits had been deliberately dumped as a result of clearance of a long abandoned settlement, though in the absence of any evidence of agriculture the reason for this is uncertain. It is also unclear why antlers were apparently stored as they were rarely used for artefacts in historical times. Nevertheless, despite possible archaeological confusion, evidence from the Dog Hole suggests that the native inhabitants of the Milnthorpe region were not greatly affected by the Roman occupation.

Apart from near Lancaster few Roman remains have been found around Morecambe Bay, and there is an almost complete lack of

The Kent and Bela estuaries from St. Anthony's Tower.

them in Furness. This is not surprising as north west England was on the very fringe of the Roman Empire. Indeed, the area was only conquered about 80 A.D. in order to preserve the peace and prosperity of the south. Roman civilization was little more than a veneer and the military occupation peripheral. The main Roman Road from Ribchester via the upper Lune valley to Kirkby Thore and thence on to Hadrian's Wall, by-passed the Lake District altogether, but a spur road to the fort of Alavne at Watercrook, just south of Kendal, probably went through Hincaster, a couple of miles north-east of Milnthorpe.

Left in peace and more or less to their own devices, the Cumbrae generally accepted Roman rule, though a revolt of the Brigantes occurred in A.D. 207 and they participated in Octavius' rebellion of A.D. 380. Soon afterwards the imperial armies evacuated the wall and the southern forts like Watercrook and Lancaster were abandoned long before the final withdrawal from Britain in c.410 A.D.

By far the most enduring legacy of late and immediate post-Roman times is Christianity. Possibly the first Christian to enter the area was an unknown Roman soldier tramping along the military road through Hincaster with perhaps the symbol of Christ crucified surreptitiously scratched on his armour. Even so, the district was probably too disturbed for the faith to take root even though it was legal and encouraged during much of the fourth century. Hence it was left to missionaries from the Celtic Church of Ireland to evangelise north west Britain. Beginning with St Patrick, a host of coracled saints made their way in and out of the coves and bays of the Cumbrian coast. Where they rested, a permanent chain of churches was founded even before Augustine had begun to convert the southern heathens about 597 A.D. So significant was Patrick's influence locally that a Cumbrian legend says he was born not in his traditional birth place of Wales, but at Bowness-on-Solway. He probably founded St. Patrick's Church at Heysham (ten miles down the bay from Milnthorpe) and gave his name to Patterdale (Patrichesdale).[23] Preston Patrick, just east of Milnthorpe, is not named after the Celtic Saint, however, but after a Norman lord. Its medieval church was actually dedicated to St. Gregory and Patrick was only substituted as a result, it is said, of the ignorance of the Bishop at the Consecration of the rebuilt church in 1852!

Other Saints followed in Patrick's wake. Kentigern headed a mission to Cumbria in A.D. 573 and somewhat later the area was covered by St. Ninian (also called Mungo). Possibly Ninezergh on the Kent, just north west of Heversham, is a local reference to Ninian. More importantly, at some time before 700 A.D. the only Anglian monastery[25] known to have existed in the north west was established at Heversham. This indicates Heversham's strategic position at the head of the bay pointing towards Ireland and also, if the normal Celtic monastic preference was followed, the area's relative isolation.

Until c. 650 A.D. Cumbria and North Lancashire were part of the Celtic principality of Rheged.[26] A few Celtic names such as Kent and Kentdale and possibly also Levens and Cark, have survived the subsequent Anglian and Nordic linguistic overlay.

According to Bede's *Historia Ecclesiastica* the Angles entered the district via the overland route across the Pennine passes. This was not until the reign of King Aethelfrith of Northumbria (A.D. 592 – 616). Anglian settlement did not result in genocide for when King Sigfrith founded a monastery in Furness about 680 A.D. the endowment included "Cartmel and all the Britons with it."[28]

Even so there are traditions that the local population resisted the invaders by force. In Cumbria, as throughout the western mountain refuges of the Britons there are stories about King Arthur. It has been claimed that the Segantii, a sub-tribe of the Brigantii, had a port near Lancaster and here they "fought many desperate battles against the Angles or Saxons under the leadership of King Arthur, one of which is supposed to have been near Beetham, a village on the Kent estuary in Morecambe Bay." It is just possible that this could be the first reference to the Port of Milnthorpe, historically the only one in Westmorland.[29] Certainly the legend confirms place name evidence that the Milnthorpe region was an area of primary settlement by the Angles who went on to spread out over much of north and central England, leaving the south and east to the Saxons.

One of the earliest Anglian place elements is the suffix "ham" meaning a village, estate or farmstead. Heversham is generally considered to be named after an Anglian Chief Haefar. Beetham might also be derived from a personal name Beadahelm.[30] More probably it comes from Betha the original name for the Bela. Camden in c. 1535 wrote "By Bytham runneth Byth water, a pretty river"[31] and Nicolson and Burn concluded that "Beetham may be understood to signify the holme ground adjoining the river." An equally early suffix is "Ceaster" found in Hincaster, a rare example in Westmorland of a name signifying Roman remains. The most common element is "tun" or "ton" meaning an enclosed piece of land, a farm, village or town. Within a few miles of Milnthorpe there are a dozen places with this ending. They include Burton[32] (in-Kendale) from O.E. Bura burge, a dwelling; Farleton[33] from O.E. personal name Faerweald, Faralf, Faerwalf; Old and New Hutton[34] from hoha, a mound or the personal names, Hod and Hoda. Hutton Roof – the "Roof" might be from a personal name Rolf. Levens[35] is also, most probably, derived from an Old English personal name of Leofwine.

From about c.650 – 850 A.D. the mixed population of Angle and Celt around the head of the bay were under the generally lose rule of the Kingdom of Northumbria. Though this Kingdom was smashed by the first onslaught of the Vikings during the ninth century the region seems still to have been under English rule at the time of the death of Alfred the Great in 899.[36] Shortly afterwards the full fury of the Norsemen was unleashed along the entire north west coastline. Having earlier settled in Ireland and the Isle of Man, Viking bands came first to plunder, then amalgamated to conquer and settle in much of Cumbria during the tenth century. An early victim was the Anglian monastery at Heversham, overwhelmed by c. 920.

The *Historia de Sancta Cuthberte* records how during the reign of King Eadward (901 – 925 A.D.)[37] Tilred, Abbot of Heversham, bought land at South Eden in County Durham as an endowment for the religious houses at Lindisfarne and Norham, to which Tilred escaped shortly afterwards. This reference of c. 910 to Tilred's expensive removal is the first specific record of any place in the Milnthorpe area and, incidentally, makes Heversham Westmorland's oldest recorded church.

The very names of the Viking leaders like "Eric Bloodaxe" and "Thorfin the skull cleaver" are redolent of violence and cruelty. Yet despite their undoubted taste for rapine and massacre they were already Christian, a legacy of their stay in holy Ireland. The church survived in the north west and by the eleventh century Heversham and Beetham were part of the Archdiocese of York to which they belonged until the Reformation. Moreover, the term Kirkby –

demonstrated at Kirkby Lonsdale and until the eighteenth century, in the name "Kirkby Kendale" – come from the Norse word Kirkga[38] (later Cherkeby) meaning a church town or farm.

The Old Norse "Byr" for farmstead is not as common in South Westmorland as in the north of the county, but other nordic names are common. They include: "eigh" for summer pasture or shieling as at Ninezergh; "holm," an island, water meadow or small eminence as at Oxenholme,[40] The Helm and Holme;[41] heafod – a "summer pasture" – from which such modern names derive as Arnside[42] – "Arnulf's heafod" (Arnholvisheved in 1244) and Burneside, "Brunulf's heafod"; Slackhead[43] near Beetham comes from Slackki meaning a hillside or slope and is found also in Witherslack[44] (from personal name Wider) and Hazelslack[45] (either from tree name haesel or pesonal hest); Brack or Brekka also means a slope – so Haverbrack[46] indicates a sloping field of oats (haver).

Thwaite is a particularly descriptive Nordic term. It comes from Pveit, meaning a clearing in a wood or a farmstead. Hence Milnthorpe's own hamlet of Ackenthwaite[46] comes from either of the personal names of Acca or Hakon; Deepthwaite near Heversham might come from diki meaning a ditch or deep stream from which also comes the word dyke and the name of the Dixies near Sandside; while the old name for Levens village, Beethwaite[49] Green probably comes from a personal name like Beaduh. Other Nordic names in the district include Hale[48] probably from halh meaning a corner, or hlio, a slope, or hlaoa a barn; Ulpha[49] from personal name Ulf or from a similar word meaning a wolf – and Meathop[50] from mior, a creak or ravine.

The derivation of Milnthorpe's own name is one of the most puzzling. The Miln[51] element comes clearly either from the O.E. Mylen or the O.N. Mylna both meaning a mill. As such it indicates that there was an established place around the lower stretches of the Bela by the tenth century. Thorpe comes from "porp" meaning a group of farms or a village. Though present in the district at Clawthorp (near Burton) and at Millthrop (near Sedbergh) this ending is most common in the Danelaw settlements of Yorkshire and the east coast. As such it could imply that the first Milnthorpians were of a slightly different Nordic stock than folk from the surrounding communities. Until c. 1860 the spelling of Milnthorpe was not standardised. Common variations include: Mylethrop (1605), Myllthrope (1669), Milnthrop (1642), Millthrop (1661), Milthrop (1713). Milnthorpe appears[52] quite commonly after c. 1732 but could nevertheless still be written as Millthorp, Milnthrop etc. even by the same writer. In the late twentieth century it is still common to hear Milnthorpe pronounced as "Millenthorp" or "Milthrup."

St. Anthony's Tower

Inevitably, within a generation or two of the initial settlement of the "Mylen porp," nature had taken its course and so by about the year 1,000 A.D. the inhabitants had fused in their veins the blood of Celt, Angle, Norwegian, Irish and Dane.

Ethnic confusion mirrored the political situation of the region. The tenth and eleventh centuries were probably the most turbulent in Milnthorpe's history. For much of the period the area was on the borders of the Kingdom of Strathclyde whose Kings, taking advantage of the collapse of the English state, had pushed their frontier over the Lakeland dome. A hoard of coins found at Beetham in the eighteenth century contains both English and Scottish coins, the latter engraved with the St. Andrews cross. The hoard had probably been collected for Dane geld, the generally futile bribe intended to keep the Vikings at bay. Certainly such payments did not prevent "Thored's Gundon's son" ravaging the north west in 966 A.D., nor a later Danish invasion which led to a battle at Cnutsfield[53] near Melling in the Lune valley about 1030 A.D.

Whether the district was still reeling or not from repeated invasion, it was sufficiently settled in the mid-eleventh century to be included (according to Doomesday Book) in the lands of Tostig, Earl of Northumbria, brother of Harold Godwinson, the King killed at Hastings in 1066. Tostig's lands covered much of Kentdale and included Biedan (Beetham), Fareltum (Farleton), Preston (Preston Patrick and Richard), Berewic (Borwick), Hennecastre (Hincaster), Evreshaim (Heversham), and Lefvenes (Levens).[54] There is, however, no mention of Milnthorpe, implying that it was either of little importance or that, being of later foundation than surrounding "vills," it did not form part of the legal or traditional

Haverbrack and Dallam Tower from St. Anthony's Tower.

units of land tenure.

Tostig was deprived of his earldom in 1065 and his consequential revengeful invasion of Yorkshire in 1066 led to his own death at Stamford Bridge and so aggravated the situation of his brother King Harold that the Normans were victorious at Hastings.

Not for some time after the conquest of southern England and the harrowing of Yorkshire did the Conqueror turn his attention to the north west. Faced with a capable Scottish King, Malcolm Canmore, in possession of nearly all of Cumberland, William I appointed one of his strongest marcher lords, Roger de Poitou, to rule from Lancaster the border territory of Furness and Kentdale. That South Westmorland was regarded almost as No Man's Land, however, is indicated by the omission in Doomesday Book of any propertied inhabitants in the region. Doomesday does record that a Scotsman called Duncan or Duvan was in possession of Kendal Castle – which indicates that the King of England's Writ hardly ran here.

Only in 1092 did William Rufus firmly and finally tip the balance of power in the western marches in favour of England. Supporters of the King of Scots were subdued or swept from Cumbria so that within one campaigning season the English frontier had moved from South Lakeland to Carlisle.

Rufus' feudal henchmen were well rewarded for their part in enlarging the realm. Accordingly in c. 1092 Rufus granted to Ivo de Taillebois much of Kentdale including the Manor of Heversham. Within a year or two Ivo, for the sake of his immortal soul, granted one third of the manor as an endowment to the newly founded Abbey of St. Mary's at York.[56] This third, known as the Rectory Manor, was ruled from the Abbey's headquarters at Heversham Hall and in time came to be called the Manor of Heversham. The remaining two-thirds constituting the "Lord's Manor" continued to form part of the Barony of Kendal and was ruled from a caput or manor house at Milnthorpe.[57] Eventually these lands were called the Manor of Milnthorpe.

The lord's manor passed in the direct male line for five generations respectively from Ivo to Eldred, to Ketel, to Gilbert to William de Taillebois. The latter changed his name to William de Lancaster and it was under this name that in c. 1260 he transferred the manor, along with the rest of the Kendal Barony to his daughter Agness as a dowry on her marriage to Alexander de Wyndesore. It was his son, another Alexander, who about 1280 granted a charter which established the Market and Fair at Milnthorpe within the Parish of Heversham. On the basis of the confirmation of this charter by William de Wyndesore in 1334 Milnthorpe Parish Council in 1982 established in the high court its right to conduct Milnthorpe's Friday market: such is the long arm of our history.

The Wyndesore's possessed Milnthorpe until 1398 when John Duckett, husband of Marjorie the daughter and co-heiress of the last Alexander de Wyndesore, sold the manor to Ralph, Earl of Westmorland who granted it to his third son, George Nevil. Though they made little impact on the immediate district the Nevilles held Milnthorpe until c. 1577 when the male line failed on the death of John Neville, Lord Latimer. His daughter, Dorothy, inherited and on her behalf her husband Thomas Cecil, Earl of Exeter sold the manor to Thomas Bradley of Arnside. According to the conveyance Thomas acquired "the manor of Eversham and Milnethorpe, with 100 messuages, 20 tofts, one mill, 100 gardens, 1000 acres of land, 600 acres of meadow, 1000 acres of pasture, 100 acres of wood, 600 acres of heath and furze, 200 acres of turbary, 20 rent, and one fair and market; to hold of the Queen in capite."[58] In 1597 Thomas Bradley sold the manor to James Bellingham of Upper Levens. From the Bellinghams and by various means the property and rights have passed via the Grahams and Howerds to the Bagots of Levens Hall who, conjointly with the Wilsons of Dallam, remain in the 1980's Lords of the Manor of Milnthorpe.

The Rectory manor of Heversham passed to the Crown at the Dissolution of St. Mary's Abbey in 1534. In 1557 King Philip and Queen Mary conveyed this manor to three local gentry: Edmund

*The Tower Steps
with Farleton Knott
in the background.*

Moyses, Richard Foster, and Richard Bouskill or Buskell. In time
Richard Buskell bought out the bulk of the other purchasers shares
in lands "holden of the manor in Eversham, Milnethorp,
Aughtinthwaite, Rowell and Woodhouse."[59] His grandson in 1614
in turn sold the manor to Edward Wilson of Nether Levens who
soon installed his nephew and step son-in-law Thomas Wilson in
the Rectory manor house. Thomas eventually inherited Edward
Wilson's large estates and his descendants moved the family seat to
the newly re-built Dallam Tower about 1720. Ever since Dallam
Tower has been regarded as the manor house of Milnthorpe,
though it is in fact within the Parish of Beetham.

Until 1896 Milnthorpe itself formed part of the joint township of
Heversham-with-Milnthorpe within the larger parish of Heversham.
It did not possess a church until the consecration of St. Thomas'
Church in 1837 and the ecclesiastical parish only became
independent of Heversham in 1924.

Having been carved out of Heversham the parish of Milnthorpe
is one of the smallest in area within the old county of Westmorland.
Inevitably, therefore, a history of Milnthorpe from time to time has
to stray beyond the narrow bounds of the parish. Milnthorpe's
historic importance and local pre-eminence is perhaps implied by
the name "Milnthorpe Sands" having been given to much of the
upper reaches of Morecambe Bay.

2

Milnthorpe Sands

Morecambe Bay is the biggest bite made by the Irish Sea in the coast of North West England. Its indented and frequently craggy coastline contrasts with the straighter and flatter shores of much of Furness and Cumberland to the north and of the Lancashire Fylde to the south. At the head of the bay, representing the sea's final eastward thrust, is the estuary of the river Kent into which also flow the rivers Gilpin and Winster and Milnthorpe's own river, the Bela. From the wider bay between Hest Bank and Kent's Bank the estuary curls north eastward to the upper tidal meanders at Heversham and Halforth. It is the inner stretch east of Blackstone Point and Holm Island that has long been called Milnthorpe Sands.

After an initial sweep into Arnside bay the estuary so twists round the hills that the open sea can rarely be seen. Often strangers glimpsing the tidal reaches from the A6 on Milnthorpe hill think they have seen the first of Westmorland's lakes! This is not really surprising because, the northern skyline is dominated by the Lake District massif, the battered remnant of a many-layered dome which on cracking let the sea in to form the bay and, by exposing a varied strata, provided a foundation for the landscape.

The bedrock is predominantly carboniferous limestone, a sliver of which forms Summerhouse Point at the mouth of the Bela. Across the river loom the cliffs and screes of Whitbarrow, whilst behind the Bela is Haverbrack, now truncated by a huge limestone quarry. Lesser outcrops occur lower down at St John's Cross, in the ivy covered cliffs at Carr Bank and in the sea cliffs fringing Arnside Knott. Meathop Crag on the northern shore is also of limestone and was once quarried but to its east is Ulpha Crag composed of silurian Bannisdale Slates, the same rock as the Cartmel Fells. From behind Whitbarrow the knife-edged Cartmel range runs southwards towards the open sea dividing the Kent and Leven estuaries. At the

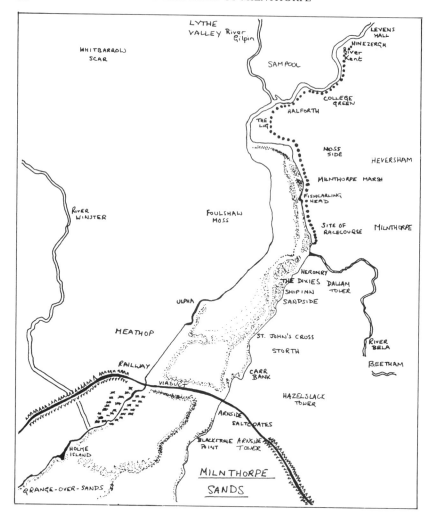

end of the Cartmel peninsula the whale-like silhouette of Humphrey Head closes the seaward view when seen from the narrow strand between the marsh dyke and the Bela which constitutes the shore of the civil parish of Milnthorpe.

Concurrent with the erosion of the uplands is the process of deposition of waterborne silts in the bay, that will, in time, return it to dry land. Both processes were accelerated by the Ice-Age. The oceans were frozen before and after the land was covered by ice. This caused the local sea level to drop to produce a step at the mouths of the Kent and Bela. Subsequent cutting back formed the low water falls, or nick points, at Force Falls and Beetham Mills. The deepening process also made the Bela navigable as far as Milnthorpe and created a rocky bank ideal as a site for Milnthorpe's water mills. Later scouring by glaciers deepened the bay and on

*'Milnthorpe Sands Westmorland' from The Dixies at Sandside
by Thomas Allom c.1820*

their retreat glacial debris was laid down on the bed. Boulder clay drumlins were formed around the bay, one of which, Fishcarling Head, sticks out from Milnthorpe Marsh into the upper estuary.

Infilling has continued: the first stage, salt marshes, is seen at Fishcarling, Carr Bank and Arnside. From them sea-washed turf has gone to suburban lawns and playing fields, though unlike the product from Silverdale, not to Wembley or Wimbledon.

The second stage is the mosses which stretch from Milnthorpe right up the Lyth Valley. Until recent times these consisted largely of peat, formed by alternate growth and decay of vegetation aided over the 10,000 post-glacial years by several climatic transgressions.[1] Peat was the main local fuel, used in homes and by such industries as the turners and dyers of Kendal, until the nineteenth century. Every house in Milnthorpe had its peat shed and many villagers had cutting, or turbary, rights on the marsh. After the enclosure of the commons about 1815 the practice seems to have continued. Many tiny allotments are specified on the enclosure awards. Clarke's field, just south of the main drain, was split into lots 108-126, the largest being of only three furlongs. These were probably peat beds. Further peat beds on Heversham Marsh, a mile to the north, belonged to Milnthorpe inhabitants: William Audland, Margaret Foxcroft, William Johnson, Edward Kitching, William, Emma and Philip Bindloss, and to the trustees of R. Crampton and R. Cragg.[2]

The Audlands lots, overgrown by woodland, continued to be held by the family until the late twentieth century. Between the Bela and the Dixies is Peatstack Hill, where peats were dried safely above the tide line.

The peat trade was a useful part-time occupation which has existed on and off for many years. Peat was supplied to Milnthorpe Workhouse until about 1890. Peat cutting continued on Milnthorpe Marsh at the turn of the century as several peat stacks were reported to have been washed away in the floods of 1907. In the 1930s the Pearson family brought peats in high wheeled carts from across the estuary at Foulshaw and they were again sold by Harold Peel during the fuel crises of the 1940s.

By the turn of the century however, most peat gatherers preferred to splash through the channels to Foulshaw to gather the fuel. All took part in clearing away the covering of bracken, heather and saplings and the upper spongy layer. After the first trench was opened the men and older boys would attack the peat wall with a wooden, metal rimmed or iron spade. This had an inverted "L" shaped handle, not the usual "T," so that a close cut could be made. At right angles to the blade a kind of flange protruded which was used in turning the turf before it was flung out of the trench in front from where it was wheeled away on flat broad-wheeled barrows to be stacked by the women and children. A depth of up to eight feet could be reached but the common height of the peat bank was about five feet.[3]

Milnthorpe villagers also had grazing rights on the marsh. When the path leading from Grisley Myers Lane over the hill to the marsh was closed about 1899 it was recalled that it had been "very much used in former days by men on their way to herd the sheep on Fishcarling Head out of reach of the tide."[4] Until c.1850 a cottage, at one stage occupied by the Huddlestone family,[5] stood about a quarter of a mile from the south end of the Marsh Lane, opposite the Sand Road. This might have been a home for the marsh herdsman or shepherd. The Grisley Myers path was said also to lead "to the old race course on the marsh before the enclosures."[6] The course was probably between the present dyke and the sewage farm but, unfortunately, little is known about the probably sporadic and informal meetings.

Following enclosure, dykes were cut to drain the marsh and form excellent arable land. The main dyke runs from Haysteads moss north of Heversham for over two miles to the mouth of the Bela where the waters are controlled by tidal gates. These seem to have been effective generally though after the severe "Mothering Sunday" flooding of 1907 the force of the retreating waters tore one of the 8 foot high doors from its hinges.[7] Towards College Green delicate drainage management is required as the fall is towards the

Kent, away from the main drain, and is of only two inches in a quarter of a mile.[8] On Milnthorpe Marsh the fall is steeper causing the dyke alongside the marsh lane to be nearly ten feet deep.

In May 1897 Robert Nelson, a 49 year old farm labourer at Waterside was drowned in this dyke while returning with James Quail and Frederick Lancaster from "The Ship Inn" at Sandside. All were drunk and when Nelson fell in his companions, seeing him standing up in the water, laughingly went on their way. When he had not returned the next morning his brother Stephen went out and found Robert's body in the dyke. He had 11s 7d on him and his stiff hands still clutched a pop bottle half full of whisky. There was talk of prosecuting Quail and Lancaster for manslaughter. Eventually, however, a verdict of "drowned while drunk" was brought in, though the Coroner did condemn "the heartlessness of action of a most reprehensible character" on the part of Quail and Lancaster. An attempt to prosecute the landlord of The Ship for allowing drunkness on his premises also failed as it was claimed that Nelson was not drunk when he left the inn but merely "staggering."[9]

The sands themselves provide much interest for the historian, both local and natural. Nowhere do the mudflats constituting Milnthorpe Sands resemble the golden sands on a sea-side post card. On a sunny day when dry and windswept they can shine bright and silvery; when overcast and wet their leaden greyness only adds to the gloom of the day; but generally they are light khaki, of a slightly less dull hue than the estuary waters. They provide a habitat for much of the district's notable wild life. The most common species – the crustacea – is generally unseen. Of these the most numerous are *Amphipod Crustaceon* and the *Corophium Longicorne* which produce a rash of worm castings on the rippled sands after the ebb tide.[10] Once shrimps were to be found and Hutton in 1770 said great quantities could be dredged from Bomersha Bay at St. John's Cross.[11] Machell in c.1691 noted that the estuary also contained "Sallam (sic) morts, sprats, trouts, eels, smelts, fork tails and the like. . . pikes are a yard long."[12] The most numerous fish mentioned in the early twentieth century were sand eels, sea trout, immature herring, spotted gobies, sprats and flounders, the latter always being known locally as flukes.[13]

Flukes were once a valuable supplement to the local diet. Even so, at a Public Meeting in Milnthorpe during the General Election of 1885 the Liberal candidate Mr Baron declared that "all live under the shadow of Dallam Tower and we were not permitted to take as much as a fluke from the sea; he questioned whether the Almighty had decreed that all fish should belong to Dallam Tower."[14] Although the owners of Dallam held firmly to their game rights the evidence is that they did stop short at flukes!

Salmon were another matter. Quite often dozens of the fish

could be left stranded in pools by the ebb tide, their presence indicated by the swirl and swoop of the gulls. The would-be poacher had to run a race against the birds, tidal currents and the Dallam "beck watcher" to get his catch. Netting, an art long cherished by the Ormrods, Pearson, Baldwins and other estuary families, was more certain but carried a heavier penalty than "pooling", which was often felt to be fair game.

In 1887 Chris Shepherd was caught red-handed with net and chloride of lime, (for use up river) by the beck-watcher Hugh Brown who asked "What is thou doing theah?"

Chris: "Nowt."

Hugh: "I thowt thou'd plenty of that afoor."

Chris: "A man must have a living."[15]

Milnthorpe magistrates thought otherwise and Chris got six weeks hard labour.

There were some official fishermen. In July 1843 "the fishermen of Milnthorpe. . . caught in Morecambe Bay upwards of three cwts of live salomon."[16] Another large catch was made in 1849 when morts and sprats were sold in Milnthorpe at 1s or 1s 1d per lb.[17] The finest catch of all was made in September 1904 when on the opening of the Bela sluice, Milnthorpe fishermen and the Dallam Tower house party netted 399 salmon, many of 8 and 9 pounds, with thousands of mort and roach in addition.[18] Perhaps the heaviest salmon caught off the Bela was a 27 pounder landed in 1867.[19]

A number of rare and curious creatures have appeared in the Estuary from time to time. In November 1843 Mr. Burrow of the King's Arms, Milnthorpe put on show at "1d a look" an eel caught on the sands which was five feet long, 20 inches in circumference and weighed 32 pounds.[20] A hogworm, over two feet long, was found at Foulshaw and shown round the village in April 1913[21] while in 1940[22] "a larger relative of the sea horse was caught. It was 18 inches long and had the slender fish shape of the eel but having a long bony snout connected to the gills." More easily identifiable was an octopus which came to the edge of the sands in 1942.[23] Porpoises, quite common off Arnside, rarely get up to Milnthorpe but two were seen off Summer House Point in 1905.[24] Strangest of all was a 20 pound shark, five feet in length, caught in 1946, by Tom Smith at the Dixies. It was put on show at Coulterts Garage, Sandside.[25]

Milnthorpe Sands provide homes for native and, temporarily, for waves of migrating birds.[26] In winter the permanent waders are joined by flights of mallard, up to 1,500 shellduck, a few knot, 30 or so peregrine falcons and cormorants. Later they make way for oyster catchers, ringed plover and redshanks. In summer come curlews, plovers and a few sandpipers en route between artic breeding grounds and their African winter quarters. All kinds of waders, dunlin, redshanks and oyster catchers abound at this time, and as the summer nights draw in the curlew comes with his haunting note to compete with the ever present howls of the gulls, repeatedly rising and settling on Foulshaw Moss and on the mudflats over towards Halforth.

The King (or Queen) of the estuary is the heron. Throughout summer and often into winter up to a dozen can be seen stalking the channels for flukes or crouching together in groups in ungraceful contrast to the smooth swoop and languid flap of their flight. Many a Milnthorpe child has received a Hitchcock-like fright after a toddler high heron has dived into a garden to investigate a bird table or fish pond.

The herons' main haunt is, however, around the Bela and the Dixies close to the famous Dallam heronry, one of the earliest recorded wild-life habitats in Cumbria. It was first mentioned in 1775, when there was a classic battle between the herons and their enemies the rooks. Some elms in which the herons had roosted had been cut down,[27] so they tried to evict the rooks from the remaining trees nearby. The rooks won but only after heavy losses on both sides. In 1817 there were only 11 herons' nests at Dallam but numbers grew during the nineteenth century to reach 50 or so in 1875, when their roosting trees were felled again. Thomas Gough of Arnbarrow, author of *The Herons and Heronry at Dallam Tower* – noted that the herons often refused to leave their nests even when the woodman was chopping away below. Another battle followed the loss of the roosts and again the rooks, who had the advantage of greater numbers, won. The heron population again went down. There were only 30 nests in the 1920's. By 1940 there were 45 nests but three successive hard winters and the arctic winter of 1947 halved the numbers. Recovery was quicker than after earlier calamities and there were between 30 and 40 nests in the 1950's which rose to 50-60 in the 1980's.

Wild fowl have not been as fortunate as the heron. Machell in c.1691 said that Milnthorpe had a "great store of duck, mallard, tiel, widgeon and wildgeese."[28] At that time most catches were made by traps and nets. Later fowling pieces took over and the "sport" was jealously guarded by the Dallam estate. Even in the conservation conscious 1980's the crack and put of the wild fowlers' arsenal regularly punctures the winter stillness on the marshes. Most of the "sportsmen" belong to the Westmorland Wildfowling Association who lease the shoots from the Dallam estate. Conservation measures have helped increase numbers of some species. Bittern – unknown in the upper estuary in the 1950's – appeared regularly in the 1980's. When a swan nested in the Bela below the New Bridge in 1959 it drew crowds, who regarded this as a novel spectacle. In later times other equally conspicuous nests hardly induced comment.

Long after the fowls of the air had been preserved by the squire or conserved by the legislator their eggs were regarded as fair game. In 1929 Thomas Dawson, gas works manager, and Clifford Holmes, were summoned for taking the eggs of the black-backed gull at Foulshaw and also of the Redshank and Green-plover. Dawson was fined 10s but Holmes' case was "dismissed under the first offenders act."[29] The priority of man's need was cited as a defence in a case brought before Milnthorpe magistrates in 1921 when two boys from Storth were charged with taking 89 eggs of the "lesser-back gull." Their father "pleaded for consideration on the grounds that they had been out of work for some weeks and the boys were sent to obtain these eggs as they were badly needed for food and were most useful in these hard times." Nevertheless they were fined 7s 6d and 12s 6d, the magistrate stressing that they had been liable to a fine of £1 per egg.[30]

The sands have been an age-long challenge for man. Traditionally their depth is unfathomable and it has been claimed that Arnside Viaduct rests on a foundation of sheep skins suspended in the sands. In fact the engineer of the viaduct, James Brunlees, discovered that below the first yard or so of loose river silt there was between 50 or 70 feet of dry fine sand. A more ingenious engineering device than sheep skins was required – "a broad iron disc at the bottom six feet in diameter like the top of a large circular dining table" was sunk under each pile which spread out like an inverted umbrella. The viaduct was, therefore, "supported like a camel in the sands of the desert by the mere breadth of its own feet."[31] Nearer to Milnthorpe the sands are almost as deep and in the Lyth Valley the bedrock is 61 metres below peat, loam and clay.[32]

Most of the sea-borne deposits in the estuary are brought in by the first surge of the tide, within thirty minutes. Sedimentation takes place as the tide falls. As the ebb tide is much slower the quantity of silt deposited is greater than that removed by the tide's scouring process. Arnside viaduct greatly accelerated deposition. Before it was built the channels were allowed to meander freely from shore to shore and the ebb tide was much stronger, which meant that the silting up process was slower. Barely half a century after the viaduct's construction in the 1850's the sands at the mouth of the Bela were said to be 11 feet[33] above sea level and to be only covered by the tide for 3 and a half hours a time on a few days each month.

There have been several schemes to hasten nature's work of land formation. In 1786 the *Gentleman's Magazine* reported "a design to inclose the sands and to turn the course of the river Kent, and others of less note, which are to go in the river Lune near Lancaster."

£15,000 was subscribed but nothing came of the project.[34] Railways later provided the incentive for reclamation. George Stephenson in 1837 planned a railway embankment from Hest Bank to Kents Bank which would lead to 40,000 acres being drained. More ambitious was John Hague's scheme (of 1838) which would have created 46,000 acres behind a bank running from Morecambe to Leonard's Point at Aldingham. Before Arnside viaduct was built the railway company again tried to interest investors in an outer bay embankment. This time 70,000 acres would have been created, "a county in itself will be added to Lancashire and Westmorland. Looking at it only in the light of grazing land, it will add materially to the wealth of our district and give us advantages which few counties or localities enjoy."[35] When the viaduct was built the Brogden and Meathop banks were constructed to its north east and with straightening of the channels, Holme Island was firmly attached to the Lancashire shore. Formerly, if the channel moved between it and the mainland the island became officially part of Westmorland! The banks were reconstructed in 1902 and 1903 after severe storm damage, but they were again breached in six places in 1920, after which they were abandoned during the inter-war period and the grazing land reverted to marsh. During the Second World War when food production was at a premium the Meathop marsh, along with Foulshaw Moss opposite Milnthorpe, were converted into arable land.

It was not agriculture, however, but estimated water needs that led to the Morecambe Bay Barrage scheme of the 1960s and 1970s. The main barrage, taking also a truck road, would have followed earlier projected lines from Hest Bank to west of Aldingham. Behind the barrage various polders to hold water were projected, the largest being off Silverdale and west of Humphrey Head, while a reservoir was also planned on Foulshaw Moss. The scheme roused a storm of protest from conservationists.

An incentive for work on the upper part of Milnthorpe Sands came with the "Barrow Link Road proposed River Kent Crossing" of 1968 which would have run from Hale to Carr Bank where it would cross the sands to join a new road over Meathop Moss to Lindale. Fortunately, a well-concerted protest campaign, involving public enquiries and national media coverage, succeeded in stopping this insensitive scheme. Wild life habitats and the naturally changing character of the sands were conserved, at least until the end of the century.[35b]

The main riddle of the sands is the channels. At high water few can be detected with accuracy as their shifting character puts charts and ordnance survey maps quickly out of date. The Kent can, for example, sweep round the Foulshaw side of the great meander at Halforth, swing inshore at Fishcarling, then head straight across the bay to The Ship Inn where it might either zig-zag via Ulpha Crag to Arnside or scour the St. John's Cross shore and then cut into the Carr Bank salt marsh to gain access to the open bay at the south eastern end of the viaduct. Sometimes the Kent and Bela can meet close to the Milnthorpe salt marsh and expose several rocky arms at Summerhouse Point and boulders at Fishcarling Head. Here at its eastern extremity the bay can vary in width from three quarters of a mile to a few hundred yards. In c.1800 it is said a stone could be thrown from shore to shore at Fishcarling.[36] Lower down, the salt marsh at Friar Cote has a similar variation. Nearby, what was Bomersha Bay is now a meadow cut off from the estuary by the embankment of the Furness Railway c.1870. Generally the Kent "swings" from bank to bank at Sandside in cycles of ten years. Beyond Arnside the cycle is much slower and indeed the main channel has recently taken seventy years to move from the northern shore to the southern.

Particularly insidious hazards of Milnthorpe Sands are the quicksands. Often they occur when a hollow is formed by an odd eddy round a piece of debris or perhaps by the bump of a boat's prow, which then fills with slimy water as the tide ebbs. The normal sands dry quickly to the extent that a B.M.X. bike hardly leaves a track half an hour after the sands have been submerged. The batter-like mixture in the hollow cannot escape from the surrounding sand which is as impervious as a pudding basin. The surface can dry and though it is smoother than the drier rippled sands the unwary or unknowledgable can be caught. At Halforth in February 1946 Lt. Louis Birkett was swallowed up to his shoulders and it took one and a half hours of continuous effort before he was extricated by Arthur and Hervey Nelson. In the next few years Arthur rescued several more bathers from the quicksands, for which he received many awards from the Royal Humane Society.

When, in earlier days, there was a regular route from the Dixies to Ulpha, Meathop and Grange, accidents happened regularly to pedestrians and to horses. Thus, in 1847, "Mr. James Harrison, his wife and her daughter were travelling over Milnthorpe sands in a gig opposite Mr. Green's house (at St. John's Cross) when the horse fell into a large hole many feet deep and they were immersed in water with no assistance near to help them from their perilous situation but. . . Stephen Carr a carrier who was coming up the sands with two horses and carts came to the rescue and threw ropes to draw them to land. Mr. Green supplied clothes. Mr. Harrison who is an independent gentleman rewarded Carr for saving their lives with three shillings."(!)[37]

Once they have been swallowed by the sands the estuary often takes long to disgorge its victims and several lots of unidentifiable human bones have been found. In June 1842 the body of the wife of "the man Smith a nailer" who had drowned at Ulverston at the previous Christmas was found at Halforth. "Part of the head and one arm were missing" and she was recognised by her boots.[38]

An even more hazardous feature of the sands is the tidal bore whose fatal work is captured in the well known saying:

"Kent and Keer
have parted many a good man and his mare."

The gradually narrowing shores of the estuary causes a funnel effect on the incoming tide and as the bay points into the prevailing south westerly winds the first wave – the bore – can reach a considerable height. At Arnside, in the nineteenth century, thirty foot bores were recorded. Twelve feet tides are common at Arnside viaduct and the late twentieth century tidal range is 8.4 metres.[39] The building of the viaduct reduced the bore on the upper sands so that nowadays it exceeds two feet only when stormy. Even so it can be strong enough to sweep a man off his feet and fatal accidents still occur.

The upwardly bob-bob-bobbing swilling effect of the tawny foamed waves has been likened to "a squadron of cavalry at the charge with the white plumes of riders cresting the brown line of the horses."[40] To a modern onlooker the flurried line of leaders racing ahead up the channels leaving bobbing myriad waves behind suggests perhaps the earlier stages of an athletic marathon.

In a frosty winter the battering of bore and tide can produce arctic scenes when the ice, formed on the rivers' edges and in the estuary shallows at low water, is shattered and piled high on a floating raft which grows at subsequent tides to form an "iceberg." During the hard winter of 1880, when Arnside viaduct was damaged by ice, and in 1940, 1947 and 1963 some "icebergs" were between twelve and twenty feet high. December 20, 1981 was the coldest day ever recorded locally when the thermometer at Robert Woods' Garage, Sandside, read 10°F. As the tide ebbed the whole bay from Milnthorpe Marsh outwards was a crazy paving of ice sheets and frozen sewage, the latter being vigorously attacked by famished gulls and shags.

Crossing the sands was always dangerous. In the north aisle of Beetham church is a marble tablet to "Jonathan Bottomley clothier of Staineland near Halifax, Yorkshire who unhappily perished on our sands and was buried here Dec 31st 1787 Aged 32." The upper bay could be crossed by the Sandside ferry. This ran between the Dixies Inn and Foulshaw. Traditionally it was maintained as a manorial obligation by the Lords of the Manor of Haverbrack, to whom the ferryman's cottage belonged. Until c.1800 this was the detached cottage on the rise slightly behind the main Sandside houses at the start of Lovers' Lane. Later the ferryman moved to a low building at the end of the houses shown in the engraving of c.1820 as having a thatched roof. The ferry never seems to have been much used as most travellers could cross the sands without the need of a boat for up to two thirds of each day.

But walking and driving were risky. On 21 June 1815, for example, Thomas Barker of Cartmel aged 18 was drowned on Milnthorpe sands and became the subject of a particularly florid epitaph in Heversham churchyard. "Amiable, lamented youth: Heaven endowed thee with a strong comprehensive mind, and a guileless simplicity of Disposition. In thee we thought to have seen the Man of Worth but thy course was brought to a sudden Period by Him whose desires are sometimes insemlable yet ever merciful. . ."[41] In 1847 a group of men were caught by the tide while crossing from the Dixies and one man was drowned. They "were all on the tramp" and "his companions who were called back did not know his name or place from which he came."[42]

The Hornby's, an old estuary family, ran the ferry in the mid-nineteenth century and Bella Hornby's "perilous situation" was reported in February 1855. "During the past few weeks the water of Morecambe Bay has frozen over to a considerable thickness but began to break up with a high tide. On Friday the 11th Instant Bella Hornby a poor woman who gains a livelihood by ferrying passengers across the bay at High Sandside Milnthorpe and was returning after taking passengers over when the tide came rolling up at great speed, sweeping the ice and the boat with the poor woman into the middle of the bay and no assistance could be rendered the poor ferry woman, from the shore. There she had to remain in her miserable and perilous situation for upwards of five hours exposed to a cold north wind till after the receeding of the tide when two men went to her assistance and succeeded in bringing her safely to shore but very benumbed with cold."[43]

In the 1860's and 1870's Thomas Swindlehurst was the "Sandside guide and ferryman" and "conducted the Post Cart across the sands to Dixies Inn."[44] The opening of the Furness branch line stopped this service and the ferry came to be rarely used. In 1905 it was moved down the shore to sail between the Ship Inn and Foulshaw. Two years later a "heartrending disaster," the most fatal in the history of the sands, put a stop to the ferry for ever. The landlord of The Ship, John Pearson, rowed across to pick up sixteen people who had been staying with the Ormerods at Low Foulshaw. It was their intention to catch the afternoon train from Sandside station to Hollingworth in the West Riding from which they all came. They were George Samuel Littlewood, a grocer aged 52, his wife Sarah 54, Sarah's brother-in-law and sister Mr and Mrs Oldroyd, both aged 55, their two sons Samuel, a piecer, and John, a spinner, John's daughter Elsie 2-3 years, their son in law James Taylor and two sisters, (perhaps their grandchildren) Polly Gower aged 11 and Dora Gower aged 7 and five others all, apparently, related. Pearson divided the party into groups of 11 and 5, the larger number including the lighter adults and three of the children. At the subsequent enquiry it was pointed out that boats of a similar dimension (15ft. 8ins by 4ft. 3ins) on Windermere were only allowed to carry five passengers and, notwithstanding Pearson's claim that the estuary salt water was more buoyant, it was "a somewhat light craft for such a heavy sea." Polly Gower maintained that when she got in the water was only six inches from the gunwhales and when the heavily built older Littlewoods got in it sank even lower.

On setting off from the shore the incoming tide swept it up and outwards into the bay. A moderately sized wave soon engulfed the boat and in the resulting panic it capsized. Melodramatically, Polly related "the water came in and seemed to take my breath away. I was dazed, I never saw the others go into the water. I remember being thrown into the water myself but I remember nothing after-wards. I thought I was dying and I said to myself 'Goodbye Mother' and then I seemed to see the light again and I got hold of the boat and stuck to it. Sam Littlewood was behind me, he stretched out his arms and said my Mother and Father's gone. I saw his mother. I remember the boat turning over and the men righted it and put me inside." For a few moments Mrs Littlewood was seen struggling waist deep in the water until the waves and her sodden voluminous Sunday best dragged her under. No-one could remember what exactly happened to Mr Oldroyd and Mr Littlewood or to Dora and Elsie Gower. Help came quickly from both shores and the Ormerods quickly fished out the bodies of Mr and Mrs Littlewood and Mrs Oldroyd. Mr Oldroyd's body was swept half a mile upstream to be spotted by Mrs Hudson of the Dixies as the tide ebbed. This was recovered by her husband. Dora Gower's body was found the next day by the Dallam Tower huntsman Mr Jackson at Summerhouse Point – over a mile from the scene of the disaster. She was "tenderly laid out at the Dixies." No trace could be seen of the toddler Elsie. Her father, who had lost both his parents, an uncle and an aunt, repeatedly "started off along the shore vainly scouring the broken water for ... his little one as he had already scores of times."[45] The search continued into the night and, it is said that one group of gallant rescuers, no doubt well fortified, seeing what appeared to be a head floating in the tide commandeered a boat and rowed out into the bay to secure a – turnip.[46] It was not for three more days that the little corpse was found lying in the channel between Summerhouse Point and the Dixies. By this time the other corpses had been taken back to Hollingsworth where the mills were closed so that the whole town could see the funeral procession go by. Prior to departure from Sandside the Vicar of Beetham read the first part of the Commital service in the flower-filled railway carriage and there were special services at Beetham, Milnthorpe and Witherslack churches. Much indignation was expressed in Hollingsworth about rumours in Milnthorpe that some of the victims had been worse for drink – the Littlewood's having been staunch non-conformists. A town councillor called Mr Oldham also drew the attention of the Westmorland County Council to the fact that thought the county "had five miles of coastline there was not a single regulation." [46]

This bureaucratic omission was surprising as Milnthorpe Sands had long been a popular bathing resort – an amenity often proclaimed in property advertisements. Thus on 6 September 1823 Plumtree Hall at Heversham was described "as a Modern Built Mansion from Market Town of Milnthorpe about one mile, within which Town there are excellent and convenient SEA BATHING." [47] On 15 March 1826 "a genteel Residence new built at Hazelslack belonging to George Wilson esq." was advertised to let "situate within half a mile of sea bathing distant about two miles from the market and Port Town of Milnthorp." [48] Sea Bathing facilities were also mentioned prominently in the prospectus of Heversham Grammar School and of Milnthorpe's Young Ladies Seminaries.

Sadly, bathing was often a fatal pursuit. Perhaps the most tragic epitaph in Heversham Churchyard is that to "Jane the loving and beloved wife of Mr John Dickinson of Milnthorpe, She departed this life April MDCCLXX (1770) aged 43 years. As also Four Children Agnes 9th December 1763, Richard 12th August 1767, Elizabeth 25th March 1768, Birbeck 10th August 1770 Drowned in bathing aged 1½ years, 6 years, 14 years, 11 years (respectively)..." [49] Within the church in the south west corner is a tablet to "John Hudson second son of Robert Hudson Esq., of Tadworth Court Surrey and also Isaac Hudson of Long Sleddale his School fellow who were drowned bathing on the Sands, the 24th of June A.D. 1792 both Aged 16 years."

In the yard another Grammar School tragedy is commemorated in a sandstone cross set up "by their schoolfellows to George Cowell of Lydgate aged 18, here buried Edmund J Goodwin of Manchester aged 19 and Richard T M Rigby of Chorley aged 15, drowned while bathing on the sands August 30th 1855."

The *Westmorland Gazette* of July 1824 gave details of a tragedy which was repeated on several occasions. "On Tuesday last Mr Amos Hodgson, dancing master was unfortunately drowned whilst bathing at Milnthorpe sandside. Mr Hodgson is a native of Cumberland, we believe, and was teaching a dancing school at Milnthorpe at that time. He had entered the water at the Saw Pit beside Dixies and had swum across nearly to the Summerhouse; But on coming to the eddy at the junction of the Kent and the Bela it is supposed that a cramp had seized his limbs. No assistance could be rendered him as he was nearly a quarter of a mile from the side. Mr Gandy of Milnthorpe soon after arrived, and dived for the body; but his humane exertions were in vain. The body was recovered at the ebb of tide."[52]

An even more poignant tragedy occurred in May 1828 when a "woman Gerard lost her life while bathing" also at "the sandside". She had "two children with her which she had bathed and she went in..the tide was ebbing she stepped off a break in the sand and was carried away...she was a widow and the children are left destitute.. Each summer one or more perish at this place from bathing."[53] The Gazette recommended that "stakes be provided" as a warning but these would not have helped much as most nineteenth century bathers could not swim since they had neither the swimming pools nor school swimming lessons in which to learn the art.

Each year from about 1840 to the 1870's a sports meeting called the Sandside Regatta was held in August at The Ship Inn at which wrestling was a main attraction. An attempt was also made to emulate the facilities of more genteel resorts, as announced in the *Westmorland Gazette* in 1853: "We are glad to inform our readers that a spirited young man in Milnthorpe has been in the course of building a large bathing van which will be ready in a few days; such a machine has been much wanted in the locality."[54] The larger proportion of "bathers" were far from genteel, being mainly villagers or labourers from Kendal. In 1815 the vicar of Heversham, Dr George Lawson, stated that a Church should be built at Milnthorpe as it was "much resorted to during the bathing season by the multitudes from the country around." An opportunity for visitors to hear a sermon would, he believed, "prevent much of the Disorders and Profaneness which are often attendant on such associations."[55]

Bathing on Milnthorpe sands was particularly well reported during the 1850's. Thus in June 1855 it was noted that "this beautiful and delightful sea bathing place begins to fill up with visitors."[56] There were some attempts to control drinking on Sunday's and in June 1852 "Many hundreds were disappointed on reaching the sands in not being able to obtain admission to the Public Houses which were closed on account of the new Beer Act."[57] In August, however, it was noted "the landlords along the shore reaped a bountiful harvest..there were no serious accidents but in the evening great disturbances and fighting took place."[58] The season was generally restricted to high summer though as early as 28th May it was reported that "the delightful sea bathing resort of Milnthorpe Sandside is fast filling up...many lodgings however are already taken up."[59] In 1909 bathing was noted as going on at Sandside on 17 October. The peak time was the "exceeding high Lammas tides" of August. In 1847 "many thousands visited

Westmorland's Little Blackpool.

Milnthorpe Sandside: the tide was a fine one and many enjoyed a dip in the salt water."[60] On 18 August 1855 it was reported that "during past few days the town of Milnthorpe has been unusually busy owing to so many strangers passing towards the Sands. The tide having been running high and all the lodging houses along the shore are quite full of visitors and bathers."[61] Similarly in August 1858 was the report that "during the present week we have had very good tides and the weather being fine brought a large company of people to the sands every day. The water was salt and good and bathing became very general among the visitors we are happy to say without any accident although there were two narrow escapes."[62]

In later times hoards of visitors still descended on the sands. Just before the First World War Sandside Station was a popular venue for excursions, especially Sunday school parties. Over 1000 adults and children from the Mount Street Primitive Methodist Church in Barrow visited Summerhouse Point in June 1914. Bathing was prohibited but within an hour of arriving on the sands an eleven year old boy Stanley McNamee was drowned. He went under in full view of hundreds of people yet the body could not be found though the search went on through, Saturday night until Sunday when "P.C. Good of Kirkby Lonsdale sent an underwater telescope to assist the workers." Four days later at 6 a.m. on the Wednesday morning it was discovered in the channel with "black backed gulls devouring it."[63]

Milnthorpe Sands - at St. John's Cross c.1934.

A similar tragedy nearly occurred in August 1939 when two teenage girls, Elsie Sumpton 17, the daughter of the landlord of the Coach and Horses, and Florrie Bond 15, also of Milnthorpe, got into difficulties. Fortunately two strong swimmers, Police Sergeant John Owen M.M. of Kendal and Robert Woof, the Netherfield goalkeeper, were on hand and brought them safely to shore.[64]

During the 1920's and 1930's almost every heatwave produced reports in the Westmorland Gazette about "Westmorland's Blackpool", but Morecambe and other commercial resorts had by then creamed off all but local visitors. A temporary revival of popularity took place during the petrol starved 1940's when on hot days the Dallam 'buses frequently seemed to carry twice the permitted number of passengers to Sandside. In the post-war years several accidents, and growing concern about sewage pollution (which might have been the cause of an epidemic of infective hepatitis in 1959) as well as the superior attractions of more sophisticated leisure pursuits led to the sands being abandoned by all but a handful of bathers, even on the hottest days.

Whether lapped by a lazy tide on a summer's day or lying damp and desolate under a heavy sky at other seasons, stillness and safety are rare and deceptive features of the sands. As Constance Holme wrote in *The Lonely Plough*: "the sea was always there and though it came quietly perhaps and inoffensively there would be many a night when it would come like a beast of prey, ravening its path between narrow shores, devouring the watery desert."[65] Often an uneasy and literally illnatured alliance of high tide and equinoxal gale has surged up the bay to meet - perilously near to the Milnthorpe embankment - the waters of the Bela and Kent swollen into flood by heavy rain. Every recent generation has had its tale of the breaking of the protective banks and the spread of the sterilizing salt water over arable and meadowland. Always there has lingered in the back of the minds of the marsh farmer the fear that a single furious tide could destroy the work of a season or even a life-time.

In the nineteenth century high tides caused alarm in Milnthorpe because many villagers had marsh allotments and grazing rights on the shore. In the New Year of 1831 it was reported[66] that "at Milnthorpe never was such a tide remembered, although by the table it was less by four feet than some have been calculated to be; but the wild and rattling storms had driven the water up the bay in such force that many of the houses on the shore were inundated. At Dallam Tower the flood rose to such a height that the usual road was rendered impassable so that those coming from or going to the Hall were compelled to go round by Beetham and in the farmyard several pigs perished by the overflowing of the water. The Mosside bank was down and during the height of the storm the Issabella, Captain Greenwood of Milnthorpe, was driven ashore at the place high and dry. In Dallam Park 23 large trees bowed their head to the sweeping fury of the blast."

The 1852 flood also came between Christmas and New Year, the banks breaking first at Fishcarling. Within "two hours the tide had overflowed the whole marsh extending betwixt Milnthorpe and Lyth several feet deep. Nothing could be seen except the remains of floating stacks of peat, etc." The wind unroofed the houses at Sampool while at Foulshaw the water rose in the farmhouse of Mr Alexander Webster to within a few inches of the downstairs ceiling. Upstairs terrified women and children believed their last had come as five feet high waves tore away the porch and broke in the doors and windows. The 'round parlour table was found washed into Milnthorpe.'

Although there was three feet of water in the shippon at Birkett's farm the farmer Walter Berry, who was also the Milnthorpe and Kendal Carrier, set out in a boat to rescue his goods in the shoreside warehouse at Sandside. As he got there several hogsheads of sugar and casks of tallow swept out, the flood carrying away the door of the warehouse. Attempting to stop the door he climbed into the building through the roof only to be knocked off his feet three times by the waves and if he had not managed to hold on to the wreckage he would have lost his life.[67]

Repairs to the bank began immediately;£1,370 13s 6d was collected by Milnthorpe subscribers for a compensation fund set up by the Mayor of Kendal. On February 5th 1853 it was reported that "a great number of men are at present employed in repairing the banks along the shore at Milnthorpe and the Foulshaw side of Morecambe Bay which the late floods have washed down and it will be some time before their tasks are completed."[68] The work was successful for when in 1874 the water rose higher than in 1852, the bank held except at Halforth where a breach was mended before the next tide. All round the bay sea defences were badly buffeted in September 1902[69] and the Meathop and Brogden banks were destroyed. At Sandside the tide covered the lawn at Arnbarrow house and reached a point only equalled in 1977. Arnbarrow suffered again in 1903 when the peach house was destroyed.[70] At Sandside roof timbers as well as slates were carried away while in Milnthorpe people were "rocked in bed by the wind and articles hanging on interior walls were made to swing and jingle together."

The meeting of storm and tide in the early hours of Mothering Sunday, 23rd March 1907, caused one of the most cataclysmic of[71] floods and also provided the climax in Constance Holme's story *The Lonely Plough*. Constance Holme based the story on the Lancasters of College Green, where on the disastrous night in question the water reached the mark cut on the dairy showing the height of the 1852 flood. Farmer Lancaster who was 84, two ageing sons, one of whom was ill, and two servant girls retreated upstairs. From the top of the stairs the old man "watched the water wondering how long it would continue to rise and listening to his wife's lamentations over the parlour carpet. He let her alone, though he knew all the provisions in the house were gone and that they were cut off from help on all hands. What he did not know was that in the bank outside was a gap a quarter of a mile wide but if he had known he could have done nothing. He could only watch the water creeping up."

Help was in fact on hand. Major Argles of Eversley himself led a party of house guests, servants and villagers to rescue two horses which were taken to Levens Hall. Getting to the house to help the frightened and sick folk upstairs was more difficult and they were only rescued as dawn broke. All that Sunday the search for stock continued:"They formed a human chain and groped, with the big sticks scouting before them, in imminent danger all the time, and more than once utterly bewildered and all but lost. Wading often to their waists, trapped by deep holes, by wire fencing wrenched into sunk snares for their stumbling feet, blinded, dripping, breathless and stunned, buffeted by the wild gusts and clouds of spray heaving in through the mighty breaks in the bank, they yet held on until there seemed to them a limitless expanse, and they knew that the floodgates at Ninehyrkes (Ninezergh) must have been smashed."

Lancaster, in fact, lost 59 lambing ewes and nearly all the poultry but a kitten was found sitting safely on a bale floating in three feet of water in the yard. Further out on the bank of the Kent, Mr Todd at Waterside only lost two sheep and the water barely touched the yard which was several feet higher than that of College Green. On the far

Tidal Sluicegates, the Marsh Dyke with the Embankment or 'Lug' behind.

bank Sampool was flooded for several days and 17 sheep were lost.
Mr Barnes of Park House (Pippin Hall in the novel) lost 36 sheep
and almost all his stack of turnips and huge quantities of manure
and fertilizer. In the Tattersall sheds (Marsh Farm) which he rented
from the vicar 10 valuable cattle were only rescued when the water
was up to their necks. For years afterwards John Handley of
Heversham Hall recalled sailing for half a mile from Moss Side over
the meadows towards Marsh Farm only to be swept upwards by the
current. In the end a boat had to come two miles from The Ship Inn
to effect the rescue.

   At Milnthorpe such was the force of the tide that the Bela rose six
feet in half an hour, flooding the cottages on the Strands to the
height of a piano keyboard and "ruining a time piece, valuable
ornaments and a much prized case of stuffed birds." Just after
midnight the gas works were flooded to a depth of four feet, the
retorts were extinguished for the next 24 hours and "tar and
ammonia barrels were carried away like play things."

At Sandside three cows were rescued in the shippon at the Dixies within inches of being drowned, almost every house was flooded, and the roadside wall and that of Woodlands were destroyed. Over at Foulshaw, Ormrod, the farmer, only just reached the safety of the house as a ten foot stretch of bank collapsed letting in a devastating tidal wave. This episode was captured by Constance Holme who transferred the scene to Ladyford (Halforth) on the Heversham side of the estuary.

"In the kitchen, the frightened women and the roused hands were busy moving food and valuables as the sea came in at the door until presently it was standing two feet deep on the flags..."The banks are giving on all sides" he said, as the household crowded around him. "We were near caught time and again as we came along. The water kept bursting through behind us before we were barely clear. The Marsh Road's gone - ay, an' the main road an' all I doubt. There's a gap like the mouth o' hell...."

In the next few days the full extent of the damage was seen as the waters fell and "the scars of the land crept shudderingly into sight. Great holes five and six feet deep where had been metalled surface, uprooted fences and railings twisted like cord; and everywhere dead things, rabbits, hares, poultry - and always, sheep. The peaceful, cared-for country lay broken and horribly disfigured, as if by the riving hands of a maddened giant." Almost all the embankment for two miles from Fishcarling to Ninezergh had gone with two gaps of 900 yards and 1,510 yards.

Major repairs followed the disaster. The bank was raised by three feet, the hedge which had been alongside it was replaced by wire fences as it had encouraged the burrowing of rabbits. An extra rate of £3 per acre on land not affected by the flood and 30s per acre for marsh land was levied on Heversham and Milnthorpe. The Dallam and Leven estates bore the cost of repairing fences and replacing the many damaged gates. Canon Gilbert, vicar of Heversham also waived two years' rent on the 100 acres of marsh glebeland.[72]

During the "war floods", in 1917 when John Handley "saw water where he had never seen it before" and in September 1918 when four inches of rain fell in twenty four hours, the banks held. Heavy September rains in 1925 rendered the marsh fields in a pitiable condition with 100 acres of corn, due for harvets, under water but it was not until the autumn of 1927 that disaster struck again. As in 1907 a high tide and river floods were accompanied by a hurricane which destroyed the windows in Houghton's Garage on the shore at Sandside and destroyed many valuable specimens in Dallam Tower Park. The gas works were flooded and the whole village was without gas over the weekend, the "congregation of St Thomas Church bringing their own illumination to the evening service." On the Strands the floods again reached the height of the piano keyboard but then suddenly dropped by as much as a foot "caused by the breaking of banks lower down the bay." A gap was forced on the Milnthorpe side of Fishcarling where fortunately the stock in the fields had been driven to higher land, but at Halforth and College Green Mr Nelson and Mr Bennett each lost 18 sheep.[73] A week later, on the 5th November, the tide rose even more alarmingly, causing wider flooding and over £300 of damage in the Comb Mill at Milnthorpe.

This time the Palmer and Fell families living in the Strand cottages were in a worse position and eventually they had to be rescued by a party led by Police Sergeant Cass. He had to prop ladders up to the bedroom windows as the downstairs rooms were impassable. Having made a perilous descent in the dark they were taken on Casson's high milk float (which almost lived up to its name!) to the National school, where they spent the night.

After 1927 over £1000 was spent on strengthening the banking, the cost being met by the river board. More extensive work was carried out after the east coast floods in 1953 so that a banking twenty feet wide at the base and ten feet high in parts ran continuously round the bay from the Dallam weir to Ninezergh and making an excellent promenade. Even so it could not withstand the storms of November 1977 which repeated the pattern but without the casualties of 1907 and 1927. Again the sea wall at Sandside was destroyed, six foot coping stones being carried across the road. Most of the houses and cafes were flooded, coal was washed away from Clarke's yard, carpets and the deep freeze were ruined at The Ship, and paper and stores drenched at Holdsworth's printers. In Robert Wood's garage the water rose to the top of the work bench, six feet above normal high tide level and destroyed the garden walls of the newly built bungalows on Dallam Drive. On the Strands the cottages were again flooded, though, as piano's had gone out of fashion, the height was not recorded!

Out on the Milnthorpe Marsh the bank broke at Fishcarling, (as always during the night) and the waters rushed across the fields to the edge of Ellers Wood, half a mile away. The bank was also damaged at Halforth but it was on the Fishcarling breach that emergency work was concentrated. Here as night fell was a scene worthy of Constance Holme. A gale force wind relentlessly whipped barbed wire from the broken fences into the faces of the workers and also threatened to force the ebbing tide over the brink of the hasty repairs. Out in the channel, often waist deep, Nelsons, Barnes and Handleys - all grandsons of those who had fought the floods of seventy and fifty years before - struggled with sandbags and straw bales to stem the breach.

Just as the tide was about to rise again the breach was healed. Later the shore was strengthened with tons of limestone and

Constance Holme in 1914
- the year of publication of
'The Lonely Plough'.

brushwood groins were set in the sands to deflect the tides. No doubt time and tide will in due course wreck these latest efforts but moments of drama might be less in the future.

Generally the Milnthorpe shore is quiet. Traffic noise and even the clump and clang of Sandside quarry seem muted by the sands. A few walkers, golfers and bird watchers come in summer and there are wildfowlers in winter, but in spring, as the soil is being turned, the tractor driver, alone in his cab with his transistor, scans an empty landscape: this is still the land of *The Lonely Plough*.

3

The Port
of Milnthorpe

The best known historical fact about Milnthorpe is that it was
Westmorland's only sea port. It is also widely believed that evidence
about it is limited and that this indicates the port's insignificance.[1]

Certainly there is little evidence on the ground. Lying in its
shallow valley and hidden from the estuary by a line of drumlins the
village of Milnthorpe lacks a view of the sea. Only two pre-twentieth
century houses, Belvidere Cottage (now The Vicarage) and
Harmony Hall, have even a glimpse of the bay. Both these houses
had connections with the Port. Belvidere Cottage belonged to John
Postlethwaite, a merchant whose interests embraced shipping.[2]
Harmony Hall was built by Joseph Fayrer, a notable sea Captain.
When during its construction "he ran short of money he set out on
another voyage in order to meet the exchequer."[3]

There are very few relics. Ships timbers are said to form the roof
of Bank Farm at Heversham and might also be seen at Crosby
Lodge, Ackenthwaite; Carlton House, Whasset; Harmony Hall and
some of the oldest cottages in Park Road, Milnthorpe. There was
never a harbour or a stone quay, though part of a stumpy wharf
survives at the Dixies. The port's many warehouses were scattered
round the village and, randomly, along the estuary shore. Probably
most would cater also for the needs of land-transport, industry and
agriculture. The warehouse of one Sandside sea-merchant was
always called Rodick's Barn.

Along with a large warehouse of Wakefields, Gunpowder
Manufacturers, and many lesser store places, it has disappeared.
Only three warehouses can be identified positively: the "Red
Warehouse" on Harmony Hill, the so-called Customs House[4] by
the Playing Field in Park Road and the large warehouse, used in the

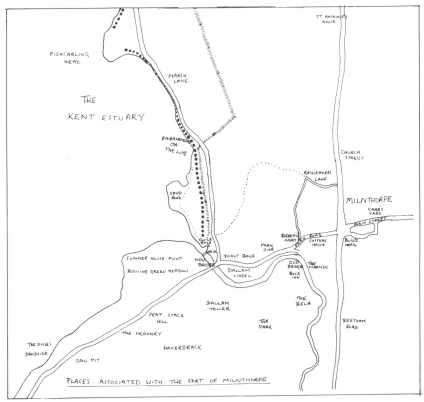

PLACES ASSOCIATED WITH THE PORT OF MILNTHORPE

nineteenth century by the Berry family, on Quarry Lane at Sandside.[5]

Inevitably many inns served the port. In Milnthorpe itself the Bull's Head, held in the eighteenth century by the Scaife family, who were also customs officers, "was the main resort of sea-faring men."[6] Westward from the village down the estuary to Arnside there were at least 10 hostelries; the Buck Inn just south of the Old Bridge in Dallam Park, the Dixies and Ship Inn at Sandside, ale houses at Rose Hill and on the site of Woodlands at Storth lane end, the Flying Dutchman at Storth, an inn at St. John's Cross, taverns at Guard Hill and at Carr Bank and, across the moss, the Fighting Cocks Inn at Arnside.[8]

Until c.1800 vessels could get close to Milnthorpe by sailing up the Bela which is tidal almost to Beetham Waterfalls. Normal tides, however, only penetrate as far as Bela Mills, and their site might have been determined by shipping consideration. Indeed Machell in c.1691 stated that iron bars were brought by sea to the forge which occupied a site close to Bela Smithy (now the garage of J Douthwaite & Sons).[10] The river bank walk from the Mill to the Old Bridge is called the Strands which, apart from The Ship at Sandside is the only nautical name in the immediate district. The use of the

Strands by shipping must have been limited at least from 1542 when the first recorded Bela Bridge was built,[10] 20 yards up stream from the present bridge of c.1730.[11] Even so, Eva Scott in 1924 stated that her grandfather could recall cargoes being shipped under the bridge direct to the Mills.[13] As the apex of the arches is only five feet above a usable depth of water only low hulks and short sailors would have been able to clear the bridge! According to Neddy Stones, the river bank, before the present Sandside road was built in c.1813, sloped down to the river and ships regularly moored close to the Old Bridge at the place where horse troughs were later installed.[14]

The Bela widens and deepens west of the bridge. Many of the port's activities were congregated here at the Dallam Wheel, where the river turns to flow a quarter of a mile north to Summer House Point and the estuary proper. Until 1813 the Sandside road crossed the Old Bridge and ran south of the river to the north of Dallam Tower from where it ran over the bluff of Haverbrack to reach the estuary at Sandside.[15] Neddy Stones recalled that at Dallam "the land betwixt the Road and the River was open and was used for Timber Yards (with) Ship Building at Dallam Wheel, and other portions of it for Rafts of Timbers and discharge of vessels."[16] On the northern bank above the Wheel was the hamlet of Scout Bank, the home of fishermen who used to dry their nets in the meadow between the Sand Road (leading from the Marsh lane) and the river. The timber and ship yards were swept away when the New Bridge and the north-bank road to Sandside were built about 1813. Over the next 20 years Scout Bank also was re-moved completely in order to improve the view from Dallam Tower. All this Stones claimed was "one of the worst arrangements for Milnthorpe by which the whole advantage to the locality was destroyed and this for the sake of Land Monopoly (by the Wilson's of Dallam) the Trade and Commerce were so limited that the parish has gradually sunk into obscurity." Yet the port flourished well into the nineteenth century. Stones himself could remember seeing in c.1845, at the mouth of the Bela, the "Old John," The "Tickler," The "Hope," The "Isabelle" and The "Elizabeth" all riding at anchor and "(I) have assisted Walter Berry in unloading them 70 years ago." He also recalled that "the Old Lighthouse (or Summer House) had a Loop in its roof to hold a flambeau to guide vessels. One light faced the outlet and the Bela, another faced the approach of the Kent and another faced the Irish Sea." In 1895 John Burrow who had lived for seventy years at Sandside said that in "his re-collection he had seen on old maps" that there was on Haverbrack bank "the beacon for the Port of Milnthorpe."[18]

Traditionally the Wilsons collected tolls from Summer House Point from shipping entering the Bela. In a dispute between the

The 'John' of Milnthorpe
from Tea-pot, now at Abbot Hall, Kendal.

Lords of Dallam and Levens in c.1660 it was stated "that every boat comes up the river pay four pence for unloading."[19] A map of 1733 also shows a building which might have been the light/toll house. By 1770 it was in ruins for William Hutton wrote "a quarter of a mile below Dallam Tower stood formerly a litte House upon a Rock with a good Bowling green near it. The sea has now work'd away most of the Latter, but the former retains the name Bowling Green Point." All signs of the green in "light house meadow" have gone but Bowling Green Point remains as an alternative name for Summerhouse Point. The Summerhouse itself was pulled down in 1898.[21]

The port's busiest part was always along the Haverbrack shore, called until the 1860's "The Milnthorpe Sandside," when it became simply "Sandside." At the shore's eastern end, nearest to Milnthorpe, is The Dixies. Many attempts have been made to explain the derivation of the name. Hutton stated that "Another quarter of a mile below this point (Bowling Green/Summer House) is the Dixies so called from a Person who liv'd there . . . Mr Richard Simpson curate of Mount Sorrel, Leicestershire was born at Dixies."[22] In the 1950's Milnthorpe was visited by an American quasi-scholar bent on establishing a link with Dixieland, U.S.A.[23] No major contribution to scholarship resulted! Most probably "Dixies" comes from the Old Norse Diki[24] meaning a trench or channel. If so, this Scandinavian name might imply that Viking long boats beached here. Opposite the wharf was the Dixies Inn, kept by the Hudson family from at least c. 1800. As a boy the last landlord sailed with Captain Bush on board the "Old John," the port's best known ship.[25]

Sandside and the Dixies had a somewhat sleezy reputation. Along with the Strand Walk it is said to have "witnessed many strange transactions when slave trading was a legitimate trade"[26]

while there is a story that "one local family was set against using
sugar after a Black Baby was landed in a cargo of sugar near Dixies
Inn in the trading days of old." There are, indeed, some hints of
local dealings in the "black cargo." Captain Joseph Fayrer of
Milnthorpe traded with Africa and, in fact, died at Cape Coast
Castle in 1801.[28] The Heversham parish registers record in 1793
the baptism of "John Burral aged 22 born in Whydah in Africa"
and also the death through "water in ye brain" of Henry, son of
Henry Tindal of British West Indies.[29] Another Carribean connection is contained in the will of Joseph Grigg of "Milthrop,"
Distiller, died 1701, for, along with shares in two boats "Phoenix"
and "Primrose" worth £14 he also left "Part of a Ship called the
Imployment with part of the cargo now fitted for Barbadoes etc.
£58 0s. 0d." Somervell comments "It would be interesting to know
whether the "Port of Milnthorpe" shipped direct to Barbadoes etc.
It probably was so."[30] There is also a tradition that the Huddlestone
family of maltsters built Glasgow House c.1820 out of the profits of
rum distilling.[31]

Sandside's bad reputation was earned more probably by the
annual bouts of drunkenness during the bathing season and from
other ordinary misdeeds. Thus the Roman Catholic Thomas
Hilton of Beetham bemoaned how in c.1720 "on a Sunday in Lent
he vowed to abstain from three things during the course of the
ensuing week viz. eating flesh, drinking wine and the use of women.
But alas the frailty of good resolutions, I broke them all, was
tempted to eat the wing of a fowl, got drunk at Milnthorpe and laid
with a girl at Sandside."[32]

A workaday appearance is portrayed at the Dixies in the well
known engraving of c.1820 by T.A. Allom of "Milnthorpe Sands
Westmorland." It shows the two old houses (one of which is dated
AIT 1728) and also a low thatched building on the site of the
present Ferry Cottage. Out in the bay is a rowing boat, while against
the banking, a single masted vessel appears to be being unloaded
on to high wheeled cards, some of which are making for the sloping
wharf.

Lower down the estuary were wooden jetties at the Ship Inn, St.
John's Cross, at the Fighting Cocks, Arnside, and later, as the upper
bay trade failed, at Blackstone Point. Generally, however, vessels
headed for Milnthorpe on the tide and on going aground were
propped up on the sand bank where the cargo was transferred to
waggons which rested on planks or pallets. The obituary of John
Mashiter of Crosby Lodge in 1900 stated that in his youth c.1840 he
had helped Ben Tattersall the maltster from St. Anthony's load
ships in the bay – "there was no proper quay, when unloading the
vessels, the carter had to keep moving round the ship to prevent the
wheels sinking too deep."[33] For this muddy method, and also

because its activities stretched right down the estuary, the Port of Milnthorpe might more properly be called the "Port of Milnthorpe Sands."

The Port's origins can only be conjectured. In their coracles the collectors and fisherfolk of ancient times might have paddled around the coves and creeks on either side of the bay bringing with them salt and handicrafts to be exchanged for what scant agricultural surpluses the primitive communities could spare. Later, traders could have followed in the wake of the Celtic missionaries and the Viking invaders and settlers. Quite probably the sandstone of the eighth century Anglian Cross and the masonry of the fifthteenth century Chancel at Heversham Church were borne by sea from Heysham or Furness to the head of the Bay.[34]

Medieval commercial expansion is shown in the establishment in c.1280 of Milnthorpe Fair, and its trade could have included shipping. The fair was confirmed by Alexander de Wyndsore in 1334.[35] With others of his family Alexander claimed lands at Kinsale, Inchiquin and Toughal in Ireland and he might have used Milnthorpe as a supply base for invasion. In 1368 there was an order for "Irish Vessels between 20 and 200 tuns be sent to Lyverpool, County Lancaster in England by the feast of St. Helary and his men at arms and archers for service in Ireland." Milnthorpe is not mentioned in this order but, "it seems only reasonable to suppose that part of the food and munitions (sic) supplied to troops employed by the Irish campaigns by a local leader passed through a port in his own territory...." There might have been reciprocal imports, for in 1376 John de Kendal was licenced "to buy wheat in Ireland and ship the same to any part of that land and bring it to Kendal, Westmorland and to make a profit of it."[36]

More conclusive proof of the estuary's importance in the late Middle Ages is shown by the pele towers. Arnside Tower on the southern shore and Wraysholme Tower, to the north, guard the seaward end. Further up were Hazelslack, Dallam, Heversham Hall, Nether Levens, Levens Hall and on the route to Kendal, Sizergh Castle. At the Bela's mouth was Dallam Tower to which Machell in 1691, said "the tide comes up almost to the Gates. Near to this place is the foundation of a castle." Most of the peles were built after the last serious Scottish raids of c.1322 and it is possible that they were built not for defence against the distant border reevers – but to protect the region from local bad neighbours and from Irish and Manx pirates. In the mid-sixteenth century Roger Piele, last abbot of Furness, in a vain attempt to justify his position as a protector of the King's peace to Thomas Cromwell, stated that he had recently imprisoned a pirate. Furness Abbey was dissolved but the pirates remained. In 1565 Commissioners were appointed to superintend "all ports, creeks and landing places in the realm." Milnthorpe does not figure in their returns but as many operative ports were stated to have "no shippes, vessells nor any maryners" it does not necessarily mean that the port was in abeyance. Moreover in c.1589 the Duchy of Lancaster Index of Patents states that "Barnabye Bennyson hath the colleccon of all such groundage and wharfage and other dutyes as shall grow due to her Matie, for castinge Anker appon her Maties soyle of the comon, called Haverbrack or Milnethorpe haven and landings of wares there."[38]

In South Lakeland the early seventeenth century was a period of prosperity based on expanding agriculture, the woollen trade and textile manufacture. This was the golden age of the pack horse and there was not as yet a great demand for bulky sea borne goods like coal and machinery. That the coastal trade was probably slack is indicated by Camden's *Brittanica* "on the south side lies Milnthorpe, the only sea-town in this county: tho' the commodities which are imported, are brought hither only in small vessels from Grange in Lancashire." Again in 1672 when the Earl of Carlisle, as Admiral, tried to impress 400 seamen he was told by Sir Daniel Flemming that no recruits were available from Milnthorpe, all of whose seamen were said to be living in Lancashire at Grange. At the same time Edward Wilson of Dallam tower said that there were no seamen at Milnthorpe "only two brothers who are boat carpenters." Perhaps they were being reticent in order to evade the Press Gang and Excise Officers for in 1671 Flemming himself had indicated that the Port was in use when he wrote "Milnthorpe is the only sea town in this county whose fair is Mayday. Here are wine and other commodities brought from beyond the sea, and brought in small vessels." Moreover the Wilson's would not have asserted their rights to port tolls if the port was inactive.

Thirty years later Milnthorpe ships were classed as belonging to the port of Lancaster. Only two Milnthorpe ships were connected to Lancaster compared with 32 from Liverpool and 12 from Poulton, while even Penny Bridge – a similar estuarine port, round the coast near Ulverston – had three ships.

Local trade with the port of Whitehaven was of some importance in the early eighteenth century. Coal and grain came into Grange and flour was exported. On 13 March 1729 the Corporation of Kendal petitioned the Lords of the Treasury for a remission of duty stating that "the River Kent is navigable for small Boats to Milnthrop, a town abt. six miles distant from Kendale but ye navigation of this River would be much improved if ye town of Kendale might be supply'd with coals from Wthaven if the Duty laid upon Water Born Coals were taken of." In support they claimed that "Kendal has been a place of great trade by the manufacture of several sorts of woollen stuffs and tanning for leather; that turf (peat) hitherto their fuel being exhausted, the expense of firing has caused the almost entire loss of their trade." The petition was rejected; the commissioners of customs reported to the House of Lords "that there has been shipped at Whitehaven and discharged at Milnthorpe in five years past upwards of 368 Chaldrons of coal, and if coals landed at Milnthorpe be exempt from duty, Grange, Pennybridge and Rampside may demand the same." Despite this set back, however, the sea coal trade continued until the nineteenth century.[39]

Salt was always a major item in the coastal trade; it was probably also one of the first. Products of local salt pans at Saltcoats, Arnside and elsewhere might have been exported by the earliest traders and they probably met the district's demands until the eighteenth century. Supplies from Liverpool and Cheshire then began to flow in and destroy production around the estuary, so that by about 1770 Hutton wrote "formerly along this south side of the sands (near Arnside) there were several Salt Steads, or small salt-works for Bay Salt. They were ruin'd by the Great Works at Liverpool & Warrington."[40]

Excise duty was charged on the export of salt and to guard against untaxed cargoes coming in Milnthorpe had its own customs officer. In 1711 "the baptism of Christopher son of Mr Clarke officer in Millthropp" was registered and again in "1721 James son of Mr William Clarke officer in Excise at Ackenthwaite" was baptised.[41]

If the cargo was damaged or lost in transit the duty was recoverable after an affidavit had been sworn before a magistrate and a petition sent to the quarter sessions. The relevant documents provide a useful source of information about navigation at Milnthorpe. Thus in 1741 "John Whitwell of Kendal stated that he had shipt on board the Prosperity, James Dowson Captain bound from Milthrop, 20 Bushels and 4 gallons of salt, duty paid, received only 12 bushels at Millthrop before a storm arose and the rest was cast away – desires a Certificate." Also "Christopher Russell of Kendal: his cargo was brought from Liverpool to Milnthorpe on the Prosperity the Captain being James, all duty paid unloaded only 2 bags before the Storm destroyed remaining 8 bags, desires certificate to buy equal amount duty free."

The first reference to a ship called "The John" occurs in an excise certificate of 24 November 1774 when Robert Saul the Master and James Swainson claimed refund of duty after a storm had damaged a "cargo on the ship John, at anchor in port of Milnthorpe." Similarly in 1780 an Excise Certificate for salt damaged on board the "Emma" was claimed by "John Burrows Master from Liverpool to Milthrop 8 – 10 May 1779."

Details of weather conditions are given in the two longest certificates.

"Be it known unto all whom it may concern that on the fourteenth day of November 1776 Robert Saul Master of the ship John belonging the port of Milnthorp in the said County, burden forty eight tons and James Swainson of the said ship, came before me, John Moon esq., one of his Majesty's justices of the peace for the said county and do on their oath say and declare that the said now lays anchor at near a place called Dickses within the said port of Milnthorp, loaded with several sorts of perishable goods, and that yesterday being 12th of this instant month of November 1776 and the said vessel laying on her side and after an end and the tide running violently at her ebb and wind being high they are afraid she was strained, as she shipt in a quantity of water whereby they are apprehensive some damage may be done to the cargo of the said ship, which said damage, if any should be, they, the said Robert Saul and James Swainson on their oathes say, was no ways occasioned by any default or neglect in the said ship, its riging, tackle or furniture, or for want of care of diligence in them, or any of the crew of the said ship but solely by means of the tide and winds as aforesaid all which being so declared and sworn by the said Robert Saul Master and the said James Swainson of the said ship the said tule and winds are protected against for any loss or damage the said cargo, or any part thereof may have sustained of also the owners and freighters of the said cargo protected and Sworn at Kendale in the said County the day and year aforesaid before me John Moon:
  Robert Saul
  James Swainson."

On 28 April 1786 Thomas Bowskill and Thomas Waring both of Lancaster swore that "on or about the twenty third Day of January 1786 there were put on board the said sloop or Vessel called the Thomas and Issac of Milthrop afore said Eighty Bushells of refined salt from the salt works of Messrs Crosbie and Urmston at Liverpool in the said County of Lancaster to be from there conveyed in the said vessel to Millthrop aforesaid That His Majesty's Duties for the said Eighty Bushels of refined salt was duly paid... that the said vessel on or about the twenty ninth Day of January 1786 being firm tight and staunch sailed from Liverpool aforesaid with the said salt on Board in order to proceed with the same coastwise from there to Millthrop aforesaid and that after the same sloop or vessel had so sailed, the weather coming in and very thick and dark and the wind blowing strong she struck upon a Sandbank about half past severn o'clock in the Evening of the said twenty ninth day of January by which the said vessel made a great deal of water and from which the mariners could not keep her free and from that cause only sixty four Bushels of the said Salt so shipped as aforesaid were entirely lost and spoiled... not through any neglect or Default of the mariners on Board the said Sloop or vessel... and that the said Eighty Bushels of salt belonged to Natham Tylor of Kirby Kendale aforesaid Grocer who is subject of this Realm of Great Britain."[42]

Coastal trade around the wooded creeks and inlets of a romantically beautiful estuary, customs officers and sailing ships all contributed to vague but strongly held notions that Milnthorpe Sands were rife with smugglers in their eighteenth century heyday. In the 1950's a radio serial on Children's Hour concerned an imaginary gang of smugglers who held their loot in Arnside Tower and the story was quickly believed to be based on fact.[44] When in c.1900 a vault carved in the rock was discovered behind the former St. John's Cross Inn it was immediately claimed to have been a smugglers lair. In the same vein the Women's Institute history of Arnside of 1956 states that "from Carr Bank a flight of steps leads up the Cliff to what has been called the smugglers cottage, which still stands on the outskirts of Storth."[45] Sadly there is no documentary evidence to support these fables. There is, however one quarter sessions Presentment recording how the customs officer was involved in a fracas along with other respectable citizens, some of whom acted as Parish Constables, and it is tempting to imagine that the incident occured during a search for contraband: – "Presentment of John Scaife officer of excize, Robert Gibson yeoman, Peter Towers yeoman, John Smith yeoman, William Carr yeoman, Richard Crampton paper maker all of Millthrop broke into the house of Thomas Walker and asaulted him and Eleanor his wife and broke and destroyed divers goods and chattels. A true bill."[46]

Certainly in the early nineteenth century the Customs Officer, Robert Marshall, who was based at Arnside, had little to do – so, according to J.A. Barns "some mischievous spirits once decided to provide him with work. They put out to meet an incoming vessel and received from it a large heavy cask with which they rowed rapidly up towards Sandside. The officer hurried along the shore and met them landing with their cargo but found it to contain only innocent salt water."[47]

There is much more evidence concerning the Port after 1800. Ironically the nineteenth century saw its decline and death – but it was a long time a-dying.

The expansion of Dallam Park and the obstruction of the Bela by the Weir and the New Bridge diverted all activities to the wider estuary. In 1829 the *History, Directory and Gazeteer of Cumberland and Westmorland* stated that Milnthorpe was classed as "a dependent sea port of Lancaster and has belonging to it 4 or 5 vessels of nearly 100 tons burden each but they seldom can get nearer to the town than Arnside or Haverbrack."[48] G. Tattersall in

The Lakes of England in 1836 attributed the decline to Liverpool which "had swallowed up the trade of all the adjacent (sic) country, and spared not Milnthorpe! Milnthorpe fell" and – he crowed – "the ships of Sardis are sunk all: in the depth of ages! but Milnthorpe still glories in two coal brigs and a sauceboat."

Robinson's Guide to the Lakes of 1839 paints a busier picture – "Milnthorpe – Vessels belonging to this port trade to Liverpool carrying hoops and casks, limestone, gunpowder etc. and returning with wood, merchants goods etc. Others sail to Glasgow and Annan in Scotland, carrying thicker leather, Kendal manufactures etc. bringing back grain, potatoes, etc."[50]

Many of the casks would be made in Milnthorpe. Stones recalled that "in the Large Field commonly called the Town Field was a large building used as a Hooper's shop. It supplied Goods for Liverpool by Shipping. Literally thousands of casks were required for Gunpowder, one of the main exports from 1790 when John Wakefield established gunpowder works at Sedgwick."[51] There are no other early references to the export of limestone. It is, however, claimed that in the mid-nineteenth century "at landing places along the shore such as Arnside and Sandside stone was shipped to Blackpool for constructing the promenade."

Cask timber, with charcoal and swills etc. came from local coppices. Some hard woods, especially oak, were exported mainly from Ulpha Cragg e.g. 1843, "Pieces of oak wood shipped on Board the Alex (Fleetwood) at Ulpha Cragg at Yd."[52] Moreover the Sisson Family of Leasgill are known to have carted timber from as far away as Sedbergh for export from the estuary.

Longer lengths of soft wood were imported either on board or pulled behind the vessel – as on 13 March 1854 "82 Larch Poles Dragged Alongside of the Thomas at 1d per pole 6s 10d."[54] The Foxcrofts invariably rafted timber to and from their yards at Sandside.

There were several other timber merchants. Thus in December 1810 *The Lancaster Gazette* announced "Daniel Walling begs to aquaint the publick in general. That he has opened a Timber Yard at Dixies near Milnthorpe, where he has now on Sale on favourable Terms. Pine & Pitch Pine Timber, Red & White Swedish Deals. Also Heart & Sap Laths. For further particulars apply Daniel Walling keeping sawyers the Timber he had Sawn in bulk."[55]

The saw-pit was between the present Hudson's garage and the shore, its site being covered now by the main road. It figures prominently in many descriptions of the area.

Other goods were sold along with timber. Thus the very first edition of the *Westmorland Gazette* of 23 May 1818 announced "on sale at Dixies, Sandside near Millthrop A large quantity of Red Pine Timber. Apply Mr John Burrow Dixies; or Robert Atkinson and Son of Holme; who have on Sale, Best Home made sun bleached Sheetings, and skirlings of various widths: white and Brown Sail Canvas, Linen and Cotton Candlewicks; show Threads and Green Hemp for Shoemakers, Grey Sheetings, sacks, sacking, Twine and White Ropes of all descriptions all made from best materials, and may be had at the lowest prices."

The following year (1819) the opening of the Lancaster to Kendal Canal caused alarm especially when plans were announced "to erect wharfs and warehouses at Hest Bank near the canal – thence to Kendal. As a port for the reception of vessels Hest Bank is in every respect superior to Milnthorp, there is sufficient depth of water even at lowest neap tides. . . Milnthorp will no longer possess any pretensions to the Charade of a sea port."[57] Large scale development at Hest Bank did not occur and the canal wharf at Crooklands, three miles from the village, never obtained a monopoly in transporting bulky goods. In April 1842 it was reported that "three fine vessels arrived at Milnthorpe Sandside near Dixies Inn laden with St. Helens coal where were sold at 7d. a cwt." In February 1843 under the heading "Cheap Coals" it was stated "that a cargoe had arrived at the high tide at Dixies Inn which were cheaper than those shipped by Canal. At 13s. per ton they were the best sample of coals that have been imported on the Sands for many a year." On 7 April 1849 two years after the opening of the Railway, low prices were maintained for sea coal for "a quantity of Wiggan coal has arrived at Milnthorpe Sandside at 7d. or 7½d. cwt. The owner of the same vessels intends to make regular trips up the sands which will greatly reduce the price paid at the station and the canal."[59] Nine years later, at the navigation enquiry, it was stated that "coals are sometimes brought up by vessel to Sandside and sold in the neighbourhood for miles around"[60] – but by then the port had for all intents and purposes closed.

Navigation would always have been difficult owing to the shallow depth and shifting character of the sands and channels. Apart from the ferry boat disaster of 1905[61] there appears to have been no major loss of life, though many ships ran aground. During the height of a storm at the dawn of the New Year 1834 "the Isabella, Captain Greenwood of Milnthorpe, was driven ashore at that place high and dry." Perhaps this, or a similar incident, is the origin of a still extant tradition that a large vessel was wrecked opposite "The Ship" at Sandside. Greenwood was one of the few captains based in Milnthorpe. Most Seafaring families like the Sauls and Bushes lived in Arnside. A reference of 1819 to a "boat on the Kent and Morecambe Bay" called the "The Elephant" built by George Berry might have belonged to the Berry family of Milnthorpe.

All the vessels were small and shallow drafted, having evolved from the Elizabethan pickards and sailing barges of "VII to IX

Tunnes or thereabouts occupied by III of VI men onlye in fishing of herrings and Killinges."[62]

Details of the "Eliza" built at Lancaster in 1816 are given in an indenture made on the 21st December 1819 between Saul Taylor "Mariner" of Milnthorpe and Isaac Braithwaite "Dry saltor" of Kendal. She had one deck and two masts; her length was 63 feet 5 inches, breadth 18 feet 1½ inches, the hold 9½ feet and the "Galliot has no Gallory (sic) and no Head."[63]

In 1856 Captain Richard Bush stated that the 70 year old "John" was of 52 tons new measurement and being of shallow draft "it could sail to Greens just below the Ship Inn, and it could land as safely at Dixies as at Fighting Cocks and never neuped but once or twice." Indeed when Thomas North was drowned while crossing from Foulshaw in August 1824 his horse and cart were saved by the crew of a sloop of 100 tons burthen.[65] Most vessels had only a single, fixed sail. The mast of the "John" was 30 feet high, that on Mr. Fernside's pleasure boat was 21 feet.[66] Whether an even longer mast mentioned as forming a footbridge over the Bela in 1890 was from a Milnthorpe ship is not known.[67] Sails were sometimes assisted by oars and in 1835 it was recorded that Captain Whittle's galliot "Dee," which had a mast, was brought up the bay by "16-20 rowers."

Unlike the ship captains most of the carriers of shipping goods were based in Milnthorpe, of whom the most important were the Carrs and the Berrys. Both families were resident in the area from at least the seventeenth century.

The Carrs were said to be rough and disreputable. They lived at the top of the village close to Captain Fayrer's and the Red Warehouse and gave their name to Carr's Yard, around which their unsavoury reputation lingered for generations. A violent dispute involving the family was reported in July 1823 after Edward Carr "carrier, was indicted for an assault upon Miles Sawrey carrier of the same place. Mary Sawrey wife of the prosecutor Miles stated she went with her husband to bring two cart loads of hemp for Mrs Coates from on Board the ship John on the 18th April then lying on Milnthorpe Sands. When they had nearly loaded their carts Edward Carr his brother Stephen Carr came to them and insisted upon having the goods stating that they had a general order from Mrs Coates to carry her goods. Sawrey refused (and) some very abusive words were used.

Carr struck her husband over the face. He also struck her several times over the head and breast. When Sawrey was down Carr punched him and hit witness over the leg on which occasion she was lame for a fortnight. Carr threatened to murder her. Sawrey got Carr by the mouth and tore it. Carr did not defend himself as he did not practice fighting."

*The Red Barn
Harmony Hill.*

Stephen Carr, who behaved better, managed to get his brother away, but Sawrey then struck Carr "with a whip the lash of which tore defendant's handkerchief." In the ensuing scuffle "Sawrey struck the defendant several times." Carr was found guilty and he had to pay costs and give securities to keep the peace.

The Berry's were more respectable; much given to Church going and good works. As with most successful local families they were said to be tight-fisted. Walter Berry (the third) did however have the occasional flutter; for in 1854 he noted "Wm. Minikin Sandside Dr. To a wager Bett at Cross Keys Inn £10." He lost and paid up in instalments.

In the eighteenth century the Berrys lived at Gandy Nook and occupied the premises lower down the Square later used by the Clarkes, another carrying family. (Still, incidentally, in business, 1987).[71] In about 1826 they took over Bridge End (Birkett's Farm and various shipping concerns from the Foxcrofts. Here they kept a stable of 30 horses for carrying, hiring to local inns and, to the Wilson's of Dallam for wood drawing.[72] For four generations the head of the family was called Walter. The Day Books of the third Walter Berry provide the valuable details about the shipping trade and show conclusively how busy the port was. This is confirmed by notes made from the Berry's papers by Edward Stones called an "abridged collection of Vessels which sailed betwixt Liverpool and the Port of Milnthorpe." Stones mentions six ships the "Dee," "James," "John," "Thomas," "Tickler" and "William." In 1839 cargoes were taken from the "James" in February, from the "Tickler," "James" and "John" in March, from the "Thomas," "James," "John" and "Tickler" in April, from the "Tickler" and "John" in July, from the "William" in August, from "James" in

Berry's Barn, Sandside.

September, "Dee," "Tickler," "William" in October and the "Dee" in December. All vessels carried mixed cargoes, the most numerous goods being: 20 consignments of sugar, 6 of soda, 5 sheets of lead, 5 of paint, several loads of iron bars, rice, coffee, "chists" of tea, 15,600 Horns and 7 sacks of vetches. He also stated that there were "always Hoops, swills, Basket rods ready to be removed by Foxcroft and Jeremy Evans the Timber Merchants and Ship builders of Milnthorpe."[73]

There were, on average, 3.4 sailings per month between 1839 and 1844, 14 per month 1845-46, 14.5 1846-47. During this period nearly 60% of goods were carried to Kendal as against 20% to Milnthorpe; about the same proportion being brought back for export.[74] A decline set in 1848 after the railway was opened. The Berry's were quick to jump on the locomotive band wagon for on 5 October 1847 is the account "1 Horse to Railwy station 8d." and "To Lancaster and Carlisle Railway Co. 4 Horses 12s." but it was not until 1854 that trips to the station at 35 in the year exceeded those to the port at 33.

In addition the vessels noted by Stones, Berry mentions frequently the "Hope" and the "New Thomas" and occasionally the "Elizabeth," "Alice" (of Fleetwood), "Amelia," "Victoria," "Dove," "Eskham," "Isobelle," "Empress," "Acorn" and "Windermere."

Cargoes were always mixed. Among the first noted were, on 24 October 1838:-

"To 15 Barrels of Flour to Kendal and 15 to Milnthorp   11s8d.
To 1 Barrel of Hrings to Kendal and 1 to Milnthorp from board

Windermere   1s.

To 5 Bags and 10 Mats of sugar from Board Windermere To John
   Ireland, Kendal   8d.

To 2 Casks of wine from Board Windermere 8 and 2 galls   6s.10d.

To 1 Cask Cream of Tarter from Bd. Do. 3 and 4 at
5d.   2s.11d.

To 1 Cask of Tin from Board Do.   1s.3d.

To 11 Bags of Wool from Board Do. 19 and 14 at 3d.

   George Whittaker Milnthorp

To 6 Boxes of Raisens from Board Windermere   1s.

30 Bars and 27 Bundles of Iron from Bd. Do.   16s.3d.

185 Bars and 6 plates of Iron from Bd. Do.   19s.6d.

To Robert Dent 1 Cask lead Pipes from Board Windermere."

Food accounted for about a quarter of all imports. Thus on 28
August 1839 from on board "William" Messrs Rigby & Banks of
Kendal obtained "12 lumps of sugar, from Board Tickler, 2
Punchions of Treacall, from Bd. do. To 1 terce of Bastard sugar Bd.
do." and "1 sack of nuts, 9 Half Chist of Lemmons from Bd.
Isabella to Windermere."

Occasional fish imports included in 1842 "1 Barrel of Red
Herrings for Huddlestone of Milnthorp from Board Dee."

Liquor came regularly by sea:

"October 1838

To Mr R Thompson of Milnthorp
   1 Cask of Gin from Board John 20 Gals.   10s.

In 1840:-

"To Mrs Hudson
   To 7 Barrels of Porter from Board John   2s.
      1 Cask of Ginger Beer from Bd. Do.   1/6
      1 Hogshead of Gin from Board James
                       47 at ½d. 1/4
   To 1 Cask of Cider from Bd. Windermere   8d.
      1 Cask of Porter and 1 Box of Cegars
                       2 for 8 9d."

Raw material amounted to about one third of imports and
included saltpetre for Wakefield's Gunpowder Works (e.g. 300 Bags
from Board Thomas on 28 August 1839), Bobin Squares, generally
for Jacksons of Holmescales, and primitive chemicals for the textile
industry and apothecaries like "5 Casks of Bleaching Powder from
Board tickler to Burneside" and "1 Hogshead of oil from Board
Dee and 1 pipe of sperm oil from Board Tickler" in December
1838. Metal came in rough loads like 160 Bushells of Rods, 85 Bars
and 15 Bundles of Iron in 1847. Milnthorpe Workhouse imported
materials for twine and harden manufacturing and for oakem
picking and in 1839 the Governor received "10 Bales of Jute from
Board Dee, 31 cwts of White ropes from Board John, 1 Trufs of Flax

and 31 cwt white Ropes from Board Dee" 1842.

Regular miscellaneous goods were Furniture, often measured in "Parchels," Grates, paint and whitening, marble for Helsington works and for G Webster of Kendal. Odd items included "To 20 Bundles of Rushes from Board John 1/- June 1841 and "To Trustees of Late James Briggs Cargo 1 Tombsone in 13 Peices from Board Dee Freight 14s.5d."

In the last days of the port large quantities of bricks were brought in. The Rev. Robert Wilson Evans obtained several consignments when building Heversham vicarage in c. 1842-4, while in 31 January 1857 "the Hope arrived here with 800 Fire Bricks (paid) from Richard Ashton and Co Liverpool at 27/6 per 1000 £1" and on 13 July 1860 1500 Fire Bricks shipped from Board the Acorn (Capt. Thomas Foreshaw).

Exports were equally varied. Thus on 26 May 1843 was the account

"To 10 Peices of Bagging Shiped per Dee 10/3

5 Peices of Sacking shiped per Dee 2/6

John Dent Hutton Roof 12s.

John Clement Liverpool Dr.

To 13 Bags of Brush stocks from Stenton shiped per Dee 7/ 7d.

To 6 Grindstones Shiped per Dee"

and later in the year

"To 12 large Grindstones from Thomas Dent Hutton Roof shipped per Tickler 4s. also item picking Tickler ladder up 1/6d." Wood products were quite frequent like "1400 Baled rods shiped per Hope 2/- 30,000 Basket Rods Shiped per Hope at 2/- £3."

In quantity and value salt and gunpowder predominated. Thus in February 1843 62 "Tons of salt from Frodsome to Milnthrop Sandside at 5/-" while in January 1848 the Hope brought in "10 tons of Dirty Salt and 2 tons of Salt Rock from Northwick" followed by further imports in April, August and November. Average cargoes ranged from 45 to 65 tons. The last salt imports come on 8 December 1851 when the Elizabeth brought in 15 tons of Lump Stowed Salt. By March the following year the railway had taken over the trade. The main "salt ship," the Hope, continued to trade with Milnthorpe for on 14 January 1854 it was reported that "this trading vessel from Liverpool to Milnthorpe was wrecked upon Milnthorpe Sands some time ago. She was yesterday raised up again and is now afloat once more and is to proceed to undergo her repairs."

As well as being potentially dangerous, gunpowder must have been an awkward cargo to handle owing to the number and varied size of barrels and casks. Thus on 8 August 1837 Messrs Wakefield and Bainbridge day book notes:-

The Dallam Wheel with Scout Bank on the left.

"To 240 Half Barrels of Gunpowder shiped per John   £2
To 5 Tons of Brimstone from Board John at 6/-   £1 10s.
To 8 Empty Casks from Sidgewicke to vesal   3s.6d.
Paid to Sailors for filling Brimstone   2s.6d.
To 100 Bags of Salt Petter from Board John
       7 tons 7 cwt 2 at 6   £244"

Another cargo shipped on the Alice in 1848 consisted of 40 whole casks, 210 half casks and 620 quarter casks, while in 1854 the Elizabeth took on board 165 whole casks, 396 half casks, 1020 quarter casks and 1580 fifths casks. The very last shipping account in Walter Berry's Day books was on 9 January 1861: "To 1150 fifths of Powder from GateBeck to Board John £3 16s. 8d."

By 1861 the port was as good as dead. The John continued to trade from the outer estuary using the Blackstone Quay until some years later it was wrecked at Garston and William Tattersall's yacht the Barleycorn sailed from Arnside during the 1870's. The death blow, delivered finally by the Lancaster to Ulverston (later the Furness) Railway's Arnside viaduct had long been forseen. Amongst the dozens of toasts proposed at the Milnthorpe Friendly Society's Whit Monday dinner at the Cross Keys in 1852 was one from Mr Lee to "all connected with the trade of Liverpool and the greater ports" While Mr Grocott thundered that "their town and

Pile Driving at the mouth of the Bela c.1900
Walter Berry (in Top Hat and Whiskers) fourth from right.

trade depended on the navigation of the bay and the man who proposed to cut it off must be insane and the victim of fraud and malice to an extraordinary degree."[76] *The Westmorland Gazette*, taking its cue from the Corporation of Kendal, championed the shipping interests. In December 1856 it enquired "Are the Westmorland people (who are) deriving positive and prospective advantages from the existing navigation at Milnthorpe to be sacrificed to obviate the presumed laches (sic) of the Ulverston and Lancaster Company's Officials? . . . within 12 miles of the port of Milnthorpe are 10 woolen mills, 2 flax mills, two gunpowder works, 4 paper mills, 3 snuff mills, 6 or 8 corn mills, 8 bobbin mills, 3 mills for preparing dye wares, five iron foundries, two extensive breweries, several tanneries, wholesale grocers, flour dealers, wool staplers etc. besides an agricultural district using largely of manures as may be supported from the skilful and enterprising character of the farmers of the neighbourhood."[77]

By February 1857 it was feared that the original requirement made by the Lords of Admiralty "that the navigation of the Kent should be left free for vessels through an opening space in the railway"[78] was going to be amended in favour of a fixed viaduct. The resulting controversy led to an enquiry conducted at the Cross Keys in March 1857 between Admiralty Commissioners, the railway company and representative of the local interests headed by the Mayor of Kendal John Whitwell. Local opinion was barely mollified by claims that between 20,000 and 40,000 acres could be reclaimed, for this would only benefit existing proprietors, while the hope that a 50 foot span in the closed bridge would "of course offer no impediment to a screw steamer with a movable funnel" did not console captains of sailing ships.[79]

The captains were led by Richard Bush (of the John) who spoke of the "great disadvantages to have a closed bridge instead of an open one. It would remove Milnthorpe more than two miles more from the port – more than double the present distance." He admitted that the trade varied as "when channel was on the other side no landings could be made at Sandside."[80] Walter Berry explained that the channel had been on the Foulshaw side for four years – even so he had imported 100 tons of salt and twenty tons of bricks within the last 12 months.

For the Sandside traders Miles Thompson, who had lived there all his life said he had seen 26 vessels within the last 10 years out of Fleetwood and Sandside and Mr Fearnside argued that the viaduct would prevent his rafting timber at Sandside and as a result it would cost ½d per foot more. Moreover he often went in his pleasure boat to Morecambe and Arnside. George Whittaker, grocer, iron-monger, and general dealer, Milnthorpe, who imported on average 130 tons a year, stated that carriage would go up from 2s. to 3s. from Arnside. Walter Berry went further and said his charges were already 2s. 6d. per ton from the Fighting Cocks to Dixies and 3s. 6d. from The fighting Cocks to Milnthorpe. All the carters agreed that "Arnside was a very long way down. . . the road was very difficult along the shore and almost impassable. . . and . . . no doubt, it was for the railway company's advantage to increase the expense of the sea route." Indeed the railway had already reduced its rates by a third and Mr Foster of Bela Mills admitted that 300 tons of his goods were already being transported by rail as against 42 tons by vessels.[81]

There was no sentiment in business in the Victorian age and hard economic facts such as these destroyed the case of the Corporation, the captains and the carriers. The Admiralty allowed the fixed bridge – and Milnthorpe ceased to be a port.

Some of the port's facilities survived. No carrier went out of business. The branch line built to connect Arnside to the main line at Hincaster resuscitated Sandside and though the railway itself has gone, in the late twentieth century Ormrods and Clarks coal yards and Broombys and the Builders Supply timber yards occupy the same, or adjacent, sites as those belonging to the port's merchants. Of the port's taverns however, only The Ship and The Fighting Cocks remained. When in 1882 the Dixies Inn was being sold the auctioneer, Mr Derome, predicted that Sandside might become a rival to Southport and change its name to Northport[82] He was wrong; because of lack of trade the Dixies Inn itself, closed. By the turn of the century the Port was only a memory. When in 1902 J. Barnes mentioned the old ships in a Milnthorpe barber's shop an elderly man replied: "I knew 'em; I knew 'em. There was Tickler, and Hope and Old John. They used to come up to Sandside and unload at that aald warehouse beside the limekill."

Then with another chuckle as old times rose before his mind "What, aald Bellman used to be yan an 'em; poor aald fella, he deed i' Millthrop Workhouse last week."[83]

KEY

1.	Haverbrack	17.	Royal Oak, demolished c.1925
2.	Dallam	18.	The 'Painters' penthouse
3.	Kent estuary	19.	Main Street
4.	Cartmel Fell	20.	Cross Keys
5.	Birkett's Farm	21.	White Lion (later Daffady's shoe shop)
6.	Probably keg and barrel workshop in Town Field	22.	Fish Shop, demolished 1880. Site of Institute
7.	King's Arms (Barclay's Bank)	23.	Strands Meadow (playing field from 1900)
8.	Old Flowerden, demolished 1860	24.	Strands Cottages, formerly Lower Mills
9.	Fleet House, demolished 1966 (Nat West site)	25.	Paper Mill, demolished 1850
10.	Cottages, demolished c.1872 on site of Stoneclough	26.	Bull's Head (original site)
11.	Mallow House	27.	Malt Kiln, later Fawcett's
12.	Green Cottage	28.	Large house in square, later Midland Bank
13.	Barn/warehouse	29.	Royal Oak Barn, later Assembly Room
14.	Coach and Horses	30.	Market Cross
15.	Bodkin Hall, demolished 1866 and replaced by St. Thomas's School	31.	The Square
16.	Vine House	32.	The Green
		33.	Ash tree, cut down in 1875

The picture was almost certainly taken from the look-out platform on the roof of Harmony Hall. Note that the Market Cross is without the lock-up which existed beneath it from 1845-62. Traditionally the picture was taken in 1845 - a very early date for a photograph. It cannot be later than 1866.

4

Markets and Fairs
of Milnthorpe

The Market and Fair are Milnthorpe's closest links with the Middle Ages. Though they gained official recognition at the same time in the fourteenth century their origin and purposes differ. Markets aimed to supply the basic needs of the population settled in the district. Held weekly, they had a limited circle of attraction, drawing most custom from less that five miles away. Some traders would come from slightly further afield, and to serve them markets were held in neighbouring places on different days. Hence Burton-in-Kendal's market was held on Tuesday, Ambleside's on Wednesday, Kirkby Lonsdale's on Thursday and Kendal's on Saturday. Milnthorpe market was at first held on Wednesday; later it was transferred to Friday.[1]

Milnthorpe was an ideal market centre since it was situated at the junction of the main street leading from the port to the old High Road at Crooklands and the minor, but locally important, north-south routes. The existence of the port and of mills from early times provided a broader and more consistent base for commerce than in most other local communities where dependence was mainly on subsistence agriculture. Shops and, hence, shopping, did not spread from bigger place to small market towns like Milnthorpe until the eighteenth century. Until then markets and pedlars supplied the sparse and scattered population. Even in the nineteenth century Milnthorpe market was not totally eclipsed although the village had up to 20 shops by that time.

All Directories and Gazeteers call Milnthorpe a "market town" and state that Market Day was Friday. Garnett in 1912 noted the decline: "the weekly market, though still held on Friday, has never been of importance."[2] The regular weekly market disappeared during the First World War. Even so stalls, often selling garden and orchard gluts; fish vans and potato carts appeared from time to time. In the inter-war period a regular visitor was an oriental gentleman who sold "genuine antique Persian Rugs" from the Market Cross.[3] He and other traders were charged either a shilling or a half-crown by either the Manor bailiff or (after 1930) by the Parish Council toll collector.[4] Hence the market rights never lapsed and so when the demand arose again the market could be revived.

By contrast to the purely local functions of markets, fairs were periodic meeting places for prosperous merchants and for wholesale exchange. Most old English fairs date from the re-birth of commerce that occurred throughout Western Europe in the thirteenth and early fourteenth centuries. Quite often they were associated with the wool trade and there are some 35 fairs in Cumbria which date from the peak "woolen period."[5] As trade developed fair and market dues and/or the sale of rights provided a lucrative revenue for Monarchs and Lords. The latter had first to obtain a charter from the Crown either by purchase or as a reward or inducement for service. Epidemics of Charter grants coincided with critical times for the King and Kingdom.

The early fourteenth century saw Westmorland and Furness involved in helping Edward I hammer the Scots; later under Edward II they were responsible for defending the north western marches from the retaliation of Robert the Bruce, and lesser raiders. Though Edward III turned the Scottish tide Charter grants continued. Locally Edward I granted Ulverston a charter in 1280, Edward II granted one to Beetham in 1311 and Edward III gave one to Brough in 1331, Kirkby Stephen in 1352 and Morland in 1363. An older Charter originally granted by Richard I to Kendal was confirmed by Edward II in 1310.[6]

The Heversham Charter is the one that founded Milnthorpe Market and Fair. Several sources state that the first charter was granted to Alexander de Windesore (or Wyndesure) by Edward I in c.1280 and that the one granted to another Alexander, his grandson, in 1334 was just a confirmation. Nevertheless it is on the 1334 Charter that the subsequent, and still operative, rights are based. It stated: "Grant to Alexander de Wyndesore Lord of two parts of the vill of Heversham and to the Kings Clerk John de Wodehouse, parson of the Church there and lord of the third part of the same vill that Alexander and his heirs and John and his successors, parsons of the said Church, shall have a weekly market there on Wednesday and a yearly fair on the feast of St Peter and St Paul the Apostles."[7]

Although granted to the Heversham manor both the market and fair seem always to have been held at Milnthorpe. It was probably

the fair that determined the site and size of the market square.
Lying west of the slope of the Milnthorpe Green Common (a
convenient grazing ground for fair stock and a pitch for travellers)
the area of the square was fairly level and lay close to the main
roads. It is comparatively large: even the paved area of about 2000
sq. yards is larger than the market places of Kendal, Kirkby
Lonsdale and Burton. Adding the greens to the west and north, the
market and fair areas were as large as those found in the nucleated
"green villages" of Yorkshire and the Midlands. This size surely
illustrates the ancient importance of Milnthorpe Fair.

An advantage for fair stock was a supply of fresh running water
on the green. The main village well, always known as the Fountain,
was at first opposite the Sun Tavern close to where the old road from
Beetham crossed the green near the present south-west corner of
the church yard. In c.1830 Henry Smithies paid for its being
culverted to a more central position east of the Market Cross,[8]
where the outlet was sunk in a circular paved area, part of which still
survives below later tarmac. At first the fountain was marked by a
single stone until (it is said) Miss Rawlinson fell into it when coming
from Evensong on a dark night in c.1895. It was then partially
fenced round with a row of rockery stones which survived (though
much damaged by traffic) into the 1980's. Until piped water from
Lupton Reservoir reached the village in c.1910 the Fountain was the
chief water supply for the village. The water was claimed to be of the
purest quality although in c.1900 the Medical Officers of Health
feared that it was contaminated because the feeder streams ran
under the churchyard. Each household had its 'pump-stick' to
thrust up the pipe and dam back the water so that it would flush out
after a moment or two to fill the bucket or jug quickly.[9]

Underneath an ordinary drain grating the spring can still be seen
bubbling away today. Even in the drought year 1976 it never ran
dry. It has not been accessible since September 1942 following the
visit of an elephant. The Parish Council minutes noted that "the
reinforced concrete cover of the outflow water pipe was broken into
fragments in the first instance by an elephant attending a travelling
circus."[10] Apparently the animals had been paraded from Milnthorpe
Station en route to the circus field on Beetham road and they
naturally called at the traditional watering place used by showmen
for generations. Unfortunately, the school was just coming out and
the crush of spectators caused the elephant to fall over the stones
and smash the outlet. Solemnly the Parish Council decided that to
avoid "future re-currence" the whole spring should be concreted
over. The solution worked – no elephant has come to grief
since.

It is possible that the earlier weekly markets might not have used
the square which would be used only by the fairs. Neddy Stones

recalled a tradition that the original Market Cross was opposite the Cross Keys at the cross roads and indeed what appears to be a cross is marked on Jeffrey's map of 1770 at that point. The Cross Keys was re-built in c.1821 and in 1823 the market square cross was described as "the new cross."[11] It is, therefore, possible that the cross was moved when the inn was rebuilt. Certainly the sandstone base, capital and the regularly vandalised and replaced ball finial (there is in fact no "cross") appear to be of the late eighteenth century. The more weather-worn column is of a different, lighter coloured stone and is probably earlier. In it is a socket – perhaps for shackles used when the cross served as a whipping post. Round the hexagonal limestone steps were iron fetters for securing felons. These unfortunately disappeared in the 1960s, nobody knows where or how.

The cross was also the village crying stone. Here markets, fairs and monarchs were proclaimed, official notices from excommunications to the banning of movement of stock during cattle plagues were read; village tub-thumpers have had their say from it in every age and in the 1920s and 1930s socialist and fascist[12] orators used it as a platform. Various Christian ministers ranging from Anglican vicars, eulogising at the accession and death of sovereigns, to the Quakers, Salvationists and, in modern times, Revivalists of "the Full Gospel Church" have preached from it; drunks have propped themselves up on it and on several occasions exponents of the temperance movement were derided by a mob paid by the innkeepers. For several years in the 1980s the village Carnival Queen's Coronation took place at the cross. It was, therefore, fitting that in 1953 the cross became the first structure in the village to be scheduled for preservation as an ancient monument and that its silhouette is used as a badge for Milnthorpe Corinthians football team and as the logo on Parish Council stationery.

Although the 1334 charter stated that the annual fair should be on 29 June the feast of St Peter (patron of Heversham Church) it was held on 12 May from at least the seventeenth century. This might have been to assist stock farmers, for Milnthorpe Fair was primarily a mart for cattle and sheep. In the nineteenth century, apart from the May fair, there were "butchers markets" in May and Christmas time and a "back end" fair in October. The latter, for a time, was well attended, but the May fair was always "The" Milnthorpe Fair. Though "Twelfth of May – Fair day" was the rule (except when it fell on Sundays) trading covered several days before the twelfth. In 1833 and 1849[13] nearly all the stock had been sold by the twelfth. In 1884 most dealing took place on Saturday the 10th but those who held back got better prices on the Monday.[14] A reason for early dealing was that dues were paid on all cattle and sheep leaving the market on the Fair day; trading on other days was not chargeable.

'Backend' Fair c.1900.

Although one third of market dues belonged to Dallam, the Levens manor controlled the Fair and the Levens steward collected them. Even allowing for waves of inflation the dues were not high: 1 penny per head of cattle, 2d per head for bulls, 5d. per score for sheep.[15] In 1890 Captain Bagot "considerately determined to forego them. Thus another remnant of the old feudal custom has become a thing of the past."[16] Nevertheless a free fair day did not prevent early trading and the next year heads of oxen began to fill the meadows several days before the twelfth.[17] In 1902 50 sheep were sold while being driven from Sandside station,[18] in 1903 "only a few score were left on the green" on fair day and in 1904 only 100 were sold, the rest having gone in the previous two days.[19] Again in 1910 it was noted "that the day fixed by statute has been ignored... which frequently causes unnecessary trouble to buyers from a distance who are guided by an almanack."[20] Even so, in 1913 dealing began on the eighth, whilst in 1915 large amounts of business were done on Monday the 11th so that on the Tuesday there "was absolutely nothing doing though more stock had been shown than for some years."[21] At the turn of the century considerable business was done at Sandside and the Parish Council twice complained to the manager of the Furness Railway about what amounted to a rival fair being set up in the station yard and on the nearby roads.[22] Yet it was on the central village that the droves of cattle and sheep converged, "the hubbub pulls to the market square eddying round the old stone steps in the middle and surging up to the railings of the church at the end."

The hustle and bustle of the fair began with the arrival of stock in the meadows. Cattle tended to be penned in Riley fields, in the Town Field and in the Strands meadows. As compensation for sleepless nights caused by bellowing of disturbed cattle, villagers were free to milk the cows.[24] Before the cattle were driven into the square, fences were put round the main houses and the iron slots into which they were fixed remained in the pavement outside Fleet House and Stoneleigh until the 1950's. Sheep were kept on the Firs and on Rigney Bank before the flocks were offered for sale on the green. Smaller stock, including geese, which sometime were tethered to the railings of Laburnum House, were also on sale in odd corners.[25] More spectacularly, Milnthorpe Fair was noted for its show of horses. Stallions and other horses were put through their paces by panting grooms running along Park Road, deals being struck at the Cross Keys and the King's Arms.

A few accidents are recorded: a "hardly driven cow" entered Daffady's shoe shop in 1894[26] and broke a glass case with its horn, while in 1900 Mr W. Thexton was knocked against the wall of Mrs Knight's shop by a runaway horse and ended up with a badly bruised shoulder and his face covered in blood.[27] Some beasts were either abandoned or lost. In 1859 Mr Tyson announced "Found at Milnthorpe Fair. A small black and white cow with Irish Horns, in calf and apparently will calf about July next. The owner may have it restored upon application to Mr Tyson (at the Blue Bell Heversham) and payment of all reasonable expenses."[28] The lost column reported in 1874:- "Lost at Milnthorpe Fair: Three Yearling Bullocks marked with a knife on the off side huggars and a mark with riddle on the near side. Anyone restoring same to Mr. Walter Berry Farmer of Milnthorpe will be rewarded."[29]

Something of the flurry of the fair was contained in a rather fanciful account of 1880: - "Everything breathed of Spring, from the level waste on the left came, as Longfellow put it, 'an odour of brine from the ocean' which was particularly invigorating. Milnthorpe reached the ideal designated by the real. The Fair was at its height and the little town had a very much overcrowded appearance. Whether one liked it or not one's observation of the spot where (sic) continually being interfered with by an indiscreet somebody or nobody (it didn't matter which if they were of equal bulk) stepping on ones pet corns."[30] In the *Splendid Fairing* of 1919 Constance Holme, who having been brought up at Owlet Ash must have witnessed many a Milnthorpe Fair, described the "tides of life swept" into the streets at fair time as "life at its fullest, as it is known to the northern farmer and his kind, the public recognition in a given place of the great and intimate system of which he is part. . . Into every conversation before so long some grand bull-calf or pedigree shearling was sure to push its way. Moving among the warm human tides was like moving in a flood, while overhead, low almost as the roofs, the mist drifted and the sky drooped." This was probably the back-end fair for in the autumn a smoke haze regularly drifts over Milnthorpe's shallow valley – though the sky also "droops" at other times.

Some indication of the size of the fair, market changes and prices is provided by nineteenth century press reports. Thus, in 1819 in the *Westmorland Gazette's* first report of the fair "a great show of cattle was noted"[32] but in 1824[33] the fair was "only tolerably attended" – even so cattle were 'in demand', there were "good things in fat, there were many large bulls both long and shorthorn and many sheep were sold to traders from Ireland'." Also in 1833 stallions were in abundance, one dealer buying seven at a time.[34] A dozen stallions were shown at the "splendid fair" of 1851[35] and again in 1857[36] but by 1863[37] the number had dropped to seven. By the 1880's the parade of entire horses was said to be "almost a thing of the past." The highest price recorded at Milnthorpe was ten thousand guineas paid "for Mr Moffatt's 'Laughing Stock' by Mr Hutton bone setter of London and late of Milnthorpe" in 1874.[38] Probably the most prestigious sale occurred in 1893 when Henry Johnson disposed of several hundred head of cattle at good prices, "several being purchased for the Prince of Wales at Sandringham."[39]

The most serious threat to the fair occurred shortly after the opening of the railway. A wool fair was started at the Station Inn in 1850 and on July 12th one buyer paid nearly £1000 for wool which brought 9d to 1/- per pound.[40] It soon declined, however, when the dealers realised they could get a better price by transporting their wool by rail to the textile towns. A fortnightly cattle fair at the station was founded in April 1849 following a meeting at the Cross Keys when subscriptions had been collected to defray the expense of pens and stalls.

This alternative market might have caused the reported drop in the number of cattle at the May Fairs of 1852[41] and 1853. This was compensated by more sheep, though they only attracted dull prices. By 1857 there were more people than for many years at the May Fair and as there were "fewer cattle" prices were high. The station fair seems to have disappeared by c.1860. In 1863 and 1865 the greens were crowded again, though the latter year was wet. Bad weather marred the 1871 and 1874 fairs but generally Milnthorpe Fair was one of those lucky events which always seem to get good weather. One of the last fairs, however, in the 1920's was struck by a freak snow storm followed by frost which "froze the swallows to the telephone wires."[43] In May 1929 a brief paragraph appeared under "Milnthorpe News" in the *Westmorland Gazette*" reporting that the Annual Spring 'show' on Friday was remarkably slow owing to the backwardness of the season. This was the last report of the May Fair.

By 1929 the Back End Fair was also a thing of the past, apparently dying during the Great War. It was much newer in origin than the May Fair, only starting in c.1818. Autumn Live Stock Sales to provide fresh meat in winter reflected the great agricultural improvements of the late eighteenth and early nineteenth centuries. Until that time most stock had been killed at Martinmas and the flesh salted down or "dried". As late as 1822 J. Briggs stated that "so strong, however, are ancient habits that beef is dried in this county even when fresh meat can be obtained at all seasons, though dried beef is allowed to cost double the price of fresh." This conservatism might have accounted for the relatively slow growth of the Back End Fair which reached its height only in the 1850's and 1860's. Even then it never received as much publicity as the May fair though in 1852 it was noted as being "very busy with sheep good and plentiful but gilt cows scarce and dear."[54]

The fair was still of sufficient importance in 1902 for the Parish Council to ask the Rural District Council to transfer its date from the 17th October to the second Thursday in October; it being proposed to move the May fair from the traditional twelfth to the second Thursday in May. Nevertheless the customary, if flexible, dates continued.[59]

There had long been a butcher's market prior to the May fair but a Christmas market was started in the 1840's. In 1847 the *Westmorland Gazette* commented that "if the farmers in the neighbourhood would only bring their fat to the market they would dispose of them and it would become a first rate market for fat."[60] The hope was realised by Thomas Briggs of Milnthorpe who displayed in 1850 and 1851 "very fine wether sheep probably the finest on the market which were fed by Mrs Hudson of Fir Tree Cottage Milnthorp and reflected great credit on the feeder."[61] In succeeding years Mr J. Smith of Haverflatts and Thomas Clemens and Thomas Mashiter of Ackenthwaite displayed fine Christmas fat stock. Briggs however, continued to have the finest stock, offering beasts weighing 15 stone a quarter and 18 weeks calves at 48lbs a quarter in 1859. On the same market G. Squires of Haverflatts offerred 4 half bred ewes averaging 35lbs a quarter.[62] Milnthorpe butchers were still noted in the 1870's W. Middleton and W. Mason being repeatedly praised for "splendid" carcases of beef and Mr R Clarke for "a lot of excellent sheep."

Unlike Kendal, Ulverston and Penrith, Milnthorpe did not have a hiring fare for general agricultural labourers. The harvest hiring fairs, made notorious because of the Rev. Nicholas Padwick's opposition to Sunday hiring, were more informal and flexible events - and could take place from the end of July until the second week in September depending on the state of the crops. In poor years gangs of men, including many Irish labourers, could turn up for three or four weeks before being taken on. Many of the disturbances, like the occasion in 1841 when several pugilists, stripped for action, met on the green before morning service, were probably prompted as a way of alleviating the boredom of hanging around.[70] As at the half year hirings, the custom of the unhired men either wearing or chewing a straw to indicate their availability was observed, the very worst labourer being "the last straw." Once hired the bargain was always sealed in the ale houses which opened at dawn for the purpose.[71]

Wages fluctuated according to the availability of labour. Thus in 1839 the *Westmorland Gazette* sympathised with the lot of some employers "for the wet season militates against the farmers as on Sunday last as far as 28s or 30s a week wet or fair with victuals and drink into the bargain - was called for - a severe and heavy tax in impoverished weather."[72] This rate was exceptional. In the 1890's 25s a week was the usual rate and in August 1914, when quite a number of men had already joined up, the "best men" were only getting 30s. When in 1915 some men, prompted by a very real labour shortage, demanded 50s a week they were met with laughter and had to settle for half as much. Normal rates were much less.[73] The lowest recorded was 7s 9d per week in 1843 whith "a farmer in the neighbourhood only giving 1½d per hattock for shearing."[74] In 1847 when some hundreds of men but only twelve masters appeared in a "dull market",[75] the rate was 11s but dropped in 1851 to 9s rising to 10s to 13s in the late 1850s[76] and, thereafter, varying between 15 and 21s with a low top rate of 16s in 1904.[77] In addition to cash the men got their board and in theory "lived-in" although few would be lucky enough even to share an attic bed; most slept in the barns.

For brief periods Milnthorpe had a corn market on the square. Curwen states "that it started in November 1810 when wheat sold at 56s per load of 14 score; oats at 28s6d per load and barley at 20s per three winchester bushels; the market came to an end when the canal to Kendal was opened in 1819."[77] Also killed was the greater market at Burton which already in 1819 was described as being of "very small importance."

Milnthorpe's corn market, however, revived. In 1837 the *Westmorland Gazette* stated that "at Milnthorpe a new grain market was opened on Friday yesterday December 14. That its effects will be felt as highly detrimental to our market in this town

(Kendal) is equally certain."[79] Prices noted were 30 loads of wheat sold at 40 to 30s, 100 loads of oats at 5s10d per stone. Other commodities included pigs at 5s10d each, potatoes 6d per stone while meal and beans were also on the market. In March 1839 the *Westmorland Gazette* "subjoin(ed) the following articles with the prices to show the importance attached to this market but recently established:

English Wheat per load...46s to 48s
Irish Wheat per load...41s to 42s
English oats per stone...14d to 15d
Irish Oats per stone...15d to 17d
Copenhagen Flour per barrel...46s to 47s
English Flour per stone 3s10d to 4s6d
Oatmeal per stone...2s8d to 2s10d
Barley per windle...15s to 16s
Veal per lb...5½d to 6d
Butter per lb...11½d to 1s
Onions per stone...2s8d to 2s10d
Potatoes per stone...7d to 8d
Eggs...24 for 1s"

Great things must have been expected for a market shelter was erected in the south-west corner of the square close to the market cross and a market hall was proposed. The high hopes were not realised and in 1842 it was reported "the quantity of grain brought into the market on Friday last was very limited as the temporary market house has been disposed of by private treaty."[81] On New Year's Day 1847 "a few farmers in the neighbourhood of Milnthorpe brought a quantity of grain into the market in order that the corn market might again be reopened...it is hoped other farmers might follow the example... Mr. Richard Dennison of Whasset showed an excellent sample of Dunnus corn and 20 stone loads met with ready sale."[82] Nevertheless, cheaper canal, and soon railway, transported corn meant that local farmers in what was primarily a stock area could not compete, and Milnthorpe corn market was abandoned.

Though of considerable economic interest it was the fun, and pageantry, of the fair that was mainly important to most of the crowds who flocked to it. On fair days school children were given, or took, a holiday. Boys from the National School got an extra holiday a week or so before the May fair in order to "help" with rook shooting. Rook pie was a traditional cheap delicacy in the inns and taverns at fair time, most of the "black-game" being donated to the landlords free or for the price of the shot. In 1869 15½ dozen rooks were taken up by the inn keepers[83] and an unspecified number "greater than for many years past" in 1871 when broods were said to have hatched ten days earlier than normal.[84] May rook shoots continued into the twentieth century for in 1907 it was noted "that the larger colonies of ten years ago" had been dispersed and had been split up into a dozen smaller colonies.[85] Though all were within a few miles radius the dispersal made the informal shoots less practicable.

The fun of the fair reached its peak after the main business had been concluded. Even so it seems strange that the fair was not, in fact, proclaimed until mid-day on the 12th of May when many traders had left. The proclamation was read in great style by the steward of the Manor. For three generations until c.1910 the stewards were all from the Huddleston family from the Malt Kiln at Glasgow House. Traditionally the Mayor and Corporation of Kendal attended. In 1843 the splendid noon-time procession was "headed by the Borough Mace and sword bearers and excellent brass band and also accompanied by the head steward at Levens and a numerous suite of at least 60 gentry walked the fair. A gayer sight had not been seen at Milnthorpe for a number of years past."[86]

A new proclamation was drawn up annually but it followed the form recorded in 1702 when the fair was held under the auspices of Colonel James Graham:

Manerium de Milthrop in Comitatu Westm'Land. A Proclamac'on for Milthropp Faire primo May Anuatim:

The Honble James Grahme Esquire, Lord of this Manour doth in her Majties name strictly charge and Comand all manner of persons of what degree soever which are here present or shall be here assembled dureing the time of this present Faire or Markett that they and every of them doe keep her Majties peace. And that none of them doe make Affrays, Tussles or Hubleshews, Pick any Quarrells or use any disturbance of the Peace upon paine and Forfyture of Forty shillings for every party soe offending within this Towne or the Liberties and precincts thereof and for every partaker Twenty shillings and their bodies to prision there to remaine dureing the sd James Grahme's pleasure. And also it is hereby Comanded that noe manner of person or persons doe bear or carry at any time within this Fair or Markett here kept this day Any unlawfull Weapons as Halberts, Pitchforks, Bills or any other Invasive or defensive weapons, Saveing such persons or Officers as by the said James Grahme are assigned, and for good Order to be kept dureing this said Faire time upon paine of forfeiture of such weapons and their bodies to Prison as aforesaid. And further it is Comanded by the said James Grahme that noe manner of person or persons whatsoever shall dureing this Fair time sell or exchange or offer to be sold or exchanged any Goods or Chattells, Wares or Marchendises but such as are good lawfull and Marchandizable without fraud or Collusion and that in

Proclaiming George V from the Market Cross May 1910.

open Fair or Markett and not in any private house Backside or Secrett place upon paine to forfeit such Goods or Wares Chattells or Marchendizes so sold or exchanged or offer to be sold or exchanged. And also that noe manner of person or persons within this Fair or Markett doe buy or Sell any goods Wares or Marchendizes by any false Yards, Ellwands weights or Measures but such as are. lawfull usuall and allowable by the Ordinances Lawes and Statutes of this Realme. And that no manner of person or persons doe conceale convey or defraud the Officer or Officers authorised and appointed to Call for and collect any of the Customes and Tolls usually due within this Fair or Markett upon paine for every peny soe wrongfully purloined or deteined to forfeite Twenty shillings. And lastly if there be any person or persons that find themselves greived injured or wronged for any matter or offence to him or them done or comitted dureing this Fair time Let them repair to the Officers of the said James Grahme appointed for that purpose there to open and declare their wrongs And they shall have the same duely heard and examined and determined According to Justice And the Ancient Custome here used. God save the Queen and the Honble James Grahme Esquire Lord of this Manour.

The "strict charge and Comand" not to make "Affrays Tussles or Hubleshews, Pick any Quarrels or use any disturbance of the Peace" seems on the whole to have been observed, although drunkeness was common. In 1862 an incorrigible beggar who had begged from 15 men at the fair got two months hard labour.[88] The next year there was case of cruelty to animals at which the defendant stated that he had hit the victim - a horse - only by accident as "he was leaning over to strike the ostler." In imposing a fine of 1s and costs the bench "intimated that they would not entertain any charge against him for an assault on the ostler."[89] For a more serious offence of horse stealing Michael Knowles aged 18 was sent to prison for 11 months in 1899. He had taken the horse from off the fair in broad daylight and sold it on the same day to Mr Dobson of Arnside for 35s, a fraction of its real value.[90]

After the fair had been proclaimed the steward, gentry, and "respectable townsfolk," rode the bounds of the fair. From at least the 1830's when the Kendal Cavalry band took part, the procession was always headed by a band, with traders, children and anyone else tagging on behind.

The more select of the company then dined in fine style, usually at the Cross Keys. With the steward, Isaac Wilson Esq. of Kendal, in the Chair, 58 gentlemen sat down in 1822. "A punch which the Gods might have tippled for nectar" followed the "excellent dinner" for 52 in 1833 including "G.B. Tovey Esq. of Kendal and other gentlemen", but the absence of Kendal aldermen was condemned - "if we cannot find an observance of our old custom and kindly interchange of feeling among the municipal representatives of the Borough where are we to find them?"[91] In 1856 the service was at fault for "dinner was excellent both in quantity and quality but we would remind Mr Robinson (landlord of the Cross Keys) to provide a larger supply of waiters for next year's dinner."[92] This rebuke led to a furious denial of the charge by Mr Robinson, printed in the *Gazette* the next week. Pleas for any defence could not be made after the Back End dinner of 1867; "which had been fixed for three at the Royal Oak but the diners got it at 5; the embarassing delay of fully two hours caused some dissatisfaction though perhaps nowhere so much as in the culinary regions of the Royal Oak."[93]

The company generally spent "several hours in cheerful conviviality" (in 1855[94] the meal was protracted until 5pm) and always ended with numerous toasts. These invariably included "Luck to Levens while the Kent Flows" and sometimes, depending on who was there "Luck to Dallam as long as Bela Flows", the "Steward of the Manor", the "Mayor and Corporation of Kendal" and the sovereign. In 1837[95] "God save the King" (William IV who died a month later) was sung as a solo by Mr Scariswick. The Lord of the Manor of Levens, for most of the nineteenth century, the Hon. Mary Howard, frequently received fulsome acknowledgment. In 1869 it was declared "that if God only gave Milnthorpe a successor half as worthy of holding that position we should be well satisfied. She was always trying to find some fresh quarter in which to bestow her bounty. She gave freely of what she possessed...there was a double blessing to those who gave and those who receive."[96]

The high point and culmination of Milnthorpe Fair was the Levens Radish Feast. Its origins are obscure but it probably dates from at least the early seventeenth century when the Bellingham's were lords of Levens. About 1690 the Wilson's of Dallam tried to outdo their rival at Levens and "invited every person who attended the Fair to partake of the good cheer lavishly provided in the Park and so great was the success that the time honoured festivities at Levens were deserted entirely that year. Whereupon Colonel Graham of Levens swore a huge oath that he would have a more splendid company the following year. And he kept his word by inviting the august Mayor and Corporation and by giving them such a royal reception they were pleased to comply with his invitation in the succeeding years."[97]

Those who went to the Cross Keys "Fair Dinner" were always invited by the Steward to go on to Levens along with about 200 others. To avoid gate crashers tickets were issued from the 1840's onwards. Behind the band the whole company rode or walked in bucolic procession over the hill and through Heversham arriving at the Hall, two and a half miles distance, at about 6pm. "One very notable feature of the feast was that it was entirely confined to the male sex."[98] Even Mrs Howard did not attend, nor it seems did her husband and when her, heir General Upton, attended in 1875, Mr Wakefield who had been at every fair for over fifty years said it was the first time that he could recall a member of the Levens family being present.[99] Threats to this male bastion were predicted in 1873 "as the times were full of agitation for change when women have already attained seats on School Boards and, if ratepayers, are eligible to vote in municipal contests and who knows that they may succeed in breaking down the barriers that have been effective against them at Levens."[100] The 1873 feast was well attended for in addition to 200 men and youths from Milnthorpe and Heversham "Grammar" boys, between 500 and 600 townsmen of Kendal and gentlemen including Major Bousfield of Parkside attended.[101]

Accounts often waxed lyrical in praise of the feast. Apart from radishes the Fare always included oatcakes (called haverbread), butter and the celebrated black Morocco beer, brewed at Levens, "come from the gloomy tun with merry shine."[102] Thus in 1822 the parties adjourned to Levens Gardens where "punch and Morocco were handed liberally around and bread and butter and reddishes (sic) vanished with great rapidity. The various sports which are regularly kept up on that day as remnants of the feudal times, gave great pleasure to the respective parties. After the sun had retired, and the shadows of the evening drew on, a variety of songs and numerous tracts kept the gardens alive till nearly ten o'clock when the company separated highly gratified with the day's amusements."[103] In 1833 "the gentlemanly bearing of Mr Milne, the steward, was complimented as it denoted feelings of respect while the gardens and bowling greens were a scene to lovers of nature improved by art which aroused the pleasures of the day." Although it was early in the season the radishes always appeared because they were specially grown on flannel strips over hot-beds under glass frames. So many were required that it took four men all the previous day to gather and wash them.[105] In 1873 Mr Gray, the gardener, was especially congratulated in enabling the "long capacious tables to groan under the weight of an immense show of long, short, white and red radishes."

The sports began with "colting." A colt was someone who attended for the first time and to gain full membership of the feast the colt had to stand on one leg and drain in one draught about two pints of Morocco from a Levens Constable - a special glass, rather like an elongated lager glass - to toast the house. Defaulters or those who failed had to pay a fee of 5s. For a bit of fun, older men often forced young lads who didn't have the wherewithal to try and try again until they were unable to stand on both legs let alone one and so "after the severe exercise might at a more agreeable reception study mathematics as they retired home." The sports which followed were generally held on the bowling green but in the 1860's they were transferred "to the west side of the moat (sic)." Bowls, wrestling, races and jumping were the main events. The latter became more sophisticated in 1852 when a "judicious improvement had been made in the apparatus for instead of rough posts two deal staves had been manufactured by the joiner",[108] and the strange device managed to measure a jump of five feet by Mr W. Huddlestone. It was also noted that in the 150 yards "a young gentleman from Heversham Grammar School" tripped another one up. The Radish Feasts were only interrupted occasionally, as on the deaths of Colonel Howard in 1846, Lord Templeton in 1863 and Mrs Howard in 1877 and it seemed that they would be "perpetuated from year to year perhaps from age to age." However it was suspended in c.1880 and in 1888 the 'Radish Feast was said to be a thing of the past." No one knows why; it probably was not on the grounds of expense, as the squires of Levens dispensed equal bounty on other occasions. It might have ended because Captain Bagot, a budding politician, was anxious that the often drunken revelry in his grounds might lose him support.

Though the Radish Feast ended, amusements provided by "the diverting vagabonds whose music has no charm" continued at Milnthorpe. In 1888, however, the showmen did not attend, while in 1896 the pleasure part of the fair was represented by a few swings, shooting galleries, stalls for sweets and toys which received a fair patronage.[109] Although Levens no longer levied cattle dues, fees were still collected from showmen, two thirds going to Levens and one third to Dallam. Swings were placed on the green and shooting galleries along the south side quite close to the house. In c.1899 a youth called Handley Woods was struck in the eye by glass from shooting at a bottle stall.[110] A memorable clash occurred in 1905 between "Hobby Horses and Switchbacks" when two rival showmen, Mr M Hoadley and Mr Charles Marshall, claimed the same pitch. Hoadley had got there first and on the principle of first come first served demanded a monopoly. Marshall, however, held that he had booked the pitch from Mr Daffady the manorial bailiff. "A wordy warfare with the promise of more delighted onlookers."[111]

Local residents were not so amused when two different steam organs began playing different tunes to a late hour and a petition went round which led to the showman being given 24 hours' notice. In 1930 a showman by the delightful name of Crimea Price got into trouble. Along with a party of gypsies he had pulled onto the green and attempted to light a fire. When P.C. Hully tried to stop this, Crimea, who was drunk, "pretended he was French and talked a lot of gibberish" before being arrested and ending up in court where he was fined £1.[112]

Until the 1950's crowds continued to flock to Milnthorpe for the fair, but gradually the number of attractions fell off as the old travelling families disintegrated or found other occupations. By the 1980's it was rare to see more than a waltzer, or dodgems, a roundabout and a few shooting stalls.

Soon after its inception Milnthorpe Parish Council expressed concern about the state of the green and market square and began to make enquiries as to whether the Lords of the Manor would transfer their rights to the council. A green committee consisting of all the council was set up and regularly reported delays in getting repairs carried out by the two Manors. Demarcation of responsibility caused difficulty.[113] Generally Dallam looked after the square and the green in front of the church, Levens odd patches, Police Square and Harmony Green. It took several months to get kerbs replaced on Harmony Green in 1918 and caravans stayed there for five weeks in 1922, partly because no-one in authority was immediately available. In 1925-26 it took two years for an ash heap of several tons dumped on the green to be removed.[114] Photographs also show that about half the area in front of the church, now grass, was just bare earth and stones; in summer it often looked like a hay field.

Radical parish councillors like Neddy Stones regarded manorial control of the village green as an anachronistic relic of feudalism. In all fairness Levens and Dallam never impeded any of the common or other rights on the green. There is no documentary evidence to support a contention that at one time householders on the south side of the green had "to pay Dallam to come out onto the square."[115] Indeed in 1905 when John Fawcett was charged with "unlawfully and wilfully obstructing" the road in the south west corner of the square, his case was dismissed on the grounds that 11 feet of the highway belonged to him and that "the Lord of the Manor had not stopped him."[116]

Trees sometimes caused problems. In 1875 a huge ash tree on the green, reputed to be three or four hundred old, was said to be in danger of being blown down. The Manor steward ordered it to be felled but the Manorial Court decided to keep it. However, despite protests from villager, it was cut down – large crowds turning out to watch half a dozen men perform the execution, which took five hours to complete.[117]

When the Parish Council wanted to plant the sycamore trees to commemorate Queen Victoria's Diamond Jubilee in 1897 it had to ask permission from the Manors. On the other hand Captain Bagot of Levens provided the trees and Maurice Bromley-Wilson of Dallam tower paid for their being planted and for the metal cages to protect them.[118]

The Parish began negotiations to take over the greens in c.1920. Negotiations were protracted as both Dallam Tower and Levens Hall were in the hands of trustees and the permission of the Ministry of Health (at that time responsible for such local matters) and the Rural District Council also had to be obtained. They had in fact been completed when at the Parish Council of 1st November 1929 Mr A. H. Read proposed "that enquiry be made to the Lords of the Manor of Levens and Dallam Tower who are the joint owners of the village green as to the terms on which they would cede control of the green and Market Place (sic) to the Parish Council and at the same time drew their attention to the urgent need for the ground to be put in a reasonable state of repair." At first the trustees of Levens believed that they could only make the green over for 60 years (the predicted life time of the tenant for life) while an annual rental of £2 was proposed; but, at length, the green and square were handed over free of charge to the village. The Dallam trustees even donated £10 towards the legal fee of £28. 7s but, having rather cheekily been asked by the Parish Clerk to give a similar amount, Mrs Gaskell on behalf of the Levens heir, refused to make a contribution.[120] By the Deed of Dedication of 1930 Milnthorpe Green (including the square) became the absolute property of the parish council and its successors. It was, however, subject to certain restrictive covenants. All encroachments, for example, required the consent of the Lords of the Manor. The Council was required to covenant that "they will forever hereafter leave open and unbuilt upon the said green and that the same shall be for the use and enjoyment of the inhabitants of the village of Milnthorpe in perpetuity. That they will for ever thereafter maintain the said green in a sightly and orderly condition. That they will permit the portions of the green situate between the old fountain and the school and between the fountain and the old Market Cross to be used as a parking ground for the motor cars of persons having business in the village." The Parish Council drew up a long, involved and either irrelevant or unenforcable set of bye-laws.

(8)(b) "A person shall not on the ground – use any net, snare or other instrument or means for the taking, injury or destruction of any bird.

(9) A person shall not in any space elsewhere on the ground play or take part in any game so specified in such a manner as to exclude persons not playing or taking part in the game from use of such space.

(11) A person shall not on the ground (a) beat, shake, sweep, brush or cleanse any carpet, drugget, rug or mat, or any other fabric retaining dust or dirt."

Although their feudal lords had, in effect, not charged fees for years the Parish Council instantly drew up a scale of fees as elaborate as the bye-laws.

Traction engines and caravans were to pay 1/- for the first night and 6d thereafter, Shooting saloons 3/- and 2/-, Roundabouts 20/- and 10/-, Swings large 2/6, small 1/6, Dutch auctions 2/6, Ice Cream 1/- and Public Meetings 1/-. In 1939 car parking charges were imposed, the attendant being paid 10/- for the first 25/- of the takings and ten per cent of the rest. The scheme soon fell through, however, and since then the Parish Council ensured that parking has been free.

A regular financial wrangle concerned the Dallam buses. Messrs J. Fawcett and Sons claimed that as rate payers of Milnthorpe they were entitled not only to have a bus stop in the square but also to allow their vehicles to stand there when not in use. In 1939 Fawcetts were induced to pay £6 per annum for using the square, renewable annually and their successors Ribble continued to pay a fee, eventually of £25 per annum.[122] In 1955, largely at the instigation of the Chairman of the Parish Council Dr. P.S. Byrne, two concrete bus shelters made by Blackley's of Sheffield were installed at a cost of £55 each, at either side of the approach to the church. Dearer but more appropriate structures had been considered but had been turned down after the Rural District Council had refused a loan of £200. As it was, the cheap shelters were partly paid for out of funds left over from the Coronation celebrations of 1953. Even before the brass plaque stating that they were Milnthorpe's commemoration

The Square c.1920.

of the Coronation had been installed the shelters had been vandalised. They remained a disgrace to the village until replaced by a limestone and slated shelter in 1983 at a cost of some £4,000.[123] The masonry of the new shelter incorporated stones from demolished chimney stacks of Stoneleigh, Laburnum House, the Cross Keys and grave kerbs removed during levelling of the churchyard.

In 1935 Public Conveniences, designed by J.F. Curwen and Sons were erected by the Rural District Council in the Market Square following long agitation for "urinals" from the Parish Council. Sited next to St. Thomas' School they had been opposed by the school managers and by many local people. As they were an encroachment the Levens trustees should have given their consent for the building. This was not obtained although Sir Maurice Bromley-Wilson of Dallam Tower had agreed to "anything the Parochial Committee would suggest."[124]. Technically they were illegal structures. Though they were built and maintained (generally in a rough and ready manner) by the Rural District Council, the Parish Council apparently had some rights for in 1939 the British Automatic Company asked permission from the Parish Council to install a machine in the men's public convenience. Even though the Council was offered a rent of £2 per annum and twenty five per cent of the profits on the goods dispensed the councillors illiberally decreed that "the idea cannot be entertained."[125] After 50 years service the old conveniences were replaced by South Lakeland

Inthorpe.

The Square c. 1930.

District Council in 1986. In return for an extra area of ground required for a disabled person's toilet the District Council acknowledged the Parish Council as being the ground landlords. Costing over £57,000 the new conveniences were said to be vandal proof. Nevertheless, two nights after they were opened one of the cubicle doors was dumped in the church-yard.

In 1966 the weekly market was revived. The story goes that Arthur Nelson, a farmer from Halforth, Heversham, having failed to get a ready sale elsewhere for his potatoes, brought a load down to the square and put them on the market. A brisk business commenced, Arthur brushing away objections from the village green grocer, who had called in the police, on the grounds that his "grandfather had stood there." In July it was reported that the Clerk and Chairman of the Parish Council had given Arthur permission "to sell potatoes and other vegatable (sic) from his van on the square providing he cause no nuisence (sic) or litter."[126] In October J. and A. Patterson of Kendal asked for permission to do the same. After the Chairman had asked a Mrs Ashworth who had objected noisily to the proposal, "to put her complaints in writing to the Clerk" it was agreed to write to the Parish Councils Association on this matter. The Association reported that if the council owns the square it cannot prevent the persons from coming to sell there on Fridays, but may charge them for the right to put up stalls or similar stands for sale of goods." In November "after discussion it was agreed that the ancient practice of Market Day on Friday be established and that the charge per stall be 5/- on the proposition of Mr. J. T. Cookson, seconded by Mr J. D. Davidson. Mr Pickthall proposed an amendment that the charge be 7/6 but had no seconder. Clerk was instructed to inform Mr Nelson and Mrs Patterson."[127] Within weeks half-a-dozen other stalls had appeared. Soon the very shopkeepers who had feared for their livelihood found that on Fridays they had to engage extra staff to cope with the increased custom attracted to the village by the Market. The Market grew haphazardly. In 1971 it was agreed that "the allocation of places be left as a gentleman's agreement"[128] with the result that in a few years stalls had spread over the green. It was even suggested that the resulting quagmire should be replaced by tarmac. Fortunately this was contrary to the Deed of Dedication and in 1981, at a stormy Parish Council meeting, it was decided to eject the stalls on the green and to accommodate them on the square by requiring delivery vehicles to be parked elsewhere. By that time there were over 40 stalls and a long waiting list.

The revived Market was a double blessing for the village. Not only did it restore Milnthorpe' position as a local trading centre, it provided revenue for the Parish Council. Although rentals were less than in other local markets, surpluses from the market account contributed to the costs of resurfacing the square, re-turfing the green, building the new bus shelter, providing play equipment on the playing field and for refurbishing the old 'cookery rooms' for use as a public library. For many years market income enabled the Parish Council to forego raising a precept (which could be up to 4p in the £) on the rates.

Market rights led to the most important legal case involving the Parish Council since the days of the Haverbrack and footpath disputes of the 1890's. The case of "Duxbury v Milnthorpe Parish Council" arose after George Duxbury had been allowed, for a small fee, to sell hot dogs on the square on certain evenings when the fish and chip shop was closed. When he persisted in trading on other nights and left his van for days on end on the square the Parish Council asked him to leave. He refused, because he claimed Milnthorpe was a 'free' market and the Parish Council had no right to order him around. Strong feelings were aroused on both sides. As the market had been in abeyance when the Deed of Dedication granting the square to the Parish Council had been drawn up in 1930 the Council had to resort to the law. Eventually in 1982, after two separate hearings in the County Court (involving Q.C.'s), the Parish Council obtained an injunction and costs (of £1000) against George.[129] At the same time its rights to "control the conduct of the square" were deemed to embrace market rights. That this could involve wider benefits was proved in 1985 when a village traders association put it about that South Lakeland District Council, which had imposed parking charges on the Kirkby Lonsdale square, was about to do the same at Milnthorpe. Car stickers urging "Keep Parking Free in Milnthorpe" appeared and there had to be a public meeting to inform anxious traders that South Lakeland Council had no rights whatsoever over Milnthorpe square. It surprised many that the Parish Councils' rights could be traced back to the charter granted to Alexander de Wyndesore in 1334.

5

Roads, Transport and Inns

Milnthorpe sits astride the A6; the main north-south road for the western half of Britain. Farleton Knott rises three miles to the east while the estuary and mosses, equally bad for roads, are less than a mile away to the west. Roads, canal and railway have to squeeze through the gap which is left.

Prior to the opening of the M6 extension in 1970 Milnthorpe was one of the busiest places in the Kingdom, and frustrated travellers must have thought that the main road had always run through the village. In fact the A6 route dates only from the building of a Turnpike Road in c.1818-1820.[1] This was the first road to run over Hale Moss (three miles to the south) which previously had diverted the main route to the east via Burton. Before the nineteenth century the road to Milnthorpe from Carnforth went via Wharton, Yealand Redmayne and Yealand Conyers to Leighton Furnace, then over Slackhead to drop down into Beetham at the Wheatsheaf. Another track ran from the north west of the Moss via Hale and Beetham Hall to Beetham.[2] These roads were so bad that Celia Fiennes in c.1690 was grateful to be allowed to go through Lady Middleton's Park at Leighton Hall for "it saved the going round a bad stony passage on to the road againe much of which was stony and steep and, far worse than the Peake in Darbyshire."[3]

By contrast, the alternative route close to the eastern hills via Borwick to Burton-in-Kendal and thence through Crooklands, Endmoor and Natland to Kendal was less rocky and more direct. Moreover, Burton being approximately 11 miles equidistant to Kendal and Lancaster was better placed for changing horses on stage coaches, the first of which is recorded as leaving Kendal in 1658.[4] Though the Burton Road was better, Milnthorpe's position as a port and market town always attracted travellers in its own right.

The Roman road running from the foot of Farleton via Hincaster to Watercrook had by-passed Milnthorpe.[5] In the post Roman period the pre-natal paths around Milnthorpe were developed into a rough and ready net work of tracks connecting both the "Mylen porp" and the important Anglian monastery at Heversham with the wider world.

Though its monastery is presumed to have been destroyed by the Vikings in c.900 A.D. the church and its contiguous community survived at Heversham. Certainly the area was sufficiently peaceful in the 940's to be visited by a Scottish Prince Cattroe from Strathclyde, en route to Rome. As Milnthorpe probably existed by this time Prince Cattroe is, therefore, its first visitor to be known by name.[6] Throughout the Middle Ages Heversham Church was an important stopping place for pilgrims and clerics travelling from York and other places to Furness and Shap Abbeys.

Beetham is marked on the so called Gough's Map of the fourteenth century; one of the few places in Cumbria to be so recorded.[7] This implies that the Beetham, Milnthorpe, Heversham, Kendal route existed and was of some importance. Nevertheless throughout the Middle Ages and until the eighteenth century Milnthorpe's main road was Main Street linking the port and estuary with the high road.

Milnthorpe is rarely mentioned by any of the notable early travellers. The cartographer John Leland, for example, went from Lancaster to Kirkby Kendale via "Bytham" in 1533 but did not record Milnthorpe though he must have gone through it. Similarly, subsequent map makers Christopher Saxton (1573), William Camden (1586) and John Ogilby (1675) ignored the village.[9] Robert Morden's updated version of Cambden's maps in c.1690 includes two routes from "the Carnford" to Kendal.[10] One clearly goes through Burton and a western loop appears to touch Milnthorpe. It was probably Morden's map that Celia Fiennes used when she passed through Milnthorpe c.1696. Both in 1715 and 1745 Milnthorpe was in the path of the Jacobite invasion from Scotland.[11] Fears that the main force would come through Heversham and Milnthorpe led the churchwardens to pay one shilling to hide the church plate. Fortunately (or for later romanticists, unfortunately) both rebel armies passed along the high road through Crooklands. More sadly in view of the village's long connection with Methodism, John Wesley, who rode on at least a dozen occasions from Lancaster to Kendal between c.1748-1790 did not mention Milnthorpe in his journals. It would, however, be surprising if he or his immediate entourage ignored Milnthorpe altogether.[12]

Even in Wesley's time the north-south road from Beetham to Heversham followed the circuitous tracks of the medieval pack horse. From Beetham the road swerved across the Bela east of Beetham House and then divided, the eastern branch joining Pool Darkin Lane leading to Hang Bridge, the western going up Cappleside Hill to join Paradise Lane. A minor lane went to the west to reach Beetham Mills and then went along the river bank to Bela Mills at Milnthorpe – avoiding the present A6 route over Belasett hill altogether. Paradise Lane was the main road. After a few hundred yards it forked: the eastern fork followed the surviving lane to Ackenthwaite and the western main track ran along the footpath to the east of Belasett and reached Milnthorpe behind Firs Road where it touched the Green at the Sun Tavern, once Milnthorpe's main Inn.[13]

Heading north across the Green the road went through Police Square up the ginnel between Rock Cottage and Sunnyside and thence over Riley Field passing the east side of Riley Field House. Its track over Milnthorpe Hill has been obscured by later roadwork but on the far side it ran through the site of St Anthony's House –the site being formed when an odd roadside triangle of land was left when the Turnpike was built. The western garden wall of St Anthony's is that of the old road. From St Anthony's the road crossed the meadow to join the lane which now goes to Park House farm. Though grassed over the old road can clearly be seen just west of the disused railway track. It is barely five feet wide – about the same as the older part of Paradise Lane. This would indicate that a stipulation laid down in 1691 that main roads should be 8 feet wide had been ignored.[14] Indeed an order of 1822 stopping up the "highway" between the Ackenthwaite Road just north of Buttsyeat (High Cragg Yeat) states that it was only four feet wide. Elsewhere horse "causeys" were only three feet wide.

From the 1660's bad road maintenance increasingly concerned the authorities. At the July sessions in 1669 it was ordered that the "owners of lands adjoining the high ways of Beetham and Milnthorpe and Heversham that they shall butt and flash their hedges hanging into the saide way before the next sessions under pain of 10s each; and that the inhabitants of Milnthrop shall stop up the Lime Kilne in the high wayside at Acquenthwaite on pain of 40s."[16] When in 1712 and in 1730-31 George Browne, High Constable of Kendal ordered a survey of Bridges and Roads in the district "he had nothing good to say about any of them."[17] The narrowness of the road was the chief complaint. Many of them are simply described as "bad" and "covered with ye hedges."

The line of the east-west road has hardly altered since the eighteenth century. According to Jeffery's map of 1770[18] the Burton and Crooklands roads came to a fork roughly at the Heater

Jeffrey's Map 1770.

Field (at that time an open common) just east of Owlett Ash. The tracks across the common connecting Paradise Lane with the Woodhouse Road and Kirkgate Lane were more irregular. One track probably crossed the yard between Ackenthwaite Green House and the Smithy and then went over the rough common called Ackenthwaite scroggs, where the Workhouse was later built, to Kirkgate Lane. Another track could have gone from Paradise Lane via Ackenthwaite Farm to the Woodhouse Road. There were in addition a number of less delineated tracks across Milnthorpe

Green. Part of a correspondence exists concerning the refusal of "Old William Audland Blacksmith" in 1797 to pay for maintenance of a road over Milnthorpe Green leading to his field Longhogs. "Old William," who had owned the land for 50 years, refused because he did not use the road since the field was adjacent to the main road (Paradise Lane) which led directly to The Smithy.[19] The original east road ran straight past the front door of Owlett Ash House and then north of the Red Barn past Carr's Yard, Harmony Green, Windy Hill to Haverflatts Lane and the Greens. Main Street continued as far as Harmony Hall and joined the main road west of the Red Barn. The road to the south of the barn was not built until after the Enclosure Acts of 1803-1813 when the road past Owlet Ash was set forward to the south to provide the present garden. This also separated Harmony Hall from its coach house and outbuildings.

The western end of Main Street, known since at least c.1840 as Park Road, but also called "Bridge Street," was continuously built up by the mid-eighteenth century, except for a gap at the Strand Meadow (Playing Fields).[20] Just past Birkett's Farm the main road turned sharp left over the bridge – with a minor track running along the north bank of the Bela via Parkside and the hamlet of Scoutbank to join the Sand Road and Marsh Lane. The southern road ran along the waste land – called "the thorns"[21] – following roughly the present footpath to the Dallam Wheel. It then crossed the Dallam Drive and went, according to Neddy Stones, almost through the present Stable yard of Dallam Tower and then up through the shrubbery and wood to the Kennels before dipping down Peat Stack Hill via Hollins Well to the Dixies.[22] The line of this road can still be clearly seen running along the field wall.

The first reference to the western route from Milnthorpe to the estuary comes in the will of Edmund Pearson – a Tanner from Beetham – of 1542... "Also it is my will to make the cost of the mason work to the supportation and making of a bridge at the end of Milnthorpe..."[23] This bridge was some yards upstream from the present "old bridge," a position marked by a flight of steps going down into the river. It is possible that Pearson's bridge was not the first. "Supportation" implies repair and possibly there was a pedestrian or "packhorse" type bridge. At most times the river is sufficiently shallow for carts to be able to splash across without danger. According to Neddy Stones, Edmund Pearson was the ancestor of the Pearson family of Holme, Burton, Crosthwaite and Milnthorpe. Stones also stressed that Pearson's will "proved that the Old bridge is a Public Bridge and is not the property of Dallam Tower... I claimed this when on the Parish Council but the matter of right is still in obeyance."[24] Later councils have not pressed this claim, preferring to allow the Dallam estate to maintain the bridge.

Nevertheless Stones was probably right. An order of 24 June 1667 from George Browne, (High Constable of Kendal Ward) ordered public funds be used to pay "unto Mr Edward Wilson the sum of £13, out of the 9d in the pound lately assessed for the reparation of bridges, for the repair of Milnthorpe Bridge."[25] Machell in c.1690 referred to the bridge "Passing the bridge whereon there stands a dial stone, with the inscription upon (it) much like an altar of the Romans. . . "Fear God and honour the King 1684."[26] As 1684 is not an important date in national or royal affairs it is possible that the inscription refers to repairs carried out at that time. That any such work cannot have been adequate is shown by several references in the Kendal Order Book:

1701/2 16 January. Milnthorpe Bridge over the Bela is presented as ruinous and in decay: "Order to the Chief Constable to call some sufficient workmen to view the said bridge and give an estimate for the repair on 14 February, and that John Cragg and John Gibson be viewers."[27]

1709 30 July "the Chief Constable. . . to attend the justicies at Milthorp on 10 August to view the bridge at Milthorpe in decay." On 10 October 1712, an order was issued to contract for repairs and on the 7 November Christopher Woodburn of Milnthorpe contracted to make a new pavement from the north end of Milnthorpe Bridge up to the horseing stone above Richard Dowker's dwelling house door, such breadth as shall be necessary for making the way good and to make the said pavement of thin stones. . . "[28]

Eventually on 16 January 1729-30 Benjamine Browne and Mr Robert Greenwood, the High Constable,advertised for a contract for rebuilding of the public bridge called Milnthorpe Bridge. . . "now in a ruinous condition." On 6 April following Robert Robinson, free mason, and Robert Bindloss of Hincaster, waller, entered into an agreement to pull down all and every part of the common and county bridge, called and known by the name of Milnthorpe Bridge, now being in very great decay and very incommodiously situated for all travellers and passengers with carriages, and to erect and build about 80 yards below a new firm stone bridge to consist of two bends or arches of at least 23 yards and one foot betwixt the springer, and 4 yards broad, and maintain and keep the same in good and sufficient repair for seven years from and after the 25 July next ensuing. . . On 10th July 1730, Robert Robinson, free mason, gives receipt, for £30 being the remainder of £90 for the new building of the bridge. . . "[29] In 1763 £18 was assigned for the "rebuilding" of Milnthorpe bridge – but considering the cost of the new structure in 1730 the term probably refers to substantial repairs. Nicolson and Burn in 1777 stated "the river Betha, coming from Beetham runs by the place (Milthorp);

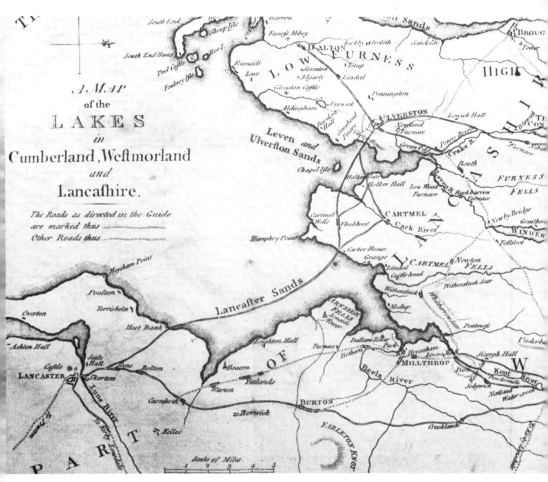

Map from Benjamin West's guide to the lakes fourth edition 1789
showing main road through Burton, pre 'A6' Turnpike through
Yealands to Milnthrop and Over Sands Routes.

over which there is a good stone bridge."[30]

Significantly the area's first Turnpike Act, passed in 1759, concerned the route connecting Kendal and Burton with the Port of Milnthorpe and aimed to improve the road from Nether Bridge to Dixies and "Milltrop" to Hangbridge – about a mile and a half to the south east.[31] No realignment of the older roads seems to have been attempted, the tolls being used merely to repair and maintain the surface. By contrast the Turnpike Act of 1818 planned an entirely new route from Beetham to Heversham, corresponding with the A6. A new Beetham Bridge was built west of Beetham house and the new road cut over Belasett to reach Main Street at the Cross Keys.[32] Here no attempt was made to widen the extremely narrow street between the Old Bull's Head and the cottages opposite on Beetham Road. At less than twelve feet this was believed to be the narrowest part of the whole road from St Albans to Carlisle. Equally awkward was the sharp bend round the Cross Keys and up Church Street, past the King's Arms, caused by the buildings projecting west from Flowerden as far as the present traffic island. Before this property was cleared in c.1923-27 the traveller approaching from the south along Beetham Road would have his line of vision closed by a continuous row of buildings which effectively masked the Cross roads. The road over Milnthorpe Hill required extensive excavation and the embankment on the lower part of Church Street enabled the houses on the Blue Row to have cellars. The embankment can be seen clearly at the allotment gardens at the end of Church Street. Much of the Turnpike was built speedily and seems to have been opened by the middle of 1820. However, it was not until 11 August 1822 that the following announcement appeared in the *Westmorland Gazette:*

Millthorpe Turnpike Roads notice is hereby given That in pursuance of an Act passed in the present Session of Parliament, intitled "An Act for now effectually repairing the Roads from Netherbridge to Levens Bridge and from thence through the town of Millthrop to Dixes, and from thence to join the Heronsyke Turnpike Road near Clawthrop Hall, in the County of Westmorland"[34] a meeting of Trustees appointed for carrying the same Act into exection (sic) will be holden at the Cross Keys Inn in Millthrop on Tuesday the 28 day of May instant, at Eleven o'clock in the Forenoon for the purpose of fixing on a convenient situation for the new Tollhouse and Tollgate authorized by the said Act to be built and erected by the side of and upon and across that part of the said Roads which is between a certain Lane called Greavygate Lane, and the town of Millthrop aforesaid, And notice is also further given, That at the said meeting a Treasurer to the said Trustees and also a surveyor of the said Road will be elected. Dated this 9th day of May 1822. Thomas Reveley Clerk to the Trustees of the said Road[35]

This tollhouse, known as the Leasgill or Beethwaite Green Gate was built at the end of Levens Hall Garden opposite the entrance to the old Greavygate (Grievegate).

South of Milnthorpe the toll house was at Beetham and part of the building was incorporated, in 1904, in the Queen Victoria School. The right to collect tolls had been advertised in January 1822 and the next year the Leasgill Gate was worth £108 2s 3d p.a. compared with £158 for the Burton Gate on the Old High Road, £180 for Cow Brow Gate on the road to Kirkby Lonsdale and £358 for the Nether Bridge Gate. Tolls were 1d per mile for Two wheeled carriages with 1 horse, 2d for two horses, 2d for a spring carriage with one horse, 3d for two horses, and 4½d per mile for three or more horses. Pedestrians were free and riders and stock paid varying sums depending on the type of beast.[36] Provision was also made for stray animals and in 1823 Agnes Garnett of Sizergh Fell was "committed to the House of Correction for three days... for rescuing from the Pound a horse belonging to her husband which had been found straying on the Milltrop Turnpike. . ."[37]

Despite this the road was either not officially or fully open until 1824 as on 27 March 1824 the *Westmorland Gazette* reported "the workmen have at last cut through the hill between Heversham and Milnthorpe and the new road is expected to be open to the public before Whitsuntide. . ."[38]

No one seems to have been satisfied for long and even Britain's most famous civil engineer came in for criticism. . . "at a recent meeting of the Trustees of the Milnthorpe and Heronsyke turnpike. . . the superintendent of the roads (had been) left to men perfectly ignorant of the very rudiments of the science. . . sometimes the parings of grass and earth are thrown upon the roads for the purposes of filling up the vacancies between the stones. To convince the men of the error of their plan is impossible and should Mr Macadam attempt to convince many of the Kendal road makers that stones would themselves bind and that any other substances added would prevent their binding when laid upon the road they would not believe him."[39]

Deficient surfaces did not deter traffic. By 1819 60 coaches were leaving Kendal each day. All had names and the "Dandy," "Defiance," "Independent," "Invincible," "North Briton," "Robert Burns," "New Times," and "New Prices" all rumbled through Milnthorpe.[40] A regular service based on the "Cross Keys" was in operation, though in January 1822 it was reported that coaches due at 10.30 a.m. at the Inn arrived at 7 p.m. and those due at 2.30 p.m. arrived at 10 at night owing to "the worst snows for 60 years."[41] A little later, on the road to Burton, 3 horses on Mr Webster's coach were struck by lightning and killed. In 1824 another Milnthorpe coachman, Henry Cotton, was injured on Cow Brow when his horses broke their traces, one was caught but "we can find nothing of the other three."[42] Drivers were regularly condemned by the *Gazette* for overloading their coaches and for "driving to the manifest danger of the outer passengers." However, "no blame could be attached to Mr Jas. Bryden Driver" for a coach accident south of Milnthorpe in 1844 when "by a sudden jerk, the pole of the front part of the coach was separate from the hinder part which caused it to be overturned and threw the passengers with great force to the ground."[43] The pole was broken and the horse was so injured that it had to be shot. A bad accident occurred in June 1841 when a gig running away down the hill, ran over a child, crashed into the Cross Keys where it broke its shafts and then careered into a cart of furniture belonging to Mrs Jane Wilson who had stopped to feed her horses. She was knocked down and her legs were run over but though she was left in "a precarious state" no bones were broken.[44] In 1845 one of the horses pulling the Mazeppo coach up the hill

Mashiter's Pantechnicon at Heversham c.1910.

dropped down dead but no one was hurt. A more prosaic accident accurred in "Bridge Street" in November 1844 when a "cart of turnips emptied on a little boy belonging to Mr Richard Lupton and broke his legs."[45]

It was not surprising that there were so many accidents. Neddy Stones told of one James Martin c.1818 "who used to ride a Black Pony and attended Daniel Wilson of Dallam Tower as Bodyguard. He was a tall stout man and in for all sorts of frolic. If he did not know the quality of good ale no one did. He was well known at the Blue Bell and Eagle and Child at Heversham, at the Black Bull and Cross Keys at Milnthorpe and at many other hostelries betwixt Penrith and Lancaster. He was always at home at the Ring O' Bells at Kendal but he finished at the Rainbow and The George and Dragon. When he got beyond the carrying trade he became the landlord of the Dixies Inn and The Ship Inn, Sandside afterward the Fox and Goose in Kendal, The Blacksmiths Arms, Endmoor and lastly the Carnforth Inn."[46] Stones also recalled the tail end of the coaching period when Milnthorpe was one of the busiest places in the north of England. Up to a dozen coaches and chaises could at one time stand outside the Cross Keys and round the corner into Church Street by the Kings Arms. More humble vehicles and horses lined up outside the Royal Oak, The Bulls Head and White Lion, while pedestrians and outside passengers made do with the Jolly Waggoners and the Coach and Horses. All these premises were congregated round the cross roads and up to a couple of hundred passengers, drivers, couriers, grooms, ostlers, pot boys

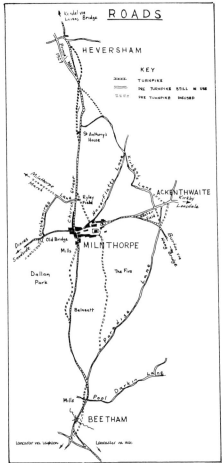

The Turnpike roads around Milnthorpe.

and messengers, to say nothing of hawkers, beggars and boys clammering "Mind your horse for a penny", bustled between them.[47]

In July 1842 the *Westmorland Gazette* noted simultaneously at the Cross Keys door, two mail coaches each with four horses, one mail with two horses, a carriage with two horses, a chaise with two horses and a carriage with four horses."[48] Amongst those halting at "the Keys" were "Lord Muncaster, Lord Sefton, Lord Howard, Colonel Nicholson etc." Similarly in the summer of 1844 Milnthorpe was particularly "busy and bustling in consequence of tourists passing through and changing horses at the Cross Keys" and at "one stage" Lord and Lady Newport and Captain Washington were noticed.[49] All the main Inns and taverns were involved in staging or in carrying. Neddy Stones[50] recalled that at the Cross Keys, Robert Hudson and his wife (Elizabeth) kept 26 horses in the stable for

Main Street, Milnhorpe.

Main Street about the turn of the Century.

posting and lending or exchanging betwixt Lancaster, Burton, Lindale, Newby Bridge and Ulverston; Mrs Robinson at the White Lion kept 3 or 4 horses, Thomas Bainbridge at the Kings Arms 6, James Redhead at the Bull's Head Inn 4, Issac Clemmett of the Royal Oak 4 while J. Postlethwaite at the Coach and Horses, (which despite its grand name was a mere tavern) kept 3 horses. There was also a large number of carriers. Some like the Carrs and Berry's were concerned mainly with Port trade. Others like the Clark's were involved in more general work. In 1829 Edward Clark carried goods to Kendal at 8 a.m. every Monday to return by 9 p.m. while on Wednesday's and Saturday's Joseph Clark and Mary Lupton went on the same journey at 8 a.m. to return by 8 p.m.[51] "In addition most of the tradesmen in the town who had a hack had horses suitable and used to lend them out for journeys, every boy was a rider and was requisitioned for riding leaders four in hand. The roads were never clear of Mail Coaches and other coaches came there every day."[52] They left the Cross Keys for Lancaster via Beetham at 7 a.m. and via Burton at 9.30 a.m. There was also a daily coach at 6 p.m. for Kendal. The Burton Road, however, still claimed pre-eminence and in 1823 a "Post Mail Gig was provided to connect the Furness Mail with the main north south running coaches" at Burton.[53] This arrangement was reversed in April 1844 when it was announced that "the Old Night Mail will run through

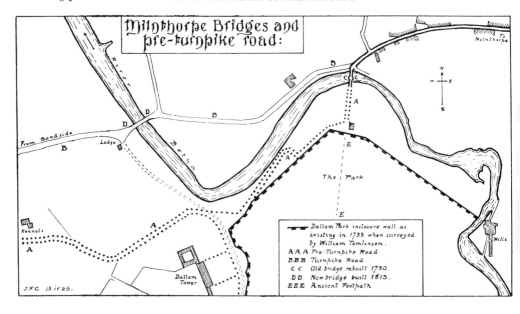

Milnthorpe. The Post Gig will run from Burton to Milnthorpe and not from Milnthorpe to Burton."[56]

Alas, Milnthorpe's coaching heyday would soon be over. Ominously in June 1844 it was advertised that "the Mazeppa Coach will meet the train at 2 p.m. at Lancaster to run through Milnthorpe to Keswick...it leaves Keswick at 6 to reach Lancaster for the 1 p.m. train to Liverpool, Manchester and Birmingham."

The worst blow fell with the opening of the main line north to Oxenholme in 1846. For a time there were false hopes that the Railway would enhance the coaching trade. In September 1847 after William Robinson had become the landlord, the *Gazette* reported that "since the reopening of the Cross Keys Hotel posting has continued very brisk through Milnthorpe considering the opposition of the Railways; a great many respectable families have changed horses and sojourned at the above hotel during the past week. Arrivals at the Cross Keys Hotel: During the past week the following distinguished families have passed through Milnthorpe - Frederick Howard Esq., Hon. C. Cavendish, Lady Fanny Howard, Rev. Mr Dunford, G Braithwaite Esq. C Bagot Esq. etc. etc."[56] In December Lady Fanny and suite arrived at Milnthorpe from Holker Hall and took the train for the south.[57] The following February they again arrived at the Cross Keys "by Mail train for Holker Hall." After an apparent break it was noted on 26 May 1849 that Posting began through Milnthorpe again. "Lord Forbes, Sir - Fletcher, changed horses at the Cross Keys...as did...tourist travellers in their carriages to the Lakes." Nevertheless only three years later a report

Old Bridge c.1910.

Detail of Old Bridge with Deer Fence.

of the May Day celebration harks back to a vanished golden age - gone so recently but gone for ever: "Saturday last being the 1st May as in olden times the Royal Mail, the New Times and the Royal Mail post gig between Manchester and Ulverston were each gaily decked with ribbons etc. The Royal Mail had four splended horses, each decorated with rosettes etc. the coach was beautifully painted and varnished and in fact it was as good a show of the kind as has been seen in Milnthorpe for a number of years."[58]

Coaching was over but carrying and the carriage trade for short journeys continued. One carrying family - the Easons - came to Milnthorpe when William Eason was in charge of the L.N.W.R. horses being used on the construction of the railway. They and others maintained a regular service to the railway station, 1¼ miles away - though this distance was always minimized; many gazeteers saying "the town was but half a mile away." For 40 years until c.1890 Old Ned Mashiter drove the Cross Keys bus. This or a similar vehicle dated from at least 1849 when the "buss" was reported to have "run over the legs of Mr Hudson, landlord of Endmoor, but no bones were broken."[59] It survived until the First World War when it was used during the petrol shortage.

In the later nineteenth century horse traffic was sufficiently busy in Milnthorpe to yield a regular crop of accidents, fully reported in the press and nearly always concluding with the doleful news that the victim was in a "precarious state." If bones were broken the condition became "very precarious", as in the case of Mr North of Lyth who in 1852 was knocked down by a cow in Church Street and broke his arm.[60] In May 1855 John Fawcett ("Happy Jack") "general dealer of Milnthorpe was descending the hill into Milnthorpe with his horse and cart when the horse took fright and set off with a gallop. Fawcett was thrown out of the cart, the wheel passed over him but he escaped without much damage."[61] Less fortunate was a "young lady" on a visit to Mr Swindlehurst, Greenside, who in 1874 was thrown from her horse in Beetham Road and broke her arm and cut her face. She was carried to Mr Forster's Bela Cottage, "but some time must elapse before she can be safely removed."[62] Also in 1874 but at the other end of the social scale was William Knowles, son of Ellen Knowles, hawker, aged 3 years but very strong and intelligent for one so young and fond of imitating those who exceeded him in years "who, while grooming a pony (at 3!) was kicked and had to have 13 stitches in the face" - without, incidentally, anaesthetic.[63] At the general election in 1880 several people were hurt, but none seriously, when Thomas Llewellyn, coachman to Mr Wilson "drove straight into the crowds with yellow ribbons streaming." He was charged with "furious driving" and fined £3.[64] Ten years later Tom Argles of Eversley had to cope with a furious horse, which got the bit into its mouth and being frightened bolted from the top of Milnthorpe hill, right through Heversham and Leasgill before depositing Mr Argles bruised and bleeding from a gash across his face and a broken jaw onto the gravel of his own drive. By a lucky coincidence Dr Leeming was on the drive and so immediate treatment was given.[65] Perhaps it was no coincidence that Mr Argles was one of the area's first motorists! It was not just horses and drivers who could be furious, for in 1894 George Langstreth drove into John Grey with a wheel barrow - doing 16s 6d worth damage to a cart. He was ordered to pay the costs and was fined 6d.[66]

The effect of the coming of the railways in 1846 was reflected in the declining value of the toll gates. Whereas in 1845 the Milnthorpe Turnpike Gate was worth £495 in 1846 it "was put up at £300 but got no takers." Receipts in 1847 at the Beethwaite Green Gate were £308 10s 4½d, and £305 in 1849[67] and declined continuously until the Turnpikes were abolished in the 1870's.

The railway actually led to a further restriction for travellers because in 1855 a Toll Bar was erected on the Crooklands road

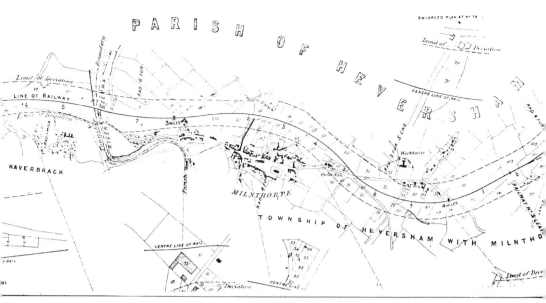

Map showing the Original Proposals for the line joining the Furness to the Carlisle Railway.

opposite the gable end of the station. It led to vigorous complaints and several prosecutions. In November 1855 John Smith of Haverflatts, a farmer, was summoned to the petty session for non-payment of tolls, having carried his goods from just before the bar to the station. Mr Gregg prosecuting conceded that "the defendant had the impression that he had the right to do what he had done..he should not press for heavy penalties...the case was to shew that the defendant was not justified;"[68] John was fined 1s.

The bar remained as an "intolerable nuisance" despite demands that it be moved back one mile on the Crooklands road and that tolls should be reduced by 1d. In 1867 the case was taken up by the local press when a "Milnthorpian" wrote that the "Railway was a very important part of the social system of Milnthorpe, it brought their friends, their letters and their parcels and yet to drive to the station they were taxed 6d or if a cart went to fetch a hamper it cost 3d at the Bar." Another correspondent stated "Whilst the remaining Bar on the Kirkby Lonsdale Road should also charge one half toll rather than being cleared as at present by payment at Milnthorpe. Thus the absurdity of taxing those who travel only 200 yards to the Railway Station with the repair of ten miles of Turnpike Road for the good of Kirkby Lonsdale would no longer exist." Though "the Cerbereus who guards this gate says 'Oh but the payment may clear you to Kirkby Lonsdale it may' but I don't want to go to Kirkby Lonsdale nor does one out of twenty of us, so why should we be taxed to save Kirkby Lonsdale people THEIR fair payment for repairs of THEIR roads."[69] The complaints came to nothing and in 1870 a farmer was summoned for passing cattle through the "chain or bar on the east side of Rivy Bridge" without paying. The Bar was removed in c.1875 and the Tollhouse in c.1938.

Just by the tollbar and station was the junction of the Gatebeck Tramway with the main line. An application to construct a light railway was made to the Churchwardens and to the Trustees of the Kirkby Lonsdale Turnpike by Messrs W.H. Wakefield & Co, gunpowder manufacturers, in October 1874. The company wished to "make certain alterations to the width, height and curve of the road" and "after taking into consideration and some discussion the trustees acceded subject to certain conditions."[70] These included an undertaking to use animal power only with a speed not to exceed five miles per hour and there was a way leave charge of £1. The tramway was taken up in c. 1930 but until the Rowell Green bridge was rebuilt in the 1980's the supports for the tramway bridge could be seen by the beck.

Enquiries as to whether the main line from Lancaster to Carlisle should take the Lune Valley or go over Shap began in 1838. Eventually the surveyors chose the latter route - though the terrain was, if anything, more difficult - and the line opened in 1846. The longest continuously level stretch on the whole line is from Burton to Milnthorpe, about 2½ miles, but just to the north of Milnthorpe station a deep cutting had to be dug at Rowell and for three years there was a large camp for navvies at Woodhouse. Two workmen were killed while building the Milnthorpe stretch of the line. In February 1844 Robert Wills a "small farmer living at Hale"[72] was carting materials when his spirited horse bolted with the waggon. He was thrown under the wheels and decapitated. The following December George Townson,[73] a native of Caton and only married a fortnight, was killed when three waggons ran into him. Three other navvies were hurt, one of whom was scalped. At the beginning of 1846, with the main line well on the way to completion, a branch line from Milnthorpe was projected. A meeting of the North West Railway Group was held at the Cross Keys, but the opposition from local interests was so great that it was abandoned.

The first train used the line on August 29 when "to many of the good folk here a railway locomotive was an unknown monster and many more were naturally desirous of witnessing among the hills and valleys...the iron highway which forms so remarkable a feature of modern economics."[74] The opening of the railway from Lancaster to Kendal on Monday 26 September 1846 was "kept as a general holiday, most shops being closed in honour of the occasion" and at Kendal flags flew from the Town Hall and from the ruins of Kendal Castle. The up line, (i.e. south) was opened first. A new engine named "Dalemain" travelled the two miles from Kendal to Oxenholme in eight minutes. "The train after stopping at Sedgewick for a minute or two to take on several gentlemen proceeded to Milnthorpe Station, the second on the line which is a handsome structure about half a mile (sic) from the town. After taking the directors and other notabilities to Lancaster for Luncheon the return journey was made to Kendal." Proudly for Milnthorpe, the engine this time was called "Bela".[75] There were similar festivities on 19 December 1846 when the down (north) line was opened.[76]

Shortly after the opening a notable accident occurred when the engine driver and officials left a goods train standing on the main line while they indulged in liquid refreshment at the neighbouring inn. It was hit by a train laden with cattle from Scotland and there was "fearful damage" to rolling stock and carnage to cattle - but good pickings in cheap meat were made by 'Happy Jack Fawcett'.[77]

Very early in the New Year of 1847 a platelayer, Joseph Mason, was seriously injured when "unloading coal alloted to a luggage train" at Milnthorpe Station. "The wheel passed over his leg and arm which were crushed and broken in many places" leaving him with "little hope of recovery." At the same time a railway policeman had a narrow escape when he fell "betwixt the rail and the carriage passed over him."[78]

That railway's were safe and here to stay was shown on October 7th 1848 when Queen Victoria and suite passed through Milnthorpe.[79] On that, as on most other occasions, she made the journey at night. In 1852, however, just as the congregation was leaving the Consecration Service of the rebuilt Preston Patrick Church, the Royal Train was seen steaming through Milnthorpe Station.

As a route centre for the surrounding district the Station was of considerable importance especially before the opening of the Furness Railway. In 1853 when Alfred Binyon moved to Grange-over-Sands, all his goods and furniture came through Milnthorpe Station. As a mark of his appreciation he gave a dinner at the Cross Keys for all the workmen with Mr Monks the Station Master in the chair.[82] Monk's had succeeded the first Station Master Stephen Dixon in c.1850. When he left in 1856 he was presented with a gold watch and chain costing £29 8s and a purse of gold worth £34 10s. Later came Thomas Mashiter, Master from 1864-73. He left for Carnforth and he also was presented with a watch and purse, this time for £61 4s 6d. Thomas Arkwright (Master 1873-1883) did less well, receiving a mahogany cabinet and a purse containing £22 4s. His successor was Francis Bond. His daughter "Jane, aged 9, had a marvellous escape from death. She was playing with a friend on the other side of the line and when returning was knocked over by a passing train. Fortunately she fell in the 4 foot and being stunned lay quietly till the whole train had passed over her - and though severely bruised was none the worse for her perilous adventure."[82] Inevitably there were some fatal accidents. Ned Garnett of the Coach and Horses was decapitated in 1855 after lying down to put his ear to the ground to listen if the train was coming. It came and he went.[83]

In May 1882 John Shepherd, a platelayer, was hit by a buffer and killed instantly. His father had been killed at Sedgwick six years previously.[84] Ben Whittaker the post messenger survived with broken bones after the letter retrieving apparatus hit him in 1895. Remarkable acrobatics occurred in 1902 after a new track had been laid and three waggons jumped the line delaying the Euston express by two hours. The next day several more waggons jumped the lines but after a few yards recovered themselves before overturning at Holme.[85]

A quarter of a century after the start of the Lancaster to Kendal line the construction began of a branch of the Furness Railway from Hincaster, on the main line, to Arnside. A branch line had been under consideration for some time. One projected line would have crossed Owlett Ash fields and the land behind Haverflatts Lane to bridge Church Street just north of Ryley Field before cutting through the hills above Birkett's farm and going on to cross the Bela at the Dallam bridge.[88] By an Act of Parliament of 10 July 1867 the Furness Railway Company received power to abandon this project and to dissolve the company set up to build it. In return it was granted way-leave to build the Arnside - Hincaster branch and to use the London and North Western Railway to Kendal and Tebay.[89]

Although the new line was only 5¼ miles long it took several years to build, the work being held up by three exceptionally bad winters, a trade recession and by the difficulty of the terrain. Deep cuttings through the limestone had to be made at St John's Cross, Sandside and through Hawbarrow and Dug Hill at Heversham. Just east of the Bela at Milnthorpe there was a deep cutting through boulder clay and embankments on either side of the Bela. The river and salt marsh was crossed by a beautiful viaduct constructed of limestone quarried on the site, with red sandstone pediments and copings brought up the line from Furness. The three arches over the river were of open box girders resting on stone faced piers.

The cuttings and viaduct claimed several victims. In 1873 John Metcalf of Milnthorpe, a joiner employed on the formation of the arches, fell to the ground and fractured his shoulder. Despite reported hopes that he would be back at his work in six to eight weeks, he succumbed to his injuries.[90] On the other hand when William Griffin fell into the deep cutting while building the road bridge at Heversham, he was brought home on a stretcher and though he received a severe shock to the system, no bones were broken and he recovered.[91] Even luckier was James Middleton who was working on the furnaces being built in conjunction with the railway at Sandside by the North Lancashire Iron Company.[92] He

Bela Viaduct c.1959 with British Railways passenger train. At this period it was mainly used for goods and mineral traffic.

fell 60 feet but landed almost unharmed on some canvas sheeting.

The navvies brought the usual crop of drunkeness prosecutions but generally they created less disturbance than those of the 1840's. However "ample food for the gossips of the neighbourhood" was provided by one workman in 1873. According to the press "it appears that the Gay Lothario hails from the Emerald Isle and that he had been employed for sometime as a bricklayer at the viaduct on the new line of railway and lodged in Milnthorpe about two months, but during this time he had been observed to frequently neglect his work and remained at home in the company of the landlord's wife. The erring couple (eventually) went to Milnthorpe Railway Station, the woman taking her 8 year old son to assist in carrying her luggage and afterwards giving him a shilling and letting him return home. Great sympathy is felt for the deserted husband, a steady industrious working gardener and his two children."[93] He certainly deserved the sympathy. If he failed to get back his wife, obtaining a divorce would be beyond his means in those days, but if he found consolation informally elsewhere he would have been as condemned and pilloried as had been the "erring couple."

Far more worthy was Richard Powell a labourer on the viaduct. One Monday he finished work early and "repaired to the Coach and Horses to have a glass with friends." With only 1s 4d in his pocket he left at 3 o'clock and walked all through the night to Liverpool, arriving there at 9 a.m. on the Tuesday morning. He crossed over to Wirral on the Birkenhead steamer and continued on his journey to his home at Wrexham, which he reached on the Tuesday evening. He had walked 96 miles in 27 hours, an average of

Furness Railway Postcard c.1910.

3¾ miles per hour.[94]

The Furness Branch opened on the 26th June 1876. Passenger trains were at first limited to three daily so as not to impede the iron and coke trains running between Barrow and the North East via Tebay. In July 1894[95] a special train conveyed Sir Henry and Lady Bromley to Sandside Station from their seat at Ashwell in Rutlandshire on a two month visit to Dallam Tower. With them came "servants, horses, carriages and dogs." In 1890, when the passenger service had been extended to four daily, a station was opened near the railway bridge at Heversham. For many years from just after its opening the Station Master was Thomas Walker, who was also at various times, Chairman of Milnthorpe Parish Council. As Heversham was nearer than Milnthorpe station the service - and especially the long remembered engine "Kendal Tommy" – became popular, but it never paid and ceased during the Second World War. The mineral and goods traffic continued. Twice in the 1950's the Royal Train containing the Duke of Edinburgh, who had engagements in Barrow, stayed overnight on the line just up from the Bela viaduct, overlooking the estuary – and the sewage farm!

Despite being relaid with new concrete sleepers in 1960 the branch line was axed by Dr Beeching in 1963. Up came the new track and down came the viaduct. Most of the rubble from the viaduct was dumped in the cuttings but some of the dressed limestone blocks were used in the retaining walls of the Wheatsheaf

Demolition of Viaduct, 1966.

car park at Beetham and behind the Bela factoring house on Beetham Road. Dr. Beeching also closed Milnthorpe Station, but the stopping trains had become so infrequent that few Milnthorpe people noticed and there were no protests.

Having stagnated for half a century, Milnthorpe's road traffic increased in the 1890s during the cycling craze. There were already some cyclists in Milnthorpe. The first person to own a bicycle is said to have been Thomas Baldwin who about 1865 "possessed a bone shaker with wooden spokes and iron hoops, a linear descendant of a hobby horse owned by a doctor in the village."[96] A later enthusiast was John Mashiter of the Post Office, who used his bicycle for business as well as pleasure. On one occasion as he was taking the night mails to the station, he was injured after riding into a gate left by vandals on the Ackenthwaite road. In 1903 he was found lying unconscious on the Dallam Drive, having been thrown against a wall after a pair of skates hanging on the handlebars got entangled with the wheels.[97] Around the time of the First War villagers were treated to the spectacle of Mr. and Mrs. Mashiter, always notably dignified and conscious of their importance, setting out for a ride – he on the bike and she in a side-car resembling a bath chair. On one occasion they got as far as Blackpool. Later still after he had retired

*John Mashiter on
Bone Shaker c.1890.*

to "Maymyo", villagers were sometimes alarmed to see the septuagenarian John speeding down the hill with his brightly polished boots perched on the handlebars!

In 1894 a cycling club was formed with Mr. T.A. Argles as president and it immediately organised a major event at Milnthorpe – a road race from Bela Mills to the Canal Bridge at Skerton, a round trip of 25 miles.[98] However there was only one competitor, P. Unsworth, who completed the round trip in one hour and twenty two and half minutes on a 24lb Beeston Humber. At the end of the event one of the Milnthorpe stewards was thrown from his bicycle and broke his wrist. It was decided not to repeat this race because of objections from the police rather than lack of support.[99]

Others were not deterred and "swarms" of cyclists converged on Milnthorpe during Easter, 1895. "There were the usual crop of spills at the corner of Church Street. They appeared to be none the worse beyond a few lumps and soiled garments and spoilt temper." Casualties included Dr Alexander whose "conveyance was crushed out of shape" and one went through Woods' shop window and destroyed a machine only a few days old.[100] In July 1898 Mr Nickel, of Waterloo in Liverpool, who was staying at Sandside, received severe injuries to his face and neck when the station omnibus suddenly turned across his track on Harmony Hill.[101] He was carried unconscious into the vicarage and took some time to come round. Later that summer "Mr Burrow, who is no light weight, was taken sharply in the rear." He was badly cut and bruised but the cyclist got away "scot free."

Much worse was to follow.

As regards accidents, the motor age began for Milnthorpe on 1st October 1901 when an Argyle voiturette, made in Glasgow, collided in Beetham Road with Mr J Clark's butcher's cart whose shafts were broken. Mr Clark was thrown from his cart and the motor was damaged, but, though it careered across the road, it "remained upright." At first the occupants refused to give their names until the advent of the police after which they were allowed to proceed on their journey. The resulting "Motor Car Prosecution at Milnthorpe" was treated as a cause celebre. Joseph Fisher Hodgson of Etterly View Carlisle was charged "with driving a motor car on the 1st instant at a speed greater than was reasonable and proper having regard to traffic." John Webster of Beetham Hall and other witnesses estimated the speed to have been between 20 and 30 M.P.H. Hodgson denied this on the grounds that his vehicle was incapable of going at such a speed. He had left Preston at 9.30 a.m. and reached Milnthorpe, 37 miles away, at 1 p.m. and although he had not had a breakdown until he reached Lancaster he had decided to drive slowly in order to get the car to Mr Croft's garage in Kendal. It was a 3 horse power model and was geared at 18 M.P.H., and took over 1½ hours to drive the 8 miles to Kendal. The voiturette was, moreover, "the smallest car that is made." Outfaced by all the newfangled technicalities the magistrates dismissed the case and also Mr Clark's claim for £2 damages.[103]

Great excitement was caused in 1903 when a famous motoring pioneer, Mr Cecil Edge, broke down at Milnthorpe. He was bent on winning a record for the first 2000 mile run from London to Land's End to John o' Groats and back to London. Even John Fawcett could not do the necessary repairs and Mr Edge had to telegraph to London for spares. Such was the effectiveness of the railway at that time that the right parts arrived, were promptly fitted and he was on his journey again, within 24 hours. Without further incident he completed the run in 136¾ hours.[104]

By 1906 the Milnthorpe bench had found its teeth. One of the first motorists to be successfully prosecuted was a magistrate, T. A. Argles of Eversley. Along with Mr Geoffrey Howard M.P. he was found guilty of exceeding the 25 M.P.H. limit at a speed trap at Beetham.[105] The Chairman recommended that speedometers should be fitted as stop watches were of little use. Captain Bagot of Levens Hall, another early motorist, was luckier in 1907. On payment of 2s 6d costs his charge was dismissed of driving at 20

Charabanc in the Square c.1914.

M.P.H. and ignoring the 10 M.P.H. speed limit signs.[106] In 1912 three motorists were acquitted of speeding after the bench accepted that they had been unable to see the speed warning sign half way up the wall of the Institute. Later special County Council "10 M.P.H." signs were set up in Beetham Road and Church Street.

Notwithstanding strictures and restrictions motoring became increasingly dangerous. During "prodigious traffic" at Whitsuntide 1906 a Minerva and a Packard car ended up "Hors de Combat" and two cyclists were injured at the Cross Keys corner.[107] The noisy engines often caused horses to bolt. Woods' window suffered again in August 1909 when a carrier's cart, whose horse had bolted from Ryley Field, threw a load of "eggs, butter and a huge can of milk into the shop."[108] In 1911 a confectioner's van was dragged by a frantic horse from Hawbarrow into Milnthorpe. George Lancaster, the driver, was dragged the whole length and ended up with his broken thigh bone sticking through his leg and "in a pitiable condition."[109]

That travel was still a novelty for the urban working class was seen at Whitsuntide, 1914. When a charabanc containing 30 Blackburn mill workers broke down in the morning the repairs were not made until 8 p.m. Even so the party continued on their "day trip" to Windermere.[110] There was little reduction in what was called "joy riding" in the first summers of the Great War and with many experienced drivers at the front there were hosts of minor accidents. In 1915 a car was a write off after crashing into a wall "by the elbow on the Crooklands road."[111] The outbreak of peace led to the first enormous queues through the village and one passenger, Mary MacIlvain Mercer "of Hong Kong," died in her car while jammed at St Anthony's in 1920.[112]

Traffic control was amateurish and inadequate judging by the increased number of road accidents which in proportion to vehicles on the road was much greater in the inter-war period than at any other time. On Fair Day (May 12th) 1924 a lorry driver had his case of driving recklessly dismissed on the grounds that the noise of the cattle in the streets made it impossible for him to hear the shouts of the policeman, ordering him to slow down.[113] In 1933 Donald Bernard Shepherd, a driver's mate from Scotland, was killed when his lorry hit a telegraph pole at night on Beetham Road. Thomas Nicholson of Carr's Yard was killed at the cross-roads in August 1937 having failed, while going to work at 6 a.m., to observe the halt sign. He left a widow and two small children.[114] A rather similar accident, aggravated by the black out, occurred in 1940 when Miss Ellen Burrow was killed by a lorry as she dashed out of Bull Lane to cross over to the Institute. Curiously, she was stated to have been carrying not the usual battery flashlight but an archaic candle lamp. Miss Burrow, a retired school mistress, was given a grand funeral, with three other former teachers, Mrs McNabb, Mrs Sheldon and Miss Scott, acting as Pall bearers.[115] Numerous children were injured on the roads and in 1941 five year old Gillian Mary Roberta Kerr was killed on Milnthorpe hill while crossing the road to post a letter. The child's distraught grandmother, with whom she lived, refused to have the body brought home and so it was laid out in the wash-house of Marsdene, Milnthorpe, where the autopsy was performed.[116]

Without the aid of the breathalyser there were few successful prosecutions for drunken driving in the early days. Drink was behind an alarming incident in 1920 when the drivers of a "Charabanc and lurry" (sic) tried to out-race each other, repeatedly colliding and crashing, as they tore through the village and up the hill, providing "light relief in the interested amusement of the villagers who had watched the endless procession all day long."[117] Eventually the lorry driver was fined £17 for dangerous driving but the magistrate also condemned the behaviour of the enebriated passengers of the "Chara" who had booed and hissed the Constables trying to apprehend the drivers.

At Christmas 1931 a woman, Nurse Lucy Thompson,[118] was fined for drunken driving and the following year Mary Curzon, wife of the Bishop of Stepney, was fined by Milnthorpe Magistrates for not having a driving license.

Danger to life and limb was not the only consequence of the motor age. Dust was the first and worst. At Easter in 1910 it was reported that "the greatest drawback to the pleasure of foot passengers and cyclists on the roads was the dust which was stirred up in clouds by the great number of motors ever passing and repassing. The houses in the main street and Church Street appeared as if some gigantic flour dredger had been besprinkling, it being necessary for all self respecting housewives to keep doors and windows fast shut."[119] Numerous complaints were made by the Parish to the County Council and a chemical called "Dustabo was sprayed on the limestone gravel roads.[121] It was more or less a failure so a water cart had to be used.

The only real solution to the dust problem was a new type of road surface, and in 1911 "great interest was evinced by the tar spraying operations which are now in progress in the town and one side of each street has already been completed. It has proved not to be an unmixed blessing, as in addition to the housewive's complaints of dirty floors, horses do not like it. On Wednesday a horse and a dog cart landed on the pavement opposite Mr Daffady's shop – smashing badly a gent's bicycle which was standing against the wall. A few minutes later a horse and a laden coal cart came down near the same place."[122]

The village youngsters loved the commotion caused by gangs of workmen sweating behind the huge tar kettle followed by the elephantine steam rollers. One group of boys who had been camping in the Lakes – where they had "beaten the Langdale lads hollow"[123]– had lasting regrets that they missed the first tar stretch being laid between Harmony Hall and the Square. The work seemed to go slowly. G. D. Abraham in *Motor Ways of Lakeland* of 1913 commented that "there was ample evidence that ours was a popular route: agressively ugly stock signs were tiring to the eye and the budding hedgrows lay thick in dust. It was only near the speed limits at Beetham, Milnthorpe and Heversham that the countryside showed its full beauty. Milnthorpe with the cross roads of tragic memory where even '3 miles' limit may be dangerous... gave a final glimpse down and across the sandy strands of Morecambe Bay..."[124]

Tar spraying followed no consistent pattern. In 1914 a request to tar roads to the station was refused though "two miles by Belaside Hill were sprayed yet scarcely a house."[125] Nevertheless by 1916 the whole A6 had been tar sprayed from Kendal to the Lancashire boundary.

Road widening followed in the 1920's. In 1927 it was reported that "the structural alterations now in progress gives the village quite a different appearance. On Main Street the Royal Oak has been demolished to make way for Mr Fleming's business premises." These included the cafe/bakehouse on Beetham Road, the Midlands Bank at the corner and a small shop for George Flemming's Saddler's business – later occupied by Sheldons and then Rushton's chemists and later still used as a snack bar. "As a result of the roadwidening the shops and warehouses on Church Street and the old premises of the bank of Liverpool/Martins Bank Limited and the adjacent confectioners shop are now being demolished."[126] With the western end of Main Street gone Flowerden was left standing on the corner, its gable end revealing in exposed undressed stone (formerly hidden) the building line of its vanished neighbours. There were no roadside buildings on the east of Church Street at this time and so opposite the Blue Row a grass banking was formed when the Flowerden garden wall was set back thirty feet. Many of the trees which gave Church street an avenue-like appearance also went and the survivors, a line of beeches between the Blue Row and Grisley Mires Lane, were felled in 1945.

With the demolition of the Bull's Head, Beetham road was widened and the new Bull's Head (erected on the Royal Oak garden opposite the Institute) was set back by ten feet. The new Bull's Head made use of the Royal Oak Assembly room as a dining room while part of the Royal Oak brew house was incorporated in the bakery of the cafe. During the building of two small shops in the yard behind the bakery in 1986 the Royal Oak well was rediscovered.

The greater and faster flow of traffic did not improve road safety. Sergeants Downing and Aikrigg while directing traffic at the cross roads, often had to jump for their lives. Elderly and young pedestrians found the wider street difficult to cross quickly. In 1926 the police were provided with a wooden platform and in 1934 the Parish Council demanded the provision of an island lampost refuge or an "electric robot" to safeguard pedestrians. The Ministry of Transport refused on the grounds that "automatic signals" (used for the first time in London only in 1932) would cost £800 and the volume of traffic, of only 340 vehicles per hour, was insufficient. Four traffic islands were provided in 1936 but these proved to be controversial.[127] Both pedestrians and motorists said they were confusing and dangerous, a claim substantiated when Thomas Nicolson was killed there in 1937. They did not prevent the "world's longest lorry" of 76 feet passing through Milnthorpe conveying an accumulator from Arran to Rotherham.[128]

Nevertheless after a few months they were removed and automatic lights were considered to be the only solution. As an interim measure one large island near Thorpe House (Martin's/Barclay's Bank) was created. Finally, in 1937, Milnthorpe obtained its famous, (or notorious) traffic lights. In 1939 several motorists summoned for disobeying the lights said they had "never seen anything so ridiculous with one stream of traffic being held up on the main road while from the opposite direction only a few are proceeding."[129] Thereafter, the Parish council and others have

*John Fawcett and family outside premises in the Square,
shortly before the fire of 1910 (See Chapter VII).*

regularly grumbled that the priority given to the A6 was too long
and since the removal of Belisha Beacons about 1950, have
demanded a zebra, pelican or any other sort of animal crossing to
safeguard human life. Only in 1987 did the County Council finally
provide proper pedestrian crossings.

For most Milnthorpians the motor age did not dawn until the
advent of the Dallam Motor Bus Company in 1924, belonging to
the firm of John Fawcett and Sons. Long after the company was
taken over by Ribble in 1950 older residents of South Westmorland
would speak of the Dallam buses; the "Duchess," the "Bedford,"
"Percy's bus" and the "Old Lion" with a nostalgia reminiscent of
the yarns told in the 1890's about the Port of Milnthorpe's ships.
The Fawcett's had converted a couple of military vehicles into
charabancs for occasional use after the Great War[130] but it was not
until John Fawcett and his elder sons John (Jack) and Harold saw a
"new type of luxury bus on show at the Wembley Empire
exhibition" of 1924 that they organised a regular service. The first
bus had a "hot water system piped round the interior of the bus for
the comfort of passengers,"[131] but still had solid tyres and gravity
petrol feed. At first the bus made two hourly trips between Kendal,
Milnthorpe and Arnside and during a rail strike later in 1924 was

Dallam buses, staff and crew in the Square, December 1950 -
on the eve of John Fawcett & Sons Motor Bus Company being taken over by Ribble.

regarded as "a great convenience for school children going to
Heversham Grammar School and Kendal High School and for
business people." After the toll road at Silverdale became free in
1927 a service was started between Lancaster, Carnforth, Silverdale
and Arnside. Other routes took in Hincaster, Sedgwick and
Natland and in 1940 the company acquired the Grange to Kendal
route.

After the death of John Fawcett in 1927 the sons Jack, Harold and
Percy, with their mother Jessie, ran the firm and by 1930 their fleet
consisted of 16 vehicles. The family boasted that in over a quarter of
a century they never had a successful insurance claim made against
them. Nevertheless in 1932 one of their drivers, Albert Peet, was
gaoled for 2 months for drunken driving. After a Keystone Cops
chase from Beaumont Bridge, Lancaster, via Silverdale, the law
caught up with Albert when he crashed the bus at the Old Bridge in
Milnthorpe, demolishing 7 yards of wall and wedging his vehicle
across Park Road.[132] In 1933 Harold was fined the princely sum of
1s for employing an unlicensed conductor and in 1934 Percy was
fined 10s for carrying 34 passengers on a 31 seater bus.[133]

Petrol rationing and then the ban on private motoring during the

Second World War made "the Dallam" the life line for much of South Westmorland. Legendary stories were told of overloading and of how mothers were instructed to let their children hang out of the windows to gain more room. Many would have agreed with Harold when, on being summonsed in 1940 for driving a bus with tyres worn down to the canvas, he told the Magistrates "I think that instead of imposing a fine you should give us a medal."[134] Disregarding the letter of the law, but with a fine sense of justice, the case was dismissed. In July 1949 the 8.30 a.m. "school bus" was badly damaged when it was hit by a heavy lorry at the Cross Keys corner, four children and two women, including the Leasgill School teacher Miss Davidson, were cut by flying glass. As far as is known they were the only passengers ever to be injured on the "Dallam." Displaying a renowned business accumen the Fawcett's sold the bus company in December 1950, just as petrol came off the ration and the age of universal private motoring began.

1950 also marked the beginning of Milnthorpe's 20 year martyrdom by the motor car. At Whitsuntide 1954 an estimated 1500 vehicles per hour crawled through Milnthorpe. The opening of the Lancaster by-pass on the M6 in 1960 only added to the problem. Throughout the 1960's Milnthorpe's bank-holiday traffic jams were considered to be second only to those on the Exeter by-pass. According to County Council records, in August 1967 the average daily traffic flow on the A6 south of Levens Bridge was 23,000 vehicles per day.[135] Day time average for the whole year, including the quieter winter months, were estimated to be in excess of 2000 per hour. Moreover much of this traffic was heavy lorries, including the first juggernauts, which could only growl up the hill at 15 m.p.h. Amongst several attempts to mitigate the problem was one which involved stopping of traffic at the north end of the village for ten minutes to allow the morning holiday rush from the south to go north in a double lane. At night the process was reversed. A similar scheme was employed in summer between Brussels and the Belgian coast but to Milnthorpians it was beyond all reason and happily it was soon abandoned.

Milnthorpe was pulverized and polluted and cut in half by a noisome vehicular snake seemingly without an end. Life became intolerable. Property values stagnated; Park Road business folded; the Cross Keys and Bull's Head lost their residential trade because night time traffic kept visitors awake. Even the police court held at the Institute was curtailed because the constant grind and grunt at the traffic lights disturbed the magistrates.

As early as September 1936 a Milnthorpe-Beetham by-pass had been suggested. The first line proposed would have left Hale Moss, south of the King's Arms Inn, crossed the Bela east of Beetham House and then taken the Paradise Lane route to the east side of the

Heater field. It would then have followed Kirkgate Lane through to Heversham where a new railway bridge (to replace one already dangerously weakened) would be built close to the junction with the Princes Way. A tentative line had been agreed when all such works were postponed for the duration of the Second World War. In 1945 Hodgson, Nelson and Scott were told to take into account the by-pass route when building houses on the Heater Field. By this time the original route had been amended so that there would be one bridge over the eastern roads at their junction west of the Heater Field. By 1947 a 1 in 19 gradient was planned for the cutting through the limestone and boulder clay hill south east of Heversham station and the road was to be 150 feet wide, about twice that of the Princes Way. Nothing then happened. When Milnthorpe Secondary Modern School was built the Education Committee was ordered to site the school to take account of the by-pass. Also in the 1960's there was talk of lavish compensation for local landowners. However the opening of the M6 in 1970 and the Barrow Link in 1974 eased the problem. A decade later, in April 1984, the average daily flow through Milnthorpe was estimated at 9324 axle pairs, less than half the 1963 flow. For the time being there was no more talk of a by-pass.[136]

Milnthorpe's historic importance as a route centre was reflected in the large number of inns and taverns established to meet the needs of travellers. At the peak of the coaching period c.1800-1840 there were at least eleven licensed premises in the village. They were the Jolly Waggoners tavern in Park Road, the Buck Inn south of the Old Bridge in Dallam Park, an unnamed ale-house in Main Street near the site of Stoneleigh, the Malt Shovel (or just "the Shovel") on Windy Hill, the Coach and Horses on Haverflatts Lane, the Sun Inn (or Tavern) in the square and at the cross-roads the Royal Oak on the south east corner with the Bull's Head just south on Beetham Road; on the south west corner, next door to each other, the White Lion and the Cross Keys and on the north west corner the Kings Arms. There are also the odd references to "a Bridge Inn" but this could be just another name for the Buck Inn, and also to a "United Friends Tavern." The latter was kept by someone called Atkinson and might have been another name for the Sun Tavern or Tavern Loft next door.[137] On St. Catherine's Day, 1843, Mr Cornthwaite's men were treated to bread and cheese at "Mr Atkinson's United Friends' Tavern."[138]

In addition to the Milnthorpe inns there were two hostelries – the Dixies Inn, the Ship Inn – plus other ale houses at Sandside and three inns, the Ship, the Blue Bell and Eagle and Child at Heversham – all within a mile or so of Milnthorpe square. No wonder Milnthorpe earned a reputation for hard drinking! Very little is known about the smaller houses and most of the

The crossroads c.1910. On the left a horse is tethered to the painters of the Royal Oak. Left centre is the Cross Keys and right centre the King's Arms. On the right is Flowerden and the cottages attached - the latter were demolished c.1927.

information about the rest is after 1800.

The Cross Keys was by far the most important inn, both for travellers and local people for whom it served as a centre for every type of public and private function. It was the headquarters of the Friendly Society, the court room, the place for inquests and the polling station. Traditionally the original inn was a low building with an awning or pent house jutting out into the cross roads. It might have dated back to the middle ages. For a long period the inn belonged to the Hardy family. Robert Hardy was both owner and licensee from 1781 until 1818. His daughter Agnes married Edward Kitching in 1793[139] and they became the parents of Dr Kitching and Mrs Elizabeth Bindloss whose names live on in the Kitching Memorial Reading Rooms and the Bindloss Homes. Robert Hardy retired in 1818 and in August of that year Richard Nelson announced his transfer from the White Lion to that "large and convenient inn known by the sign of the Cross Keys." The Hardy family retained ownership and in 1821, the year when Robert died, the inn was rebuilt. While the work was in progress the license was transferred to a house on Harmony Hill. In October 1821 Nelson announced the reopening of the Cross Keys which was greatly enlarged both in house and stabling, and anticipated a "share in the patronage of the nobility and gentry etc." His high hopes were not realised and in February 1824 it was reported that Richard Nelson had "assigned all his goods, credit and debts to John Postlethwaite, liquor merchant." At the same time the owner of the inn, Richard Hardy, a surgeon of Whalley, advertised "to be let with immediate possession, All that old established and well accustomed Inn known by the sign of the Cross Keys with the Barn, Stables, Gardens and other Appurtenancies thereunto adjoining and belonging and now in the possession of Mr Richard Nelson together with about 50 acres of excellent meadow and Pasture Land.

"The above Inn is situated in the centre of the Market and Port Town of Milnthorpe – at the junction of the Lancaster, Burton, Kendal and Ulverston Turnpike Roads and from its contiguity thereto, forms a desirable and advantageous situation for any person wishing to carry on an extensive coach and posting concern, and is in every respect well adopted for the reception and accommodation of commercial and other genteel Travellers. Proposals in wrinting will be received by Mr Clapham Solicitor Burton-in-Kendal until the 24th instant when the taker will be declared at the said Inn at Six o'clock in the evening.[142] On the 25, 26, 27 all the valuable Hosehold Furniture belonging to the said Richard Nelson was sold along with Horses, Harness, Chaises, Gigs, farming Stock etc. etc." Despite the earlier advertisement the Inn was again advertised on 28th February when it was stated that it was "much frequented by commercial and other Travellers and genteel parties visiting the Northern Lakes and Mountains for whose reception and accommodation it is well adopted."

By 28th March 1824 Robert Hudson, like his predecessor, had moved in from next door and advertised "his thanks for the liberal encouragement he has met with during his residence at the White Lion and take the earliest opportunity of informing the Nobility, Gentry, Commercial Travellers, Public in general that he has taken and entered on the above inn. . . N.B. Choice wines and Spirits. Neat Post Chaises and Careful Drivers."[143]

Robert Hudson died in December 1828 and his widow Elizabeth carried on the business until she retired in May 1847, just as the coaching trade suffered its greatest blow with the opening of the main railway. In August 1847 William Robinson, following precedent set by his two immediate precedessors, "begged respectfully to announce to the gentry, commercial gentlemen and the public that he has entered upon the Cross Keys Hotel late under the superior management of Mrs Hudson. . . and . . . it will be his study to conduct in such a manner as to merit the continuance of the favours so liberally bestowed on his predecessor. Good Stabling with Lock up Coach Houses – Conveyances attend the station daily. . . wines and spirits of best quality."[144]

The sale of Mrs Hudson's equipment lasted four days – 12 to 15 April – 1847. Lots included mahogany, carved and plain four posters, tent and camp beds, an antique oak carved chest dated 1705, an immense number of culinary requisites and "a Family Mangle."[148]

Robinson seems to have been an enterprising landlord for in 1849 a band of 'Ethiopian Grenadiers' gave two entertainments at the Cross Keys to a respectable audience of 166.[149] Business was still quite brisk because before the Furness Line was built the inn was still used by the coaching trade. Among the arrivals at the Cross Keys in 1855 were Lord and Lady Muncaster, a newly married couple en route to Muncaster Castle but "on their arrival at Milnthorpe his lordship received a telegraphic message stating that his brother was going out to the Crimea and after sojourning at the hotel for the evening Lord and Lady Muncaster returned to Portsmouth."[150]

Robinson stayed until 1861 when the inn was taken successively by John Hutton and his daughter Isabella – who was a great benefactor to the workhouse. Miss Hutton left in 1876. She was followed quickly by James Bell, T. Relph and George Piper. By this time the Inn had been purchased by the Dallam Estate. When advertised under the heading "Morecambe Bay, Westmorland" in May 1878 it was described as a "hotel and posting house with stable, coach house and 26 to 30 acres of rich meadow and pasture land."[151] From 1880 the landlord was William Hodgson who with his family played a prominent part in local affairs and who did much to support football and other sports in the area. He retired to Woodlands at Sandside in 1915. Many lots in the Cross Keys sale of 1915 harked back to the pre-motoring age with black horses bringing 57½ gns., 40 gns., and 25 gns. a char a'banc £25, a Rolli Cart £9 2s 6d, a dog cart £7 10s, silver harness 14 gns and a hearse £57. He was followed by Alfred Hind Read, formerly manager of the Winter Gardens at Morecambe, who continued the residential side of the business.

For over twenty years from the Second World War the license was held by Miss Cairns under Hartley's Brewery of Ulverston. In the 1940's and 1950's it still had some pretensions to be a hotel; annual dinners for local associations were held there and there was a restaurant for non-residents.Unlike many other local inns, however, the Cross Keys did not develop its catering standards and became just another beer house. Few of its present clientele would realise that the Cross Keys was for two centuries the most prestigious, as well as the largest, hostelry between Kendal and Lancaster.

The Kings Arms on the opposite corner to the "Keys" was for long it's main rival. The original inn was just to the west in Park Road, in the house occupied in the twentieth century by Jacksons and then Gunby's, the solicitors. Between 1814 and 1821 Edward Dixon was the landlord. He was followed by Thomas Bainbridge and in 1824 the new Kings Arms was built next door.[152] On May Day "the license was taken thro' an opening into the Bar of The New Premises without ceremony and interference."[153] The owner seems to have been a Mrs Hardy, whose family also owned the Cross Keys - but in 1824 it was advertised for sale as consisting of "4 parlours, a large Bar with kitchen etc. on the ground floor, nine bedrooms on the first floor and five bedrooms on the second floor; together with a farm, two stables, shippon, peat house and other appurtenances thereto belonging."[154] Shortly afterwards, according to the *Westmorland Gazette*, a potentially dangerous accident occurred when "One of the servants having set down a candle very carelessly...the flame communicated to a curtain...anxious to extinguish the fire without alarming the house she had nearly fallen a victim to her folly when her cries drew some other members of the family to the place barely in time to preserve the premises from destruction."[155] Thomas Bainbridge left in February 1858 when the Inn was stated to have "an excellent brewhouse, ten stalled stable, barns and garden." After several tenants, including a Mr Bland, William Tyson was the landlord from April 1868 to May 1873. During his occupation the following curious incident was reported; "Sagacity of a Retriever, A Fortunate Recovery. Friday the 19th inst was Candlemas Day at Milnthorpe when many farmers and tradesmen met to settle their accounts. After dinner was over Mr Tyson of the Kings Arms had retired to the bar to smoke his pipe. He keeps a large black dog of the retriever breed known as "Sam" who is a dog of much intelligence. Amongst other accomplishments when they give him a penny and tell him to fetch a newspaper he goes off to Mr Fryer's, walks into the shop, puts down the penny on the floor, puts his foot on it until Mr Fryer gives him the paper which he immediately takes home. On Friday, however, Sam had something in his mouth which was not a newspaper and placed it on the bar table. The landlord took it up and saw it was a purse and on opening it found the contents to consist of seven five pound notes or thirty five pounds, with no trace to whom they belonged, neither had Sam the ability to tell where he'd got them. The affair was a complete mystery for two hours or more when the second son of Mr A. Webster of Beetham Hall arrived at Milnthorpe stating that his father had lost his purse and enquiring if anyone had found it. He was soon referred to the King's Arms and found all right. Sam for his trouble was presented on Saturday night with a new collar but is anything but in love with it as yet."[157] Despite "Sam" business did not prosper and in October 1870 the Inn was advertised to let: "the house might at light expense be converted into a good private residence."[158] William Tyson was followed by John Maudsley and then by William Constable who stayed until 1880 when the Inn lost its licence. In 1881 Dr Hanson Evison moved his surgery to the old inn, now renamed Thorpe House. His eventual successor Dr Seagrave moved from here to Stoneleigh in 1894 when the house became a temperance hotel. From c.1926 a branch of Martin's Bank (later taken over by Barclay's) has been established there.

The White Lion was probably almost as old as the Cross Keys but nothing is known of it until Thomas Huddleston took over the inn when he came from Dent in 1758. In the 1820's, along with the Cross Keys and the Kings Arms it was owned by the Hardy family. After William Thompson left for the Cross Keys in 1847, Isaac Rowlinson was the landlord until 1854. Several tenants followed until the inn closed its doors for the last time in 1873 when Arthur Atkinson was the landlord.[159] The property was purchased by Joseph Daffady, the boot maker, and eventually it passed to his daughter and then to her husband Roland Sharp who continued the shoe business until the 1950's. The shoe shop remained latterly belonging to Mr & Mrs Mason until c.1977 when the premises were put to a variety of short-lived uses.

The Bull's Head was originally just west of the Memorial Hall. From the eighteenth century it belonged to the Scaife family and was a popular haunt for mariners.[160] The last Scaife left in 1829 and was followed by J. Redhead until 1840, Joseph Birkett to c.1843, a Mr Airey to 1847, Arthur Atkinson c. 1852, Mr Sawrey to 1858, Henry Tyson to 1866, and then Mrs S. Moorhouse. She was succeeded respectively by John Wilson 1871-1885, James Brennand to 1894, Edward Moorhouse to 1921 and then by Philip Mackereth who was there until the old inn was pulled down and transferred to its new site, partly adjoining that formerly occupied by the Royal Oak.[161]

Old photographs show the Royal Oak to have been a long low building with its main frontage on Main Street but with two attached butcher's shops and a cottage on Beetham Road. On the corner facing Main Street was a penthouse or "painters", ostensibly a point for tethering horses but more generally a vantage point for "Standers" as "street corner johnnies" are called in Milnthorpe. In 1875 William Hodgson applied to the road surveyor for permission to pull down the "painters" and enclose it. This was refused but he was paid £10 compensation. William also rebuilt the stables and the Assembly room (designed by Eli Cox in 1871) which survived respectively as the Bull's Head Garage (converted into shops in 1985) and Dining Room. Though undoubtedly an ancient establishment, the earliest recorded inn keepers are Edward Grayston in 1814, John Postlethwaite in 1820 and Isaac Clemmet between 1826-1842. Isaac was a great supporter of wrestling and organised a match in Mrs Hudson's field behind the Cross Keys in

Crossroads c.1920, Royal Oak S.E.corner.

September 1842. Unfortunately, after the young lads had had their throws and the ale was flowing, Isaac, although aged 50, agreed to challenge his rival Joseph Birkett of the Bull for the bout - and, falling badly, "came to his death."[163]

His widow quickly made way for Edward Johnson, but in December 1843 the Inn was advertised for sale as "All that well Accustomed Excellent Inn or Public House known of the sign of the Royal Oak situate in the centre of Milnthorpe...with the stabling, yard, Gardens and other convenient outbuildings thereunto adjoining now in the possession of Edward Johnson; together with that Small Dwelling House or cottage adjoining now in the possession of Mr Henshaw...also Two Cottages with part of the garden."[164] Johnson was followed by Thomas Rawlinson and then Thomas Gee who made way for the Hodgson family who held the house until 1923, Mary C. Hodgson being the last licensee. Eleanor Hodgson, daughter of William (landlord from c.1870-1897) married Ben Airey, the swill maker, and named her house on Harmony Hill "Oakleigh" after her old home.

By the early twentieth century the Royal Oak's useful days were over, a victim of changing social habits and of rivalry from the other Hodgson family across the road at the Cross Keys. Curwen described the premises as being derelict[165] and at the licensing enquiry in 1922 Sergeant Downing described it as "being in bad repair, structurally worse than other (public) houses." Although the brewer, A.J. Miles, said the inn was sufficient for the trade it did, he admitted that the shippons, stable and out offices were bad and was prepared to let it go.[166] Accordingly it closed down in 1923 and was demolished the next year just before the old Bull. Much of the stone was incorporated in the new buildings and the surplus was used to level the A6 road at Bela sett.

The new Bull's Head was quite an elaborate structure with mock oak panelling, leaded lights, "H. & C." and electricity laid on. In more modern times a notable landlord was Bill Watts, reputedly a former cowboy in Canada, who held sway in the 1940's and early 1950's. For a while he was Chairman of Milnthorpe Parish Council.

From having been an important inn The Sun in the square had degenerated into a tavern when it was advertised in 1816. Along with the usual barn, stable and garden it was said to have a Bowling Green; all in the occupation and ownership of James Woodburn. Mary Huddleston owned the house in c.1826 and William and then James Robinson in the 1840's.[167] In Feb 1843 James' 3½ year old son was burnt to death after being left for only a few minutes in the parlour after the maid had lit the fire at 8 a.m.[168] In 1850 it was announced that "a match of shooting for a goose at a lead will come off at the house of Mr Stephen James Sun Tavern."[169] After several tenants the license was lost about 1870 and the house - known as the Traveller's Rest - became a boarding house and also provided accommodation for the Mechanics Institute. In the 1920's the Rigney Bank houses were built on the Sun Tavern's garden and former bowling green.

Across the greens the less respectable Malt Shovel on Windy Hill survived until 1906. Having been the workhouse until c.1815[170] it bears several features of the eighteenth century. Just when it became a beerhouse is not certain, but it was for long owned by the Huddlestone family who also owned the Glasgow House Malt Kiln just to the north. In 1869 the house was nearly destroyed by a fire which badly damaged a shop and peat house next door belonging to Mary Mitchell.[171] The landlord, Anthony Huddlestone, made a daring rescue of cows from the smoke filled shippon. Anthony and Ann Huddlestone left the house in c.1881. In 1884 Thomas Hartree was the licensee and he was followed by Edwin Daws who was drowned at Grange in 1889. John Proctor then kept the house until 1906 when he went bankrupt for £314 with assets of only £22 2s 4d. He blamed his penury on high medical fees required for his wife and on declining trade. By 1905 he was selling only 50 barrels per annum at 30s per barrel. At the same time the licensing magistrates judged the house surplus to requirements and closed it down. Proctor got £150 compensation but the money all had to go to pay Mr Dilworth of Ulverston for rent.[172]

Traditionally the lowliest public house in Milnthorpe was the Coach and Horses in Haverflatts Lane. In 1846 it was put up for sale with a four-stalled stable, in the occupation of Thomas Rowlinson. Again in 1848 it was to let as "all that excellent and well accustomed Beerhouse, with stabling, brewhouse etc., in good repair." Apparently it was purchased by Robert Fryers and let to Edward Garrett whose widow Dorothy was still the licensee in 1873. Between 1881 and 1914 the house was owned and occupied by Isaac Wilkinson who fought off an attempt to close it down.[173] He was followed by James Moss who came up three times before the magistrates in 1915. They were bent on declaring the house redundant on the grounds that the population of Milnthorpe was falling (in fact 1051 in 1901 and 1019 in 1911) and that there were 11 public houses within 3 miles, equivalent to 1 per every 203 people. At £17 p.a. the rateable value of "The Coach" was lower than the other licensed premises: the Cross Keys and Bull at £40 and the Royal Oak, at £38. Sergeant Park, the village policeman, agreed with the magistrates that "there was not as much drinking as formerly, but the house had a highly respectable working class trade." It moreover had good sales of "supper beer and local people preferred to go for it there as some of them do not like to fetch it from public houses in the main street." The *Westmorland Gazette* commented: "They shrink from letting their right hand know what their left hand doeth. By their jugs ye shall know them." Moss explained that he sold at least 4 barrels a week and that he also earned a good wage as a mason.[174] The house was allowed to stay open and was granted, eventually, a full license. Gradually becoming more genteel, the premises were modernised in the 1920's then again in the 1960's For some 20 years until 1984 Robert Hoskinson was licensee.

Though Milnthorpe since the 1920's has had only 3 inns - the "Bull" the "Keys" and the "Coach" - by the 1980's there was no shortage of licensed premises, the sale of alcohol being allowed in eleven premises, the same number curiously as in the heyday of inns and coaching at the turn of the eighteenth century.

6

The Land

According to Campden, writing in 1611, Westmorland was not to be "commended either for plenty of corne or cattle neither being clothed with arable grounds to bring forth the one nor pasturage to bring up the other."[1] Nicolson and Burn, in 1777, confirmed the unproductive nature of the county's agriculture, "the soil was barren and unfruitful, there being much uncultivated waste ground and much of it incapable of cultivation as this county abounds with mountains."[2] There was, moreover, "no great plenty of wood."[3] Lack of trees was not, they believed, caused by the harsh climate and terrain but because, they "seem to have been industriously destroyed to prevent (them) affording shelter to the Scotch invaders."[4] A mixed blessing was caused by the region's "lying near the Western ocean it is much exposed to Rain brought by the South West winds which blows in this part two-thirds of the year. Hence their crops are later by three, four or in some places six weeks than in some other parts of the Kingdom."

On the other hand there were many fruitful and pleasant valleys; and "the bottom of Westmorland (as it is called) hath a considerable quantity of level ground, though surrounded on every side with high mountains." The air in the County was "somewhat sharp and severe (especially in winter) but withal very healthful and people live commonly to a very great age...and though barren as the soil is in many places the county is very populous in proportion to the value of the lands than any other county in the Kingdom."[5]

Lying, certainly, in the "Bottom of Westmorland" Milnthorpe was well placed for agriculture. The surrounding countryside was composed largely of boulder clay drumlins which, though sticky in winter and hard whenever there was a drought, could produce a friable tilth as well as excellent pasture. As the valleys long remained wet and choked with vegetation the earliest farming communities were on the hillsides which were also better for defence. Evidence from the late Romano-British Dark Age site around the Dog Hole on Haverbrack suggests that sheep and cattle were kept supplemented by the, non-lupine, products of the hunt, fish and molluscs from the estuary and the wildlife of the mosses.[6] To these the Normans added rabbits; and in 1335 John de Wodehouse King's Clerk and parson (of Heversham) and Alexander de Wyndsore received a grant of free warren on their desmesne lands in Milnthorpe and Heversham.[7]

The names Haverbrack[9] (first recorded as Hal Freheh in 1094) and Haverflatts, probably refer to agriculture. "Haver" is Old Norse for oats; hence the local name for oatcake, "Haverbread"[10] might well go back 1000 years to the time when the Scandinavian settlers near the "Mylenporp" began to scratch a living from the soil. Haverbread, also called calp cake or yat bread, was still a major food item in the early nineteenth century. The lumps of black mealy dough were cooked on a gridle - a disc usually 26 inches in diameter set on a three-legged brandreth - rather like a stool - placed in the embers of a peat fire.

No clear evidence survives as to where Milnthorpe's early and medieval corn fields were. It is reasonable to suppose that the shallow slopes of St. Anthony's Hill, Kirk Gate and Cappelside were cultivated, though few traces of old crop marks remain. Rig and furrow undulations however, can be seen clearly in Dallam Park where the top soil has not been disturbed by modern agriculture. Until the expansion of the Deer Park in c.1820 these slopes were cultivated by the villagers of Milnthorpe. Neddy Stones recalled that the "land over the old bridge up by the Buck Inn and on the east side of the foot path to Haverbrack was in fields, arable and pasture. My mother used to go out with the team and led the horses whilst ploughing; a customary matter in the common sense days of old."[12] By that time it was probably only the plough team which was held in common. Open field cultivation on the pattern of the Midlands and the South was not general in the North West partly because of the lack of large areas of level land and of compact communities necessary for the purpose. No doubt the hillside ploughed land was cultivated in common in the Middle Ages. The name Town Field (behind Church Street) might also refer to community use. Even so names surviving into modern times like The Firs (Furze = Gorse), Foggy Hole, Crestolang Mires and Grisley Mires indicate considerable areas of waste land.

Early documents relating to agriculture are as scant as the evidence on the ground. Stock is mentioned in a summons issued to William de Courcy in 1336 "to answer Alexander de Wyndsoeur of a plea that he took his cattle and unjustly detained them, namely 8 oxen and 8 cows at Heversham in a place Called Milnthorpe."[13]

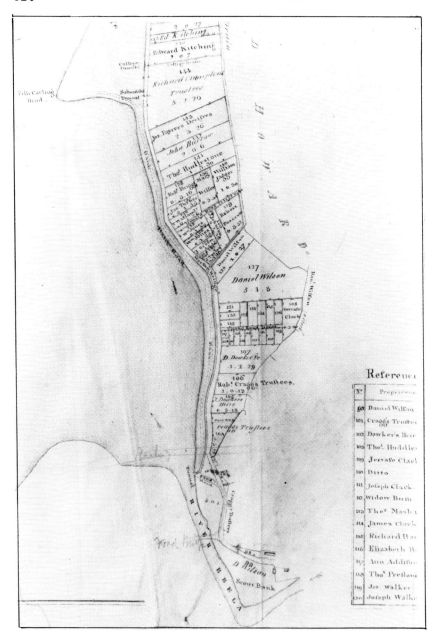

Enclosure Award 1803.
The Marsh.

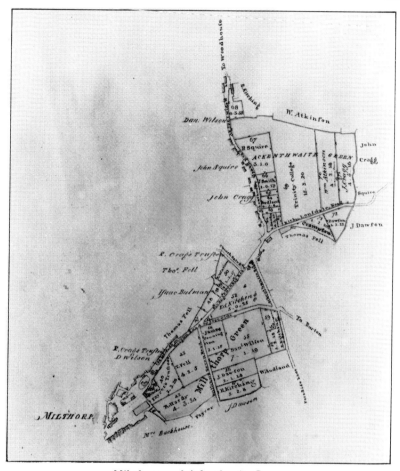

Milnthorpe and Ackenthwaite Greens.

The oxen would be used for ploughing. In 1356, Alan, son of Hugh de Heversham, impeached John, son of Nigel Coysons, for reaping and carrying away his corn at Heversham to the value of 100s. A wide variety of farm products are related in the grant of a living of £20 per annum by William Booth, Archbishop of York to the vicar of Heversham. To provide the income the parson was to receive "the third part of the Mill of Milnthorpe, anciently belonging to the said church, also the tithes of fishings, mills, foals, calves, pigs, brood geese, hens, ducks, bees, eggs, pigeons, lint, hemp, leeks, onions, and garden products of the whole parish."[14] Until c.1800 part of the vicar's tithe was collected in kind - and a tythe barn is indicated on a plan by the road[15] between Owlett Ash and the Red Barn on Harmony Hill.

Wills and inventories provide some evidence of stock and crops. In 81 Westmorland Wills dating from 1686 - 1738 J. Somervell found that animals were very few in number.[16] The value of sheep rarely exceeded £5 (less in many cases than wearing apparel) and cattle £10. Thus Thomas Preston of Milnthorpe, Husbandman, left in his will of 1700 "one little Horse, two kine and a little Heifer valued at £10." His furniture and equipment were assessed at twice as much despite low values e.g. "Trade utensils etc. carts and wheels 5/-, Harrow Barrow 2/6 Gavelock 1/- Wheel Benches, shelves, Guilded Balls (sic) 15/-." Joseph Grigg of Millthrop, Distiller, (Died 1701) was more opulent, leaving "Live stock etc. Four Horses and Mares and two Kine £14 10s. Cart Wheels, Swine, Poultry and dunghill £5." There are few references to pigs, and bacon only occurs once in Summervell's Wills.

Judging from the inventories, oats was by far the most important crop, with regular references to Barley (often called Bigg) and Hay. Wheat, Rye and Peas are rare but Flax and Hemp, probably grown for domestic spinning and weaving, occur several times. Thus, Thomas Preston left stores of Barley, Hay, Hemp and Flax valued at £11 2s.6d. and Meal and Malt worth 14/6. Will Croft's Meal and Malt were worth £7, Hemp £1, Hay in Barn £3, Straw £1 and oats £12 10.00.

Until the nineteenth century farmers seemed to have concentrated on grain despite the unsuitably wet climate and cool summers. The main reason for this was the poor roads which meant an area suitable for grain like North Yorkshire could not readily relieve less well placed regions. The milder winters of South Westmorland did enable flocks from harsher areas to be wintered. Turnips and other root crops were very slow in coming in, while even hay was limited owing to small fields as much as to the wet summers.[24]

Milnthorpe was an area of early enclosure. There were tiny plots called "parrocks" near to the village and farmsteads with larger closes further out. Most enclosures are irregular in shape indicating piecemeal reclamation of the land, but the narrow north-south rectangular fields on the southern slopes of St. Anthony's Hill are typical of the seventeenth century. The St. Anthony's Hill fields might, however, be even older as their name is derived from the lands forming a portion of the estate of William Shepherd who in 1542 left an endowment for a priest serving a Chantry in Kendal Church dedicated to St. Anthony. It is from the St. Anthony's lands that Milnthorpe's most conspicuous landmark, St. Anthony's tower, takes its name, as does St. Anthony's House and a bungalow on the east side of the hill called Little St. Anthony's. There was actually a field of 1 acre 1 rood 16 pecks known as "Little St. Anthony's," which in 1831 was in the occupation of Ewan Rawlinson.[25]

Elsewhere, the well known test of counting tree species in a field hedge indicates, (on the principle that the greater variety the older

Haymaking in Dallam Park, by T.Allom c.1820.

the hedge) that many boundaries are several centuries old. The
Paradise Lane hedge, for example, shows a dozen or so varieties
including several types of slower growing holly.

The names and area of old enclosures is indicated in many
surviving conveyances and in Manorial records. In 1742 John
Cragg of Cragg Yeat, Ackenthwaite, sold to John Smyth for £100
"The Close called The Pickle at 4a 1 Rd., Holling Hill meadow 2a
3rds. Gandy Bank 1a 1 rood, Law Close 4a, High Close 1a 3 rds." An
earlier deed relating to Cragg Yeat refers to the house or two houses
and "..Closes called Brunthwaite, The Parrock or Cragg Parrock at
Rowell Lane End Containing in all 3 acres."[26]

A larger estate was purchased for an unspecified sum by John (?)
Chambers on 24 October 1746, consisting of Marsh Close,
Atkinsons Croft, Arnthwaite, Back Croft, Gate Croft, Four Acres,
Stiles acres, Great Lythalls, Gate Lythalls, Back Lythalls, Cornthwaites
Croft, Walter Cross Clease, Pease Land containing in the whole by
Estimation 28 acres 3 rood 30 perches at a Customary rent £1 14 7½
in Millthrop in the Parish of Heversham.[27]

Some conveyances indicate common and other rights. In an
indenture of 1717, William Cornthwaite of Scout Bank, Yeoman,
sold to Robert Cornthwaite, Yeoman, "for three score and Thirteen

pounds 10 shillings a house at Scout Bank holden under the Rt. honourable James Grahme Esquire and of the Manour of Millthrope by yearly rent of Three Shillings and Sevenpence halfpenny all and singular edifices buildings barns stable out houses folds, fronts, forthparts, commons of pastures and Turbary Mosses marshes moors ways waifts easments hedges fences ditches Rights Liberties previlieges."[28] Similarly the will of Samuel Towers of 1740 specified "a cottage dwelling house in Millthrop, outbuildings, orchards, gardens, fronts, folds, backsides and one little fold or parrock lying on the north side of Milnthrop."[29]

Most Milnthorpe land until the nineteenth century was held from the manors of Levens Hall or Dallam Tower, and was not therefore, free hold. Unlike tenants of rented property the occupants could sell the property rather like the holders of modern leases. Customary lands were, however, subject to annual rents and other obligations. These were fixed and levied at Manorial Courts held around Old New Year's day (Lady Day) 25 March, Mid Summer, Michaelmas and St. Thomas Day (21st December). The Levens Court met at the Cross Keys from c.1800 and the Dallam Court generally in the large court room at Heversham Hall. Summons to attend the Dallam Manorial Court in 1699/1700 are typical of the form used:

"Whereas by ye custom of ye Manno of Heversham by all the time whereof there is no memory of man to ye contrary, only the customary tenants of ye sd. manor have agreed to pay an orbitrable & reasonable fine ouvry of their customary tenements within ye said manor at the exchainge of Lord & tenant now I James Barchouse for & on behalfe of Edward Wilson, Lord of ye manor & by his appointment due upon ye chainge of Tenant demand of you William Cragg for ye customary Tenants right within ye said manor of ye Rent of one Shilling & for ye...fine of one pound & ten shillings. And you will pay ye said upon ye 26th day of March next being Tuesday at the house of James Becke in Heversham aforesaid betweixt the toimes of one or two of ye Clock in the afternoone of ye same day Demand ye first day of March 1699. Demanded at the time of William Wilson for his Customary Tenant right estate within the said manor of Heversham of the yearly rent of three shillings and fower pence the sume of one pound and ffifteen shillings for a ffine for the said Estate and to pay the same att the house of the above named James Beck, upon the aforesaid 26th day of March 1700."[30]

Rents and entry fines were not high. (An entry fine was a fee payable by new tenants). In 1729 Robert Woodhouse paid George Wilson an annual rent of 1s 10d for three Closes; Woodgate Close, White Close and The Rood. In 1729 Robert Dickonson paid 10s for a parcel of meadow called Crestolay Mires following alienation of

John Elleray customary rent 3d. In October 1741 Joseph Dickinson was admitted as a manorial tenant by paying a Fine of 13d in Grisley Mires; in 1749 Jas. Preston paid on admitting fine of £1 2s.6d. for Scoutbanks, by will of Isobel Preston; 1750 Rich. Bork paid a fine of £2 10s for Blayshaws and Hogg Holme, rent 1s 9d; 1758 James Dowker paid £1 1s for Kirstal Mires and Ornethwaite "both lying near Millthrope" from Jo. Dickinson, rent 10d.[33]

Fines called Heriots were levied on the death of the tenant. Originally this meant rendering up the best beast or chattel of the deceased but by the sixteenth century fines were usually commuted for cash. A memorandum states that "Gabrial Croft his wife showed a Deed of ye flatts being 3 acres of 2s rent bought of Rich Bufskell by Leo Wright 1599 to bee ascertained to an Herriott of 8s in money. I had ye another Herriot of £3 from ye sd. wife."[35]

That rents were low is shown by the Dallam returns of fines for Ackenthwaite and Milnthorpe in 1686.

Ackenthwaite	*Mid Summer*	*St Tho. Day*
John Saule	2 (pence)	2 (pence)
Tho. Cragg	8	8
Jon Jackson for The Craggs	8	8
Tho. Baxter for Edmond Hines	24	24
Sarah Middleton for a tenement	28	28
Robt. Gibson for Cornthwait	7	6
Hinds & Briggs	-	-
Jon Audland	6	7
Tho. Baxter	8	8
Milnthrop		
Jon Benson	4	4½
Robt Gibson for		
Atkinson	5	5
Widdow Clarke	43	47
Widdow Geldert	1	1
Widdow Cragge	9	9
Widdow Tunstall	2	2
Rich Clark	2	2
Jon Dowthwait	2	2
Edw. Carcus	2	2
Tho. Troughton	4	4[36]

Milthorpe and Ackenthwaite rentals were cheaper than other hamlets in the parish; Heversham rentals averaged 2s 4½d, Rowell 1s 9d. Excluding Widdow Clark, Milnthorpe rentals averaged only 7½d and Ackenthwaite 10d. The reason was probably that there were more small cottages and parrocks in Milnthorpe.

Fines payable on the death of the Squire are shown in "General ffine due upon the death of Edward Wilson Esq., late lord of the sd. Manor."

Ackenthwaite

Rent		Fine
4 pence	Lanselot Jackson	6 0
1/4	Chr. Bellman	1 5 0
4/4	Rich Baxter	-
1/9	Henry Baxter	1 1 0
5/4	Tho.Hutton & Tenant & parsell	4 10 10
1/1	Wm. Audland	10 0

Millnthrope

9 pence	Ffrancis Benson	6 0
6/0	Elizabeth Elleray	12 00
1/10	Elz. Elleray	Admitting fine 15s
3d	Rich Simpson	0 6 0
-	Robert Dickinson	12 00
10d	Ruth Cragg	16 0
4d	Myles Towers	6 0
4d	John Atkinson	3 6
4d	Ditto for Carus	3 6
9d	Geo Noble	10 0[37]

Release from manorial obligations could be obtained. In 1743 Richard Cragg got release from boons (labour dues) on 18 acres of closes of several names: "High Close, Low Close, Wheat fold, Meadow Goody Bank, Far Branthwaite, Far Bryan, Brunshaws, Hollinghill and a close called the pickle."[37]

By the eighteenth century most landholders were - in practice - independent of the squires. Those with 20 or more acres like the Craggs and Audlands of Ackenthwaite, who would also have common rights, belonged to the "statesman" class, the local equivalent of a yeoman; the traditional back bone of Old England. As late as 1777 Nicolson and Burn stated that "every man lives upon his own small tenement and the practice of accumulating farms have not yet here made any considerable progress."[38]

Many of the surviving farm houses and building go back to the high period of the local statesmen in the seventeenth and early eighteenth century. Birkett's or Bridge End Farm was held by the Dowker family in the seventeenth and early eighteenth centuries. In 1712 Richard Dowker held the farm and the executors of his descendants still possessed the property in c. 1826 when Walter Berry II took over the tenancy from the Foxcrofts.[39] The name Birkett's comes from an even older family, resident in Milnthorpe from at least the sixteenth century and who appear to have been the landlords of the Dowkers. It was a Mr Daniel Birkett who sold the farm on 14 February 1843 to George Wilson of Dallam Tower, the Berry's remaining the tenants until 1906.[40] It says much for the resolution of smaller landowners or statesmen that not until the mid-nineteenth century were the powerful Wilsons able to obtain such a property within sight of Dallam Tower. It comprised over 60 acres strategically placed between the tower estate on the marsh and the Park and other Dallam holdings in the village. After Walter Berry IV died the property was tenanted by Thomas Ferdinand Casson from 1906, who farmed about 168 acres. Since 1932 the farm has been occupied by Thomas Whitfield and his son John and expanded to some 180 acres. It was under the Wilsons that the original Birkett's Farmhouse[41] was demolished and rebuilt in 1877.

To the north of the village the Squire family were in continuous occupation of Higher Haverflatts from the early eighteenth century to the 1870's. The present villa-like farmhouse was built in 1882 after the farm had been sold to William Tattersall the Maltster in 1872. The earlier house is said to have been built by two brothers called Squires. In 1755 William Tyson sold to Robert Squire Goody Bank and in 1767 he took over 5½ acres of the Brunthwaites, to the south of the farm.[41] Under the Tattersalls, John Bell was the tenant from 1894-97 and he was followed by James Melling who remained after Tattersall's daughter Alice Whiteley sold the farm to Thomas Ward in 1913. In 1916 Ward took over the farm himself.[42] From 1920's to March 1987 the farm was occupied by the Burch family.

Lower Haverflatts has an older farmhouse dated 1691. It seems to have been a smaller property. When the family of John Smith tenanted the farm from c.1806 to 1867, 46 acres of land went with the place. They were followed by John Kidd and his widow until 1904. From 1906 to 1920 John Alderson was the tenant. After 1920 the farm was tenanted by Thomas and then Bernard Dowker, descendants of one of Milnthorpe's earliest farming families.[43]

Parkside and Owlett Ash, which retain features from the sixteenth and seventeenth centuries, also had land attached to them. From c.1800 Parkside was generally farmed along with the Dallam Estate. Owlett Ash, although one of the largest residential properties, never seems to have had more than thirty acres.

Ackenthwaite Farm, whose house is externally of the mid-eighteenth century, was probably always a larger holding. In 1826 Fell and Pennington were owners of the farm and Robert Clark was the tenant. When it was sold to the Dallam estate William Ormerod took over and farmed 100 acres. From 1888-1900 and from 1900-1915 William Bateman and William Edward Barnes were the

Crosby Lodge, 1907.

Detail of roof, Crosby Lodge.

tenants. In 1915 James William Garnett entered in to be followed eventually by his son William and grandson Wilson.[44]

Crosby Lodge, whose datestone inscribed RTC 1749 is the oldest in the Civil Parish of Milnthorpe, has continuously retained independence from the great estates, as has the neighbouring property of Cragg Yeat, of which at one stage it formed part. In 1826 the farm was owned by John Cragg and John Mashiter was the tenant until his death in 1849. He was followed by his son until 1885 when John Hewetson became the farmer. In 1897 John Mashiter, grandson of the earlier tenant, took over. He only lasted until 1905 when John Wilson rented the property eventually buying it in 1925 from the trustees of John Bownass, nephew of William Smith Cragg. Since 1936 Crosby Lodge has been farmed by John Wilson's son-in-law, James Melling and grandson Edward Wilson Melling.[45]

The (Low) Cragg Yeat estate has perhaps the largest archive attached to it of any local property independent of Dallam Tower and Levens Hall. The Craggs were certainly domiciled here from the early seventeenth century and their prominence in local affairs is revealed in manorial records and conveyances e.g. in 1742 "John Cragg, grocer of Milnthorpe, granted to Robert Squire all that his cottage dwelling house wherein Francis Lund now inhabited with all the out buildings, orchards, gardens and draw-well situate at Ackenthwaite."[46] By the mid-nineteenth century the Craggs were absentee landlords, the farm having been occupied by Richard Ormerod in1885, followed by Benjamin Cornthwaite and then from 1912 by Richard Holliday.Since the 1940's it has been farmed by the Barnes family.

In addition to the larger yeoman properties there were many smaller landholdings. Buttsyeat (High Cragg Yeat) at Ackenthwaite, with about 16 acres, was a typical smallholding. Most of the smaller farmers had other occupations. James Clark, who farmed 40 acres at Hillside, Ackenthwaite, in 1860 was a boot maker by trade. "Here the farmers with their men come to be shod with good strong leather boots, made to special order and measurement."[46] Similarly, Edward Sanderson who held Ryley Field from 1826-1842 was a clog and pattern maker. When he died the property was advertised as having a large garden and orchard and with or without a shippon and five acres of good land.[47] The next owner, Martin Whittaker, expanded the property but was mainly interested in his large ironmongery and guano importing business.[48] After his death Ryley Field went to his nephew John Holme who let the house and land to various tenants. His son sold it to H.C. Hodgson in 1919. In 1945 Percy Wrightson, a poultry farmer, purchased the property but when much of the land was acquired by the local authority for the Ryley Field Road and Kirkhead Council housing estates it ceased to be a viable unit. Between 1979-1986 much of the remaining land was acquired for private housing.

The lower (southern) part of Ryley Field was probably farmed from Sunnyside, a small farmstead on Haverflatts Lane. Its adjoining barn had already been converted into cottages by 1930. It is possible that the five acres, two roods and 38 perches advertised in 1864 as belonging to Rock Cottage, to the east, were farmed from Sunnyside.[48] In 1885 John Jackson Kirby of Rock Cottage was described as a farmer. Twine Walk to the west of Rock Cottage, though mainly an industrial unit, was also a small farm. In 1840 it was advertised as having an adjoining barn, stables and garden while in 1870 Martin Whittaker of Ryley Field bought 8 acres of land belonging to the property called Low, Middle and High Bucks. Nevertheless Thomas Hodgson farmed the Twine Walk land in 1885.[49]

Though most of the smaller farmsteads had only a little land adjoining their buildings, many had outlying holdings plus

Johnny Wilson and bull c.1910.

common rights. As late as the 1980's the Audlands, who until
c.1800 combined the occupations of smiths, farriers and farmers,
retained fields at Heversham,Woodhouse, Ackenthwaite, along
Paradise Lane and on Milnthorpe Marsh, which altogether
amounted to less than thirty acres. This scattered pattern was
typical of the area and may have originated to enable farmers to
share out wet land (generally on the mosses) with higher ground
(called "hard land") and wintering closes.

For the inquest post-mortem
taken upon the estate of Richard Gibson, late of Rowell, in 1630,
showed for example that he was "seised in his demesne of one close
of land, called Newlands on the south side of Milnthorpe Green,
and of a close called Crostonlaugh, of another called Eskrigge, of
another called Branside, of another on the west side of the last, of
another called Farclose, of a parcel of land in a place called
Todholes, and of another parcel in Sylecroft and of another parcel
called Foggyholme, all of the last in Ackenthwaite amounting to 12
acres."[50]

For all villagers, whether they possessed much land or none,
common rights were important. Commons provided grazing for
sheep and beef cattle, or if near in, for dairy cattle and geese. It was
probably for the commoners that the village pin-fold, for stray
stock, was strategically placed on Grisley Mires Lane - a road that
originally led to the common grazing land on the marsh. Turburry,

or fuel rights, to cut peat and gather kindling, were particularly prized by the very poor. With little open fell land available, Milnthorpe commons were not extensive. By the eighteenth century there were three main commons, Ackenthwaite Green, Milnthorpe Green and Milnthorpe Marsh (the mosses).

Ackenthwaite Green ran along the east side of the Woodhouse road from opposite (Low) Cragg Yeat to the junction of the Kirkby Lonsdale road. From the south its boundary started close to the water hole corner on the Kirkby Lonsdale road and ran for a quarter mile north to the head of the common, in all about 30 acres. Milnthorpe Green was larger with about 40 acres. Its eastern base was a line along the end of Paradise Lane across to the start of Kirkgate Lane; it then swept westward over the hill on which the Bindloss Homes now stand down to Milnthorpe square. Its south boundary was over the top of the Firs, a couple of fields beyond the present cemetery. To the north it also included a ragged area along the north side of Kirkby Lonsdale road which was bordered by several parrocks. One was called Willans, a name now used by a house built on the Heater Field nearby. The main common of over 300 acres was on Milnthorpe Marsh which stretched from the north of the Bela two miles north to the River Kent, just before it whirled round its final meander at Halforth. By the late eighteenth century peat cutting over almost the entire area had aggravated flooding and the unproductive extent of the commons aroused concern especially amongst the greater landowners, who held the main rights to improve wastes by enclosure. As the owners of four-fifths of the land they had to give consent prior to legal powers being granted through a private act of Parliament, which rather like a later twentieth century motorway act, could override objectors. Nationally, most enclosure acts occurred in the late eighteenth century, but locally they came later: the Kirkby Lonsdale Act being passed in 1808, Hutton Roof and Witherslack in 1815 and Beethwaite Green (Levens) not until 1837-38.[51] The Heversham Act dates from 1803.[52] The main landowners who sponsored it were the Lords of the Manors of Levens and Dallam; Viscount Lowther, who owned large tracts in the Lyth Valley, then part of Heversham Parish; Trinity College, Cambridge, which owned the Rectoral lands of Heversham Church and most of the corn tythes. The Vicar of Heversham, Dr. George Lawson, was also deeply involved. He required compensation for common rights which were part of his glebe. The former common land would also provide compensation for commutation of tithes which would be included in the Enclosure Act.[53] Lesser landowners and possessers of common rights had a statutory right to be informed and details of procedure and plans were posted at the church and read publicly. Often, however, smaller and frequently illiterate claimants were baffled

into submission before the whole process began.

The Act which "divided, collated and inclosed the commons, wastes ground and mosses in the parish of Heversham" was passed in 43 George III i.e. 1803. It caused the enclosure of some 6000 acres throughout the Parish as a whole and so the three to four hundred acres concerning Milnthorpe were relatively small. However, as the Milnthorpe commons were potentially good farming land, not merely fell pasture, and were used by a substantial population close at hand, they were important and valuable. The Awards granted under the act were eventually bound in a massive volume, five inches thick. It details exactly how the commons were apportioned, and who got what. The plots were numbered and varied in size from less than one acre to over fifty acres.

The commissioners first specified that new roads had to be laid over the former commons. A Marsh Road 21 feet wide was to run for two miles north from the Bela to the College Green, crossing near Heversham new roads running from Moss Side and from Leasgill. At the southern end the Sand Road was specified as running from "the Bela along the shore to Fishcarling Head to join another tract west of the new sea wall called Bank road." Several field access roads were specified including Clark's and Howard Road off which were many smaller plots. On Ackenthwaite Green a new road was laid out starting opposite the realigned end of Paradise Lane and connecting with the Kirkby Lonsdale Road. It was to be called Ackenthwaite Green Road but later became known as Smithy Lane as it cut across the yard between Audlands House and the ancient smithy. It was to be thirty feet wide including grass verges. The realigned Burton and Kirkby Lonsdale Roads formed with Smithy Lane a triangular field, of 5 acres 24 perches, soon called "The Heater Field" because it resembled both the shape of a flat iron and the limestone coping on the field walls also known as "heaters." To the south of the junction with the main road (close to Owlett Ash) another narrower lane led up the enclosed common to the new enclosures. It was to be called Milnthorpe Green Road, but was soon called "Pig Lane."[54] Later it led to the cemetery. The major construction ordered by the Enclosure Commissioners was the sea bank, the famous or notorious "lug"[55] of the Constance Holme novels 'against' the River Kent. To protect it brushwood and 'paving' were to be laid on the sea-ward side, along the whole length from the Bela to Ninezergh, in all about two and a half miles. A public drain, always called "the dyke", was to be dug "the width of 6 feet at the bottom which we deem to be called Millthrop Marsh Drain, beginning at the River Beela near the south end of Millthrop Marsh extending northward to the east side of the bank against the said River Kent to the Bridge over the said drain called Marsh Bridge thence north east over Millthrop Marsh then to the side of the ancient inclosed lands to the allotment no 198 herein awarded to Richard Howard Esquire thence north..to a drain across Moss side Road to..a drain on Leasgill Marsh." Other smaller drains were also created including Vicar's Drain, between a 58 acre allotment awarded to the vicar and fifty acres awarded to Trinity College, both on the west side of Marsh Road. Both the lug and the dyke must have given work for scores of men. Unfortunately neither the numbers involved nor the costs have survived.

Fences and ditches between allotments had to be constructed within three calendar months of the award. The ditches had to be two feet six inches deep at the bottom and quick wood was to be planted one foot from the sides, to form, eventually, a four foot high hedge. On higher land stone could be used and walls, always called "fences", were to be five feet high, two feet thick at the bottom and 14 inches at the top.

Several walls were erected on Milnthorpe Green, using field stone removed during clearance, but hedges were more usual. The provision of stock-proof bounds was notoriously expensive for poorer folk. Fences were proportionally dearer the smaller the plot and many, like plot no 112 awarded to Margaret Park on Clarks field of 26 perches, were scarcely bigger than a cottage garden. At the south end of the marsh there were 28 allotments of less than one acre, on Heversham Marsh twenty more. The majority of allotments were less than 2½ acres. But most of the bounds decreed by the commissioners were in fact eventually formed and many tiny plots survived until the 1950's. Often holdings were scattered. Allotments at the south end went: Dowker, Cragg, Dowker, Cragg and further up the Dowker's got plot 169 at 4 acres 2 furlongs 6 perches and the Cragg's no 150 at 6 acres 0 furlongs 5 perches. Larger plots awarded to other Milnthorpe inhabitants were Plot 145 of 5 acres 2 furlongs 26 perches to Edward Kitching; Plot 144, 5 acres 2 furlongs 26 perches to Richard Crampton; Plot 196, 5 acres 0 furlongs 21 perches to Emma Bindloss.

The larger landowners who had induced the act got the lion's share. The vicar got Plot 175, 58 acres 1 furlong 0 perches, on the Marsh; Trinity College, Plot 176, 50 acres 3 furlongs 4 perches and Plot 193 of 50 acres 2 furlongs 8 perches; Daniel Wilson, Plot 127, 5 acres 1 furlong 3 perches, Plot 152, 6 acres 0 furlongs 20 perches and 152a, 6 acres 2 furlongs 13 perches; Richard Howard, Plot 151, 6 acres 0 furlongs 20 perches and 151a, 7 acres 0 furlongs 2 perches (adjoining the Park House Estate).

Awards on Ackenthwaite and Milnthorpe Greens were smaller than the larger moss allotments and involved parrocks numbered 44-50 and the north side of the Kirkby Lonsdale roads. Closer to the village smaller plots were laid out that soon provided sites for Laburnum House (plot no. 39), Belvidere Cottage and for St. Thomas's Church. Daniel Wilson got the largest allotment, Plot 55 of 7 acres 1 furlong 19 perches on Milnthorpe Green and Trinity College the largest (Plot 69) of 15 acres 3 furlongs 20 perches on Ackenthwaite Green, which is still known as "the College." Close to the realigned Woodhouse Road opposite the old cottages were several small plots including no. 64 of 0 acres 5 furlongs 8 perches awarded to Audland's, which went with Ackenthwaite Smithy.[56]

Whereas on the Marsh the awards were made without payment the green allotments were often sold and brought good prices. Daniel Wilson paid £690 for the 7 acre plot no. 53; Thomas Fell, £408 for 4 acre plot no. 43 and Edward Kitching, £324 for the 5 acre

Heater field. When some of these lands were sold in the 1920's they did not bring as much as they had a century earlier!

Close to Paradise Lane, plot no. 59 of 3 furlongs 2 perches was laid out round an old sand hole and called Milnthorpe Green Quarry. Sands Bungalow, on the opposite side of the road takes its name from it. In the 1980's Milnthorpe Parish Council regained control of this public property from the District Council and let it as paddock for £70 per annum - perhaps the last permanent benefit of the Enclosure Act to have come down to the landless villagers of Milnthorpe.[57]

Enclosures were part of a general change in farming methods. Locally the improvements were so gradual that the term "Agricultural Revolution" seems an exaggeration. Old Field names survived and Tavern Croft, Low Long Tail, Thornbriggs, Barn, Brow and Well Closes, Hogg Holme and Crestolang Mires appeared in nineteenth century advertisements.[58] Enclosures remained small. Compared with most of Cumbria the Milnthorpe district was important for arable farming, and cultivated land actually increased as a result of the drainage and enclosure of the mosses and commons. It is significant that Constance Holme called her novel about the farming folk of Heversham and Milnthorpe, *The Lonely Plough*.

Oats continued as the main crop though Haverbread, according to G. Atkinson, had been replaced in c.1850 by Mashelden; a coarse wheat and rye mix.[59] Oatmeal was used for porridge or if flavoured with treacle, beer or cheese for "hasty pudding."[60] Oats were sown about the 1st of April; 7½ winchester bushels per acre were expected to provide a fair crop of about 60 bushels. After harvest, 80 to 100 carts of manure were applied per acre supplemented by imported guano. Barley or "bigg" was more productive realising for four bushels of seed per acre a crop of about 54 bushels."[61]

Judging by old names like Wheat Close at Ackenthwaite, some wheat had been grown in earlier times. It had increased only slightly by 1819 when Adam Walker commented that around Milnthorpe, Burton and Farleton"..it was not quite so rare to see a few acres of wheat." The seed was sown in September at 4 bushells per acre on land previously manured and limed. The seed itself had either been soaked in brine or dried in lime. A good crop harvested in August/September was about 40 to 50 bushels per acre - but most farmers did not think it was worth the bother.[62] In 1890 only 1½ per cent of local arable was down to wheat and in 1917, at the height of war time famine scares, only 82 acres were grown in South Westmorland.[63]

Flax ceased to be grown after c.1850 when the local textile industry disintegrated.

Apart from the name Ryley field no details of Rye production have come down.

Roots were not very common. In Walter Berry's accounts rare references include (1842) "3cwts carratts at 4/10 per cwt," (1853) "1lb Mangale Warsall seed 1/– (1858) "12 stone (sic) Mangle Wurzle seed for 1/6d."[64] Five acres of turnips were advertised in Robert Jackson's Ackenthwaite sale in 1866.[65] By the 1880's there were usually about 40 entries for roots in local shows -compared to over 100 for horses and cattle.

Potatoes became more common and as seen by Workhouse records gradually ousted porridge as the staple diet of the very poor. In the 1840's, judging by cart loads of potatoes supplied by local farmers, Milnthorpe was spared the worst effect of the blight suffered by parts of England, as well as Ireland, at that time.[66] Indeed, there was much competition amongst gardeners to produce early or abundant crops. In May 1849, Mrs Hudson of Fir Tree House, offered new potatoes for sale at 6d a lb,[67] but in 1855 the first earlies were not on sale (at 1s a lb) until July 10th and "we are sad to say disease is prevalent amongst them."[68] Rather later a few curiosities were noted. In 1873 H. Dobson of Parkhouse grew a potato weighing 1lb and measuring 16ins by 10ins; about the same time a Hincaster gardener produced 8lb of mature potatoes from 3oz of seed.[69]

Local implement makers were more enterprising than most of the farmers and their products even achieved international fame. Pringle in 1794 stated that the South Westmorland ploughman used a light, neat wooden swing plough drawn by two or three horses.[70] In 1815 John Moor said a two horse plough "led by a third" was common. Between 1820-1850 'Westmorland" ploughs were developed by Francis Harling of Sedgwick, William Garnett of Endmoor and especially by John Stenton (or Stainton) the blacksmith of Milton who first advertised his equipment in c.1829. His light iron curved ploughs were ideally suited to the stoney boulder clays of much of the new land opened up after the enclosures. Stainton also produced other implements - in 1853 his parallel expanding drill grubber was said to be the most perfect ever seen. In 1858 he was reported as "that noted mechanic Mr Stainton of Milton near Milnthorpe whose manufactures are so well known in this county and we are glad to perceive that our transatlantic farmers are beginning to appreciate its (the Stainton plough's) merits."[71] *The Belleville Hastings Intelligencer* of Canada spoke highly of the "Merits of the Stainton Plough, the judges passing a high eulogium on its qualities," and awarded the plough a prize of 150 dollars. In 1862 the *Intelligencer* reported a ploughing competition where "People looked with delight and scarcely knew which to admire most, the beautiful plough or the dextrous and easy manner with which it was managed. Mr Bennet used a plough of Mr Stainton's Manufacture...this is the second year he has carried off the prize with the same plough."[72]

By this time other manufacturers were prominent locally and a new implement invented by F. Wilson Esq., earned high praise at the Milnthorpe Agricultural Meeting in 1854: "the peculiarity of this implement is that the handle is bent two inches to the foot out of perpendicular to one side of the labourer to guide it into the ground. The hand is then applied to the long lever handle thus bringing greater power to bear. The fork can be used by the left and right hand as the prongs are flat. The object of the implement is to losen the subsoil after the spade has gone over it. This implement is sharp at both sides, curved backwards so as to throw the weight behind in cutting. It has a hand at the handle so as to defend the cutter."[73] A "cottage allotment" barrow made by Halliwell of Milnthorpe was also mentioned - "the weight is thrown on the wheel which is sunk into the floor of the barrow" and so could carry twice the usual quantity.[74]

An indication of the equipment owned by a small farmer is revealed in the account of the Buttsyeat fire of May 1874 in which the barns, shippon and stables were destroyed, the horse being saved by cutting beams from the barn above. As well as losing 50 yards of hay, the tenant Mr Lancaster "lost an excellent threshing machine nearly new, a quantity of sacks, grass seed, winnowing machine, straw cutter, turnip cutter, rakes, forks, hooks and a variety of other implements." The fire was believed to have been caused by a trespasser. Fortunately both Mr Lancaster and the landlord Mrs Bindloss were covered by insurance.[75]

In the nineteenth century ploughing matches were an important feature of rural life. The Milnthorpe Ploughing Association was founded about 1849[76] - but had been preceded by occasional 'Matches'. At the 1847 match, held in Mr Burrow's field on Milnthorpe Marsh, thirteen men and two boys took part. The winner was John Walker of Sampool who got £2 10s. the runner up, Thomas Powley of Beethwaite Green, £2, and the winner of the boys' competition, Thomas Stott, son of T. Stott of Preston Hall, £1, and Robert Ashburner, ploughboy to Mr Scott of Farleton, 15s. "The 8 (sic) unsuccessful competitors each received 2s.6d."[77] There was a lull in the association during the 1860's but it revived in 1872 and in March 1874, 700 spectators attended the competition in William Tattersall's marsh field, followed by a dinner for 100 at the Cross Keys, where William Powley was presented with first prize for double ploughing and James Barker, ploughman to Ransome, Sims & Co of Ipswich, with a plough made by the same firm, won with a single plough.[78] The Milnthorpe Ploughing Association advertisement of 1880 gave precise details:-

Steam threshing, either at Ackenthwaite or up the Lythe, c.1900.

"A TRIAL of DOUBLE and SINGLE FURROW PLOUGHS (open to all comers) will be held on Thursday the 4th day of March next on Land at Low Foulshaw, near Milnthorpe, well adapted for the purpose. The following Prizes will be offered: silver cup value £5 5s or £5 5s in money, for the best work by a Double Furrow Plough and a Second Premium of £2. Silver Cup, value £5 5s or £5 5s in money for the best work by a Single Furrow Plough; £2 for second Best; £1 for Third best; and 10s for the Fourth best.

£2 for the best work by a single Furrow Plough, held by a Youth under 19 years of age; £1 for the second best; 10s for the Third best. To produce Certificate of birth when making entry. £1 1s will be given to the best work on the ground. Entrance Fee for Men 3s; Boys 2s 6d each. Entrance Fee to be paid at the time of making the entry to the Hon Sec which must be on or before Monday, the 1st day of March next. H.G. Roddick Esq. Beela Mills Milnthorpe will give a pair of Cart ropes and a Pair of Plough cords for the best opening made. Also a Pair each of the same articles for the best Pair of Horses (working together) the property of a Tenant Farmer. Mr John Woods, Saddler, Milnthorpe, will give a whip for the best Finish made in the Competition. Visitors to the Ground (except subscribers 2s for this year) will be charged 1s each.

N.B. The Tides being low there will be no difficulty in crossing

the sands at any time of the day..
The field is within ten minute's walk of the Sandside Station on
the Arnside to Hincaster Branch Railway - For further information
apply to John Cottam Milnthorpe, DINNER at the Cross Keys
Hotel Milnthorpe at Five p.m.."[79]

Great crowds braved the channels and sands of the estuary to
attend the competition in which double ploughs had to plough 1
acre and single ploughs half an acre. "The famous ploughs of Mr
J.B. Stainton of Milton Milnthorpe were again in the ascendant, the
greater number of ploughs being of that gentleman's make - it was
observed that the work done by these ploughs left a very clean
furrow." The winning plough was, however, by Hornsby of
Grantham. T. Atkinson won the prize for the single ploughing,
Joseph Lancaster for the double and J. Leather won the prize for
the hedging - which generally accompanied the ploughing
competition.[80] In 1882 charges of favouritism led to a change in the
rules so that judges "should not inspect the fields until the
ploughing is finished and that no name should be given, just
numbers."[81] This must have been an impossible rule to enforce for
when the match was held on Mr Lancaster's College Green Farm
the winner of the £5 silver cup was his son James Lancaster!
Most of the Milnthorpe ploughing matches were held out of the
township - Beetham Hall in 1890, College Green 1892 - but it was
land on Ackenthwaite Farm which, in 1894, was said to be such as to
"delight the hearts" of the 13 ploughmen and 11 boys who took
part.[82] There was renewed controversy in 1899 when the winner,
Thomas Dobson of Holme, was said to be a relative of the judge
A.Dobson from Temple Sowerby. It was also said that the half acre
was too much for the under 19's to plough in a day and that,
contrary-wise, prizes should not be awarded to those who had not
completed the work, so that "dilatoriness" should not be
encouraged.[83] The First World War stimulated change, Mrs Argles
of Eversley - "suitably attired for the purpose" and other ladies,
tried their hands at ploughing. In January 1917 great crowds and
"hosts of seagulls who hovered about restlessly" flocked to Mr J.W.
Garnett's Ackenthwaite Farm to see a demonstration of motor
ploughing. Resembling a caterpillar tractor and built on the lines of
tanks being developed at the time, it was judged to be far too bulky
for the local fields and would only be of use on flat, non-stony
ground. "Certain parts of the Plough by Ransoms gave way under
the strains of stones." Operating at a fair walking pace it would be
50/- faster and cheap (at 10s per acre). The kindest thing reported,
however, was that it was "likely to be varra useful but furrows not
deepy defined.."[84]
Post war attitudes were no different, for at the South Westmorland

Bringing tea to competitors, Ploughing Competition, Whassett c.1934.

Association's Match (as the Milnthorpe Competition had become in 1919) of 1920 intransigent conservatism was relayed by "Jacques." "T'tractors interested me terribly but I wondered if t'drivers knew es mich aboot the ploos es they shud eve; if sou why in the werld didn't they set em to ploo boath forrers t'saume size instead c'first a tell en es tiddler quite differn't. The nobbut was yan ploo oat et five et did ploo equal..Ensway they showed what a lot of wark cun be dun in a lile time on a gert farm whar lands farely level but they wod be of lile use on a smo spot as they wad waan't maast part et field fer headriggs."[85]

There were no tractors at the next few competitions. In 1923 drenching rain showed the worth of the heavy shires and also the saying "A red morning, Shepherd's warning." Even so work went on till 4 p.m. when the chorus of "They're all jolly men who follow the plough, was heard from the end of the meadow."[86] At the competition at Rowell in 1926 one farmer was heard to say "Give me a swing plough, wheeled ploughs are apt to want a bit of their oan way at times - Ay a gay lot sometimes...wheeled do not allow a tried furrow stitch next a good furrow to get a clean cut turnover to produce a good arridge."[87] One of the last, and also most numerously attended old time matches was held at Paradise Field, Ackenthwaite, (belonging to Cautley Farm, Whasset) in February 1934. The fair slope slanting into the bright sunshine was a "severe

Ploughing competition 1940's, Ackenthwaite Farm.

test" not having been ploughed for 20 years. For once no one seems to have minded when the first prize went to John Atkinson, son of the farmer.[88]

Developments in animal husbandry accompanied developments in cultivation. There was certainly room for improvement. The gaunt goat-like sheep and bony angular cattle of the eighteenth century bore little resemblance to their descendants two hundred years later. As late as 1794 Pringle[89] said "no attempt has yet been made to improve either the carcase or the fleece. They are horned dark or grey faced...with coarse strong hairy wool." Fed on ling (heather), fell sheep were highly esteemed for the fine flavour of the flesh, terseness of the wool and tendency to fatten. In October 1769 it was stated that "local mutton is now in season, for about 6 weeks it grows fat and nearly resembles venison." Lowland sheep were even fatter.

Mutton fat was used for rush lights. In 1827 Briggs recalled that "several poor people in the neighbourhood of the mosses make a tolerable livelihood by peeling rushes for candles and making besoms and bears (mats) with the peelings."[90]

By 1800 the sheep of South Westmorland and the mosses were of local Silverdale, Limestone or Wharton Crag breeds which were joined in c.1830 by Black faced "moir" sheep and, a little later, by longer wooled Leicesters or South Downs.[99] At the end of the century Swaledales and Suffolks and their crosses were common, with the hardy Herdwick reigning supreme on the fells.

Around Milnthorpe larger sheep, prone to multiple births were prized. A ewe belonging to Mr Richard Ormerod of Ackenthwaite[100] was reported in 1874 as having had five lambs on 22nd March. With tupping in October and lambing in February, Spring lamb was usually available in Milnthorpe. On Good Friday, 24th March 1861, a lamb offered by Mr R. Clarke of Whasset and slaughtered by Mr G. Garnet, butcher of Milnthorpe, was the first offered in the season.[101]

By 1891 there were no less than 8,933 sheep in Heversham Parish and sheep sales, lambing and dipping involved the wider community, as much as did cattle fairs, hay time and harvest. Sheep were dipped in the Bela at the watering place by the Mill on the Strands, in the meadow by the new bridge and at Whasset.[102] In 1899 a foot bridge was ordered to be built over the Bela at Whasset "near to the dub used by Mr Webster for sheep washing."

However, it was cattle which attracted most interest locally. Stock improvement was encouraged by Daniel Wilson of Dallam Tower, first President of the Kendal Agricultural Society in 1799. He introduced Black Galloway Cattle to the area and in 1820 enclosed the foreshore at Peat Stack Hill for them.[104] In 1821 he won the prize for the best cow at the Kendal show. With Irish Killoes crossed with the local varieties of longhorn the area became "the stronghold if not the fountain head of the original Longhorn breeds." But by 1810 "the graceful horns, white back and brindled sides of the Lonsdale short-horn" had become a common sight. Until the Fresian began its half-century reign in the 1930's the shorthorn dominated the local herds.

Generally speaking, fresh milk could only be sold in the immediate district until motor transport and refrigeration came in, though some was kitted and taken by railway to the big towns. Crosby Lodge had a good trade in this. Even so, as late as 1934 when Libby's Milk Factory was planned, it was said that 60 per cent of local milk went into cheese and butter.[106] Many other houses besides farmhouses had a dairy. Usually facing north and often at a lower level than the rest of the property, it was equipped with churns, cheese press (made of cubular limestone), massive three foot wide cheese pail, 56lb wooden firkins for the butter and slate or free stone slabs lined with earthern ware settling bowls. Until the 1880's lead cisterns were used for settling and before c.1820 wide wooden dishes.[107]

Johnny Wilson delivering a milk kit to Milnthorpe Station, c.1934.
In float, Christopher (later Sir Christopher) and Elizabeth Audland.

Butter varied in price according to the season as it did in colour, being 'buttercup yellow" in summer and lard-white in winter. Butter prices per pound recorded by Walter Berry at Birkett's Farm, Milnthorpe from June 1855 to May 1856 included June 10d, July 9½d, August 1/-, September 1/1½d, September 1/0½d, October 10½d, November 1/1d, and 11½d, December 1/1d, January 1/2d, February 1/1½d, or 14d, March 1/3d, April 13½d, and May 1856 1/2d. Cream was sold at 6d a pint. Cheese, which was of a soft Lancashire type, was less consistent in price and was sold by Berry in larger quantities. "Dec. 1842 to Wm. Kidd of Kendal, 9 cheeses, 1cwt 0lb.4ozs. £2 0s 6d...July 1845, 6½d per lb...June 1856, 23lb, 13s 5d."[108]

Local dairy products were not of high quality. In 1869 Lady Bective tried to encourage butter-making by offering annual prizes, but after 30 years' struggle gave up as the prizes had "entirely failed." Her ladyship claimed that most Westmorland butter would not keep for 50 out of 52 weeks. By then, however, the County Council had begun to replace petulant patrician patronage by education. Migratory Dairy Schools had been started in 1889. Instructresses came for a month to a village centre, which at Milnthorpe was generally the Agricultural Hall at the Public Rooms or the Royal Oak Assembly Room. When Miss Frost, the instructress, brought the school to Milnthorpe in October/November 1891 the 16 places for trainees were allocated by ballot. 425 gallons of cream were turned into butter and the prize winners were Miss Webster of Low Levens with 86% and Miss Atkinson of Overthwaite who won a Silver Medal. Though inspected by Captain and Mrs Bagot and other gentry it was reported that "very few townspeople had visited the rooms at all."[110] Even so, the visiting schools continued until after the First World War when they were replaced by residential courses at Newton Rigg Farm School.

Perhaps the traditional insignificance of pig meat might be attributed to the poor physique of the beast. At a dinner at the Cross Keys in 1814 William Ellinson commented that "a few years ago the pigs had big ears and mishapen snouts, their ears so big as to cover their eyes nor were they blessed with fat."[111] The latter alleged deficiency was made good later in the century. In 1859 Walter Berry noted "1 Fat Pig, 20 stone 10lb at 6/s lb."[112] Fat porkers though popular were not particularly numerous. Surviving Victorian sties on the larger farms suggest that there was accommodation for less than six pigs. Pigs do not appear in accounts of Milnthorpe Fair and only numbered about 10 in Milnthorpe Show entries in the 1880's.

There were always hens around the yards and on the greens. In 1855 John Fawcett's hen hatched a dozen chickens from six eggs,[113] but in general little attention was paid to poultry until the 1880's. Geese, traditionally reared on the commons and mosses, were fattened at Christmas time but in surprisingly small numbers -roast beef being the main item of seasonal fare. The most geese sold by Walter Berry were 10, sold at 8½d per lb in 1856. In 1848 a 9½lb goose brought only 6d lb. After 1858 there are no more references to geese in Berry's day books.[114] In the 1880's a Poultry Society was formed and began to put on shows; that of 1889 had 700 entries and was considered to be perfect in every respect except that "the only oversight being the absence of water in the pens for pigeons."[115] Captain Bagot, who opened the show, said that "£3m. which went into the pockets of foreigners could be saved if English men kept poultry." In 1894 there were 550 entries at the Show held in St. Thomas' School but attendance was down in 1895 and 1896, though in the latter year Edward Stones was reported as having a hen's egg "seven inches round and eight inches lengthways."[116] An Egg and Poultry Industry Society was started in 1901 at the instigation of Captain Bagot who at the inaugural meeting returned to an earlier theme saying "that 2000 million (sic) eggs were imported annually."[117] As a result of his activities a depot to collect 4000 eggs each week was opened, which continued until larger egg marketing schemes came in during the inter-war period.

Improvements in stock stimulated and were accompanied by greater attention being given to grass. Thus in April 1853 Walter Berry bought:

20lbs cow grass seed at 8d...13s 6d

10lbs Trefoil at 5d...8s 6d
10lbs Red Clover seed at 8d...6s 8d
2 measures Italian Rye Grass...6s 8d[118]

If sold, hay was not expensive for Berry got only 9d per stone for 72 stone of hay. (The measure is unusual - even in the barn it was generally measured by the yard and not by weight). In 1846 Mr Richard Saul of Milnthorpe was reported as having begun cutting his hay on the 1st June but this was unusual. Hay time normally lasted from mid-June into July. Two hay crops a year were rare. Haymaking methods changed little since the middle ages. In the well-known engraving of Dallam Tower, Milnthorpe by T. Allom,, haytimers are seen at work on the north west slope of the park facing the Tower. In the centre foreground a group of men are seen, two have wooden rakes while another, wearing a smock, is turning the hay with a pitch fork - an operation more essential and frequent in damp Milnthorpe than in drier places. With artistic license a hunt (unknown in July) is seen in the background and a smaller group, perhaps of women and child labourers, are seen waving to it.

Some haystacks were built on the marsh[120] but by the mid-nineteenth century hay was stored in barns, often of the bank barn type over cow byres. The unhealthy nature and poor ventilation of shippons was being recognised and during the later part of the century many single storey shippons were built, quite often round an older barn.

Farm Sales advertisements give a useful impression of stock and tackle belonging to local farmers of the last century. Robert Jackson of Ackenthwaite's sale, conducted by Mr Hodgson in 1866, included "5 Calving stock, 5 spring calving Cows, 8 gilt Cows, Heifers in forward condition and other spring stock. 25 Herdwick ewes, 20 Leicester ewes, 2 good work horses. One Bay mare 6 years old by Smuggler, one Brown Colt 4 years old by Contract, one Brown Filly 3 years old by Idas - 5 acres of turnips to be eaten off by Sheep."[121]

A regular summary of agricultural interests is provided by accounts of the Agricultural Shows. The Milnthorpe Agricultural Society was founded in the 1830's and at the 1836[122] show there were twenty-one classes for long and shorthorns, but two classes for pigs and seven sweepstakes! The field adjacent to the town field behind Church Street is called the Show Field; but the show moved around – it was held in "a field adjacent to the Cross Keys" in 1853 and in "a field contiguous to the Railway Station about a quarter of mile (sic) from the town in 1869."[122] By the 1800's it had amalgamated with Burton and Carnforth to form a joint show, eventually always held at Burton and becoming known as "Burton Show." By the 1860's the Burton and Milnthorpe Shows compared well with its neighbouring rivals.

	Cattle	Sheep	Pigs	Horse
Kendal	98	132	13	133
Lancaster	44	78	--	95
Bentham	93	105	10	69
Lunesdale	89	75	11	76
Burton & Milnthorpe	54	83	13	86[123]

In October 1870 "notwithstanding the alarm created by the spreading of foot and mouth disease throughout the country and a slight outbreak of the malady in the two townships, the annual show of this society was held on Wednesday at Milnthorpe."[124] Though cattle were inevitably down there was a good show and the famous short horn bulls of William Handley of Greenhead Farm, Hincaster, were on display. It was an unusually hot day for the season, the Milnthorpe brass band played at intervals during the afternoon and among other attractions a horse handler (Gymkhana) competition was won by Rowland Parker of Moss End. Show entries were published annually in the *Westmorland Gazette*. A random selection shows the varying popularity of the classes.

	1880	1884	1886	1889	1891	1893	1895
Cattle	39	77	84	82	79	99	82
Sheep	90	160	111	94	136	121	104
Horses road	220	130	78	89	70	121	80
Horses field		99	73	58	56	57	87
Butter	8	38	37	32	40	39	28
Roots	108	40	32	49	48	50	41
Pigs	8	9	8	8	9	10	12

There was a decline in the late 1890's with 532 entries in 1896, 412 in 1897, 371 in 1898, 364 in 1899. It gradually revived though the figures never reached the level of the earlier years.

	1902	1903	1904	1905	1906
Cattle	46	13	68	84	59
Sheep	106	119	67	96	60
Horses	171	205	139	184	151
Butter	19	22	18	19	22
Pigs	2	0	6	0	6
Total entries	429	505	409	459	375[125]

(including classes not specified)

Entries stabilized at around the 400 mark in the immediate pre-First War period.

Many farmers supplemented their income with other occupations like milling, lime burning and general dealing. Walter Berry at Birkett's Farm was a principal carrier in the 1840's. He also let out horses.

He also often let grazing for a few shillings to tradesmen such as Edward Stones the cobbler, who kept a cow e.g. 1842. Despite odd jobs Walter Berry's income dropped with the decline of his carrying trade when the port closed and though he continued in farming he was almost bankrupt when he died in 1906 and everything had to be sold.

Many landowners were ruined in the agricultural depression preceding the Great War. No local failure was more sensational nor longer remembered (in a garbled form) than the bankruptcy of Milnthorpe's Squire, Sir Maurice Bromley-Wilson of Dallam Tower. When he faced the Official Receiver in January 1913 the bankrupt baronet's debts amounted to £51,069 2s. Declining landed income was only partly to blame; the rent roll of about £7,500 p.a. could have met the estimated upkeep of £3,000 on Dallam Tower, with a further £1,000 for estate maintenance, pensions and charitable obligations. Other expenses had included £600 on motor cars and stables, £300 on hounds and, above all, "losses by betting and money borrowed at high interest rates" amounting to a staggering £24,000. There was laughter in court when Sir Maurice told the Receiver "the more he borrowed the more they seemed to enjoy lending money" and "the only time when I did make a coup the fellow went."

All Milnthorpe thought "the tower would have to go" and that the long sway of the Wilsons of Dallam would come to an end. Fortunately Dallam Tower was a settled estate and except for some outlying portions, disposed of to secure annuities, the land could not be sold. The trustees also saved the bulk of the Dallam pictures and, at a cost of £50, the Dallam deer herd.

All the rest of Sir Maurice's chattels had to be liquidated. The three day furniture sale was said to have brought only "give away prices." Mrs. Howard of the Wheatsheaf at Beetham bought two sets of embroidered bed curtains for half a crown, an Elizabethan table brought £8 5s, 20 mahogany dining chairs in morocco leather £60 and 25 stags heads £4 10s.

Even sadder was the disposal of the contents of the famous Dallam conservatories. On a teeming wet December day 3,000 plants were brought from the hot houses and sold from the market cross in the square: "valuable orchids disposed of for a few pence. . . flowery foliage plants of beautiful growth going off at 1s a dozen." "Exotics" were sold at the Institute and included "palms of 40 years growth, 12 feet high" which went for "a few shillings." The highest prices were £19 paid for a mare and foal and £16 for a garden cob cart.

The Tower was let, firstly to the Peart-Robinsons (1914-1920) and then to the Heatons (1921-1930). Sir Maurice retired to the family properties in Nottinghamshire but regularly visited his mother, Lady Bromley, at Parkside, the Dallam dower house. Eventually in 1932 he returned and for the next 25 years resumed the role of squire, though shuttered windows and ragged lawns proclaimed his straitened circumstances. After a life-tenancy of over 60 years Sir Maurice died in 1957 and was succeeded by his nephew Brigadier E.G. (Teddy) Tryon-Wilson. Almost immediately the estate was modernised, and Dallam Tower and its grounds immaculately restored.

Early evidence about horticulture in Milnthorpe is restricted to occasional reports of oddities, and of shows. In September 1878 a "Lyburnum tree" was reported as being in full flower and a pear tree was bearing its second crop. On the 8th July 1843 William Dennison, Coachman to Mrs. Blewart of Harmony Hall, picked from the hot bed a cucumber measuring 22½ inches long by 6 inches round, and weighing 2½lb. When Henry Moore lived at Harmony Hall from c.1870-1885 and Dr. Carden from 1885-c.1900 the conservatory, which had a powerful furnace in the cellar, contained orange trees and other exotics.

Late season crops are regularly recorded. On 27th October 1906 an apple tree was in full bloom - while it was also said that three swallows had been seen and a goose had laid eight eggs. In November 1936 John Mashiter at "Maymyo" picked several measures of peas while roses were still in bloom. Regarded as notable curiosity was the vine which grew outside the house now called Vine Cottage from about 1880. In October it was reported "Mr. T. Hyde cut the last grapes from the vine outside his cottage on Harmony Hill. This vine is an old one, the fruit being usually no bigger than good sized peas but this year there had been a record quantity and the grapes have been more than twice the size and flavour quite acceptable though rather acid."[128]

Village gardeners began to organise horticultural shows in the 1870s. At the 1878 show a marquee 90 feet long was used to display 200 entries, and a display of ferns collected by Roger Mashiter. "These shows must," claimed the reporter, "engender a love and taste for flowers that cannot fail to have a refining influence on the growers."[129] Obviously the bitter infighting, claims of malpractice and long, far from friendly feuds had not been envisaged! Roger Mashiter travelled all over Britain and Europe collecting ferns, and also snakes and toads which were kept in the greenhouse at Fern

Cottage.

Mashiter's ferns were again displayed at Milnthorpe show in 1882, along with an exhibition put on by Mr Isaac Woods, gardener, Greenside (Hincaster) whose "gardens held all manner of store."[130] The seventh show in 1884 attracted 400 to 500 entries. Nevertheless in the January following, came the news that "the Milnthorpe and District Flower and Horticultural Show has ceased to exist. Its career has been comparatively brief. It is, however, somewhat in the character of the town... that its institutions should be shortlived."[131] Thereafter although occasional shows were held in the Institute no great horticultural tradition developed in Milnthorpe.

Allotment gardens were first provided by Captain Bagot on Beetham Road in the 1890's but in 1894 "the idea of a show was deferred in order to get the ground into better order."[132] Small scale vegetable shows were held from time to time but never amounted to much. Other allotments were situated in the south east corner of the Square near the Padding Can and at the end of Church Street which survived into the 1980's. In the early twentieth century the Rev. Reade and some of the gentry, notably the Argles, arranged lectures and there was a massive potatoes growing campaign during the Great War. It was not, however, until the Second World War that the village acquired on Ashpire Field, behind Summerville Road, the large number of allotments for which Neddy Stones had agitated in the 1890's. In 1941 Milnthorpe allotment holders were given free seed and blackcurrant bushes provided by the War Relief Committee of New York. Encouraged by Joseph T. Cookson, the village headmaster, then secretary of the County Horticultural Committee, the Milnthorpe and District Allotment association was formed and its first show was held in the Bull's Head Garage in August 1941.[133] Later the show moved to the Memorial Hall and then to the Community Centre. Unlike its Victorian predecessor it survived happily for the next forty years – and perhaps more.

7

Industry and Trade

Milnthorpe is literally the village near the mill. Whether it comes from the Old English "Mylen" or from the later Norse "Mylna"[1] the place name suggests that there was a mill on the Bela from at least the tenth century. The main reason why a large village grew up close to the mill probably owes more to Milnthorpe's situation as a route centre rather than because the mill was of great importance. Mills on the Kent at Sedgwick and Force Falls were possibly of similar economic value but because of their relative isolation nothing larger than hamlets grew up near them.

Water mills were known to the Romans and were common in Southern England in Anglo–Saxon times.[2] The Domesday Book of 1086, for instance, shows hosts of water mills south of the Humber – but there were only seventy in the Northern counties. Milnthorpe Mill does not appear in the Domesday Book and unfortunately later documentary evidence, even in modern times, is sparse. Unlike agriculture and land tenure which were subject to deeds and manorial agreements, industry required few records. Written bills of sale and receipts were useless in a society where the miller and his customers were, until the eighteenth century, more or less illiterate. Moreover, unlike farms, mills were rarely in the same occupation for long. At Milnthorpe the three generation tenure of Bela Mill from the 1880's to the 1950's by the Dobson family of comb manufacturers is the longest traceable period of possession by one family. No doubt as one miller gave way to the next any paper work was thrown out. Mills also rarely appear in cash rent rolls because mill dues were normally paid in kind. The mill rights were "farmed" out; the miller or "farmer" gave a proportion of flour to the lord and in return for his services kept some back for himself. For example, between 1237 and 1248 Ralph de Ayncurt granted liberties to John Gernet at Viver Mill "the granter will find the mill

and the miller to grind John's own grain there without multure...
further it be known that John and his heirs should give food to the
miller when he grinds his corn."

The first of Milnthorpe's mills was undoubtedly a corn mill.
Place names and ground evidence indicate that there was sufficient
arable cultivation before 1000 A.D. to make grinding corn viable.
At Milnthorpe the Bela was well suited for milling. Between
Beetham Waterfalls and the old bridge, a distance of just over a
mile, the water is swift and has cut into the limestone bedrock
providing firm foundations for wheel houses, while the overlying
thin layer of boulder clay can easily be cut for mill races and other
essential earth works.

Though the place name suggests that Milnthorpe's mill was one
of the oldest, by early medieval times it was only one of many
similar local mills. John Somervell in his *Water Power Mills of
South Westmorland* notes that Kaker Mill at Crooklands was
recorded in 1119, Holme Mill in 1184, Milton Mill 1220, Heron
Mill (Beetham) 1220, and Viver Mill 1237. At least 40 water mills
existed in South Westmorland before 1500 and another 10
appeared in the sixteenth century, including Sedgwick in 1554.

Milnthorpe Mill belonged to the part of the Manor of Heversham
granted by Ivo de Taillebois to St. Mary's Abbey at York in 1094. In
the same way that Milnthorpe Market was referred to as belonging
to Heversham Manor, so too it seems that reference to a
Heversham Mill means those belonging to the church on the Bela
at Milnthorpe. Thus in 1302 Robert de Wessington (Washington) of
Kerneford (Carnforth) recovers by replevin "24 messuages, 200 a.
and 5½ bovates of land, 5 a. meadow, 14 a. wood and ⅔ of a Mill in
Heversham, lately seised for his default against Walter (de
Strikeland) son of Elizabeth, daughter of Ralph Daincourt." In
1332, under Heversham and Milnthorpe, appears a subsidy of a
fifteenth from "Richard of the Mill 7/6."[5]

By the fifteenth century nomenclature was more precise. In 1460
William Booth, Archbishop of York, appropriated most of the
revenue of Heversham church but conceded to the vicar an annual
stipend of £20 – provided from "the annual sum of the third part of
the Mill of Milnthorpe anciently belonging to the said church also
the tithes of fishings, mills...lint, hemp...of the whole parish." The
"Mill of Milnthorpe" suggests that there was only one mill at
Milnthorpe, while the "tithes of mills" refers to others elsewhere in
the parish. Mill dues remained part of the vicar's glebe and tithes
until the commutation act which accompanied the Enclosure Act(s)
of 1803–1815. During a protracted dispute with Levens Hall the
vicar of Heversham, Dr George Lawson, claimed £4 – per annum
for mill dues for the period 1798–1805. He estimated this to be
worth £24 by 1815.[7]

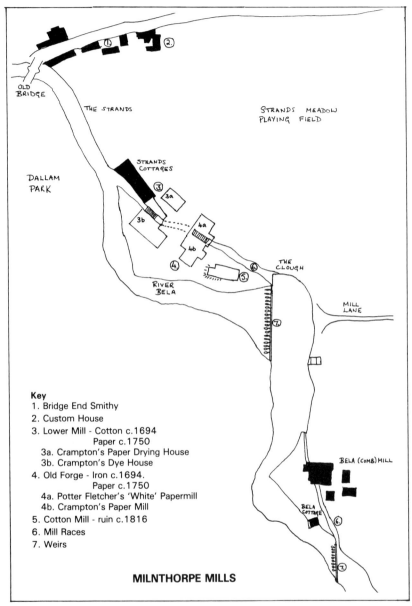

Key
1. Bridge End Smithy
2. Custom House
3. Lower Mill - Cotton c.1694
                 Paper c.1750
   3a. Crampton's Paper Drying House
   3b. Crampton's Dye House
4. Old Forge - Iron c.1694.
                 Paper c.1750
   4a. Potter Fletcher's 'White' Papermill
   4b. Crampton's Paper Mill
5. Cotton Mill - ruin c.1816
6. Mill Races
7. Weirs

MILNTHORPE MILLS

The lint and hemp mentioned in the 1460 deed are the earliest reference to textile raw materials, other than wool. Later they appear in wills. Hemp and flax belonging to Thomas Preston,[8] who died in 1700, was assessed for probate at £11, the largest item in his estate. In 1701 along with "meadow ffogg, Line and Onyons," Agnes Preston's hemp was valued at £12.00.[9]

Until the early nineteenth century most local spinning and weaving was done at home. Fulling, the beating of loosely woven cloth to produce fulled or shrunk material, could only be done efficiently by power – and there were, indeed, several fulling mills on the Kent. There are no references to a fulling mill at Milnthorpe – but owing to the immediate district's presumed importance for textiles the possibility of there having been a fulling mill on the Bela cannot be ruled out.

It seems there were several Milnthorpe mills by the seventeenth century. Machell in c.1694 said that there was a "paper mill a little above the (old) bridge, before that at the same place was an iron forge." Presumably the Bela mill was already in operation. This information was quoted by Nicolson and Burn in 1777 who added that "there are (now) two paper mills at the place."[10]

It is impossible to give precise sites of all the mills, though there are traces of industrial activity on the east bank of the Bela from Bela Cottage (south of Bela Mills) to the Old Bridge. The oldest maps[11] show buildings behind Bridge End Smithy (Douthwaite's Garage) and along Park Road as far as the Strands Corner. Perhaps the forge mentioned by Machell was here. The Strand Cottages which are now (1987) the closest riverside buildings to the bridge were definitely part of the Lower Mill, shown on Blount's map of 1826. To the east of the cottage buildings was a larger structure dissected by a mill race and wheel house. The race survived until the cottages were altered in the 1970's. This lower mill was probably one of the cotton mills mentioned in several sources. It could have existed by 1701 when "cottun wooll" is mentioned in the inventory of goods belonging to Joseph Grigg whose ships 'Phoenix' and 'Primrose' traded with Barbadoes, where cotton was grown.[12] If so, Milnthorpe's cotton industry pre-dated that of most of Lancashire.

Across the Strands to the north of the cottages is a single storeyed, hipped roof structure of perhaps c.1780. For most of the twentieth century it has been used as a changing room by the footballers. In c.1800 it was the drying house of Crampton's Paper Mill.[13] Crampton also used the southern part of the Main Mill building, but the northern half was Potter Fletcher's White paper Mill mentioned in a dispute of c.1760.[13] This mill complex occupied part of the present Strands footpath; the old path ran through what was later woodland to the south. Partial erosion by the river has revealed over the years quantities of coke slag and course lumps of iron and though the site is perhaps rather too far away to be described as "just a little above the bridge" this could be the site of the forge mentioned in c.1694. By 1826, according to Blount's map, it was a ruin. Apparently it was burnt down; a disaster referred to in the *Topographical and Historical Description of the Co. of West'd*, by Rev. M. Hodges of c.1816, "Milnthorpe. Here are two paper mills, one of them on the site of a cotton mill burnt down some years ago: the other about 100 years old and before that time

Mill at Milnthorpe 'Lancashire'! c.1800.

employed as an iron forge."[14]

Having skirted the "forge mill" the old path ran on for 100 yards or so before crossing a footbridge over a pond–like enclave of the Bela formed by a weir diverting the water down the race to serve the lowest mills. This part of the Strands is called The Clough. Here the weir/lodge still survives, its protecting upright flags in place, but the sluice gate and arch were removed about 1977. The mill–race itself was filled in on the orders of John Garnett, the Parish Clerk in 1983, using soil removed when the road at Harmony Hill was widened. Sadly, it erased an important relic of industrial archaeology.

Just round the bend from the Clough, as the river straightens out to run north – south, the buildings of the Bela Mill start. Until c.1950 there were cottages at right angles to the road, just by the south boundary of the Strands bungalow (built in c.1977). Their positions indicated strongly that they had had an industrial use, although at the time of their demolition there was no sign of a wheel house. It is possible that this structure was converted into housing about 1810 when the main mill building to the south was largely rebuilt by Henry Smithies. The mill itself has been little altered; it consists of a three storey rectangular limestone block with a pigeon loft in the east gable. Half a century earlier Somervell noted that "the present mill is thought to have been built about 120 years ago (c.1810). It is still run entirely by water power...".

The 80 yards long Bela Mill race starts just below Bela Cottage to the south. It is particularly broad and in 1930 still turned a wheel 12 feet wide by 14 feet diameter and weighing 19 tons. (It is still in place and capable of being used occasionally). A similar wheel measuring 16 feet high by 6½ feet wide at Waterhouse Mill,

Weir and Sluice at Bela Cottage.

Beetham, was advertised in 1843 as being capable of driving two Roy engines, two callendars, one chopping machine and other machinery.

Water rights were jealously guarded and were the cause of several disputes. A disagreement of 1700 between the Manors of Dallam Tower and Levens Hall appears in a manuscript at Levens: "1700. One Edward Wilson of Dallam Tower esq., being seised of the demesne of Heaversham and of some few customary tenants, pretends to keep a Court Leet and taking all opportunities to incroach upon the liberties of this Manor. And that in time to come it might appear that he is lord of the water of Bethay...and now pretends to be joint lord of the said Manor...now that the mills upon the water called Beethay and the mill dams that quite cross the water, belonging to Mr. Grahme (of Levens) and were part of the purchase from Bradley."[16]

It can be seen that there have been at least six mills along the Bela, apart from the conjectural forge close to the bridge, behind the Smithy, of which nothing can be found. They were respectively Crampton's Dye mill on the site of the Strand Cottages, Crampton's Paper mill on the site later occupied by the Gas works and Potter Fletcher's white paper mill to its north, then the larger forge followed by the main Bela Mill with the smaller mill at Bela Cottage

Bela Mill c.1930. From 'Water Power Mills of S.Westmorland' by J.Somervell.

beyond.

Most evidence comes from the later eighteenth and early nineteenth century and would support a contention that Milnthorpe's busiest industrial period was between 1740 and 1840.

Some information about industry, craft and trade at the end of the eighteenth century is contained in the Heversham Parish Registers[19] because after 1780 these give details of occupation. Richard Oliphant, and William Hird were respectively described as of the "Cotton Works in Milthrop" and of "the Cotton Manufactory Milthop Blacksmith." Other cotton manufacturers were James Brigg, William Catterl, William Railton, John Walker, Anthony Burrow ("of the High Mills"). Two less respectable members of the Smithies milling family are mentioned. "1798. James Beck Smithies, natural son of Richard Smithies, Cotton Factor. 1808. Susan, natural daughter of Thomas Smithies, Cotton Spinner." Perhaps because there were several cotton "manufacturers" there are only a few cotton spinners recorded, including James Carr, Peter Parkinson and Robert Peat. Issac Rothram and Robert Parker appear as millwrights. Rope makers included Robert Cragg, Charles Hodgson and Edward Robinson. In 1781 William Battyson and, in 1793, Thomas Brigg appear as twine spinners; – other twine workers were John Ashburner, Thomas Brigg, John Clementson,

Joseph Gouldon, William Jackson and Benjamin Mason. Of the paper makers the only Master specifically mentioned is Robert Hardy in 1794; other papermakers (whether employees or independent workers cannot be determined) include Edward Addison, Thomas Busby, Robert Brian, John Caton, James Halliwell, James Holloway, Nathaniel Howard, John Towers and Peter Wier. Weavers were the largest employment category mentioned involving over 40 separate surnames including Beck, Braithwaite, Cork, Clark, Cornthwaite, Garnet, Foxcroft, Graham, Grime, Heaps, Huddlestone, Herring, Johnson, Lupton, Towers, Moss, Punch, Wearing, Wainhouse and "Cumberland William Pennington." In 1796 Lancelot Johnson was the first to be recorded as a harden weaver.

Many innkeepers or "Innholders" are mentioned (but not the inns) including: Thomas Atkinson, John Brown, Robert Garrard, John Rawlinson, James Newby, Robert Mowson and Richard Thornton. Thomas Huddleston was described as "Innholder and Weaver." In the burials section, Mathew Cleminson was registered as "Innholder and huntsman to George Wilson Esq. of Dallam Tower." He had died of "mortification of the Bowels." The christening of a posthumous daughter Isobella is also recorded.

Joint occupations, apart from agriculture, were quite common and John Squire of Haverflatts was registered as a clogger and ropemaker. No other footwear makers were mentioned in the 1780's and 1790's though there were tailors like Thomas Beck, Issac Bulman and Anthony Burrow, two skinners William Thompson and Joseph Pearson, a hatter John Baines, cordwainers John Coatman, John Cook, Joseph Johnson and William Thornton and a staymaker Henry Fox. Para-agricultural craftsmen included John Burrow, saddler, William Turner, maltster, and Samuel Taylor, a mole catcher – but only one butcher, Richard Nelson. Blacksmiths included John Audland, Robert and Christoper Philipson – all of the Smithy, Ackenthwaite – William Sewell and Robert Wilson. William Hird was a whitesmith. Construction crafts were not particularly numerous; wallers/masons were William and John Brown, John Bainbridge, Edward Dixon and John Woodburn; sawyers/housecarpenters were Robert Birkett, John Richardson, John Shaw and John Thomas; glazier, William Mills; joiner/cabinet makers, Edward Taylor and Richard Wearing. Grocers were often linked with tallow chandlers and included John Johnson, Robert Mansergh, Martin Wood, Thomas Skelling and Edward Turner. (One of the tallow candle houses stood on Beetham Road near where Candle Lane now is. According to Neddy Stones the old candle house was demolished about 1860 to provide materials for farm buildings required by Dallam Tower. In 1834 two cottage houses called Candle Houses were advertised to let with a yard, stable and garden and the 'inclosure' called Candle House Field of 1a 2r 12p, the lands being occupied by Mrs. Hudson and the cottages occupied by John Metcalf and Miss Orselin.) In 1790 Thomas Bullman and Betty Wainhouse (who had a natural daughter christened Ann) were spirit merchants. There were four hoopers: James Foster, Thomas Redhead, Henry Topham and John Sinkinson, and Thomas Ashburner was a turner.

Craftsmen were trained under the traditional seven year apprenticeship system. A youth between 14 and 21 generally lived with his master where in return for being constantly at his beck and call for only a tiny, though progressively increasing wage, he was taught the "secrets of the trade." The apprenticeship indenture of 1754 of "Patrick Darnson, son of Patrick Darnson, charcoal burner of Skerton, Lancs, to James Hall of Milnthorpe tailor for 7 years" lays down that young Patrick at "Cards Dice or other unlawful Games He shall not play, Taverns or Ale Houses shall not haunt or frequent, Fornication He shall not commit, matrimony he shall not contract...," James had to "cause or procure to be sufficiently taught and Instructed after the best way method or mannour that He or they can and in due manner correct and chastize Him."[21] However this apprenticeship fell through after two years and Patrick was transferred to Joseph Bigland to complete his apprenticeship.

Indentures did not alter much for the next century and a half. The indentures made between Roger Mashiter, tailor of Milnthorpe, and Thomas Knowles son of Robert, Licensed Hawker, in 1865 stated "the said apprentice his said master shall faithfully serve, his secrets keep, his lawful commands everywhere gladly do, he shall do no damage to the said master nor see or suffer it to be done by others... he shall not play at cards, or dice tables or any other unlawful games whereby his said master may have any loss, with his own goods or other during the term without licence of his said master he shall neither buy nor sell, he shall not haunt Taverns or Playhouses or Public Houses nor absent himself from his said masters service by day or night unlawfully."

Roger Mashiter had to train him in the art of a tailor which he "useth by the best means that he shall teach and instruct." he was to pay Thomas 1s a week for the first year, then 2s, with similar annual increases – and also "finding unto the said apprentice sufficient meat drink washing and lodging and also wearing apparrel during the whole of the said term." Even in 1865 it is interesting to note that neither Robert and Thomas Knowles, nor John Kirby, a witness, could sign their names but merely made a X for "his mark."[22]

As well as gaining the status of a journeyman a good workman on completing his apprenticeship could be given a party. On Friday 13th January 1854 "being the loosening of Thomas Brennand who

Employees of Mashiter and Son 1900.

had served his apprenticeship with Mr Robert Brockbank, mason of Ackenthwaite, near Milnthorpe, was celebrated by a tea party and ball at the house of Mr Robinson, Cross Keys Hotel. An excellent quadrille band was in attendance on the youths of both sexes from the town and neighbourhood."

Milnthorpe's water mills survived for at least half a century after steam power had been applied to the textile industries of Lancashire and Yorkshire. Water power from the Bela was swift, virtually inexhaustible and above all free. Milnthorpe only began to suffer when the canal and later the railway, could bring raw materials such as coal cheaply and, just as cheaply, take the manufactured goods away.

Milnthorpe was at the crest of its industrial wave about 1820. Based partly on his fathers recollections, Neddy Stones noted that in c.1818 there were "thirty journeymen twine spinners besides apprentices in the town. Mr Edward Cragg sent most of the Twine to Liverpool."[24] There was also a large trade in sackcloth shipped to Liverpool and at this period we find the following manufacturers, Mr Henry Smithies and Son, Bela Mills; James Williamson Paper manufacturers, The Strand; Francis Cragg, F. Inman (?), Waterhouse Mills; James Briggs, Twine Spinner and Sacking; John Boyd, Twine Spinner; James Davis, Rope Maker; Thomas Huddlestone, Twine Spinner and Weaver; John Cleminson Twine Spinner. Briggs's twine works were at the end of a short lane off Main Street still called Twine Walk.[25] A ridge formed by the levelling of the walk could be seen quite clearly in the 1930's but it has been erased by later

building. The warehouse at the end of Haverflatts Lane (belonging
in the 1980's to James E Rushton Ltd.) was built as a warehouse for
twine and was later used for meal and malt storage. It was never a
mill. Huddlestone's twine walk was behind Glasgow House and
traces of it survived until the Ryley Field Road estate was built in the
1950's. Higher up Haverflatts Lane – perhaps in the barn used in
the 1980's by J Proctor and Sons builders – was Huddlestone's
weaving and ticking shop. On the opposite side of the road John
Ashburner had a twine spinning shop behind the cottage between
Summerville Road and Wyndsore Avenue. The Huddlestone's
were typical of Milnthorpe's entrepreneurs and manufacturers. As
well as holding the license of the White Lion from c.1784 Thomas
Huddlestone was soon engaged in rope making, sacks and cloth
weaving, in two twine walks and a large weaving shop. Neddy
Stones also recalled numbers of looms in the weaving shop on the
corner of Police Square and Haverflatts Lane. "The weavers waited
outside for materials and then wove it. Mr Foster of Bela Mills
(c.1853 – 1880) was the last that gave work out and took it in
again."[27] The last small scale hand-loom weavers belonged to the
Mayors and Beck families who gave up in the 1880's In the obituary
of Thomas Whiteley in 1912 it said that he had been a wool spinner
when he came to Milnthorpe 23 years before.[27]

John Boyd's twine walk was in Park Road on the site of Oaklea
built by Joseph Storey in 1890.[28] Approximately behind Boyd's was
the large Hooper's shop "which operated in the Town Field for the
shipping trade." Stones also noted that John Postlethwaite was a bag
and sail manufacturer and that Lancelot Johnson was a linen
manufacturer, but did not state where these premises were. It is
possible that they and "other manufacturers were merchants who
carried on their businesses in this trading centre."[29]

The Parson & White Directory for 1829 confirms the picture
painted by Stones. "Milnthorpe. In the town and neighbourhood
are several extensive flax mills and large quantities of excellent
twine and linen thread are spun, a considerable portion of which is
made into sheetings, bed tics, wrappers, sacking, bags, sails etc.
. . . and on the Bela also are two paper mills."[30]

At Bela Mills – described as "Milnthorpe Mills" – was the firm of
Henry Smithies and Sons, "flax and tow spinners, rope twine, bed
tick, wrappers and sacking manufacturers."[31] By 1840's Richard
Hardy's and James Williamson's mills had closed down. In 1842
William Turner's Waterhouse Mill went bankrupt. To the initial
relief of the many Milnthorpe workers Turner's concerns were soon
taken over by Richard Batt (also spelt as Bott) but soon there was
trouble at the mill. The workers went on strike when there was a
reduction in wages and the skilled men were told to provide their
own felts. A representative from the Paper Makers' Society of

Maidstone, Kent came (literally) post-haste to tell a meeting at Milnthorpe that "the society will not allow its members to take a reduction from regular pay." Nevertheless, poverty soon forced the men back.[32]

Although he was given to charitable work of an improving nature, Batt seems to have been a hard task master and something of a rogue. In October 1851 Batt was taken to court by a foreman Edward Hastings who stated that he had only been paid one week's wages for a fortnight's work. Batt explained that he had done this as "a cheque upon his forman" but when this procedure was found to be "contrary to the rule and custom of the place" the magistrates ruled against him with costs.[33] More shady practice came to light in 1854 when J Smith proved that Batt had sold a "paper quire short" while in 1855 the court ordered him to pay an unkept contract of £3 0s 4d.[34] In April 1869 the Milnthorpe magistrates heard a case between Batt and an apprentice Thomas Lishman who had refused to take out ashes from a grate, as not being his duty. On the indentures being read out the case was dismissed, both sides paying costs.[35]

The death of Henry Smithies in 1842 was a great blow to Milnthorpe as Bela Mills immediately closed down. The blow was softened partly by the Smithies family giving a dinner of roast beef and plum pudding in the National School for the dismissed workers. As a result of this disaster the 1842 celebrations for the feast of St Catherine (the patron saint of mill wrights) were not observed.[36] In 1844 after two hungry winters, the *Westmorland Gazette* announced that Messrs Atkinson, Flax and Tow Spinners, had taken the mill – "this will be a great boon as the mill has been empty since the death of Mr H Smithies three years ago when a great many hands were thrown out of employment." But the Atkinsons only lasted until 1847 when a makeshift firm of Taylor and Briggs took over. By 1849 an Irishman, Mr Vero, had joined the firm which was now called "Thomas Briggs, Taylor and Vero. Sacking, rope and twine manufacturers." New machines arrived from Liverpool for the better working of the mills[38] but nevertheless in October the whole business was ordered to be sold to meet unpaid rent.

After another hungry winter for the mill workers it was announced in February 1850 that "Messrs Waithman of Holme near Beetham... the party who have taken the mills... have sent people to put the mill in repair and make what alterations may be required. It is expected that in a short time the mill will be at work and give employment to numbers of poor families who are at present out of work."[39] The alterations and repairs cannot have been very adequate for in December 1853 "a floor collapsed on the work people... one of the men known as Captain Garth, a pensioner with a wooden leg, as he fell was caught by his apron strings to a hook in the wall and was there suspended swinging in the air until he was released from his perilous position."[40] The following June serious damage was caused by a fire in the warehouse when a lighted match was dropped in a heap of tow.[41] Finally, to crown the bad luck the mill was closed in September, this time by order of the Kendal Bank. It was not until the end of the next year (1855) that there came happier news. "During the past week the mill has commenced running by Messrs Foster and Sons after standing upwards of 12 months since the failure of Messrs Waithman and Co. It is to be hoped that the revived mill will do good to the poor people of the neighbourhood."[42] The hope was justified. When the 1861 Census was taken, John Foster; Flax, hemp and tow manufacturers, was employing 96 hands. Some diversification followed for in 1873 the firm was described as "Corn and flour sacks and bag manufacturer and rope and twine spinners."[43]

Despite various Factory Acts mill work was chronically dangerous. Shortly after Foster took over Bela mill (about 1855) a young worker called John Blair "broke his arm and had the flesh torn off" the *Westmorland Gazette* reported. "This is the fourth boy who has had his arm caught in the machinery of this mill within a few months and it is high time that something should be done to prevent such accidents."[44] Nevertheless, in 1878 it was reported that "James Young, a boy working as a 'halftimer' at Bela Mills met with a lamentable accident on Monday last while feeding a machine called a 'tummer'. It seems that while packing some hemp through the rollers his right hand was drawn into the machinery and that some time elapsed before it could be extricated. Dr Royle and Mr Evison were soon on the spot and advised his removal to Lancaster Infirmary where the hand was amputated."[45]

By 1881 the mill was declining and there were only 20 workers. On the 6th May 1884 the whole contents of the mill were put up for sale. Then for a few months Mr Roddick of Arnside attempted to carry on – but failed. Eventually in 1886, Milnthorpe's textile days were over and the premises were taken by the firm of John Dobson and Son, comb makers. The firm had been founded in Bradford in the late eighteenth century and had moved to Ann Street in Kendal into a mill formerly belonging to James Sisson and Son. The Milnthorpe premises having "the additional advantage of water power" were apparently ideal for the purpose because comb making did not need the heavy machinery required by then for textiles and for which the buildings were unsuited.

Until 1927 combs were made from horn provided by local stock farmers and also from further afield. Stinking wagon loads arrived at Sandside Station and were then brought by cart to the mills, often

Bringing horns to Comb Mill c.1910.

by Dick Pearson and his family who had to be careful not to be infested by the fat 'sloughs' (or maggots) which thrived on the shreds of decaying flesh and skin remaining on the horn. In addition to the smell and the chance of disease, horn making could be dangerous. With the cry of "Oh Dear!" on his lips John Pickthall Wilson, aged 19 was killed instantly in October 1888 when he was struck on the forehead by a shattered grindstone. This had been revolving at 500 to 600 revolutions per minute. The broken stone smashed the window and landed outside.[47] A similar accident occurred in 1894 to a 20 year old young man named Shaw who was also struck on the forehead and died within five minutes. He was working on a stone 18 inches in diameter by three inches broad and it was revolving at 900 revolutions per minute "a greater speed than normal as there was a fresh-out in the river."[48]

John Dobson, the elder, lived into his 91st year and died at Bela View in 1907. He was survived by six of his thirteen children, five sons and one daughter. His son took over the business which continued to employ about twenty people until after the First World War when the business nearly foundered. It was rescued by his son W. P. (Percy) Dobson who in confounding the traditional notions of "rags to rags in three generations" became one of Milnthorpe's most successful entrepreneurs. New processes and synthetic material were used but Percy, a skilled craftsman himself, could still produce traditional work in ivory, horn and tortoiseshell, some of which was even presented to royalty. Though the Dobson's ceased to run the mill in the 1950's the firm continued and a hundred years after it moved to Milnthorpe employed some 20 people.

In 1860 the site of Crampton's Paper Mill was obtained by the Milnthorpe Gas, Coal and Coke Company Limited. This had been set up at a public meeting held on 24th February.[49] There were to be 250 shares at £5 each but even at the inaugural meeting £810 was subscribed and by March of the following year share capital amounted to £1500. Gas was first seen on 1st February 1861 "when three of the inns and a few of the shops were lighted with gas for the first time and Mr J Perks (the contractor of the works – from Burton) entertained a few friends to supper at the Bull's Head Hotel to commemorate the introduction of gas into Milnthorpe. During the last week the Cross Keys, several more shops and a few private houses have been lighted up but through excessive leaking of the pipes in the street the work has not made that progress which it otherwise would have done." Nevertheless the reporter conceded "the inhabitants can now find the Post Office (which is often wanted for last mails) and other places at night without fear of accident."[50]

By November the church and many houses had gas laid on. Within a year or two the mains went as far as the station to the east (taking in the workhouse, the smithy and Audlands on the way) and to Heversham Grammar School to the north. Twenty street lights were provided immediately and others followed. A lighting inspector was at first appointed by the Directors and then by the Parish Council, who levied a rate in the lighting area. There were always complaints about the supply; the pipes often corroded and leaked; occasionally the supply was intermittent and sometimes the Bela rose and put out the retorts. In 1885 Neddy Stones told the lighting inspector (his enemy Joseph Daffady) that even between 31st October and 31st March the street lamps were only lit for two hours and then "half of them were faulty."[51] Often quite obvious places lacked lamps; there were only three on Church Street and none was provided outside the almshouses on the hill until the 1920s. A gas lamp was provided for the church steps only in 1915 through the generosity of William Dobson – a Methodist!

During the 1920's when a lamp in the Park Road was out of action for many weeks, the directors were induced to order repairs only after a Chinese lantern was hung on the standard!

Milnthorpe Gas was always measured in feet and not in therms. In 1916 it was stated that sales were down by 1000 feet owing to introduction of summer time and the directors decided to increase charges from between 3d and 5d per 1000 feet.[52] The biggest interruption in the supply came in January 1925 when, soon after Tom Wheatman took over as manager of the works, the stone chimney was struck by lightning. As it fell it narrowly missed

Milnthorpe Gas Works 1970.

Mrs Wheatman and her baby son Ronny and destroyed much of the building. After nearly three weeks of gloom throughout the area it was reported that "the energetic body of workers have been able to get into order a temporary gas making plant."[53] The next year three new retorts were installed at a cost of £445 but were soon not working fully owing to coal shortages, caused by the General strike. As a result gas went up from 6s 8d to 7s 6d per 1000 feet.

Late in 1926 there was an acrimonious public meeting at which "Ackenthwaite objected to being included in the rating area but could not get gas for domestic purposes." Farmer John Wilson of Crosby Lodge stated that "in the quiet country village only one gentleman had asked for the whole area to be included and he did not represent the village. They are simply minding their own business. He might only be small in stature but he was pretty big when rates were being paid and he did not want anything to do with Milnthorpe. In the last 20 years he had gone out with his milk floats in the dark and had never failed to find his way back."[54] When it came to the vote 15 men were against the proposal to include Ackenthwaite in the area – but nonetheless it still had to pay the rates. A slight alleviation occurred in 1931 when charges were reduced 5d per 1000 feet following an increased demand "owing to the popularity of appliances for cooking and heating."[55]

A general electricity scheme was late in arriving in Milnthorpe, though as far back as 1902 Fawcetts generated power to light a lamp wired to the Market Cross during the Coronation Celebrations of Edward VII. In the next 20 years several businesses and larger houses installed their own generators. Even so, when the modern houses were built on Milnthorpe Hill in the early 1920's they could only have gas lighting. In 1923 Mr T Wilkinson, who had introduced a successful electrification scheme in Arnside, addressed a public meeting in Milnthorpe. He proposed that an £800 semi-diesel 30 H.P. generator should be installed on the Bela behind the gas works and went on "to enlarge on the saving in the drudgery of housework in using electric irons and other appliances."[56] At the meeting Mr Miles, the brewer, said that if a general scheme was not adopted he would have to have his own engine at the Bull's Head which was currently being rebuilt. He was supported by Dr Fuller who said the scheme would have to come. Ten years previously, said Dr Fuller, it had been difficult to get 10 subscribers to the Telephone service "but now there were over 40."

Despite all this urging Milnthorpe did not get its own generator and it was not until the area had been connected to supplies from Lancaster in 1929 that people began "to get the electric." Even so, in 1950 there were still dozens of houses with only gas. More suprisingly Alice Ashburner's cottage on Harmony Green did not have electricity until the 1980's, although at the time of conversion to North Sea Gas in the 1970's she had been offered a free installation. The old Gas Company was nationalized in 1948 and the works operated until 1974; the last in England to be stoked by hand and to measure its supply in feet. Such archaism led to the machinery and masonry being taken to Beamish Hall Folk Museum in County Durham where they will be re-erected in due course. In 1987 the parts were still in store – nevertheless it is nice to know that one of Milnthorpe's smaller industries will be preserved.

The most important of the smaller textile works – the large weaving shed on Haverflatts Lane – had a dramatic end, for at 11 o'clock on Tuesday morning, 8 April 1844, "fire broke out in the weavers' shop situated nearly in the centre of Milnthorpe. The building was a thatched one and contained six weavers' looms, their trappings, weft and yarn. It was caused by a weaver lighting his pipe with a lucifer match which caught hold of some threads hanging from the roof of the building which soon ignited the dry thatch and in a few minutes the whole building was ablaze... it soon communicated itself to the dwelling house next door, burning it to the ground before much of the furniture could be saved... but for strenuous exertions of individuals to stop the fire much greater damage would have been done to property."[57] The weavers lost all their work tools and as the rudimentary insurance system had not touched them the Rev. Padwick got up a subscription which the next week was stated to "be proceeding satisfactorily." The workshop might have been revived for a time but by 1859 it had been abandoned and the site was obtained for a police station.

By the mid nineteenth century the twine industry was on the way out. In 1849 a report under the heading "St Catherine's Day" stated "Sunday last being the anniversary of the above Saint Mr Thomas Briggs, Twine Manufacturer, the only person left in the town of Milnthorpe carrying on twine spinning, treated his workmen to plenty of brown stout which they enjoyed in a jovial manner. The wheel turners he regaled with each a cup of elder wine and currant cake."[58] A decade later Briggs was no longer in business as a twine spinner having become a highly successful butcher. In 1859 the premises in front of the twine walk (now the butchers and vets) then in the occupation of Benjamin Foster and Ann Moseley, were sold.

By that time all the sacking makers except the Becks and Mayors had disappeared. In 1849 Issac Jackson, weaver of Milnthorpe, "who had sold sacks at Kendal"[59] was robbed of £1 5s at Helsington Lathes. Perhaps this misfortune put him out of business for he does not appear in any trade directory after that date.

Throughout the nineteenth century trade and smaller craft industries were spread round the village. There were shops and workshops on Church Street, on Harmony Hill and Park Road, which in the twentieth century became mainly residential. In c.1840[60] Neddy Stone's father's shoemaker's workshop was at the far end of Park Road opposite Bridge End Smithy run by the Tyson family; going up the street was Johnson's, Grocers, Corn and Flour merchants, and Tallow Chandlers; beyond Park terrace was the house of Joseph Flemming, a tanner and skinner who also sold brown pots, whilst next door old Betty Halliwell had a toffee shop. Then came the twine walk of John Boyd whose wife "established and conducted the dress making and general drapery business subsequently carried on by Miss Dodgson and afterwards by Miss Burrows and Mrs Elburn." Miss Burrows married Lewis Elburn in 1862. He was a traveller for Messrs Hooper and Sons,[61] and a Londoner who had been born overlooking the Fleet Ditch. When the Elburn's moved in 1872 to the large house on the corner of Main Street and Haverflatts Lane, (now the site of the National Westminster Bank) he renamed it Fleet House. His wife died in 1875 but Lewis continued the business and became closely associated with the social and political life of Milnthorpe for half a century. In 1900, at the age of 72, he married Miss M E Pridle and the elderly "happy couple" were greeted by a crowd of over a 100 as they returned from honeymoon. [62]

On Park Road beyond Fir Tree House (now Park House Coach Works) the cottages (belonging to the Langhornes in the twentieth century) belonged to two brothers called Mills; one was a painter and

gilder, the other a cabinet maker. On the site of Fern Cottage – built
by Roger Mashiter in the 1890's – "was the property of Thomas
Briggs, an auctioneer, grocer and bread baker. The sign board was
Bread and Flour sold here, by Thomas Briggs the Auctioneer."
Stones said that he was "the founder of the Briggs of Manchester,
whose grandson was twice Lord Mayor of Manchester."[63]

On the site of the Post Office (re-built by John Mashiter in 1897)
was "the tailor and draper's shop conducted by Edward Walker and
owned by his descendants." Two advertisements (of 22 March 1819
and 13 April 1822 respectively) reflect his business acumen:
"Edward Walker, Woolen Draper Tailor, Millthorp. They beg to
recommend to the notice of the Public a choice assortment of
Goods in the above line which have been personally selected in
London and will be glad to wait upon any one favouring them with
their wishes and commands."

On the south side of Park Road, about where the Co-operative
Stores were later built, was George Whittaker the seed merchant.
Nearer the Cross Keys (probably at number 9) was a beer house
called (in 1847) the "Jolly Waggoners" and occupied by a Mr.
Atkinson. Round the corner into Beetham Road past the Cross
Keys and the White Lion were two Butchers' shops (about where the
Institute was built in 1880) and in front of these fish was sold from
pavement stalls. In the yard behind was the blacksmith, Robert
Gibson. He had a cottage behind the White Lion and nearby "lived
Stephen Armstrong who had a mangle and was a descendant of the
Horsebreaking family."[67]

On the Blue Row in Church Street (See Chap. 10) were several
dressmakers and a chemist. On the east side of the street (all of
which was demolished about 1926) was a baker's shop, two
warehouses and on the corner John Fryer's draper's shop which
was later a bank, then the co-operative stores and finally a cafe.

Obliquely opposite, the Royal Oak buildings contained several
businesses including a saddlers. On the south side of the square
apart from a malt kiln, the post office, two carriers premises and the
Sun Tavern, was Edward Wilson's butcher's premises, which later
became Clark's butcher's and eventually the Flying Dutchman
snack bar and Monarch Guest House.[68]

The central block in the square, now belonging to Messrs
Crossfield and Sons, had multiple uses. At the west was Vine
House, so "named after the flourishing vine that spread itself over
the whole southern front, [and] was for a long time Edward Stones'
Grocery Store." The block also contained the premises of Martin
Whittaker, ship importers and guano merchants. Behind it to the
east was an ancient property called, perhaps because of connections
with textiles, Bodkin Hall.[70] Here, according to Curwen, "one
Hearnshaw used to bleed horses for the cure of certain ailments."[71]

Milnthorpe's oldest photograph, (and early by any standards), of c.1845 shows that Bodkin Hall had a stout cylindrical chimney on a cross wing which jutted southwards into the square. Later this site was occupied by St Thomas's school. Across Main Street was a tommy shop for navvies and another smithy, the shoeing shop being at the end of the back yard – and adjoining the Coach and Horses on Haverflatts Lane. To its east was a Beerhouse with the sign of "the Gee O'Dobbin."[72] This old and attractive property, latterly divided and occupied by Toffee Johnny Grey and the Griffin family, was pulled down about 1920.[73]

One of the area's most famous nineteenth century craftsmen was Frederick Burrow, born in 1815, a member of an old Milnthorpe family. After being educated at Beetham Grammar School, Frederick was trained as a plumber after which he went to London where he met a Frenchman who taught him the art of making stained glass. He did work for Salisbury Cathedral among other places before returning about 1850 to Milnthorpe Sandside, where he created windows for the churches at Milnthorpe, Heversham, Arnside, Great Asby, Beetham and Holme, as well as for the Tattersall Almshouses, Owlett Ash, the Smithy at Ackenthwaite and other private houses. Perhaps his work deteriorated after his Cathedral embellishing days: Milnthorpe church's east window by Burrows has been called "bad."[74] If so it might reflect Burrows' strong prejudices. "He was a reader and deep thinker, though somewhat imbued with the doctrine (Atheism) of the late Charles Bradlaugh (of whom he was a great admirer.) He reserved the keen edge of his sarcasm for anything of the nature of cant, yet few there were who could not admire his honesty of purpose."[75]

The most enduring of Milnthorpe craftsmen families were the Audlands; blacksmiths, whitesmiths and farriers of the Smithy at Ackenthwaite and of the adjoining Ackenthwaite Green House. At various times they also had smithies at Woodhouse, Lupton and at Bridge End, Milnthorpe, as well as being small-time farmers. Brigadier Gordon Edward Audland (1897 - 1976)[77] believed the Audlands were descended from the medieval de Astenthwaites (Ackenthwaites) but the earliest references to the Audlands as blacksmiths date from the late sixteenth century. The accounts of the repair work to Heversham Church following a serious fire in 1601 mention to "William Aydland for ironwork 4d."[78] In 1735/6 John Audland IX was paid £1 11s 1d for ironwork about the bells and again in 1750 he was paid 1/- "done at ye Bells, Lock for the vestry chist, mending Gavelock about Church Yard Gates."[79] In 1733 the jury of the manor declared that John Audland "shall inclose at ye south side of ye sd Smithy twelve yards bredth and twenty four yards long, he and his heirs and assigns paying to ye Lord of ye manr ye yearly rent of one penny and that he and his

The Smithy, Ackenthwaite 1910.

heirs and assigns shall be debarred from building any dwelling house upon the ground above mentioned."[80] This plot is almost precisely the area of the garden at The Smithy, Ackenthwaite, the home of the author.

This John Audland's son (William Audland VIII) lived for a while at Bridge End Smithy but later returned to Ackenthwaite. In 1761 he was paid £9 7s 3d for making a weather cock for Heversham Church.[81] It was during the lifetime of his son John (XII) 1771 – 1853 that the gentrification of the Audlands began. He was an ironmonger in Kendal, but developing the traditions of his family worked for Thomas Cornthwaite, considered by the Royal Society to be one of the greatest mechanical engineers of the day. Subsequent Audland generations produced a worthy crop of clergymen, doctors, army officers, a diplomat and experts in subjects as diverse as dry stone walling and hispanic equitation. The house at Ackenthwaite Green was retained but the Smithy was sold in 1866 to Abraham Langhorne. He rebuilt most of the property transferring its main entrance from the Crooklands road to Smithy Lane. From at least the 1830's the Smithy was let to the Douthwaite family. A deed of 1862 by which the Audlands purchased the freehold referred to "Smithy Cottage, Smithy, Cowhouse, Hayloft, garden, orchard in the occupation of William Douthwaite at a customary rent of 1s p.a.[82] William's son Abraham was born at the Smithy in 1837 and lived there all his life until his death in 1907. having been apprenticed to the forge under his father "he was generally esteemed and prided himself on his work especially of machinery. His opinion on any subject under discussion when given had considerable weight though often obtained with difficulty."[83] The Douthwaites were also agricultural engineers and it was while an engine of Mr Ormerod, the thresher, was standing on the road by the Smithy that a fatal accident occurred to Charles Bell, the 7 year old son of P.C. James Bell. Apparently, along with some 30 other children the little boy had followed the machine and as it slowed down climbed on to it. The jerk as it stopped caused him to fall off right under the wheel – a portion of scalp from the right side of the head was found lying on the ground. The Audland's maid who rushed out thought she heard him say "Oh Dada" but within 5 minutes Dr Audland pronounced him dead.[84]

Abraham's second son, William Cragg Douthwaite, took over the business and around the time of the First World War employed five men. In 1932 Willy built a new house – called the Homestead – and a small smithy in the field next door which he used until his retirement in 1952. The old property was then let to the Woodend family of log merchants and general dealers. During their tenancy in 1942 the Smithy was bought back by the Audlands from Francis Langhorn Douthwaite of Storth for £540. They retained it until 1978 when it was purchased by the author for £22,200.

Throughout the nineteenth century vets occupied an indeterminate position between tradesmen and the learned professions. Many combined the functions of farrier and stock breeder and by twentieth century standards were not to be regarded as "veterinary surgeons." Certainly they were not constricted by rules against advertising as this one shows:

"Milnthorpe, Beetham, Hale, Holme and their vicinities. T. E. Robinson Veterinary Surgeon, Druggist, Late assistant to R. E. Parkinson, Kendal, Respectfully informs the Gentry Farmers and Public generally of the above places and their respective vicinities that he has commenced business in Milnthorpe.

From his experience during the course of the last sixteen years in the treatment of various diseases incident to horses and cattle to trust he will be able to give every satisfaction to those whose patronage he now respectfully solicits and by an attentive punctuality to business to maintain their continuous confidence and support. MEDICINES FOR COWS. March 17 1858."

Apparently Mr Robinson did not flourish long in Milnthorpe, because from the 1850's to his death in 1888 William Knight was the veterinary surgeon for the area; both he and his family playing an important part in village society. His house and premises are believed to have been in the Old King's Arms on Park Road, (now Gumby, the Solicitors). Amateur practitioners also remained popular: the Mashiters who held Crosby Lodge from c.1826 to 1884 were said to be adept in treating horses and in the 1870's "Dr Hutton, the celebrated sportsman and bone setter" kept his horses and greyhounds there.[86]

Much information about nineteenth century industry and commerce is contained in the Census returns for 1861, 1871 and 1881. Returns prior to 1861 were limited, more or less, to names, ages and addresses. (Those from 1891 onwards could not at the time of writing be inspected under the 100 year rule.) The three lists available show that mid-nineteenth century Milnthorpe was clearly an industrial and trading place. Only 20 people, plus farmers' families, were directly employed on the land. Rather more were employed in para-agricultural activities.

Nevertheless, it is possible to trace the decline of Milnthorpe's industrial base by 1881. Whereas John Foster had close on 100 hands in the 1860's, Henry Roddick and John Robinson, respectively owner and manager of the flax mills, employed only 20 hands. In 1881 there were only 22 other industrial workers but ten years later even this had dropped by half. The small textile works persisted and William Ashburner was a "Rope twine overlooker," his brother John was the spinner overlooker at the Flax Mill while Glen Ashburner was also a spinner and Martin Ashburner a weaver. Three members of the Towers family were engaged in sacking weaving and three Towers were in the Rope works. William Spedding was a weaver of flax. Other smaller craftsmen were William Teassall, a cooper, and Ben Airey and John Barrow who were basket makers.

As regards crafts Milnthorpe was still basically a self-sufficient community in the 1870's and 1880's. There were eight shoemakers, four tailors, about ten seamstresses, two saddlers, (Ben Gillbank and John Woods). There was only one full time butcher, John Clark, one baker, John Johnston, one fishmonger, Elizabeth Mayor, one brewer, James Gerrard (Rock Cottage). William Dodgshon combined the trade of joiner and butcher and John Berry was both an ironmonger and grocer. There were four other grocers.

Blair, the builder, seems to have flourished for in 1881 he was employing 20 men and 1 boy. The joiners listed in the 1861 census were still mainly in business. At Ackenthwaite, William Ormerod was both a sawyer and a steam thresher while Robert Barnes, also an engine driver, ran the sawmill. There were still five blacksmiths in the village but in 1881 William Constable was described as a "mechanical engineer."

One notable feature of the 1871 and 1881 Censuses is the number of hawkers who included Ann Smith, Michael Delaney, Ellen Gibson, Jane Thompson, John Herriman, Robert Knowles and Hannah Garnet. Emma Derham was a muffin baker and hawker. One great character was a water-cress seller called Betty Varey - a member of the Knowles family, which according to her obituary of 1915 "had been recognised for generations as among the most successful of hawkers in the days now gone by."[87] Some of the hawkers lived at the common lodging houses kept by Tamar Healde, Deborah Garnett and by "Paddy" (Michael) Connor. It was Paddy Connor's house at the top of the square which was known as the "Padding Can." In the south west corner of the square, at the old Maltkiln, lived (from c.1865) "Happy Jack" Fawcett who was described in the Censuses as a hawker or as a "machine breaker." His instinct for trade of any kind was so well developed that he was more than equal to the more respectably described tradesmen. It was rumoured he also out did them all in wealth!

Fawcetts are named in the parish registers of Heversham and surrounding parishes from the seventeenth century. According to village tradition this branch of the Fawcetts were gypsies.[88] It is said that Happy Jack had a traditional horse caravan and that the place where he first camped in the Milnthorpe area was by the Bela at Hang Bridge, Whassett. Several fantastic tales tell how Happy Jack's wife and daughter-in-law (who died in 1949) preferred to give birth in the open air, generally on Haverbrack. Such myths, though recounted by otherwise respectable sources, probably reveal more about village attitudes to prosperous offcomers than historical truth.

John Fawcett was born, in fact, about 1817 at Skerton in Lancaster, which still has a large community of travelling folk. In his obituary, December 1909,[89] it was stated that he spent little or no time at school and that he bought his first donkey as a boy, and equipped it with two panniers on either side.

A well-known story concerns an encounter between Jack and the Levens toll gate keeper. Jack arrived with laden donkey at the tollgate [90] late one night and he rang the bell for the bar to be lifted. The toll keeper merely stuck his head out of the window and told Jack to throw the toll of one penny for the donkey up to him. Jack, though scrupulously honest, hated laziness in any form. He refused to pay on the grounds that he was a pedestrian who could go free - and while the toll keeper was struggling into his day clothes Jack unloaded his panniers, dumped them over the bar and then taking it on his shoulders carried the donkey over as well. The feat was more remarkable because although Jack was as tough and wiry

The Square c.1905. 'Happy Jack' Fawcett on left of group on Market Cross.

as they come, he was only five feet high.

Later he got a horse and cart and used it to take salt to Kendal from ships unloaded at Sandside and even bobbins from Crooklands Mill to Manchester. While travelling he was always singing "as if he were the happiest man alive - his ballads and folk songs being heard up to half a mile away - making him a general favourite with the public and earning him, (as Curwen put it) with the kindest of memories the soubriquet of Happy Jack."

Jack remained a 'traveller' until quite late in life. In 1862, when he was 45, he was camping on Rowell Green when two trains crashed. One of them had a cattle wagon and many of the beasts were killed, Jack instantly obtained the carcases and "salt beef was cheap in Milnthorpe for many a long week."

He was a great friend of auctioneers and always could be relied on for a bid and at the end of a sale he would buy up remnants in job lots and sort them out to retail at a profit at home. He also purchased bagging and waste materials from Gatebeck Mills and machinery, scrap iron and implements from elsewhere. He rarely employed anyone else (other than his own family later on) and yet by middle life he had become the "owner of a nice little property of land and houses" - and had he not preferred a simple life might have become very rich indeed. Though he never drank - believing that the "best side of a public house is outside" - one of the photographs of him shows a clay pipe stuck between his whiskered lips. Moreover, he adhered to the lore of all travelling folk and held that fish, fur or feather were fair game, having a particular skill at "grappling for trout before dawn." Long after mains became illegal Happy Jack continued to deal in fighting cocks – though unlike other protagonists of the "sport" he never gambled.

Happy Jack's family prospered exceedingly in the early years of the century. His son John inherited his father's business acumen and developed a mathematical skill which he applied to engineering. In 1890 at the age of only 19 he established one of the first motor works in the country if not the world, as the internal combustion engine had only been patented in 1888. Later he took his own sons John, Harold and Percy into the business and the slogan of John Fawcett & Sons was "As Old as – as up to-date as – the Motor Industry." In its early days the firm built motor cars and also produced a bicycle called the Gem. Later on, in addition to repairing every kind of vehicle, they produced specialised parts for the motor industry. In the First World War the firm did important munitions work, the two elder Fawcett sons being exempt from war service on this account.

Between 1924 and 1950 the Fawcetts ran the Dallam Motor Company's bus service; an important aspect of Milnthorpe transport history. After the death of John Fawcett his redoubtable widow Jessie, with the sons, ran the business until her death in 1949 when the partnership was dissolved. John kept the motor garage and name of John Fawcett & Sons; it is still run by John Fawcett IV. Harold founded the Bela Factoring House (in the former Bela Garage) as a wholesale motor parts warehouse, which he ran until his death in 1979.

Even the ingenuity of the Fawcetts did not equal that of the Stainton family, the famous ploughing engineers of Milton and Milnthorpe. Until the 1930's Thomas Stainton ran a motor business in the garage behind Thorpe House (Old King's Arms) on Church Street. In 1908 he was hailed as "Milnthorpe's Inventor." According to Cross Fleury's Journal he had patented a steam engine two years earlier, when he was 17: "the distinguishing feature of which consisted of improvements in the slide valves...."[91] Alas, although Stainton's inventiveness was praised – if not understood by most Milnthorpe folk – it did not bring him a huge fortune though his garage and small works did well enough.

At the turn of the nineteenth century a series of Art and Industrial Exhibitions were staged in the Public Rooms and the Kitching Memorial Rooms. Rather than pointing to future developments these exhibitions seemed to hark back to a notional period of handicraft work. The first exhibition was held in August 1885 and had 76 classes. Most of the exhibits were on sale and a quilt by Mrs Sanderson of Heaves brought £10. It contained 7000 pieces and even more remarkable was the fact that Mrs Sanderson had begun it when she was 90 and finished it when she was 92! There was also a loan exhibition of china and needlework from Levens Hall and other stately homes whose stately owners, headed by Countess Bective and the two Westmorland M.P.'s Messrs Cropper and Lowther, attended the opening ceremony. At the 1889 exhibition the main loan display was woodcarving of the peroid 1660 – 1720 "when as much carving was done in Westmorland as would have blessed the whole of Europe." Of contemporary work there were several hundred craft entries and the Rev. H.D. Rawnsley, the chief judge, said the decisions had nearly given him grey hairs.[92]

Inspired by the 1889 exhibition wood carving classes were started in the village and at the 1891 exhibition the first prize in the under 16 section was won by W. Arkwright for an elegant carved wood box. There were 200 more entries than in 1889 including 450 entries for carving, 400 for needlework (in 70 classes) and 800 other entries. The best overall exhibit was again a piece of carving: a Renaissance wood panel by A.F. Barnes who had "manifestly put his soul into the work."[93] This exhibition had been opened by the Earl of Derby, the next, of 1898, was opened by Sir John Hibbert. At the opening ceremony the Rev. F.R.C. Hutton appeared to touch a popular note by saying "there was no doubt a great number of things made in Germany. He believed that if we had these (handicraft) classes established all over the country we should before long find those things made in Old England and not in a foreign country." Applause![94]

The 6th triennial exhibition was judged the most successful with exhibits from 20 townships in the Milnthorpe area and new classes for painting, metal and leather work and for photography. An exhibition of Irish products including much fine drawn thread work and embroidered lace had been personally arranged by the Countess of Bective from Kirkby Lonsdale and the Marchioness of Landsdowne, mother of Lady Effie Cavendish of Holker Hall. Opened by the Duchess of Wellington, great contingents of Cavendishes, Bentinks, Stanleys, Bagots and Wilsons attended this exhibition, providing the greatest display of blue-blood ever seen in Milnthorpe.[95] More to the point there were 1500 entries, greater than ever before. This figure was exceeded by 100 at the 1908 exhibition which included a section for crafts made in workhouses "under the Brabazon scheme." Across in the Institute was an exhibition of "600 Scotch fabrics" which made £230, the entire exhibition raising £400. Sadly the only local prize winner was Mrs McNabb for crochet work.

Despite ostensible success, the exhibitions had perhaps outlived their purpose. In 1908, Mr C.R. Rivington in opening the exhibition, instead of uttering the usual gracious platitudes "criticized at some length the wood, metal and needlework sections, the designs of which he styled as the most incongruous and unsuitable as many of them were useless for their intended purpose." He then went on to object to the horicultural section, stating that the "Heversham lanes" provided finer blooms than the castor oil plants and other entries (including a huge banana plant) which were on display. In vain did Mr Hibbert protest that the bananas were "local," having been grown in the greenhouses of Levens Hall![96] In any event this was the last Milnthorpe Exhibition.

The quickening of economic life in the nineteenth century was reflected in the development of the postal service. Milnthorpe's position on the main turnpikes meant that by c.1830 it had an important post office, established by John Postlethwaite[97] at Belvidere Cottage (later the vicarage). He was succeeded by George Whittaker, who took the office to his tea and seedsman business on the south east corner of Church Street and Main Street; a far more convenient position with four coaching Inns almost adjacent. Even after the opening of the main railway line in 1847 the Milnthorpe postmaster was responsible for delivery and collection of mail from Ulverston and Grange – and they were often brought over the sands by mail gig. Only when the Furness Railway arrived in 1854 and the Hincaster branch line in the 1870's, did the trans-estuary service cease.

Whittaker was followed by Issac Rawlinson, a retired Chelsea Pensioner[98] and also Assistant Overseer for the Parish. He moved the office first to Church Street and then to a cottage on the south side of the square. In 1855 the British Telegraph Company laid wires through the village for a service to be operated by the post master. It was not a success because the wires were laid underground in wooden pipes which broke or rotted and the service was eventually replaced in 1870 by overhead wires. This led to the main road through Milnthorpe being lined for almost a hundred years with huge and unsightly telegraph poles. In Rawlinson's time the Savings Bank was introduced in 1861, Postal Orders in 1881 and the Parcel Post in 1883. "Old Issac" retired in 1884 and on 1st November following – his golden wedding day – he was presented with a silver tea service "by his numerous friends." [99] Rather ostentatious gifts were bestowed on the equally hardworking post-man (or post-messenger as he was called). In 1863 John Vipond, post-messenger from Milnthorpe, through Heversham and Leasgill by Sizergh and Sedgwick to Stainton, was presented with £5 3s 10d "collected by a few friends who reside in different parts of his daily(!) route."[100] Twelve years later he was given a waterproof Inverness Cape and a pair of leggings in appreciation of his punctuality and good conduct during 24 years during which time at 16 miles a day he had covered an estimated

Mashiter's Window Sill 1910.

160,000 miles. When in 1883 he had done thirty years he was given an extra 3s per week and the privilege of wearing three stripes on his arm.[102]

On Issac Rawlinson's retirement Milnthorpe's status as a Head Office was reduced to that of a R.S.O. – a Railway Sub-Office. The new post-master was the tailor Roger Mashiter, who transferred the business to the corner property on Park Road where, after 103 years it still remains. His son John took over in 1890 and rebuilt the premises in 1897. He enlarged the retail side of the business as well as having a finger in many other village concerns, both commercial and social. The introduction of Old Age Pensions (1905) and National Insurance (1911) and a telephone exchange in 1913 added to the work.

Even so, there were three collections and at least two deliveries daily. Special deliveries would be made to outlying places, John Mashiter personally taking them by bicycle lest the claim that any letter could be delivered to any place in the United Kingdom within 24 hours was not met. John Mashiter also collected the early mail at 5 a.m. at the Station. Dispatch from Milnthorpe was made easier by the installation of a cage apparatus in c.1880 which could collect bags without stopping, though occasionally it failed and Milnthorpe's mail was scattered down the line as far as Elmsfield.[103] In May 1895 Benjamin J. Whitten the night mail messenger whose duty hours were 9 p.m. to 4.30 a.m. while "effecting the exchange of bags by the apparatus, was knocked down by the fish train at 2.08 a.m. Mr Dunderdale the Station Master, who had just obtained a St. John's certificate, set poor Ben's arm which was broken in two places and "copiously bleeding." Apparently he recovered and John Mashiter and the District Superintendent had the device amended to avoid a recurrence.[104]

During the First World War the Post Office had a pivotal position linking Milnthorpe to the horrors of the wider world. The increased work led to a temporary breakdown in John Mashiter's health in 1922 and to his retirement to his splendid new house, Maymyo. In the following January Mr and Mrs Mashiter were presented with a sterling silver service at a ceremony in the public rooms.

He was succeeded by Joseph Proctor and then in 1924 by Samuel Barr, who continued the traditions of the business. In 1934 the Parish Council solemnly gave permission for a stamp vending machine to be installed on the Post Office door. In 1939 Mr and Mrs Greenwood took over. They left in c.1945 and were replaced by Dick Carruthers, a jovial young man who along with Post Office work – expanded still more by Welfare State benefits – sold china, specialising in chamber pots with scandalously scatological rhymes! Sadly he was forced into retirement at the early age of 35 and was replaced by Jim and Pat Lord, during which time the retail side of the business was much reduced. In 1981, following Pat's death, Jim Lord retired and was followed by Colin France until 1987, when Ian Fraser took over.

Banks were late in being established in Milnthorpe. Most businesmen apparently were prepared to attend the banks of the Wakefields and Crewdsons in Kendal. Only in the 1880's do part time sub-branches appear in the Gazeteers. "John Cottam, bank manager and seed merchant, Main Street" was noted in 1885 and in 1894 appeared "Lancaster Banking Co. (sub-branch) (open Tues. & Fri 10 a.m. to 2 p.m.); draw on Barclay, Bevan, Tritton,Ransom, Bouverie & Co London E.C." By 1905 Cottam's sub-bank on Main Street west of Flowerden had become part of the Bank of Liverpool (Kendal Bank) and John Webster was manager. "The Lancaster Banking Co. Ltd. open Mondays, Wednesdays and Fridays 10 to 2, Charles Hoggarth manager" was established in the shop in the Institute. Here it remained, having become the District Bank, until it removed in 1966 to new premises built on the site of Fleet House on Main Street, where it eventually became part of the National Westminster Bank. The Bank of Liverpool having become Martin's Bank (and then Barclay's) moved to Thorpe House in c.1920. The old Main Street bank was demolished during the road widening scheme of 1926. A Midland's sub-branch opened in the new property built on the site of the Royal Oak in the 1920's where it stayed until c.1965 when it moved to the big house on the south side of the square.

During the first half of the twentieth century the pattern of numerous small retail and craft shops persisted. Around 1905 there were at least 13 shops, of which bakers, confectioners, grocers etc. were the most numerous. There were sweet shops belonging to Mary Baines at the corner of Main Street in the Royal Oak buildings, and to Mrs M. Truman at number 12 Park Road. Grocers etc. were Richard Eason in the Public Rooms shop in the square, Johnny Gray in Main Street, Mary and Agnes James, (who were also excellent confectioners) at Hillside (Jasmine Cottage) on Main Street, George Helliwell next to the Cross Keys on Park Road – later the Bon Bon sweet shop. Across the road was Christopher Knight who was an "agent for Gilbey's patent medicine dealer." On the corner of Church Street (west of Flowerden) was the Kendal Co-operative Store run by Mr William Millward.

Edward Stones had been reduced to a small shop in his Church Street house, from where he also sold bacon from home-reared pigs, for which his daughter trailed the streets collecting pig swill. The main grocers were by this time T. and H. Richmond in the square. They had a large delivery business and by 1914 had a motor van driven by Charles Mashiter which took goods as far as Barbon, 15 miles to the east. The tailor's shop of Mashiter and Son, run by Walter Mashiter on Park Road, employed five or six men and was the largest craft shop in the village. Up Church Street, Thomas Dobson also worked as a tailor. Abbatt & Son of Kendal had a draper's and dressmaker's shop in the Institute shop nearest the Cross Keys; other, home based, dressmakers were Miss Douglass on the Strand and Annie Blair next door, Miss Margaret Holmes of 1 Park Terrace (customers had to go up the back ghinnel to the side door) and next door to each other on Main Street, opposite the school, were Eleanor Langstreth and Miss Alice Wilkinson.

George Francis Atkinson was a boot and shoe maker whose retail shop was in the front room of his cottage (now the vets) while the workshop was on the site of what later became the newsagents and, later still, a health food shop. Joseph Daffady in the former White Lion on Beetham Road, Albert Hayes in the shop under the old chapel on Haverflatts Lane and William Hind in a building next to Fir Tree House in Park Road were also cobblers. Between Atkinson's workshop and house was Alfred Peter Claughton's butchers and, across the square (at what became the Monarch Guest House) was Robert Clark's butchers shop. His slaughter house was on Beetham Road, to which a back lane connected, though at other times carcases would be dragged up the square to the front of the shop.

Milnthorpe was still well supplied with builders and joiners.

Christopher Scott, who had come to the area from Gargrave when he was foreman during the restoration of Heversham church in 1869, was still in business with his sons, the eldest of whom, William, amalgamated with Hodgson and Nelson of Heversham in c.1920. The other son Christopher, killed at the Dardenelles in 1915, had carved the date stone (1910) of the Police Station. Scott's yard was next to the slaughter house on Beetham Road. Joiners included James T. McNabb of Ackenthwaite Saw Mills, Edward Coward of Thorpe House and W.G. (George) Wilson whose yard was in Park Road at the end of Grisley Lane. Higher up were the premises of George Semple who also sold oil and ironmongery. The longest established painter was John Thompson of Park Road.[108]

The inter-war trade directories look little different from those at the turn of the century. Daffady's boot makers, Clark's butchers, Wilson and Scott builders, Eason the grocer, Mashiter's gents tailors, Semple's and Thompson's painters – were all still in business. Joining them, Isaac Coward had set up as a 'Surgical and Practical Boot and Shoe makers'. Bobby Langhorn had a (rather somnambulant) joiner's shop on Park Road and H.B. Battersby another at Gandy Nook which did not last long. By contrast Frank Holmes – "Interior Decorations a Speciality Personal Attention to all orders" – lasted for nearly 50 years. T.T. Richmond had now been taken over by Daish's Ltd. while the Co-operative Stores was being run by Henry Atkinson, son of G.F. Atkinson the boot maker, who had retired. The old front room shoe shop was used as a chemist's shop by G.F. Atkinson's son-in-law, W.H. Sheldon M.P.S. before he moved across the road to a new shop which for a time had been used as a saddlers by George Flemming. Atkinson's cobbler's shop had been extended by George Brown to form a sweet and newsagent's shop. On Park Road Handley Woods and his family ran the Bon Bon sweet and newsagent's shop, while another newsagent was the Moss family of Sun House. There were two draper's shops on Church Street; E. Newsham at the bottom and Mrs Mary Bosworth's at the top, the latter finally belonged to Walter and Jessie Thompson before closing in 1939.

Milnthorpe had by this time three ladies' hairdressers: Miss Grace Barr on Park Road, Miss Elsie Pricket on Main Street and Cottam's "Saloon" on Beetham Road and two barbers, Charles Bosworth of Main Street and Harold Whiteley's in the cellar of the Tavern Loft on the square. Frank Dunford at Thorpe House was a fruiterer and greengrocer, while in the square was "Fishy" (Thomas) Whitehead's fishmongers. On Main Street Mrs G. Heath opened her fish and chip shop; a service which made Milnthorpe famous to thousands of passing motorists. The combination of petrol fumes, smokey drizzle and fish and chip odours became the

The Co-op 1906.

ubiquitous smell of Milnthorpe.

A general trend after the Second World War towards the creation of larger units, with a total eclipse of the "corner shop" was accelerated in Milnthorpe by traffic congestion on the A.6. which effectively cut off Church Street, Park Road and Beetham Road from the main business area. In c.1950 there was still Newsham's drapers and Walker's greengrocers on Church Street. In Park Road there was the Bon Bon, Mashiter's outfitters, the Post Office, Mrs Whip's second-hand shop, Co-op butchers (formerly Clark's), Co-operative Stores, Mr Teriblee's ice cream shop and a small grocers run at first by the Teriblees and then by others including Eileen Fothergill. On the west side of Beetham Road there was Daffady's boot store (Rolley Sharp) and Mrs Gould's Grocers. Of these only the Post Office and Joan's ladies' dress shop (formerly Mashiter's) remain. Elsewhere in the village, the grocers on Harmony Green belonging to Audrey Hyde in the 1940's and 1950's closed about 1960. Ethel Spry's grocer's shop in Fleet House closed in c.1965, Dixon's (formerly Eason's and then Gillam's) in c.1970. By 1987 Messrs Crossfield and Sons (known generally as the Spar) was the only remaining grocer. There was still a greengrocer's run by Jackie & Marie Cordukes at the former Eason shop, a butchers – calling itself Ye Olde Butcher's Shop – on Main Street, a health food shop and, in the premises formerly occupied by Fawcetts, a large N.S.S. newsagents. The pharmacy of James E. Rushton Ltd, having taken over from Sheldon's in 1945, is now the oldest of Milnthorpe's retail outlets – such has been the transitory nature of commerce.

Concurrent with the decline of the old retail trades Milnthorpe in 1970's and 1980's saw the expansion of service businesses stimulated partly by the easing of the traffice problem after the opening of the M.6 and Levens Link and by the "suburbanisation" of most of the surrounding villages. In 1986 there were four estate agents, a vet, two dentists, two insurance businesses, a video shop, an architects, an opticians and three hairdressers. There is a business equipment supplier and, surprisingly, a well known publisher. Though trades are different Milnthorpe remains an important and thriving trading centre.

Milnthorpe also survived as an industrial place. In the 1920's and 1930's the area was spared the worst effects of the depression. An unemployment exchange was opened but there were rarely more than thirty people on the books. Even so, there was much sympathy for 250 workless marchers from Glasgow who halted in Milnthorpe for refreshments in October 1931.[109] Five years earlier, during the General Strike, Samuel Johnston of Storth, James Dodgson of Green Cottage and John William Riley of Windy Hill were prosecuted in Milnthorpe's Magistrates' Court for trying to prevent Joseph Ponsonby from working at Falls Mill, Beetham. Strong feelings were expressed on both sides when they were all given short prison sentences.[110]

*Libby's Milk Factory
1936.*

In April 1934[111] the American firm of Libby McNeil and Libby established the strangely named "Milk factory" close to Milnthorpe Station – and it was hoped that it would employ 100 men. Along with an American manager, Jenkinson, came American management methods, including a thriving social and sports club as well as what were ultra-modern premises and working conditions.

Libby's were taken over by Nestle's in the 1970s and shortly before the Milnthorpe factory celebrated its half centenary milk processing was replaced by fruit canning and sauces as the main products –fortunately without causing any redundancies.

The preservation of Libby's, the expansion of transport services on the adjoining site and of computers, comb making, coach building (at Houghton's Parkhouse Coach Works) in the village and also several construction and plant hire concerns, including two firms run by the Rockliffes – one of Milnthorpe's older families – meant that Milnthorpe's economy still had an industrial base. During the recession of the 1980s unemployment was generally below 6 per cent – less than half the regional average. Milnthorpe at the end of the twentieth century, therefore, appeared to be relatively more prosperous than at any time since the 1830s.

8

Homes

Milnthorpe is an ancient place overlaid by newer development. As such its buildings reflect the continuous evolution of human society. Mankind and, when it comes to homes especially, womankind, have rarely been content with the artefacts of earlier times. Most old houses, therefore, bear marks of every period of occupation. In any case no building can be permanent. A wet and windy climate like that of South Westmorland has meant that even solid looking slate roofs hardly last for more than a century and a half. Chimneys – a prey to the elements, wind and water without and fire within – are especially vulnerable, but doors and windows need to be replaced frequently too, though here fashion, or upgrading in the householders' status, often dictates a change. The installation of "neo-georgian" or aluminium framed opaque glass doors in former council houses have shown how such features proclaim to the passing world the upward mobility of the owner. For the same reasons mullions were replaced by sashes in the eighteenth century, which in turn were replaced by Victorian plate glass and, perhaps, a century later by patio doors.

In less conspicuous places older or less sophisticated features often remained. Thus Hillside Cottage on Harmony Green, family home of the Semples, has well cut sandstone quoins of c.1780's painted rendering and Victorian sashes and a lead covered porch of c.1880. Round the back the limestone rubble walls are exposed and an original window with leaded panes has survived.

Similarly, Ackenthwaite Farm has small casements of c.1750[1] to the upper storey while on the north wall is a sash of c.1800. The lower windows of about the same date now have modern glazing while the cellar retains stone mullions of at least 1700; the only mullions left in Milnthorpe. In the Blue Row, on Church Street, the double glazing salesman wreaked such aesthetic havoc in modern

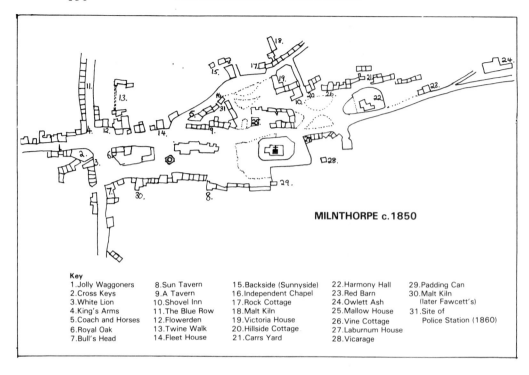

MILNTHORPE c.1850

Key

1.Jolly Waggoners	8.Sun Tavern	15.Backside (Sunnyside)
2.Cross Keys	9.A Tavern	16.Independent Chapel
3.White Lion	10.Shovel Inn	17.Rock Cottage
4.King's Arms	11.The Blue Row	18.Malt Kiln
5.Coach and Horses	12.Flowerden	19.Victoria House
6.Royal Oak	13.Twine Walk	20.Hillside Cottage
7.Bull's Head	14.Fleet House	21.Carrs Yard

22.Harmony Hall	29.Padding Can
23.Red Barn	30.Malt Kiln
24.Owlett Ash	(later Fawcett's)
25.Mallow House	31.Site of
26.Vine Cottage	Police Station (1860)
27.Laburnum House	
28.Vicarage	

times that by 1987 only one house was left with its original sashes of c.1820. Elsewhere in the village even some of the larger houses, like Glasgow and Victoria Houses, have been similarly "modernised."

Road widening in the 1920's and "slum" clearance in the 1950's removed about a quarter of Milnthorpe's older cottages. Many more were amalgamated to form larger units. Most of the houses in the Blue Row were originally divided,[2] but only one pair of "half-houses" still existed by 1987. They share a common front door and the individual entrance is from a tiny triangular lobby via a door set diagonally across the corner of the living room.

Carr's Yard now contains about half-a-dozen cottages mainly for single people or couples, but in 1900 it was a teaming slum of about twenty dwellings and over 100 habitants. Such changes explain, partly, why although Milnthorpe's built up area has quadrupled in the twentieth century its population has not even doubled.[3]

Much of the newer development is behind or apart from the older village, whose core could possibly be recognised by a reincarnated stage coach traveller. Milnthorpe probably contains more buildings of the eighteenth and nineteenth century than any other place in South Westmorland except Kendal. Certainly it has escaped much of the bungaloid sub-topian sprawl which has despoiled neighbouring "residential" villages.

There is little that can be verified from before the eighteenth

*Park Road c.1920. Spring Cottage on right; Park View on
left, built on site of Milnthorpe's last thatched cottages c.1871.*

century. Local limestone is difficult to carve. Unlike other
limestone villages such as Wharton or the Yealands datestones
made from sandstone imported from adjacent areas were never
fashionable in Milnthorpe. Lower Haverflatts is dated 1691, but
within the village the oldest date is 1726 on a renewed stone in
Carr's Yard, Crosby Lodge is dated 1749, and there is a worn datestone, BRM 1727(?), in the outbuildings at Harmony Hall. A stone
built into the yard wall of Flowerden reads "E + Kitchen 1807" and
an iron rain-water spout on Fir House (Park House Coach Works)
reads EH 1850. Of the few other date-stones all are later.

   The very first homes in the area would have been constructed of
turf, timber, wattle and thatch. Field stone might have been used as
well and a substantial slab would have been provided for a hearth.
Nevertheless, not even around the Dog Hole on Haverbrack, a
recognised area of ancient settlement,[4] has anything survived of
these essentially temporary dwellings. Nothing remains either of
the Scandinavian "Mylen Port" nor of its medieval successor. The
rectangular shape of the "long house" of the Middle Ages,
however, might have determined the plan of many of the older
buildings. The long house generally had two rooms, one for the
humans, the other for the animals.[5] Low Croft at Ackenwaite is a
descendant of the simplest of these structures and might itself date
from before 1700. Chestnut Villa, a similar dwelling off Main
Street, dating at least from the eighteenth century was originally a
harness room and stable. Later developments of the long house
included an upper storey, originally a mere loft approached by a
ladder or outside stair, a "through passage" to divide human and

Vine Cottage.

animal occupants and an "outshut" or other extension.

Vine Cottage on Harmony Hill contains many of these features. It is only one unit deep, its low upper storey is partly contained in the roof and there is a through passage separating the house from what were originally farm buildings. A similar ground plan exists at Lower Haverflatts farm and Low Cragg Yeat. No.3 Main Street (now Estate Agents and Solicitors) and Ivy Cottage have prominent outshuts of at least the eighteenth century. The former has deep eaves, an attic casement and first floor sashes of the mid-eighteenth century.

Most of the older houses have flues contained within the gable end walls. Crosby Lodge has a partly corbelled external chimney breast, containing a space for smoking hams. High Cragg Yeat has a corbelled square base (now obscured by recent additions) for the traditional "round" chimney. Parkside has a group of three original cylindrical chimneys midway in the ridge, two at the west end, one on corbels at the east, and there are two circular flues in the north wing. Most of the lesser dwellings would not at first have a fire place in the upper storey where the chimney would be made of studds lined with clay and gathered together in a hollow half-pyramid to join the chimney stack. Several such flues have survived in the Park Road Cottages. Some of these cottages and also Ivy Cottage, Ackenthwaite, have "hecks": short walls at right angles to the main door designed to deflect draughts away from the fire.

That most houses had only one or two chimneys is demonstrated by the hearth tax returns (as recorded by Curwen):

On referring to the roll for 1669, under the civil parish of Heversham with Milnthorpe, we find that there were only fifty-two houses enjoying a fireplace; that Mr. Wilson had seven at

Dallam Tower and five in another house; that four residents had the luxury of three; that the Rev. Thomas Bigg, vicar of Heversham, had one in the kitchen and one in his study; whilst the majority of the others had only one fireplace apiece.

Mr Wilson	.. ..	7	Tho: Cocke	 1
Mr Bellingam	.. ..	2	William Atkinson	 2
Tho: Kitchine	.. ..	2	Arthur Hudson	 1
Widd: Dickinson	.. ..	1	Math: Adlington	 2
The same	.. 1 wald up		Tho: Wright	 2
Myles Croft	.. ..	1	Mr Wilson	 2
Robert Preston	.. ..	1	Mrs Duckett	 3
Robt Becke	.. ..	2	John Saull	 1
James Murthwte	.. ..	3	The same	.. 1 wald up
Mr Bigg	.. ..	2	Rich: Cragg	 2
Mr Wilson	.. ..	5	Robt Gibson	 1
John Wilson	.. ..	1	Tho: Barton	 1
James Harrison	.. ..	1	John Cornthwte	 1
Edward Barrow	.. ..	2	John Hadland	 2
Peter Cowper	.. ..	1	Rowland Bickas	 1
James Jackson	.. ..	1	George Atkinson	 1
Robt Woodhouse	.. ..	1	John Hudson	 1
Willm Parker	.. ..	2	Robt Dickinson	 1
Symond Watson	.. ..	1	Widd: Clarke	 2
Henry Preston	.. ..	2	Thomas Bellingam	 1
Rowland Parke	.. ..	2	Belchar: Wright	 1
Leonard Croft	.. ..	3	Willm Docker	 1
James Moone	.. ..	1	Tho: Powe	 1
Tho: Cragg	.. ..	2	Widd: Parke	 3
Mr Wilson	.. ..	2	John Gregg	 2
Robt Cornthwte	.. ..	1	Willm Ridley[6]	 1

Peat was the main fuel until c.1800. An article of agreement made on 11 May 1687 between "Mary Hinde of Auckenthwait Spinster and Thomas Cragge of Cragyeat in Auckenthwait" concerning "a dwelling house and garding," states that Thomas should buy the property for £8 providing "that Mary Hinde shall use occupie and possess ye Chimney and ye body stead of ye aforesaid house during her naturall lyfe... and that ye said Thomas Cragge shall give and lead cart to ye doore of ye said Mary Hindes house five cart full of peats or turfs and in every yeare during her natural lyfe."[7]

Increased imports of coal via the port of Milnthorpe during the eighteenth century inevitably led to more chimneys being installed. Coal was better suited for parlour and bedroom grates even though peats might still be used in the kitchen or "fire house." Until cheap lead flashing came in during the nineteenth century the joins between the roof and chimney stack were particularly vulnerable to rain so to give some protection stepped slates were often built into

Parkside Chimneys.

the stacks. These can be seen at Laburnum Cottages, on some Carr's Yard cottages and at the Dallam Tower cottages in Park Road.

The port records show that fire bricks for chimneys were used in c.1840[8] and occasionally building bricks were imported. Little use seems to have been made of the local clay deposits for brick making. In c.1820 a brick works was in operation at Moss Side, Heversham, but after it had provided bricks for the Hincaster Canal Tunnel it closed down. Stone remained the main building material until the First World War. In c.1905 it was still cheaper to build a shed in Heversham church yard of stone rather than of brick. Jeff Scott's first job as an apprentice for his father's firm of Hodgson, Nelson and Scott about 1925 was to dig a "stone hole" to provide material for rebuilding a cottage in the square. Where on-site stone was not available the nearest outcrop was used. That in the Town Field behind Church Street was quarried to supplement stone already available from earlier buildings on the site when Oaklea was built in Park Road. Many walls and houses display re-used material. The wall of Harmony Hall contains flag stones from Harmony Hill House which adjoined.

Field stone of all kinds and colour was also used and adds variety to the pinkish hued limestone from Heversham and the slightly buff shaded stone from Sandside used in most buildings. From whichever quarry it came the local limestone cut into roughly angular blocks of a greater thickness than the thinly stratified stone from Levens, for example. Though difficult to cut it was easily "coursed" in the thick lime mortar which replaced clay as the main bedding material by c.1600. Most walls were of coursed rough stone or rubble. A feature of such walls is the use of "throughs" which protrude from the exterior of the building. These can be seen at Lower Haverflatts, Gandy Nook and at the Presbytery on Haverflatts Lane. Because limestone is porous houses were invariably weatherproofed by rendering and then lime washed as at Parkside, Ackenthwaite Green House, Ackenthwaite Farm, and Crosby Lodge. Even when they adjoin the house, however, as at Low Haverflatts, farm buildings were often not rendered.

Main windows and doors generally bore straight limestone lintels traditionally obtained (along with gate posts) from Farleton Knott where the stone could be hewn directly from the scar or from limestone pavements. The eighteenth century Laburnum cottages have flat arched window openings and several Park Road cottage windows have wooden lintels protected by plaster or slates. To avoid cutting square quoins the corners of lesser buildings, like the cottage on Windy Hill, were often rounded as were garden walls. A similar corner off Harmony Green was probably built just to save space, however. Most lintels were smoothed in order to take rendering, but after c.1860 rock faced features were seen e.g. the old police station, the Smithy at Ackenthwaite and Thorpe Cottage. Occasionally dressed limestone detailing was used, as at Victoria House, Fountain House and Rock Cottage which all have limestone ashlar plinths. The Vicarage (Belvidere Cottage) and Laburnum House (also of c.1820) have good limestone ashlar though that at Laburnum House was described in 1851 as being of "limestone lately erected."[10]

Sandstone, though not indigenous to Milnthorpe, is nevertheless fairly conveniently available from Hutton Roof, Lancaster or Heysham. Except, however, for dressings in the larger houses like Harmony Hall and Flowerden it is used sparingly. Rock Cottage has an arched sandstone architrave, Mallow House a square cut rusticated doorway (without fanlight) architraves and sills. Next door at Ivy House the window details are of sandstone but limestone has been used for the doorstep, gate posts and the porch which supports an attractive Victorian oriel. Two cottages in Milnthorpe Square of c.1905 were faced in sandstone carted from Lancaster by the brother of Edward Mashiter the builder.[11]

The roofs of all the older houses are of local slate. This is generally Westmorland green slate laid with the larger pieces on the lower rows, gradually becoming smaller towards the ridge coping which is usually of sandstone. Park Terrace, built in c.1870 on the site of older cottages which had been demolished by G.E. Wilson twenty years earlier,[12] and Stoneleigh of 1875 received Welsh slate roofs that proved to be less durable than local slate. Unlike the Welsh slate, local slates have a rounded end (which is overlapped by the upper layer) so that it need only be secured with one peg. Number 13 Park Road has a slated gable end apparently roughly contemporary with the c.1780 date of the house.

Many of the roof timbers in the older houses are rough hewn and some in the Park Road cottages are unsquared limbs, even retaining bark. Oak or other hard woods were used for principle rafters and purlins, softer woods for joists and for floor boards. Several houses, including Ackenthwaite House, Ackenthwaite Green House, Low Crag Yeat and Crosby Lodge have some oak floor boards and stairs.[13]

The steep pitch of many roofs notably Crosby Lodge and the Dallam Tower cottages in Park Road was probably designed for thatch originally. Slates were used on larger properties like Ackenthwaite Green (c.1735) from the eighteenth century and frequently came by sea from Cumberland to the Milnthorpe port. Even so at the turn of the eighteenth century many houses were still thatched and the well known engraving of Milnthorpe Sands shows two thatched cottages at the Dixies. By the late nineteenth century cheaper slates carried by rail had replaced thatch. According to a press report of May 1870 "the last thatched property in Milnthorpe consisting of two cottages and a barn situated at the low end of the town and believed to have stood for 200 years, having lately come into the possession of Mr James Bury of Manchester he determined to pull them down and rebuild. They were, therefore, evacuated for this purpose on the eighth instance and the foundation stone for three new houses (now Park View, 1871) was laid by Mr Bury on Saturday the 13th instance, after which Mr Bury gave the workmen and other friends a supper at the Cross Keys Hotel which was served up in Miss Hutton's usual style."[14] A similar "bountiful spread of good things" was provided in the Agricultural Hall in October 1874 for workpeople employed by Mr James Blair in erecting a new building on the outskirts of Milnthorpe.[15] Such feasts generally followed "topping-out," a ceremony still surviving in rudimentary form when workmen fly a cement bag or tattered cloth from the scaffold pole immediately the highest point of the new building has been completed. Over 60 workmen sat down for the topping-out dinner provided by Canon Argles in 1900 after the shell of his summer residence at Hawbarrow had been completed.

Very few houses display distinct architectural features, though there are a few neo-classical doorways. The slightly bulbous ionic columns of the blocked up doorway in Vine House (Crossfields grocers) could be of c.1740 and Glasgow House of c.1820 has slender columns. Other properties having well-cut moulded porchways of the period 1790-1840 include the Midland Bank, Fountain House, Thorpe House, Victoria House and Ackenthwaite House.

Of the larger village houses the basic type is the "double-pile house" i.e. of two rooms depth,[16] common in the north west from

Mallow House c.1820.

1680 to after 1800. Such houses normally comprised two full storeys with four main rooms on each floor, a spacious garret and often a small cellar. Except for a peat house, stabling etc., all offices were contained within the main structure. Ackenthwaite Green House, substantially rebuilt about 1735 by the Audlands, (who had occupied the site from at least 1580) is typical. Plainly rendered, except when painted pink in the 1950's, devoid of architectural pretension and standing four square and solid, it exemplified the qualities of the moderately well-to-do yeomen for whom it was built.

A larger and earlier house is Owlett Ash which retains five original narrow window openings on the upper storey, though these now contain Victorian sashes. The bay windows on each side of the front door are also Victorian, c.1870. The doorway itself has a distinctive pediment architrave and ironwork of c.1740-1780, and inside the house the turned balusters of the staircase also appear to be of this date. In 1834 Owlett Ash was advertised as consisting of "a handsome and commodious Dwelling House with suitable outbuildings such as Coach House, Stable and Cow House with Garden and Orchard and about 27 acres... immediately adjoining the house."[17]

Other houses of the same type include Crosby Lodge, Fir Tree House, Fountain House, Mallow House, Bela House and Ackenthwaite House – all probably belonging to the second half of the eighteenth century. Rather later are Ryley Field, St. Anthony's

House, Rock Cottage and Laburnum House.

Built about 1827, Laburnum House incorporated as the "breakfast parlour" part of the older cottage to the north. In 1832 it was advertised to let as being "a good Dwelling House newly erected situate at the high end of Milnthorpe and suitable for a small genteel Family. The House consists of on the first floor two good parlours, kitchen and pantry with excellent cellars and Brewhouse attached on. Second floor 4 lodging rooms good attics over. Handsomely furnished, now in the occupation of Mr Towers the owner."[18] When put up for sale by Mr William Turner in 1841 it was described as containing three living rooms, kitchens, beer-house, with six bedrooms above. By 1851 when John Morland put the house on the market it had expanded to four living rooms and eight bedrooms.[19]

Belvidere Cottage – the Vicarage from 1840 – is a departure from the basic plan. Its main entrance is in the south gable, though a vestigial "blocked" doorway was incorporated between the drawing room and dining room windows on the main west facade which was faced with beautiful limestone ashlar. The house also possessed a full range of cellars and spacious attics that had dormer windows until c.1956. Belvidere was probably built by John Postlethwaite who advertised it for sale in 1821 "as a newly built dwelling house."[20] Before it was eventually sold to the Rev. N. Padwick it was advertised, unsuccessfully, on several occasions. An advertisement of June 1833 gave full details:

"Freehold Mansion House and Premises in Milnthorpe. To be sold by Auction by Mr. Thomas Bainbridge at the house of Mrs. Hudson the Cross Keys Inn in Milnthorpe in the County of Westmorland, on Friday 14th Day of June next at 6 o'clock in the evening All that excellent messuage or Mansion House called Belvidere Cottage with the Garden, Yard, Barn, Stable, Coach House and other out buildings there unto belonging. The House is modern built with limestone front well calculated for the reception of a genteel family and pleasantly situated on a gentle eminence on the east side of the Town of Milnthorpe is replete with Conveniences consisting of an Entrance Hall, Dining Room 17ft by 16ft, Drawing Room 15ft by 14ft, Breakfast Room 12ft by 8ft, extensive Kitchens, 3 pantries, on ground floor five comfortable and commanding bedrooms and water closet on the first floor with attics above the whole divided into 4 rooms and excellent and convenient arrangements of cellars beneath the whole comprising wine cellar, and 4 others. The Coach House and other out offices are well arranged with every accommodation. There is a beautiful Pleasure Ground in front of the House and immediately behind the House a Kitchen garden nearly ½ an acre in extent bounded on the north by a wall

Procession down Main Street, probably the Peace Procession of 1919. A rare picture of Harmony Hill House (left), once attached to Harmony Hall, whose bay window can just be seen. The road was surfaced in 1911.

one hundred and twenty yards long well stocked with Fruit Trees.

The premises command a view of a fine richly wooded country to the west immediately over the Town is seen an Estuary of the Bay of Morecambe an arm of which reaches within less than a mile of the House and in the distance appears a beautiful and extensive display of the Lake Mountains. The neighbourhood is much resorted in the Summer Season. Mr. Postlethwaite of Milnthorpe aforesaid Post Master, the owner, will appoint a person to shew the premises."[21]

Milnthorpe's finest house, Harmony Hall, is sufficiently different in scale and quality to be distinguished from other larger houses. Both the R.C.H.M.[22] and Pevsner[23] ascribe it to the early nineteenth century and this would accord with the tradition that it was built by Captain Joseph Fayrer who flourished at the turn of the eighteenth century. However, in style it belongs more to the period around 1780 and is not unlike work by the Carrs of York. Unfortunately no original plans nor the name of the architect have survived. Harmony Hall, also known simply as Harmony Hill, occupies a commanding position at the head of the Green. At some stage in the early twentieth century an adjoining, possibly older property to the south called Harmony Hill House[24] was demolished so that

Harmony Hall.

the house is now appropriately detached.

The main west facade of the house is of sandstone ashlar cut in thin rectangular blocks, accentuated by protruding chamfered quoins and cornice. There is a low lipped roof. The side and rear walls are rendered without ornamentation of any kind. Harmony Hall's finest external feature is the main doorway which consists of two columns with plain bases and cornice capitals bearing adamesque plaques supporting a triangular pediment into which the rounded door head containing fan light is carved. On either side are mid-Victorian bay windows, above which are the three original sashes.

Inside, the house contains good contemporary plasterwork, one plain chimney piece of c.1800, another of c.1870 and in one bedroom an original cast iron grate of Regency style. There is a graceful curving or flying staircase, redolent of the age of elegance, lighted by a high paladian window containing the original slightly curved and slightly blurred panes.

Following the death of Joseph Fayrer his trustees, in order to sort out his affairs, had to resort to a private Act of Parliament which received the Royal Assent of the Prince Regent on 8th July 1819. The Act refers to a will made by "Joseph Fayrer late of Milnthorp, Master Mariner" dated 19th September 1800. By a codicil he requested that his loving wife Bridget... should be secured in the

Harmony Hall Staircase.

Possession of the Testator's House in Milnthorp called Woodburn's House."[25] Whether this name refers to an earlier home of the Fayrers is not known. As a result of this exceptional legislation the 'heir at law' was determined to be Joseph Fayrer's grandson, John Fayrer Coates, son of John Coates of Huddersfield (Manufacturer) and Hannah Fayrer. Apparently by this time all of Joseph Fayrer's seven children were dead and John Coate's trustees immediately put the property on the market as "a capital Messuage or Mansion House called Harmony Hill delightfully situated at the head of the Town of Milnthorp with the Coach House, Garden and premises all on the south side and contiguous to the Highway betwixt Kendal and Burton now in the occupation of Mrs. Blewert."[26] The accommodation included a drawing room 22ft by 16ft, dining room 16 feet by 15 feet, a butler's pantry, kitchen on the ground floor and many good bedrooms and dressing rooms, excellent cellars and suitable offices. "The situation in point of eligibility can hardly be exceeded as it is in a genteel neighbourhood and commands delightful views of Dallam Tower Park, Whitbarrow Scar and Millthrop Sands. A small garden, Well built barn with two stables and harness room on opposite of Road to Lot 1 together with a close or parcel of land called Milnthorp Green Allotment as now staked out all lying together containing by estimation 1 acre 1 rood 12 perches...." One of the 14 remaining lots refer possibly to

Harmony Hill House; "a neat and commodious dwellinghouse
and garden adjoins, pleasantly situated in front of Milnthorp Green
and occupied by Effingham Howard Grant Esq. This is well
adapted for a genteel family residence. The house contains on the
Ground Floor a Drawing Room and Dining Room each 15ft 9in by
12ft, 6 bedrooms and other conveniences. . ."[26]

Milnthorpe's only notable Victorian houses are Stoneleigh and
Flowerden. Stoneleigh was built in 1873,[27] on the site of several
older cottages[28] by Mary, Elizabeth and Sarah Saul. Sarah the last
Miss Saul, died in 1883 when the house was advertised to let as
containing three entertaining rooms and seven bedrooms with
domestic offices and servants' quarters. It had in all some 20 rooms
but almost no garden until the ancient cottage adjoining to the west
was demolished in the 1920's. It is, however, a handsome structure
in dressed limestone with an attractive porch and windows. In 1983
the eastern corbelled chimney stack collapsed and the debris only
narrowly missed falling on two men lodging in the house. Salvaged
stone from this disaster was used in the Parish Council's bus
shelter.

Flowerden, at the western end of Main Street stands on the site of
the home of the Kitchings who were based here by at least 1794. It
was built to Eli Cox designs by Mrs. Agnes Bindloss, daughter of
Dr. John Kitching, in 1881.[29] It is a tall house of three complete
storeys plus a turreted porch crowned with a Frenchy pavilion cap,
not unlike the much larger tower of Kendal Town Hall donated by
Alderman and Mrs. Bindloss and designed by S. Shaw.

Documentary evidence about older houses is slight and
confusing. Deeds rarely go back beyond the eighteenth century and
then only prove title. Often they do not name the property, or
specify its site, nor is the age given. Old property, therefore, might
only possess deeds going back half a century or so, while newer
property might retain deeds relating to previous buildings on the
site. Thus, although it is known that a Caput or Manor house of the
de Wyndesore's existed in Milnthorpe, its site is not known. In any
case it probably would only be referred to as being situated in the
Parish of Heversham, a typical example is recorded in 1281: "Peter
de Kendale complained against William de Karliol for pulling
down his house at Heversham and taking away the timber of the
same to the value of 50s."[30] Similarly in 1318, "Ranulf, son of
William de Windesore of Heversham in Kendale, grants to William
son of Ranulf Payfoote of Heversham a dwelling house in
Astenwhate with 20 a of land within the praedolium of Heversham."[31]

Seventeenth century deeds are rather more precise. Hence in
1657 a conveyance by "Edward Wilson, gent, of Heversham Hall
and Roger Sill, yeoman of Milnthorpe to Richard and Isabella Fell,
yeoman, Broughton in Cartmel of a Mansion House etc. in

Milnthorpe and certain Closes (and) a Moss at Heversham and Brackendale on Rowell Green"[32] states the price as £171 but does not mention the address. However, attached to this deed is one of 1641 which includes a reference to a new house called "The Taverne" which then belonged to Roger Sill, who, fairly unusually for the time, could sign his name. It is possible that these documents refer to the former Sun Tavern in Milnthorpe Square, which traditionally was the oldest house in Milnthorpe, and whose general dimensions and "T shaped" plan resembled that of seventeenth century Low Cragg Yeat.

Vagueness persisted in nineteenth century advertisements. Thus "All those two messuages or dwelling houses with the gardens, piggeries, dunghillsteads and other appertenances thereunto situate on the north side of Milnthorpe occupied by Benjamin Foster and Ann Mosseley"[33] was advertised in 1851 without mentioning the address. Similarly, an advertisement of May 1875 gave every detail except the name of the property:

"A dwelling house and eight cottages together with the drying ground, Gardens, Orchard, Yards, Stables, Cart House, Hay Lofts, Barns Shippons and Conveniences thereto belonging all pleasantly situated at the high end of Milnthorpe at present in the occupation of Mr. John Foster, Messrs. Eason, Wharton, Toulman, Knowles, Woods, Barnes, Woof and Sandham as tenants at very moderate rentals.

Milnthorpe possesses a salubrious climate and is near the seaside and the property possesses one of the best positions in the Town, it possesses very beautiful sites for new buildings to which can be attached suitable gardens and Pleasure Grounds. There is a good Pump on the property and the water has never been known to fail. Owned by Thomas Briggs esq., of the Homestead, Richmond, Surrey."[34]

The provision of water and drying ground was an important amenity in a period when washing occupied much of the housewives' time. A local rhyme urging domestic diligence ran –
"Those that wash on Monday have all the week to dry,
Those that wash on Tuesday are not far awry
Those that wash on Wednesday are not much to blame
Those that wash on Thursday for very shame
Those that wash on Friday for very need
And those that wash on Saturday they are sluts indeed."[35]

Before the passing of the 1832 and 1867 Parliamentary Reform Bills, freeholders' voting rights were saleable amenities. Thus an advertisement in 1832 reads "of two very desirable Freehold Messuages or Dwelling Houses, with the out buildings, Garden, Orchard, and one close or parcel of land thereunto adjoining... the above premises are pleasantly situated on the north side of the street leading through the town of Milnthorpe aforesaid and are well worth the attention of persons desirous of becoming freeholders of the County of Westmorland. Mr. William Turner, Paper Maker will appoint a person to shew the Premises."[36]

Documentary evidence is all we have of Milthorpe's lost hamlet of Scout Bank, removed because it overlooked the Dallam Wheel and spoilt the view from Dallam Tower. For example the Heversham Manorial roll records that "Will Atkinson of Scout Bank"[37] paid for two Herriots in December 1729.

Though the ground, subject to low customary rents, belonged to the lord of the Manor, the actual properties were purchased by the Dallam estate only around 1800. The Dallam archives include reference to "a freehold messuage or dwelling house and the out houses, Garden and orchard thereto belonging situate at Scoutbank aforesaid within the liberties and precincts of the Manor and holden of the Manor of Heversham aforesaid by payment of the yearly customary rent of eight pence and heretofore the customary estate of the said Allan Briscoe now in occupation of William Chamly."[38] This was purchased by the estate about 1800 along with another Scoutbank house belonging to John Burrow, saddler, two closes called Watchmoss (4 acres 2 roods) and Brackendale (1 acre 1 rood). Also purchased was a "freehold dwelling house, Barn, Stable, Backside, Littlehouse" (the privy)[39] and all other appurtenances belonging to Thomas Kitching.

These properties still stood in the 1820's. According to Neddy Stones, "approaching Milnthorpe from the new bridge the gardener's cottage stood in the Little Park and 3 cottages stood on the high side of the road which is now a plantation. One man of the name of Chamley was one morning cursing because the frost had nipped his potatoes and a Methodist parson was passing at the time who remarked, "Oh, Chamley you must trust in Providence" "Trust in Providence," says Chamley. "Look at my taties all frozen! Taken Providence yan times with another he does more harm than good."[40]

On the river's edge at the end of the plantation were three more cottages occupied by Henry Halliwell, Ann Hind and Betty Hodgshon. "The Dog Kennels were opposite the water trough, (just west of bridge) on a site where Foxcroft's carts and waggons used to stand. Parkside field belonged to Richardson's Farm. The Rt. Hon. Fulk Greville Howard built the Bridge House upon a piece of waste ground. It has been occupied by the coachman of Dallam Tower and others ever since..."[41]

In contrast to the obscure references to house sites, the information from wills and inventories from c.1600 is often detailed and precise.

In 1681 Richard Cragg of Ackenthwaite left to John Cragg his "goods movable and immovable brass powder beddings, wollings, linnings, bedsteads, cupboards, tables, chists..."[44]

The will of Thomas Preston of Milnthorpe, Husbandman (died 1700) itemised his personal possessions as "His Purse and Apparrel £6.0.0. Furniture. Two chists and two Boxes 10/–. A clothes Press and little chest 12/–. Lining (Linen) £1.0.0. Bedding and Bed Stocks £2.5.0. Meal Chest 6/8. Chaires and Stools 5/–. Tabel and formes 10/–. Cupboard £1.0.0. One clock and two cases £6.0.0. (? from Son's stock). Vessels etc. Brasse and Pewther £1.10.0. Wooden and Earthern Vessell 6/–. Raken crook Grid–iron tongs and brandreth 4/–."[45]

The will of Richard Johnson of c.1741, (contained in the papers of the Squire family of Haverflatts), again indicates the importance given to beds and the relative lack of other furniture. "My said wife (Jane) shall and may also for and during the full Term of her natural Life and no longer have the full and free use privilege and advantage of wearing, keeping & Peaceably & Quitly enjoying of my Clock and Case, my Joynor Chest my meal chest two pair of my best Bedstocks with Bedding of all sorts Sufficient & Suitable for making up two Beds – withall, my cupboard & Dresser in the House, my best Looking Glass, my Warming Pan, and my two best Tables together with as many other of my Household Goods as she my said wife shall be mindful, willing and Desirous to have or keep for her own Use and Wearing.."[49]

By Milnthorpe's standards the Craggs, Crofts, Griggs, Kitchings and Prestons were rich. The possessions of most other villagers were too paltry to justify wills and inventories and their homes were almost worthless. Five dilapidated cottages on Harmony Hill were sold in 1873 for £255 on the understanding that a sixth would be given to the purchaser (John Mayor) by way of bonus.[51] The highest bid for Sunny Villa, with its shippon, offices, large garden, a close of land and five cottages in Carr's Yard failed, in 1894, to reach the reserve of £500.[52] Even after the First World War despite a shortage of homes for heroes, Milnthorpe's cottages were of little value. Several cottages in Carr's Yard with a rental of £75, on the market for £180, remained unsold throughout 1925. The next year Mr H. Battersby purchased for £26 a cottage near the church with a rental of £6 10s p.a.[53]

Not until the turn of the nineteenth century did the notion dawn in Milnthorpe that the living conditions of the poor were not necessarily part of the station in life to which it had pleased God to call them. Some of the conditions were appalling. In 1896 a child was reported to have suffocated at Milnthorpe while sleeping in a bed with five other people. The father, son and two daughters also shared the same bedroom. Later, the *Westmorland Gazette* described a cottage at Milnthorpe "occupied by a bed–ridden woman with nine cats and an unknown number of rats where filth is allowed to accumulate until the stones themselves almost cry out with the foulness thereof..." The paper wondered whether the situation was a "nuisance under the meaning of the Public Health Act or an innocent diversion within the rights of an Englishman, whose house is his Castle?" It was pleaded (at an enquiry) on behalf of the bed-ridden woman that "the cats helped her to pass the time cheerfully and also that the rats helped the cats to pass their time cheerfully."[54] The woman's husband Fredrick Hey, a comb maker, admitted that "the house was much infested with rats and that sometimes they found 6 or 7 dead ones on the floor in the morning when they got up." The situation "could not be helped because he had no daughter and so there was no one to clean up." In those days, as man of the house, he would never have considered doing it himself.

It was not, therefore, for nothing that Neddy Stones (about whom there was a pointed reference in the report) cried out about village housing. "Thirty-one cottages," Neddy said, "had been demolished since about 1860 and replaced by a few larger ones: those which remained were of the meanest and had sanitary conditions scarcely fit for dog kennels." Some houses, he claimed, were only 12 feet square with bedrooms opened to the slates and with ashpits and closets abutting onto the living apartments."[55] Stones and the Parish Council tried to have modern cottages built for workmen but met with little encouragement from landowners. Maurice Bromley-Wilson in replying to the council's request for building land declared that "he was much surprised to hear that your council are of the opinion that all the remaining cottages in Milnthorpe are mere slums and unfit for habitation" and "the overcrowding and insanitation (is) a disgrace to the age in which we live. I hope and believe that such a description does not apply to the few that belong to me.. and apart from other questions, as I am not aware that Milnthorpe Parish Council are able to acquire land for such a purpose, a negotiation with them would be meaningless and I cannot enter upon it." Captain Bagot was willing to sell a little field near Bela House – which having "a long frontage to the high road is very eligible" but doubted whether the Parish Council could have cottages erected on such a site with prudence "unless they were likely to secure a class of tenant who could pay probably 4/- a week or thereabouts."[56] Mrs. Whitely (daughter of William Tattersall) was willing to sell land on Beetham Road for the purpose but the scheme came to nothing owing to the opposition of the tenant, William Dobson – who, as a Parish Councillor, had supported the housing scheme! Similarly a scheme just after the First World War to build 6 cottages opposite the Blue Row on Church Street came to nothing. Later in the 1920's two houses on Milnthorpe Hill (numbers 58 and 60 Church Street) were built with subsidies provided under the Housing Act, 1924 of the first Labour Government.

Older property continued to cause problems. In 1917 Dr. Fuller complained to the Parish Council about a derelict cottage next to Mrs. Griffin's, adjoining his house Stoneleigh "it was full of rubbish and a visit would make it quite evident for what purpose it is occasionally used."[57] This was the cottage formerly occupied by "toffee Johnny" Grey who hanged himself following the mysterious visit by two men whom villagers believed were detectives investigating an unsolved murder in Liverpool. For a few years the cottage was repaired and used as a warehouse, but was eventually demolished about 1920: a pity as old photographs indicate it probably dated from at least the seventeenth century.[58]

Few could object, however, to a closing and eviction order granted in 1935 on behalf of the landlord George Brown on a cottage tenanted by Richard Pierson in Twine Walk. The ground floor measured only 16 feet by 20 feet, divided into kitchen and pantry; it had no back door and only two bedrooms. Pierson, however, protested vigorously, stating that he had lived there for over 30 years, had brought up 8 children there and still had 4 at home. His rent was only 11s 9d per month and when Brown stated that Pierson could buy a new house on a mortgage of 12/- per week the judge exclaimed that no working man should be called upon to pay 12/- per week.[59]

Low rents were also quoted in an enquiry about 8 cottages scheduled for demolition in 1938. John Tugman and Mary Nicholson paid 5/3 per week and Archie Ashburner 2/6 per week for cottages on Haverflatts Lane. Numbers 42, 43 were let for £3 5s p.a. while for No. 44, Fred Thompson, paid 2/1d per week.[60] In 1939 there was a five hour hearing concerning the demolition of five houses in Haverflatts Lane which had "a roof pretty useless" and ceilings only 6 feet or 6 feet 2 inches high. Despite the landlord's being willing to pay for repairs amounting to £77 9s 6d. the cottages were condemned. Some of their occupants were rehoused on the Wyndsore Avenue Council Estate. The cottages themselves were not demolished until c.1950.

Poor water supplies and sanitation bedevilled village life and even touched local politics. Many larger houses like Harmony Hall, Laburnum House, Stoneleigh, Flowerden, Owlett Ash, Rock Cottage and the Inns had their own wells. Audlands at Ackenthwaite Green had to share theirs with the Smithy even after they had sold it to the Langhorns. At Harmony Hall the well in the cellar still functions and is over 25 feet deep and rarely has less than 4ft of water in it. Round the Square, apart from the Fountain, there were pumps at the Padding Can, at the Mashiter's cottages in the centre

Audland's Pump
at Ackenthwaite Green.

of the south side, at Fawcett's (now the N.S.S. store) at the Bull's Head, the Royal Oak, at the bottom of Twine Walk and at Thorpe Cottage, now the chemist's. There were pumps or wells at Scott's Yard, the Slaughter House and at the Candle House on Beetham Road and at Fir Tree House, another opposite the Dallam Tower Cottages and a well in front of Spring Cottage, (Douthwaites Garage) in Park Road. Church Street was served only by a pump behind the King's Arms and by Grisley Well several hundred yards to the north. At Ryley Field there was a pump and also a well in the orchard – where a maid servant is said to have drowned herself in about 1870. Water closets were advertised in sale notices of Belvidere Cottage and Laburnum House in the 1840's and Ackenthwaite House in the 1850's but until the mid twentieth century most houses had earth closets, known when being polite, as privies or petties. The larger houses and also those on Park Terrace and the Blue Row had superior affairs often combining ash pit, pig sty, lilac tree and rhubarb patch. Elsewhere privies were either tucked into odd corners close to the houses (as in Windy Hill) or sometimes quite a distance away. The cottages next to the Cross Keys had a walk of 300 yards to their conveniences by the piggeries behind the stable and midden!

At Christmas 1891 an outbreak of typhoid led Dr. Carden to condemn the fountain in the Square as having been contaminated

*Wilkinson's Water and
Night Soil Cart, c.1900.*

Privy, Ackenthwaite Farm.

by seepage from the graveyard. He also pointed out that ismatic disease in Milnthorpe was 90% above that of other areas in the Kendal Union. At the same time the old rain water sewers made of porous limestone and dating from the eighteenth century were in poor condition. That at the bottom of Church Street was found to be obstructed by a gas pipe. A newer sewer running across it had silt 18 inches deep.[61] Later the Parish Council proposed a new sewer to discharge into tanks in the Cross Keys meadow at a cost of £300, in preference to a more elaborate scheme envisaged by the Rural District Council. It also considered bringing water from the canal reservoirs at Lupton and Killington but this would cost £1,500 and would take over 30 years to pay off. The landlords did not want to pay for the scheme and tenants did not want to pay water rates. Neddy Stones said that the whole scheme had been pushed forward in the interest of 10 or 12 who had W.C.'s and "water was next exploited by the same set for the same reason." He proposed

Laying Water Mains.
Elmsfield, nr. Milnthorpe 1908.

engaging Mr. Gatey, who had represented the villagers in the Haverbrack Common dispute, "to fight against the water lobby."[62]

More furious protests blew up in 1906 when the R.D.C. proposed a lavish £15,000 water scheme to cover the whole district including Milnthorpe, Arnside and "out of the way places like Hale." As the rateable value of the area involved amounted to £12,955 p.a. it was not prohibitive but[63] Neddy Stones did not think so. Neddy kept the controversy going for years and in 1910 the *Westmorland Gazette* responded with a veiled reference to Neddy

"Milnthorpe never shrinks from the noble duty of being Judge in its own cause. In the present instance it not only acquits itself but casts liberal (Neddy was a Liberal) reflection on its' neighbours. How it asks can the dish water of a wholesome innocent spot like Milnthorpe be detected in the Beela when the drainage of Holme, Hale and Beetham goes into the river. People talk about leaving no stone unturned in a good cause. The Milnthorpe Parish Council turns the stones every time and leaves its persecuters to cry...where is the truth?"[64]

In 1913 a sewage farm was planned for the plantation just south of the Bela viaduct. The cost of £3,900 was again considered to be prohibitive and this scheme was rejected. George Wilson spoke for most villagers when he said that "people who had W.C.'s in their homes should be prosecuted because it was these dirty devils who were causing all the bother." Ten years later John Fawcett threatened to withold part of his rates as a "protest about a new sewer being built to serve the new houses on the hill because his house (also quite new) was not on the Mains." Adequate sewerage was apparently not necessary before a house could be built and in the 1920's Mr. Cropper, Chairman of the R.D.C., said that "owners of bathrooms had every right to demand discharge into the stone drains even if unsuitable." Between 1920 and 1936 over 100 new houses were built in Milnthorpe, putting further strains on sanitation. Seepage from a makeshift cess pit on the Strands led to the closing of the Park Road pump. The inhabitants were forced to use a stand pipe for over a year, until the Dallam Estate and other landlords had water laid on to the cottages. Not until 1938 was a sewage farm approved north of the railway arches on the marsh, at a cost of £4,500: "J. Mashiter thought it would contaminate the paddling place."[65] The scheme was then postponed by the Second World War.

Mains water from Lupton Reservoir arrived in Milnthorpe in 1911 and made the inter-war housing schemes practicable. The pressure was not good for many years and in August 1944, when owing to wartime demands it was increased, it led to a plague of burst pipes. (The flood water destroyed at least one householder's hoard of rationed sugar!) In the 1960's Lupton water was supplemented by a larger scheme and since then water supply and sanitation problems have become a thing of the past.

Higher hygienic standards, a measure of prosperity, easier mortgages and the start of council housing led to Milnthorpe's built-up area expanding in the 1920's and 1930's. Tentacle like, the expansion followed the main roads in classic ribbon development. Maymyo, a house in the neo-vernacular style, was completed by Messrs Ion of Slackhead for John Mashiter in 1922. It was the first house on the hill but was quickly followed by the two larger semis to the north, built by George Wilson. The story goes that George Wilson and John Mashiter were never the best of friends and just after John moved into his fine house George dumped a pile of bricks in the field in front. In order to preserve his view John was forced to purchase this land at an inflated price. To get his own back he arranged that no house could be built immediately behind Maymyo either. George was not to be outdone. He bought the land and built the two houses The Mount and Malvern right on the edge of the bank overlooking the road which was in fact west of Maymyo's building line.

Two pairs of semis and four detached bungalows followed in the 1920's. On the west side of the road The Rise was built for Chief Constable Burrow when he retired from the York City police force in 1920. The builder, Willy Scott, then erected Overdale next to the Almshouses. He used materials salvaged from The Knoll, a wooden

Maymyo, first house on Milnthorpe Hill, 1922.

pavilion on Woodhouse Lane, Heversham, including five different types of windows. Willy's firm, Hodgson, Nelson and Scott built nine more houses and four bungalows on the Kirkgate field in the 1930's, and the final houses followed in the 1950's. In the lower part of the village Bela Avenue, half a dozen houses on Beetham Road and Summerville Road, off Haverflatts Lane, were built in the 1930's. Bela Avenue houses all sold for less than £600 and Summerville Road were even cheaper. At Ackenthwaite The Homestead was built for Willy Douthwaite when he left The Smithy in 1932. The proposed cost was £520 but Willy only had £500, so costs were cut by omitting a bay window to the sitting room. The idea of borrowing the difference, let alone having a mortgage, never occurred to the Douthwaites.[68] Just as the Second War broke out 20 council houses on Wyndsore Avenue were completed by Nicholson and Wright at a cost of £7,536 8s 10d[69] – or not quite £380 each.

All housebuilding ceased in September 1939 and Stuart and Nan Harper, recently returned from Canada to Milnthorpe, were forced to abandon plans for a new bungalow on Milnthorpe Hill "just as the first sod was about to be lifted." It was, however, the first house to be completed in the district after the war and the first to have a stainless steel sink, though building controls compelled the Harpers to make do, for a time, with concrete floors.

Faced with the worst housing crisis in our history, post–war national and local building effort was focussed on council housing. In the pre-war years when Wyndsore Avenue was built, a Rural District Councillor, the Rev. F. Dean, had "hoped that it did not mean that those people who were turned out of their houses at Beetham would have to go to live in Milnthorpe."[70] In the post–war world his fears were more than realised. Firs Road of 100 houses was completed by 1951. It spread along the contours and included a large green. The estate was much admired at the time, though later planners would criticize its low density as a waste of land and with the advantage of hindsight, the lack of car parking and garaging space. Ryley Field Road followed in the 1950's and was extended to Kirkhead in 1963. The latter development included old peoples' flats situated on the far edge of the estate, up a steep hill and approached by precipitous steps. Finally, just as the nation began to move over to the expansion of private housing, a large council estate was erected at Owlett Ash Fields. Partly financed by the Liverpool Housing Authority as part of an overspill scheme, Owlett Ash attracted a number of families from outside the district, some of whom quickly contributed to the local community and some who did not. As a result of this scheme more than half of Milnthorpe's residents were by 1980 occupants of council houses.

The demand for lower priced private homes in Milnthorpe met with difficulties owing to a shortage of available land and the stricter planning regulations. The development of the Workhouse site and Sycamore Grove at Ackenthwaite and Dallam View on Beetham Road only partly met the needs. At a public enquiry in 1984–5 the Parish Council successfully opposed the development of the summit of St. Anthony's hill as it would spoil the landscape and "obscure the view of the tower on the hill: Milnthorpe's best known land mark." As a concession some development on the lower slopes was accepted, though not without controversy. On one thing everyone was agreed: in the next decade Milnthorpe would require more new houses for all age and income groups, a sure sign of a living and thriving community.

9

The Church
In Milnthorpe

One of the oddest facts about Milnthorpe is that for most of its long history it lacked a church. Even after St. Thomas's Church was opened in 1837 Milnthorpe remained, until 1896, part of the joint township of Heversham with Milnthorpe within the much larger Heversham parish which also included Levens, Crosthwaite and Lyth, Crosscrake (Sedgwick and Stainton), Barrows Green, Preston Richard (Endmoor) and Hincaster.[1] Only in 1924 was the ecclesiastical subordination of Milnthorpe to Heversham ended and even then the vicar of Heversham remained patron of the living.

There are many reminders of former links. The civil parish of Milnthorpe, having been carved out of Heversham is one of the smallest in area within the old County of Westmorland. The ecclesiastical parish is even smaller and excludes all the houses on the west of Milnthorpe Hill and also all of Ackenthwaite east of Smithy Lane and the road to Woodhouse. Contrary to normal village practice the main place of worship is often referred to not as simply "the church" but "St. Thomas's," a reference perhaps to the days when it was but a chapel of ease to the parish church at Heversham. Similarly, until the 1950's many older inhabitants addresssed the parson as "minister," a usage typical of the strong protestantism of the place but harking back perhaps to the days before 1875,[2] when the incumbent of Milnthorpe, as "a perpetual curate," could not use the title of "vicar." For over 100 years "leading families" like the Holmes and Audlands continued to worship at Heversham or at least were married and buried there. As late as 1900 George Francis Atkinson, though Clerk and assistant overseer for Milnthorpe and a staunch worshipper at St. Thomas's, took his family to Easter Communion at Heversham for "it was the parish church."[3]

Many tracks and footpaths led to the old parish church; that from Ackenthwaite to Heversham is called appropriately Kirk Gate, a name also used on the west side of Milnthorpe Hill, the east side being called Kirk Head. More confusingly for visitors, the A6 road leading from Milnthorpe to Heversham (and away from Milnthorpe church) is called Church Street. Perhaps the Cross Keys Inn at the start of Church Street gets its name from the Cross Keys badge of St. Peter the patron saint of Heversham Church.

Within Heversham parish Milnthorpe seems always to have been the most substantial place. Unlike Levens, Stainton, Preston Richard and Crosthwaite and Lyth it did not constitute a separate hamlet and accordingly did not have its own church-wardens. From c.1660 the name Milnthorpe was substituted for Heversham in the list of Church Wardens in the Heversham Vestry book.[4] In 1827 the area was redesignated Heversham with Milnthorpe or Heversham and Milnthorpe.

Until the twentieth century Churchwardens were generally landholders or farmers and as there were more of them in the Heversham part of the "hamlet" that part provided more of the Wardens for Heversham with Milnthorpe. Of families commonly resident in the Milnthorpe part of the hamlet the Craggs provided 9 Wardens between 1687 and 1819, the Saules 4 between 1703 and 1794, the Bindlosses 5 between 1756 and 1814, the Squires of Haverflatts 5 between 1752 and 1842 and the Audlands of Ackenthwaite Green 9 for a similar period. From 1880 to 1891 Dr. John Audland was continuously Churchwarden for Milnthorpe at Heversham and the Audlands' house remains part of the ecclesiastical parish of Heversham to this day. Generally until the late nineteenth century it was rare for the office of Churchwarden to be held by the same person in succesive years. Instances of longer terms for Milnthorpe wardens include William Audland 1704 to 1706, George Taylor 1758 and 1759, James Saul 1793 and 1794, Ewan Rawlinson 1816 and 1817, John Frearson 1823 and 1824, John Wilson 1825 – 1831, Ben Tattersall 1844 – 47, Issac Rawlinson 1858 – 1860, Martin Whittaker 1865 – 74 and William Bond 1875 – 1878.[5]

From about 1730 it became common for landholders, whose turn it was to provide a churchwarden, to nominate a substitute to fill the office. These are recorded in various ways e.g. 1752 Thomas Scott for Audland Estate, 1769 James Redhead hired Robert Cragg, 1775 Mr John Machal Issac Cragg serves for him,1786 Robert Dinely for Mr Dowker Estate at Scout Bank. As a rough "who's who" of the middling ranks of Milnthorpe society from the seventeenth to the nineteenth century the Churchwardens' list provides a guide to the decline of families like the Preston's, Cornthwaites and Craggs who disappeared in the nineteenth century or, as in the case of the Audlands and Bindlosses, of advancement which took them far afield though they remained parish property owners. Some families of longstanding like the Ashburners, first recorded in the seventeenth century, never attained the rank of warden while Dennis Shaw who became warden at St. Thomas's in 1981 was the first member of an almost equally ancient family to hold the office.

Milnthorpe Hamlet also chose members of the Council of 24,[6] who helped collect the church rates and acted as stewards at morning service, responsible for a "side" hence the derivation of their modern name of "sidesmen." As far as the records show from the Reformation onwards most Milnthorpe people accepted the worship of the Church of England as by law established. There were some dissenters in the seventeenth century and the area was traversed by George Fox and some of the earliest members of the Society of Friends. Thus "on the 13th October 1678 Edward Wilson, a Justice of the Peace, sent several Informers to a Meeting held in the House of Edward Cragg of Ackenthwaite in the Parish of Heversham, and upon their evidence convicted divers Persons without being brought before him, and issued Warrants for Distress, by which was taken:-
From Joseph Gregg, a Young Cow worth £3 10s. Later Joseph Gregg of Milnthorp, was prosecuted for non payment of Tithes in the Bishop's Courts, by Thomas Wright, Arthur Hudson and other Tithe Farmers there, and was committed to Appleby Goal (sic) on the 26th of the Month called May 1682; where he was a Prisoner almost five years. At length Thomas Wright, the Chief of his Prosecutors, being sick sent for him and signifieth his Uneasiness of Mind for detaining him so long in Prison. The Patient Innocence of this sufferer had so Mollified the Heart of this Prosecutor, that he became an Intercessor in his Behalf with the others concerned, and persuaded them to discharge him. Accordingly they sent a Writing under their Hands to the Sheriff and Justices who committed him, and they released him from his Long Imprisonment about the Beginning of the Month called March 1686." Moreover Jane Gregg "wife of Joseph G. Distiller of Milnthorpe" was twice fined for attendance at Meetings at Hale and Farleton during her husband's imprisonment.[7] Members of the Preston family of Rowell and Ackenthwaite were also Quakers. In 1684 Agnes, wife of Thomas Preston, was imprisoned for absence from National Worship and Thomas was fined "2 young steers value £5" for non-attendance at Church and non-payment of tithes. In his will of 1700 Thomas Preston of Milnthorpe, Husbandman, "stated that should his grandson John the heir die before he was 21, the remainder shall be

distributed amongst the poorest sort of my ffriends commonly called Quakers and the poorest sort of my Relations by my said Trustees as they shall think most fitt." There are few later references to Quakers partly because having their own burial grounds and refusing to be married or baptised according to the Anglican rites they are not recorded in the church registers. Even so it was noted in 1700 that "Margaret Pearson was buried amongst the Quakers."[9]

Presbyterian and Independents, active during the Civil War Period when the vicar of Heversham Thomas Bigge lost his living, survived for a generation or so.[10] Thus on 28th October 1672 Edward Briggs of the Parish of Heversham obtained a license for his house to be used for divine worship. With the withdrawal of Charles II's Declaration of Indulgence this license was soon withdrawn. The Toleration Act in 1689 made non-conformist worship legal and in August 1691 the Presbyterian Fund to assist students for the country ministry made a grant of £8 per annum "towards the propagation of the Gospel at Milltrop in Westmorland." Thomas Jolly was the preacher until June 1693 when the grant was discontinued.[11] In the eighteenth century the deaths of a couple of Presbyterian ministers are recorded, implying some local support for dissenters, but by and large they seem to have been in decline. In 1778 the Rev. Henry Wilson stated that there were only 9 families of Quakers in the Parish. They had a meeting house at Stainton but "no duty is done in it as there are only two families near it. . . there are only a few Methodists and I do not think the number increases."[12] By 1804 there were at least 60 Methodists in Levens and their strength was one of the official reasons why the Hon. Mary Howard built Levens church. The unofficial reason was that she had quarrelled with the vicar of Heversham, Dr Lawson, who owed her money. Milnthorpe was visited neither by Wesley, Whitefield nor by their main followers though "as the number of inhabitants has greatly increased of late years (c.1780) owing to various manufactorys established here" social conditions were rife for evangelism.

There were only a few Roman Catholics. In 1778 the Rev. Henry Wilson answered the question "Are there any papists in your Parish". . . "We have not more than 6 or 7 Roman Catholics Families in the Parish and these extremely poor. Their Priest resides at Kendal."[12] In 1789 there were six Roman Catholic families, mainly labourers "who had neither school nor chapel," while in 1804 Dr Lawson was aware of no papists whatever in the parish "except a poor family consisting of two people" and again in 1814 and 1824 there was still only one family.

It was however, national fears that prompted a report on 1st June 1822 that "A Petition to the House of Peers against the Bill to authorize Roman Catholic Peers to sit and vote in that house now remains for signature at the Cross Keys . . . we have no doubt will be numerously and respectably signed as a universal feeling prevails in this neighbourhood against granting any further political power to persons avowing themselves amenable to foreign jurisdiction and particularly to that of the Pope of Rome." A generation later, in 1850, anti-Roman feeling surfaced at the time when territorial titles were given to Roman Catholic Bishops and a meeting of the "Milnthorpe and District Clergy met at the Vicarage House, Milnthorpe, to petition the Queen against Papal aggression."

Local problems were more prosaic. In 1778 the Rev. Henry Wilson gave a full and significant answer to the question "are there any persons who profess to disregard Religion?"

"Milnthorp and Ackenthwaite form, as it were one large village, consisting of near two hundred families, the nearest at more than a mile's distance from the church, and bad weather, therefore, in winter is their excuse then, for absenting themselves from public worship, but hence is contracted an habit, by which they become more careless and indifferent about Religion in general. But in the country if a clergyman cannot draw His Parishioners together on Sunday to instruct them in their Duty to God, their neighbour, and themselves, it will be in vain to look after them in the week following, being for the most part engaged then at a distance from their own houses and in so extensive a parish their houses so far from the Vicarage. But if a chapel was built in this part and a sermon preached every Sunday afternoon by the vicar there (who can scarce get a congregation (of) them at the church) it would be a means to prevent the spread of irreligion and profaness among 'em.

Yet how this good matter is to be effected I know not, the inhabitants are themselves poor and gentlemen who have property there, too indiferent about Religion to think of erecting a Chapel at their sole expense. Your Lordship, perhaps some time, hereafter, may be able to put us in a way to effect it – By the assistance of the present Lord BP. of Ely we got a chapel and a sallery of ner fifty pound a year to the curate at Crosscrake where a chapel was not equally wanted – nay I suppose, the odds may be as seven to one in favr of Milnthorpe. N.B. Milnthorp from its situation being the only seaport in the county is a very improving village, and since my coming hither (i.e. 1757) has received an increase of twenty familes."

The briefer answers in 1789 stated that regular absentees from service are "the lowest and worst part of the parish and their number increases with that of the inhabitants." In 1804 there were "no instance of continued absence" other than two cases caused by infirmity while "we have none who profess disregard of religion." However in 1814 Dr. Lawson returned to the question of a chapel for Milnthorpe – but stated "that my neighbour Mr. Wilson of Dallam Tower wishes to build a chapel at Milnthorp." He supported this plan because "I derive from thence the principal part of my audience." He would be prepared to preach a "sermon there in the afternoon only and prayers read in ye morning." A further reason for building a chapel of ease was derived from the circumstances of "Milnthorp being much resorted to during ye bathing season by Multitudes from the country around." An opportunity for the visitors to hear a sermon would, Dr. Lawson believed, "prevent much of the Disorders and Profaness which are often attendant on such associations."[13]

Continued anxiety did not lead to an immediate provision of an Anglican church. It was the non-conformists who first established themselves. The Methodist's local preacher, Stephen Brunskill (1748 – 1836), is believed to have lived at Owlet Ash in 1809. Towards the end of his life, in recalling his 62 years ministry, he noted "Our next removal was to a farm about seven miles from Kendal, which brought us considerably nearer those places I usually preached at. Here we collected a small society, but the work of God did not make much progress. During my residence on this farm, I superintended the workhouse at Milnthorpe, about half a mile distant."[15] As the workhouse was built in c.1816 it is reasonable to suppose that a Methodist Society existed in Milnthorpe by about 1820. Nevertheless it was an "independent" Henry Hewetson who erected the first church building in the village on the site of some old cottages in Haverflatts Lane.

It was licensed at the Quarter Sessions on 12 July 1819 and opened for worship on 18 March 1820."[16] The chapel measured 37 feet by 22 feet and there were two tiny ground floor cottages. Though typically plain with undecorated round arched upper windows it had a handsome porch set on limestone doric pillars. The first Minister was Rev. Giles Hoyle. He was followed about 1842 by Rev. H Riddle and then by the Rev. Mr Yeates who preached his farewell sermon "to the sorrow of his congregation in August 1845."[17] For the next 22 years the Rev. Richard Jones was minister. He established Bible Classes, Missionary Societies and with less success, the temperance movement. Shortly before his death in 1869 the Rev. Jones and his independents were evicted from the Chapel and in 1866 Henry Hewetson advertised "all that building now used as an Independent Chapel and also those two dwelling houses situate beneath... with Gardens and offices and appertenances thereunto belonging. The Building... might at a trifling cost be converted into a substantial and desirable residence."[18]

In fact Methodists took over the chapel and continued to use it until the Wesleyan Church was built in 1904. The Methodists had held meetings in rooms above the Sun Tavern from about 1816.

The Pillars, Haverflatts Lane -
The Independent Chapel
1820-1904.

Long before the Rev. Jones came they led the campaign for temperance in the area. Sometimes their efforts were not successful: in July 1835 a "Tee total meeting of orations on the Cross and Green" was convened by Methodists from Holme and Yealand as well as Milnthorpe "but the non-temperance men would not stand it and were determined to have a flare up. Three barrels of ale were brought out and given freely to the thirsty group – coppers were thrown among and around the speakers and the idle boys rushed in to scramble for them – while the renowned Joe Stubbs trundled a wheel barrow round and round the stone steps of the Cross and men, women and boys shouted, hooted, hurrahed so the speakers could no longer bear the horrible yells and deafening dins so they marched off amid this human created storm."

Fears that nonconformists based in Milnthorpe might lure Anglicans, faced with trudging over Milnthorpe hill to Heversham church, away from the church probably spurred on efforts to build a new church. Initial funds came from the less well off. A printed invitation to attend a subscribers meeting in 1835 which was sent to Edward Stones has survived.[21] As he was a boot and shoe maker this indicates that the initiative was not solely taken by the gentry. By May 1835 plans were well advanced and it was announced that the "new church at Milnthorpe – an object so long desired by every resident and friend of the establishment is at length likely to be accomplished. The same benevolent individual who came so handsomely forward to aid the friends of the new church at Kendal... has aforded another distinguished instance of Christian liberality and has again munificiently subscribed £1,000 (with) two new temples erected in our own immediate neighbourhood... it is particularly gratifying to record these instances of devotedness to the interests of true religion when our national church is threatened with danger and its resources sought to be extinguished."[22] (There was currently an attempt to divert some church endowment into education.)

The benevolent individual was Mrs Thomasin Richardson of Stricklandgate, Kendal who had endowed St. Thomas's in Kendal whose "noble example" earned her "the expensive words, she loved our nation and built as a synagogue."[23] Nevertheless, hiding her light under a bushel was not one of Thomasin's virtues, for it was after her, rather than the doubting disciple that both new churches were named.

Mrs Richardson's gift prompted the reconvening of the committee and on "Friday 12th June 1835 a public meeting was held by adjournment at the Cross Keys Inn in Milnthorpe for the purpose of consulting about the building of a church in this town and of making other arrangements preparatory thereto."[24] In the chair was the Rev. Carus Wilson, Rector of Whittington and founder of the Clergy Daughters' school just removed from Cowan Bridge to Casterton. Wilson was also the "Mr Brocklehurst"; the "Black Marble Clergyman" savagely caricatured in Charlotte Bronte's *Jane Eyre* as "a bad man, mean and hypocritical." As regards Milnthorpe he was neither. Not only did he assist in the worthy Christian act of building a church in a place with which he was unconnected, he contributed £20 to the funds – he was also a trustee along with Mr Wilson of Dallam Tower, the vicar of Heversham, Dr. Lawson and the Rev. Mason, vicar of Normanton. Dr. Lawson, chronically impecunious, made no financial donation, though his son, Rev. B.R. Lawson gave £1. More open handed, were George Wilson who gave £200, (according to Edward Stones junior this was later increased to £500),[26] Hon. Fulk Greville Howard and the Hon. Mary Howard of Levens Hall a further £100. The Rev Mason only gave £20, but his mother Mrs Blewert who was owner of the Harmony Hill School and his sister Mary Ann Mason, each gave £50 as did J. Gandy Esq. of Heaves. Mr Holden, the village doctor, and Mr Armistead each gave £50.

They successfully obtained contributions from most local landowners, professional people and tradesmen. Major Swain of Old Hall, Endmoor, gave £10, his wife £5, children £2 and servants £1 3s. One wonders if the latter contributions were entirely voluntary. Joseph Thexton and William Hutton of Beetham each gave £5, Richard Hardy, owner of the White Lion Inn, gave £10 and his brother Dr Hardy another £10. Mrs Hudson of the Cross Keys gave £5 5s, her daughter £1, Mrs T Huddleston the maltser £5 5s, James Briggs, twine manufacturer, £5 5s, Henry Smithies and family of Bela Mill £27, the Audlands £5 5s and Farmers Croft and Berry and 18 other contributors gave £5.

Neither the Bishop of Chester nor Trinity College Cambridge, the patron of the Heversham living, gave anything. The half-acre site on Milnthorpe Green was given by George Wilson of Dallam Tower.[27] Slightly elevated at the east end of the square in the very centre of the village it could not have been bettered. It had previously been a garden and until 1813 had formed the apex of the common land of Milnthorpe Green. "In order to gain an exact position it was found necessary to take a certain portion of the Green on the low side and to sacrifice a portion of the garden on the high side."[28]

By October 1835 the building and endownment fund amounted to £1906 12s. The trustees were therefore in a position to let contracts. Messrs. Brockbank of Milnthorpe were responsible for the stonework, Mr Castle of Kendal for painting and glazing, Messrs Nelson of Hutton for carpentry and Messrs Rushton and Taylor of Lancaster for plaster work.[29] No bills or specifications have survived, nor have the plans drawn up by George Webster of Kendal, who concurrently designed St Thomas's Church Kendal which it closely resembles.

St. Thomas's church is not a great work of architecture. Even contemporaries could say little more than that "it is a very neat edifice, situated in the centre of the town and has a beautiful cemetery. It will seat about 600 Hearers."[30] In the 1880's it was stated that the building in which divine service was conducted before the restoration... was a reproach to the district. It was unworthy of the purpose of the place and for the spiritual wants of which it was to provide."[31]

Pevsner bestowed on the church one of his most scathing and brief accounts. "St. Thomas, 1837, except for the chancel which is of 1883, w. tower, lancet windows in pairs, thin buttresses i.e. the commissioners' type, no aisles of course, but a w. gallery with iron posts and thin geometrical tracery. Stained Glass in the E. window by Frederick Barrow (in fact Burrow); 1872; bad."[32]

It was a plain building put up on the cheap in the manner of those erected by the church commissioners following a parliamentary grant in 1818. But it was large, the warehouse like nave measuring 72 feet by 38 feet with a small seven foot deep recess forming a chancel.

As at Grayrigg (also built 1837) there was originally a flat plaster ceiling below the barnlike roof. Outside the five windows on either side were paired lancets; inside they were set in a wider round headed aperture, rather like those found in feebly classical non-conformist chapels. Three stepped lancets formed the east window while there were single lancets on either side of the west tower. Jutting out from the main body the tower is the finest feature of the church, its height being apparently increased when approached from the lower green up the broad steps that have provided a useful platform for various church and village celebrations and a setting for wedding groups. The main body is supported by thin buttresses, those on the tower are set diagonally giving an element of strength to a basically thin structure. Above the pointed and studded door a single lancet lights the ringing chamber, while above the clock (installed after 1837) are twin belfry lights. The whole is surmounted by corner pinnacles and instead of a weathercock is a fifteen foot flag pole. One of the more cheerful Milnthorpe traditions is that the church flag is flown more frequently than on the usual ecclesiastical and royal occasions. During the Falklands conflict, in which two Milnthorpe men were serving, the Rev. John Kelly insisted that the Union flag flew for the entire six weeks of the campaign.

From the start the church aroused much interest. One vendor of potential building sites sought to cash in on its proximity by advertising "for sale the inclosures of land the Tavern Croft, Tavern Meadow and Armthwaite. The said lands overlook the Town of Milnthorpe and are near the site of the intended new church and afford eligible sites for building commanding delightful views of rich woody country immediately surrounding and the interesting shores of the Bay of Morecambe in the background."[33] The project failed and the land remained meadow land for over a century.

The foundation stone of the church was laid with great ceremony on the 2nd December 1835. "Mrs Richardson, the munificent benefactoress towards the church, and who had so liberally endowed it with the sum of £1,000, was unable to attend through indisposition." The vicar, Dr Lawson, was also absent and it was left to the Rev. William Stephen, curate of Levens, to preside. James Gandy of Heaves laid the stone but its position has not been recorded. "Under it was deposited in a copper case a number of coins of the present reign (i.e. William IV). A very numerous and respectable assembly of persons attended which commenced with a short but impressive address by Mr Gandy" who after stressing once again the "munificence of Mrs Richardson" hoped that the stone was "the beginning of a work which would lead to the spiritual welfare of the inhabitants and the praise and glory of God. The National and Sunday Schools scholars then led the assemblage in singing the 100th psalm.

After prayers by the Rev Stephen all the children were presented with 1s each from Mrs Richardson. Later in relays they and a large number of widows were "regaled with coffee etc. in the National school." With due regard to social distinction the trustees and "a few gentlemen who were present adjourned to the Cross Keys Inn where they partook of an excellent repast."[34] Eighteen months later the *Westmorland Gazette* went into raptures about "the various churches and chapels which have sprung up round us so recently." Levens church had been opened in 1829 though it was not consecrated until October 1836 while Selside and Grayrigg chapels both "rebuilt and forming neat little Temples dedicated to the worship of God were consecrated on 22 April 1837."[35] In June it was announced that "the new church at Milnthorpe is to be consecrated on the third of July next and that the elegant structure erected in this town (Kendal) will be consecrated on the fourth."[36] In fact the Kendal church was consecrated on the fifth of July, the change of date being announced in the same black-edged paper which reported the death of William IV and the accession of Queen Victoria. For no known reason Milnthorpe's consecration was postponed, though it was opened for worship in July. (Walter Berry was born on the same day – a fact he later used as a final argument as to why he should always have his way in church affairs!)

It was not until the late autumn that "the Reverend Mr Nicholas Padwick, late incumbent of Linthwaite in the West Riding of York, has been nominated by the trustees to the newly consecrated church of St. Thomas Milnthorpe in the County of Westmoreland to which he has been licensed by the Lord Bishop of Chester."[37]

Padwick was present at the consecration service and signed the Consecration Deed along with the Bishop (J.B. Chester), Henry Raikes - Chancellor of the Diocese, George Lawson, William Stephen and James Gandy. A printed invitation from the trustees had been circulated previously and inserted in the press:- "The Consecration of St. Thomas's Church Milnthorpe will take place D.V. on Sunday 1st October when the Right Reverend the Lord Bishop of Chester will preach. After the service a collection will be made. Divine Service will commence at Half past ten o'clock in the morning, and half past six in the Evening."[38]

The "largely attended" and "interesting solemnities connected with the consecration" began with the solemn reading of the Sentence of Consecration. This outlined the need for a church "as the existing churches or chapels not being sufficiently capacious to afford accommodation for more than one third of the inhabitants... which facts are verified... by a certificate signed by George Webster, Architect, upon actual admeasurement and attested by John Postlethwaite and J.L. Holden, two respectable house-holders."[39]

No mention was made of Mrs Richardson's donation though the

contribution by "divers pious and well disposed Christians" was acknowledged in providing the building and endowment of £1,000 to which should be added income from a Pew rent amounting to £75 15s ("less £3 17s for repairs"). A third of the seats were to be free for the benefit of the poor, while pew number 19 was to be reserved for the church wardens – who in the first instance were William Hird and Richard Saul. They and the trustees were to be responsible for allocating pews. Later it became the practice for one of the wardens elected at the Easter vestry meeting to be the "pew rents warden." Precise details were given about the churchyard which "contains in the whole 2600 square yards... provided nevertheless that no corpse or dead body shall at any time be interred in or under any part of the church nor in or under the said yard within six feet of the wall of the church."[40] (This latter provision was broken by many internments including that of the Rev. F.T. Raikes, the only vicar to die in office.) In the morning service the Bishop preached on the text both optimistic and gloomy "For a great door and effectual is opened and there are many adversaries." In the evening the Rev. H. Raikes's text was drawn from the fifth verse of Psalm 87 "And of Sion it shall be reported that he was born and the most high shall stablish her."[41]

Conviviality and seriousness continued. After one shilling had once more been given by Mrs Richardson to the school children and to 80 poor women they had to hear another address, this time from the Rev. H. Padwick who spoke of "the responsibilities involved in and the privilege to be enjoyed from the opening of a new church."

St. Thomas's immediate "low church" tradition was reflected in the interior of the building. There were 49 box pews of yellow pannelled pine with doors and sides high enough for the occupants to be unable to be seen by the rest of the congregation. In best preaching-shop fashion they were arranged in a central block with two narrower rows on the north and south sides. This meant that the church lacked the usual Anglican nave aisle so the tradition at weddings arose that the bride went up the north aisle a spinster and down the south a wife. There were seven large family pews, four in the centre block, one on either side at the east end and one (No. 49) a third of the way down on the south side. These pews had benches on all sides so that the worshippers faced each other.

There were also 6 "poor" benches on the north side and 19 on the south. Extending over the whole west end as far as the first window was the gallery, furnished only with forms for the school children, to which access was gained via a ladder stair in the tower. Contrary to Pevsner's account, the gallery rested originally not on iron piers but on trefoil wooden columns. When these were replaced in 1883 they were reused on either side[42] of the front door of the bay-windowed house on Church Street but were removed in the 1960's.

Valuable information about the early days of the church is contained in some notes by Edward Stones (1838 – 1920) made towards the end of his life.[43] He recalled how the Sunday School children (about 150 of them) assembled in the National School every Sunday morning at 9 o'clock for a hymn, a prayer and the hearing of the collect for the day – then two abreast they were escorted to the church at 10 o'clock. In the afternoon they were all assembled again at 1 o'clock and retained until four in the afternoon.

"thus keeping the children employed instead of rollicking about the streets and getting into mischief as they do at the present day. In 1854 a Fund was subscribed by the children and their parents for an organ for the Sunday School. I first learned the Rudiments of music and I continued to play it for Mr Padwick and for the school for a number of years upon all occasions. The music in the church was firstly conducted by a choir of men and women and girls conducted by Geoffrey Bentham the Schoolmaster at the National School. The Clerk gave out the Hymn and each verse, and the singers were started by a Pitch pipe. This went on for a considerable time until the choir broke up and Thomas Inman, the Superintendant of the Sunday School, collected together a class of Boys and Girls – and we sat in a square pew, just under the Pulpit singing to an accordian, after some years a Seraphim was obtained and was placed in the centre of the Gallery, overlooking the body of the church, the singers occupying the Pews on each side of it. In 1853 a Subscription was got up for the purpose of buying an organ. As there was no funds available for an organist a set of Barrels was fixed in behind the organ to be played in the event of no organist being available. Thomas Inman performed the ceremony as organist (Free Gratis) but relinquished it in August 1855 and placed me in his position."

Though it was purchased in 1854 the organ was not installed until January 1855, when it was reported that the "sweet toned instrument would reflect great credit on the builder, Wilkinson and Sons of Kendal." After only 15 years this instrument was replaced by one built especially for St. Thomas's by Messrs Forster and Andrews of Hull. It was opened with Divine Service on Friday 19 March 1869. Being in the "modern style with a swell front on the venetian principle" it contained 336 pipes and was erected in the gallery and described by the adjective ubiquitous to the church as being "very neat."

The Sunday School was one of the first and most important inaugurations made by Nicholas Padwick. In 1838 the Milnthorpe

and Heversham Sunday schools combined to celebrate the
Coronation of Queen Victoria when Padwick addressed them on
the theme "Be ye faithful unto death and I will give thee a crown of
life." The scholars then sang;
All Hail Great Emmanuel's name
Ye Angels proclaim the fall
Bring forth the Royal Diadem
Crown him Lord of All."
    Afterwards the children and the 80 poor widows were again given
a shilling each by Mrs Richardson and, with 160 other inhabitants,
coffee at the school.[46]
    The first confirmation was held in the church in July 1841 when
the Bishop of Chester confirmed 110 males and 121 females.[47]
    Annual Sunday School treats and processions in the manner of
the Lancashire walks were also held. These always included
marching to Dallam Tower behind the Holme or Gatebeck Brass
Bands. The older children carried banners bearing such aphorisms
as "Train up a Child in the way he should go" and "True Religion
and ever-lasting life." Despite Neddy Stone's memories some
"rollicking" on Sundays did occur. On 21 January 1842 "a great
disturbance was reported by a number of vile and disorderly
persons assembling themselves in the centre of the town and
throwing snowballs at every person that was passing to any place of
worship."[49]
    Only a fortnight earlier the effects of the winter weather had been
mitigated when stoves were installed in the church for the first time,
paid for by public subscription. The stove pipes can be seen
protruding from the roof in the earliest sketch of the church.[50]
These, however, fell victim to a gale in January 1845 which
succeeded in "interverting many chimneys and at St. Thomas'
church it destroyed nearly all the windows in the neat little
building."[51]
    A more conspicuous addition to the church was the clock. In July
1846 it was reported that "the inhabitants of Milnthorpe are about
to erect a clock in the tower of St. Thomas's church in that town, a
meeting having been held at the parsonage house at which Messrs
Weston and Son of Cartmel were commissioned to make one after
the beautiful model of the one under construction for Dr Dawson
of Wray Castle by the same firm. The addition to the tower will be
both useful and ornamental to the town."[52] It cannot, in fact, have
been very useful because it was replaced in May 1868 as an
"anonymous gift by Mrs Proudfoot of Laburnum House" by one
made by Messrs Scale Bros. of Kendal – the Gazette enthusing
"what with the new organ... and ornamental tower clock, the
church of Milnthorpe may be described as particularly flourishing
both as regards its external and internal appearance."[53] This clock

lasted even less time than its predecessor, for it was reported in March 1878 that the clock "made a few years ago by Messrs Scales Brothers, is for sale – no reasonable offer refused." This led to acrimonious correspondence in the press between the clock winder and repairer, Mr Postlethwaite of Kendal, and the churchwardens. The latter claimed the clock had been broken by a man who did not understand his work – i.e. Postlethwaite – while the hands of the four foot dial were crusted over with rust from long neglect. Postlethwaite blamed the neglect on the Clerk "who was in very delicate health and not able to give the attention which all large Clocks require." He had offered to send a man down weekly for the cost of the rail fare but this had been refused. Moreover "no ladder could be found tall enough to enable him to reach the hands and the Churchwardens declined to go to the expense of a scaffold."[56] On 23 March it was announced that the "Clock supplied to Milnthorpe church tower by Messrs Scales of Kendal in connection with which there has been so much unpleasantness lately has been acquired for the Tower of Natland church to which building it was transferred this week. . . a subscription is on foot for purchase of a new clock." [54]

The new clock was made by Messrs Rhodes of Kendal and had a diagonally set five foot square copper dial on the north side as well as the west. Judging from a photograph of c.1860 the diagonal setting was taken from the smaller first clock. Why the face bears horological masonic symbols cannot be explained. In 1945 chimes were added to the clock by the Rev. Dean in memory of his son James Fraser Dean. In 1953 there was an attempt to add a third face to the clock on the south side as part of the village commemoration of the Coronation of Elizabeth II. This plan failed – the Chairman of the Parish Council, Dr. P.S. Byrne, apparently ignoring the inhabitants of Firs Road, claiming that only a few[56] Frisian cattle on the hill side would benefit! In the early 1960's there was renewed controversy over the clock when the painters, without authority, changed the colour from a royal blue to an opaque gold tinged colour. Only after great difficulty was the brighter original colour reinstated.[57]

The new church encouraged evangelism and reform. Not all efforts were successful. When in 1845 "the clergymen of the neighbourhood of Milnthorpe resolved to hold a series of weekly lectures in the national school room for the railway labourers. . . not one labourer attended. It was probably too near the monthly pay day."[58] More successful was a special service held in August 1856 when the Bishop of Carlisle (to whose diocese the church had recently been joined) "preached extempore on Ezekiel and a collection of £10 1s. 9d. was made towards the Society for the promotion of Christianity amongst Jews by a numerous and respected congregation."

Nicholas Padwick's most notable achievement during his incumbency was his success in abolishing Sunday hiring fairs for harvest workers. He was not alone in this work for similar hirings were stopped at Burton in 1832 and Dalton in 1839. Apart from breaking the fourth commandment, hirings involved drinking, fighting and noisy disturbances. Even before Padwick arrived in Milnthorpe an appeal had been published "to arraign the conduct of the better part of the community at Milnthorpe and in the neighbourhood for suffering the wicked and awful sinful practices committed there on the Sabbath to pass unnoticed . . . and should it be too late this year will they not provide against the next? If they don't the very stones in the streets will cry out shame! shame! . . . In our last we told the public it has been a glorious harvest week and that the country had a rich golden appearance but we forgot to add that the farmers about Milnthorpe devote the day appointed for them to offer up thanks and praises to the Author and Giver of all these good gifts to hiring, buying and selling; all of which naturally and of course are attended with drunkeness, fighting and swearing."[59] After 1837 these abuses took place on the green in front of the newly erected church; the hirings being in full swing during morning service and the fighting getting into full swing around Evensong. From 1838 for the next eleven years Padwick had a broad sheet printed outlining the abuse, as well as writing lengthy, and often repetitive, letters to the press – addressed to "the Farmers, Labourers and all other Sabbath breakers" who should "bear testimony to awful warning of the law embracing the blessed invitation of the Gospel."[60] Labourers were also reminded "to avoid the temptation to spend on unnecessary drink as this would prevent their fulfilling their other responsibilities, for those who provide not for their families are worse than infidels."[61]

The next year Padwick managed to get most of the farmers, along with gentlemen, to attend a meeting at the Cross Keys at which they agreed to ban Sunday hiring, but there was mixed opinions as to whether it should transfer to Saturday or Monday.[62] Inevitably labourers and farmers turned up on Saturday, Sunday and Monday. Finally in 1843, Monday was fixed as the hiring day and on August 19 the *Westmorland Gazette* published its congratulations "the merit for having done away with this disgraceful and most unnecessary desecration of the Sunday is exclusively due to the Reverend Mr Padwick, the highly respected incumbent of the town."[63]

The appeals continued, nevertheless, with a view to ending the practice elsewhere. Even by contemporary standards the eleventh appeal was excessive; after emphasising the evil of Sabbath breaking Padwick thundered: "God may yet punish us for our national sins for it is said that there is scarcely a doubt the Asiatic Cholera is steadily promising its march to this country. Should it seize us in such intense malignity and frightful extent as at St. Petersburg. . . who can conceive or describe what the consequences will be?" Rather wearily the Editor apologised "Our limited space precludes us from giving more than an extract from the appeal from the Rev. Mr Padwick."[64] He took the hint; his work was accomplished and this was his last appeal.

One legacy of Nicholas Padwick for which his successors have had cause to be grateful (and sometimes on the part of their wives to curse) was the acquisition in 1844 of Belvidere Cottage, for use as a vicarage. It had been built for John Postlethwaite in c.1820.[65] The church's founders did not provide a parsonage, so when Padwick was appointed he lived for 6 years at Fountain Cottage on the south side of Milnthorpe square. Padwick seems to have received some help for the new house but there was a deficiency and "Mrs Padwick had a sum of £400 which they paid for the purchase. . . and when they retired they were compelled to sacrifice this sum as it was not recoverable."[66] Whether this loss reduced the Padwick's to a poverty-stricken retirement is not known, but if so it might have been the cause for his subsequent re-appearances. There is a long tradition that the vicarage is haunted and that the ghost, first seen in the days of the Reverend Raikes, is that of Nicholas Padwick. The story was current in the early twentieth century and he was seen by Miss Jennifer Gamble in the 1920's and by the daughter of the Rev. Walsh, also called Jennifer, in the 1960's. She was only a child at the time and it was thought she must have been dreaming when one morning she asked "Daddy, why did you come into my room wearing your robes last night?" Only when her enquiries were repeated on subsequent occasions did her parents learn the story of the haunted vicarage. To be on the safe side John Kelly, shortly after he became vicar in 1979, asked the Bishop of Penrith to conduct a private communion service in the vicarage. Since then 'Old Nicholas' has not been seen.[68]

It is in fact doubtful whether Padwick cared about money. Although his stipend barely exceeded £200 he allowed a fifty per cent rebate on the rents on his tiny glebeland and was generally charitable in the community.[69] In 1841 he sent one of the new-fangled New Year's greeting cards to every family within his charge, though the message can hardly have been regarded as convivial, even by the early Victorians:

The Sabbath Night
Another Sabbath Day is past
To many it will prove the last
If this should be the case with me
How stand I for eternity?

There were five more verses in a similar vein.

Padwick's health had never been good and as early as 1853 because of illness he was being assisted by a curate, the Rev. W. Parry. From 1855-56 the Rev. Thomas Benton and between 1856 and 1860 the Rev. William Morton were curates, paid £50 p.a. from the Pew Rents and £50 p.a. by the vicar of Heversham for assisting at afternoon and occasional services at Heversham. In July 1860 Padwick was forced to resign "owing to long continued failing health.[71] As soon as his resignation was generally known an effort was set on foot by some of the congregation to present to their late pastor some testimony of their esteem and affection. The result has been a presentation to Mr Padwick of a purse containing the handsome amount of 70 guineas. . . ." Taking with them Margaret Daffady[72] as their housekeeper, the Padwick family retired to Petersfield in Hampshire where Nicholas died on 30 November. Sometime later a marble scroll to him was set up in the chancel by "parishioners and friends who valued his ministry, esteemed his memory and mourn his loss; and in grateful remembrance of his zeal in abolishing the Sunday hiring at Milnthorpe."

Except for a tendency to be a Job's Comforter as revealed in surviving extracts from sermons and various addresses, Nicholas Padwick's successor was unlike him in almost every way. He was, moreover, untypical of most mid-nineteenth century small town parsons. Frederick Raikes was born in 1819, the same year as Queen Victoria, Raikes belonged by upbringing and early life to the elegant world of the Regency upper class, being the son of Richard Raikes, Governor of the Bank of England – a position which was held uniquely by *both* his grandfathers, Thomas Raikes and Samuel Thornton. He was nephew of the Earl of Leven and Melville and by marriage of Lord Stratford de Redcliffe, (the famous ambassador to Turkey) and of Admiral Fitzroy, the famous captain of the "Beagle." As a youth he had belonged to the notably impious court of the Duke of Clarence, who shortly before he came to the throne as William IV obtained a commission for him in the 62nd Regiment. After ten years service in India he left the army and went in an official capacity to the Island of St. Thomas in the Bahamas and on returning lived for several years in Kent.

After his "comparitively humble clerical lot was cast"[73] in Milnthorpe he lived comfortably and his daughters were regarded as the belles of the district. Census returns[74] show that there were generally three or four female servants at the vicarage and a governess; the coachman, groom and gardeners lived out. Like the Gilbert's of Heversham, the Raikes kept a fine carriage which Mrs Raikes used, it seems, on quite short journeys in the village. Mr Raikes himself preferred horseback and often used the steps at the corner of Green cottage as his mounting block; until these were removed in the 1920's they were known as the Vicar's steps. As late as the Jubilee exhibition of 1977 two old villagers could recall as infants seeing the septuagenarian vicar wearing a tall hat sitting astride his horse on Harmony Green. Raikes was middle aged before he joined the ministry but his ecclesiastical connections were impeccable, as one can well imagine. He was a relative and friend of Montagu Villiers, Bishop of Carlisle, who enabled him to become curate of St. Georges, Kendal, in 1859 and he was a nephew of the Henry Raikes, Chancellor of the Diocese of Chester, who had played such a prominent part in the foundation and consecration precedures of St. Thomas's church. Most interesting of all he was the great nephew of Robert Raikes (1736-1811)[75] the mill owning founder of Sunday Schools – a fact his flock were often reminded about, as at the Sunday School festival in 1873 during which "in the course of a powerful sermon Mr Raikes stated that it was 95 years since his uncle (sic) Robert Raikes instituted Sunday Schools and no one would now dispute the utility of Sunday Schools which gathered their thousands and thousands of children to be instructed in the truth of the Gospel on the Lord's Day."[76]

From the start Raikes was concerned about general education in the parish especially for the girls. In c.1859 there were 50 boys at the National School but only 15 girls, although for Sunday Schools the respective figures were 55 and 70.[79] When he compiled his answers for the Bishop's questionnaire in 1861 Raikes could already state that a site for a school was available, for girls and infants.

For many years there had been part-time classes organised by the Friendly and Bible Societies but these had lapsed by the 1860's while, according to Nicholas Padwick, in 1859 there was also "a private Evening school which I think but few attend." By 1861 Raikes had resuscitated the Mechanics Institute and there were 24 [80] pupils attending in the winter months. In 1888 notice was given that church rooms had been opened for the men's Bible Class which had previously met in St. Thomas's school and "the vicar appealed for old newspapers etc."[81] Where the rooms were cannot now be recalled.

Despite Raikes' militant Anglicanism the Nonconformists were active. In 1875 the London Missionary Society held Divine Service on three evenings at the Market Cross "when the plain spoken manner" of Messrs Gavin Kirkham and Robert Craig attracted "a large concourse including many who never attend either church or chapel."[82] Two such meetings were held despite wintry weather in January 1883.[83] The Methodist temperance band of the Rev. Mr. Pickersgill led singing in the market and 95 people signed the temperance roll.

A week later the village was visited by a Salvation Army detachment. As "at Tel-el-Kebir (a recent British victory in Egypt) a night march was made from the Kendal Barracks and the inhabitants were aroused from their lethargy by the arrival of the army patrolling the streets and singing hymns. The effect was electrical. People turned out of their houses, public houses emptied themselves, the excitement seemed intense. Soon a large crowd had crammed the chapel where the army man gave a stirring address, founding his remarks on the parable of the foolish virgins. He exhorted his hearers to be 'in time.'"[84] At a subsequent Blue Ribbon meeting the Rev. Pickersgill in a long address sought "to emancipate the sons of toil from the thraldom in which they were held by drink." As a result Mr. McNabb enrolled 140 into the Blue Ribbon organisation while 106 pledges were also taken. Not to be outdone the church choir contributed "melodies from Moody and Sankey" led by Mr. G.F. Atkinson – although he himself was as frequent an attender at the Royal Oak, Cross Keys and Bull's Head as he was at the church![85]

Frederick Raikes was comfortably off and unlike most contemporary clergymen he did not have the problem of managing glebe land nor of levying church rates. Nevertheless, for the sake of any less affluent successors, he devoted much time to augmenting the benefice of Milnthorpe. With the income from the original endowment, pew rents and a grant of £41 p.a. made by the church commissioners in 1846, this only amounted to £245.[86] In order to obtain a further grant of £50 p.a. from the church commissioners it was necessary to augment the living by £1500. By 1865 the augmentation committee, chaired by G. F. Argles of Eversley House, reported that the fund amounted to £1150. This was despite a disappointing response from Trinity College, Cambridge, which had promised £100 but in fact sent only £70. By 1870 the £1500 target had been achieved.

An assured income from investments and declining land rents led to the sale of the church's miniscule glebe in 1888. There were three fields involved: "Ash spire" of 3 acres, (now the allotments on Haverflatts Lane), Kirk Yeat and Willan Close, both of just over 2 acres and now covered respectively by the Owlett Ash[88] Fields Estate and the playing field of Dallam School. They were bought by William Tattersall of St. Anthony's for £1200, an extremely good price. After legal fees, £1165 9s 3d. was invested in 2¾ per cent stock.[89]

Raikes was also responsible for ending the financial subordination to Heversham. Until the death of Archdeacon Evans, (vicar of Heversham until 1866) the Heversham Sexton was entitled to receive 2/- and the Clerk 6d for every internment at Milnthorpe although they did not perform any duties there. These continued for a time when the Rev. Gilbert became vicar of Heversham but in 1869 Raikes informed the Heversham vestry meeting that "nothing would serve more than anything else to cement closer that bond of union which there should be between the mother church and Milnthorpe... if they... would take up the case of their poorer brethren here and obtain for them, if possible, the right of burial in their own district churchyard without their next of kin being insulted in the penalty of 2 shillings and six pence." The vestry then agreed to abolish the fees at "the next vacancy" which occurred in June 1875. In return the Rev. Raikes agreed "not to take any steps, with a view to the separation of Milnthorpe from Heversham without the consent of the Milnthorpe vestry, during my incumbancy." Gilbert also told Raikes that "as you now have the Fees you may style yourself vicar though technically there may be a doubt about it."[90] The technicality was that the title of "vicar" implied that the incumbent did not get all the income belonging to the living. At Heversham the vicar got less than half the income, the main portion being taken by Trinity College, Cambridge, which owned the rectorial rights. When Milnthorpe became fully independent in 1924 its Parson possessed all the tiny endowed income and as such he could have taken the title of "Rector," but by that time the title of vicar (originally just a courtesy one) had been confirmed by faculty.

With church endowment increased Raikes turned next to the enlargement and "restoration" of the building. Some 'improvements' had been made since 1837, as for example when two chairs with uncomfortable straight backs and mutilated Egyptian feet were provided for the sanctuary in 1857. Huge and hideous, they must have filled the tiny original chancel! Then in 1872 the East window was given by Martin and Robert Whittaker in memory of their parents, George and Margaret. Designed by A. Burrow and called "bad" by Pevsner, it shows in bright purples, greens and reds seven scenes from the life of Christ.

In 1879 stained glass was installed in the third window from the east on the south wall. A brass plaque below it reads: "In memory of Caroline Morland Wilson who died at Brussels of Typhoid Fever 1 December 1871 in the 18th year of her age, only child of Robert Wilson of this town who died in 1856. This window is erected by Her Bereaved mother Elizabeth (nee Morland) to whom Her Loss is Irreparable." The tableaux only fills the middle half of the window. It shows Christ apparently healing James's daughter, who wears the flowing locks of a Victorian schoolgirl and a disapproving expression, no doubt copied from the deceased. There are three haloed apostles in the background, also a turbaned levite and a clumsy looking servant. Above is a garlanded motto "My God Knows what is blessed. If he plucked His Lily soon it was to save it some rough blast." At the base beneath a row of golden lilies is the more usual "Blessed are the pure in heart for they shall see

God."

Gas lighting was installed in November 1861 but this was a mixed blessing for along with a "very damp and flagged floor, very wet to the feet, the ceiled roof gallery is oppressive when the gas is on."[91] Later, tall steeple-like ventilators were installed on the nave and after the restoration, on the Chancel. Apart from making the roof line more interesting their effect was limited and they were removed even before electric light was installed in 1937.

For over thirty years the church had only one bell until "Henry Moore presented two bells of steel and Richard Saul another which were pealed first on 9 May 1869,"[92] according to Curwen. However, the *Westmorland Gazette* reported on 21st April that the town had been enlivened by the ringing of the new bells on the previous Sunday.

These bells led to one of the best remembered hoaxes in the village's history. The story goes that the verger, Johnny Graham, (who rang the bells for the evening service) was in the habit, after bowing the vicar into the pulpit, of popping out to the Royal Oak for a quick-one before rushing back to chime the final peal. One February 20th, which was both his birthday and that of vicar Raikes, when Johnny got into the pub he was treated to a few extra pints, and since he had already been celebrating he nodded off. Later he was rudely awakened by a friend who pointing to the clock which showed the time as 7.30 shouted "Ay-oop Johnny tha's ga-ing ta bi laite. Git a move on an give't bell a rite good pull as its tha' birthday ant parson's." Johnny did better than he was bid for instead of ringing just one bell he pulled indiscriminately on the ropes of all three. The resulting cacophany was long, loud and above all alarming for Johnny's drink and the pub's clock had both been doctored. Johnny's birthday peal had gone forth over the village at three in the morning.[93]

Shortly after they were installed the bells – and Johnny's daughter – had a lucky escape. On 16 July 1870 at about half past five when a "violent thunderstorm was at its height the tower of St Thomas's church was struck by lightning on the South East corner and some of the displaced masonry broke through the roof on which it fell. A girl named Graham, who was in the church at the time, received a severe shock and must have had a narrow escape as the subtle fluid had evidently entered the body of the church leaving a mark on the wall near the entrance on the north side. The damage to the tower though not great was sufficient to prevent the bells (which are of steel and but lately placed in the steeple) from being rung on Sunday as the vibration might have caused more of the loosened stonework to fall."[94]

By the 1880's the church was considered "to be a disgrace to the neighbourhood, dating from a time when ecclesiastical architecture

*St. Thomas' Church from the south, c.1900
taken from site of Firs Road, built 1946-50.*

was at a low ebb."[95] In 1882 the Rev. Raikes set up a restoration committee. As with the earlier augmentation fund it had a lay chairman in Henry Moore who lived at Harmony Hall from c.1870-1883. Moore himself gave £150 to the cause while E. H. Wilson gave £200, Mrs Wilson and the Misses Wilson £30, Canon Gilbert of Heversham £100 and the Whittakers of Ryley Field £50. The two local M.P.'s, Hon. W. Lowther and Earl Bective, sent £10 and £15 respectively. When over £1000 had been collected a faculty was obtained (at a cost of £1 10s) to hold services in St Thomas's school during the alterations and the church was closed in October 1882.[96] The architect was Bintley of Kendal.

The blandness of the original building was retained except for the enlarged chancel, where the architect coped adequately with marrying it to a more varied and historically more correct Early English style. This was lower than the nave but almost as broad. In its north west corner went a small organ chamber under which was a boiler house. Three narrow single lancets were on the north wall and a single one on the south. The three lancets on the east window were reused (as was Burrow's glass) but refaced in sandstone/ freestone; the same material used in quoins, lintels and in the paired stepped buttressess on the corners. The chancel roofs swept down to half the height of the nave walls giving the church its most attractive aspect.

Inside the church the architectural problems of the original building were only partially solved. The old plaster ceiling was removed and the nave roof was panelled in red pitch pine, the chancel in oak. The gallery was rebuilt, using iron piers and was 18 inches lower than the original. It still had to be entered via the west porch. The chancel was raised a couple of steps because of the lie of the land and opened into the nave through a wide mouthed arch adorned with two identically ugly plaster head stops.

All the original furnishing, except some of the benches re-used in the gallery, the holy table and sanctuary chairs, were thrown out. The box pews were replaced with open pews, made despite the extra expense from pitch pine, the additional money being provided by an anonymous gentleman. Rented pews were numbered with brass name plates, the rest – all at the back – were labelled "free." The cost of the pews is not recorded, but the carpenters Wright and Son were paid £800 4s 1½. This was the costliest item of the reconstruction. Other contractors were J. Dixon (masonry work) £701 19s 0½, W. Jackson (painter and glazier) £103 7s 9d, H Goulding (slater) £60, Mansergh and Co. Lancaster, two chairs for vestry, £5 1s 6d and Whitwell and Co. for vestry linoleum (which lasted until 1950) £3 15s 4d. Bintley's bill was £106 but he gave 10 per cent back towards the general costs amounting in all to £2,204 1s 11½d.[97] Though large for the time the sum should be compared with £6,557 spent on Heversham church during the 1870's.[98] Amongst many donated items were the brass lectern from the Rev. Raikes' son-in-law and daughter, Mr and Mrs Stavert of Helsington Laithes; a communion cloth from Mrs Wilson of Dallam Tower; the Holy Communion kneeler embroidered with lilies, the result of six months' labour by Mrs Raikes and the brass communion rail provided by the Rev. Raikes. Miss Saul of Stoneleigh paid for a new Caen stone pulpit. Unfortunately this was soon daubed with "brush grain" and then in the 1940's distempered pale pink!

The church was re-opened with great style on Tuesday 12 June 1883. The packed congregation included all the gentry, Canon Gilbert and most other local parsons, the Rural Dean, Canon Ware of Kirkby Lonsdale and the Archdeacon of Westmorland and Furness. In his sermon based on Hobbakuk, Archdeacon Cooper spoke of the Anglican belief that "the Lord delighted in reasonable service in intelligible worship. Wood and stone were not essential but only . . . common sense . . . and natural perception of fitness and decency . . ."[99] Despite all these congratulations the church was not quite finished; it was not until 1884 that it was reported that "the church has undergone a complete transformation during the past fortnight the walls having been coloured and painted and given a very comfortable appearance. . . Mr George Semple was the contractor. Behind the communion table is a rich and artistically executed design illustrating the True Vine, the Bread of Life and in the centre a Cross."[100] This would imply that the old wooden reredos inscribed with the creed, commandments and Lord's Prayer had already been dismantled. They were hung at the back of the church and later on the north wall.

Further embellishments included more stained glass windows. In 1885 Sarah Saul "erected" a window in memory of her sister. Equally bright and banal is glass, again by Burrow, set in the Chancel side lancets, to members of the Whittaker family.

Rather better are the figures of Matthew, Mark, Luke and John in the most eastern window of the north wall of the nave, erected by former friends and parishioners to the memory of Frederick Thornton Raikes in 1897. No better, but far more cheerful, is the next window and the newest in the church, installed in 1928 to the memory of Joseph Daffady – for many years a churchwarden – and his wife Elizabeth.

Some of the south windows were filled in 1886 with a geometrical pattern of coloured Victorian front door glass which was considered "to be a useful addition to the church in subduing the sometimes fierce rays of the sun."

The Rev. Frederick Raike's death on 26th March 1895 received maximum publicity. "When the mournful sound of the passing bell was heard. . . announcing to the inhabitants of the parish that their vicar had departed to his long home it called forth sincere expressions of regret; and the news came as a shock to many, who, although they knew he was seriously indisposed still had hoped he might be spared for a time."[108] On Saturday 30th March he was given Milnthorpe's grandest funeral. None of the panoply of Victorian mourning was omitted; "all the shops in the town were closed, flags were displayed half-mast and the bells of the church rang muffled peals. A large concourse of people of all classes assembled outside the gates of the vicarage, the children of the National school and St. Thomas's Girls' school lining each side of the road, whilst lower down were the masters and boys from Old College, Windermere." The headmaster of Windermere College was the vicar's only son A.H. Raikes. One of the pupils who attended that day was the young Arthur Ransome, later the famous journalist and author, who never forgot the journey by special train to the funeral.

Nicholas Padwick and Frederick Raikes were straight-laced low churchmen. By later standards Holy Communion was infrequent. In 1858 it was celebrated only 8 times a year, and there were never more than 30 communicants though between 250-300 worshippers attended Sunday matins. This figure, considered good at the time, should be set against the church's capacity of 570 seats and Milnthorpe's population of about 1500. Though the church "had a very decided predominance in the neighbourhood" and, Padwick believed, only poverty and indifference kept some folk away,

Victorian church attendance was not as high as later myths suggested.

Raikes introduced "cottage lectures in a small School Room which belongs to Miss Mason during those months when there is not an evening service on Thursdays... they are especially for the poor – but they are not so well attended as I could wish." He also feared that family worship "in the middle class... is not so generally adopted as I could wish but amongst the lower orders it is neglected to a great extent."[112]

Collections were taken only at Communion and a few special services. Until about 1870, 20s. worth of bread was given annually to the poor, increased to £5 p.a. but by c.1910 tickets for "bread money" were given out instead of loaves. The vicar also administered two private charities based respectively on bequests of Mrs Agnes Bindloss (d.1895) and Dr George Henry Seagrave (d.c.1910.) Recipients had to come to the vestry door after the service or submit their names to the wardens. This system did not meet with the approval of Arnold Greenwood, the solicitor to the trusts, and 10 acrimonious letters on the subject between him and the Rev. Pickering have survived. Eventually it was conceded that the vicar need not obtain the trustees permission for doles of about 2/6d.

The only notable innovation during Raikes incumbency seems to have been the introduction of Harvest festivals about 1875. Until the 1950's these were held on a week-day evening and a neighbouring parson was invited to preach. With opportunities for decoration, music and a harvest supper, they were instantly popular and disappointment was recorded when because of the restoration work a festival was not held in 1882. So that "folk could go round" the festivals the customs arose of holding them in succeeding weeks – in Milnthorpe on the last week in September, Heversham on the first week in October and so on.

During the interregnum following the death of the Rev Raikes the Rev W.R. Hopper was responsible for a major innovation – the foundation of a Mothers' Union branch, at "a numerously attended meeting" in the Public Rooms, in April 1895.[115]

To follow a respected, long serving and recently deceased incumbent is a notoriously difficult task for any cleric. There are, after all, always those who think the only good vicar was the last. In 1895 the patron of Milnthorpe, Canon Gilbert, seemed to have chosen carefully by presenting a well known local clergyman to the living. He was Edwin Pearsall Reade, Vicar of Skelsmergh from 1872-95. Like Raikes he had reached "safe" middle age when he came to Milnthorpe; like Raikes his background was a little unusual. He was a Scotsman, born at Paisley in 1841, educated in Ireland at the University of Dublin (B.A. 1860, M.A. 1864) and was married (eventually for 68 years!) to Lydia Theed Dearden, a Manx woman. He was fat and jolly and a lover of the countryside who gave lectures on beekeeping.

He got off to a good start, but at the next Easter (1897) a ritualistic bombshell hit the church, and led to the fiercest dispute in its history. The cause was a plain brass altar cross donated by Sir Henry Bromley of Dallam Tower similar to the one he had previously presented to Beetham Church. Bromley must have known he was detested locally because of the still smouldering dispute over access to Haverbrack (see Ch 13). Even so he was as open-handed to the church as had been his predecessors, the Wilsons of Dallam. Palms and "exotics" from the Dallam glass houses were loaned to decorate the church and the gift of the cross (along with an oak framed notice board for the hymns) must have seemed to him as a minor, if overt, act of piety.

The cross was placed on the Holy Table for the 8 a.m. Communion on Easter Day. In the interval between Communion and Morning Prayer at 10.30 it was removed. Immediately its loss was noticed the police were called, so delaying the start of the main service. With half the congregation inside and half out "every hiding place in the sacred edifice" was searched and eventually the cross was discovered in the churchwardens' pew at the west end. It also turned out that the vicar had not consulted the churchwardens about the cross which many regarded as 'Popery'. "A profound sensation was caused in the town when the matter got wind."

Inevitably, the Easter Vestry meeting held a few days later was reported fully and verbatim. Walter Berry led the attack, "I am as old as the church – I was born the day it was opened and in the last 40 years I have paid many a broad pound towards its expenses but what I want to say is that if these things are going to continue I'll not pay another cent towards it. We see plenty of such like works at Beetham and at Kendal. I have always considered it was a Protestant church, and I want to know what it is to be? Are you going to make it Roman Catholic? . . . and I think if there is money short now there will soon be a greater lack."

Mr. Elburn, "For myself I must say that when I entered the Church on Sunday and saw the cross on the table I was so shocked that I could not pay attenton to the service. Last August a wood platform was placed at the back of the Communion Table ostensibly for the display of vases of flowers. Now this cross has been placed on it! Next thing it will be candlesticks followed by candles. I can see we are only in the early stages but bit by bit we are on the way to Popery."

When the Vicar pointed out that the cross was perfectly legal and that there had been one at Skelsmergh for 25 years Berry yelled, "Away with your Virgin Maryism, we want no aids of that kind here. These things may do for a few Skelsmergites but you're not amongst Skelsmergites now." An attempt was made by the Dallam Agent Mr Cary to calm things down – "I object as much as anyone can to Romanish practices but not to the cross." Whereupon Berry declared, "We will not worship the images which thou hast set up." Cries of "No! no!" Mr. Flemming went further and said that the vicar was a "Jesuit in disguise" and neither he nor the other sidesmen would vote for the vote of thanks for the vicar "while that thing remains." Poor Rev. Reade said he felt "rather like a man walking in the dark who puts his foot in a hole which lets him down suddenly." Humiliatingly he had to promise that it would go no further. "Nevertheless when the vicar was proceeding to say that he could not think of removing the cross now without forfeiting both his own respect and that of his parishioners the meeting abruptly broke up."[117]

The cross in fact stayed but so did the anti–popery sentiment. In 1902 the Easter Vestry refused the offer of local woodcarvers to provide a chancel screen, lest this might give undue mystery to the sanctuary and altar. Even as late as 1979, when the Rev. John Kelly (having obtained the consent of the P.C.C.) placed candlesticks presented to him by his former parishioners in Barrow,[118] on the altar, he was asked by one indignant lifelong worshipper whether she should have to go to confession as well. Apart from St. Thomas's, Kendal, Milnthorpe was at that time the only church in Westmorland without altar candlesticks.

A more practical concern soon involved both vicar and congregation. This was the churchyard which was almost full. Since it opened in 1838 there had been 683 burials and it had now become impossible to dig a new grave without disturbing human remains. There were also fears that a recent typhoid epidemic had been caused by contamination of the stream which ran under the yard to the Fountain in the square.

Milnthorpe churchyard has mercifully avoided being cluttered with gravestones, partly because the more opulent internments continued to take place at Heversham. In 1982 nearly all the gravestones were laid flat in order (it was claimed) to make maintenance easier. Surviving this debatable act are 60 monuments, out of an original number of about 80. There are no attempts at sculpture. The most elaborate (and still in situ) monument is an open table tomb just south of the main path. It is to "Alice wife of William Robinson who departed this life on 29 day of July 1854 aged 40" and, sadly, to many of her children who died young: Isabella, 7 months (22 June 1842); John, 14 years (5 July 1842); James, 16 years (April 1857); Robert, 8 years (20 June 1853); John, 18 years (22 Sept 1861). Her husband William died aged 70 on 20 November, 1876. Another son Thomas, is also recorded as dying at the age of 22 at Newcastle–on–Tyne on 18 March 1866. Also in the grave (making nine in all) are the bodies of John Brockbank who died aged 82, March 18th 1866, and his wife (no name) who died August 25th 1870, aged 82.

The largest and most elaborately inscribed grave is a ten foot square slate over a vault in the north west corner. It is inscribed "In Memory of Robert Preston Rodick of Woodclose Arnside West— moreland who died December 29 1859 aged 37 years. He was one of Her Majesty's Justices of the Peace for the County of Lancaster and eldest son of the late Thomas Rodick of Beachwood Arnside and of Garston near Liverpool J.P. and D.L. for the County of Lancaster."

Having been reduced in 1982 to a sterile patch of turf the churchyard is redeemed by 11 splendid lime trees round the walls and by several yews at the west entrance. In 1986 hundreds of daffodils and crocuses were planted as part of the 150th Anniversary celebrations.

The need for a larger churchyard was not easily met. In 1898 a piece of ground offered by Maurice Bromley-Wilson at Rigney Bank was rejected on health grounds. Similarly Jepson's Field on Beetham Road, later occupied by Dallam View, was also rejected.[120] It was not until 1902 that a hillside field east of the Bindloss Homes and 600 yards from the church was chosen. Mr. Bromley-Wilson[121] gave the site but 160 yards of Pig Lane leading to it required macadamising and gates, new walls, and drainage would cost £250. If a mortuary chapel was built another £300 would be required. When the fund accounts were published in 1903 only £93 18s from 25 donors had come in and it was not until 10 August 1904 that the ground was consecrated by Rt. Rev. Henry Ware, Bishop of Barrow. A chapel was not built but in 1948 after £1,000 had been left by Sidney Scott Greaves of Morley to provide a fund to maintain the grave of his mother Eliza (d. 1940) it was decided to allocate a quarter of the legacy for the erection of a cemetery shelter. Despite post-war shortages of suitable material, which led the P.C.C. even to consider using artificial stone, a rather basic limestone shelter was built by Sept Rockliff for £240 in 1951.[122] The remainder of the legacy of £750 was invested in 3½ per cent war loan and a "Greaves' flowers" rota drawn up for the graves.

Despite a preference in the last quarter of the twentieth century for cremation, some 224 memorials were erected in the 80 years since the cemetery was opened, the majority since 1950. Unlike the churchyard it has not been entirely spared green marble chippings and the like, while even after the diocese suggested that only local stone should be used, a number of polished black, pink and white stones were set up.

The twentieth century fashion of limiting inscriptions generally to names and date of death (and sometimes not even the latter) reduces considerably the potential interest of a modern graveyard.

So far the only person of more than local importance to be buried at Milnthorpe is Constance Holme. Her grave in the north western part of the cemetery by the laurel bushes is marked by a limestone cross. It is inscribed "In loving memory Frederick Burt Punchard of Underley, Kirkby Lonsdale and Owlet Ash, Milnthorpe. Died April 25, 1940 aged 78. Also of his wife Edith Constance Punchard (Constance Holme). Died June 17, 1955 aged 74."

One of the pleasantest customs of the cemetery is that relatives are generally buried close together. Thus there are groups of Ashburners, Atkinsons, Dowkers, Fawcetts, Garnetts, two lots of Mashiters, Frears and Dunfords, Wilkinsons and many more. This arrangement seems to have encouraged the families to maintain several graves, with the result that the cemetery is always attractive. Moreover, after 80 years it is still surrounded by open farmland and it commands good views of Farleton Knott and the Pennines to the east and, beyond the tower on the hill, of Whitbarrow and the Lakeland fells to the north and west.

The Rev. Reade resigned in 1910 on the grounds of ill health, a convalescent trip to Lake Lucerne in 1907 having failed to effect a cure.[123] All his main antagonists had either mellowed or "passed on" and his going was regretted. He concluded his final sermon "by asking for forgiveness if there had been any grievances, for now cometh the end." But it was far from the end: he was vicar of Ings from 1910–1919, became an Honorary Canon of Carlisle in 1914 and after retiring to Windermere he lived hale and hearty, dying in 1937 after his ninety–fifth birthday.[125]

Milnthorpe's most unusual religious personality was probably John Taylor who followed the celebrated Brigham Young as second head of the Mormons in 1877. His obituary in 1887 stated that he had had few educational advantages having been born to a poor family, generally said to have been based at Stainton. It was, however, from Milnthorpe that he emigrated to Utah at the age of 21. Many years later, on the death of Brigham Young, he was elected in his place as "head of the Mormon Twelve Apostles."[126] Just before the First World War Mormon missionaries made a pilgrimage to Milnthorpe, but they were warned off by the vicar who described Mormonism as "simply a species of white slave traffic under the guise of religion and he earnestly warned parents and others to be on guard against the wily arguments of these men."[127] Even so there are supposed to be some Mormons who regard Milnthorpe as a second Bethlehem.

By far the most important product of the nineteenth century Church was the growth of Methodism. Whatever its detractors might say the Chapel provided far more than a turgid diet of psalms, sermons and sanctified stinginess. There were always

Laying Foundation Stones of the Wesleyan Chapel, Beetham Road, 1904.

chapel treats and the Independents held regular summer sports in the field opposite the chapel. Afterwards, in 1842, "upwards of one hundred healthful and blooming youths of both sexes sat down to an abundant repast."[128] Around the middle of the century primitive Methodism gained ground under a locally famous leader "navvy Joe" Pennington. One of Joe's early converts was Thomas Whitwell of Milnthorpe, who having led a wild life when young became a respected shoemaker in Main Street and took to preaching in barns and cottages throughout the district. Thomas and his wife, who died the day after him, were amongst the first to be buried in the new cemetery in December 1906.[129] They had lived to see the opening of the Wesleyan church on Beetham Road which replaced the old Haverflatts Lane chapel in 1904.

The building fund for the new chapel opened in 1903. A splendid bazaar raised £100, and a good site was obtained on Beetham Road, next to the old Bull's Head, formerly the garden of the White Lion Inn. The Foundation Stone laying ceremony, presided over by the Rev. Samuel Miles of Kendal, took place on September 5 1903. Miles laid the first stone followed by "seven appropriated for some time with the names cut" by Mrs. Walker of Whitehaven, Miss Handley of Greenhead Farm, Hincaster, Mr. R.

The New Chapel.

Clark of Milnthorpe, Mr F.J. Crossfield of Ulverston, Mrs. Howetson of Kirkby Stephen, Mrs. Miles (on behalf of Kendal Friends) and Mr. Jas. Tyson of Staveley. A sum of nearly £230 was either placed on the stone or collected during the ceremony...each one who laid a stone was presented with a silver trowel. Afterwards a tea party was held in the Public Rooms; the profits from the tea of £5, plus £10 from an evening meeting, raised with other donations the sum collected to over £250 in one day.[130]

The chapel was designed by John F. Curwen and built by the firm of W. Scott of Milnthorpe. Curwen called the style "Queen Anne" but in fact it bears almost no relation to the architecture of the early eighteenth century. With sloping buttresses in limestone, a red pantiled or "Roman–tiled roof" graced originally by a high ventilator, it is very much in the villa style of the period. Light and not too large it was admirably suited to its purpose. The chapel measures 54 feet by 22 feet and has a narrow west gallery. The floor slopes downwards towards the communion table with the pulpit/reading desk behind. To the north is a school room 46 feet by 22 feet which can be thrown open to the main chapel through large oak doors.

At the opening ceremony on 27 September 1904, the Rev. Miles again presided.

Longevity of service has been a feature of the chapel. Miss Jane Dobson, who played the organ at the opening ceremony, cut the Jubilee cake in 1954, while Miss Doris Mashiter who was also present at the opening ceremony, only retired as organist in June 1986.

For most of its history Milnthorpe Methodists did not have a

New Church Bells, 1912.

resident minister, the local society being under the pastoral care of ministers stationed at Kendal, Kirkby Lonsdale and Arnside. The first Milnthorpe based minister was the Rev. J.W. Ladell (1938–1941), who married Miss Elsie Wilson of Crosby Lodge in 1941. Tragically a promising ministry in Northumberland was cut short by his early death. His widow, having returned home, became (with their son) a leading member of the church.

In 1910 the Rev. Reade's successor as Vicar of Milnthorpe was the Rev. Christopher Pickering. He stayed for 14 years, then he became Vicar of Arnside. He encouraged greater participation by the congregation and in 1912[132] Joseph Storey and in 1917 John Mashiter were inducted as lay readers. Spanning the years 1914–18 his ministry was engulfed by the First World War.

New bells were obtained in 1911, and the *Westmorland Gazette* noted that "the sour campanology of Milnthorpe will now be changed for something sweeter."[134] There had been many difficulties. At the end of 1910 £276 17s 10d had been collected towards replacing the bells and the chances of raising the required total amount of over £400 seemed a long way off. The Rev. Pickering suggested buying only the 10cwt tenor bell and Dr. Fuller, a churchwarden, even suggested dispensing with the whole project and just having chimes – but perhaps he had an ulterior motive because his house Stoneleigh, opposite the church, would receive the full campanological force.

Nevertheless matters went ahead and the architects Austin and

Paley were summoned to confirm the tower as safe. A three day bazaar with evening "cafe chantant" was then organised and it was a great success. After £50 had been spent on materials there was a net profit of £220.[135]

The new bells were brought in procession from the station and solemnly photographed on the church steps before being hung. Suggestions that the old bells would make good plant pots were rejected and they were given (not sold) to Levens Church, on the understanding that "if no longer required there for church purposes they should be returned to the churchwardens of Milnthorpe."[136] They were not hung in a belfry at Levens but placed in a wooden frame in the churchyard where they were sounded by being struck with mallets. Though the bells are rusting and apparently underused, Milnthorpe has never asked for them back.

A deficiency of £62 10s in the accounts in 1917 led to the suggested economy of replacing the bellringers (who cost £10 p.a.) with the chimes by the caretaker (at a cost of £2 10s p.a.).[137] This scheme was abandoned after Will Scott forcefully pointed out that £500 had quite recently been spent on new bells and when the wrath of George Wilson (head bellringer from 1895 to 1945) had been vented.

Sadly, as in many other places, the Milnthorpe bells have had a chequered history. They were rung at both morning and evening services and on special occasions in the 1920s. Having tolled out the old year and rung in the new the bellringers were throughout the inter-war period entertained at Mallow House by Mr. and Mrs. Hadwin Allen. The passing bell was rung for every death, including those at the workhouse, until the Second World War. It was rung on the death of Mrs. Emily Gamble, wife of the vicar, in April 1948 but in 1951 it was decided not to restore the practice.

Silenced from 1940 the bells were rung again after the Eighth Army victory at El Alamein at the end of 1942, but the team was depleted by war service and considerable publicity was given when a 15 year old school girl, Jean Proctor, took up the ropes in 1944. For a time around 1948 Jean was even the head ringer. In the late 1950's the team consisted mainly of teenagers but when many left for university ringing declined. By 1977 the bells had not been rung for many years because, it was said, there was no-one to ring them and in any case the tower was unsafe.[138] In the late 1980's minor repairs were carried out under the Rev. John Kelly since when they were rung regularly but perhaps not as often as people would have liked.

With the wider world falling apart Milnthorpe in 1917 took steps to end its remaining legal links with Heversham. Negotiations, carried out by the churchwarden Dr. Fuller, continued for many

*The First Girl Bellringer. L to R. William Thompson, George Wilson,
Jean Proctor, Rev. J. L. Gamble.*

years and it was not until 1923 after the retirement of Canon
Gilbert, Vicar of Heversham (1866-1921), that a full marriage
license was ratified for 1924.[141] Dr. Fuller was also concerned with
augmenting the living to bring it up to £350 p.a. through a Church
Commissioners' grant. The problem was that Milnthorpe's
population had fallen from the 1,250 estimated by the Rev. Raikes
in the 1880's, to under 1,000 in the 1920's, and the Commissioners
would only make a grant if it was 1,000. Attempts to include Rowell
in Milnthorpe's ecclesiastical parish having been resisted, they had
to wait for a natural increase. This came about in 1925 when the
Miles family, numbering 7, moved into Laburnum House; Joan
Miles being number 1,000. By 1940 there had been a slight increase
of stipend to £365; not supplemented much by the Easter offering,
which never exceeded £16. In 1944 the Church Commissioners
pointed out that Milnthorpe's living was £60 below the accepted
minimum and the P.C.C. had to make good the deficiency, Harold
Fawcett guaranteeing personally the extra amount.[142]

It was in the 1920's that the Parochial Church Council was
inaugurated to replace the old Vestry meetings. Unfortunately no
records before 1936 appear to have survived.

Both the Reverend and Mrs. Pickering were popular. He for his
good humour and for his pastoral care; on Mondays he always
visited the homes of regular worshippers if they had been absent
from the Sunday service. She was long remembered as being smart
and good looking and, though herself childless, for her active
involvement with the Girls' Friendly Society whose meetings were

always held at the Vicarage.[143] When they left for Arnside in 1924 they were presented with a cheque for £60 collected, according to the churchwarden J. McNabb, as a token of "appreciation and esteem of all classes."[144]

John Leonard Gamble, the new vicar, had local connections. His father had been Vicar of Loweswater for 27 years; he himself had been at college with Mr. Pickering and he had been Canon Bardsley's curate at Ulverston and Lancaster from 1901 to 1909, and then of Wyresdale from 1910 until 1911 when he became Vicar of Yealand. His removal from Yealand was prompted by the death of his only son in 1921. Though quiet and rather shy, "little Mr. Gamble" and his wife, two daughters and their aunt Miss Crabtree, who acted as housekeeper, were active in the village. As well as conducting church affairs Mr. Gamble good-naturedly presided at the various Jubilee, Coronation and Victory celebrations and at the flower shows and sports. Though his living was scandalously poor, and his clothes remembered as being green with age, he was generous and he kept up the practice of "leaving a vicar's half-crown on the mantlepiece"[145] when visiting his poorer parishioners.

An unusual request in 1929 for Sunday funerals could not, on legal grounds, be turned down, but was effectively discouraged by a decision to charge double fees. Old anti–popery notions must have rolled away by Whitsuntide 1933 when the choir was robed for the first time.

To celebrate the centenary of the church it was decided to install electric light on "the Holophane Scheme No/1601/5" system at a cost of £137.[149] At the same time the church was redecorated and (a big surprise) the Anglo-Catholic English Hymnal Books obtained. To help meet the cost of all this Mrs. (Frances) Miles with her family offered to be responsible for 100 shillings – a suggestion which was only copied, however, by Mr. Scott, Mrs. McNabb and the Vicar. Even so, the gas lights were removed, though four brass switches by the pulpit and the bases of the standard gasoliers remained. Electricity was switched on in time for the Centenary services. Held on the 2nd October these included sermons from the Bishop of Carlisle and from his assistant Bishop Danson. A parish tea, costing 1/- each, was also held in the Public Rooms.

As at Heversham and elsewhere the P.C.C. records hardly hint at the impact of the Second World War. Evensong was transferred to 3 p.m. in winter because of the blackout. When rules were relaxed in November 1944 and the service went back to the old time of 6.30 p.m., the police complained about the lights, only to be told they "would be better employed by keeping their eyes on Wop prisoners and local girls and leaving our overworked clergy with complaints that lights are too bright." Many members of the congregation were drawn away by war service. Leslie Powell's resignation as organist was refused though the P.C.C. "are prepared to release him for the duration of the war." Mrs. Hayes replaced him at a salary of £30 p.a. and though perhaps not as accomplished as her predecessors she was as loyal.

By the deaths of John Mashiter, lay reader and life long choir member in 1942, and Bill Garnett, the long serving verger in 1945, the church at a difficult time lost valuable servants. A lectern Bible was presented by his family in memory of John Mashiter and a verger's chair by the P.C.C. in memory of Bill Garnett. Wartime shortages caused problems and it took nearly five years to obtain replacement cassocks for the choirboys. As regards numbers the church was still in good heart. It was still the done thing to go to church, though social gradations were maintained. Typical of the old school was Mrs Elburn. Until her death in 1937 Mrs. Elburn would leave her home, Fleet House, as the five minute bell sounded, and make her way across the square followed by her dutiful maid Beatrice. Inside the church Mrs. Elburn sat 'up–front' in one of the rented pews along with others of the middle classes; Beatrice occupied one of the free pews at the back. As late as the early 1950's there was a noticeable stir between 10.15 a.m. and 10.30 a.m. as people walked to church and older residents recalled that on special occasions the end of services was "like a football crowd turning out."[150]

At Easter 1948 Mrs. Gamble died and her husband, after a total ministry of 48 years, decided to retire. He was given a cheque for the unprecedently high (for Milnthorpe) sum of £263 4s 6d[151] and like Nicholas Padwick before him, retired to Hampshire where he lived at Basingstoke until his death in 1966.

Before Mr. Gamble left the P.C.C. had already told the Bishop that they "would like a young married man, not a high churchman and one who is acquainted with and interested in the rural way of life. It is felt that the church work among the young people should be continued and strengthened."[152] For once they got what they wanted – for the Bishop and the patron Rev. W.R. Cleghorn appointed Cyril Lee.

Cyril and his wife Alice, who had two little girls Susan and Rose Anne, threw themselves wholeheartedly into youth work of all kinds, forming Cub and Brownie packs, reorganising the Guides and encouraging the already well–established Scouts. For the former the vicarage barn was renovated using funds left over from the defunct Girls' Friendly Society. Alice Lee possessed a good commercial instinct well borne out in the organisation of bazaars which because of clothes' rationing and other shortages attracted both customers and acrimony! A bazaar organised in 1950 by a working party of Mesdames Dalton, Rushton, Sheldon, Thompson, Mason, Hyde and Miss Scott raised £500.[153] This sum was spent on redecorating the church in fashionable but clinical pastel shades, and at the same time the altar dorsal curtains installed in c.1912 to designs by Austin and Paley were removed. A more important change was that pew rents were abolished by a unanimous vote of the P.C.C. on 5 April 1949. The position of pew rent warden was replaced by that of a "people's warden" to be elected at the annual meeting. The P.C.C. also agreed to contribute £50 towards the parson's stipend, but even so it only reached £480, by 1950. Not surprisingly, the Bishop pointed out that ordinands were failing to come forward because of the lack of a living wage. Despite continued pressure Milnthorpe barely met the minimum stipend requirements before the immediate responsibility for paying the vicar was taken over by the Diocese in the 1970's and replaced by increased Diocesan Quota.

In 1951 the P.C.C. acquired the former St. Thomas's School. (See Ch.14) By 1937 the school was on the Westmorland County Council's "blacklist" and as the Church could not afford the estimated £4,000 to replace it, the P.C.C. agreed to its being taken over as a maintained school.[154] After the opening of the County Primary and Modern Schools the Church had the option of buying it back for £420. A quick decision was taken and the building was obtained for use as a church hall. Much of the money was raised by Henry Atkinson, the Treasurer and Booking Secretary, through Olde Tyme Dancing evenings. Later when the Management Committee banned "Rock-'n'-Roll" music from the hall, the youth of the village was allowed to borrow the Olde Tyme records; so a generation which by rights should have jived to Hayley, Steele and Elvis, split the Willow, dashed with the White Sergeant and contorted with the Gay Gordons instead!

In 1950 the Diocesan authorities (represented by the curiously named Messrs Bottom and Ball)[155] condemned the existing sanitation at the Hall. After six years of effort, £1,200 was raised to install toilets and cloakrooms (which never had hot water) and to create a primitive kitchen with a serving hatch to the main room. Even so, the Church Hall never became either a convenient or an attractive venue, although it was well suited for jumble sales, for the W.I. market and for the weekly coffee morning started by Mrs. Walsh and the Mothers Union when the Friday market was re-established in 1966. The initial difficulties in obtaining furniture for the hall were solved when the Rev. Lee bought 70 old chairs from York at a cost of £16 10s.[156] but these, with 12 nursery school chairs, tables left over from the school and the flotsam and jetsam of parish attics, plus various trestles and benches, did not create a comfortable impression. Moreover, in 30 years the knotted and nail-studded floor never received lino; while the walls, despite regular redecoration, ran with dusty tear-stains of condensation

*Over-Sixties Club, Church Hall, 1962. Mrs.Harris cuts the cake
assisted by Rev. Bernard and Mrs.Kitts.*

thanks to ill-chosen gas radiators.

Possessed of youthful high spirits, both the Lees were popular
and successful. Cyril Lee's successor in 1955 was Bernard Kitts
from Manchester; not unknown to the area, having done summer
duty at Heversham. Though like Cyril Lee he only stayed seven
years Bernard Kitts did much good work. As well as supervising the
completion of the Church Hall project he started the popular Over
Sixties Club, which continued to flourish for the next thirty years.
More transient was a Youth Club founded for the confirmed youth
in 1958. This dispensed a bland but jolly mixture of ping-pong,
prayers, alcohol free parties and fell walks. Soon after its foundation
57 young people (including 12 from Holme) were confirmed, and it
is pleasant to record a number of these had kept, or regained, their
faith when middle-aged.

With Tom Wood, one of the village bank managers as Treasurer,
the church finances were yet again re-examined and a stewardship
campaign inaugurated. This was over optimistic and by 1962 only
£650 of the hoped for £1,200[157] per annum had been promised, so
the pattern of coffee mornings, bring-and-buys and jumble sales
came back.

When the Kitts, following the precedent of the Rev. and Mrs.
Reade, left for Ings in the spring of 1963 the living was accepted by
the Rev. Eric Walsh, Vicar of St. Helens, Churchtown near
Garstang. His, and his hardworking wife's, first task was to

supervise the refurbishment of the vicarage. In 1924 a bathroom had been installed for the Gambles, electricity had been put in in 1937 and when the Lees arrived in 1948, £133 had been spent on redecoration and £5 18s on a Rayburn cooker. A telephone was only installed in 1950. In 1957 the attic dormers were removed.[158]

By 1963 it was a shabby, uncomfortable house. Though large by modern standards it occupied the ideal, and indeed only possible, site. Therefore it was refurbished at a cost of over £4,000 while the vicar and his family lived at Hawbarrow House, Heversham. Although the Walshes contributed to some of the costs and the Rev. Walsh's father gave £100, the scheme, involving full central heating, a new cloakroom, demolition of outbuildings and a new kitchen, was regarded locally as extravagant. The Secretary of the P.C.C. was compelled to write to the press refuting some allegations.[159]

Eric Walsh was a good man whose conscientous manner and piety compensated for a rather reserved disposition, and a slight speech impediment. It was his fate to serve at a time when apathy to the Church and opposition to traditional standards reached their depth. Twice during the "Swinging Sixties" Milnthorpe P.C.C. debated the impact of a – short-lived – casino which opened on the square.[160] His position was aggravated by a changing population with many middle class families preferring to live in other villages and the arrival of a largely "un-churched" population of strangers on the housing estates.

Despite much good work it is impossible not to detect decline and disillusionment in the church at Milnthorpe in the 1970's. Attendance at services dropped sometimes even to single figures. Remaining worshippers were engulfed in retrenchment and make-do-and-mend. In 1970 an "inside toilet for the church would not be practicable but it was decided that a glass and receptacle suitable for dealing with emergencies should be provided."

In September 1978 Eric Walsh resigned, and went to live in Morecambe, where he died in 1983. The Catholic and Methodist ministers were very active in the village, and it was felt that the new vicar must show an immediate willingness to become involved in the life of Milnthorpe.

These requirements were fully met in the Rev. John Kelly from Barrow, who arrived in March 1979. He immediately announced that Series II Prayer Book would be phased out, Series III would be adopted and then (in 1981) the Alternative Services Book used for all worship; the bells would be rehung and rung; Sunday School would be held in the mornings with the result that the number of children and parents attending services went up; candles were placed on the altar and he celebrated facing the congregation on a table placed under the chancel arch and a lady, Miss Joyce Glover, the first of several lay administrants, was appointed to assist with the chalice. Within a month of his arrival he asked the P.C.C. for the church to be left open during the day for a trial period of 6 months, and, when the fears for the new red carpet were not borne out by events, it remained open. The effect was instant. Whereas there had been 40 communicants at Easter 1978 there were 143 at Easter 1979.

With one sweep two major problems were to be solved with a bold plan. The decaying and depressing church hall would be sold and the over-large and expensive-to-heat nave would be reduced by building a new hall in the long redundant gallery. With a floor area of 1,750 square feet the new hall would in fact be larger than the 1,700 square feet of the old hall, plus a similar area for a modern kitchen, cloakrooms, coffee area and narthex. It was estimated that the old hall would fetch on the open market between £10,000 and £15,000 and the new work cost between £20,000 and £25,000. Cheerfully ignoring all protests, mainly from the "Smarties-pennies" brigade, a gift day was held on All Saints Day 1979 when some £4,000 was donated.

The original estimates were both wrong - for when the old hall was sold, to Messrs Crossfield & Son, the grocers nextdoor, it brought in £47,500. With the proceeds of the gift-day and other fund-raising, including a series of coffee evenings, and an almost unprecedentedly high Diocesan grant of £15,000, all expenses were more than covered. The main contract of £48,625 was awarded to J.E. Proctor & Sons, a local firm, as were all the other contractors. Even the architects, Alison Hutchison and Partners of Edinburgh, had a local connection for Mrs. Mackay was formerly Ruth Powell of Ackenthwaite! So successful was the scheme that the only persistent complaint was the new colour of the church doors – purple. The consecration of the Church Centre on 20 March 1982 marked a fine achievement for John Kelly and his helpers, principally John Leighton, James Melling and Richard Townley.

In May, 1982 John Kelly also became Priest-in-Charge of Beetham, it being agreed that two-thirds of his time would be spent in Milnthorpe.

During the 850th Anniversary celebrations of the Diocese of Carlisle in 1983 Milnthorpe came first in "the Most Welcoming Church" competition.

John Kelly resigned both ministries just after Easter 1985 and moved to Cammerton in West Cumbria at the end of June.

After an unusually short interregnum, the Rev. Michael Simpson was licensed to serve both parishes on 19 September 1985. Beetham was chosen for the induction service as the Bishop had been at the Confirmation at St. Thomas's the previous Sunday. Undaunted by his five previous years' ministry in Hong Kong, Michael Simpson soon showed that he would continue well the work of the Church of England.

Roman Catholicism was only re-established in Milnthorpe as a result of the Second World War. A Mass centre was set up in the cookery rooms to serve Catholic evacuees from Liverpool in 1939. Later in the war the evacuation of a convent to Levens Hall and a monastery to Sizergh Castle and the arrival of the Italian prisoners of war at the Bela River Camp in 1943 gave further impetus to Catholicism. By 1945 there were about 30 non-POW worshippers and for their benefit Dr. P.S. Byrne arranged for mass to be celebrated in the garage attached to his surgery at Stoneleigh Cottage. "A trestle set amidst oil and petrol cans served as an altar and worshippers dodged raindrops seeping through the roof."[164]

In 1946 the congregation moved into the old malt kiln behind Glasgow House. At first worshippers had to kneel on the concrete floor, the cold being aggravated by the lack of doors and windows. Led by Rev. Dr. J.J. Salter, the "unpretentious exterior matched by the puritan simplicity of the interior"[165] was renovated and when the building was consecrated in 1947 as the "Church of Christ the King" the altar was adorned with a crimson and gold backcloth a cross and a set of fine candlesticks. It was lit by fluorescent lighting and heated by "electric braziers." A parish serving the area south of Levens Bridge to Beetham and from east of the Kendal-Crooklands road to Arnside in the west was attached to the church. In 1953 Barn Hey, a house converted just after the war out of the barn attached to Glasgow House, was obtained for a presbytery and Father Whelan moved in shortly afterwards.

In the 1950's the church was embellished with an Italianate sandstone portico, much plaster statuary and a colourful lithograph of Christ, donated in the memory of Private Patrick McVeigh. As such it might have met adequately the needs of the local congregation for many years.

However, largely through the munificence of Mr. and Mrs. Ronald Somervell of Haverbrack, the foundation stone for a new church was laid in 1969. It was sited on Haverflatts Lane and designed by Weightman and Bullen of Liverpool and built by Messrs Thom of Lancaster. The building is an unusual seven-sided shape "derived from the pattern of movement turning in a facetted spiral up a slightly ramped approach arriving at a point of stillness in the round interior." Certainly the uncluttered interior with Westmorland slate floors, white roughcast walls and very simple altar, harks back to early monastic simplicity. The only colour is provided by a stained glass abstract at floor level in the south east corner. At the consecration by Rt. Rev. T.B. Pearson in November 1970, the cost was stated to be £45,000. The church's first funeral was of Francis Burchall, landlord of the Bull's Head and the first wedding was of Imelda Moore to Christopher Allan, the following

April.

No official representatives of other branches of the Church were present at the consecration of the new building though Father L.J. Kelly was popular in the village. But fortunately this situation changed before long and by the late 1980's clergy and congregations of all denominations met regularly and occasionally worshipped together. On Good Friday, Christians of all persuasions take part in an open-air service on the green which is followed by a procession of witness round the market on what is generally the busiest day of the year.

10

Politics, Good Works and Welfare

For most of Milnthorpe's recorded history society was unevenly divided between the haves and the have-nots. The male haves ruled and the have-nots did as they were told with an odd grumble or two. After 1842[1] the loud mouthed poor had the privilege of jeering or cheering the landowning electors as they arrived to declare their vote at the hustings set up at the Cross Keys; for the rest of the time they too touched their forelocks to the gentry, parson and plutocrat. In a largely illiterate society most folk knew nothing of national affairs and so could not care one way or another about the world at large.

Only from the early nineteenth century was Milnthorpe touched noticeably by the outer ripples of the political whirlpool. The movement for the reform of Parliament is more conspicuously marked in Milnthorpe than in many of those places where Reform Bill agitation is recorded. St. Anthony's Tower, the village's most notable landmark, was built by Henry Smithies[2] to commemorate the passing of the First Reform Bill of 1832. This fact is little known. A. Wainwright in *Westmorland Heritage*[3] states that "it was built in early Victorian times as a summerhouse for St. Anthony's House on the main road nearby, and served as an observation post for the Home Guard during the last war" (i.e. 1939-1945). John F. Curwen in his *History of Heversham With Milnthorpe* admitted that "we can learn little about the tower – beyond the fact that a fox hunt passed by it in the year 1844 and that subsequent to 1832 Mr. Wilson of Dallam Tower stopped the continuation of the "Blue Row" in order that he might continue to see this tower on the hill."[4] To Curwen the tower was part of the contemporary craze for follies and summerhouses. The Wilsons' of Dallam did not own the tower

The Blue Row in 1910.

or the St. Anthony's land until long after the tower had been built. Neddy Stones, appropriately Milnthorpe's greatest radical, put the matter straight by noting that "Bela Mills were almost rebuilt by H. Smithies and Son. He made a fortune at it, bought the land, built St. Anthony's and erected The Summerhouse; a descendant sold it to Mr. Tattersall. The last of the family died at Riley Field."[7] G. Tattersall in the *Lakes of England*[8] (1836) states that it was built as a monument to the passing of the Parliamentary Reform Bill in 1832.

This would also confirm Curwen's record[11] that it was in 1832 that Mr. Wilson sought to preserve the view by buying land at the end of the Blue Row. The purchase might in fact have occurred in 1834 when there was advertised "all that piece of ground staked out behind the same intended for gardens 890 square yards adjoining the west side of the road leading to Kendal being parcels of the herediments late belonging to the Kendal Union Building Society."[10]

The Blue Row is the old name given to the terraced cottages on Church Street. They were built by the Milnthorpe Union Building Society which later amalgamated with the Kendal Society. Blue was the local colour for the Whigs, the exponents of parliamentary reform; the local Tories used yellow borrowed from the Lowthers, Earls of Lonsdale, who either provided or nominated Westmorland's Tory M.P.'s.[11]

The Milnthorpe and Kendal Building Societies were sponsored by the Whigs to provide voters. The Blue Row houses carried with them the voting qualification of a 40 shillings freehold. There were 20 full houses but most could be divided, and even in 1987 one set of "half houses" remained. Generally the Blue Row could provide about 30 voting heads of households. Six advertisements quoted by Curwen show that the houses were built before-the Reform Bill of 1832.

The radical tradition of the street survived various franchise reforms, for in the 1910 elections when most of the village was draped in yellow bunting (for Captain Bagot) from "the Blue Row fluttered blue banners"[12] for the liberal Stewart-Smith. At the end of the street the white front door belonging to Mrs. McNabb, who though a Tory supported Votes for Women and was known (behind her back) as "Mrs. Pankhurst," was painted blue in the night by some Liberal urchins. In the middle of the street lived the village Hampden, Neddy Stones. Further down, the Sarginsons espoused the radical cause, and even as late as 1956, Mary Walker nee Sarginson, announced to the author (a suitably enraged schoolboy royalist) that she would not put up any flags in preparation for the visit of Queen Elizabeth II. One small flag was eventually put out of her window but, it was rumoured, only after one of the customers of Mrs. Walker's greengrocer's shop threatened to take her business elsewhere, asking the proprietor whether she would shame the village by flagrant republicanism?

Henry Brougham.

Despite the Blue Row radicals most villagers were Tories. When the "Lion of the Day," Lord Brougham, the Lord Chancellor and the "biggest of Whigs," changed horses at the Cross Keys on Tuesday 19th May 1834, the following incident was recorded:- "A friend of ours Josy F--n, in joy at the great event, had been drinking not only skin deep but pottle deep and after many a bee-lurch he reeled up to the carriage and thus addressed the noble Lord 'hoo Harry, me lad, hoo is ta? What thoo sits thare as cloaze as ta does a top et woosack, en the ases nea gittin the out er off'. One of the suite intervened and Josy was beckoned within to drink the Lord Chancellor's health again or the event might have proved serious."[13]

It was not until the approach of the Third Reform Act of 1884 which, in effect, gave the vote to all male householders, that organised political activities reached Milnthorpe, although the Tory, Colonel Lowther M.P., had addressed occasional meetings in Milnthorpe in the 1860's. Liberal attempts to oust the Tories were dampened by the Tory Milnthorpe correspondent of the *Westmorland Gazette* who in 1884 stated "I have never heard so much clap-trap and audacious, impudent assertions as fell from one gifted with gab as at the Milnthorpe Liberal Meeting." Moreover he went on to declare that "Liberals here are at a discount. It is possible that wide awake Liberals might endeavour to proselytize but I venture to say that if other parts of the country attend to their work and follow the example of Milnthorpe the battle may be said to be won ere it has been fought, and the Conservative leaders may with confidence look forward to share in the enthusiasm which comes of a great and signal victory."[16] Nationally he was wrong, for Gladstone's Liberals won the General Election, but locally the Tories won. A Conservative meeting at the Agricultural Hall had been crowded. It must have been a marathon occasion for addresses were given by Hon. W. Lowther M.P., Mr. J. Holme (in the chair), the Earl of Bective and most of the gentry and the clergy including the Reverends Raikes and Hutton and Canon Gilbert.

Milnthorpe was one of the first places to have a "Habitation" of the Primrose League, founded to uphold the Conservatism of Disraeli after his death in 1881. The League certainly supported the political activities of Captain Josceline Bagot as he made his way to becoming the "beau ideal of a country M.P." At a Levens rally in 1895 Mrs. Bagot announced that there were 389 associates and 26 knights. Later in the year the League supported an anti-Home Rule meeting. Captain Bagot thought "such matters as pauper immigrants, the competition of foreign prison-made goods and the aged poor could be dealt with more effectively than going in for changing the great system under which we had lived happily so long."[18]

Captain Bagot won the election and his popularity increased as result of his and Mrs. Bagot's work in the Boer War. He served as press censor and she, along with other fashionable ladies, ran a hospital. At an exultant meeting held at the Public Rooms on their return in 1903, Capt. Bagot successfully defended the imperial policy and denounced Liberal proposals for increased expenditure, but he had difficulty in justifying to local Tories the 1902 Education Act. This Act seemed to weaken Church schools as well as increasing the rates, in order to pay for raising the school leaving age to 13. More popular, in such an over-pubbed place as Milnthorpe, was his opposition to the licensing of ale houses on the basis of the population per acre. This did not save him, however, and in 1905 for the first and only time, Westmorland got a Liberal M.P. The *Westmorland Gazette* announced the result under the headline "Conservatives beaten but not dispirited. Stewart-Smith (Liberal) 2,899, Bagot 2,662."[20] At Milnthorpe 474 men voted out of a total electorate of 530, and the yellow flags prevailed except in Carr's Yard and the Blue Row. All day the streets were "busy with motors and other conveyances" including carriages from Levens and Dallam and Canon Gilbert's brougham.

In 1907 the Tory fight back involved a meeting at the Public Rooms for 500 Conservatives presided over by Sir Maurice Bromley-Wilson and a newly appointed agent, Mr. Danbury. This was the high period of the public meeting and even more – 600 to 700 people – flocked to a "Cinematograph exhibition staged by the Dallam and Levens Primrose League Habitation" in January 1908 – "a number of those present had not previously had the pleasure of seeing a first class exhibition of this sort and it was received with much appreciation. The programme of pictures included the anarchists' fight with the London police." This was used to illustrate Captain Bagot's latest warnings about pauper immigration. Less successful was a lecture on Free Trade v Protection when a box of slides illustrating the lecture had gone astray on the railway and so could not be shown. Instead, the audience were told how employers were being taxed beyond endurance and tariff reform was the only answer.

In 1910 there were two general elections and in the first Captain Bagot (under the slogan "vote for Bagot and better times") recaptured the seat. All but 44 of Milnthorpe's electorate of 577 voted, some including Rev. John Audland who had come from Salisbury, travelling great distances to do so. Political meetings were calm – the Liberals being "too crowded for fighting, though the Chairman could not be heard" but at Captain Bagot's "there was very little of a discordant nature."[21] Later in the year Milnthorpe was treated to a women's suffrage demonstration by a group of "County ladies" including Mrs. Gandy of Heaves and Miss Rayden of the National Union who "begged every man who voted for

Captain Bagot to send a post card demanding votes for women."[22]

No doubt impressed by its "yellow" strength, Captain Bagot honoured Milnthorpe by arranging his pre-polling day rally in the Public Rooms before the December election of 1910. He might also have decided to do so in order to avoid Kendal, where the Liberals were strong. Unfortunately, his meeting was ruined by what the *Westmorland Gazette* called "Politics and Fire." Just as Captain Bagot had reached the middle of his speech, some of the audience on the balcony in the Public Rooms saw through the window flames flickering in the yard behind Fawcett's motor works, barely ten yards from the wall of the hall. Within seconds there was an explosion as the first of several oil cans ignited. Instantly, the speeches stopped and the hall emptied into deserted streets.

Even Sergeant Park on the door had failed to notice the fire. Mrs. Fawcett and her children had to be woken out of bed, although it was only 9 p.m. and taken to a place of safety. Mrs. Fawcett remembered to bring with her a bag of sovereigns!

Meanwhile, over at the works the gentry and volunteer fire brigade, aided by appliances brought in from the Comb Mill and the Workhouse, were falling over themselves to put the fire out. They were hindered by a large motorcar, minus wheels, which resisted all efforts to move it. Major Argles sent his motor for hose pipes from the Eversley greenhouse while Sir Maurice Bromley-Wilson directed the chain of buckets – "but they might well have spit on it for the good it did." When the Eversley hoses arrived Mr. T. Wilson of Kidside took over and was "agreeably surprised to find that the water went twice the height of the house."

It appeared that "the whole block of buildings seemed doomed and Mr. T. Arkwright's house on the other side was dismantled with all speed, much furniture being thrown outside anyhow." Mr. Roland Sharp, however, managed to retrieve the Conservative papers from the Arkwright's parlour which was being used as a committee room. Mr. James Wilkinson had to climb through a broken window to rescue the dog from under the bed. Next door, Mr. Eason's stock in trade and furniture were moved to neighbouring houses. Only after the roof had fallen in did Colonel Weston (who as the highest ranking officer present, had taken charge) allow his wife to telephone for the Kendal fire brigade. This took some time to assemble as the Chief Constable, Mr. Smith, and Fire Superintendant Norman, were on duty at the Liberal Meeting. When two 'manuals' with four horses each arrived at Milnthorpe they found only a glowing ruin and Sir Maurice Bromley-Wilson standing guard, soaked to the skin, to prevent "salvaging." Mr Fawcett who with an assistant had left home at 3 p.m. to deliver a car was "completely stupified" when at 8 a.m. the next morning he returned to see "his premises gutted, his valuable machinery and

Dunlop tyres destroyed." The damage was estimated at £3,000 and was only partly covered by insurance. Both Parliamentary candidates visited the scene the next day and a collection was organised,[23] but this did not amount to much after more of the Fawcett sovereigns were found under piles of smouldering rags in the yard. As always after such occasions, the village thought that "Fawcett's never looked back after t'election fire."

In the excitement Captain Bagot's re-election seemed of secondary importance, but his death three years later was treated with the highest solemnity. The coffin arrived at Milnthorpe station by special train from London and the cortege – a full muster of gentry and clergy – went through the village en route for the grandest funeral ever staged at Heversham Church. Flags were half mast, the passing bell tolled and blinds were drawn even on the Blue Row.

Bagot's successor, the fire fighting Colonel Weston, had a walk-over by-election. There was only a "moderate attendance" at the Public Rooms when the Liberal Mr. Somerville explained that the Lloyd George National Insurance Act of 1911 would take 4d or 6d from a family each week but they would get at least 8d back! An Insurance Protest Meeting presided over by Canon Gilbert was well attended.[24]

War brought a party political truce until the 1920's. In 1921 at a meeting in Milnthorpe, Colonel Weston, once an ardent anti-Home Ruler, actually supported the creation of the Irish Free State, as the best means of settling the problem "and on more than generous terms." Even after the disintegration and virtual disappearance of their national party the Liberals remained the strongest opposition to the Conservatives in Westmorland, but by 1924 the Labour Party had also entered the local fray. The *Westmorland Gazette* was as anti-Labour as it once had been anti-Liberal. A report on a meeting in the Public Rooms addressed by the Labour candidate, Mr. P. Burnett, was headlined "A Socialist Fiasco." "Not one remark was greeted with a hear, hear from the body of the hall, the only visible appreciation of his speech being accorded by a supporter on the platform who occasionally clapped his hands. A Kendal youth of about 18 years of age presided. Uproar greeted Mr. Burnett's announcement that a new agreement with Bolshevik Russia could open up new markets and Mr. Burnett was obliged to hurry away. A collection was taken amounting to a handful of small change. One member of the audience was heard to enquire from another whether they did not pass a vote of confidence at Labour meetings but by this time the platform was deserted."

On election day "a few red flags were exhibited which seemed to lend variety to the prevailing yellow and some Union Jacks which were welcome. . . Just as 7 o'clock struck a group of ladies headed by Mrs. W.E. Mashiter presented themselves to exercise the franchise for the first time in their experience,' (votes for women were introduced in 1918). In the evening the Tory candidate, Oliver Stanley, received "rounds of cheers from large crowds which had assembled." No one in Milnthorpe was surprised when he beat "Bolshie Burnett" by 10,694 votes.[25]

With Levens Hall and Dallam Tower temporarily abandoned by the Bagot's and Wilson's, the Primrose League Habitation was not resurrected after the First War. A junior Imperial League set up in 1924 by Captain Barnes from Headquarters, with Lawrence Nanson as Chairman, actually attracted 60 members at first but declined in the 1930's.

By then a more sinister attraction had reared its ugly head. Support for fascism was not negligible in Milnthorpe and black shirts were donned by several local men, one of whom had his movements restricted under Regulation 18b when war broke out. Sir Oswald Mosley, the Fascist leader, addressed meetings in Kendal in May 1934 and April 1937. William Joyce – the "Lord Haw Haw" of the German wartime propaganda machine – also visited the area and on one occasion spoke briefly from the Market Cross at Milnthorpe. This event does not appear to have been recorded in the press at the time, but it was remembered by several villagers including Hedley Sheldon, the chemist, who actually left his counter to go out into the Square to hear the speeches. Tradition also has it that Joyce or another fascist addressed a gathering at Ackenthwaite, the speaker standing on the steps of the field stile opposite Ackenthwaite House. [26]

On a May Monday evening in 1936 a company of Blackshirts from Lancaster took the village by surprise and held a meeting in Harmony Square. There was a fairly large attendance of young people and three addresses were given after which enrolments were invited – but no one joined the movement.[27] On the other hand, no one seems to have objected at the time either. So sure of themselves were local fascists that in June 1937 W.G. Eaton, the Lancaster District Inspector of the British Union of Fascists, declared that "Westmorland will be fought at the next General Election. We have a man in mind; he will be allocated to the division in due course."[28] But the next election was in 1945 and by then fascism was just a skeleton in a cupboard.

As in other places, political activity in Milnthorpe, even at election time, dwindled in the face of national media coverage. For a time in the 1940's and 1950's there was a Labour Party branch in the village and the Liberals survived in a quiet way also, but by the 1960's the two other parties rarely organised tellers or committee rooms at election time. The Conservatives remained active and a long existing women's branch expanded into a full branch of the association in 1976. Throughout the 1970's and 1980's Milnthorpe paid the second highest quota in the constituency to central Conservative funds. Both Colonel Geoffrey Vane, Conservative M.P. 1945-1964 and Michael Jopling, M.P. from 1964, visited Milnthorpe and at election times addressed political meetings – but these meetings were only shadows of the exciting occasions at the turn of the century.

Until the brave new world which followed the Second World War most Milnthorpe people came into the "have nots" category of society. In welfare, hygiene, housing and health they were poorly off and liable to be submerged altogether by the onset of illness, by agricultural or trade depressions, by old age or by large families.

Private charity was always regarded as a more acceptable palliative than the Poor Law and sometimes received official endorsement. For example, in August 1848 a petition went round addresssed to the "Benevolent Christians of Milnthorpe" asking help for Daniel Berry, a poor industrious, labouring man with a wife and seven small children, to purchase a Horse and Cart to carry on a little trade as a Carrier to support his family."[29] Notwithstanding Daniel's several convictions for drunkeness, George Wilson of Dallam Tower gave him £1 although the Venerable Archdeacon Evans only managed half-a-crown.

There were occasional bequests to the poor in local wills. In 1701 Joseph Grigg left "to the poor of the Hamlett of Milthrope £5."[30] Larger sums were managed as Parish charities by the Churchwardens. Of these, Bread Money paid out of collections made at Holy Communion (celebrated about five times a year) was the most important. Bread Money was supplemented by the Woodhouse Charity Estate. This was a small farm purchased in 1793 for £350 with money from an accumulated amount of poor stock belonging to several townships of Heversham parish and £84, the residuary legacy of Agnes Martindale. The poor stock was made up partly of £98 Apprentice money, a fund used to equip youths when put to a trade. This originated from the will of Robert Gibson who in 1701 left a rent charge of 40s p.a. "to give to some poor child in Heversham and Milnthorpe when going out apprentice." Also in the stock was £12 left to the six poor widows of Milnthorpe town and £17 Communion Money.

The Churchwarden's also administered Atkinson's Charity – applicable to Heversham with Milnthorpe and Levens resulting from the bequest of £21 by Thomas Atkinson in 1811.[31] When Heversham and Milnthorpe were divided in 1896 the charities continued, and biannual meetings of the trustees still continue. On a population basis Milnthorpe received about three-fifths of the proceeds, and about 40 senior citizens were given a small sum of about a pound at Christmas.

The well-to-do regarded as an inescapable obligation the relief of poverty without, at Milnthorpe, seeking to change any of the conditions which made poverty inevitable. Unemployment, for example, was regarded as a consequence of a free economy: if there was no work, then the working man would be laid off. When scant savings were used up only charity prevented the sad trail up the hill to the workhouse. Thus in 1842 and 1843 Mr. Kitching distributed potatoes freely (as) "there are at present many poor weavers in the town in great distress from want of employment."[32] A ladies soup kitchen was also "set up at Milnthorpe for the benefit of the many poor families."[33] but charged them a ½d a quart. (The last soup kitchen operated on three days a week in 1894-95). Mrs. Wilson of Dallam Tower introduced a Clothing Club for poor families which, like the soup kitchen, charged small sums. Whether this was to remove the stigma of "Charity" or to remind the labouring classes of their personal responsibilities, cannot now be determined and probably could not at the time.

The labouring classes themselves contributed to a fund set up by Rev. Raikes and Martin Whittaker to relieve the cotton districts during the cotton famine in the 1860's. £56 4s ½d was collected in Milnthorpe including 5s 3d from the Sunday School and 15s from Mrs. Lund's School.[34]

Christmas donations often had to wait on the convenience of the bountiful. For example, it was not until the middle of January in 1826 that Mrs Wilson "distributed to poor families in the neighbourhood 30 pairs of blankets, 30 pairs of shoes, 28 pairs of stockings and various small sums."[35] In 1841 Master and the Misses Wilson "due to severe weather gave out soup and a large quantity of coals."[36] Later in the year a "loaf of fine bread and ¼lb of tea was distributed among the poor men of Milnthorpe to celebrate the marriage of Mr. Wilson to Miss Hulton of Hulton Park."[37] Gifts of blankets, sheets, duffle or cotton were given by the clergy, and minor gentry followed the example set by the Wilsons for in 1849 as well as a fine carcase of beef being received with great thankfulness by the poor of Milnthorpe, Beetham and Storth from the Wilsons, Miss Smithies of Ryley Cottage gave away a quantity of coals and Miss Mason of Harmony Hall gave out to the poor a quantity of meal.[38] In 1867 Mr. Wilson gave out fat beef, Mr. Forster of Bela Mills, 4 tons of coal and Mrs. Proudfoot "with her usual kind liberality to the poor, sent presents of money and provisions suitable to the season which all went to comfort many a household." In 1882 Dr. Carden gave out 3 tons of coal to the poor.

In good times, employers could be bountiful. On Good Friday, 1846 "Mr. Dean of Bela Mills gave a treat of currant cake, coffee, bread and cheese and ale and with many a flowing bowl of punch passed round, God Save the Queen was sung and many toasts drunk."[39]

Self-help was organised at a relatively earlier period in Milnthorpe. The Milnthorpe Friendly Society was founded in 1787 to protect its members against ill health, old age and to provide death benefits. According to Neddy Stones it was founded by James Raven, the head coachman at Dallam Tower and the insignia and banners were kept at the Cross Keys until c.1917. By the 1830's there were several similar societies covering Milnthorpe, including the St. Peter's Lodge of Oddfellows and the Ancient Order of Foresters No. 644. The "Friendlies" met at the Cross Keys, the Oddfellows at the Blue Bell (at Heversham) or the White Lion and the Foresters at the Bull's Head or King's Arms. Despite their meeting places, members were pledged to sobriety, although this was not always kept. The funeral of Oddfellow Mr. W.R. Harry in March 1843 was "more like an Irish wake than the funeral of a respectable man". The member's quickly got to fighting and "one unfortunate shoemaker had his nose bit off by a brother member and the sober fellow is suffering very much from his loss."[40] At the 56th Annual Dinner held at Mrs. Hudson's Cross Keys, ten toasts were drunk. The next year Major Hutton, who had chaired the dinner for 40 years, proposed "the Queen, Prince Albert, Prince of Wales, all the Royal Family, the Lord Lieutenant of the County of Westmorland, the Army, the Navy and George Wilson Esq. of Dallam Tower and many other singular toasts."[41]

The other societies were not to be out done in their patriotism by "the Friendlies." At the combined dinner of the Foresters and Oddfellows at the Blue Bell, Mr. J. Reed of Milnthorpe sang a patriotic song to the tune of the National Anthem.[42]

Rivalry between the societies was pointed and the annual balls were held on the same night in adjacent Inns. The Foresters' ball was preceeded by the Court of the Youthful Queen, a pageant from which, no doubt, all of Milnthorpe's successive Rose Queens, May Queens and Carnival Queens have stemmed. 150 members attended the Court held at the Bull's Head on Wednesday 26th December 1855 the room being "decorated with banners, evergreens, horns and insignia appropriate to the order." "Jollifications began at 8 o'clock with a good old fashioned country dance which continued until 12 o'clock when upwards of 70 Foresters partook of the cup which cheers but does not inebriate together with a plentiful supply of eatables provided by our host and hostess Mr. and Mrs. Sawrey."[43] In 1858 "the evening being fine, brought a good many young people to town and 200 entered the ballroom," dancing going on until 4 a.m.[44] "The Friendly Society Ball at the Cross Keys in 1865 began with a tea party at 6 p.m. and went on until 6 a.m."

All the societies conducted Club walks which reached their apogee between 1860 and 1870. The processions formed at their home base pubs and led by a band, wended their way to Heversham or Beetham churches with a service at St. Thomas's Church or the Vicarage as well. The return journey was via all the principle residences including Ryley Field, Owlett Ash, Ackenthwaite House, the Vicarage, quite often Ashton House and Beetham House, and of course, Dallam Tower. The Oddfellows' Dinner in 1857 was spoilt by bad service but in 1858 a "sumptuous dinner was provided and Mr. Robinson not being a man to be caught napping twice there were plenty of waiters."[45] Sometimes the religious element was damned with faint praise as in 1874 when the Rev. Raikes preached for a "considerable time" on 1 Cor. 10:31 "whether, therefore ye eat or drink, or whatever ye do, do all to the glory of God." He praised the Club's strict measures taken to keep out bad characters and concluded by urging all to show the same zeal in obeying the laws of God." The fellows then trouped off to Ryley Field where Mr. Whittaker delivered a speech, explaining how the societies had saved the rate payers two million pounds per annum.[46]

For a few years in the 1870's the societies organised summer sports. 1,500 people attended an Oddfellow's Gala at Dallam Tower on Whit Monday 1875. Mr. Stones supplied refreshments at a nominal charge and there was a grandstand for the gentry and clergy. There were 12 races and in the sack race "considerable amusement was caused... as the men started from a sitting position R. Blair being unable to rise was found at the post when the race was over. Others came to grief on the course and J. Dawson, who appeared to have the race in his own hands, suddenly collapsed but dextrously turned a summersault, alighted on his feet, and came in winner amidst deafening applause... lovers of the terpsichorean art had a quadrille band to which music its youthful parties continued to move until the shades of evening foretold the time of departure."[47] These sports ceased after 1880 when the meetings held in Kiln Croft were deemed to be a failure as only (sic) 300-600 people turned up owing to the superior attraction of an "excursion to Bowness." By 1881 the Whitsuntide processions were nearly a thing of the past. Only 8 men turned up for the Mechanics' Institute Walk which set out from the Coach and Horses and the Rev. Raikes had to shorten his address on the theme "Bear each others burdens."[48]

Funds and payments were small. In 1858 the old society was stated to be in a flourishing state with a balance of £25 6s 1d besides paying for a new flag during the year. Friendly Society subscriptions included Child, 1-10 years of age admitted for 2½d per week, 10-14 years 1d per week and 14+, 1½d per week. After the age of 10 children, if members for 12 months, would be recognised as "funeral men" and be entitled to £3 death grants. Sickness benefit would be 2s 6d per week for those over 10 for 26 weeks, 1s 9d for next 26 weeks, 1s per week thereafter on a payment of 1d per week.[50] In 1881 it was announced that Milnthorpe Friendly Society No. 94 established on 22nd May 1787 had a balance of £739 3s 9d. Times were changing, however, and in November 1882 it was reported that "last Saturday week there disappeared from the list of Friendly Societies one of the oldest probably in this part of the country; the Milnthorpe Friendly and Sick Club was 95 years old."

The Oddfellows and the Foresters survived longer but their membership declined after the introduction of National Insurance in 1911. Meetings ceased about the time of the First World War but in the 1930's and into the late 1940's the Tenacity Lodge of Oddfellows held half yearly meetings at the Coach and Horses

The non-conformist temperance movement also embraced general village life. In the 1870's the Star of Hope Lodge of the Independent Order of Good Templars was set up. With a penny a week subscription and seasonal celebrations it followed the pattern of the Friendly Societies – except that alcohol was never served. At a Good Templars' Tea held in the chapel in 1874 members were urged to check our national vice and Junior Templars wearing scarlet and white badges regaled the company with "Come friends and brothers all unite" and "Merry, Merry little spring."[51] The summer picnic on Haverbrack was a little too merry for after the Templars had had tea provided by Mr. Tongue he began "to sell cigars and cigarettes." An outraged reporter retorted "How this would harmonise with the feelings of those who condemn the weed . . . we do not know." The Templars were encouraged by the Forsters of Bela Mills and in 1880 the Rev. Pickersgill presented a work box to Miss Sarah Armstrong, "the gift of Miss Forster, late of Bela Mills, for best attendance at the juvenile Templars." At the same time £3 was donated to the Sir Rowland Hill Memorial. A Blue Ribbon Club was also formed and in 1883 95 members wearing their sashes of sobriety held an open meeting at the Market Cross. The Templars' Movement ground to a halt at the turn of the century but as late as 1950 it was reported that Harold Fawcett, "who never drank anything stronger than Communion wine," had chaired a meeting of the Temperance Union.

In addition to temperance the Forsters tried to improve the minds of the working classes. A Young Men's Improvement Society was established in 1849 with "hopes of getting a library but there is only a news room as yet"[53] – but the young men of Milnthorpe having more traditional pastimes resisted improvement and the Society came to nothing. Mr. Forster then set about getting a reading room but tactlessly invited the Vicar of Heversham, the Ven. Evans, to contribute to the funds before asking the Rev. Padwick of Milnthorpe.[54] Meanwhile, Mr. Bott of Beetham Mill proposed opening a lecture room. Forster, resenting his business rival getting in on his charitable act, instigated a letter writing campaign to the *Westmorland Gazette*. One letter signed by W. Berry and others (none of whom were working men in the sense of labourers) stated that "for more babbling stump oratory than he (Mr. Bott) advances it would be scarcely possible to conceive... and perhaps Mr. Bott thinks the working men of Milnthorpe are not fit for a reading room." Bott replied to this, with a dig at Forster's tee total habits, "he that touches filth let him be defiled and that only under the influence of unhealthy stimulant could they have written as they did." The result was that no purpose built reading room was provided for 20 years.

A Mechanics' Institute with a savings bank was established in November 1861 and in 1862 put on a reading from Dicken's Christmas Carol by T. Wilson Esq. They probably met at the Independent Chapel for it was not until 1881 that a separate Institute and Reading Rooms were opened.

These were provided as a memorial to Dr. John Kitching, who had died in 1879 aged 83. At the same time a Cottage Hospital was built on the hill above Owlett Ash, which was once part of Milnthorpe Green. The precise form of the benefactions are confused, but it seems that Dr. Kitching's sister, Mrs. Elizabeth Bindloss, widow of Alderman Thomson Bindloss of Kendal, built the rooms. His daughter Sarah, who was married to Alderman William Bindloss, (nephew of Thomson Bindloss) built the hospital. The foundation stone of the Rooms was laid on 3rd September 1880 on a[55] "site of a row of houses... in the very heart of the town" in Beetham Road. Eli Cox was the architect of the building described as the "Gothic style freely treated. It cost £2,000. Certainly the arched pillared doorway with head stops is Gothic and the mansard roof has a touch of sixteenth century France about it – Norman Nicholson singled the Institute out for praise in his *Cumberland and Westmorland* of 1949 with "its dormer windows, pointed gables all of limestone, khaki freestone with delightful drainpipes twisted spirally like sticks of barley sugar."

Inside, the accommodation was elaborate. After entering through linenfold doors into the "spacious entrance hall" on either side respectively, was a coffee room, and a reading room. Upstairs was a library above, in the roof were rooms for "chess and bagatelle." No survey seems to have been taken as to the demand for this latter facility. All the rooms had magnificent plaster cornices and centre pieces by Bonehill and Co. of Manchester, carved dados by A.W. Simpson of Kendal; paving was by S. Compton and walling by R. Troughton.[56]

The foundation stone of the Cottage Hospital was laid on 19th May 1880. Inevitably the Rev. Raikes gave an address and expressed the thanks of "the people of Milnthorpe and especially the poor" to Mrs. Bindloss for her generosity. Eli Cox was again the architect who used what was called a "mixed, medieval, early, modern style." Mixed it certainly was with hummocky Coniston slate roofs, machine cut Prudham sandstone trimming including the Coat of Arms of the Kitching and Bindloss families and rock faced limestone walls. There was to be an out-patient's room with bath and lavatories, a men's and women's ward, surgery, kitchen and mortuary. A verandah facing straight over the estuary, the Lakeland fells and the Gulf Stream – for above all, alone on the hill, the hospital would be well ventilated. At the gate went a two storey lodge for the caretaker. The walling was by J. Dixon, joinery by S. Compton, slating by H. Goulding, plastering by Mr. Chippendale of Grange. A memorial plaque stated "this hospital was erected by Mrs. William Bindloss in remembrance of her dear papa the late John Kitching, surgeon, formerly of 61 South Audley St, Grosvenor Square, London. He returned to Milnthorpe his native place in 1830 where he practised for 30 years where he died May 26 1879 aged 83 years."

Both the Memorial Reading Rooms and the Hospital were opened on 20th October 1881 when the "quiet little town was a scene of great rejoicing – being – literally draped in flags and bunting." A carriage procession conveying Alderman and Mrs. Bindloss, Mayor and Mayoress of Kendal, with other Aldermen in their robes, mace bearers and all their officials left Kendal Town Hall at 2 p.m. and arrived at 3 p.m. After luncheon at Flowerden "recently erected by Mr. and Mrs. Bindloss" in Main Street, the company then went on to the hospital over whose gate banners proclaimed "Long live the founder, God helps the afflicted." After a prayerful ceremony the processions went down the hill for the opening of the Memorial Reading Rooms. A "splendid banquet" for 100 guests was spread on a table handsomely set with flowers and after further speeches the toast to Alderman and Mrs. Bindloss, and Mrs. Thomson (Elizabeth) Bindloss were "made with musical honours." On the next day, Thursday, the Bindlosses gave a tea for the work people and on Friday a tea for all the village children.

While Mrs. Sarah Bindloss was at the children's party her Aunt met with a fatal accident at Flowerden. She had been born in the older house on the site. The old lady, who was 78, apparently pushed open a tight fitting door to the barrel vault of the cellar which did not have stairs. Although the cook, Mary Ann Jones, caught hold of her she fell six feet, broke her ankle badly and died of the shock within three days. The flags in Kendal, put up for Milnthorpe's grandest opening ceremony were then lowered to half mast.

Even sadder than the inaugural tragedy was the fact that neither the Reading Rooms nor the Hospital successfully accomplished their objectives. The fault lay partly with the lady founders who wished to approve all hospital patients admitted and censored the reading matter in the Library. A new management committee for the rooms was set up in 1883 "to do their best in selecting a good supply of literature and daily and weekly newspapers etc. Hitherto this has not been the case. If they are a failure they will add nothing to the credit of Milnthorpe."[57] The scheme failed. A new committee formed by the Wilsons of Dallam and Canon Gilbert did better but it never seems to have occurred to them that if they gave freedom of management to its users the institute might have been a success. A billiard room was opened and the unused bagatelle and chess sets thrown out. Thereafter, "going up 'stute" to the billiard room in the roof has been a pseudonym for a mis-spent Milnthorpe youth. The opening of the Public Rooms in 1885 reduced demand for functions and by 1893 even the billiard room was closed.

The use of the lecture room as a Magistrates Court brought a regular income eventually and "up t'leaden steps," named after the covering on the Institute stairs, meant in Milnthorpe, getting into trouble. The Bindloss family seemed to have retained control for the next 40 years. Although they had "given the rooms" to Milnthorpe their trustees apparently had to be bought out. A plaque in the lower room reads "this tablet commemorates the generosity of Major Argles and T.D. Eversley who gave £500 towards the purchase of this Institute for the people of Milnthorpe, May 1921." In 1934 it was resolved that the name be no longer Kitching Memorial Institute but to be simply "the Milnthorpe Institute."[58] The Reading Room continued to operate until c.1960. Norman Nicholson related in c.1949 how "a notice tells you the use of the room is free to residents but that visitors are requested to place one penny in the box provided. You drop your penny as loudly as possible when you hear someone coming, and you hope that they will be impressed with your honesty."[59]

In the 1960's the Institute was again in the doldrums; better education, more money and television had removed the need for a reading room; the County Library got a van and so no longer needed the old library room and the Magistrates removed themselves to Kendal. Eventually, yet another re-organisation led to the granting of Club licences and the Institute became a venue mainly for beer and billiards – the working men of Milnthorpe having resisted as firmly as their forefathers any further attempts made for their "improvement."

The hospital had an even shorter life. A Miss Townshend had been appointed Matron in 1881 but she did not last long and other attendants came and went. Most people preferred to be ill at home, especially as a maintenance charge was made at the hospital. The aged poor, the long term sick and unmarried mothers, in anycase, received free care at the Workhouse. By 1893 the *Westmorland Gazette* commenting on the Kitching/Bindloss bequests stated "first and foremost there is one of the neatest and prettiest little country hospitals that ever was erected. It looks very pretty on a little hill behind Milnthorpe but part of it is to let."[60] The reason for this the *Gazette* concluded was that "conditions for entry were too harsh." Shortly afterwards the hospital was converted into the Bindloss Cottage Homes. It was rather a makeshift conversion, many of the rooms being tiny and awkward yet retaining the high, sick ward ceilings.

From the start anxiety was expressed in Milnthorpe about nomination rights to the Homes. In 1898 the Parish Council was told Milnthorpe had no priority.[61] According to a press report in 1931 the candidates for the homes at that date, had to be qualified by birth or 30 years' residence in Kendal, Milnthorpe, Heversham or Beetham, to be of at least 50 years of age and be of good character.[62] In response to further enquiries, prompted by unconfirmed criticism that no Milnthorpe person was a resident, Milnthorpe Parish Council was told in 1986 that the trust had been changed in 1966 so that any resident of two years' standing of Milnthorpe, Heversham, Beetham or Kendal who was over 50 years of age could be considered. Strangely the 1966 trust did not, it appears, include the Lodge House.

The Tattersall Almshouses, built and endowed by William Tattersall the brewer from St. Anthony's House in 1884, were more successful. They were purpose built and moreover their management has not aroused controversy. Called "elaborate structures" by Curwen[63] they cost £10,000 and were designed by Bintley. Perhaps the only thing wrong for old peoples' dwellings was that the site was out of the village and almost at the top of the hill. Even so, they enjoyed "an extensive view of the landscape embracing a richly diversified prospect looking across the town to the fair domain of Dallam Tower and Haverbrack Common." Rather like Cox's Reading Room and Hospital, the architectural style was imprecise being called "an adapted, early, middle, pointed style of Gothic conventionally treated." They were built in an 'L' shape with three single storey houses facing south, two facing east and a corner one with an upper storey which had delightful carved features. All rooms had mottled pine dados by Simpson, the windows had upper panes of stained glass by Burrow of Sandside, and paving by Love of Harmsworth. Proctors of Heversham excavated the land

Tattersall Almshouses, c.1890.

and dug the well, Pattinsons of Kendal were responsible for the masonry. An attractive feature was the spacious glazed porches amounting almost to small conservatories. In the yard behind the buildings was a pump house with a stone cistern for hard and soft water and a privy block. The latter became redundant only in the 1950's when the pantries were converted into bathrooms.

Furniture was provided and included gas fittings and three sets of fire irons. Chairs, tables and a sofa were supplied in the parlour. The bedroom was fitted up with pin rails, and other conveniences, a closet, spring beds, dressing table and looking glass. In addition to the sumptuous building, Tattersall also laid aside £5,000 out of which each resident received 10s a week and a double allowance at Christmas. Not surprisingly election to the Almshouses was seen in the same light as later generations regarded a football pool's win. Residents had to be over 50 years of age, be resident of the old parishes of Heversham or Beetham and not to have been in receipt of Parochial relief for two years.

The foundation stone had been laid on 25th April, 1884 and the Almshouses were opened on 23rd April, 1885 – St. George's Day – "when the whole area was bathed in the glory of a perfect April day." After Mr. Tattersall had handed the keys to Canon Gilbert representing the trustees "thanks were expressed on behalf of the decayed farmers, labourers and traders. . . in the hopes that others would follow the noble example of Mr. Tattersall. . . as those eligible for such homes will increase in numbers by reason of the

Detail of Tattersall Almshouses.

fierce competition and keen struggle for bread and water."[64] The
first resident chosen was Mrs. Isabella Atkinson, widow of the
parish clerk. She certainly came into the defined category as
"having once occupied a better position in life but such who have
been reduced through circumstances over which they had no
control." In fact, quite a proportion of residents always seemed to
have been farm workers (who had had tied cottages) or "living in"
domestic servants who had been "reduced" merely because their
accommodation was required by their employers, some of whom
were actually trustees of the Almshouses.

Almost all the residents were highly respectable. A possible
exception was one old dear who entertained a stream of Italian
prisoners of war in the 1940's, and not long afterwards bought one
of the village's first television sets. When reproached for what
appeared to be a flagrant breach of the good character rule she
replied that the "Eyeties could not do her any harm and she might
do them some good."

A more conventional lady was Mrs. Clapham, the fictional
charwoman heroine of Constance Holme's *The Trumpet in the
Dust*, set at the "Hermitage Hill" Almshouses that looked "towards
the Marsh and the park and the dim blueness of the bay." With a
mixture of Mills and Boon bathos and practical domestic detail
Constance Holme touched on the pride and bewilderment felt by a
new inmate as she took up residence.

"At last she was in the temple to which she had climbed so
long... she went first into the kitchen (where)... she could
know definitely whether the smell of the house-soul was all
right... she could hardly contain her delight at the sight of the
closed range, the handy pot-rails and cupboards, the stout
dresser and strong chairs. She laid an awed touch upon spoon

and forks, on dishes and plates, and stood back to gaze through excited tears at the pans, shelf-high on the coloured wall. It seemed to her as she passed enraptured from find to find, that she would never want anything more as long as she lived. In the thrill of the moment it seemed to her like a September-time Santa Claus."[65]

If the Almshouses represent the best of the contemporary charity, the Milnthorpe Mutual Co-operative Society established in 1862, represented the supreme nineteenth century virtue of self-help. At the first meeting the Chairman, Mr. F. Wilson, announced that membership fees would be 1s. per family but "those who could not afford this sum could pay 1d."[66] Under the management of J. Nicholson the society soon paid a dividend of 1s. per £2 capital. In 1865 Mr. T. Cornthwait "very minutely laid down" financial details: in three years and 9 months the value of goods sold was £4,566 2s 6d, interest on capital borrowed £25 7s 10½d, dividends paid out £177 0s 3d, the highest "divi" being £16 3s 9½d at 1s 3d in the pound."[67]

Despite a good start the society seems to have lapsed in the 1880's only reviving in 1896 when a store was opened in the cottage just below Park Terrace. From 1899-1906 the stores were at the corner of Main Street and Church Street before moving to new premises in Park Road, adorned with imitation Westmorland round chimneys and plate glass windows. Grocery was sold downstairs and clothes and haberdashery upstairs and there was a Manager's house. Later the stores took over Clark's butcher's shop next door. From the 1920's to 1960, Henry Atkinson, a local man was manager. He was followed by George Ellwood who stayed until 1982 when the branch closed, a victim of changing retail practice.

Emigration, a favourite nineteenth century social policy of combining relief of domestic poverty with imperial expansion, found little support in Milnthorpe. One early emigrant was James Booth who, influenced by Geoffrey Bentham at the National School, joined the Church Missionary Society and emigrated to Wanganui in New Zealand in 1852. Here he became a local magistrate and militia leader. Once he was captured by warlike Maoris but managed to escape after three days.

Just before the First World War a number of local farm workers sought a better future abroad. In 1911 the *Westmorland Gazette* reported that 50 people had emigrated from the Milnthorpe area in the previous five years, compared to 60 or 70 from Windermere and 25 from Endmoor. "Strange to say the U.S.A. is behind as an attraction" and "very few go to Australia or South Africa as the journey is too dear." The most popular venues were Brandon in Manitoba and Saskatchewan in Canada, which had attracted 25 to 30 local people, mostly in their early twenties.

Until the nineteenth century places like Milnthorpe did not warrant their own doctor and none are included in professions entered in early parish registers. The border line between barbers, apothecaries, surgeons and physicians and other trades and professions was blurred until c.1880. The Audland family of blacksmiths from Ackenthwaite also acted as farriers and veterinary surgeons and this inherited experience might have contributed to some of their descendants becoming doctors.[69]

At the turn of the eighteenth century Richard and James Hardy were doctors in Milnthorpe. By 1829 they had been replaced by William Jackson and Isaac Mossop.[70] The following year Dr. John Kitching established himself at Flowerden. Other mid-Victorian doctors were William Harrison of Kidside and Robert Hutton of Ivy House. Dr. Hutton's practice was joined and eventually taken over by Dr. Octavian Newcombe Royle [71] who practised until 1883 when, on retirement, he was presented with a purse containing £62 10s – "as recognition of his 25 years of medical work in the town." He left his practice to his son-in-law, John Condell Carden who removed from Ivy House to Harmony Hall in 1885.

Dr. Carden was at the centre of a controversy that same year, following the death of 8 months' old Llewellyn Hartree, son of the landlord of the Shovel Tavern. Hartree claimed that the child had "refused the breast for two days and when a little port wine, warm water and milk was dropped on the lips it had not the strength to swallow." Dr. Carden had declined to attend "unless I sent him an account of £4 4s." Dr Evinson did "not refuse to come but said he could not interfere with Dr. Carden's patient." The result was that the child was only seen by Alice Wilkinson, the midwife. After a long hearing the Coroner accepted Dr. Carden's opinion that "I was sent for at the last moment and was informed that I could do no good but was only wanted to pass my opinion. . . and to give a death certificate when required." A day or two later the inconsolable mother, Elizabeth Hartree, committed suicide.[73]

Dr. Carden continued until 1898 when he sold the Harmony Hill practice to Dr. William Purves who stayed until about 1914, being assisted in later years by Dr. Joseph Black whose surgery was at Ivy House. Later Dr. Malcolm McLeod took over, practising first at Laburnum House and then, following his marriage to Mrs. Ethel Davy at Flowerden, where he died in 1934. His catch phrase to patients was "I will not leave you until I have found you better."

In the 1870's and 80's Dr. Evison had a practice at Thorpe House which was taken over by Dr. Irving in 1884 and then in c.1890 by Dr. George Henry Seagrave who, after his marriage to a Miss Arnold of Arnbarrow, Sandside, moved to Stoneleigh in 1894.[74] Dr. and Mrs. Seagrave played a prominent part in the social life of Milnthorpe while Dr. Seagrave won a reputation for conducting operations at home – and also for extracting teeth! On his retirement in 1906 he gave up the practice to his son-in-law William Anderson Fuller.

On Dr. Fuller's death in 1927, John R. Caldwell took over and created a group practice of all the local doctors. With Dr. James Kenneth Cameron (until 1934) and then with help of various assistants including Dr. Patrick S. Byrne and Dr. A. Kenneth Bingham, Dr. Caldwell made this Milnthorpe practice one of the most up-to-date in the north of England. The surgery at Stoneleigh Cottage was equipped with a laboratory, facilities for minor operations and an X-Ray unit. Dr. Byrne became senior partner in 1945, on Dr. Caldwell's retirement, and partly helped by the introduction of the National Health Service in 1948, the practice expanded still further with surgeries at Endmoor, Levens, Burton and Carnforth, as well as having three consulting rooms at Milnthorpe. Though the newly available anti-biotics almost cleared the district overnight of its biggest medical scourge, tuberculosis, and so eased the burden, this was still the period when regular home visits were expected. On occasions, driving always at great speed, Patrick Byrne would visit in one day patients as far afield as Heysham to the south and Newby Bridge to the north. This was in addition to two or three surgeries, late "Morphia visits" for cancer sufferers and remaining on call for nights on end for confinements and emergencies, including innumerable road accidents.

For many years Patrick Byrne was assisted by his wife, Dr. Kathleen M. Pearson, then by Dr. Phillip N. Holmes from 1945-57, by Dr. Neil Hargreaves (1953) and Dr. Harry Proctor (1957). Dr. Hargreaves became senior partner and Dr. Michael Warren came as an assistant when Patrick Byrne moved to a post at Manchester University, where he became the country's first professor of General Practice. Before his death in 1980 he had been President of the Royal College of General Practitioners and had received numerous awards including the O.B.E. and C.B.E.

A second Milnthorpe practice was founded by Dr. Edward Hopkinson in the 1940's and on his precipitous removal, following the "Atomic Egg" scandal in 1954, it was taken over by Dr. Nick Carter who with Dr. Elizabeth Perham soon had a flourishing practice rivalling the older establishment at Stoneleigh Cottage. On Dr. Carter's retirement in 1987 he was succeeded by Dr. Simon Wilson: the first Milnthorpe-born doctor to practise in the village since John Kitching 130 years earlier.

Until the introduction of the NHS most health care was provided by voluntary effort. After the failure of the Cottage Hospital the local practitioners supplemented the staff of the County Hospital, and local ladies, including all the doctors' wives, ran the Linen League and there were regularly "efforts" to raise funds. In 1900

John Holme and Dr. Seagrave formed a committee to support a sanatorium for Westmorland Consumptives at Meathop.[77] Milnthorpe provided a bed there over which the local committee had nomination rights "but in the event of the bed subscribed being vacant and there being no patient available, the committee have the power to lend the use of their bed to another district." Isolated T.B. Huts were also provided locally to enable patients to escape the cramped, damp and ill-ventilated cottages of the lower and central parts of the village. Two such huts were still to be seen at Ackenthwaite in the 1940's.

Little help was given in the early part of the century to the physically handicapped. In 1922 a paralysed 18 year old, Lily Fell of Bela Cottages, was burnt to death as she lay in her invalid carriage when a spark flew out of the fire. Her mother had just gone out for a few minutes to feed the ducks. It was winter and the deceased was said to be wearing "a flannelette petticoat, a wool vest, a flannel petticoat, a print dress, a jersey and a coat."[78]

A District Nursing Association was formed by a Ladies' Committee in 1896 and Nurse Penrose of Gloucester appointed. According to Rule (1) she had to give her time, strength and trained skill to promote the recovery from illness and to relieve suffering. The sick poor were to be attended "gratuitously" but the "well to do" had to contribute according to means.

On her bone-shaker bicycle in 1899 the District Nurse made 3,131 visits including 218 to Sandside and 360 to Storth. Random figures for the next 20 years include 2,440 visits in 1901, 2,412 in 1905, 2,165 in 1914, 2,142 in 1917 and 2,941 in 1919.[79] In 1919 the nurse was also required to make returns on the number of patients suffering from tuberculosis and venereal disease. There were no reported V.D. cases but many T.B. patients – 78 visits to T.B. patients in 1927 and 72 in 1930, for example.[80] In 1929 a local committee consisting of Mrs. Duncan of Heversham, Mr. Nanson, Beetham, Mr. Dobson, Slackhead, Mr. Houghton, Sandside and Mr. R.O. Hodgson and Rev. Gamble of Milnthorpe raised money to provide the District nurse with a car. For the presentation ceremony the car was taken into the Public Rooms and the Rev. Gamble spoke of her no longer being a wet nurse and of how her good fortune tempted him to break the 10th Commandment.[81] Increased mobility enabled 4,619 visits to be made in 1935.

Most nurses were young and of marriagable age and did not stay long, but several were remembered. Nurse Helen Bird served the village for several years before the First World War, just before she left for service in Serbia she was given a bicycle with pneumatic tyres. Her successors were Nurse Nellie Moore and Nurse Roskeld to whose salary the County Council contributed £12 p.a. Nurse Mary Forrester came to Milnthorpe in the 1920's. When she left to be married she was presented with a silver tea service but shortly returned as Mrs. Sharp to resume her duties for several more years. Later she retired to the village and became a member of the Parish Council. By far the longest and most notable District Nurse was "Sister" (never "Nurse") Winifred Cummings, who bountifully bossed over village bedsides from 1944 to 1967, by which time her functions were no longer controlled by "lady superintendents" but by the National Health Service.

11

The Poor Law and Milnthorpe Workhouse

Jesus said "the poor ye have with ye always."[1] Their care has always been a basic Christian duty. Until the sixteenth century relief of poverty was controlled by the Church but with the reduction in ecclesiastical power at the Reformation there was a corresponding increase in the social role of the State. There were Pauper enactments in the reigns of Henry VIII and Edward VI and these, with later regulations, were combined in the "great" Elizabethan Poor Law of 1601.[2] By this act the care of the poor was placed in the hands of the local authorities which had to impose a Poor Rate on all holders of property.

In Heversham Parish this was assessed by the Church Wardens, levied at the New Year or Easter Vestry meetings and collected along with the Church Rate or cess, by the Council of Twenty Four Marksmen[3] or "sidesmens." The 1601[4] Act provided for various categories of pauper. Vagabonds could be whipped or have the gristle of the right ear bored through by the common hangman. Those who were deserving – "the poor in very deed" – were acknowledged to have a claim on public benevolence. An important Settlement Act of 1662 tried to discourage poor people moving from one parish to another by requiring them to obtain movement certificates from the magistrates. If they became a charge on the rates in their new parish they could be sent, or whipped, back to their native parish.

From Elizabethan times poorhouses could be set up where the able-bodied might be put to work and paid "according to the desert of their work." The poorhouse also served as a primitive infirmary, orphanage and home for the destitute and the aged.[6] The parish register for 1736 shows the death of Mary Mills in the workhouse at

Milnthorpe and is the first reference to a local house.[7] Occasional later registrations include the death of John Shaw, formerly a dragoon, in the workhouse at Sedgwick – implying that even the smaller townships in Heversham Parish had such places.[8]

Where the first Milnthorpe workhouse was situated is not recorded. In the eighteenth century it was on Windy Hill in the property which later became the Malt Shovel Tavern (now a private house, "Lea Bank"). The high garden wall of Victoria House behind "Lea Bank" was probably that of the workhouse yard.[9]

Many applications for relief and maintenance under the Poor Law and Bastardy Orders have, however, survived. For example, in 1730 Mary Johnson applied for relief "having had a bastard of Thomas Wright of Milnthorpe, yeoman, who has left the country."[11] In 1743/4 a warrant was issued against William Gerkin of Milnthorpe, husbandman, for "having begotten a bastard on the body of Elizabeth Preston." He was arrested by the Constable of Milnthorpe, Benjamin Barker, but was rescued from arrest by force – for which he was fined 2s 6d.

As so often in later times maintenance payments were low even on the basis of contemporary income. Christopher Bateman, a weaver of Milnthorpe, the alleged father of a female bastard child born to Margaret Ewen, singlewoman, had in 1744 to pay 20s. immediately and 8d. weekly. Stephen Barker who "had a male bastard child of Isobel Fisher" had to pay the same sum. Both Christopher and Stephen were put in custody until they could find sureties. A generation later, in 1779, James Tolly of Beetham was forced to pay £2.18s for having neglected to maintain a bastard child of Hannah Woodburn of Milnthorpe.

Many of those forced to be subject to the Poor Law were respectable and in April 1739 Richard James, yeoman, asked for help as he was "very infirm and unable to support himself and a family"[12] His, and similar pleas were rejected. Even so, the old Poor Law seems to have been generally, if grudgingly, accepted by recipients and rate payers alike until the turn of the eighteenth century.

Between 1811 and 1821 the population of Britain rose from 14.5 million to 18.05 million, the steepest rise in our history.[13] Inevitably there was a similar increase in infirm, destitute and unemployed people which led to a general concern about poverty.

In 1800 the main problem appeared to be the able-bodied poor. Only a few were "incorrigible idlers" or "sturdy rogues." Many were the victims of war, trade depression and inflation, over which they could have little control. Others suffered because of industrial change which could put whole occupation groups out of work. Later in the century this group included the Kendal hand-loom weavers and the textile workers of Milnthorpe's water mills, ruined by steam powered industry on the coalfields to the south. The enclosure of the remaining commons involving the loss of pasturage and fuel rights had made it harder for the poorer cottagers to eke out an independent, if precarious, existence. Whatever the cause it was clear that the old haphazard system of the Poor Law aided by private Charity needed reform. Out-door relief for paupers was becoming expensive and increasingly was believed to encourage pauperism. As elsewhere, Poor Law Guardians in South Westmorland believed the solution was the Workhouse.

A new type of workhouse was envisaged, to fill the functions of the old Poor House in caring for the helpless but also be a genuine house of industry for the able bodied. As larger units were more efficient, rural and scantily populated parishes combined in Poor Law Unions to provide a Union Workhouse.[16] With a large workhouse at Kendal (and smaller ones at Grayrigg and Kirkby Lonsdale) Milnthorpe, the largest and most central village, was an obvious place for a Workhouse serving the remaining part of South Westmorland and neighbouring North Lancashire parishes.[17]

The site chosen was half a mile east of the village on the Kirkby Lonsdale road, opposite Ackenthwaite Smithy. It had been part of the Ackenthwaite Green Common and was known as Ackenthwaite Scroggs. On 2 June 1801, a meeting of land owners had decided to enclose "that parcel of ground of three acres at or near Kirk Yeat lately set out and allotted by the Homage juries, by and with the consent of the Lords of the Manor (from the commons and waste lands thereof) to William Bindloss, John Burrow and Thomas Huddleston for the use and benefit of the poor. . ."[18]

If the local poor had suffered as a result of enclosure it was ironical that this former common, which had been enclosed for their benefit, should provide the site for their incarceration! Perhaps this justifies the rhyme:

The law locks up the man or woman,
who steals the goose from off the common,
But lets the greater villain loose,
who steals the common from the goose.[19]

Certainly "the lord" did not suffer by the change, for Manorial dues still had to be paid to Levens Hall. Sometimes the Guardians forgot and in 1859 they paid £4 "to the Hon. Mary Howard being 7 years back Lord's Rent."[20]

Tenders for the new building (designed by Francis Webster) were let on 18 February 1815,[21] and it must have been almost ready by the following September when the Guardians advertised for a governor who would be responsible for 100 inmates. It cost £4,990[22] and was constructed of limestone whose pink hue suggests that it came from the parish quarry on Heversham Head, two miles away. Originally, all the external walls were rendered: a sound fashion because 150 years later during conversion into private housing, the original pebble dash and mortar were stripped off exposing the porous limestone to the weather and the walls were said to run like a riddle. But much of the accommodation must always have been damp as the entire lower floor was almost all below ground level, while the site was unsheltered by trees or nearby hills.

The main block of the Workhouse was 'H' shaped in plan, with a principal southern facade composed of three rows of four sash windows on either side of a canted, or bay, central feature of three windows. Connecting the north and south wings was an attractive western facing colonnade. There were separate yards for each sex; the men in the south, the women in the north, along with the privies, piggeries and laundry. Round the entire site ran a ten foot high wall. The sole entrance faced west, with a vagrant ward to the north and porter's lodge to the south. In between, the tall dark doors were studded and furnished with heavy hinges and bolts. There was a pauper-thin snickett let into the door. Inside, all except the dining room windows were barred. The workhouse was by far the largest building in the neighbourhood. Large and menacing, it is no wonder that workhouses such as this earned the gruesome title of Bastille.

The Poor Law Union was not formally established until after the Workhouse was opened. It was in July 1816 that the representatives of the townships of Heversham with Milnthorpe, Levens, Hincaster, Beetham, Burton and Holme, Dalton and Yealand Redmayne agreed to unite for the better maintaining and (significantly) employing of the Poor. Later they were joined by Meathop and Ulpha, Witherslack, Sedgwick, Natland, New Hutton, Scalthwaiterigg, Stainton and Underbarrow.[23] Each parish agreed to pay for the building according to the average of their poor rate during the preceeding three years. In July 1836 after the Poor Law Amendment Act was passed, the Milnthorpe Incorporation joined the Kendal Union made up of 58 townships. The Guardians of this Union were responsible for Milnthorpe Workhouse and for the poor of the district until 1929.

On 30th August 1836 the new guardians visited the Workhouse and found "a modern building in an elevated situation capable of accommodating 40 persons on a site of about 3 acres. The building is well constructed for classification by night and day and in this respect little alteration would be necessary as the working rooms are commodious in which the sexes may be kept apart. The lodging rooms mostly for two beds were clean and airey (sic.)"[24] Accordingly they agreed to keep the building on a 21 year lease from the Milnthorpe Union. Despite periodic attempts to build a new

The Workhouse, mid-nineteenth century.
The Painting is traditionally ascribed to a Pauper Inmate.

combined workhouse for Kendal and Milnthorpe it was kept until the end of the Poor Law.

There are very few records concerning the first twenty years or so. In December 1817 the office of superintendent was vacant and also in March 1826, following the death of John Dodgson, when the Guardians of the Milnthorpe Corporated Workhouse advertised for a new Governor at £40 per annum.[25] The successful candidate was John Rawes whose wife was appointed Matron in 1831. By this time it was clear that far from being a house of industry Milnthorpe workhouse catered mainly for the old and helpless. The *Westmorland Gazette* reported on the 5 January 1828 "there are at present in the Workhouse at Milnthorpe 67 inmates, 14 men whose united ages amount to 944, 3 of respective ages 44, 72 and 75 are engaged in weaving. One of 78 in occasional work, one of 30 an Idiot and Blind and the remainder are all infirm and unable to do anything. 13 women whose united ages amount to 958 years, 9 of whom are either confined to their rooms or unable to work; other women who are blind, one deaf, one dumb and one an idiot, 12 boys under 13 years of age, 7 under 10, 3 under 4, 7 girls, the oldest 9, youngest 2 months. The average cost of maintenance is only 2s.6d. per week. On Sunday an extra dinner and food on Christmas Day included."[26]

It was John Rawes who compiled two surviving registers of inmates. The first is dated 4 March 1829. There were only 28 inmates "viz. men 6, women 18, boys 4, girls 4," John Marshall (76) and Robert Atkinson were both "very infirm," Mary Winder (75), Betty Wells (74), Nancy Wallace (74), Jane Newby (65), all "infirm," Isobella Morris (75), Thomas Mansergh (71) "a very bad subject," Thomas Batman (69) and Sarah Gibson (63) both "lame and infirm," Agness Nicholson (66) lame, Ann Pool (90) and Hannah Caton (76) both "confined to her Bed the last 2 years," Agness Prickett (46), "not Quite Right," Jane Atkinson (42), "sick," Peter Burnley (31) Idiot and Blind, Jane Smith (30) Blind, Mary Rocliff (43) "3rd Illigitimate Child." Sarah Cornthwaite (17) "Pregnint (sic) and Not Quite Right." The only inmates not afflicted in anyway were Thomas Bellman (76), Ann Nixon (73) and five children: Hannah Waitson (10), William Langhorn (13), Robert Richardson (12), Janet Atkinson (10) and Thomas Rocliff (2½). The only able bodied pauper was 13 year old William Langhorn who was engaged on the "Roop Walk." Rawes did not record the hand mill for grinding corn apparently used in the house in 1829.[27]

On the second register, dated 6 April 1831, there were "15 men, 16 women, 11 boys and Girels(sic) 1, amounting to 43 inmates." From the previous register there remained Robert Atkinson, Thomas Batman, Thomas Bellman, Peter Burnly, Jane Smith, Jane Newby, Ann Nixon, Agnes Nicholson, Mary Rocliffe ("3 child") Ann Batty and Agnes Prickett now "Insane at Times" and William Langhorn – no longer on "the roop walk" but just "a very Bad Boy."

Of the newer inmates William Atkinson at 86, Ann Wallace (89), Elizabeth Hodshon (80) were the oldest; William Wearing (71), Thomas Taylor (68), John Redhead (74), Richard Birkett (70) were all "very lame," Robert Park (49), Robert Brown (40) were "sick," Thomas Townson (51) had "a Bad Arm," Elizabeth Wilson (79) "infirm and Very Dirty," Jane Barns (26) "Not Quite Right," John Parker (51) was afflicted with "a Large Family," Mary White (70) "since died" and Hannah Wilson (20) who was "a very bad young woman" while Hannah Bainbridge (31) was "pregnint third time." The only fit inmates were William Smith (60), Samuel Stephenson (58), Mary Parker (44) and Margaret Smith (65). The children came mainly in three families: the Moores – William (10), James (8), Thomas (6); the Parks – John (11), James (8), Richard (5), Robert (3), Mary (2), the Newhouses – Thomas (12) and John (7).

There is also a note concerning the gory result of Hannah Bainbridge's third pregnancy – a girl named after her mother – "Hannah Bainbridge Died 26 April aged 31 hours. Born Sunday the 24 April 1831 and the Whole of the Intistines of this strange Child was outside of the Body and had Been so from its first formation as Reported by the Surgions who examined it – Mr Parsons and Mr Armistead."

The cost of maintenance was "average per head for provisions only 2s. 3½d. with clothing and Incidentals Included 4/2½d." The total costs for 1828-29 were provisions £365 19s.11d., Clothing £78 1s.5d., Incidentals £234, Funerals and Christenings £15 14s. 2½d. Nothing was spent on "Extra Diet" but the cost of Fish and Herrings is recorded as £2 9s. 8½d.[28]

An indication as to what the pauper's diet might have been is given in a letter of 31 Dec, 1828 from R.K. Kelham of Bleasby Hall, Nottinghamshire to his uncle William Atkinson of Burton House, one of the overseers of the Milnthorpe Union. "Breakfast every Morning Milk and Bread or Gruel and Bread, Supper every evening Milk bread or Gruel, bread or Bread and Cheese. Dinner on Sunday and Thursday Beef and potatoes, on Wednesday rice milk, on Saturday pudding or Dumplings no firmented liqiors – the cost to be adults 2/6d, males 16 – 18 and females 1s. 10½d."[29]

Typical accounts for this period included payments to Robert Browne for 20 Loads of Potatoes at 10s per load; Richard Wallace 8 stones of Rice at 2/9 per stone and 4 lbs. Black pepper at 1s.4d. Wm. Faulkner 1 Load of Flour at £1 16s. per load; Thomas Whitehead, Milk at 3½d. per gallon and butter at 10½ lb.; Edward Wilson meat at 6s. 4d. per stone (1836) and John Hartley meat at 5s per stone (1838). Apart from scant morsels put in gruel the meat was mainly for officers. There were piggeries at the Workhouse but these seem to have been a lucrative side line for the master. Not until 1859 did the Board order that pigs fed in the Workhouse "shall be consumed by the paupers and those resident in the Workhouse."

Clothing accounts include "to Mr Mallison £34 2s. 8½d. for 29 Mens Sutes at 23/6½d each, 2 Boys Sutes at 4/5, 6 yrs old 14s.8d. Thomas Rigg £3 14s. for Stockings and Nancy Turner £1 11s 8d. for Bonnets and Hats" – this is the only early reference to women's clothes.

General items in the accounts include: George Whittaker for Table Knives, £4 5s.; George Tyson, Coal Boxes 18s. 10d.; George Whittaker, Brooms £3 18s.; Straw at 10s. Richard Ratcliff was paid 19s. 6d. a year for shaving the male paupers during the 1830's and 1840's; after twenty years as barber, Edward Ashburner was only being paid £2 for the same services in 1893. There are many bills for "Dip candles, 6s 3d. for dozen lbs." and for rush lights which still continued in use after 1861 when the Guardians resolved to take gas for Milnthorpe Workhouse if the new Gas Company will "supply it at the rate not higher than what they may charge the Railway Company for Station purposes." In 1867 they purchased a gas stove for £1 10s. In 1836 there was expenditure on Mary Spooner (a lunatic) in being transferred to Lancaster Asylum. On 24 June 1837 Rawes received the Order "that Mr Edward Landy, a dangerous Lunatic, be immediately removed to his relations on the application of his brother-in-law," for which the Board allowed him 3s 7d. per week. In the same year "Jn. Moore & Co (were paid) £2 9s. 6d for Iron Shackles." The shackling of insane inmates continued until 1858 when it was ordered that "the iron instruments be removed from the Bedsteads and that in future no Iron Locks or Chains again be employed in restraining Pauper Lunatics."

There are only a few references to workhouse labour. In 1836 John Dean supplied 8 doz. pairs of clog irons of different sizes, 8 doz. toe plates and 2000 nails indicating that cobbling was done in the house. Until 1895, when 25/- was spent on men's shoes from Daffady of Milnthorpe, all inmates seem to have worn clogs.

Industrial labour seems to have lapsed in Rawes' time, for he was ordered to send four boys from Milnthorpe Workhouse of the names of, Woodhouse, Bainbridge, Dodd and Baileff "in order that the same may work." "Encouragement money" of no more than 6d. per week could be paid to inmates.[30]

Rawes' term as Governor coincided with the workhouses and Poor Law as described in *Oliver Twist*. His regime seems to have been as harsh as that described by Dickens but his eventual downfall and dismissal shows that the Guardians could be humanitarians, protecting the poor.

Occasionally inmates absconded. When Rebecca Austin climbed over the wall in 1837 she was wearing workhouse clothing and so she was charged with theft. A case concerning Mary Rooking, who had left the house with an infant, along with Jane Thompson, was reported verbatim in the *Westmorland Gazette*. The magistrate questions Thompson:

> Magistrate "You are accused of running away from the Workhouse at Milnthorpe; why did you leave it?" Jane "I didn't like it." Magistrate "You didn't like it? How?" Jane "Because he's sik a bad man." Magistrate "A Bad Man – ." Jane "Ay. He punch'd me yance or twice, up wi his foot and punch'd me." Magistrate "you should have asked leave and not taken it." "I did ax' im and he wouldn't let me go home. Rawes (shaking her head) is a bad man." Magistrate "What were you saying when he punched you?." "I wasn't saying not a wrong word when he kick'd me." Magistrate "Why did you go to the Workhouse?" Jane "Because I can't maintain myself for I can't get no work. 'Fore I went in I ax'd 'em to give me one shilling per week out, but they wouldn't give it to me." Magistrate "How did you and other women get out of the workhouse?" Jane "I got over the wall. I helped her child over, it was 3 weeks after her confinement." Magistrate "You took away clothing with you from the workhouse." Jane "Yes but I brought nothing in the bundle but what they gave me I brought nothing but a petticoat out for I brought in a gown and other petticoat."[31]

The case was adjourned for a week until 20 June when another inmate was examined. She was Dolly Daws who said she would rather die than go back and that she had not been attended to by Mrs Rawes as she ought to be. To which the Magistrate responded "There were eight or ten women together. Surely you were able to assist one another. You wouldn't have a servant would ye?" Mr Rawes said "Gentlemen, She's a bad 'un that, a regular bad 'un. She wouldn't tell us what was the matter. She wouldn't say she was going to be delivered. She wouldn't call for a doctor. She's a very unnatural woman."

Jane Thompson was again called and on being asked if she had been ill treated said "Ay he (Mr Rawes) had laid me terribly with a rod on Sunday morning" and that her daughter had been refused admission with tea and sugar. Despite these pleas Jane was sent back to the Workhouse while Mary Rooking was sent to the House of Correction for two weeks.[32]

Rawes downfall came about as a result of the treatment and death of Thomas Robinson on 21 April 1838, about which he and Robert Wilson the surgeon reported to the Guardians in May. They stated that Thomas Homes, an inmate, was in Appleby Gaol awaiting trial under a common warrant for the manslaughter of Robinson. The Guardians summed up the case as follows:

"the deceased was in a state of mental imbecility and his health appeared to be rapidly sinking under an attack of Tabes Missenterica and Consequent Diarrhoea yet the Committee found that he was not under the care of a nurse nor properly under the care of a Medical Attendant. That as far as the Committee found he had never any Medicine for the original disease nor any during several weeks before his death for the Diarrhoea – That he was placed under the care of Thomas Holmes and left with him when from weakness and disease he was totally unfit to have had anyone in the same Bed – That he was subjected to an unwarrantable exposure of cold under the plea of cleaning him and, to a shameful exposure of his person in the Washouse, and that he was treated by the said Thomas Holmes with great cruelty."

Under these Circumstances the Committee considered there was culpable neglect of duty on the part of both the Governor and the Matron:

"First as regards attention to the comfort of the deceased in weakness, sickness and death.

Next as regards Internment without due notice and enquiry.

Lastly as regards the Moral influence on the inmates of the Establishment, from the outrage on common decency, the want of kindness, and Consideration in this distressing case."

The Rawes were to be dismissed and to leave on Tuesday at the latest. As the meeting was on Monday afternoon this really was a case of instant dismissal!

When later the Rawes returned, to collect their belongings, the Board decided to "find out the number of times Mr and Mrs Rawes had been to the workhouse and the number of meals they had had there etc."[37]

Advertisements for their successors appeared in Manchester, Liverpool and the local paper which stated that the new master and matron must bear "character for humanity and sobriety." Eventually in October from a short list of six it was announced "that on Saturday last Mr Samuel McGowan and Mary his wife were elected master and matron . . . in the room of John Rawes and Elizabeth his wife whose dismissal from their situation we sometime ago noted."[38] At first the master's salary was £55 p.a. but it was raised to £75 p.a. in 1868 when the Kendal Master's salary was reduced from £100 to £80.

One of the McGowan's first important duties was to introduce a new official Dietary in December 1838. The quantities were generous, but the fare was plain in the extreme, consisting mainly of "slops." Water porridge with milk was served at 15 out of 21 meals, with rice milk and oat bread for Sunday dinner, scouse with milk for dinner on Monday, Wednesday and Friday and milk porridge and oat bread on Thursday and Saturday dinner.[39] There seems a total absence of fruit and vegetables, other than potatoes, although there was an orchard at the house. It was reported in August 1828 that there was "a tree growing in the garden in which there are a cluster of 35 apples in a space of 12 inches and another 24 in the space of 14."[40] Perhaps the staff ate them or they were scrumped by the inmates as unofficial diet!

A temporary improvement was cancelled in November 1839 when the Guardians ordered that scouse be substituted for a dinner of boiled beef on Wednesday. "The health of the inmates would not be injured and the substitution of scouse for Beef would be more relished, and that oak cake be withdrawn from the Dining Tables on the days when scouse is provided." This would save about £100 – £120 p.a.

Concessions were made: "old people, being all 60 years and upwards, may be allowed one pint of coffee for breakfast, or 2 oz. of coffee for meal. The addition of one pint of Tea at 4 o'clock each afternoon (or 1 oz. of Tea per week), 7 oz. of Wheaten Bread per day and 7 oz. of sugar per week and milk for those whose age and Infirmities it may be deemed proper and requisites (sic). Children under 9 years of Age to be dieted at the discretion, above (that age) to be allowed the same as women. Sick whatever is ordered by the Medical Officer." A year later the bread ration was reduced from 7 oz to 5 oz for men and for women and children from 5 oz to

4 oz.

In 1840 it was proposed "that the quantity of water put into milk when the paupers have porridge dinner to be reduced from five to three gallons." This improved the quality, though only skimmed, or "blue" milk was used. On Sunday the rice milk was sweetened with treacle. Surprisingly perhaps, paupers could chose how much they wanted, until 1846 when uniform portions were ordered. Though the measures were generous such a control caused "general disatisfaction." At breakfast for instance "the porridge are placed upon the table in large wooden dishes containing 2 gallons, each furnished with ladels by which the paupers from time to time help themselves until they are satisfied – so that what porridge are left can be boiled up again with the next meal, but in the new dietary what is left cannot be used up again and must consequently be wasted." A Committee of visitors also noted that "peas are substituted for potatoes now (but) as in the Workhouse the inmates consist chiefly of infirm and disabled bodied paupers and as old persons are mutually subject to flatulence, it is our opinion the peas are decidedly objectionable. . . Scouse makes a more comfortable dinner and much more wholesome." They also ordered that three dinners of barley, introduced in 1843, should be changed to rice as although barley was cheaper "it takes much more boiling and is, therefore, not an economy."

Modifications in clothing were made at this time: "instead of the present suits for men consisting of a coat and waistcoat and Trousers all of Fustian which now cost £1 4s.4d. to provide for them a suit consisting of Fustian coat to cost 9s. 6d. and the waistcoat and trousers to be made of the Harden Manufactured in the House which would be 6s. 11d. This suit would then cost 16s. 5d. . . . a round about jacket instead of a coat which would cost still less (except for old men) and that clothes brought into the house be laid till they go out again except they be very bad." Harden wore well and lasted twice as long as fustian but, being coarser, the trousers had to be lined with flannel.

Outfits were supplied for two of the officers. In 1852 the Superintendent of labour was to have a "Frock Coat, waistcoat, Trowsers, Three Calico Shirts, 3 pairs of stockings, 1 Hat, 1 pair of Shoes," while the nurse, Ann Harrison, received "2 cotton print gowns, 1 flannel petticoat, 1 shirt, 1 pair of stays, 3 calicoe chemises, 3 handkerchiefs, 3 aprons, 3 pairs of stockings, 1 pair of shoes, 1 Bonnet and Calicoe for 6 Caps." Edward Stones was paid £1 14s. for officers' shoes and Simpson and Ireland £1 10s. for a Scotch bonnet.

Considerable attention was paid to the care of the sick. In 1862, a staircase was made to the womens' infirmary and the former lying-in room was converted into a male infirmary so that men would be on one side of the house and the women on the other. "The ward for the sick and dying old men would thus be removed from the lower part of the house and made much more quieter." Operations were performed at the house and in 1843 the payment of £5 was authorised for an amputation but in future the medical officer had to have such "treatment approved by some other medical gentlemen." "A white wood leg" was made by Peter Carter for 4s. 6d.

Segregation of the sexes was not absolute. Younger couples were kept apart and in 1838 "Woodhouse and his family were ordered to be sent to Kendal and that they be separated there." It was, however, resolved that Gill and his wife be allowed to sleep together owing to his "good character"; while in 1843 it was agreed that "married couples never sleep more than one couple in a room except two very old couples who have long done so and who mutually help each other." All beds were double until 1858 when it was decided to do away with the "practice of male adult paupers sleeping two in a bed." New iron bedsteads were ordered from Messrs Basett of Bristol. They were to be "brought by sea to be put down at either Lancaster or Ulverston."

Spiritual as well as moral guidance was well regulated. At first the Vicar of Heversham or his curate, made occasional visits – but it was not until 1837, when Nicholas Padwick became the first Vicar of Milnthorpe, that regular ministrations began. Two dozen testaments were purchased for 9s. (which were supplemented by 18 Bibles from Sleddales Charity in 1860) and a harmonium installed. This survived until 1909 when it was replaced by an American organ.

Inmates could attend Church but after complaints that they also visited the public houses it was decided that "the master had to go with paupers who go to church and some other delegated person should go to the independent chapel so that a check may be made on the demeanour of paupers on the Sabbath." The master was also ordered to attend the funeral of paupers. When he failed to do so he had to be reminded that this was his duty "unless particularly engaged in the exercise of other business."

The Rev. Padwick received no stipend for his workhouse duties but in 1847 "a vote of thanks with a purse of Twenty sovereigns was given to the Revrd Mr Padwick as a slight acknowledgement by the Board for his kindness in gratuitously visiting the Milnthorpe Workhouse twice a week and performing Divine Service... from July 1837 to Aug 1837." He was given the same sum in 1857 and on his retirement the Board gave £10 "to the testimonial now being subscribed him on leaving the curacy of St Thomas Milnthorpe."

When it was proposed to pay his successer, Rev. F.T. Raikes, £25 for "visiting the inmates and administering to them religious consolation and advice" the motion was lost by 16 to 21. It was not until 1874 that Raikes was appointed as "chaplin (sic) at £26 p.a. for which he had to conduct Divine Worship every Sunday afternoon." Soon afterwards he failed to take the services on three successive Sundays and he was ordered to appoint some other qualified person to do the duties in "his unavoidable absence." He appointed Rev. J. Audland as his deputy and, later, his curate Rev. W.R. Hopper took all the services, although Raikes' stipend was increased to £30 p.a. His successor, Rev. G.C.P. Reade only got £26 but gradually the scale rose to £100 for the Rev. Gamble as Chaplain to the Mental Home.

Pauper funerals loom large in the accounts and competition for the contract was keen. In Dec. 1838 William Birkhead Harrop's tender was £1 6s. 6d. for paupers above 14 and 13s. for those below with 8d. per mile beyond Beetham or Heversham. A quarter of a century later costs had dropped; Abraham Langhorn only charged 9s. 6d. for "pauper funerals under 16 years" and 18/- for adult burials. Thomas McNabb had the burial contract from 1878 – 1919, and charged for most of the period 17/6 for up to 16 and 32/-for adults not counting the 7s. 6d. paid to the vicar of Heversham. Pauper burials at Heversham were always contentious. Shortly after the opening of Milnthorpe churchyard in 1838 all pauper burials were ordered to take place there, but when they continued at Heversham the Guardians agreed to pay 5s. each to the vicar of Heversham. Even so, objections continued because the vicar could get £5 for private burials.[41] Over a hundred paupers were buried at Heversham in the nineteenth century. An unusual one was reported in the press when "an interesting dwarf, a native of Kendal named Simpson" was buried on 15th February 1895 having died in Milnthorpe workhouse. "She was 26 years of age and stood exactly 3ft 5ins in height and her weight was four stone four pounds. She was fairly proportioned in all parts of her body but the head was abnormally large and the spine had been indented from birth which was the probable cause of the stoppage in development. She was not able to speak, but could hear and apparently understood anything that was said to her, and she was of a happy dis-position."[42]

The workhouse came nearest to justifying its name during the 1840's when the master, Samuel McGowan, was paid £10 for keeping the accounts of the harden and twine manufacturing. Good workers could be paid 3d. a week; other earnings were to be kept for "the use of the pauper when he may desire to leave the house." Able-bodied workers were never regularly available however, because most men preferred to be in Kendal Workhouse "where they could obtain leave to obtain work at the manufactures." So eventually when the space was needed the workshops were closed and the 'old twine' manufactury converted into bedrooms and furnished with 20 double beds.

More notorious forms of casual workhouse labour continued. Disentangling old rope – oakum picking – not only survived but was extended in 1861 to women "as it was desirable that a more erksome employment shall be provided for the Young Female Inmates as it (the workhouse) had become in certain cases a harbour for Females who were known to be of idle habits and fond of an easy life therein." Oakum was made into new ropes and also into doormats which were sold at 7d. each.

There was stone breaking for the men. In 1839 enquiries were made as to "whether the master could dispose of 100 yards of Broken stone to Mr Robinson the Bridge Master" and also "what would be the expense of carting to the Canal, if the Boat owners; would take them." When a vagrant ward was built (at a cost of £120) in 1851 it was laid down that in return for a night's lodging "males had to do three hours' work at getting stones or spade labour at picking oakum, or cleaning wool." Females had to do "three hours work at cleaning the vagrant wards and making the vagrant's Beds or repairing and washing clothes or cleaning wool." Vagrant rations included for supper a pint of porridge with 5 or 6 oz. of bread or scouse – 2 lbs. for men, 1½ lbs. for women."

A school was started about 1836. A cellar was provided for the school room and a female inmate appointed as a teacher who was to be allowed "6d. per week with tea and coffee for assiduity in attending the schools." In 1839 a schoolmaster was allowed £1 6s. 6d. while in 1842 a new room was provided "out of building now occupied chiefly by lumber called the Barn between the coal place and the washhouse." By 1847 there was both a mistress, Jane Ruthven, and a master, Mr Wilson, who was paid "£6 p.a. with rations for himself and family."

The school closed in July 1848 because the children "would get more supervision at Kendal than at Milnthorpe and will no longer be influenced by the evil example of adult paupers." The school room became a "Bed and sitting room for the infirm."

This implied lack of supervision might have been caused by the preoccupation of the master, Samuel McGowan, in his domestic affairs. His wife, Mary McGowan, the matron, died in 1844. In advertising for her successer the Board stated that "a widow without incumbrance will be preferred. She must be of unexceptional character combined with strict economy." The salary was £20 p.a. with rations. Mary Remington, who might have been a relative of the Clerk to the Board, Richard Remington, obtained the post and rapidly rose to become the second Mrs Mary McGowan. When her husband died suddenly in 1851 her stepson Alexander McGowan succeeded as master, but Mrs McGowan remained as matron with a salary rise to £25 p.a. Alexander stayed until March 1857 when he resigned "in consequence of having taking to rent an Inn – The Station Hotel."

He was replaced by James Todd. Todd was only 22 and his salary of £45 was £5 less than McGowan's had been. Mrs McGowan's salary was raised to £30. Todd also had to find sureties: James Todd of Halforth and Robert Hoggarth of Crosside. He left in November 1862 and was replaced by Thomas Nelson who resigned after a few weeks as he had "never felt comfortable and found the books and accounts confusing." Failure to keep the books also led to the enforced resignation of his successor, Robert Marston, in September 1864.

As Mrs McGowan was still matron, if the master was married his wife could not hold the post. Moreover, a wife could not live in the workhouse but had "not to reside at a greater distance from the workhouse than Milnthorpe and that he (the master) shall be permitted to spend two nights each week with his family, leaving the House not earlier than 8 p.m. and returning the next morning not later than half an hour before breakfast" i.e. 7.30 a.m. Moreover it was stipulated that "when the matron's office falls vacant the master's job shall become vacant within three months." Benjamin Airey accepted these conditions and stayed until September 1867 – when Mrs McGowan seems to have been in charge for a few months until, at last, she retired on a pension of £15 p.a.

Out of 30 applicants Mr and Mrs Robert Preston, formerly of Haslingdon workhouse, became master and matron, being replaced by Joseph and Elizabeth Greenwood in May 1872. They had been master and matron at Sedbergh and the Board allowed them 8s. 8d. removal expenses. When they moved to Barrow workhouse in march 1883 the Guardians would only state that they had been "on the whole satisfactory." Moreover, Greenwood demanded payment of £8 for a greenhouse, which he had built in the garden. This was considered by the Board to be "a luxury used only for flowers and cauliflowers" and the wrangle was still going on a few years later when Greenwood was accidentally killed while crossing a railway line.

Mr and Mrs Mossop, who succeeded the Greenwoods, received even more scathing treatment for they were forced to resign after only three months, when the Poor Law Board decreed that Mrs Mossop "was not suitable as a matron."[43] They were consoled by a florid address from the inmates: "We the undersigned inmates of Milnthorpe Workhouse beg to render our most grateful thanks to you for your general kindness and your wife towards us since your appointment. We also beg to express our deep regret at your retirement and hope and trust that you may succeed to a more lucrative situation and that prosperity, long life and happiness may

Mr. & Mrs.Richard Mason, Master and Matron, 1907.

attend your future endeavours is the earnest wish and prayer of
your humble servants."[44]

They were replaced by Mr and Mrs Thomas Huck who were the
longest holders of the office only retiring in 1907 when they were
given an extra year's pension and "a handsome duplex hanging
lamp by the indoor staff and a set of carvers and jugs by the
inmates." Richard Mason was the next master and his wife, who was
the daughter of Joseph and Elizabeth Greenwood, became the
matron. Before her marriage she had been headmistress of Levens
School. They stayed until January 1912 when they left to become
master and matron of Carlisle Workhouse. They went on to have a
long and distinguished career in Poor Law – for many years they
were in charge of Salford Workhouse, one of the largest in
England.[46] Charles Mathews who came in 1912 was the last master
of the workhouse. On the outbreak of war in 1914 he patriotically
withdrew an application for a pay rise. He stayed until the
institution became a Mental Home in 1919.

Since for most of its history Milnthorpe Workhouse catered
mainly for the old, the infirm, unmarried mothers and their infants
(Pauper Classes 2 and 4), nursing care gradually came to be
regarded as important. The slow development of a nursing
profession in the decades after Florence Nightingale began her
reforms in the 1850's are shown in the Board's minute books. For a
long time nursing was left to a "suitable female person from in the
Workhouse" i.e. an inmate, but when Mrs Ellen Bainbridge
became nurse to the weakminded and idiot women, it was decided

that "having to be locked up in the Ward and having the care of lunatics she would require some little renumeration" – which was fixed at £5 p.a. When sick nurses Ann Locker, Ann Harrison and Hanah Lawson – who had a pay rise to £10 p.a. – came and went in quick succession it was agreed to improve conditions. Instead of sleeping in the ward with the patients the nurse was to be given her own room "over the ward now appropriate to placing corpses in their coffins." To help in moving patients a sedan chair was obtained for £1 10s. from Edward Burton and to brighten the patients' lives the weakminded were allowed walks in the garden in which paving was replaced by lawns and garden seats and amusements provided.

A trained nurse was appointed but she only stayed a month. The next was equally soon dismissed for "acting in direct disobedience to the master and matron." Nursing help for the weakminded was provided by the porter Issac Murray but he was dismissed in March 1863 after being "found in improper communication with the female inmates." His successor John Hoaksey was no better for in January 1866, he and nurse Margaret Clark "having been found guilty of indecent and improper conduct, were given one month's notice." Margaret Clark left her position but Hoaksey, almost sixty at the time, must have made an honest women of her and kept his job because the 1881 census returns record John Hoaksey, 74, Porter and vagrant Ward Master – Chelsea Pensioner, his wife Margaret, 73, and his stepson Benjamin Clark, 30, Rural Post man. A new nurse, Ann Jane Taylor, was appointed, but she too had to go when it was learnt that "during her widowhood she had been confined of an illigitimate Child which facts she had not stated to the Guardians." At this stage Sarah Earl, the "idiot nurse" was promoted to help in the sick ward and was given a pay increase of £10 to £20 p.a. "but £10 was to be deducted for "the maintenance of her three children as long as they remain in the Workhouse"! Whether poor Sarah was celebrating her delusory good fortune or drowning sorrows is not known but she soon had to be reprimanded for being drunk and forced to agree not to leave the workhouse. After a new head nurse Margaret Nelson was dismissed for using insulting language to the matron her replacement Mrs Royle had the same weakness as Sarah and was sacked despite her pleading "I do not say I had had no drink but I had not so much that I could not do my work." She was followed by Mrs Mary Bingham, a widow from Staveley. She stayed an unprecedented five years until 1874, and gave satisfaction although there were complaints that "visits from her friends who sleep in the house are too frequent." No less than five nurses, from distant parts, came and went in the next two years despite the salary being raised to £30 p.a. After a Guardian had complained that they did not want another "young lady who had her breakfast in bed and did not get up until

10 o'clock" the "idiot nurse" Agnes Yates was promoted to head nurse at £27 p.a. After this time more experienced and qualified staff became easier to get, but few stayed very long.

The buildings as well as staff caused concern. In 1863 the Poor Law Inspector, Mr Hurst, reported that "the main Day Rooms and female lying-in room were overcrowded and capable of improvement." A new dispensary was built and fitted up for the Medical Officer Dr Royle, and a new wing at the west end of the women's ward was built at a cost of £122. The upper part of the sleeping room in the infirmary was totally divided between men and women, and new dormitories meant the men no longer slept in the cellar. To complete the series of improvements, Ralph Thompson was paid £18 6s. 6d. in 1873 for two water closets. This meant that the contract for taking night soil (human excrement used as fertilizer) fell from £5 10s. p.a. paid to Richard Ireland in 1870 to £3 p.a. paid to Richard Ormerod in 1879.

There seems to have been running water quite early as it was reported in 1852 that a stone cistern ordered from William Holme of Hutton Roof "had been delayed in consequence of the heavy fall of Rain which had caused the roads to be almost impassable." The water supply, pumped from the well, gave persistent trouble. Sometimes it ran out and in June 1880 Dick Ormerod was paid £1 6s. for carting water. In 1886 and 1891 the well was said to be polluted as it was situated either virtually under or in the immediate proximity of the building. When in 1892 the Medical Officer said it was safe the inmates threatened a demonstration; the only recorded instance of organised indiscipline.

Lack of suitable water might have been the cause for complaints made by the inspector that inmates were not bathed regularly. The Guardians protested stating "that the Clothing of inmates of dirty habits (i.e. incontinent) was changed when the occasion required, in some cases three times a week"! They also ordered that, in future, only one patient should be bathed in the same water, and a glazed stoneware bath with Hot and Cold water laid on was installed in 1894. This served the whole house until 1914 when three new bathrooms were built. These, together with new w.c.'s, required a "new cess pool near Ackenthwaite Smithy in the field belonging to Mr Gathorne Hardy." This was an elaborate affair, built of concrete and lined with white tiles. Long forgotten, it was rediscovered after the building of Sycamore Grove in the 1970's, by Mr and Mrs Bell, who thought they had unearthed an air-raid shelter.

The late nineteenth century diet tables show gradually improving standards of nutrition. In 1861 the Medical Officer at last declared that it was too fluid; even the scouse served four times a week was measured as a liquid – 2 pints per adult. A kitchen range on "the Glendining principle" was installed in 1857 so that wheaten bread could be baked at Milnthorpe and not brought from Kendal. Wheat bread was substituted for oat bread at all meals in 1864, while more cheese was allowed at the bread and cheese supper introduced in 1852. The master was allowed to buy American butter at 10½d. lb. American cheese at 6d. lb. Lancaster cheese at 8d. and Dutch cheese at 4½d. lb. "A vessel for tea to hold 14 gallons" was purchased from C. Gardner for £1 1s. in 1861 and cocoa was first ordered in 1879. Coffee appears to have been the main beverage before this time. In 1867 vagrants were given a pint of coffee together with 8 oz of bread for men and 6 oz for females "before going to bed." They had the same amount of bread and 1 pint of porridge for breakfast.[47]

Fish was introduced as an experiment in 1883 and met with approval by "all except one inmate who had never eaten fish before and didn't intend to start."[48] One Guardian, however, grumbled that the "summer fish" (haddock) was all skin and bone while whiting was little better than "curdled water." When another member of the Board suggested that the master should chose what fish the inmates found most palatable, the Chairman enquired "If salmon was in season would they be having it at Milnthorpe?" Eventually it was decided to provide 10 oz of "good, nice and clean" cod in winter and ¾lb. of haddock in summer. When Mrs Cropper – the only lady Guardian – objected that 1¼lb. of potatoes served with the fish "was rather a large dose," 4oz. of bread and a few potatoes were substituted. A light Monday supper of bacon and pease pudding in winter and of an egg, bread and butter and cocoa was introduced in the 1880's. The solid meals remained "heavy." In 1900 Dr. Carden got the Guardians to change "16 oz. of Suet without sauce" for a milk pudding for Monday dinner.

Milk remained a major item of food. In 1884 there was a debate, as fierce as that over fish, after Dr. Carden recommended that all inmates should be given new (full fat) milk and not blue (skimmed) milk. As 4,468 gallons were consumed each year, at 4d. a gallon, to provide dearer milk at 1s. per gallon would obviously be prohibitively expensive – so the Board decided to provide it for children only. Three Guardians objected even to this. Mr. Punchard said the milk would make fat and not muscle or bone . . . "even farmhouse children didn't get it." Mr Thornber said "he had stopped it for his own five year old as it (sic) was getting too fat" . . . while Mr Black said "his children had always had blue milk." The chairman suggested that Mr. Black's children "were of good stuff to begin with, unlike workhouse children."[49]

Periodically the inmates were asked if they had any complaints about the food. Although a cook was only appointed in 1879 at 10/- per quarter, plus rations, the inmates always seemed satisfied – but it was the master who asked the questions. In 1888 only five inmates complained, and this was the largest number known.

Alcohol was provided, ostensibly for the old and sick. Thomas Hodgson's account to supply liquor in 1864 is typical: Port Wine at 13/- per gall., Sherry at 13/-, Brandy at 23/-, Gin 12/-, Porter 1/8, Best Ale 1/6. When Samuel McGowan resigned as master to become landlord of "The Station" he got the liquor contract and the order increased. A notice prohibiting smoking had been put up in the house in 1880. Even so, 1 oz of pipe tobacco was given to both male and female inmates per week. An extra allowance could be given to the sick on the direction of the Medical Officer; such is the gulf which separates medical opinion of Victorian times from our own day!

Health records are relatively sparse. There were epidemics of Cholera in 1866 (when "a gratuitous supply of medecine for diarrhoea" was granted), of typhoid in 1873 and of influenza in 1891, when the master could not attend a Board meeting in Kendal because of extra nursing duties. The Poor Law Board was the vaccination authority and the workhouse was a vaccination station for Heversham, Milnthorpe and Beetham. There was concern in 1873 when it was reported that "there are nine cases of illegitimate children born at the workhouse at Milnthorpe whose mothers had taken their discharge with their children unvaccinated."[50] Thenceforward a leaving certificate had to be witheld from mothers if their babies had not been vaccinated. In 1897 Dr Carden was paid 6d. in addition to his normal fee of 5/- when vaccination with cattle, and not human lymph, was introduced.

There are many references to mentally handicapped and mentally ill patients, many of whom would nowadays be classified as spastics, stroke victims, Down's Syndrome cases, geriatrics or epileptics. In 1861 it was decided not to send out "epileptic Thomas Smith to the lunatic asylum but to keep him in the idiot ward at Milnthorpe;" in 1880 two other "idiot" patients were ordered to look after "an inmate subject to epilepsy." In 1885 the Guardians debated whether a lunatic called Balderson should be discharged from Garlands mental hospital at Carlisle and boarded out with Belle Eccles of Holme, who was stone deaf. Mr Barwise asked "if it (sic) could not make itself (sic) understood because it could not speak. . . it would not matter if she could not hear him if he could(laughter)." They decided that Mrs. Eccles should take the child at 5s per week, the father paying 2s per week "as he was a labourer at the limekilns making 18s-20s per week depending on weather and had only two or three children to support"![51]

Towards the end of the century most mental patients were put away out of sight and out of mind of the "sane" outsider. The young Norman Birkett (later the famous advocate, Lord Birkett of Ulverston) as a Methodist lay preacher, regularly visited Milnthorpe

Workhouse and was "always vastly interested in the mental state of the inmates and used to ask all about them."[52]

The 1861, 1871 and 1881 census returns show that two thirds of the inmates were old and sick.

Kendal was the most common parish of settlement. In the 1861 census 36 stated that they had been born there, 46 in 1871 and 28 in 1881. In 1871 10 inmates all born in Ambleside are listed together, hinting that they might have been accommodated in the same, or adjacent wards. This is unusual because paupers chargeable to the other parishes are not listed together. Before and after – in 1861 and 1881 – only one or two inmates come from Ambleside. There were remarkably few inmates from Heversham and Milnthorpe; only 14 in 1851 and 6 in both 1861 and 1871.[53]

Useful information about the vagrant wards are contained in press reports of the Board meetings of the 1870's and 1880's, the original returns having been lost. They show that inmates at the Kendal and Milnthorpe institution varied in both houses from about 120 in the late summer to 160 in January and February, with the highest peak of 293 at Kendal and 214 at Milnthorpe in 1879. The number of days spent in each home by vagrants were set out under four national groupings, English, Irish, Scotch (sic) and Foreign – as in March 1882:[54]

	English	Irish	Scotch	Foreign
Kendal	38	14	9	1
Milnthorpe	72	14	9	0

Invariably Milnthorpe received more vagrants than Kendal. There were always more Irish tramps than Scottish or foreign, and sometimes more Irish than English tramps. In 1863 in order to discourage wayfarers the Guardians ordered "a notice to the charitable minded not to give Promiscuous Relief to tramps and vagrants, to be printed and posted throughout the town."[55] Tramps had to obtain a ticket of relief from the Police Constable or from the assistant overseer, who was usually a prominent tradesperson like the Post Master Isaac Rawlinson, and shoemaker Francis Atkinson. In March 1875 an Irishman called John Campbell, aged 28 years, engaged on mason's work at Bowness, got a ticket for the vagrant ward at Milnthorpe Police Station but fell down dead suddenly at the lane end of a "fit of apopolexy."[56]

There were always fears that vagrants spread disease. In the early days in order to deter infection the vagrant wards did not have beds but just a wooden platform and blankets. In the 1880's mattresses of chopped straw (which could be burnt easily) were introduced. In 1913 they were replaced by hammocks after it had been discovered that the men, some dripping wet, were sleeping 5 or 6 together."[57] In 1890 a tramp had taken cutaneous scabies (known as the "itch") from Lancaster Workhouse to Kendal via Milnthorpe. At about the same time another tramp had wandered from a smallpox area in the West Riding into Westmorland. The master was ordered in future "to furnish each vagrant on his discharge from the ward with a ticket indicating where the vagrant had slept the previous night, from whence he came and whither going." Even so in 1895 two lady tramps, Armer and Bell, were found to have "borne the itch" from Milnthorpe to Kendal.

For other inmates the discharge regulations were "1) if the pauper had not previously discharged himself from the Workhouse within one month, 24 hours notice. 2) If he has discharged himself once or oftener within one month, 48 hours. 3) If he has discharged himself more than twice within two months, 72 hours."

Discharge could be witheld for a few days for minor misdemeaners; refusing work was a criminal offence for which the offender could get 14 days' hard labour. In 1867 Francis Philippson and Ann Fennick were found guilty of indecent conduct and forbidden future leave of absence, given a reduced diet for 48 hours and separate confinement for 24 hours. In 1893 the inspector, Mr Jenner Furst, suggested "that the underground cell at the Milnthorpe Workhouse might be done away with and instead substituting a portion of another room as a punishment room which was well lighted."[58]

The Workhouse was no doubt a place of misery and of well scrubbed squalor. For those never conditioned by the school bell or by the factory siren and for whom time had never been precisely regulated, the workhouse bell must have clanged irksomely. Yet the food, though plain and sloppy, was more plentiful than for many "over the wall" while, at a time when to bring up a family of eleven children in a three roomed cottage was unexceptional, few would have noticed a lack of privacy. Some might have despaired; but whether their stay was brief, the result of fleeting misfortune, or long and terminal, the result of incurable sickness or senility, most inmates seemed to have accepted their lot if not cheerfully then with resignation: it was but a consequence of the station in life to which it had pleased God to call them. It is interesting that in nearly 100 years only one case of attempted suicide is recorded: that of Billy Wilson who in October 1844 swallowed "sugar lead valued at ½d."[59]

Relieving the institutional tedium were the Workhouse treats. These are nowadays regarded as the epitome of bourgeois condescension, where patronising smiles made stingy amends for hard hearts and tight fists, but at the time they were greatly enjoyed by all. There were special treats for Royal occasions: extra rations were ordered for the Coronation of Queen Victoria in 1838, a tea of cold beef for the wedding of the Prince and Princess of Wales in

1863 and a breakfast of bread and butter, tea and an egg, dinner of roast beef, rice pudding and tea with fruit bread buttered, for the Diamond Jubilee in 1897. Certain inmates were allowed to visit local events, as in 1866 when men "were to be let at liberty at the discretion of the master to attend Whit Monday sports."

Christmas Day in the workhouse was celebrated with a dinner of roast beef and plum pudding. Later in the season the Guardians and Committee of Visitors, freed from their own domestic responsibilities, paid a ceremonial visit for another treat. From the 1870's onwards it became more and more elaborate.

Like their Elizabethan forebears the Victorian Guardians had other responsibilities than the workhouse; and as time went on these became wider. Until the advent of the County, Rural District and Parish Councils in the 1880's and 1890's they were the sanitary and highway authorities. Thus in 1854 the overseer ordered the surveyor for the Milnthorpe District "to clean the streets, lanes, passages and public ways and places and to make proper the sewers... to abate nuisances which at present exist." Attempts to get paupers to mend the roads (a time-honoured would-be solution) failed in the 1850's because of the broad area of the Poor Law District and the difficulty of transporting and housing on site the relatively few able-bodied labourers.

The Poor Law Board also encouraged the temperance movement. In the 1870's it petitioned the House of Commons to close public houses between 11 p.m. and 5 a.m. and on Sundays except between 12.30 p.m. – 2.30 p.m. and 7.30 p.m. and 9 p.m. "for bona fide travellers only.[68] Outdoor relief (i.e. outside the Workhouse) was paid generally to younger applicants, the sick or to the aged who could partially support themselves. Payments were usually little more than 3 or 4s. for each adult per week with an extra Christmas allowance of 1/6d. for adults and 1s. for children. Personal and family responsibilities were always enforced to save ratepayers' money. If an inmate was compelled to enter the Workhouse, any personal income was appropriated. For example in 1838 "the overseer of Milnthorpe brought James Garth before the Board when he assigned his pension from the East India Company of £5 per quarter to the overseer." This was excessive as, even at the end of the century, rations for a teenage child were valued at only £5 per annum. In 1865 Moses Collinson had to pay 13/- towards the upkeep of his wife in the workhouse, Anthony Blamire had to pay £4 1s. 4d. for his family, Robert Wilkinson £1 6s. for his wife while Jabez Robarts of Holme was ordered in 1877 to "maintain a female illegitimate child of Mary Jane Atkinson now an inmate of Milnthorpe workhouse." Also in 1877 action was taken for the cost of maintenance of their wives and children in the workhouse against Leonard Fell, William Haworth and William Garbutt.

Under the heading "Connubial Infelicity" the *Westmorland Gazette* reported in 1890 how Thomas Seddin had to pay 5s. for his wife (of six months) and their child from his wage of 17s 6d. per week from Lancaster shipyard.[69] Thomas Henry Robinson likewise was ordered to pay 8s. for his family's maintenance in the Workhouse from his earnings of 25s. a week on the Lancaster and Morecambe Tramway. He refused, stating that "they had a home if they'd come to it."!

As in earlier times boys were "put out" to apprenticeship by the Guardians and checks were made on both the apprentice and master (or mistress). In 1838 "the Guardians put their seal to an indenture of Apprenticeship for the Binding of Stephen Towers, a Poor Boy from the Township of Haverbrack, to Bartholomew Croft of the Township of Heversham and Milnthorpe, to the trade of a Plumber and Tin Plate worker. The Premium given being £2 10s. by the Guardians and £2 10s. by the Father." In 1856 "Stephen Lupton, bound to Mary Berry to learn the art of agriculture, appeared and gave entire satisfaction," but three years later it was resolved that "Mr Walter Berry (Mary's son) pay to Stephen Lupton the sum of £2 19s 6d. being 14 weeks and 6 day's wages at the rate of 4/-per week for having served him over and above the indenture." The period of apprenticeship was generally for the traditional seven years, as in 1870:- "James Scott apprenticed to Hannah Douthwaite of Ackenthwaite Blacksmith for 7 years and George Holme to Benjamin Airey of Milnthorpe, Basket Maker." Echoes of the 1662 Settlement Act, in which people could be moved back to their native villages, re-occurred throughout the period. In 1893 the Medical Officer, Dr Carden, certified that "James Donnelly aged 80 years was fit to move to his place of settlement at Trebullon nr Monaghan in Ireland, having lived in Milnthorpe three years and been in the Workhouse eleven weeks."[70]

By the early twentieth century it was clear that the days of the Poor Law and the Guardians were numbered. The Liberal Manifesto of 1905 said that the "Workhouse was out of harmony with the present day." Reform was approved by the Conservative Chairman of the Board Mr Weston (later Colonel Weston M.P.) who in 1907 spoke of "the pleasure afforded him by his work in connection with the Old Age Pensions Act, as the receipt of a pension would enable many old people to remain at home." Fears that the Old Aged Pensioners would spend their money on drink and then "apply to the parish" did not occur.

There were still some sad cases like that of William Graham whose death at age 83 was reported in 1910 under the headline "M.A. dies in the Workhouse." He was of good family and had been educated at Edinburgh University before running a profitable tour business on the Continent. "He once was arrested in Brussels for absentmindedly lighting his cigar on a candle carried by a Roman Catholic Church dignitary." On retirement he bought a £4000 mansion but lost this and all his fortune except £10, when the Bank of Glasgow crashed. Forced to make a meagre living as a travelling book salesman his health gave out in Ambleside and after two years, when his savings were spent, he had to apply to the Parish, spending the last eleven months of his life in Milnthorpe workhouse. "He bore his troubles patiently and read to the other inmates."[71]

There were always a few difficult inmates. In 1909 William Hall – once a noted hedger – "ran amok and fought and struggled in a most terrible manner." It required several policemen and Willy Douthwaite, the local blacksmith, to take him to the Police Station where he broke the cell windows before being certified and sent to Garlands.[72] Later, when the house was a mental home, the matron Mrs Kerr ran across to The Smithy for Willy's help when a patient, naked and brandishing a kitchen knife, had cornered Mr Kerr, who was defending himself with a chair. With a red hot iron plucked from the forge, Willy so intimidated the mad man that he dropped the knife; but he never ceased to wonder what would have happened if he had been forced to brand the unfortunate man![73]

Less dangerous but more infuriating were some of the unmarried mothers – one of whom, Jane Brownrigg, was given one month's hard labour in 1913 after throwing porridge over the Matron who had refused her a cup of tea at 7.30 a.m. – a privilege granted only to laundry workers who started work an hour earlier.[74]

The Poor Law Inspector's Report of 1909 provides detailed information about the Milnthorpe Workhouse in its last years. Bed accommodation comprised "Old men 37, male sick ward 15, infectious disease 1, male receiving ward 2, able bodied women 7, old women 37, female sick 16, lying-in 3, female receiving ward 2, Total 120." On 18 September 1909 there were in the house 45 men, 54 women and two infants – one of these was newly born. The mother had already had 6 illegitimate children. There was only one sick patient, a girl suffering from Phthisis (pulmonary TB) from which her father and sister had already died. The inspector criticized the three earth closets used by the imbeciles, the scanty provision of only one hair brush and one comb per ward and the fact that clothing "each with its distinctive smell" was kept in the same room as food. Moreover, in "the room in which disinfection is done there is one bed for itch or venereal disease, an obviously unsuitable arrangement." They praised, however, the good garden which gave "employment to the inmates and enough vegetables, except potatoes."

Some improvements were carried out. In addition to modern

sanitation, a new kitchen range, hot water systems and partial central heating were installed. The house was connected to the telephone in 1912 "provided the service did not cost more than £8 p.a."[75]

Soon after the outbreak of the Great War the vagrant ward was closed and tramps were in future directed to the Common Lodging house in the Square or to Kendal Workhouse. Local people recall that German prisoners of war were billetted in the empty wards and were taken daily up the Woodhouse Road to work at Greenhead Farm. There are, however, no records of their staying in the house. In 1917 it was decided to close the sick and old people's wards and use the premises for the Feeble Minded. This occurred just after the Peace celebrations on August 30, 1919, when the inmates had been granted extra fare for two days and out-door paupers had received an extra 2/- for adults and 1/- for children.

The Workhouse was renamed "Ackenthwaite End" and later on "Milnthorpe Hospital" but it was always known as the Mental Home, while Kirkgate Lane continued to be called Workhouse Lane. The Guardians transferred administration firstly in 1926 to the Cumberland and Westmorland Joint Mental Deficiency Committee and then, on the disappearance of the last vestiges of the Poor Law in 1948, to Manchester Regional Hospital Board.

Whatever the correct Mental Health Authority titles the two chief officers were still addressed as Master and Matron. There were only two holders of each office: Mr and Mrs Kerr from 1921 to 1938 and Mr and Mrs Foster, 1938 to 1963. They all earned high praise. The Kerr's were congratulated on profits earned from baking bread, while the standard of craftwork was exemplary. The Fosters coped manfully with war-time rationing and staff shortages. Excellent links were maintained with the village, pre-empting many similar Leagues of Friends introduced into old people's homes and the like in the 1950's. The Christmas pantomime, latterly performed by the Women's Institute, continued the tradition of the workhouse treat, while patients were always invited to the "first night" of the twice yearly production of the Amateur Dramatic Society. Improved staffing levels provided opportunities for local employment. To a child, brought up in the village in the 1940s and 1950s, the sight of a long crocodile of patients being taken for walks around the lanes was so familiar as to arouse little interest or comment. The Mental Home did, however, become the butt of savage criticism from the Medical Officer of Health, Dr. S.F. Dow, who said that the "institution is a prison... the patients go there, ring the bell; the gates shut and they are inside. Contrast that with Garlands where the patients are walking about and being looked after." The hospital's Medical Officer, Dr. P.S. Byrne, responded by saying that "these people are made more comfortable than their almost negligible intelligence can appreciate." Even so it was condemned for closure.[76]

Despite its archaic fabric it was a sad day in March 1961 when the National Health Service announced that it would not renew the lease after the retirement of Mr. and Mrs. Foster in 1963.

Having been rejected by the Milk Marketing Board, the Prison Service, Heversham Grammar School (for use as a Boarding House) and the Education Committee as a site for a Secondary Modern School, the building was advertised for sale as "a unique opportunity to purchase accommodation suitable for domestic or institutional use with walls etc. in excellent condition." Eventually it was sold to Messrs Davy of Grange for £6,750, an earlier offer of £5,501 having been refused. The proceeds were shared out amongst the parishes that had formed the original but now totally forgotten, Milnthorpe Poor Law Union. As several parishes had been sub-divided this was a long-winded and complicated process. Eventually, as their shares, Milnthorpe received £630 and Heversham £419.[77]

Improbably named "Chelsea Flats," for no obvious reason except that this was the Swinging Sixties and it sounded good, the buildings were converted into tenements and houses and bungalows were built in the grounds. After ten years or so Chelsea Flats were resold and re-converted into more attractive and more expensive, dwellings. The new development was renamed "Ackenthwaite Court" and "Chelsea Court" but some residents preferred the "Old Workhouse" to be their address; such is the charm rendered by old age to a charmless, if useful, institution.

12

Crime and Punishment

Crime and punishment have always loomed large in the verbal and written traditions of any community. As the twentieth century media has shown, most people prefer to hear about the misdoings of the bad and the antics of the scandalous, though trivial, than to be informed about the deeds of the good and the great.

Since the days of clay tablets law and its enforcement have formed a main footing to all civilizations. At village level, however, records are unreliable and slight. Folk tales rarely go back for more than a few generations. Legal documents like Quarter Session returns, Committal and Assize records are normally based on the wider area of the hundred or the county: a brief description of the crime, along with place names and those of litigants and witnesses might be mentioned – but little else. This is mainly because the ordinary misdeeds of the masses were neither serious nor extensive, though every generation seems to have worried about a crime wave. Over the centuries vagrancy, drunkenness, proletarian fisty-cuffs, domestic discord and petty theft have constituted the bulk of rural crime. Only the details change. Lads who stole horses in the 1780's might have been transported to the colonies; for taking and driving away a motor vehicle in the 1980's they might have to do community service. Of the sensational or significant crimes few details were recorded before the advent of a regular local press.

Occasionally records of what appear to have been only minor crimes have survived from the earlier periods. Hence in 1320 "Alexander de Wyndesore lord of the manor of Milnthorpe complained that Roger de Clifford and others broke his park at Qwynne Fell, Co. Westmorland and took away the eggs of his sparhawks lately nesting there, whereby he lost the profit of his aery."[1] Alexander also appears in a longer record of rustling in the wild Westmorland of the fourteenth century. In 1336:

"William de Coucy was summoned to answer Alexander de Wyndesouer of a plea that he took his cattle unjustly and detained them, namely 8 oxen and 8 cows at Heversham, in a place called Milnthorpe."

For small crimes and misdemeaners great folk like the de Cliffords and the de Wyndesouers would be fined. Of necessity the poor masses had to be treated differently. Custodial sentences in prison were rare before the nineteenth century as there were few prisons. As the poor lacked money they could not be fined. Therefore, for those without cash the law resorted to the lash. "For the stealing of goods valued at a few pence men and women were stript to the waist and marched through the open market. . . and whipt with the cat-o'-nine tails till their blood came."[2] Thus in April 1694 an order was made for the apprehension of "Thomas Postlethwaite of Heversham Head, yeoman, who stands indicted for felony, but has neglected to appear. He stole a sheep, price 1s. of Tho. Harryson, found guilty and whipped." The next year Thomas Harryson himself was lucky for he was acquitted of stealing a wether sheep price 10d. of John Burrows, though for an asault on William Fell, one of the constables in the execution of his office, he was fined 5s. Later, however, he had to pay William Fell £1 14s. for expenses "in conveying the said Thomas Harryson to the County Gaol."[4]

Corporal punishment remained common at the start of the nineteenth century. In April 1800 it was "ordered that James Simpson be taken to the House of Correction and there confined in a solitary cell until 12th day of May next (Fair Day) and from thence be taken to the market town of Milnthorpe and there be publicly whipped through the said market till his body be bloody and then discharged."[5]

Though gradually abolished for offences by adults flogging was long regarded as a soft option for juveniles. When John R. Woof, aged 11 years, was found guilty of stealing half-a-crown from Mr James Brennand in November 1884, the Milnthorpe magistrates decreed "this being the first offence they would deal leniently with him and hoped he would never appear there again. He would receive six strokes with the birch rod to be administered by the constable. The castigation was afterwards administered by P.C. Cannon in the presence of Superintendant Shields. Woof left the court a sadder and probably wiser boy."[6] In 1897 another "desperado of eleven years" was reported as having been found guilty at Milnthorpe of lifting sausages and wax candles from a village emporium. "The young thief was caught in the act, not being sufficiently artful to get away with his strange booty. . . The magistrates suggested a good whipping. That goes without saying;

because no boy who had a preternatural appetite for rich things would steal sausages and wax candles."[7] Even as late as 1920 when Norman Arkwright and Harold Pearson, aged 10, stole some carrots, ate four and gave the tops to their rabbits, they were told "they had narrowly missed being birched."[8] Instead their parents had to pay 7s. 6d. The carrots were valued at 2s.

Law and Order was a shared responsibility of the magistrates and the manor courts. In 1823 the notice appeared "Manor of Kirkland and Milnthorpe in the County of Westmoreland, Notice is hereby given To the Tennants and other persons owing suit and service or having anything to do at the Court Leet or view of Forkpledge with Court Baron of the Honourable Fulk Greville Howard for his Manor of Kirkland and Milnthorpe – Milnthorpe at the Cross Keys at 10 o'clock forenoon on Thurs 24th October – Issac Wilson Steward."[9] Later, on the 1st November 1823, it was recorded that "Milnthorpe Court Leet was held on Friday se'night when many complaints having been presented respecting the disorderly state of the town particularly on the sabbath day it was resolved that an active police should be established. Several of the most respectable inhabitants of the town very creditably came forward to be sworn in as special Constables who declared it to be their intention to visit the public houses every Sunday evening at nine o'clock and otherwise to ensure the regularity and peace of the town."

The constables were "special" because they augmented the official parish constables appointed by "Millthrop Association for the Prosecution of Felons." This body had been founded by the 1780's and was composed of most respectable householders. In 1790 the list of subscribers numbered 66 and in 1795 it numbered 88 including a woman, Elizabeth Hodgson. Their aim was "to prosecute at our joint Expense with the utmost Rigour of the Law; and if possible to convict, every Person or Persons who shall be guilty of any Burglary, Felony, Theft or any imperious Treatment or Damage against our Persons; or the Property of any or us" including all "under the Character of Highwaymen, House-breakers, Shop-lifters, Robbers of Houses, Orchards or Gardens, Takers away or destroyers of Fences Defacers of Milestones and Guide Posts..."[11]

The annual meeting and dinner of the Millthrop Association took place either at the Cross Keys or the King's Arms at the end of June, around Old Midsummer's Day. Here constables were chosen and in 1846 it was announced that "Mr E Wilson, Butcher, Mr B Croft, painter and Mr Brown, rope manufacturer, have been appointed Constables for the coming year."[12] They were not paid but got expenses and shared rewards. These were offered by the Association, as in December 1834, when the house of William Hind, Whitesmith, was broken into and a gun, barrel and ram-rod stolen. Alas, the thief was not taken or the property recovered.[13] Equally unsuccessful were rewards offered to apprehend sheep stealers who on several occasions in 1844 and 1845 slaughtered animals belonging to John Scott of Greenhead, leaving the skin, head and legs behind in the field.[14]

A professional police force was established after the passing of the County Police Act in 1840 and in 1844 "Mr Grossmith, newly appointed County police officer, paid Milnthorpe a visit and found one of the inn keepers selling during the hours of divine service."[15] There was still no resident "bobby" in Milnthorpe until 1852 (see later) and the constables had to raise an old style hue and cry after a particularly brazen tramp who "had committed three robberies at Milnthorpe in one day. He had taken three silver spoons from Mr Robert Wilson, the surgeon, a copper kettle left at the door by Miss Smithies, as she went to get the rogue some bread and a copper pan and tea kettle left out at night by Mr Bainbridge at the King's Arms. He was also believed to have taken half a load of meal (!) from Mr Robert Baines of Whasset." No doubt all the swag weighed him down for the offender was "caught by Mr Stones, Constable, on the road to Beetham." The Association Constables continued to be elected until 1872, William Constable being one of the last.[16]

Milnthorpe's position on the main road meant that it was regularly visited by tramps, who over the years committed many crimes. In 1851 two Irish girls, Ann Henderson and Mary O'Connell, "recently imported from their native soil, were seen begging in the streets of Milnthorpe."[17] Shortly afterwards a poor woman called Nancy Jackson discovered that her plaid shawl, left outside her cottage, was missing. It was found wrapped round one of the Irish girls and both were sent to the House of Correction. Just for begging, James McCann, "a surly looking Irishman," was sent down for 7 days in 1865 [18] while the next year, Stephen Beetham, "a man who walks with a wooden leg," was given three months for being an incorrigible beggar and a disorderly person."[19] A spate of vagrancy convictions in 1882 produced a letter in the *Westmorland Gazette*:

"Sir, I noticed in last week's Gazette a paragraph headed Milnthorpe Petty Sessions which after informing us about a tramp states that 49 cases have been before the Bench this year; 23 previous have been sent to prison and others disposed of by sundry fines, and twenty five times the Court has been opened. Now, Sir, this seems most formidable and Calculated to convey the impression that Milnthorpe was in a degraded state as the statistical argument is not qualified by any explanation of what the cases were. Most of them I venture to say were paltry in the extreme, being poor vagrants, who for asking for bread have been "run in" and sentenced to 14 days imprisonment. For the credit of the district I think this fact should be known. Signed, A Looker On."[20]

Sometimes fears about tramps were justified and in 1899 John Henry Churchhill, "a watercress gatherer," assaulted Mary Ann Garth and "throppled (sic) her until her tongue held out."[21] A tramp named James McDonald in March 1902 provided light relief for when charged with begging, "in broad scotch he protested that had it been Monday he would have gone to his work but as it was the sabbath he couldn't." He got 7 days.[22] More peculiar was Thomas O'Brien who in January 1904, "tore up all his clothes including his boots" and had to appear in court in a suit "new to him."[23] The magistrates ruled that 1s. 6d. found on him should be used to defray expenses. He was given 1 month in Lancaster Castle. The same penalty was meted out to Margaret Fryers, a pauper, who was found sleeping out at Owlett Ash, having refused to go into the Workhouse. More alarming were a band of German gypsies, including women and children, "who begged at every house in Milnthorpe" in 1908 before being escorted to the Lancashire boundary by the County police.[24] But the unluckiest tramp of all was John Foley, who in 1906, being unable to read the notice, inadvertently knocked at the Police Station door in order to beg for food and was run in for 7 days![25]

Drunkeness either by vagrants or residents was always common. With eleven inns and beerhouses in the village, few other recreational facilities and, during the winter months, no daylight leisure hours, this was not surprising. At a time when a dozen people could live in a three roomed cottage the sleaziest tavern was a more comfortable home-from-home.

"Tom the Barber" (Thomas Thomson) was Milnthorpe's most notorious drunkard in the mid-nineteenth century. One autumn night in 1845 Tom was so drunk that his companions were able to put him in a sack and take him round to the surgeons' house claiming that they had a body available for dissection. They got no takers and when Tom sobered up he started fighting, whereupon the would-be Burke and Hare handed him over to the police and Tom, not they, was fined 15s.[26] A year later he was committed to the House of Correction in Kendal for stealing a "piece of red Callichoe (valued 10½d) which he had stolen in a state of intoxication in order to purchase another pint of ale."[27] At Christmas 1849 he was again in trouble, this time for stealing a pair of worsted stockings from the "Eagle and Child" at Heversham.[28] All this was in his younger days, but he never learnt his lesson and his end at the age of 55 in May 1870 was tragic – but fittingly macabre. Tom had been in the Workhouse for six weeks and on being allowed out he headed for the Shovel Inn on Harmony Green where he cut the landlord's hair in return for beer. On being unable to beg or earn anymore he left. About a quarter of an hour later the landlord's 7 year old son came into the house and said that "Tom the Barber was hanging himself in the cow house." Anthony Huddlestone, the landlord, investigated and "found the deceased hanging from a cross-piece fixed against two joists by a handkerchief." Apparently the infant had witnessed unblinkingly the whole grisly act. The verdict was "hung himself during a fit of insanity."[29]

Another drunken pauper was James Garth, a skinner, who on receiving a pension of 4s. per week in 1865 from the Skinner's Society of Birmingham, celebrated too much and was given one month hard labour.[30] Similar penalties were meted out in 1873 to John Steven who was found "grovelling in the mire" and to George Cunningham and Michael Cassidy who while drunk stole a pair of boots which the owner, Edward Stones, identified by a secret mark. Also in 1873 Hannah Wilkinson, having been convicted several times for drunkenness, was given two months' hard labour though she was acquitted of stealing 10 sovereigns from James Tatham. She had been "his supposed housekeeper" and had to return to him £1 4s. 6d worth of clothing. A month later she was back in the House of Correction on the old charge of drunkenness. Other inebriate women who acquired long records were Margaret Smith and especially "Irish Ann" Haley. On one occasion the bench tried to keep her out of gaol by fining her 20s. – but when she said she only had 7d. in the world, she went down for yet another month. Her compatriot Patrick Brannon had been in the same predicament when fined 5s. for over-celebrating on St. Patrick's Day 1873.[31] He admitted he had "had a drop too much, in fact he had spent all he had and was not possessed with a single farthing. Under these circumstances he was provided with board and lodging in the House of Correction for 7 days." In 1874 William Graham, described as "three sheets to the wind," and two others "fresh from the shrine of Bacchus" were fined 10s. and their companion, an Irishman called James Connel, got 2 months hard labour for assaulting P.C. Barnes.

Sometimes those who embarked on a life of temperance failed to keep afloat: in 1873 Thomas Mayor "was one of the noble band who pledge themselves to sail in the Good Templar's ship for a life long voyage but unfortunately for him . . . he slipped cable and was once more submerged in the sea of dissipation. The result was that he broke a window pane, 6 inches by 8 inches in Hannah Garnett's house, where he lodged, and also pulled plaster off the wall."[32] Unable to pay a fine of 10s and costs of 2s. 6d. he went to gaol for six months. In 1884 William Bell, a painter, got off with a light fine after pleading "I was only singing one of Sankey's Hymns. I have been a member of the Blue Ribbon Army for several months and the drink had more effect upon me than I thought."[33]

The Lock-up, c.1860.

Public disturbances were quite common in nineteenth century Milnthorpe and were often caused by drink. Gangs of "Glasgow workers" broke into a cellar on "the north road" in 1842 and searched it for bread but found "it had all been eaten by the rats."[34] Worse was to come when shortly afterwards Milnthorpe became the "paying-out place" for the hundreds of navvies building the railway.

> "This pleasant little town has again this year witnessed the disgraceful scenes of much intoxification and fighting during Easter week. Gangs of young men with 30 eggs each, some had upwards of 60... had drunk many gallons of mulled ale. After the liquor had begun to operate upon them, fight they must... there were three separate battles at one time... a number of wives and sweethearts of the pugilists had a set to. It is high time that a lock-up should be erected in the town which would doubtless tend to stop such disgraceful scenes."[35]

The authorities acted firmly and in March 1845 the *Westmorland Gazette* announced that "we have great pleasure in stating that a meeting of the gentlemen and tradesmen of the town of Milnthorpe was held on Monday last at the Cross Keys Inn when it was agreed that plans and specifications should be prepared and that tenders should be determined upon on Tuesday next. The site chosen for the building of the lock-up is where the market cross now stands."[36] Early in June came the news that "the contractors for erecting the lock up... Messrs. J. & T. Brockbank, Masons, commenced clearing the ground on Saturday last and the building is to be finished about 6 weeks from this date."[37]

It was not before time for after a recent pay day "the (railway) labourers kept up their drunken holiday until Thursday morning but were peacable (sic) compared with some occasions."[38] At the Petty Sessions it was reported that James Rose, the ring leader, had tried to break into Mr James Burrows, cabinet makers. His accomplice Henry Johnson was found guilty of stealing onions from Mr Huddlestone's garden but Rose was acquitted as "he could not positively be identified." Rose's freedom did not last long for a week later he offered to fight his neighbour, Mr Joseph Sharples, a saddler, and was taken charge of by the police. Special police had been appointed to deal with the navvies and were paid for by the railway company. James Rose was "put in the lock up and he being the first tenant they have named the place Rose Castle after the first martyr."[39] The next day at a hearing before George Wilson Esq. of Dallam Tower, he was fined 14s. 6d., "a week's pay" plus 1s. cost. The second "lodger in the lock up" Roger Askew, got off with a 5s. 6d. fine for causing "so much disturbance in the streets that people took refuge in the public houses."[40] At the October fair in 1847 a man named Bowen was put in the lock up for fighting but it seems to have been little used after the navvies moved north with the railway. In 1862, shortly after the police station was built, the lock up was demolished, though the shackles on the limestone steps of the cross survived for another century.

Communal battles continued to break out from time to time even when the railway navvies had gone. During fighting in the streets in September 1850 "one combatant had an inch bit off from his finger... it is hoped that should a similar disturbance occur the parochial Constable will summon such parties before the magistrates."[41] In 1866 there was "a murderous affray between navvies James Allen and James Ramsbottom at the lodging house in the old School Rooms (on the square) during which one received three stab wounds, one below the left eye and two in the breast."[42] Half a century later conditions were no better: in June 1900 there was a street fight between Agnes (Aggie) Knowles and two sisters, Mary Ann Griffin and Ellen Spedding after Agnes had threatened "to rive her pluck out."[43] Not long afterwards Aggie attempted suicide by jumping into the Bela from the Strands. Though she fell in a depth of ten feet she was rescued by James Wilkinson who was carting water and given artificial respiration by Robert and George Wilson. Suicide being a criminal offence, Aggie was imprisoned in Lancaster Castle.

In 1904 a domestic row spilled out into Park Road and John Ashburner was fined 5s. for creating a disturbance lasting an hour and a half though he pleaded that "he had never insulted anyone since he came into Milnthorpe and he was born and bred in the place."[44] Carr's Yard was the most notorious place in Milnthorpe for many years. In 1904 John MacDonald of Carr's Yard was fined 5s. for obscene language, the bench commenting that "it is scandalous that in a decent and respectable place like Milnthorpe that such horrid disgusting language should be so common."[45] A year later MacDonald was involved in a general free-for-all with the Fell family which landed Julia Fell, wife of John Fell, a comb maker, in court. She claimed that she was angered because John and Elizabeth Ashburner, who lived near by, had taunted her with having killed her brother. The result was that Julia gave MacDonald a black eye and in return was fined 5s. From the First World War onwards Milnthorpe became quieter though in 1921 Leonard Dowker of Holme and George Graham of Milnthorpe were fined 15s. for carrying on a running fight in Haverflatts Lane which lasted for nearly two hours and drew a crowd of over 100 people.[46]

Serious crimes have been relatively rare in Milnthorpe though petty thefts and misdemeanours were common. In 1843 the "young mens depredations in breaking down fences and knocking on doors was condemned and it was hoped that the constables would bring the night prowlers to justice."[47] Hopes were not realised for a little later it was reported that 60 yards of winter potatoes had been stolen and "scarcely a week passes in the neighbourhood of Milnthorpe without something of the sort taking place." A cruel theft occurred in 1846 when Miss Mason of Harmony Hill advertised that "her valuable lap dog of the King Charles breed" had been stolen. It has "a black head, a white star, brown feet and answered to the name of Charley." A reward of £5 on conviction was offered but alas "Charley" was lost forever.[48] Even meaner was the theft of 8 ducks, ready for market in 1849, from Thomas Towers a poor weaver. Eventually they were recovered from the orchard of William Wilson, beer house keeper of Holme, who claimed he knew nothing of their origins.[49] In the same year a notorious thief called Stephen James, alias "Cute," was caught at Milnthorpe after taking handkerchiefs off a hedge at Clawthorpe. In October 1850 a highway robbery by footpads was reported at Ackenthwaite. It was like a twentieth century "mugging": three men threw Mr E. North, a joiner, to the ground, ransacked his pockets and robbed him even of his foot rule.[50]

A sneaky burglary occurred in December 1851 "when the shop door was bored through of Dodgson the Milliner and Linen Draper in the centre of the town of Milnthorpe but the villains were not detected."[51]

John Whitehead "a large farmer of Ackenthwaite" created a major village scandal in the autumn of 1865 when he was charged with "being about 3 o'clock this morning in a barn at Ackenthwaite in the occupation of Mr Robert Johnson for certain unlawful purposes, to wit to steal certain oats therein." P.C. Rockcliffe had hidden in the straw and witnessed Whitehead's coming and going. Shortly afterwards he was found in bed fully clothed but with his "trowser bottoms wet." Apparently he had carried on the practice for two or three months. Notwithstanding his being a "large farmer" and his "crying bitterly" on arrest, Whitehead was given 6 weeks' hard labour.[52]

Whitehead got off lightly: common felons might well receive heavier sentences as was shown by that of one month imposed on each charge in 1865 on "Phillip Smith (aged 33 and reads), charged with stealing a linen crumb cloth left on a hedge, the property of Lewis Elburn, and a pair of curtains."[53] A few weeks after the crime he had hung the curtains at his own windows only 60 yards from where he had stolen them! Rather similarly, John Wilson, a hobby horse showman, was convicted in 1903 of stealing the shirt he had on from Charles Vincent, a lodging house keeper. Though he said "God forgive me for taking it," the bench sent him down for one month.[54] By contrast in 1850 the owner of a quantity of clothing including one linen shirt, two gowns, two chemises and 1 pair of worsted stockings could not be found though "the bellman announced the find through out the town[54] (The Bellman continued to perform from time to time until c.1940, Arthur Ashburner being the last holder of the office).

More often than not any attempt at detection was unsuccessful. No criminal was apprehended when in 1898[55] the church was broken into, nor in 1900 when a thief entered the cloakroom and robbed the dinner baskets in the cloakroom of St. Thomas's School.

Even for minor offences the accused could expect to be locked up pending appearance in court. Soon after Milnthorpe's new police station was opened in 1910 James Robinson, a shoemaker, "after a night in one of the new cells, appeared on the old charge of drunk and disorderly. He had taken a drop of rum to keep the cold out which seemed to upset him."[57] In 1917 a farmer's wife, Sarah Dickinson of Black Dyke, was fined £2 for stealing a lamp but she was not put in the cells because her husband was in "a substantial position." She was summoned to the court instead.[58] Fourteen year old George Rockcliffe had not been so lucky in 1908, for having on two occasions stolen cash amounting in all to 19s. 9d. he was sent to Ashbar Nautical School at Heswell in Cheshire, the bench decreeing that "it would be no kindness to the boy to leave him in his present surroundings." The father was ordered to pay 2s. per week for maintenance as he earned 26s. a week and only had 4 children aged 23, 13, 9 and 6. He would get his "son cared for at less cost than at home." Thereafter poor George was hardly ever referred to by his highly respectable family.[59]

That punishment was not necessarily a deterrent was shown in 1919 when Robert Holt was sent to prison for one month after breaking Mr Fawcett's shop window. He was aged 61 and had just "celebrated" a 50 years Jubilee of Crime![60] In 1931 the chief witnesses against a youth called Nicholas John Halliwell were his parents – after he had stolen £7 8s. 7½. from the Poppyday funds collected by his mother. He was sent to Borstal and it was hoped that "he would benefit from the Education received."[61]

The Second World War gave a slight fillip to criminal activity. Under the cover of the blackout two robbers got a good haul from the Co-operative Stores in 1941 including "11,000 cigarettes, 2lbs of twist, 12 boxes of 25 cigars, 18 boxes of 20 cigars, 8 oz. of flake tobacco, 2 bottles of lemonade, 3 steak and kidney pies, 1 loaf of bread, ½lb. of butter, 1lb. of cheese, 10 packets of cheese, two tins of bloater paste, 1 pair of boots and 1 pair of overalls valued at £8 9s 3d."[62] About the same time a bungalow on Kirkgate was broken into and Mrs Downing, widow of the late Police Sergeant, had her rate money stolen. The thief was never found but some years later a medal kept in the sergeant's wallet, which was also stolen, turned up at a village jumble sale. By contrast, the five men who held up Mr Costello, managing director of the comb mill, and robbed him of 67 cases of combs, were all caught. The ring leader, Leonard Barretta, was given three years' penal servitude and the rest "who had lain in hiding near the Kendal to Lancaster Road by the River Bela" got 12 months.[63] An old-fashioned hue-and-cry occurred in 1947 after Mrs Metcalf saw two absconding borstal boys breaking into Miss Kilpatrick's bungalow on Church Street. Sergeant Irving was passing and he and members of the public took up the chase over the hill to the estuary, where one boy fell into a dyke and was captured, and then over Haverbrack where the other got away.

In 1951 there was a mysterious burglary at the home of comb manufacturer Percy Dobson. A quantity of jewellery valued at £1,500 was 'stolen' in what was apparently a daylight robbery. After a considerable furore the jewellery was eventually found by a maid in a drawer of their new home.[64] The mistake had occurred because the Dobson's had been moving from Fieldedge to Bela House! But ten years later the *Daily Mirror* reported "A £1000 reward was offered last night to anyone who can solve the big riddle of the A6. The burglary in the best Edgar Wallace style was at the twenty room Bela House, a lonely (sic) mansion off the A6 at Milnthorpe, Westmorland. A soft shoe gang, it is believed, tip toed around and carefully went through a £40,000 collection of antiques, miniatures, gold and silver trinkets... and opened a safe. They worked so silently that the owner, wealthy William (Percy) Dobson, a retired plastics manufacturer and his wife Margaret slept on." Altogether £6,000 worth of treasurers including a £3,000 ruby ring and a Charles II inkstand valued at £460 had gone – forever. Fortunately they were insured.[65]

Sensational as were "Percy's burglaries" they were completely eclipsed in 1954 by a case concerned superficially with an unpaid bill of £21 4s. for electricity. It led to Milnthorpe becoming a major item on the B.B.C. news and earned headlines in newspapers around the world. The main defendant was Dr. Edward Hogarth Hopkinson, aged 38. A local man who had a brilliant career at Heversham Grammar School and Oxford and Liverpool Universities, Edward set himself up in General Practice at Flowerden Cottage. For his residence he rented Laburnum House, next door to several cottages on Main Street owned by his mother. Though "Dr Hoppy" was jovial and popular his practice did not prosper and in November 1953 the North Western Electricity Board "experienced a certain amount of difficulty in collecting accounts." After the usual warnings the electricity supply to Laburnum House and the cottages was cut off.

At 8.30 a.m. one Monday morning in the following February an Electricity Board worker noticed that both the cottages and house were lit up. That evening they were lighted again. The following day after some delay caused by Dr. Hopkinson threatening to take the hapless officials to the Medical Council they gained access to the properties, where they found that the seal on the meter box had been broken and a piece of copper wire had been contacted to the fuse holder. Outside they discovered that "a brush had been wedged from an upstairs window of Laburnum House against the jumper wire connecting the live wire and in that way contact had been made."

This time the supply was cut off from the electricity pole outside and Hoppy and his tenant, Kenneth Maynard Mordy, had to use paraffin lamps. They were also summoned to Milnthorpe petty sessions for maliciously using electricity belonging to the North Western Electricity Board. When the case came up Mordy was too ill to attend and a long letter was read out from him enquiring if the Chairman of the Magistrates was a member of the Westmorland Agricultural Executive. It seemed Mordy was engaged in protracted litigation with various authorities after a business venture at Crooklands Nurseries had failed following the destruction of his tomato crop by a faulty fertilizer. This enquiry was considered to be irrelevant and after a hearing lasting several hours both men elected to go for trial by jury.

Their trial at Kendal Quarter Sessions began at noon on

Laburnum House - where 'Hoppy's Atomic Egg', was hatched.

Saturday, July 3rd, 1954, and lasted until 9.10 p.m., the latest finish ever for the court – though just in time for the Sunday papers. Lord Chorley who presided said that "it was probably the most extraordinary ever to be heard in this court" – while the case of "Hoppy's Egg" entered the folk lore of Milnthorpe.

In cross examination Dr. Hopkinson agreed with much of the evidence. "It is correct that an ordinary domestic broom was present near the wires but it was put there by me because the wall plug and bracket was coming loose and the whole thing was in danger of falling into the yard. It would have been an acrobatic feat to bring together the ends of insulated cable. I am neither an acrobat nor an electrician." He admitted that he had generated 120 volts of electricity compared to the Board's 250 volts. In reply to the question "what was the source of supply?" he answered "it came from an experimental thing called an egg. It generated electricity by a process known as nuclear fusion and is in its experimental stage. It is non-mechanical and it does not make a noise if it is brought into the proximity of another apparatus known as a hen. . . it can supply a sufficient illumination for only a limited number of lights. . ." The egg had been fixed to the meter "which he had rewired for the purpose of passing a supply from Laburnum House to the cottage." When asked why he had not divulged this information to the Milnthorpe Court two months earlier he said "I am bound by the oath of Hippocrates as a doctor that I shall not divulge anything of a secret nature. This was a secret. The egg was lent to me when it was known by the owner that I was in difficulty over my electricity supply."

Time and time again the prosecuting counsel asked him to produce the egg but Dr. Hopkinson refused on the grounds that he hoped to have the apparatus patented and so for the time being its whereabouts and workings must remain a secret. The best he could supply as an expert witness was Dr. Edwin Holmes of the Lancaster Royal Infirmary, who spoke of Dr. Hopkinson's "high character and considerable abilities which in scientific matters made him almost a genius." Of "the egg" Holmes declared "I have not seen the one he is talking about but I have seen one that operates lights for traffic control." Holmes, however, was a gynaecologist and not a physicist.

Although they only had Edward Hopkinson's testimony to go by, it still took the jury an hour and thirty five minutes to bring in a verdict of "Guilty." In sentencing Hopkinson to a "lenient" fine of £70 and Mordy to one of £15, the judge said he had chosen not to send them to prison only because of their "previous irreproachable character... perhaps the worst feature of the case is that you persisted in the story when the jury clearly believed it to be a cock and bull story."

It was the "silly season" for the media so Hoppy's egg sensation brought swarms of reporters to Milnthorpe. The fact that the term "nuclear fusion" had to be explained to the court illustrates the novelty of Edward Hopkinson's account at that time. There were some who said that if the egg was patented he might have solved the world's energy problem; others thought that if it existed and if it went wrong Milnthorpe might suffer the same fate as Hiroshima and Nagasaki.[66]

Edward Hopkinson soon closed his practice and left Milnthorpe. He hit the headlines again some years later when he was charged with cycling round a hospital while "high" on drugs. He died an early death not long afterwards.

Throughout the nineteenth century the most "rural" crime of all, poaching, occupied the Milnthorpe bench considerably – though many practitioners of the art came from surrounding villages. In 1861 William Nelson of Goose Green was sent to prison for one month for stealing a pigeon. On the other hand, after a day-long trial, a charge against Nelson of stealing a ferret from Mathew Walker, a bobbin Turner of Crooklands, was dismissed owing to difficulty in identifying the valuable live stock.[67] In 1874 "Anthony Hornby and Richard Pearson native of the far famed city of Storth" got 14 days for poaching, but William Vasey of Holme was fined only 20s. The result of a quarrel over ill-gotten gains landed poacher John Pearson of Storth in court on a charge of assaulting Mary Nelson "a woman of somewhat weak intellect who made many curtsies to the court." Mary being less valuable than game Pearson, on this occasion, was let off with a warning.[68] A brazen poacher, described as a labourer, was Thomas Saul of Clawthorpe, who when fined £3 in 1908 flung down the money saying "there's plenty more where that came from" and caused the *Westmorland Gazette* to comment "Either he is an exceptionally well-to-do labourer or an exceptionally successful poacher."[69]

Occasional cases of petty violence came up at Milnthorpe from time to time as in 1833 when John Railton was sent to prison for 14 days after failing to pay a fine for an assault on Mary Hadwin. In a rare case in 1859, Thomas Mayer of Milnthorpe summoned a boy named James Beck for an assault. The assault was admitted but in defence it was stated "that when it was committed the complainant was in liquor and had provoked the boy by using very disgraceful language about his mother and had done so several times before, destroying their peace at home. The boy believed his mother to be perfectly innocent (she bears a good character) and his temper being raised, he thrashed the complainant there and then. The defendant was fined the small sum of 6d and costs and the complainant received a very severe reprimand from the bench at his disgraceful conduct."[70]

A dispute amongst the fair sex in 1873 caused Jane Thompson to be summoned by Bridget Doodes for an assault at Mr Forster's Mill. Her daughter Nancy Thompson had drawn a large knife in the affray and threatened to give Bridget a few inches of the blade. The mother then knocked Bridget off a stool. For this a fine of 14s. (or 14 days) was imposed.[71]

A fine of only 1s. was imposed on William Hodgson, landlord of the Cross Keys, after he had got his ostler John Cornthwaite by the throat for scratching a door of his carriage after the funeral of Mrs Wilson of Dallam Tower.[72] Even more lenient was a mere caution given to a Kendal dyer who in March 1910 broke into a dance in the Public Rooms and "upset the doorkeeper and smote the professor (the MC) not wisely but too well." The "professor" was advised next time to wear chain mail.[73]

Three cases around the turn of the century show that cruelty to children is not a modern phenomenon. All three could be attributed to inadequacy and neglect probably caused by low intellect, aggravated by appalling housing conditions and probably drink. In 1895 Robert and Mary Jane Riley were summoned for neglect of their twelve months old daughter Maggie Bell. Dr. Seagrave reported that Maggie Bell weighed only 13 lbs 10 oz., showed marked wasting, was very dirty and filthy. Riley and his wife were given 1 month's hard labour. Maggie Bell subsequently survived tuberculosis but some months later the magistrates were told she was "not likely to grow up."[74]

It seems that prosecution was the only way to ensure help. Thus in January 1902 Richard and Ellen Bain of Carr's Yard were summoned by L. Gardner Thompson Hon. Sec. of the N.S.P.C.C. branch for cruelty to their children Annie, 7, Robert, 5 and Agnes, 2. Dr Seagrave said that all the children were verminous and that Agnes' head was a mass of sores. The floor in the children's room was caked in dirt. In the parent's bedroom there was a piece of carpet covered with mildew completely rotten to the floor. The children slept on a flock mattress which was filthy dirty and stagnant with urine. Completely verminous, the covering consisted of two old coats and a horse blanket. The woman had been twice drunk in Kendal and the Police Constable had seen the little girl go back and forward to the public house for beer as early as 7 a.m. "He had seen her drink from the can on the way." The father's plea that he "was not a drinking man just a glass or two with his dinner" was accepted and he received only a caution but the mother went to Lancaster Castle for a month.[75]

In the third case the more guilty parent was again the mother, Jane Fenwick, wife of John Fenwick, comb maker. In 1910 she was described as "brazen and came into Court struggling between two officers." The bench was told that the Fenwick's had six children, one girl and five boys, the eldest of whom helped his father at the works. Between them they earned "good wages of 32s per week." The other children who were all under 10, rarely went to school and lay around all day while the mother just sat by the fire while the little girl was "dull and had swollen glands with superating large scabs on the head caused by irritation of vermin." All the children went to the Workhouse while their mother did a month's hard labour at Lancaster Castle.[76] However, in the following year brazen Jane was again brought to court "struggling and making a running commentary." Nurse Helena Bird stated that she had repeatedly cleaned the scalps of the children but they remained verminous and "there was always excretion on the bedroom floor." Jane had become worse: she just sat all day by the fire but when her husband came in the fire was always out and "he had to do all the baking – and washing." This time the Fenwick's were deprived of their mother for 6 weeks and not long afterwards they left the village.[77]

Sex crimes do not appear to have been common in the nineteenth century. Because of the extreme reticence of the period sexual assaults would be less likely to be reported fully than in later less inhibited times. Even so, in 1847 Robert Hudson aged 70, stone mason of Milnthorpe, was charged by Elizabeth Brockbank aged 14, a servant in his employment, with having on several occasions attempted to commit an assault on her person. For this he was fined 40s. but "the particulars of the case were unfit for publication."[78] In 1849 a man, farmer John Grisedale of Allithwaite was the aggrieved party at Milnthorpe petty sessions. It was reported that after the May Fair as "he was leaving Milnthorpe in a state of intoxification he was accosted by two females who took liberties with him." In so doing they removed a £20 Craven note, a Leeds £5 note and 1½ sovereigns.[79] One of the females, Ann Greaves, got Thomas Warden, a tailor, and Thomas Pinn, a coach painter, to exchange the notes at the Malt Shovel and this led to their discovery. They were fighting drunk when arrested and "their apprehension caused not a little disturbance."

More serious was the case of Charles Parker, a horse driver at the railway works who in 1874 was charged "of a rape on Margaret Garnett on the Marsh Lane. He first accosted her on the main road and at length he pulled her off the bridge into the lane and tried to throw her down in the lane. She struggled all she could to get away but finally he threw her down, put his hand to her mouth to prevent her screaming, ultimately he mastered her and effected his purpose."[83]

One of the few cases of open soliciting occurred in January 1863 when Jane Bailey, a woman of loose character, was brought up into custody charged with accosting men in the streets of Milnthorpe and of using indecent language on Christmas Day night. . . she was being followed by a number of young men "who were 'saved' by her arrest."[80] Even so she only received 7 days in the House of Correction.

Elizabeth Maria Cotes was described "as a very respectable looking woman" when in 1866 she was charged with feloniously marrying Edmund Kershaw at Burton while her husband James Cotes was still alive. For this she was committed to Appleby Assizes.[81] A war-time bigamy occurred in 1942 when Amelia Eleanor Smith "married" Robert Eugene Henderson at St. Thomas's Church. He had told her that he earned £9 15s. and would take her to live in Swinton. Instead she was left in the lurch and he was given 15 months in gaol the judge commenting "there's far too much bigamy these days."[82]

A perjury case "lasting from 11 a.m. to 7 p.m. with only half an hour off" caused much interest and no doubt amusement in 1904. The case concerned Eleanor Ann Atkinson of Woodhouse. She had previously failed to get a paternity order imposed on Lancelot Langhorne, Coachman of Woodhouse but the person in the "dock" was Jane Metcalfe. She had sworn that a man named Bell was the father, as she and her daughter had seen the girl and Bell in the carthouse at Deepthwaite on top of some sacks. Moreover she had heard the girl's mother say it must be the lad (Bell) "as the girl   .

was never off his back." Canon Gilbert and his curate had both been to ask her if her evidence was true and she had said "Yes." She denied that she had ever said to Langhorne "God bless ye Lanty, I thought I'd git thee off." To support his case Bell brought a dozen witnesses who told the (not suprisingly) "crowded court" that they had taken "liberties" with Eleanor including on one occasion when she had been on the way to deliver apples to the vicarage. The case was eventually dismissed but the magistrates commented that Bell's evidence was most unsatisfactory. Mrs Atkinson said she would "discuss the matter" again with Eleanor when they got home. Poor girl![84]

In the inter war years the village was agog when in October 1934 Dr. Charles Harrison of Liverpool, aged 45, and a typist Miss Nora Banks, 37, were summoned for giving the false names of Mr and Mrs C. Harris in the visitors' book at the Bull's Head. The case was dismissed as "no offence had been committed as their nationality had been given correctly."[85] Nevertheless their "flagrant immorality" caused a stir.

Inquests into accidents, sudden and criminal deaths and suicides attracted the attention of the press from time to time. In June 1838 Margaret Townson aged about 10 was burnt to death by accident after her clothes had caught fire at the Lodging House. In her panic she had rushed out into the street with her clothes ablaze. An inquest held in March 1843 at the Sun Inn brought in a verdict of accidental death on the landlord's 3½ year old son who "fell in the back parlour fire at 8 o'clock and died at 1 o'clock."[87] Natural causes were given as the reason for the cot death of Ann Atkinson aged 4 months in 1849. She "had taken the breast before going to sleep. In the morning it was found dead in bed, its hands clenched, its lips and fingernails discoloured purple and its tongue slightly protruding through its gums. Verdict dead in bed."[88] In 1851 an inquest was held at "Mr Bainbridge's King's Arms on a little girl, Eddy Towers, daughter of James Towers, weaver, who had died as a result of being scalded by a pan of boiling toffy (sic)."[89] The inquest on William Milner Clark was held at the Cross Keys in 1855. He was aged 28 and a native of Swaledale and "had cut his throat in the River near Bela Mills. He was a private (sapper and miner) engaged in ordnance in Milnthorpe for three months."[90] So discoloured was the face and body of Miles Nicholson, a cordwainer found in Parkside field in 1866, that a murder was first suspected – but the inquest brought in a natural causes verdict after hearing that the deceased had been subject to fits of apoplexy and had been seen climbing a fence shortly before his death.[91] Over the years a number of persons drowned themselves in the Bela, including George Edward Thompson aged 53 found drowned at Bela side in 1916. He was a painter and plumber and had not been well since he had fallen and hurt his head while painting the Post Office in 1912.[92]

Not all village cases were sad or serious. Sometimes even minor cases received special attention and a verbatim account has survived of a scene in court during 1878 when Elizabeth Stephenson was accused of stealing a scarf worth 2s. belonging to Annie Akister of Milton Moor. The incident took place at the Blue Bell, Heversham.

"Defendant, not altogether a prepossessing young lady, could not pay much attention to the business of the court for the loud sobbing in which she indulged during the trial, though often rebuked by the bench. The witness Ann Ellis said the ball (at the Blue Bell) broke up at 12 o'clock. Defendant brought her bonnet out of the room. I asked her were (sic) she got the 'scarf'? She replied "I have cabbaged it." I said there might be a row about it and she replied "Hold thee noise, I's get the yan on Thursday." The witness here bust into tears, prisoner exclaiming "you don't tell the truth, it's all through your bad company; you persuaded me to go off with you." The prisoner who pleaded guilty was sentenced to one month's imprisonment."[93]

Petty as the two shilling scarf case was the most trivial case must have been that brought against five boys – William Knight, Ralph Thompson, Walter Thompson, Gilbert Whiteley and Ronald Thompson – for damaging a County Council notice board. They were each fined 6d. and had to pay the full costs of 1s. 9d.[94]

Murder in Milnthorpe – as everywhere else – has always caused the greatest sensation. On 13 November 1824 *The Westmorland Advertiser and Kendal Chronicle* announced:

A Murder Most Awful

One of the most horrid and dreadful murders has been perpetrated in Millthrop since our last publication on a person named Wilson, by trade a cooper. We are under the necessity, at present, of saying little as possible until some circumstances occur that may lead to a detection of the murderer; and until then, we think, no journal ought to give any report.[96]

This warning did not prevent the Advertiser's main rival, the *Westmorland Gazette*, from reporting the evidence given at the inquest held at the Cross Keys on 7th November, the day after the discovery of the crime. Subsequently, the Advertiser's account was even more lurid than that of the Gazette. The victim James Wilson "was a single man rather growing in years" who had recently purchased a house on the Blue Row. The house was one "up the steps" at the south end of Church Street. This position was conveniently near to the cooper's workshop in the Town Field, behind the row, where probably he worked. For over twelve months he had lodged with Mary Blackburn and curiously the night of the 5th October was the first (and last) which he spent in his new house. According to the Advertiser Wilson had gone to a neighbour, Mr William Inman's house for a light and told him that if he did not return to fasten the cellar window. Early next morning Inman heard a noise as if someone was stamping... blows were heard being repeatedly struck as if some soft body was being struck. The Advertiser then said that "an alarm of fire was given" and that William Flemming and a man named Brockbank entered the house, removed the bedclothes and discovered the deceased "who had a burnt hand and one foot... and... bruises and blood on the left side of the head above the temples." The Gazette, however, stated that:

"he was found about noon on Saturday last; his skull fractured in a shocking manner and his heat (sic) almost to pieces. A quantity of blood was upon the wall and report says the print of a bloody hand. If this be true the hand may lead to a discovery – It seems that after the murder, to conceal the act the villain or villains had set fire to the bed in which the murdered man lay. The fire, however, had made small progress; yet his feet and legs etc. were burned in a manner too shocking to describe. It was this fire that led the neighbours to break into the house; for the smoke issuing from the slates made them suspect the place to be on fire, and they broke in to put it out, when the awful spectacle presented itself of one of their acquaintance lying with his head crushed and his lower extremities in the very act of roasting"...

Equally gory was the forensic evidence of Robert Hancock the surgeon who stated that there were "several deep wounds externally upon the head... bones on the left side of the head were broken and beat into the brain to a considerable depth... the wounds were likely to be caused by repeated beatings from a small round headed hammer... the wounds on the left eye two inches deep... done by a sharp triangular instrument... the wounds on the head six inches long and lower jaw bone broken on both sides... "it was also reported that there were burnt sticks in the hearth though the deceased had never had a fire in the bedroom.

The Inquest Jury, after sitting day by day, have brought in a verdict of "Wilful Murder against some person or persons unknown." As there was no regular police force investigations were left to the amateur exertions of the magistrates and other local worthies. Accordingly "there was a numerous meeting of magistrates on Tuesday, to investigate the late horrid murder. Among the rest were present, W.W.C. Wilson Esq. M.P., Thomas Greene Esq. M.P., Rev. Henry Sill; W.W. Atkinson Esq., Thomas Holme Maude Esq., etc. The greatest praise is due to Col. Smythe (of Dallam Tower), for his vigorous exertions – exertions which will not be relinquished, we believe, till some clue has been found."

The investigators also issued a hand bill stating "In order to bring to justice the Perpetrator of this horrid deed, the magistrates will feel obliged by any Person who may have had, or known others to have had, any Money Transactions with the deceased, to give the earliest information to them or to Mr Gandy, Mr Postlethwaite, or Mr Whitaker all of Milnthorpe."[98]

For unspecified reasons Ralph Hayes, a watchmaker and friend of the deceased, was suspected for a while. Later suspicion fell on a Mr. M. Dean but soon afterwards the Gazette had to state that "after a full enquiry we are perfectly satisfied that there is no foundation for such a report." The local investigators then called in a Bow Street Police Officer, whose warrant was signed by the Home Secretary Robert Peel himself. The Gazette then hoped that with the strenuous exertions of the magistrates, aided by Tanton, one of the most vigilant of the London Police Officers, the murderer will in a short time be detected. Expectations and high hopes were not realised – no murderer was ever found – and the affair continued to mistify Milnthorpe for generations. When about 1890 a hatchet was discovered by Mr Tyson in the quarry in the Showfield behind Wilson's house it was believed to be the murder weapon though the murder had taken place nearly 70 years previously.[99]

After the Milnthorpe murder the local authorities were ready for action – and in 1828 William Mosey (calling himself William Wilson) was apprehended at Milnthorpe on a charge of murdering William Longthorne of Barnaby Moor, Nr Pocklington and brought before the magistrates at the Workhouse. They had, however, got the wrong man and issued a wanted notice describing the suspect as being "about 20 years of age, 5 ft. 1 in. lad like appearance, dark complexion, dark eyes and hair with strong features, last seen wearing short blue striped smock frock, soiled duck trowsers and a round cap and supposed to have wounded himself in one hand and his trowsers are very bloody."[100] Eventually the right villain was arrested at Workington.

A century later in 1935 Milnthorpe was drawn into the sensational murder case of the Lancaster doctor – Buck Ruxton. After dumping the dismembered bodies of his wife and maid in a Scottish ravine Ruxton was stopped at 1 a.m. by P.C. Lowther as he drove off the Square, having called at the newly opened public lavatories. Lowther was investigating a report that a car like Ruxton's had knocked a Mr Beatty off his bicycle on New Road, Kendal. Lowther later told the assize court that "the Doctor had a little boy with him and seemed extremely agitated and more so than one would have thought if he had only been involved in a slight accident."[101] Many villagers recall that after Ruxton's arrest local police, specials and Scotland Yard made a minute search of all the A6 hedgerows in case the doctor had discarded any bits and pieces of his victims locally.[102]

Occasionally Milnthorpe magistrates have had to inaugurate committal proceedings on murder charges against persons from neighbouring villages. Thus in 1909 Mary Young Robson of Burton was committed for murder by Milnthorpe magistrates. She was found guilty but insane.[103] In 1926 Mary Ann Scott, wife of John Henry Cross a labourer at the gunpowder works at Sedgwick, was charged with the murder of her eight year old son Harold. Before committing her to the Assizes the bench was informed that her husband's taunting that he was not the child's father had driven her to the desperate act.

Mental disturbance was undoubtedly behind the "case of the boy in the bath," Milnthorpe's only twentieth century murder. At a special court at the Institute in 1942 Lena Gertrude Pilling, aged 34, of 19 Summerville Road, was charged that "feloniously, wilfully and of malice aforethought did kill and murder one Bruce Pilling, aged 7 years, at Milnthorpe on Thursday, 5 November, 1942." Lena had been troubled with her nerves for some time since her husband George had been called up to serve in the National Fire Service in Liverpool.[104]

At the subsequent murder trial at Westmorland Assizes, which attracted the attention of the National Press, the jury were told that she had imagined she was being persecuted by an unnamed man who was after her money. At 10.25 p.m. on the night of 5 November Albert Jackson Goddard, who lived next door at number 17, was knocked up by Lena who though apparently calm persuaded him and Mrs Goddard to go into her house. In the bathroom they found a pile of sodden women's clothes on the floor; in the bath, submerged in 12 inches of water was Bruce, dressed in his dressing gown and pyjamas. He had been dead for some time. Mr Goddard asked "Why did you do it Lena?" She replied "I though that maniac would be coming again... I have been in twice. I got in on top of Bruce. I thought I could go as well." Without leaving the box the jury accepted Lena's plea that she was "guilty but insane." The judge made it clear that the allegations against the man were completely untrue and that "he was perfectly respectable." Lena was committed to a criminal lunatic asylum, "her mother and husband were given leave to see her before being taken away."[105] More than twenty years later Lena was eventually able to return home for some years before her death. Nowadays it is doubtful whether this homicide would have been treated as murder.

In 1952 an inquest held at Milnthorpe had no option but to bring in a verdict of murder against a person or persons unknown on the body of a newly born female child, aged about 36 hours. It had been found at Blackstone Point by boys from Earnseat School and

The Old Police Station.

had apparently had its skull smashed on the rocks. Neither the mother nor the "murderer" were ever found.[106]

Milnthorpe did not have a court room until the police station was built c.1861. Prior to that time cases were either held in the magistrates' houses or in the inns. A change took place when in 1893 it was reported that "Milnthorpe people have heard with something like astonishment that those gentlemen deputed of the county authorities to choose a room for the transaction of police business at Milnthorpe are about to decide on the Institute for the purpose. The Public Rooms were offered at £13 a year and were not accepted on the grounds that they were too far from the police cells. The astonishment comes when it is learnt that the Institute rooms are less private, are further away and cost £22 p.a."[107] Because the staircase going up to the court room was covered in lead "going up the leaden steps" came to mean getting into trouble. But it was only a makeshift arrangement. In the 1930's Colonel North, Chairman of the Bench, complained that if he moved his chair a few inches he would be in danger of falling over backwards.[108] Moreover, it appeared that the magistrates' retiring room was being used as a spare bedroom by the caretaker. Twenty years later the magistrate Henry Hornyold Strickland stated "if we are not frozen (all the magistrates were wearing coats) we have to breathe smoke fumes from a broken heating boiler."[109] When the windows were opened the magistrates could not be heard for noise of vehicles revving up at the traffic lights outside. Moreover the retiring room was so small that the magistrates could not sit down. Despite these and further grumbles the court continued to meet in the Institute until c.1970 when all local petty sessions were removed to Kendal.

The railway navvies brought official law enforcement to Milnthorpe. In April 1845 a "pair of active policemen" were brought from Liverpool "from Friday to Wednesday to cover the monthly pay day of the labourers." The next year two special constables were enrolled to assist them.[110] When the works were completed this force moved away, no doubt following the navvies to other projects. They were so badly missed that a regular policeman, James Waiting, was appointed in 1852. He stayed until 1858 when Sergeant Bertram took over. At first the police were based in their own lodgings or cottages until in April 1858 George Wilson of Dallam Tower offered premises on the site of the old weavers' shed in Haverflatts Lane: the area now known as Police Square. In order to provide a humane lock-up and other accommodation tenders were advertised. The letter from the successful contractor has survived:

5 Jan. '60

Milnthorpe
Dear Sir,
I send you an estimate for the Erecting and finishing of the Dwellinghouse, Magistrates Room, Lock-ups and other Offices Appertaining to the same, and to finish the Same according to the satisfaction of the magistrates, the Surveyor and who they may think proper to appoint to inspect the same for the sum off (sic) £221 8s.[111]

John Davison

The new station had two cells "with their strongly bound doors, heavy locks and bolts and with the necessary iron spy flaps." There was also a small high-walled yard, and even one of the larger domestic type sash windows was furnished with iron bars. This was replaced by the Police Station on Beetham Road in 1910, with a more commodious house, two cells and a shed for the police ambulance.

Following Sergeant Bertram there were six constables P.C.'s Barnes to 1881, Johnstone to 1883, Jacob Cannon to 1885, Bell to 1891, Kerr to 1896 and Thomas Goad to 1906. Since then the senior officer at Milnthorpe has generally been a Sergeant. Francis Park was Sergeant from 1906 until his retirement in 1920. His "one man band' became locally quite famous. George Henry Downing came in 1924. He died unexpectedly in 1927 and was given one of Milnthorpe's grandest funerals. There were police contingents from Kendal, Penrith, Kirkby Stephen, Kirkby Lonsdale, Ambleside and Windermere headed by the Chief Constable P.T.B. Browne.

There were also large bodies of Special Contingents of Specials. Notwithstanding all the tributes Mrs Downing, her two daughters and nephew, had to be out of the station house within ten days. They only found accommodation at Ivy Cottage in the nick of time, their furniture being carried across the square at night, to enable Sergeant Cass to move in the next morning.[112]

Though devoid of serious crime Milnthorpe was and remained an important police "manor." Traffic problems of all sorts created considerable work and extraordinary pressure came in the Second World War, especially after the Prisoner of War Camp was established at Bela River two miles to the east.

The P.O.W.'s stayed until 1948 to be followed until 1952 by "displaced persons," mainly Poles and Ukrainians. In October 1951 it was pessimistically reported that the camp would be retained for use as a "reception centre for evacuees in the next war."[113] Other suggestions were that it should be used for temporary civilian housing, or as a holiday camp. It came, however, as a considerable shock "to residents of neighbouring villages and hamlets when the Home Office announced that the "Milnthorpe Camp" would become an Open Prison.[114]

Local fears were hardly allayed when the Home Office announced that only selected types such as debtors serving short terms or others nearing the end of longer sentences would be there. "Discipline was still very strict and there would be no murderers."[116]

Geoffrey Vane the Westmorland M.P. asked questions in the House which resulted in a full scale public enquiry being held in the Memorial Hall.

It was all to no avail. While Milnthorpe celebrated the Coronation, the Home Office announced that a "prison without bars" would come to Bela River.

Nothing of what the public feared happened. The prison became an extremely popular institution. Local labour was recruited, and several Milnthorpe men became "prison officers" while local businesses, the chemist, the doctors and even the clergy, received extra income from the camp. The prisoners were soon to be seen going to work in parties or by themselves on red cycles and at a time of acute labour shortage many people employed them as jobbing gardeners. Despite all the fears, no local person was ever harmed and few prisoners absconded. What with television, dunlopillow mattresses, "a roast on Sundays and Turkey at Christmas" few would – it was claimed – wish to escape. The 'bus conductors called the prison stop the "holiday camp." Something like pride was felt when, soon after the camp opened, a well known peer of the realm, involved in a notorious peccadillo became a resident. One local officer, was said to have always addressed him as 'My lord'!

13

Neddy Stones
and the Haverbrack
Common Dispute

In nineteenth century Milnthorpe Neddy Stones was a rarity; he was a radical and, by parochial standards, almost a revolutionary. If he had lived in a city or in a growing industrial town he might have been swept into the major reform movements of the time and achieved wider recognition. Having been born in 1838 and dying only in 1920 he witnessed the economic decline and stagnation of Milnthorpe.[1]

Mirroring economic decline and the contraction of the community was the erosion of common rights and the demolition of workers' cottages. Stones himself estimated that in the nineteenth century thirteen fishermen's and labourers' cottages had been pulled down at Far Arnside, while at Milnthorpe six had gone at Scout Bank, two on Milnthorpe Marsh and about thirty others in the main village, along "with two paper mills destroyed and all the benefits arising therefrom, in the interests of the Town and Trade, two rope walks, a twine walk, three large weaving shops and the Blue Row gardens laid to prevent further building."[2] The town of Milnthorpe had degenerated into a village dependent merely on local trade and on farming, but even the landed interest was hard pressed by a world agricultural depression. Deeply involved with the minutiae of local life and with his own, generally unprofitable, concerns, Stones did not see that the decline resulted from larger uncontrolable forces. Instead, with unoriginal radical fervour, he blamed the aristocracy; his target being the Wilsons of Dallam – the "squires" of Milnthorpe.

The Wilsons had, indeed, enlarged Dallam Park and made

gardens, plantations and paddocks where there had been houses, but their remaining tenants did not have their rents increased. Moreover George Edward Wilson, his son Edward Hugh and daughters, the Misses Gertrude Mary and Gertrude Sophia, squires and successively owners of the estate from 1853 to 1892, were resident at Dallam for most of the year, patronized local tradespeople and were bountiful to the poor, the churches and all worthy causes in the best Victorian traditions. All this changed suddenly and tragically within three weeks during the winter of 1892, for Miss Gertrude Mary died on 23 January, old Mrs Wilson on 5 February and Miss Gertrude Sophia on 11 February. The cause of death given at the time was the influenza epidemic which in the south carried off Cardinal Manning and the Duke of Clarence but the Dallam family have always attributed the tragedy to typhoid caused by a faulty drain. Edward Hugh Wilson had died five years earlier.[3]

By a complicated process of the laws of entail and inheritance the heir was a somewhat distant cousin called Maurice Bromley, who derived his title from the second daughter of Daniel Wilson who had married into the Bromley family. Daniel Wilson had had two daughters, the elder marrying Colonel Smyth (who took the name of Smyth-Wilson) and they were the grandparents of the Misses Wilson. Maurice, who on coming of age took the name of Bromley-Wilson, was in America when he inherited. More importantly he was still a minor and the estate was in the hands of trustees, most of whom were unknown in local society. Until this time few had dared to question or perhaps even doubt the authority of Dallam. From the ranks of prosperous tradesmen downwards villagers either curtsied or doffed their caps to "them fra Tower."[4] At Beetham the whole congregation rose to its feet as the party from Dallam entered for morning service on Sunday, while at St Thomas's Milnthorpe, the occupants of the gallery and the free seats at the back did the same for the agent.[5] All believed it was no more than was their due – all that is except for Edward Stones.

He was personally known always as Neddy but his special antipathy to manorial rights and jealousy in endeavouring to guard the "public interest" earned him the title of the "Village Hampden," after John Hampden whose opposition to Ship Money in the 1630's weakened the power of the monarchy. Ironically, John Hampden belonged to the squirearchy, the very class which Neddy opposed.

Like most "revolutionaries," Neddy was often regarded in his time as an embarrassing nuisance, for most Milnthorpe people, like those from other places, preferred docile grumbling to action to redress grievances. At the end of his life Neddy was reduced to poverty being compelled to accept "dockets for warm winter clothing" from the Bindloss Charity[6] and to give up his rented pew in the main body of the church. Both he and his daughter Annie retreated to the gallery from where their loud and discordant voices descended, several notes and phrases behind, onto the rest of the congregation.[7] Often when Neddy and Annie emerged from their squalid house on Church Street they would be taunted by gaggles of children amused by their shabby mid-Victorian clothes and beards – Neddy's was long and straggly; Annie's, though luxuriant, was more like an "imperial." Sometimes they were accompanied by a simple minded girl, of uncertain origin, regarded as a "grand-child."[8]

Despite his tawdry end Neddy's leadership during the Haverbrack Common dispute entitles him to be remembered. The dispute was one of the most savage, long drawn out and sometimes ludicrous affairs in Milnthorpe's history. It coincided exactly with the inauguration of the Parish Council in 1894. Between 1894-96 there was only one council for the joint township of Heversham with Milnthorpe. During the affair such disparate elements as the fawning Canon Gilbert, vicar of Heversham, village traders like the Mashiters who were generally beholden to "the Tower" and many humble folk were united with Neddy. This says much for the justice of the cause but also for the stand taken by him. At the very least he dented the impression that the owners of Dallam were all well meaning as reports of their seasonal benefactions or obituary notices suggested. The main villain of the piece however, was not a Wilson but Sir Henry Bromley Bart., the chief trustee for the Dallam Estate during the minority of his eldest son Maurice Bromley-Wilson.

To the Wilson's Neddy must have seemed merely a stroppy peasant. He was neither. In village society he came about the middle. He was born in a thatched cottage at the lower end of Park Road. His father, also called Edward, was a boot maker, a craft traditionally associated with radicalism. After attending the National School under Geffrey Bentham, whose memory he revered all his life, Neddy was educated at Heversham Grammar School. He was also a keen musician and "conducted the church choir and played the organ for Mr Padwick and for the school for a number of years upon all occasions unto 1862... after which played seven years at Preston Patrick and two years at Heversham Parish Church during the alterations." On leaving the Grammar School he became a clerk and then "a traveller for Messrs Bott, papermakers of Waterhouse Mill."[9]

Like most villagers he was also a part-time farmer, rearing a few beef and dairy cattle on the marsh and in meadows nearer the village. This activity led to his first brush with Dallam Tower for in 1880 "Edward Stones was charged with stealing hurdles the property of Dallam Tower near the field belonging to Mr Raikes at Owlet Ash and also Mr Forster's field".[10] This case was dismissed but in April 1894 he was not so lucky when he was charged with adding water to milk. He claimed that the cows had been milked at 7.40 a.m. having been fed the night before on straw, turnips and potatoes grown on the low land (i.e. the wet marsh). The magistrates were not convinced and he was fined £1 10s. plus costs.[11]

Despite this contretemps his milk trade survived for in July it was reported that when "Mr E. Stones, farmer, accompanied by Mrs Stones and a child were going across the market place on their customary round of retailing milk, a wheel of the trap broke off. Mr Stones was thrown off and badly bruised... the horse then bolted, the runaway cart broke Clark's butcher's shop window before careering down Bull Lane and into Beetham Road where it over-turned outside the Bull. Mrs Stones and the child had to be rescued from underneath the wreckage".[12] Shortly after this incident Neddy's farming activities ended and he set up in business as a grocer and general dealer, at first at Vine House in the Square and then from his Church Street house. Later, during one of its periodic closures, he tried to take the lease on Waterhouse Mill, but was prevented in this undertaking, it is said, by the Tower trustees, the owners of the free-hold and water rights, who declined to do business with him.

Neddy could also be at loggerheads with other village traders. In 1890 he and Joseph Daffady, boot and shoe maker, were involved in a "violent incident and filthy language" after a meeting concerned with the Public Rooms Management. Neddy had objected to Daffady's Chairing the meeting as he was a shareholder and, it was claimed, called him an "ignoramus and factotum" and asserted that "no honest man would be guilty of sitting in the position you are". As he was leaving Daffady approached Neddy and said "Now, Mr Stones, the meeting is over and what have you to say about me?" He then stuck Neddy a blow on the left eye and another on the mouth and kicked him down. Following up this advantage Daffady then got on top of him and struck him three blows on the ground. Stones "found he was in hostile company so he put his arms around the defendant and squeezed him tightly to him to prevent any more damage", it was said at the hearing which followed. Daffady escaped from the grip by his jacket slipping away under his arms, but Stones stuck to the jacket and pulled it over his opponent's head, who got up and left. Neddy then went to Dr Seagrave to have his wounds dressed and instructed Mr Rheam to begin proceedings.

In court Dr Seagrave confirmed that Stones had bruising on the right cheek, lower lip, left eye and that there was a good deal of

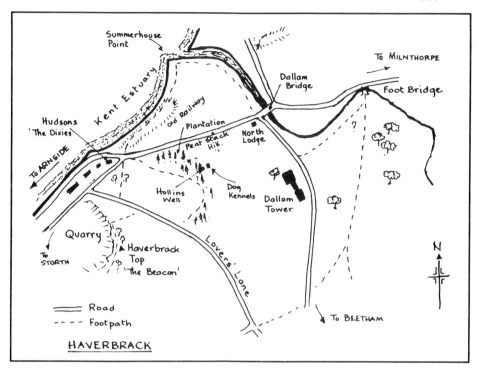

HAVERBRACK

blood on the face from the cut lip. Mr Watson defending, "Nothing very serious" "No."[13] Rather surprisingly this case was dismissed.

Notwithstanding his involvement in the bizarre spectacle of middle-aged frock-coated burghers brawling in public and his other court appearances, in 1893 Neddy sought nomination for the ultra-respectable position of assistant overseer of the parish. He came third in the poll with 45 votes as against Ben Clark with 79, George Francis Atkinson with 61 and ahead of A. Hoyle with 32 votes and J. Mashiter with 30. That Mashiter, the village post master and already a well respected figure in public and church affairs came well below Stones shows the extent of Neddy's strength in the community even before the clash with the Dallam trustees.[14]

The cause celebre began not with Haverbrack, on which it was later centred, but with the blocking of the gateway in the roadside wall opposite the north entrance to Dallam Tower. The gateway opened into the field known as Bowling Green Meadow which ran down to the estuary at Summerhouse Point. The pathway skirted the Bela and had always been accepted as a public right of way. Before the construction of the Sandside Road and the New Bridge about 1813 the whole area had been unenclosed as far as the shore, and the river bank had been used for the loading and discharge of cargoes, especially timber, from ships coming up the Bela. Even after the abandonment of the port and the building of the weir a cart track continued to be used by peat dealers and farmers crossing the sands to and from Foulshaw. More informally the summerhouse on the point had been used as a bathing pavilion by the general public with the tacit consent of the Misses Wilson.[15] Sadly Sir Henry Bromley and the other trustees were not so generous. Perhaps they were ignorant of local customs. More cynically they might have wished to demonstrate that the new brooms at Dallam would sweep away old habits, and at a time when the traditional power of the squire was about to be diluted with the imminent introduction of the Parish Council they would show who the masters still were. Always, however, they asserted that as trustees they had to safeguard the heir's rights including privacy on his desmesne and undoubtedly all the land in question (though not all the river and shore rights) belonged to the estate.

The gateway was walled up in the summer but it did not come to the notice of the general public until a letter appeared in the *Westmorland Gazette* of 23 October 1894 signed by "Pedestrian" of Kendal.

"Sir,

On Sunday last I had a delightful stroll to Milnthorpe and passing through the town I wended my way to the shore with the double object of enjoying a whiff of sea breezes and to admire the charming view from the shore beyond the railway arches at the estuary of the Bela. On arriving at Dallam Tower Lodge I was astonished to find the footpath which commences directly opposite the lodge gates had been walled up and that access to the ancient footpath leading to the shore had been stopped. This had been done I understand by the Trustees of the Dallam Tower estate. Now this footpath has been used by the writer for 25 years and has been open for as long as the oldest inhabitant can remember – probably before the land through which it passes was enclosed. Visiting Milnthorpe yesterday I was annoyed to find the obstruction still in existence. Is the public spirit of Milnthorpe dead? The obstruction should be thrown down in broad daylight and that without delay."[16]

"Pedestrian" was probably George Gatey, secretary of the local Footpaths Association and his letter elicited a reply from "Grachus," who was probably Neddy Stones, on the 3rd November.

"The writer has enjoyed the right for over fifty years" (Neddy would be 56) "for walking, bathing, picnicing, football, spell and knur and other recreations along with the rest of the public without interruption. The ground next the shore on which the old beacon (or summerhouse) is erected has always been called the bowling green and was regarded as common right beyond the sunkfence. In addition to the gate removed there was prior to the Furness Railway (i.e. built in 1873-1875) being made another gate for the use of the public when the tides were too high for passengers to pass by the shore edge and out by the old saw pit where the present Railway Bridge crosses the road at Sandside. This gate has been removed and we were told that the Railway Co. were compelled to make the footpath continuous on the outside of the embankment. This has not been done and so one right after another is lost."

In conclusion he stated that there would be "no need to petition the officials at Dallam Tower... surely they know they are wrong..."

On 10th November "Grachus" produced further evidence:

"I have had an opportunity of studying a plan or map 70 years old which shows distinctly the footpath and the inference I draw from the survey that the footpath has originally commenced at the Old Bridge by the river's edge to Dallam Wheel (where ship building used to flourish) thence to the point where the new bridge is built and continuing to the summer house and along the shore to the saw pit and so on to Dixies Inn."

The issue provided excellent propaganda for the Parish Council election which was to take place at the end of the year. The first Grachus letter had already declared that "it is a public question: - the new Parish Council when it comes into existence must deal with it" and hinted at subsequent action by suggesting "a subscription fund for the defence of anyone who may undertake to remove the obstruction." On 10th November "Pedestrian" added grist to the populist mill by issuing the challenge that "if the apathy of the people of Milnthorpe are afraid to thwart the wishes of the owners of Dallam Tower in the interests of the public at large and of other footpaths in particular the matter must not be allowed to rest."

130 electors turned up at the nomination meeting for the Parish Council at which 16 candidates were put forward. At the head of the nomination vote were John Flemming 76 votes, Edward Stones 73, Philip Rheam 71. By contrast two clergymen, the vicar of Heversham, Canon Gilbert, and the headmaster of Heversham Grammar School, Dr Hart, received but 36 and 31 votes respectively. At the meeting Neddy Stones put three questions to the other candidates:

1. "If elected a Parish Councillor will you use your utmost endeavours to protect all public rights of way in the neighbourhood and cause representation to be made to the Rural District Council that the public footpath from Dallam Tower Bridge to the shore has been obstructed and to take proceedings to establish that public right of way?"

   All candidates were "in the affirmative" except for Canon Gilbert who would support the motion "only if certain preliminaries were carried out and independent opinion decided if it was a public right of way."

2. If elected a Parish Councillor will you urge the District Council to prevent the unlawful enclosure of Haverbrack Common and to establish the public rights of recreation over the Common?"

All the nominees stated "Yes" or "Yes if found to be legal."

3. If elected a Parish Councillor will you take immediate steps to find out how much land is needed in the Parish for allotments or common pasture? Will you support the Council using all its power of producing it at reasonable rent? All answered "Yes."[17]

This last resolution, one of Neddy's hobby horses which he was to pursue for the rest of his life, indicates that rather than following Squire Hampden he perhaps resembled the seventeenth century Levellers, who wanted to return to a mythical past where society was composed of independent peasants. In this respect he was as much a reactionary as a radical.

The election on 17th December aroused widespread interest and 200 out of 370 electors voted for nine councillors out of a list of 14 candidates. Throughout the day the hall was surrounded by large crowds composed of the majority of villagers who did not have the vote. At first voting was in "a very desultory fashion until towards evening which was very brisk until closing time." There was much "pent up excitement amongst the townsmen of all classes in comparison with which the parlimentary elections were tame."

Attempts to emulate more sophisticated methods of electioneering were made: "A donkey harnessed to a barrow placarded with 'Vote for Bateman the people's friend', 'Stones and public right' and 'Llewellyn and free trade' paraded the town accompanied by a noisy crew with a horn, several voters being carried off to the polling station in this impromptu coach."

A Committee room was opened in the Institute and a great number of people assembled near the rooms talking and arguing in an excited manner. Towards midnight the results were announced: Stones 125, Rheam 124, Llewellyn 121, Flemming 121, Daffady 87, R. Mashiter 85, Canon Gilbert 77, Rev. Dr Hart 77, Hodgson 77: - not elected Dobson 67, Elburn 56, Beaton 54, Bateman 54. Subsequently "Mr Stones was seized and carried shoulder high through the streets." Crowds went to the other candidates houses and "demanded speeches from the winning candidates – but Mr Llewellyn told them to go home."

Just after Christmas came a spell of severe weather which provided grounds for mutual recrimination between Dallam and the "Stoneites."[18] There was a general stoppage of out-door work and there were seven foot high frozen waves in the bay. In the Bela "a beautiful pair of swans were frozen in the ice." Inevitably great crowds of skaters and sliders were attracted to the frozen river and equally inevitably there were casualties. Two boys fell through the ice near the weir where the water was deep and were only rescued in the nick of time by John Mashiter and George Spedding. P.C. Kerr who had recently got a St. John's ambulance certificate gave artificial respiration, even so one of the victims only recovered consciousness after several hours.[19]

The next day Mr Cary, the Dallam agent, ordered the weir sluice gates to be opened, to let the supporting waters out and the ice to collapse. Such was the ill feeling already engendered by the footpath dispute between the community and Dallam that this humane action caused Dapper Dick in the *Westmorland Gazette* to "put an obvious construction on the incident which says more plainly than words 'You may have your footpaths yonder but you shouldn't have any skating here.' So the Parish Council has found a new bone to pick with the agent and the world at large has another reminder that it was not to infants in arms that the sacred writer addressed the injunction 'Little Children love one another.' "Poor Cary did not help his case much when he wrote to the Gazette to say that "the water had been drawn off to save deer since several had drowned in Mr. Wilson's time" i.e. 1870's. The Editor did, however, comment "we are glad to state that his neighbours believe that Mr Cary is incapable of any display of childish spite."[20] Even so long after other details of the Neddy and Haverbrack affair had been forgotten the "smashing of the ice" entered the village folk lore and garbled versions of the tale were recounted by older inhabitants even in the 1950's.[21]

At the end of January the Dallam trustees, sensing the strength of public opinion, offered to come to an amicable settlement.[22] No attempts at negotiation came. Neddy, the Parish Council and the Footpaths Association, not surprisingly, contended that public rights could not be the subject of a compromise. Early in the spring the trustees retaliated by enclosing part of Haverbrack. Whether they had begun the work or had made similar moves earlier is not clear, though Neddy certainly had envisaged such action at the time of the parish council elections. The part enclosed was a two acre plot lying just to the south-east of the Dixies, bordered to the west and south by the old Sandside Road and by Lovers Lane which runs over the common via Haverbrack hamlet to Beetham. A five foot high wall 150 yards long was built to cut the plot off from the lanes and it was planted with saplings. The economic incentive must have been meagre. Even 90 years later the native trees, which included many sycamores, appear to be of little value. It seemed that the trustees were using the tiny plantation as an inch to take a yard and the rest of Haverbrack, (which certainly formed part of the Dallam Estate) would if undefended, be enclosed completely. Haverbrack, since the opening of Sandside Station twenty years earlier, had become a popular venue for excursions from Morecambe, Kendal and, especially Barrow. The "old" Wilson family had made no objections and instead had often patronised Sunday school picnics and the like on the common.

The plantation enclosure was in fact inoffensive as it neither commanded wide views nor did it obstruct the main paths onto Haverbrack. It did, however, cut off one of the paths to Hollins Well which was still in use and which lay a few hundred yards to the east by the old, and,(notwithstanding all that was said) disused track to Milnthorpe on Peat Stack Hill.

A Public Rights Association was now formed with J. Flemming as Chairman and Neddy Stones as secretary as they believed it would be better to act as public representatives to such an association than merely acting for – "a particular concourse of exasperated villagers." The result was that Neddy and his associates took the law into their own hands.[23]

On the night of 10 October at about 10 p.m. Stones with his other followers were seen by the village policeman P.C. Kerr gathering near the Cross Keys. They then headed down Park Road towards Sandside – and Haverbrack – with Kerr following, cloak and dagger fashion, some distance behind. As Kerr got to Peat Hill he heard "a rushing of stones (sic!) and heard two men say "Leave off Ned, we sharn't be able to do it all to-night." He then made up the fell but as he was getting over the wall he was spotted by Neddy who with a great display of courtesy helped him down. Neddy had removed about three feet of wall and so Kerr arrested him. Stones made "no resistance" and the next day he was formally charged with causing malicious damage to the value of 5s. He was given bail pending a trial in Milnthorpe Magistrates' Court at the end of the month.[24] Even so Neddy must have believed a greater demonstration was required and between 11 p.m. and 5 a.m. on the exceptionally dark and wild night of Wednesday – Thursday 19th – 20th October 1895 no less than 110 yards of the wall around the plantation was knocked down – and "although strong iron implements must have been employed in the demolition of the wall, the high winds; noise of the inflowing tides of the bay on the western side of the highway protected the asserters of public right from detection."

Next day the Dallam trustees offered a reward of £10 for information regarding the perpetrators of the "outrage" and, immediately ordered a temporary double wire fence to be put round the plantation. By the weekend when "Haverbrack was visited by large crowds from the surrounding villages and Morecambe the wall (had) been again built up."[25] This more serious incident in no way weakened Neddy's support and on the Saturday before the trial opened on Monday the *Westmorland Gazette* commented that

Haverbrack c.1890, with Summerhouse Point beyond.

"On the north eastern side of Morecambe Bay there is no more suitable point for obtaining a view of the wide expanse of delightful scenery than Haverbrack Fell or as it is more commonly called Haverbrack Common... for generations people have enjoyed liberty of wandering over Haverbrack Common and participating in like pleasures have been thousands of young folk who yearly take their annual treat on the broad expanse. Little by little portions of the common have been fenced off... Mr Stones... has since given notice of the following resolution to be brought forward at the next Parish Council: that the Rural District Council be requested to use its best endeavours to prevent encroachment of Haverbrack Common and to preserve the Common as a place of public resort and recreation. That the attention of the Rural District Council be drawn to the recent obstruction of four public pathways... and the shutting up of the public well by walling up the openings giving access thereto."[26]

Long before the case against Neddy Stones opened at 11 a.m. on the Monday there were "great crowds" in the streets to greet Neddy as he made his way from Church Street via the Cross Keys to the Court Room in the Institute. "Mr Stones' manner was cool, yet not defiant." On the bench were Major Braithwaite-Wilson (Chairman) and Messrs J.C. Gandy, Hulme and H. Thompson. Neddy was defended by George Gatey while Dallam Tower was represented by Arnold Greenwood of Kendal, W.B. Hutton of Bolton and by Mr Sutton Q.C. of Manchester. The prosecution case was that no public rights had been breached as there was ample access to Haverbrack and that the well water had been piped to the main road for the greater convenience of Sandside residents. Moreover the gateway leading to the well had been left open. If Stones had wanted to get to the well he could have gone through it. If he believed his action in destroying the wall was justified he should have done it openly instead of skulking down to the common at dead of night.

Neddy replied that he had given P.C. Kerr notice of his intention to "do it in daylight but finding public feeling so strong he felt that if he did the same thing openly it might lead to riot." As the Dallam trustees had remained obstinate in the face of much publicity he had not thought that much could be gained by taking the issue up with the District and County Councils as was his right under the Local Government Acts. He strongly rejected claims that the old track had been abandoned as "it was used by the public because it was more sheltered than the other way and under the lee of the old wall people constantly came down in stormy weather and that was the plain truth at the present time."

On the subject of Hollins Well he contended that it had been a public well since time immemorial and if it was a public well then the access to it must be a public highway. Using a Beetham Court Roll of 1828, he showed that public rights had not been infringed by earlier enclosures and indeed they might have been extended for the roll stated

"Mr Wilson the Lord of the Manor, having proposed to give up pasturage in respect of the whole Dallam Tower property (within this Manor) on the common whilst uninclosed on the condition that the landowners do allow Mr Wilson to inclose for his own use the part of the common on the first Flatt, from the Crow Wood on the north side of Hollings Well to the warehouse belonging to Mr Wakefield and thence to the sands as now staked out and also the south east front of the bank for planting as now staked out, but reserving to the owners of Dallam Tower property all their rights on the common in the event of an inclosure."

This was a crucial document for it showed that the Dallam trustees were acting contrary to an agreement made at the instigation of their predecessor. In any case they had acted contrary to procedures for legal enclosure which involved obtaining the consents of other landowners, possessors of common rights, the vestry meetings, manor courts and (since 1888 and 1894) the County, Rural District and Parish Councils. Even then a private act of parliament might have been necessary, and following the preservation of Epping Forest a decade earlier (which stimulated movements for conservation) this might not have been obtained.

With regard to the well Neddy rejected the suggestion that he was legally a "stranger and as a parishioner of Milnthorpe he had no rights to Haverbrack Water, and cited the fact that it had been used by ships crews from far away when the port was open. Moreover, Frederick Burrow, aged 80, of Sandside, said that before he was apprenticed at the age of 14 he had often used the old road and the well and James Beck, aged 81, of Milnthorpe "had often met the owner of the estate and never been stopped." In more recent time James Dobson, aged 61, a stone mason, remembered fencing (in 1871) Peat Stack Hill before the railway was built. "When the fence was built there was a gap left in it on purpose to leave the road open to Hollins Well."

Faced with such formidable evidence Major Braithwaite-Wilson decided that he could not try the case. Mr Sutton then replied that the trustees would take the matter to the District Council but Sir Henry Bromley and the other trustees would be prepared to discuss the whole question in a friendly way.[27]

No friendly ways being possible the whole issue was again debated at a special meeting of the Rural District Council held in the Board Room in Kendal Market Place. In all but name it was another Court case with both sides legally represented, the trustees by Mr Tilly and Milnthorpe Parish Council by Phillip Rheam. As well as the Haverbrack issue the legality of the northwards expansion of Dallam Park which had occurred seventy years previously was challenged. Eventually it was conceded that no common rights had been infringed and that although the gate on the north lodge did bar an earlier open road, public rights were not threatened as it merely replaced one 400 yards nearer to the house.[28]

The question of skating rights were complex and bitter. The Dallam trustees seemed oblivious to the mean-minded impressions they created when as the representatives of the richest family in the neighbourhood they attempted to use their considerable resources to deprive village youths of what amounted to a few hours' recreation. As it was, the rights of navigation on the Bela had to be debated. If the river was navigable (as the village claimed) as far as Park Side it might be regarded as a public highway and so the public could skate on it without permission. If it was not navigable this might be because it was obstructed by the weir built by the Wilson's near its mouth. On the other hand, the weir had been built before the Bela viaduct and the Railway Act had not mentioned navigation rights and so since c.1871 the river had not been regarded as being open to the general public. In addition to all the legal niceties, several witnesses certified that they had skated untramelled on the river over the previous half century. Further legal action seemed inevitable until Arnold Greenwood announced that the trustees wished to repeat their offer to confer.[29] The Chairman then adjourned the meeting until February – when the trustees announced that they were prepared to:

1. "acknowledge a water supply for public use from Hollins Well.
2. a footpath from the road leading to the limekilns (i.e. Quarry Lane) to the old ash trees into the highway near the Dixies Inn and thence to Haverbrack passing through the old enclosure.
3. a handgate near Sandside Station.[30]

To everyone's relief the skating issue had been dropped but the trustees still had not acknowledged public access to the well. At a joint meeting of representatives of both Milnthorpe and Haverbrack held in the "Old Toll bar" at Beetham, the Haverbrack members were opposed to having water conveyed in pipes irrespective as to the question of losing their rights and it was generally agreed that neither this committee nor yet the Rural District Council were entitled to barter away the rights of the public and so the trustees were again rejected. At a subsequent meeting of the Heversham with Milnthorpe Parish Council Canon Gilbert announced that the "Council was bound to enforce public rights." Evidence against the trustees continued to snowball. It was discovered that "when the late Mr Wilson brought water to the Dog Kennels in 1863 he obtained the sanction of the Local Authority (and agreed) that the Footpath from Lover's Lane will be kept open."[31] By this time the District Council was sick of the whole business and in March, after yet another long debate, most members agreed that if the blocked roads were reinstated or if other convenient roads substituted the Rural District Council would not contest the changes. Councillor Punchard, who as agent for the Underley Estate might have been regarded as an interested party, in particular stressed the need for compromise and if "Milnthorpe Parish Council would not accept it they should be left to fight their own battle." Again Phillip Rheam said it was not a question for compromise, but of right.[32]

Eventually after two more meetings between representatives of the trustees and the Rural District Council and special meetings of Haverbrack and Milnthorpe Parish Councils a de facto compromise was arrived at. The residents of Sandside agreed to use a stand pipe bringing water from the well a quarter of a mile nearer to the hamlet but "they did not say there was a road to the well and they did not say there was not, they merely said they did not require to use it so long as they got a proper supply of water."[33] Similarly the trustees were prepared to vest control of the well in the council but not the possession of it. When this arrangement was accepted by a meeting

The Summerhouse.

of Haverbrack residents Neddy Stones was again on the war-path "as all except two of the electors present were tenants of the Dallam Tower estate and those two were employed by tenants." Truly local government was a farce, he argued, in a letter to the Gazette,

> "if in a small parish such as Haverbrack when meetings of the tenants of an estate professes to be a meeting of the free and independent electors. The chairman artfully brought into discussion the question of expense. Sir, no amount of expense should weigh down the scales against right and justice. Do the Rural District Council seriously contend that they should be guided by the tenants of the Dallam Tower estate in giving or witholding their consent to the stoppage or diversion of footpaths on the estate? These rights of way have been closed to a patient public for 18 months and all that time the police have skirted their duty of prosecuting the obstructions before the magistrates; the Rural District Council have skirted their duty of indicating the obstruction and now we have a so-called parish meeting skirting its duty."[34]

Although Neddy did not have the satisfaction of seeing the trustees admit their fault in every respect, he had obtained for the public, the fruits of victory: the footpaths remained open, including that to Hollins Well.

In a tiny concurrent dispute over Rowell Green he was less successful. Seemingly part of the green had been enclosed by the farmer and the lords of the manors of Heversham and Milnthorpe (Levens Hall and Dallam Tower) had cleared away much brush wood and timber. As this act was merely to tidy up the area,

The North Lodge, Dallam Tower - with Wash House
built from the demolished Summerhouse on right.

Neddy's demands that the parish should be entitled to receive the value of the coppiced wood fell on deaf ears. Even so, as usual, he brought to light useful documents including a request by Messrs. Wakefield made to the Parish vestry in 1872 for permission for the Gatebeck tramway to cross the green, which proved the common rights.[35] Although now reduced further by road widening the remaining area of the green is still administered as a parish waste by Heversham Parish Council.

More regretable perhaps was the failure of Neddy and the Parish Council to secure the footpath over the hill to the marsh from Grisley Mires lane which was blocked by iron railings in 1899.[36] The path appears to have been well used and its existence was acknowledged by the Furness Railway Company when it built a bridge over the deep cutting where the path crossed the line. The matter was pursued for several years and only in 1903 did the Parish · Council pay George Gatey £3 6s for the legal expenses incurred.

It also took several years of steady pressure by Neddy and the Parish Council to compel the Dallam estate and the Furness Railway to fulfil their obligations under the Furness Railway Act, as acknowledged during the disputes of 1894-6.[38] Only at Easter 1901 was it announced that a "promenade" had been constructed "of great benefit to residents and summer visitors to that part of the

Eastern Gate of Lakeland."[39] In fact it was a cinder track running along the railway embankment, scarcely wide enough to walk two abreast, running from the Dixies to Summerhouse Point.

By 1901 Summerhouse Point no longer deserved its name for in the high summer of 1898, just when it would have been most used the *Westmorland Gazette* reported:

"to the universally expressed regret of everyone in this district the Summerhouse which has stood on the rocks jutting out into the bay at Sandside for nearly a century has been demolished during the past week. A simple one roomed circular tower built of dressed limestone its walls withstood the fury of many a wintry gale and during the higher tides the waves almost encircled it. In E.H. Wilson's time and in Miss Wilson's time it was constantly used as a dressing room when bathing. Nothing under the new regime has stirred the people so much as the removal of this ancient landmark and the beautiful panorama of seascape and landscape has distinctly suffered by its loss. The only reason given is that a wash house is needed for the gamekeeper's cottage and the stone is handy for the purpose."[40]

As it was definitely the property of the Dallam estate nothing could be done and the wash house was built behind the North Lodge; its neat comparatively small masonry contrasting with the more rocky Victorian walls of the lodge.

Minor acts of apparant spitefulness on the part of "the Tower" continued. In 1900 John Wilson was fined 10s for taking "6d worth of kindling wood, the property of the Dallam Tower Estate."

Happily, after Maurice Bromley-Wilson came of age relations between Milnthorpe and the Tower improved. Personally convivial and in his younger days far too open handed and extravagant for his own good, Sir Maurice was always a popular figure in Milnthorpe. His nephew and successer Brigadier C.E. Tryon-Wilson continued the benevolent traditions of the family. Since 1892 Milnthorpe has had only two "squires" "Serm'orice" and "the Brig."

Neddy Stones continued to champion the cause of humbler villagers, after the campaign against Dallam was over. He continued to agitate for small-holdings and, after the passing of the Housing of the Working Classes Act of 1901,[42] demanded that the Rural District Council should provide cottages to replace those "demolished to make way for a few large houses" and many of those remaining which were, he argued, "the meanest and the sanitary conditions scarcely fit for dog kennels."

Despite this plea for hygiene when the sewerage question was debated "Mr Stones objected to the drainage scheme being pushed forward in the interest of 10 or 12 who had w.c.'s in their homes. . . and water was next exploited by the same set for the same reason."[43]

If folk memories are to be believed, water when combined with soap was not exploited by Neddy. His slovenly appearance reflected, and no doubt contributed, to a decline in pre-eminence. Nevertheless Neddy literally earned a 'swan-song'. He was candidate at the Rural District Countil elections of 1905 and "a bard of Milnthorpe" who signed himself "L'homme qui sit" parodied Tennyson's *Crossing The Bar*

Monday – and striking noon,
and that clear call of old
and may there be at no rising of the moon,
No Stonite still unspoiled

But such a crowd as passes mortal ken,
Too great for hostile groans
A mighty man of moral Milnthorpe men
who vote for St-n-s

Monday and striking eight
and after that – success
Behold a Trampled Toff bewail his fate
Without redress

For soon from out this ribbed and cabined place
My founding fame shall roll
I hope to see the Council face to face
When I have topped the poll

4th November 1905

Sadly for him he did not "top the poll."

In 1914 he lost his seat on the Parish Council. According to the *Gazette* at his nomination a cry went up in the Public Rooms "Oh no! He has been there before!"[45]

As he became crabby, senile and "a pauper" the village lost interest in Neddy but he retained his interest in it. In 1916 on bits of scrap paper and old ledgers he wrote down what he could remember of Milnthorpe's history and of his own time, which via two John Mashiters, father and son, was most kindly loaned to the present author.

It was John Mashiter senior who in 1920 as the local correspondent of the *Westmorland Gazette* informed the public of the death of "Mr Stones of Milnthorpe which removes one who in his day took a prominent part in the life of Milnthorpe and district" – but the obituary was only four inches long, in contrast to the many columns which almost weekly for several years recorded Neddy's doings a quarter of a century earlier.[46]

Happily Neddy was not quite a pauper. Somehow his executors were able to find sufficient funds to fulfill one of his bequests – that the school children should be given a treat at his expense – which took the form of a picnic on Fairy Steps. It is a pity that the organisers did not choose Haverbrack.[47]

14

Schools

South Westmorland has many ancient schools. Grammar schools were founded in the late sixteenth and early seventeenth centuries to replace the education formerly provided by the pre-Reformation Church. Some, like the schools at Witherslack, Burton-in-Kendal and Beetham, disappeared or degenerated into elementary schools in the nineteenth century; others, particularly the Queen Elizabeth School at Kirkby Lonsdale, and Kendal and Heversham Grammar Schools survived, to evolve into comprehensives in the twentieth century.

Milnthorpe was served by Heversham Grammar School which was founded in 1613 by Edward Wilson, ancestor of the Wilsons of Dallam Tower. Like most other grammar schools, Heversham catered exclusively for boys, most of whom stayed only for two or three years before following the occupations of their fathers. No doubt many quickly forgot what elements of Latin and Greek had been flogged into them, but for some being a "grammar boy" was a vital first stage on the ladder of social advancement. The sons of Dallam Tower and Levens Hall never seem to have attended Heversham but until the expansion of public schools after 1820, boys from lesser landed families like the Backhouses, Chambers, Craggs and Crofts went there. They would rub shoulders with the offspring of small farmers and tradesmen. During a golden era in the 1730's, the Rev. Thomas Watson had in one class a future bishop, William Preston; a Senior Fellow of Trinity College, Cambridge, James Backhouse and the instigator of the first encyclopaedia, Ephraim Chambers. Later his own son Richard Watson attended the school before going on to become Bishop of Llandaff, professor of both Divinity and Chemistry at Cambridge and, also, the owner of Calgarth Park on Windermere.[1]

The Grammar School always provided the local communities

Owlett Ash, as a Boarding School.

with its mundane professional men, clerks, village dominies and
literate tradesmen. Scholarships to Oxford and, especially, to
Trinity College, Cambridge, enabled young men of comparatively
humble stock to grasp at higher things. Within two generations
around the turn of the eighteenth century the Audlands of
Ackenthwaite rose from being blacksmiths to the ranks of the
minor gentry partly as a result of their bright boys going on from
Heversham to the University and then entering the professions and
marrying well.[2] Rather later two Hevershamian sons of Joseph
Clark, a carrier fom Milnthorpe Square, were ordained, William
becoming Vicar of Chorlton and Joseph Vicar of Stretford near
Manchester.[3] Similarly the Hardy's and Kitching's who produced a
dynasty of early nineteenth century doctors were educated at
Heversham.[4] From the middle of the century the school became
more exclusive, with a stong boarding side and the poor boys eased
out.[5] Nevertheless the first Milnthorpe Parish Council obtained the
right to nominate two of its governors.[6] After the Second World War
Milnthorpe played a prominent part in opposing a plan to abolish
the school. Sadly the Parish Council was not consulted during the
stages when the old grammar school was amalgamated with

Milnthorpe Secondary School in 1983 to become the Dallam School, though a majority of both schools' pupils came from the parish.

Until about 1820, before they went to the grammar school boys were taught to read and write either at home, by the school usher after hours, or in a Dame school. Some of their sisters might also be taught by a Dame, but the majority of men and women were illiterate. Richard Crampton, owner of Bela Mills and of Owlett Ash, signed an agreement with Dallam Tower in 1753 by making a cross.[7] Until the 1850's half the grooms and more brides could only make "their marks" in the marriage register.

From about 1800 fee-paying private boarding schools began to proliferate. An account dated 24th June 1817 from Miss Clark's school in Stricklandgate, Kendal has survived. It was sent to William Gray of Owlett Ash and concerns the board and education of his sons.

Board and Education	£50
Washing	£ 2 10s 9½d
Shoes	£ 2 1s 10d
Tailor	7s 6d
Books	£ 1 16s 11d
Admittance and lecture on Astronomy 2 nights	6s 0d
Indian Juggler and Charitable Contributions	3s 8d
French Master	£ 1 16s 0d
Drawing paper and pencils	3s 9d
Haircutting	8s 8d
	[8]£59 15s 1½d

Around the time when Milnthorpe was a stage coach centre several private schools for girls were established in the village. Of these the most important was based eventually at Owlett Ash. This originated from a school opened by a Miss Jones at Kidside House in December 1818 which moved to Fir Tree House, Park Road in May 1819.[9] It was however, soon taken over by a Mrs Nunns and then by Mrs Hayton who in September 1821 announced that "she had taken a house pleasantly situated in Milnthorpe with the hope of re-establishing that well known school, declined about two years ago by Mrs Nunns and respectfully solicits patronage and promises the utmost attention to the health and morals of the young ladies entrusted to her care."[10]

On the 5th January 1822 appeared the advertisement "Boarding and Day School, Fir Tree House, Milnthorpe, Mrs Hayton BEGS leave to announce to her Friends and the Public, that the school will

Owlett Ash, 1987.

re-open on Monday the Fourteenth instance, on the following reasonable terms

	Per A.M.
Board, including English Grammar, Plain and Fancy Needlework	£21 00s 0d
Weekly Boarders	£15 15s 0d
Daily Boarders	£10 10s 0d
Washing. half guinea per quarter	

DAY SCHOLARS	Per Qtr.
English Reading or Grammar, Plain and Fancy Needlework	10s 6d
Writing, Arithmetic	4s 6d
Geography and Use of Globes	£1 1s 0d
Music	£1 1s 0d
French	£1 1s 0d
Persia Painting	10s 0d
Dancing	[11] 15s 0d

A year later the public were informed that "Mrs Hayton, Green House (Harmony Hall) Boarding School, has taken a larger more commodious house with an excellent play ground for the better accommodation of young ladies committed to her care."[12] Finally in December 1824 Mrs Hayton removed to Owlett Ash where its size and curriculum expanded. By August 1832 it was announced as "Owlett Ash Boarding School for Young Ladies, Milnthorpe, conducted by Mrs Hayton, Mrs Stubbs and Miss Hayton on the undermentioned terms; Board including Tuition in the following branches of Education viz the English and French Languages, writing, arithmetic, Geography with the Use of Globes, Drawing, Ancient and Modern History, Plain and Fancy Needlework for Thirty Gns per annum, no entrance or extras (washing ½ guinea per quarter excepted)." A similar school run by a Mrs Wilson at Witherslack charged 23 gns with washing at 2 gns.[13] Though high, Mrs Hayton's fees were consistent, for at the end of her career in 1854 an illustrated prospectus stated that the fees were still 30 gns and washing was still ½ gn. per quarter. Among the items in the young ladies' wardrobe "at least four night caps" were required.[14]

On 13th May 1854 "Miss Alexander (from London) begged to announce that she will succeed Mrs Hayton and Miss Bradshaw in the Management of the establishment at Midsummer next. . . N.B. a resident Parisian (sic) Teacher." Six years later the "desirable establishment for young ladies" was to let as Miss Alexander was returning to London.[16] Mrs William Lord took over and reduced the fees to 23 – 25 gns. "Without extras. Foreign Languages and Accomplishments on usual terms. A resident Parisienne." The 1861 census shows that Marienne T. Lord was aged 38 and with her lived her brother Frederick J. Gregg aged 32, a cook, Elizabeth Parkinson and a boy, William Batty, apprenticed to a tailor. There were 16 pupils, the youngest being 5 year old Emma Horrocks from Bradford and the oldest Caroline Burton aged 18 from Ossett. All except two boarders came from these towns or from Bradford and Bingley.[17]

The school was put up for sale in May 1867, but in July 1868 it was still advertising for a few Young Ladies as Boarders. Finally in March 1869, boarding school equipment was sold and the house was to let as a private house in 1870 [18] and was acquired by John Holme. His daughter Constance Holme lived there until shortly before her death in 1956.

The *Westmorland Gazette* of 3rd July 1830 which reported the death of King George IV – "One of the ablest and best of Kings" – also announced that "the Misses Burrow of Laburnum House in returning their grateful acknowledgement to their friends for the very liberal encouragement they have received, whilst with the utmost deference solicit a continuance of their patronage which it will ever be their study to maintain by the most unremitting exertions for the advancement of their pupils, the school will recommence on Monday July 26th."[19] The school is known to have been formed with 12 boarders in 1829,[20] but lasted only a few years as in 1841 William Turner put the property on the market as a private house.

Of the smaller schools, that run by Mrs Eleanor Blewart at Harmony Hill was the most important. She seems to have established it at Harmony Hill House which adjoined the south and east side of Harmony Hall. After her death in 1844 her daughter Mary Anne Mason took over Harmony Hall as well to accommodate more boarders.[21] In June 1850 she opened a class room in a converted barn on Harmony Green and, until the property was converted into "Tudor Cottage" in the 1950's a date stone inscribed M.A.M. 1850 was to be seen in the gable over a high mullioned window. (This house has a well authenticated reputation for being haunted. According to Eva Scott's essay on Milnthorpe of 1930 "the furniture in the room and the crockery on the table were reported to have danced a jig of their own volition by the banging of the doors on a still day.")[22]

The new classroom was opened in June 1851 when the 22 scholars looked "very neat" and respectable in uniform bonnets and tippets as they made their way to a special evening service conducted by the Rev. W. Mann, Vicar of Normanton, brother of the principle. Other clerical visitors of the school included Archdeacon Evans of Heversham, the Rev. Stephens of Levens, the Rev. Padwick of Milnthorpe and the Rev. Simpson of Skerton."[23]

For a long time Miss Mason was assisted by Miss Marchant. In 1862 both ladies retired together, closed the school and left the district.[24]

Little is known about the Dame schools though one existed until c.1910 in the cottage on the west side of Police Square next to Stoneleigh, now occupied by the offices of Cicerone Press. Occasionally young ladies tried their hand at teaching and in December 1844 it was reported "on both Saturday and Sunday last some wretch broke into the private schoolroom at Milnthorpe belonging to Miss Kitching, daughter to John Kitching, where she occupies and teaches a dozen poor girls gratis." The "wretch" had also destroyed a quantity of beautiful flower pots and "cut up the whole of the cloaks which that amiable young lady had purchased to keep the poor children warm during the severe weather." In the same year "Miss Seymour, a lady visitor from Blandford in Dorset, gave a treat of currant cake and coffee to the 100 children of the National School who sang hymns which the lady had been kind enough to instruct them."[26]

From 1872 – 1883 the Misses Pickersgill, daughters of the Rev. Hanley Pickersgill, the Independent Minister and "earnest advocate of temperance," had a school at Victoria House. They were said to be brilliant pianists and singers and played a leading part in the musical life of the neighbourhood. When they left Miss Pickersgill

MILNTHORPE SCHOOL.

THE Inhabitants of Milnthorpe and Ackenthwaite are informed, that the School erected by MISS MASON will be opened (D. V.) in June, 1851, for the Instruction of Thirty Girls residing in the District of St. Thomas' Church, Milnthorpe, from the ages of Eight to Sixteen.

The Children will receive a religious and plain Education in the usual branches; viz.: Reading, Writing, Cyphering, &c.; also, in Sewing.

The School is intended for the benefit of those Children whose Parents are not able to pay more than Twopence a week, which sum must be paid by each girl on the Monday Morning for the ensuing week. Only one child out of the same family will be admitted on the first opening of the School.

An experienced TEACHER from a good Training School will be appointed, whose Rules must be strictly attended to by the Scholars. A wilful infringement of the Rules of the School will be punished by expulsion.

The girls will be required regularly to attend the Services of the Church, and to wear BONNETS and TIPPETS, which will be provided for them and kept at the School-room.

The School will be under the regular Superintendence of the Rev. R. W. EVANS, the Rev. N. PADWICK, MISS MASON, and Mrs. PADWICK, and will be inspected by occasional Visitors.

All who wish for admittance to the School must apply to the Rev. N. PADWICK, who will give the names to MISS MASON, for her selection.

The Terms and Regulations of the School, also the number of Scholars, may be changed after trial, according to the discretion of the PATRONESS.

March 18th, 1851.

JOHN HUDSON, PRINTER, KENDAL.

Poster for Miss Mason's School, Harmony Green, 1851.

"who was deeply moved at the prospect of parting" was presented with a bracelet and broach.[28] The school continued under Hannah Milburn (until 1887) and Elinor Mossop, who maintained the high standard of the school till 1897, when she retired in order to marry Joseph Brown, the station master at Heversham.[29] The Misses Taylor then took over, announcing that their Boarding and Day school for Young Ladies, and Preparatory School for Little Boys would reopen on January 19th 1898. "Terms Moderate, References permitted to Lady Dale, the Head Master of Heversham Grammar School and the Chairman of the School Board Darlington."[30] A summer concert was reported annually and in July 1905 "the infants gave a pleasing entertainment with a Chinese Lantern Drill" and "the shepherd" in which M. Pickthall portrayed a snowdrop and M. Downing a thistle.[31] In 1914, Margaret and Jane Taylor retired but stayed at Victoria House, the last Miss Taylor dying in 1920.

Miss Pickersgill's school at Victoria House might have evolved from a day school connected with the Independent Chapel.

Certainly shortly after the opening of the Chapel in July 1819 there was a flourishing Sunday school. No doubt this non-conformist incursion posed a threat to the Anglican establishment and might have induced George Edward Wilson of Dallam to found a Church School, supported by the National Schools Society. Initially the foundation could not have cost much as it was situated in an attic over two cottages on the south side of the Square known descriptively as "the forty steps."[32] The first master was John Woodburn whose relation kept the Sun Tavern a few doors up the Square. Presumably he lived in one of the cottages below the school as in 1819 it was advertised as "the schoolhouse with two Turf Houses in occupation of John Woodburn and Thomas Cotton."[33] Geoffrey Bentham followed Woodburn in either 1829 or 1830. He had been formerly Master of the National School in Kendal and was "fired with missionary enthusiasm" and rigorously enforced the rule that the children should attend church twice on Sunday as well as going to Sunday school from 9 to 10 a.m. and after mid-day dinner until 4 p.m.[34] Bentham remained Master when a new school was built at the south east corner of The Strands Meadow, close to the Bela Clough. The date stone reads:

1834
This School was built by
George Wilson Esq.
of Dallam Tower.

Bentham's salary was never more than £40 p.a. nor, unlike most village schoolmasters, did he get a free house. He did, however, get small fees based on pupils' attendance and there was an usher, "who for his exertions shall each day receive a ticket of reward which ticket shall be valued at 6d per day and shall be paid in money on the Friday evening or be reserved to purchase articles of clothing as the patron and visitor may think proper. The teacher shall receive a ticket of reward of 4d per dozen but these tickets shall be given to such only as shall have kept their respective classes in order and in a state of improvement!"[35] From the start Bentham gave satisfaction. The first published report of 1830 stated that the pupils had acquitted themselves much to satisfaction of the parties present, giving great credit to the Masters and it was hoped that this "first examination will not be the last, so as to induce others to take interest, for there can be no greater pleasure in seeing the rising generation promising to surpass their forefathers in Christian Knowledge and virtue."[36] The fourth 'R' – religion – dominated the curriculum; School treats might relieve the pupils of scrivening but never from scripture. At Christmas 1841 "Miss Smith, sister to George Wilson esq, gave 6d and a little book to each child for good behaviour and for subscribing to scripture while she visited."[37] For the annual treat in September 1844 150 children led by the Holme Brass Band processed to Dallam Tower where they sang a hymn *We won't give up the Bible*.[38] In May 1844 "Mr T. Inman, senior Sunday School teacher, presented Mr G. Bentham, Master of the (National) school for upwards of 15 years with an elegant copy of the Holy Bible and a complete Church service."[39] Bentham also played a part in establishing a Temperance society which in its first year, 1841, forwarded (through the far from temperent Dr. Lawson, vicar of Heversham) £45 to the parent society in London.[40] Occasional evening classes were held at the school and in January 1846 Mr. Bird of Orton gave a lecture on Astronomy. Full and complete rules were issued in 1854, and a copy of the poster displayed at the time is one of the few original documents surviving from the early life of the school.

Geoffrey Bentham became ill in January 1856 and the managers allowed him to appoint a supply teacher called Christopher Prickett, at 10s a week. When Bentham died in March the cortege, including all the children, started from the school.

The Managers advertised the post at £40, without a house, for any person being a member of the Church of England.[43]

Mr A Swainson was appointed. He could obviously offer more than the four 'R's because it was soon announced that "if a child is taught Book Keeping, Geometry, and mensuration – to pay 8d a week, if out of the township 10d a week each – the higher branches of Mathematics to pay 1/- a week. In both these classes each child is to find his books." In 1858 weekly pence were abolished and parents were charged quarterly: "two pupils 1/6 a quarter, three 2/3 a qtr. and four 3/-." He also organised magic lantern shows, with buns and coffee.

Unfortunately Swainson soon left and was replaced at Whitsuntide 1857 by Mr Tom Cornthwaite, who was appointed without an interview as he had been a candidate in 1856. His appointment was not however, approved by Mr Murphy, "Organising Master" and in January 1858 he was replaced by Thomas Gill of Crawshaw Booth, Manchester. For him the salary was increased to £50 p.a. and it was "resolved that the Desk on the south side of the school be removed and replaced by two moveable Desks, that two blackboards and stands and one dozen first and second standard books be obtained" and also "that the Total Abstinence Society be allowed to have the school for meetings."

Gaslight, installed in 1863, doubtless made the school more convenient for evening meetings. The school still closed an hour earlier in Winter because of poor light.

The Forster Education Act of 1870 which set up School Boards to provide Elementary Education for 6 to 11 year olds, where there were no voluntary schools, did not affect Milnthorpe, as "no

MILNTHORPE
NATIONAL SCHOOL.

This School will be re-opened on the 17th July, 1854, and conducted according to the following Rules :—

1. To be under the management of a Committee of the following seven persons, viz. : —

GEORGE E. WILSON, Esq., Patron.	Mr. M. WHITTAKER.
Rev. R. W. EVANS, B. D., Visitor.	Mr. ISAAC RAWLINSON.
Rev. N. PADWICK, M. A., Superintendant.	Mr. JOSEPH TURNER.
Mr. J. HOLME, Treasurer.	

2. Any Child may be admitted being three years of age or upwards, who is recommended by one of the Committee, or a Subscriber of not less than 5s. per annum.

3. Each Child to pay

For Reading	1d. per Week, or	9d. per Quarter.
For Reading and Writing	2d. ,,	1s. 6d. ,,
For Reading, Writing, and Cyphering	3d. ,,	2s. 3d. ,,
For every thing taught in the School...	4d. ,,	3s. 0d. ,,

If the Child lives out of the township of Heversham with Milnthorpe, to pay one half more.

4. If there are three children of the same parents, to be one-third less than the separate payments would be, provided they pay above one penny a week.

5. Each Child to pay on Monday mornings for the week or quarter in advance. The sum to be entered opposite the Child's name in the Admission Book, and to be paid by the Master to the Treasurer the last Friday in the month.

6. After the Child's name is entered in the Admission Book, to pay half-price during the weeks he is absent from the School, excepting in case of sickness, notice of it having been given to the Master ; before the removal of a Child from School, one week's notice to be given by the Parent to the Master.

7. The School Hours from the first Monday in March to the last Friday in October, to be from nine to twelve, and from half-past one to half-past Four ; at other times from nine to twelve, and one to four.

8. The holidays to be three weeks at Midsummer, and two weeks at Christmas, and every Saturday, Christmas Day, Ash Wednesday, Good Friday, Ascension Day, and Monday and Tuesday in Whitsun week : when there is service on these days the Children are expected to go to Church, as on Sundays.

9. Only such books to be used in the School as are approved of by the Patron, Visitor, and Superintendant : the Children to find their own Bibles and Prayer Books.

10. The School Room to be free for the Bible Society and Church Missionary Meetings ; if wanted for Lectures or Exhibitions, five Shillings to be paid for the use of it towards the School expenses, permission having first been obtained from G. E. Wilson, Esq., or Mr. J. Holme.

11. The Annual Subscriptions to be due the first week in January ; the Book to be presented to the Subscribers by the Master.

J. DAWSON, PRINTER, KENDAL.

Poster for Milnthorpe National School, 1854.

additional accommodation is needed except separate offices for girls and boys." In 1872 Mr Gill resigned and was succeded by Thomas William Tassell at a salary of £80 p.a. At Christmas 1874 he was given leave to attend a teachers' examination inLondon which he failed, though he did pass it three years later, just before he left Milnthorpe. Partly because of the expansion of elementary education after 1870 the managers had difficulty in replacing him. A Mr Kirkbride was at first appointed but refused to come for under £100 p.a. including salary as organist. There was no national salary scale for teachers in those days, but Mr Barker from Longtown also wanted £100. Eventually Matthew Walker accepted the post at £80 p.a. with £5 p.a. for rent of a house approved by the committee. This was not a successful appointment and the school declined. In particular there was anxiety over a pupil teacher called Edward Robinson who failed his examination several times before qualifying as an assistant teacher in 1883, and the 1886 H.M.I. report was "not satisfactory." The committee considered the gradual falling off in grants (this was the time of payment by results) and was of the opinion that a change of master was desirable – "whereupon Mr M Walker resigned immediately." Thomas Bowes from Bedford was the next master from 1886 to 1895.[46] Almost immediately he made a change for the better for in 1887 the H.M.I.'s noted a great "improvement in arithmetic and gave a good merit grant."[47] Nevertheless Bowes had some trouble with pupil teachers and in 1891 George Semple was dismissed after being absent from home for ten days. His father was made to pay £5 in lieu of notice.[48]

State grants to the National Society were raised to 10s p.a. per pupil in 1891 in the hope that this would lead to the abolition of school pence. Milnthorpe charged 14s per annum, so as this "would involve a loss to the school of four shillings" it was not declared free but 1d per week was charged. Parents could demand exemption "until recently," the managers' minute book noted, "the right for exemption has not been exercised but conscientious objections have at last arisen and nearly a score of such applications have been received." Therefore, in April it was decided to take the "Bull by the horns" and make the school free.[49]

Mr Bowes resigned in 1895 and a temporary teacher, Mr Atkinson, was appointed provided "Mr Bowes stay a week to put him in the way of managing the school."[50]

The next few masters tended to use Milnthorpe as a stepping stone. A. Hassal only stayed three years. When he resigned in 1898 there were 61 applications for the post which was obtained by J. Morely for whom the salary was at last raised to £100. During his time remaining fees chargeable for books were abolished. He also appointed the first female assistant; Ellen Burrow in 1899 at a salary of £20 p.a. followed by Agnes Procter in 1901, who being younger got only £15 p.a. Later she resigned after the Inspectors held that "her teaching had not improved." The H.M.I. report for 1900 was not good. Reading was "weak" and the school roll numbered only 32. Exacting attendance regulations were laid down. To qualify for a Board of Education grant of 1s 6d p.a. a child had to put in 400 attendances in the year (two per day). Mr Mosely was, however, praised for starting evening continuation classes which had 28 students of whom the best, Kate Griffin, was presented with an album for 100% attendance.[51]

National School, c.1914. Mr. Tuson's boys.

Under T. Simmons, the next master from 1901 to 1906, the evening classes declined and in 1902 the Inspector grumbled that instead "of any flowing to the classes there is but a meagre attendance." Simmons acquired a microscope for use in botany classes and the curriculum included sketches from nature. When Mr Simmons moved to Witherslack school he was presented with "a handsome oak coal box and gun metal and copper fire irons."

R.V. Marwood, formerly headmaster of Barton school Pooley Bridge, was at Milnthorpe from 1906 to 1910. He was a vigorous young man who achieved a good attendance from his pupils; for example Harold Whiteley had 100% for four years and Jacob Taylor for five. He was also a stern disciplinarian and there were cases of "Capricious removals of pupils to Beetham school," simply because the boys had been reproved for faults (not corporally punished). Henceforward transfers were only allowed with the consent of the managers and when Marwood left for Ambleside in 1909 there were 70 pupils at the school.[52] James Tuson came from Longsledale in 1910 to replace him and stayed until 1923. Under him a lantern slide club, whose repertoire included "Jack the Conqueror" and "John Bull's money," made a profit of 16s 4d and the school garden in 1911 brought in £4.15s. Tuson also earned the approval and support of a considerable number of grown ups and the boys were reported as "Keen and industrious." At Christmas most boys received a book from the Bindloss charity fund. A further Bindloss prize went to the boy who wrote the best account of his book.

The school had less success in preparing boys for the newly introduced grammar school "scholarships" and in 1915 the managers discussed the fact that Milnthorpe candidates – "not only failed but were all at the bottom of the list. . . . Mr Tuson should take a more active interest in seeking out suitable boys. . . ." He was also criticized for "forwarding a letter to Mr and Mrs Wilson signed by 30 boys expressing dissatisfaction at the withdrawal of their son Leslie." What this episode was about remains a mystery. Soon afterwards Mr Tuson (in military class 4) was summoned to war where he was taken prisoner and did not return until the summer of 1919. Mrs McNabb (formerly Miss Gledhill of St. Thomas's school) took over for the duration. Under her the school gardens expanded as part of the war effort. In 1916 a three week's holiday was granted so that the children could help with the harvest. A months' half-time teaching was allowed for the same purpose in 1917 and 1918 with an extra week in October for potato picking. In 1923 Mr Tuson was promoted to the headship of a larger school at Kirkby Stephen.

His successor Frederick Comber stayed until 1930. During his seven years he helped to found the Milnthorpe Boy Scout branch and improved academic standards so that in 1924 two boys H. Hartwell and F. England won scholarships of £6.15s p.a. tenable for their school life at Heversham.[53] Victorian standards were still expected. At the 1929 prize-giving the Rev. Gamble, in the manner of middle-aged vicars in every age, bemoaned the fact that "the boy of the present day had greater freedom than formerly. He doubted whether it was altogether to the good for unless boys learnt habits of self restraint they could not be expected to possess this all important attribute on reaching manhood. Until he was 18 he had addresssed his father as 'sir'."[54]

It was to the vicarage that 25 year old Joseph Thomas Cookson was summoned for interview for the headship at 7 p.m. on Saturday 12th July 1930. The late hour was so that the Director of Education could attend.[55] Having been chosen out of several candidates Joe did not arrive home at Hawkshead on his motor-bike until the small hours – only to be told by his family that he had landed himself in the "arse hole of Westmorland."[56] So began a career, unprecedented in the district, of forty years as a head teacher, first at the National School and then from 1951 to 1970 at the County Primary School. Bullet headed, fat and ebullient in a "hail fellow well met" sort of way Joe was also feared by pupils (and it was rumoured by his staff) though many were devoted to him. Like all his predecessors (but not quite all his contemporaries) Joe believed that to spare the rod (or the cricket stump or whatever else happened to be handy) meant to spoil the child.[57] Yet his title "Old Joe" earned before he was 30, carried with it an element of affection. Under him no one could say that school life was dull. The time-honoured but sluggish curriculum was reinvigorated by all manner of activities and his booklets for less able pupils on local and natural history were regarded by the Inspectors as exemplary. They also praised the fact that "he practised as well as taught religion,"[58] though it was noticed that when he was no longer head of a church school his attendance at worship fell off. He believed in liberating the child from the desk – if this meant some diversion from the three 'R's it did not matter "most of his kids were not academic any-how." It did, however, mean that many middle-class parents with 11 plus ambitions chose to send their children to the more traditional Heversham Church of England School at Leasgill.

Above all the children "seemed to be forever gardening" and many old boys later stated that they went out into the garden everyday winter and summer alike.

Discipline was always strict. In 1931 the Inspectors noted a good class, not exceedingly bright but doing good work. "They had, moreover made a valiant attack on Amos and Hosea." In 1935 there was a fair amount of shyness which made it difficult to ascertain how much they really knew. The 1937 report stated that the majority of older boys appeared very unreliable when subjected to examination – hardly any could repeat poetry which they had learnt, while in 1939 there was too much uncertainty in fundamental work. On the other hand "good constructional and repair work and some painting and decorating are undertaken and the trim borders and rockeries reflect credit on all concerned."

Accommodation was always judged to be poor during the inter-war period with "51 children in two classes, packed together in a small classroom which has recognised accommodation for 40. Water is laid on but the closets (earth) are primitive."[59]

In 1939 evacuees added to the problem. Though the Roman Catholics were told by their teacher Miss Daly "not to play with the (Protestant) Milnthorpe boys" [60] and some evacuees had lice, most of the newcomers had been used to having a lavatory at school. Hence to cope with the extra numbers, water lavatories were installed, putting an end to a persistant myth that the older boys could do unquotable things with a nettle on a stick pushed through the trap behind the privy when it was being used by a lady teacher! In 1942 a bicycle shed was built and in 1943 the 7 to 9 year old boys were removed to the billiard room at Dallam Tower, loaned free of all charge by Sir Maurice Bromley-Wilson.[61] For many the time at the tower provided the strongest memories of school life made colourful by the benign presence of "serm'orice," his peppery brother, "t'admiral," a sleazy war-time staff, the Dallam Tower otter hounds and Corky the parrot, glimpsed in the kitchen by the monitor sent down the tenth of a mile long area passage"to get Miss Tallet's tea."[62]

Gertrude Tallet was a teacher at the school for over thirty years and could in her own way be as formidable as Joe. She possessed a grim hawk-like expression, dyed black hair and a penchant for telling fortunes at local events under the guise of "Madam Cantellum." Until it broke on an unyielding backside, her main teaching aid was a wooden spade – flotsam from a nature walk on the marsh. With or without it she somehow managed to marshall her class the two-thirds of a mile through the park to the school dinner held each day in the Institute annexe from 1943 – an excursion which could take up to two hours.

After the war Milnthorpe was designated a "growth area" and its new schools were given the top priority in the County. Sadly the National School Managers' Book recorded in 1946 that "this would mean the closing of the Boys' school (and the Girls' school too). The circumstance of the school being private property and no means in hand or possible to effect the government requirements, are such that the managers with much regret felt they were helpless and must bow to the inevitable and that the school must close after an existence of 112 years"(sic).[65] In fact it took five more years before the Primary and (temporary) Secondary Modern School were opened. Though Joe Cookson as headteacher now worked at the new primary school he did not leave the National School because he acquired the old building from the Dallam Estate and converted it into an attractive house called "Heronsyke" from where he was buried in 1973.

In its early days the National School was attended by girls – but they always seemed to have been in a minority, and many more girls than boys were illiterate. The possibility of the state stepping in "to fill the gaps" in voluntary education with secular board schools spurred on many churches in the 1860's to provide more places. Thus barely four years before the Board School Act of 1870 the Rev. F.T. Raikes, Vicar of Milnthorpe, established the St. Thomas's Church School for girls and infants. The site chosen was at the eastern end of the central block in the square formerly occupied by Bodkin Hall.[66] The land was given by Mr and Miss Smithies and the school, designed by Miles Thompson of Kendal, was paid for by subscription. Tenders were invited on 6th January 1866, the Rev. F.T. Raikes performed the opening ceremony on 22nd December and it was used as a school for the first time on 7th January 1867.[68] It closed in 1951 after the opening of the County primary school. Regretably none of the school's log books or other records seem to have survived. This loss, perhaps the biggest gap in

St. Thomas's Girls' School, c. 1898.

Milnthorpe's archives, can only be filled partially by verbal tradition, H.M.I. reports and the local press which though frequently lavish on school treats and concerts hardly ever noted the curriculum.

The first headmistress was Mary Atherton. When she left in May 1870 she ws presented with a handsome gilt and blue timepiece by the committee of managers and lady visitors. She was followed by a Miss Hibbert from July 1870 to December 1870, Mary Fielding January 1871 to December 1872 and Janet Cruickshank January 1873 to March 1876. The first published H.M.I. report in May 1870 was reasonable, "the Religious Knowledge is very creditable in the upper portion of the school and fair in the infants' division. The arithmetic also is improved and is now pretty fair. The reading, writing and spelling are good. Miss Atherton has received her certificate of competency in an elementary school from the committee of the Council on Education."[69] Under Miss Harriet E. Derham, headmistress from April 1876 to April 1893 the school was "carefully conducted, discipline (was) very praiseworthy, the infants pleasantly managed while much care has been bestowed on Religious Instruction and reflects much credit on the exertion of mistress and teachers." Order was excellent and "occupations creditably managed."[70] Greater provision led to a rush of school attendance cases. Although elementary education did not formally become free and compulsory until c.1891, parents in areas where there were sufficient places available were guilty of an offence if their children did not go to school. Thus in 1882 Thomas Arkwright was fined 2s and in 1884 Nancy Bouskill and Robert Newsham were both fined 5s for "neglecting to send their children to school."[71] The next year W.R. Pearson was fined a similar amount even though he pleaded that the reason for his children's truancy was that "he couldn't afford to pay the school pence."

Miss Derham's successors were Mary Alice Dobson, until 1898 and then Sarah Gledhill, a formidable character who combined staunch membership of the Women's Unionists with support for the suffragettes. At the age of forty but no longer in the full bloom of her ugliness, she left in August 1903 in order to marry Tom McNabb, the joiner and undertaker.

Miss Gledhill encouraged pupil teachers and several went on to become qualified teachers. This was an important and practical step in the professional emancipation of women, for most of the girls would either have gone into service or stayed at home until they married. The life of a pupil teacher was not easy for as well as teaching quite large classes, under the eagle eye of the headmistress, they had a lesson themselves before school and often stayed behind for two hours in the evening. They also attended a pupil teacher centre in Kendal on Saturdays having to catch "Kendal Tommy" from Heversham station at 8 a.m. At the ages of 16 or 17 the "half timer girls" then went to teach away from home before taking examinations for a bursary to a training college. One pupil teacher Mary (Polly) Atkinson, daughter of the Parish Clerk and shoe maker, never forgot "going up to Grayrigg," of which, though barely ten miles from Milnthorpe, she always spoke as if it was the end of the earth. Armed with a dressing set, the gift of pupils and teachers, and a sovereign from her father which "I hadn't to use unless I had to, so I never did" her journey involved a trap to Milnthorpe station, a change to the Tebay train at Oxenholme and then a steep two mile climb, her trunk coming on behind in a cart, up to Grayrigg which she had never previously visited. Like most P.T.'s Polly never went on to college but qualified as a "licensed uncertified teacher" and went on to teach at Maltby near Rotherham. Her marriage to Hedley Sheldon in 1914, which under the regulations in force until 1939 put an end to her teaching career, was "the last horse drawn wedding in Milnthorpe."[74]

Miss Gledhill's successor was Ellen Annie Hescroff. Her time at Milnthorpe ended precipitously after she had been involved in a dramatic row which landed one of Milnthorpe's most formidable matriarchs in court. In 1907 the *Westmorland Gazette* reported that "Jessie Fawcett, wife of John Fawcett, Cycle and Motor agent, was summoned for insulting school headmistress Miss Ellen Annie Hescroff." Apparently there had been stone throwing by her son Harold, aged 6, and by Percy Scott, aged 5, and Harold had been punished by Miss Smith – but not Percy. "At noon next day witness (Miss Hescroff) found Mr and Mrs Fawcett and all the family (including 90 year old grandfather, Happy Jack) waiting for her. Percy Scott held on to Miss Hescroff (when) Mrs Fawcett, dragging the boy Harold forward, came at her and in a very bad temper tried to get hold of Percy Scott, calling to her 'Hit him! Hit him! as hard as you can,' and calling Miss Hescroff a vulgar, low lived beast "Mrs Fawcett declared that Miss Hescroff would not touch Percy Scott because she lived with his people (Miss Hescroff lodged with Percy's grandmother, Mrs Arkwright, in the big house in the Square next door but one to the Fawcett's). At this stage Mrs Fawcett struck Miss Hescroff and it was this action which led her to be fined 1s with £1 costs.[75]

Following Miss Hescroff's departure Clara Miles was headmistress until December 1908 when she returned to Devon whence she came. Eva Scott then took over and stayed until 1939. The daughter of the Milnthorpe builder Chris Scott, she had been a pupil-teacher at the school before going on to Durham training college and teaching for eight years in Manchester. She encouraged musical activities of all kinds and as Church Choir Mistress and organist saw that it was combined with the religious tradition of the school. Non-Anglicans attended the school and Doris Mashiter, a Methodist, was firstly a pupil-teacher and then after teaching at Sedbergh and Ulverston returned to the school until her retirement in 1953. Miss Scott's successor was Mrs Sarah Beaton who stayed until the school's closure when she went as Senior Mistress to the Modern School.

St. Thomas's school had never provided ideal accommodation. For a long time the infants were taught in a gallery in the main room, but the noise was so disturbing to the older scholars that other class rooms had to be provided.[77] This would appear to have been in two cottages adjoining the school to the west. These were demolished about 1888 when a new room was added. The infants moved to the south room and were accommodated in desks rising in a steep tier, rather like those in a lecture theatre. Though these were done away with about 1920, formal teaching continued even for little ones and in the 1930's Mrs Clark and Mrs Hodgson kept long canes to crash down on the desks of infants who were not attending.[78] Evacuees in the early war years and the raising of the school leaving age to 15 in 1948, put extra pressure on the school and classes had to be taken in the upper rooms of the Memorial Hall, formerly the Agricultural Hall. A generation of children starting school in 1945-7 were in fact, taught in five different buildings before their primary education ended at 11 plus : at the Infant Class in the Square, then the "upper room," the billiard room at Dallam Tower, at "Joe's on The Strands" and finally at the brand new Primary School. Sanitation at St. Thomas's school was as bad as that at the National School, with "five privies, cleaned three monthly, no deodorizing material applied and a urinal pail with a defective tap and flushing apparatus."[79] In 1949 Norman Nicholson painted a charming picture of Milnthorpe with its church "tall and stiff as a school ma'am looking down her nose at the children playing in the Square."[80] For the children the lack of a school playground was a serious impediment to normal development. Though playing ball games on the green was permitted there were regular complaints from residents while teachers and parents worried about road accidents especially after a boy was killed in the Square by a backing lorry in 1945.

In 1939 St. Thomas's managers accepted that the school would have to be replaced by a secular County school but it was not until the end of the war in 1945 that a two and a half acre field adjacent to the new housing estate (Firs Road) was purchased for the new school. This was expected to cost £15,000 to £20,000, excluding roads and services which were to be provided by the housing department. Though there were doubts whether accommodation for 150 would be adequate, everybody agreed "that the opportunity was too good to miss as it would save the need for prefab accommodation." Nevertheless, it was not until 1950 that the school, the first new one in Westmorland for 40 years, was completed and in January 1951, 130 children moved in. Descriptions of the new school appeared in both the national and local press which dwelt on the cost (£30,000) and (this being the age of austerity) the judicious use of material and space "whilst great care has been taken in installing modern amenities there is nothing lavish or unnecessary. At many points of the interior the brick walls have merely been painted in a warm colouring. Brightness and light are the cardinal features of the new school."

On an elevated site "commanding fine views over the village to Whitbarrow" the school faced directly into the Gulf Stream. The architect had therefore, erred on the side of the optimists in providing classrooms with roofs "half of which can be opened in summer." More practically there was a drying room with a fan "for carrying out the damp air." Designed in the best Festival of Britain style the hall was the finest feature. With a good Westmorland green slate roof, supported (unseen), by what at the time seemed huge iron girders, it had a parquet floor, good stage, modernistic copper light fittings, serving hatch for school dinners, wall bars for "P.E." (no longer either "P.T." or "drill") and "a wall of glass opening onto a western terrace raised on a wall of blue (sic) limestone quarried on the site."

The nursery section, "a new departure for Westmorland," had elaborate facilities with a "room for parents to assemble for their

The Infants' Class at the County Primary School when it was opened, 1951.

youngsters, a pram shed, a paddling pool and a sand pit" –
apparently a sensational feature for it earned a separate headline in
the *Westmorland Gazette*, while the provision of jig saws and
puzzles of nursery rhymes received special comment.[81] After the
noisome earth privies of the old school, the row of miniature
toddler sized toilets with pegs for each child and towel, hairbrush
and tooth brush, seemed the height of luxury. Not surprisingly
such splendours were inspected regularly in the early years by
teachers and educationalists from all over and after 18 months in
operation, the school was visited by none other than Minister of
Education, Florence Horsburgh herself. Instead of retiring to the
privacy of Joe Cookson's office for coffee, dispensed from Percy
Dobson's silver coffee pot, the minister drank a cup poured straight
from the pan by Elsie Ladell in the kitchen. Truly everything about
schools seemed to have changed.

15

War

Milnthorpe can be said to have been founded in war. The Scandinavian settlers of the "mylen porp" might have met resistance from the Angles and Cumbrians of the neighbouring "hams" and "tons." More bloodshed accompanied the Norse onslaught on the north west coast in the tenth century and the Norman expansion of the Cumbrian Marches in the 1090's.[1] Later as the ruined pele towers testify, the district was assaulted by Irish and Manx pirates as well as by more immediate bad neighbours. Except for Bruce's incursion in the 1320's Scots' raids, so far south, were mild and sporadic. As the middle ages closed some of the combatants in the Wars of the Roses and of such subsequent risings against the Tudors as Warbeck's invasion of 1497 and the Pilgrimage of Grace of 1536-7 touched the area. In 1537 a few might have followed the example of the Vicar of Beetham, William Lancaster, and joined 500 rebels as they mustered at Endmoor. One of the local leaders was John Stones, an ancestor of Milnthorpe's Victorian rebel Neddy Stones.[2] Both Lancaster and Stones were hanged at Manchester, and no doubt most Milnthorpe folk were thankful that they had been content to be mere "lookers on."

On half a dozen occasions in the 1640's and 1650's Civil War soldiers tramped through the district. Fairfax's soldiers aided by a local mob led by Richard Sill of Whassett sacked Beetham Church in 1644. A Parliamentarian called Samuel Cole, "who could be relied upon to support Presbyterians" was imposed as Minister on the Parish Church at Heversham. Both Samuel and his brother William, who became de facto Vicar of Kirkby Lonsdale, were Londoners and had fought in the Parliamentary Army. They are said also to have "got into trouble through a struggle near Milnthorpe where a malignant was killed"[3] but whether this was just an isolated crime of violence or a clash of cold steel between Roundhead and Cavalier is not known.

Even so, these and later wars would have been felt mainly in the purses of the tax paying classes. A series of assessments "within Milthrop Heversham Haverbrack for carrying on a vigros ware against franse" (covering the years 1694-1702) is amongst the papers of the Croft family of Ackenthwaite. In the quarter ending June 13, 1702, a sum total of £5 16s 0d was collected by the Assessors Leo. Croft, John Gibson, John Cragge, John Atkinson. Edward Wilson Esq. paid 40s and the remainder of 29 including several women like "Widd Audland, John Gibson his wife, John Cragg his wife" paid smaller sums, usually 4s.[4]

Scots invaders descended on the area in both the Jacobite rebellions but faced neither open hostility nor received active support from the stolid inhabitants. Bloody clashes at Lancaster and Preston in 1715 and at Clifton Moor, near Penrith, in 1745 showed, however, that there had been a serious threat. As many a local pub sign[5] shows, the Duke of Cumberland was regarded in 1745 as an heroic saviour.[6] The Redcoats, it seems, had already had local recruits. In 1733 "Mary (Milbis) wife of Thomas (Milbis) late of Milnthorpe applied for a relief of a house to live in since her husband joined his Majesty's Service and left her with two children."[7]

Later, the larger and longer Revolutionary and Napoleonic Wars, caused little disruption of civilian life. In far away Westmorland the continental wars had almost no direct impact. Often, however, as the bellringers accounts show, victory peals drifted over the fields from the belfries[8] of Heversham and Beetham Churches to penetrate the huddled cottages of Milnthorpe and arouse the loungers in the taverns or around the Square with echoes of distant battle. Occasionally Milnthorpe was swirled into activity by the arrival of the Redcoats. With them came requisitions from the quarter master:

"To the Constable of the Township of Millthorp and Heversham in the said County (Westmorland) By virtue of an order from His Royal Highness the Prince Regent this day brought and shewn unto me Christopher Wilson of his Majesty's Justice of the peace for the said County by a Sergeant in the Royal Perth Militia Commanded by Major Craigie you are hereby required to provide twenty sufficient Carriages with one horse each, and able men to drive the same, within your Constablewick whereby to remove the arms, cloaths, and accoutrements of the said Regiment on their March from Kendal to Burton in the said County and with them you are to appear at the Markett Place in Kendal aforesaid to-morrow precisely at five of the Clock in the morning.

Herein fail not, as you will answer the contrary at your peril. Given under my hand and seal at Kendal in the said County the twentieth day of April in the year of our Lord one thousand eight hundred and thirteen.

Chris. Wilson."[9]

Martial feeling was still alive in 1822 when "the Milnthorpe and Burton troops of the Westmorland Yeomanry Cavalry under Captain Smith, Lt. Atkinson and Cornet Clapham arrived in Kendal about 4 o'clock in the forenoon amid that Bustle of the Town which so gallant a troop was sure to excite. The bells with many a merry peal welcomed the gay cavaliers."[10]

Thereafter only a few alarms and excursions jolted the civilian slumbers of the nineteenth century. After Louis Napoleon Bonaparte seized power in 1848 there were fears of attack from France. Local militia contingents were raised and in August 1851 the Westmorland contingent including 36 Kendal and 7 Milnthorpe men passed through Milnthorpe with the Furness Cavalry after 8 days training at Lancaster. "The Captain and officers made their Headquarters at the Cross Keys when many a good song and toast were given and returned."[11] No less cheerful was the welcome given in September 1855 to Colonel Upton when he returned to Levens Hall from the Crimean War.[12] A local delegation went in procession from Milnthorpe with an address of welcome. Earlier in the year Heversham and Milnthorpe had subscribed £156 16s 6d to a "Patriotic Fund".

At the time of the Egyptian campaign in August 1882 an attempt was made to form a Yeomanry branch in Milnthorpe. However, Egypt was won for the Empire without the help of Milnthorpe. A thanksgiving service for the victory at Tel-el-Kebir was held in September when the vicar proclaimed that Christianity and British conquest went hand in hand by preaching from Isaiah 19v19 "In that day shall there be an altar to the Lord in the midst of the land of Egypt and a pillar at the border thereof to the Lord."[15]

Though a drum and fife band visited Milnthorpe in December 1882 nothing seems to have come of the volunteer movement until August 1890 when under the headline "Better late than never" it was reported that "Milnthorpe is about to do what it should have done 20 years ago – form a volunteer force. I don't see (said the Editor) why our only sea port should not raise two companies: half each from Gatebeck and from Heversham and Leasgill and one from Milnthorpe and Beetham."[16]

The following April the Volunteers had received rifles, new uniforms and in February 1892 a Volunteers' Ball was held to raise funds for a band. Unfortunately, a "Volunteers Soiree" for the same cause was poorly attended in November as the footballers had held an event the night previously! Nevertheless by September 1894 "Captain" Argles with Sergeant Instructor Carr inaugurated a band – with the help of some Gatebeck bandsmen. One of the district's first Rummage Sales was held to raise funds for instruments. £20 was raised and Milnthorpe got a "full silver (i.e. tin) band."[17]

It was soon seen leading church parades of 180 men. Sometimes the combined Gatebeck and Milnthorpe contingents met at Rowell Bridge to march together to Church. Forty eight volunteers camped at Shap in June 1896 where they took part in a "sham fight" under the direction of Captain Argles.[18] The next year 8 men from the local force (who had to be over 5 feet 10 ¾ inches tall) helped line the streets of London for the Diamond Jubilee. At home there was a Church parade of 62 ranks and 32 members of Endmoor Boys' Brigade.[19]

Spurred on by Jubilee jingoism the village entered into the Boer War with gusto. At Christmas 1899[20] Mrs. Rheam and her sister Miss Constance Holme "who gave invaluable assistance as accompanist" raised £9 for the "widows, wives and orphans of the South African War" in a patriotic concert at which Sergeants Carr, Scott and Hayhurst sang "Boys of the Old Brigade" in uniform. A second performance was held in January before "a select audience of most of the best houses in a wide area." Mrs. Radcliffe of Summerlands rendered selections from the "Sleeping Beauty, a Salute of the Queen gained protracted applause, and the Volunteer Band played Rule Britannia and the National Anthem."[21]

When a contingent led by Sergeant J. Downham of Farleton with Private J. Bell, J. Towers, Issac Teasdale, J. Cragg, W. Wilson, left to join the Imperial Army they were seen off by an enormous crowd. The band, playing a full repertoire of patriotic anthems, was "led by a mounted charger borrowed for the occasion and met with ringing cheers." The men were treated to "a capital breakfast" by Captain Argles and were given a sum of money and 1 lb of tobacco. Unfortunately, Private Robinson was rejected at the last moment not being up to the standard height.[22] At the following Christmas Mrs. Rheam with perhaps rather hazy notions as to the South African climate sent out to the men woollen shirts, mufflers, vests, socks, and also pocket handkerchiefs, magazines and scent.

When Mafeking was relieved flags were hoisted on the Church tower at 6 a.m. as soon as news was received but the bell ringers refused to ring a victory peel until the news had been confirmed. In the evening at 6.30 p.m. all the village children paraded on the green, under a banner made by their teacher Miss Gledhill, proclaiming "Baden Powell and Rule Britannia," three cheers were raised for Lord Roberts followed by "For He's a Jolly Good Fellow" and the Te Deum and the National Anthem.[23]

In April 1901 Sergeant Atkinson, Corporal Milne and Private

Wallace returned home. Coming from Sandside station they were greeted by "an elaborate triumphal arch at the cross roads in the centre of the town constructed of evergreens, flags and flowers which wilted after a day." On the way from the station Maurice Bromley-Wilson of Dallam Tower treated them to some "Californian Sherry put down by the late Mr. E. Wilson twenty years ago."[24] When peace was proclaimed in June 1902 the village "presented a gay appearance." At noon 200 children processed to the Square where a telegram from Lord Kitchener announcing the peace terms was read from the Cross by Mr. Gandy, Chairman of the Magistrates, "every second child carried a union flag and there was yet another banner fluttering nearby reading "God save the King and Queen." After singing "Now thank we all our God" special prayers were said giving thanks for "not one Milnthorpe man having been killed or seriously wounded... and taking into consideration the length of the campaign there was every reason for gratitude to God who had taken and then spared their fellow townsmen."[25] A fortnight later Privates Bibby and Robinson returned home. They were greeted by the village band playing "See the Conquering Hero Comes" and were taken in procession to Milnthorpe for a service at which Te Deum was sung.[26] During the celebrations for the Coronation of Edward VII in August the Boer War Veterans were presented (on the Church steps) with gold watches.

Probably, Milnthorpe was no more jingoistic than any other place and the progression from patriotism to pugnacity in village attitudes between the Boer and Great Wars was, no doubt, typical of the time. In January 1905 Captain Argles declared that "every young man who declined to serve in the Volunteers, the Yeomanry or the Militia should be compelled to do a period of service in the regular army (applause)."[27] When Volunteer Private Henry Abbat of Park Road died in 1907 aged 21 he was given a quasi military funeral with a solemn procession led by the band playing the Dead March in Saul, the men with guns reversed.[28] At the service the hymn "The Sons of God go Forth to War" was sung. In 1909 Captain Bagot, who was hoping to regain his seat in Parliament from the Liberals, made an impassioned speech at Milnthorpe in favour of more armaments – even the Liberal War Minister "Mr. Haldane has admitted to himself that they would not really be ready for war until six months after it had been declared."[29] Bagot won the seat for the Conservatives and after his death in 1913 so did Colonel Weston although his opponent Mr. Somervell caused outrage by "going round the country working up a scare about German aeroplanes and other bogies." Late in the year a womens' Voluntary Aid Detachment was formed in Milnthorpe and soon had 33 members learning first aid. As a counter blast to the

Highland troops leaving Milnthorpe Station for a pre-First War training camp at Farleton. The Old Toll Bar is in the background.

"German scare" Mrs. Theodora Wilson, recently returned from a Peace Conference at The Hague, organised an anti-war meeting at the Cross in the Square – and a "resolution against compulsory military service was passed though there was a considerable number of dissidents."[31]

Despite all the talk and posturing when war did come it was unexpected. In the local press the assassination at Sarajevo and the initial manoeuvres were hardly noticed. More attention was given to the prospective formation of a golf club on Heversham Head and the Milnthorpe Mothers' Union's trip to Morecambe. When the oldest member Mrs. Hayes aged 83 "saw a fine flight by an aeroplane her delight was unbounded – never again would she say anything was impossible, for this beat all wonderful things come about since her young days."

War was declared on the 4th August 1914. It happened that the Territorial Army was encamped at Farleton. Within two days 3,000 men and 27 horses had entrained at Milnthorpe for the front.[34] On August 8th the first of the local reservists John Bowden, Ralph Thompson, James Wilkinson, Bob Sharples, H. Clayton and J. Robinson were given a hearty send-off following a church service at which "O God our help in Ages past" was sung.[35] The first recruiting meeting held the next week was a failure. Various speakers "were subject to a running fire of interruptions and criticism" from several men "who were not in a fit condition for admission to the meeting" and only one man – Harry Robinson – joined up.[36] A later meeting, organised by local ladies, was a total success. A hand bill entitled "Wake up Milnthorpe" had been sent round beforehand and the room was packed to hear a redoubtable termagant, Mrs. North, wife of Colonel North of Old Hall, declare that she had four brothers-in-law, eleven first cousins and one husband in the Army and if they did not come back she would not wear mourning but a white band round her arm in memory of gallant men who had given their lives to shield women and children. Endmoor had already sent 49 men but Milnthorpe only 12. The result was that when Major Rigg announced that he felt sure that Milnthorpe men thought "Honour was more important than life" twenty four men joined up.

A "sportsman's meeting" for all cricketers, cyclists, footballers, rowing men, athletes, golfers, swimmers and all sportsmen produced more cannon fodder. On Monday the 14th September "the Milnthorpe Athletic Volunteer Force" of H. Hyde, S. Shepherd, W. Taylor, R. Hudson, J. Parker (destined for the Royal Artillery), S. Barnes, T. Lloyd, W. Arkwright (for the Royal Engineers), C Hyde, B. Cowan, S. Ashburner, John Wilkinson, Fred Barnes, A. Garth (for the Border Regiment) assembled on the Green to be given a hearty send off as they left for entraining at Kendal. The National School boys sang the National Anthem, the church bells pealed, the choir sang "O God our help in Ages past" and the men received cigars from Mr. Moorhouse of the Bull's Head and cigarettes from Miss Mabel Holme.

A second contingent left the next day: R. Thompson, T. Coward, W. Knight, H. Thompson, Edward Mashiter, James Ashburner, E. Dixon, H. Sharples, Thomas Wilson, James Garth, F.R. Wilkinson, Philip M. Rheam and Harry S. Seagrave. Deliberately they were all pals together. Pals battalions were good for recruiting as the men, most of whom had never been further afield than Morecambe and Blackpool, could stay together. Serving together meant also that many of them fell together and two generations later the legend was born that Milnthorpe lost all its men in one week.[37]

Training, though cynically brief, could be cheerful. Reports came through as to how Milnthorpe lads had taken part in a Lonsdale Battalion Smoking Concert and of how some encamped at Sittingbourne had been "criticised and admired by the King."[38]

Though good for recruiting such news was not good enough. As summer made way for a muddy autumn it became clear that the men would not be home for Christmas and if villagers were not to share succeeding Christmasses with the Kaiser more men would have to go. A lantern slide lecture organised by the Imperial

Milnthorpe Volunteers 1914.
L. to R. Back Row: ?, Fred Coward, Edward Mashiter.
Front Row: Isaac Coward, Tom Coward.

Maritime League culminating in a kaleidoscope of the Crowned (Allied) Heads of Europe was followed by an "eloquent appeal for more and still more men to join the forces both naval and military.[39] No recruits offered until the vicar, the Reverend Pickering, urged the young men to be "up and doing" whereupon Mr. Fred Todd, who worked with Mr. J. Douthwaite at the forge, announced that he would join the Royal Engineers as a farrier." Still literally on the war path, Mrs. Edward North magnanimously announced that if any youths made the excuse "their mothers did not want them to go" if she was "furnished with the names she would go and see them."[40] At the October hiring fair in Kendal Thomas Atkinson Argles, now promoted "Major," induced the farm lads to "come and be trained" and many answered the call to fight for "King and Country." To replace them the Westmorland Gazette announced that the Church Army was recruiting "boys for farm service at £4. per annum."[41]

That truth is the first casualty of war was shown by an atrocity story in, of all journals, the *Methodist Recorder* which reported that three trained nurses, two of them being sisters, had left "Milnthorpe near Kendal to work for the Red Cross. All three are dead. One was killed when the hospital was shelled. Another came home to Milnthorpe to die as a result of having lost a leg and an arm cut off by a soldier who molested her while attending the wounded at Mons amid falling shells, while the remaining one had her ears cut off before being killed."[42] Sensibly, the editor of the *Westmorland Gazette* called such stories "madness" but failed to see any insanity in the pages of photographs of recruits and casualties which he published regularly for the next four years.

Milnthorpe did not have a nursing martyr but it did have a nursing heroine when its District Nurse, Helena Bird, volunteered for war service in Serbia. After a horrific journey through the battle-scarred Balkans, Nurse Bird worked for several months during 1915 at a hospital at Skopje where eight of her colleagues died of typhoid. On the advance of the Austrian Armies she retreated with the ragged columns of refugees and camp followers, trudging for 300 miles over mountain passes behind the dispirited ranks of the defeated and squabbling Serbian forces. Often she had to be hidden in a bullock cart to avoid the attentions of the soldiers and local bandits. By the time she reached the coast and British rescue forces at Brindisi she had lost several stone in weight and all her luggage, but not her virtue. She arrived in London on Christmas Day 1916 with nothing but the clothes she stood up in, but after a short convalescence, she went back to Serbia for another 18 months. Loaded with Serbian decorations, she was honoured at home by having her photograph hung in the Girls' School and by being the only woman to be treated as a war veteran at the village peace celebrations. Her health was permanently impaired by the War. She served as District Nurse at Levens for two years and at Crosthwaite for some months but was forced to retire to Bewdley in Worcestershire where she died in February 1926.[43]

Amongst the first to go to war were the fourth territorials who replaced regular troops in Burma in 1914. By 1915 a contingent of Milnthorpe men including R. Sharples, R. Thompson and Lt. Ernest Mashiter (son of John Masiter, the post-master, and just down from Oxford) were established at Maymyo.[49] It was John Mashiter's lot to relay the dread news contained in the War Office telegrams but, fortunately for him, it was always to other families. Ernest Mashiter survived though, later, he too fought in Flanders. When his father retired from the Post Office in 1922 he called the fine house he had built on St. Anthony's Hill overlooking the village "Maymyo." When other houses followed the community on the top of the hill was called for a time "Maymyo Town."[50]

While at Maymyo several Milnthorpe men nearly succumbed to poisoning after eating nuts gathered in the jungle and were only saved by surgeons using stomach pumps. Otherwise the local lads survived their far-flung soldiering unscathed.

Fireman Carter's grave,
Milnthorpe Cemetery.

Milnthorpe's first casualty was Chris. Scott injured and probably killed at the Dardanelles in 1915. Eventually his family accepted his death but there were recurrent rumours that Chris had not been killed but had been seen on an ANZAC hospital ship bound for Australia. During the war no report of his death was published nor was a memorial service held although his sister Eva, the village schoolmistress, played the organ at most of the other memorial services. Moreover the list of casualties published at the end of the war concluded with "Chris Scott 1915" although in theory it should have been the first.[51]

A strange casualty also occurred in 1915 when a naval fireman, Arthur Carter, aged 33 from Scotland, was killed on the main railway line. His body was found at Elmsfield Bridge. Apparently the only witness was a "Chinaman" and in the absence of local interpreters a verdict of accidental death was brought in – but there were rumours that the unfortunate Carter had either committed suicide or that he had been trying to abscond. His grave in Milnthorpe Cemetery is marked by an Imperial War Gravestone.[52]

The first memorial service in Milnthorpe was not to a local casualty but to Nurse Edith Cavell a popular heroine, held a month after her execution by the Germans in November 1915.[53]

Even before the decimation of village youth in the battles of 1916, anti-German feelings and fears were high. When an airship flew over the bay just before Christmas it was immediately believed to be a German spy zeppelin as were others which landed at Moss End, Farleton, though these were found to belong to the British War Department.[54]

On Saturday morning the 30th April 1916 the villagers were aroused by the church bells being chimed by the vicar, the Reverend Christopher Pickering, to the tune of "Days and nights quickly flying".[57] They announced the death of James Garth, killed on the Western Front. Formerly a comb maker he had been one of the first to join up at the "Ladies' Recruiting" meeting in August 1914. A few days later his parents received a letter from Ralph Thompson who was serving with him stating that "the bullet went right through his head so you have the consolation of knowing that he died quite painlessly. Jim is the first one we have lost from our platoon. We all felt it very much." A day later news arrived that his brother, John Garth, had been wounded. To the sound of muffled bells a packed congregation attended a joint memorial service for Jim Garth, Stanley Knight Bates (grandson of the village vet), and Robert Hudson of Sandside.[57]

Mourning was accompanied by demands for more fighting men. Under the headline "Milnthorpe found wanting" came a report that Captain Long had heard "a great deal of talk at Milnthorpe about young fellows who had not gone but ought to go, spending their evenings lounging about smoking cigarettes." Conscription began in April 1916 and with it came pleas for exemption, nearly all of which were dismissed. Some claims were apparently trivial – as when a Milnthorpe grocer's son stated that he had to remain at home in order to carry goods to the shop from a warehouse sixty yards away. In 1917 a 38 year old married man from Sandside who farmed 21 acres, kept 6 cattle, a horse and had 2½ acres of wheat had to go but a single man, who drove Major Argles' motor plough had his appeal allowed![59]

Throughout the "Somme Summer" casualty telegrams came in almost every week.

Waiting was perhaps even worse in this war than in any other. In earlier wars relatives generally did not know the fate of their menfolk until they had been dead or imprisoned for some time. In 1914-1918 they could be informed almost immediately if a relative was wounded or "missing" but without the wireless or the efficient telephones of later wars they were still dependent on the post or telegraph which could take days or even weeks to percolate through the military machine. Thus in July 1916 Jack Wilkinson's parents were told that he was wounded. After getting no news for a fortnight they got a letter from him stating "I don't know whether it was a bullet or a piece of shrapnel but it went through my steel helmet and stuck in my head and I must thank God to have come through all right... I shall have some strange things to tell you when I

RFC Balloon, Moss End, 1915.

return if I am spared."[64] He wasn't and on a fateful Wednesday
morning in autumn the mournful peal of "Days and moments
quickly flying" announced that he too was dead. Jack, who was 32,
had been a great village footballer.

At about the same time the village lost another footballer, Fred
Barnes aged 36, William Knight, one of Mr. Tuson's old boys who
had managed his parents' carrying business, and John Spedding,
though few details were forthcoming. Something of what the
hoped-for victory was costing was contained in letters from Richard
Prickett of Hincaster Hall and of Harold Hyde of Milnthorpe who
had just been awarded the Military Medal with ribbon for "doing a
little bit extra" with the Border Machine Gun Corps. In his letter
Dick stated that "one boy from Milnthorpe who used to drive
Dr. Fuller's motor car, named Wilson, told me that he was one of
six who were left of 36 who enlisted with him. You would never
imagine what the country looks like where the battle (has) been
going on. To say that it had been visited by earthquakes or volcanic
explosions is putting it mildly. There is not a tree, bush or hedge
that is not blown to fragments."[66]

From the Somme, Harold Hyde wrote "our platoon were in the
trenches and on the 21st we made an attack on Fritz and that was
where I got the wound which is just a nice one and I expect to get to
Blighty. I got hit in the left jaw and left hand as I got to the barbed
wire. Jack Sennick was with me and he took over the gun and I got
back to our trenches and was getting bandaged up when he landed
up too, having got it in the arm. When I was coming down the line
from the dressing station I met Sennick, Willie Taylor from Leasgill
and another lad out of our platoon and all four of us had our left

hands up in a sling. When we got off the train we were all sent out to some hospital and three of us are in the same ward. Willie Taylor is in another ward but we will look him up today." He added ironically: "I have not heard how Jack Wilkinson and Bob Smith who were left with the gun got on. So if you hear anything let me know. There is no need to worry about me as I am feeling champion but just a little bit sore. P.S. I am just leaving for Blighty."

As the Somme offensive fizzled out in the autumn rains the casualties lists grew shorter and the village prepared for the third Christmas of the war. A ladies' committee sent 80 parcels and St. Thomas's school 55 parcels to the troops. Along with the usual chocolates and tobacco each parcel contained a jar of vaseline.[70]

Then from a forgotten front came news of Private Harry Bond. He had been captured by the Turks at the fall of Kut in Mesopotamia in 1915, having previously served with the Borders at Poona in India. His wife Fanny had received no news of him for 16 months until a note came saying that he was well and was being well treated. In fact by that time he was dead. His name is one of several not on the war memorial. The reason given was that he came originally from Endmoor. On the other hand James Punchard from Kirkby Lonsdale was commemorated as he was the brother in law of Constance Holme.

Despite the grief and gore the terrible year for the village was brightened by the weddings of two of its most notable citizens. In February 1916 Constance Holme "who has done much to brighten life by her dialect plays *Duck Egg Dick* and *Womps*", was married to Frederick B. Punchard. As her beribboned carriage drew up she was greeted, pre-war fashion, by all the school children and by a merry marriage peal. She was attired in a "gown of white chiffon taffeta, the skirt bordered with white fur being caught up over a lace underskirt, the bodice was of taffeta and a wreath of white flowers held in place a Brussels veil lent by the groom's mother. Her white and gold satin shoes were the gift of Mr. Rowland Sharpe, village shoemaker."[72] At Christmas 1916 Sir Maurice Bromley-Wilson, who like Connie Holme was past his first youth, was maried at St. George's, Hanover Square, to Mrs. Godfrey Armitage, widow of Major Armitage of Nab Wood, Bowness. Though he had not been much in the village since his personal bankruptcy of 1913, Sir Maurice and Lady Bromley-Wilson were presented with a gold cigar case from the tenants and a silver loving cup with walrus ivory handles from the Dallam Tower Basset Hounds (sic).[73]

There was a six months' gap in the catalogue of battle casualties until the start of the "Passchendaele" offensive in May 1917. A few soldiers actually came home on leave though rarely for more than 3 days. Though almost every family had had their losses Christmas was celebrated.

At the Christmas Service special prayers were said for John Parker of Park Road who had been missing on the Western Front since October.[82] Jack's fate had still not been confirmed by the following April when his brother Edward was killed, and it was only on the 25th May that the family heard that Jack was presumed killed on October 26th.[83]

The final "pushes" claimed a full share of Milnthorpe men. In April and May Walter Thompson[84] and James Tuson (Head Master of the National School)[85] were taken prisoner and Geoffrey Jackson, son of T.O. Jackson, the Solicitor, was wounded in the head and though he lived never recovered his health. One May night the Ashburner family were awakened by a crash of Edward Ashburner's photograph falling to the floor. Next day a telegram informed them that Edward had been killed by a shell instantaneously.[86] His brother Martin's death on the Somme 18 months earlier was confirmed only about the same time. A day or two later Mr. and Mrs. Edward Clarke of Chestnut Cottage were informed that their son, Percy, had been killed "outright" by a shell. "When called up the business carried on by his father had to close down."[87] Next came confirmation that Charles Hyde who had been missing since April had died as a result of shrapnel wounds. His brother John was also wounded in the same battle but was back at the front in a fortnight.[88]

The fourth anniversary of the war came and went, having been celebrated with a parade of the newly formed Girl Guides, an address from the Cross in which Rev. S.W. Wheeler, Chaplain in France, "spoke of maintaining a third line of defence at home" and a special hymn "God bless our soldiers" sung.[89] With war's grimmest irony Fred Clark from the Market Place, was killed in October 1918. He had joined up in October 1914 and while going for a year's service in Egypt his vessel had been torpedoed. Though he had fought for the four full years of the war he was just 21.

A fortnight later it was over. "A telegram from the Secretary General of the Post Office stating that hostilities had ceased was received shortly after noon on Monday and the news spread with great rapidity so that the village was in a very short time decked with flags and the new St. George's ensign presented by Mr. W. Allan of Mallow House for the long expected event was run up on the flagstaff of the Church tower. Peals were rung on the church bells at intervals until late at night and the Church clock once more struck the hours which seemed to take the popular fancy more than anything."

As the first peals sounded Polly Sheldon who was staying with her parents, Atkinson's the shoemakers, in Main Street, rushed out to be told by Jack Black – grocer's boy at Richmonds (and who ever afterwards claimed to be the first person in Milnthorpe to know of the armistice) – that the war was over. Abandoning for a moment her normal "schoolmarm" air, she yelled the news out only to realise instantly that she had addressed Ben Clark who was pushing his hand cart into the Square. Ben dropped the cart and said quietly "It won't bring Fred back." He went home and the cart stayed in the gutter for the rest of the day.[92]

Christmas 1918 was celebrated with pre-war cheer though the services had a "memorial character" with the names of the fallen being read out and Captain Ernest Mashiter reading the lessons.

The war's last victim was Lt. Fred. R. Wilkinson, son of Mr. and Mrs. James Wilkinson, who, after leaving Heversham Grammar School, had gone to Keble College, Oxford. He was killed in south Russia while engaged in the allied intervention against the Bolsheviks. His death was not witnessed and it was presumed that he received fatal injuries by a fall from a horse. However, rather suspiciously, he was found with his "head bashed in" propped up against a tree. He was given a full military funeral.

His coffin was carried to its final resting place in the Crimean Cemetery at Hyder Pacha under the shadow of the Florence Nightingale Hospital by three British, three Sikh and 3 Dublin Fusiliers officers; a firing party of 100 men was drawn up from his own regiment.[93]

In March 1919 a War Memorial Committee met. Seven proposals were rejected:

1. A tablet in the Church and the Methodist Chapel – "too insignificant."
2. A children's playground – "too expensive."(!)
3. A mortuary chapel to cost £700 – "not worth the expense as there were only eight burials a year."
4. A lych gate was wanted by no one except Dr. Fuller.
5. Seats – "too ordinary."
6. A village club – the Institute and Public Rooms were already under-used, and finally,
7. A suggestion by Chris Knight, just demobilised, that the memorial funds should be shared out amongst those who had returned home.[94] This was rejected on the obvious grounds that it would ignore the fallen. Finally it was decided to erect a memorial cross. After considering various sites, including one at the Fountain in the square it was decided to place the elegant Portland stone cross (16 feet high "designed on simple lines without meretricious ornament" and enclosed by chains and 8 stone pillars) on the green opposite Police Square.

It was unveiled on Sunday afternoon, 11th September 1919. Flags were at half mast on the church and other public buildings, the church bells rang a muffled peal and the re-formed town band under C. Knight led a procession of demobilised men under

Sergeant J. Slimon from the National School along the Strands and up Park Road to the Main Street where a service was conducted by the Vicar, the Rev. Pickering, assisted by six other clergymen. Col. Weston M.P. unveiled the Cross as the choir sang "When I survey the wondrous Cross." During the singing of this hymn "the vicar never took his eyes off the top of the Cross." The base of the cross was almost buried under wreaths from wives, mothers and orphans. In addition to the Cross six memorial seats were placed at selected points – four of which survived 70 years later.[95]

Peace celebrations, 1919.

Two months earlier, "Peace Day," Saturday 19 July 1919, "a day ever memorable for the present generation," had been celebrated in fine style with a procession of decorated cycles, carts and "fancy dress" pedestrians from Owlett Ash via the Square (where the customary service was conducted from the church steps), to Dallam Park. The efforts included a 60 yard race for 4 year olds and a blindfold wrestling and boxing match at which the final bout between Mr. John Alderson and Mr. Ferdy Casson caused great excitement.[96]

The last serviceman to come home, Henry Atkinson, did not return until Christmas 1920, having served in India and Mesopotamia for nearly six years. He never forgot how he was unrecognised for several minutes when he went into the "Royal Oak."[98] By coincidence, having been the last to come home, Henry was the last of Milnthorpe's "Old Contemptibles" to die, in June 1985, a week after his 90th birthday.

It was not until Tuesday 12th January 1921 that 99 ex-servicemen and one woman, Nurse Bird, were treated to a "Welcome Home."

Nurse Bird was given an umbrella and "each man a rattan partridge walking cane, bearing a silver band with the initials and dates 1914-1918 engraved thereon. The belated celebrations were marred, however, when Walter Thompson fell descending the balcony steps and striking the back of his head on the stairs, suffered severe concussion. Despite Dr. Fuller, who was also the master of ceremonies, being at hand it was several hours before Thompson regained consciousness.[99]

The 1920's in Milnthorpe were neither "naughty", nor "roaring". Most war veterans seemed to have sunk thankfully back into civilian life. Even if their homes were not fit for heroes to live in most were just glad to be home: almost none ever set foot out of England again.

Some veterans groused a little. At the meeting held in 1925 to form a British Legion branch, Mr. R.E. Sumpton grumbled, "the war memorial which cost £300 was erected without the ex-servicemen having any say in the matter and the money, in his opinion, would have been better spent helping to provide a club room for the men. All they got was a supper and a walking stick." Albert Hayes said "it was a slander to say the men were neglected." He became secretary of the new branch whose committee consisted of J. Atkinson, R.E. Sumpton, H.F. Flemming, H. Hyde, J. Sliman, W. Moorhouse and F. Comber with G. Cooper as Chairman. The Rev. Gamble agreed to be chaplain and Mr. A.J. Miles, the brewer, though not an ex-serviceman "since he had taken his discharge from the navy about 20 years ago" agreed to help in every possible way.[101] Within a short time the branch had 76 members and far from being a quasi-military corps, the legion concentrated on social activities and on organising an annual Old Folk's treat.

During the worrying thirties the "post-war" increasingly made way for "pre-war", although at the Milnthorpe Unionists' Hot Pot Supper in September 1937, the Westmorland M.P. Oliver Stanley dismissed any war scare: "it is quite true that one certain way of avoiding war in the future is to have a war today. We must never let ourselves believe that a war in the future is inevitable and forestall it and have a war today."[103] Two and a half years later Oliver Stanley was Minister for War.

In 1938 the *Westmorland Gazette* (at first as postscripts to the usual village news), reported practical preparations in Milnthorpe for war. In June 1938 a committee to plan air raid precautions was set up by Mr. Frederick Astley of Greenside and Mr. A.J. Miles.[104] Willy Scott took charge of the A.R.P. contingent and by March 1939 the fire brigade had received new equipment including an electric siren – supplemented, in 1940, by a fire bell hung on the Public Rooms gable.

In August 1938 plans for receiving 2,500 east coast evacuees in

Westmorland were announced and Milnthorpe was to be one of the six main reception areas. A month later, during the Munich crisis a peace service was attended by 80 ex-servicemen. Though war did not break out defence planning continued, although Milnthorpe did not get gas masks until March '39. In the following month a large number of people attended a National Service meeting addressed by the Chief Constable of Kendal, Mr. P. O'Neil. As evidence of local preparedness a bren gun was displayed and the audience was told that the Home Office would telegraph the Post Office when to extinguish lights.[106]

In 1939 there was none of the jingoism of 1914. With National Service implemented in April 1939 and a controlled "call up" there were no recruiting meetings and no "pals battalions." Instead of being bade farewell by a cheering crowd and the town band, the 1939-45 conscript merely received a card in a brown envelope telling him where to report for a medical. If he passed, then armed with a travel warrant and a postal order for 4 shillings, he got on the bus for Carnforth station to make a lonely journey, not to a battle front but to a training camp where immediate danger (and glory) were nil. Reserved occupations reduced military call-up and there were many moans about men who had "dodged the war" by getting jobs at Libby's Milk factory. No white feathers were handed out and conscientious objectors, a number of whom were drafted to work at the Mental Home, were respected even though their views were not generally shared. On Milnthorpe Hill lived two such "conshies" both highly qualified civil engineers. One was reduced to living on his savings and the "£1 a week plus rations" nurses' pay. The other, son of a Labour M.P. and son-in-law of prosperous local business people, was drafted to "work of national importance" on the Haweswater Dam. He received a full salary and a petrol ration to take him on a 50 mile round trip to Haweswater.[107]

Women, instead of organising ladies' recruiting meetings as they did in 1914, were fully occupied. Many, like Edith Powell, wife of the solicitor, did men's work at Libby's. Others coped with evacuees. Between 30th August and 10th September 1939, 10,000 evacuees arrived in Westmorland. Over 100 came to Milnthorpe on the 1st and 2nd of September, arriving by special trains between 2 and 5 p.m. In "the first glorious week children chased butterflies, gathered blackberries, got stung, lost and other exciting adventures all under glorious sunshine. Providence weary of seeing these little mortals penned up in concrete tenements has given them a holiday in the fields."[108] Most of the children came from working-class homes in Todds Nook, Newcastle. Almost all were housed in the cramped homes of Milnthorpe's own working class. Teachers and adult evacuees, whether private or official, went to the better homes. Two of them – Mrs. Harris who lived with the Mashiters in

Milnthorpe Square, and Miss Gibbard who stayed with Miss Dobson on Church Street – never went back.

Most of the children stayed only briefly. 1,300 Westmorland evacuees had gone home by November. By Christmas 1942 only 280 were left in the whole county.[109] A few children stayed and made lasting friendships with their "aunty's" families; some did not. One group of children billetted at Flowerden with Mrs. MacLeod, who, despite living grandly with servants and a chauffeur, kept a notoriously poor table, had to be taken away because they were "hungered." There were the usual horror stories of untrained, bad mannered children for whom "evacuation" seemed to have two meanings, and in December 1940 an evacuee boy was put on probation after stealing a gold ring worth £50 and a watch worth £20 "from the large house in the Milnthorpe area where he was billeted." Generally, however, there were few real problems. The "strangers were received in the parish for the most part with genuine sympathy and settled down in good homes."

Air raid precautions created a semblance of war and there was a rash of prosecutions for blackout offences – thanks to the diligent constabulary.

By the first Christmas of the war all sorts of voluntary organisations were in full swing. Christmas parcels for the troops were organised by the vicar, the Rev. Gamble, Methodist Minister Rev. J.W. Ladell and the National School Headmaster Mr. J.T. Cookson. The British Legion sent 10s. notes for "all men in the forces" (i.e. from Milnthorpe) and Mrs. Harold Hyde began a series of weekly Whist Drives in the Institute which she ran throughout the war in aid of forces' relief. There was no lack of support for more active work. At a Christmas social Mr. J.F. Ramsbottom spoke of the "100 first aid workers who stolidly tramped miles on wet, cold nights last winter in order to train for voluntary duty in the Milnthorpe area." Undoubtedly, many people had "the time of their lives" enjoying to the full the enforced sociability of war without, in Milnthorpe, any of its dangers.

Chief amongst the well remembered aspects of war time Milnthorpe was the fire service. Though equipped with a new engine, the gallant brigade fought almost no fires. The only serious incident was a domestic fire at St. Anthony's Cottage, the home of the Masons, in November 1939. At night a clothes maid fell into the fire and the resulting blaze gutted the house. Mr. and Mrs. Mason, their two children and the new baby escaped down a ladder from the upper floor. Mr. and Mrs. Shepherd's cottage next door was also badly damaged and part of the roof fell in but they were able to save much of their furniture.[113] Despite war-time shortages the cottages were repaired within a few months though charred roof timbers had to be re-used. Villagers rallied round to provide clothing and other necessities for the Masons who had lost virtually all they possessed.

Early in 1940 Milnthorpe received a direct naming from Lord Haw Haw of Germany (the traitor William Joyce) who in a German broadcast actually singled out the garrison town of Kendal and the village of Milnthorpe "when the time arrives." It was a common ploy of these broadcasts to name specific towns – even streets – to reduce morale but that this occasion was not just far fetched propaganda was revealed in 1946 when Ronny Somervell of Haverbrack House was in the team which interrogated General Von Runstedt. One of the documents produced showed the later stages of a German invasion plan to land troops in Morecambe Bay from Ireland and nip Britain in two at its narrowest point between Teesside and Milnthorpe. Dr. P.S. Byrne later claimed that the dossier included an O.S. map of Milnthorpe showing his house Stoneleigh as the first aid post. This archive cannot, however, be traced.

In 1940 Milnthorpe, along with the rest of the nation, prepared to repell the invader. Men between the ages of sixteen and sixty volunteered for the Home Guard and the Observer Corps. The Home Guard began as the Local Defence Volunteers (LDV) and does not appear to have been as makeshift an affair as later legends suggested. By 1941, when Eric Proctor added a year onto his age to join, it was fully equipped with .303 rifles, a Sten gun firing 15 rounds, a Browning automatic pistol and a projectile mortar. The latter was fired at Fishcarling Head where target practice was also held, especially "when the wild fowl were in." Parades were held outside the Headquarters (the large house in the Square, at the time the home of the Roe family) and, after the H.Q. moved to Bela View, on the playing fields where there was also bayonet practice. Night exercises included cross-country manoeuvres from a camp at Hazelslack, attacking the Summerhouse (St. Anthony's Tower), sentry duty at the Levens Bridge road block and inspection of similar defences at Kirkby Lonsdale. On one night the guards' lorry driver Henry Hodgson changed the detail from inspection of the Lune bridges to the bars of the Royal Hotel and other hostelries, much to the disgust of Corporal Godfrey Sadler, a leading teetotaller and rechabite.

At its peak the Home Guard numbered about forty men and boys under the command of Captain Micky Moyse, Lieutenants John Outhwaite and John Dawson (all reserved occupation men working at Libby's or the Paper Mill), Lt. Kenneth Jackson, village solicitor, and Jim Wilson who pulled himself up the ranks via sergeant to become, just before "stand-down," a second-lieutenant. Other ranks included the Sergeant Major Charley Crayston and Corporal Alf ("Pious") Wilson. Quite how they would have

Bomb crater, Overthwaite, 1942.

performed had the Wehrmacht intervened no-one will ever know.

The Royal Observer Corps did less strenuous but, as it turned out, more useful work. A band of observers including Robin Wallace, Bob Cottam, Arthur Ashburner and Reg Benson spent endless cold nights scanning the skies for enemy aircraft from the Summerhouse and from a specially built look-out on Haverbrack. During the bombing of Barrow and Belfast the Luftwaffe flew directly over Milnthorpe in both day and night raids. Once a party of picnickers on the sands swore that they could see the "nasty Nazi face" of the pilot of a "spy plane" swooping low to investigate Arnside viaduct!

Though spared direct participation in the Battle of Britain Milnthorpe was included in anti-invasion plans. Place names and sign posts were removed in the summer of 1940 and not replaced until 1943, pill boxes were built round the bay, there were road blocks at Levens Bridge and the church bells were silenced until after El Alamein in October 1942. This latter restriction put an end to a noon angelus rung by the Rev. Gamble to call all who heard it to pray "at work or wherever they happened to be."[114] The salvaging of metal was regarded as important but only in 1943 were iron railings removed from round buildings, by which time their propaganda, let alone their practical value, was limited. Away went the chains round the War Memorial and, by accident, the litter boxes in the Square!

At the end of April 1941 Milnthorpe was shaken by an air raid when Grange-over-Sands was bombed. A crowd gathered at the top of Laking Steps to watch Yewbarrow Lodge burning.[118] The closest any bombs fell to Milnthorpe itself were in Slackhead and "a stick"

John Balmer, B.E.M., with his sister(L) and wife(R) outside Buckingham Palace after the Investiture.

which punctured the meadows at Overthwaite in 1942. Almost certainly they had been unloaded to lighten planes returning from raids on Barrow. Alternatively, they might have been surprised by the anti-aircraft search light mounted at Whassett in order to illuminate potential attacks on the railway and on Libby's.

In complete contrast to the First World War it is the impact of the War at home that dominates contemporary accounts and later memories. Milnthorpe did, however, have its share of heroes and casualties. In June 1941 John Balmer was awarded the B.E.M. for gallantry in recovering the crew from a crashed aircraft. He had been delivering mail near his training camp when he saw the plane spin and crash two miles away. Using his motor bike he crossed ploughed fields and then jumped a fence and a ditch and found the plane a few minutes after it had landed just as it burst into flames. "Gunner Balmer tried to reach the cockpit to get the pilot out but the flames and intense heat drove him back. He thereupon put on his motor goggles, took off his great coat and holding it in front of him went into the cockpit. Assisted by Gunner Williams he tried to drag the pilot's body out but his feet got jammed. He then got him by the shoulder and got him out."[120] During this time the plane was burning fiercely, burning petrol was splashing on the ground around the plane and the machine gun ammunition was exploding with the heat." Though far from reticent about other exploits "Ponny" Balmer could never be drawn on this gallant act; even so there were many who thought he should have got more than the B.E.M. The award was, however, presented to him personally by the King at Buckingham Palace, who wished him "the best of luck in the world" to which Ponny replied "Thank you, your majesty." Those presented had been told not to look the King full in the face lest it brought on the royal stammer. Twenty years later Ponny was involved in rescuing bathers from a Scottish loch which was widely reported though no award followed.

Milnthorpe's most highly decorated war hero was Squadron Leader Richard Arthur Miles of Laburnum House, son of the Parish Council Chairman, A.J. Miles. He was awarded the Distinguished Flying Cross in September 1942 for a daring and unusual exploit over the English Channel in June 1941. On 11th of that month he participated in a sortie against enemy shipping off Le Touqet during which the attack was pressed home in the face of intense anti-aircraft fire. Sq. Ldr. Miles dived his aircraft almost to sea level whilst taking evasive action but it was apparently hit. The port engine propeller struck the water but the pilot, displaying great presence of mind and exerting great effort, succeeded in keeping his machine airborne. With all but one engine out of action he managed to climb slowly to 800 ft, and skillfully flew the aircraft back to an aerodrome in this country, where he made a safe landing with undercarriage retracted.[121] An account appeared in *The Sphere* and Miles broadcast about the operation in the main propaganda spot after the evening news.

Sadly, Richard Miles was killed while training other officers in Canada in March 1943. His widow Margaret and year old daughter Janet had to make a perilous journey home by convoy. Richard's ashes preceded them and were buried in the churchyard, the last internment to take place there. Bravely, Arthur Miles presided at the Parish Council a week after his only son's death and "spoke of the hopes he had had for Richard after the war." A year to the day of Richard's death Arthur himself died. He had, however, been consoled by the birth in October 1943 of Richard's posthumous son – Hugh Richard.

At first battle claimed few Milnthorpians. In 1940 many local men serving with the Territorials had been captured at the fall of France and so for them the really dangerous part of the war was over.

Many local warriors served in North Africa.[113] In August 1943

Richard Miles winning the D.F.C.

Brigadier General Gordon Audland was awarded the C.B.E. for his "organisation of victories in North Africa." In the same month came news that Sergeant M.A. ("Sandy") Atkinson of Cautley Farm Whassett had died of wounds in North Africa. As in the case of Edward Ashburner in the First War his mother had woken up in the night with a premonition of his fate.

Another "desert hero" was Milnthorpe doctor Kenneth Bingham, who was twice mentioned in despatches for gallantry. His hospital at Tobruk was visited by the official war reporter and peace-time Society photographer Cecil Beaton, who, in *The Years Between* described an operation and the doctor: "Major Bingham with his bright eyes, looked little more than a schoolboy."[125] In fact Bingham was one of the first doctors to use penicillin which initially was in such short supply it had to be recycled from the patients' urine. One of his publications on the "use of penicillin in the treatment of compound fractures" was highly regarded for some time. In 1944 as the war moved on to Italy, Bingham found himself working in the same hospital as Captain R. Fuller, son of Dr. W.A.C. Fuller and grandson of Dr. Seagrave, both of whom had previously owned the Milnthorpe practice to which Dr. Bingham belonged.

Also serving in the Mediterranean theatre was Able Seaman George Richardson from the Square. George was in Malta when the famous convoy got through and witnessed the relief of the islanders "who despite tremendous suffering were intensely loyal to the British Empire."

In 1942/3 a prisoner-of-war camp was built at Hang Bridge south of Whassett. The first prisoners were Italians who though unanimously regarded as being lazy and dishonest were well liked. German prisoners who joined the "Ities" in 1944-1946 were harder working but not as popular. There were few curbs on "fraternization" and soon legends grew up about camp followers "trading with the enemy" in the Ackenthwaite hedgerows! Many P.O.W.s stayed on after the War and two Milnthorpe girls, Pamela Arkwright and Sheila Wheatman, married respectively Henry Peterson (ne Pitzkowesh) and Arnold Tauber.

Vacated by the Italians the camp became "home" for 600 former paratroopers, sailors and S.S. Most of the German P.O.W.s said it was their worst camp mainly on account of the cold. Coal ran out in the arctic winter of 1946-47 and even after fields for miles around had been scoured for branches, posts and fences it was impossible to fuel the hut stoves. Food was meagre and monotonous. P.O.W.s got the basic civilian ration of 2oz of butter, ¼lb of margarine, ¼lb of lard and 4oz of meat a week, but the menu was always the same: two slices of bread and marge, perhaps a spoonful of jam, a brownish liquid "a cross between tea and coffee for breakfast" and hot pot for dinner. Supplements included jacket potatoes (when the stoves worked) and always Libby's Condensed Milk provided in such quantities by P.O.W.s working at the Milk factory that whole walls were insulated with cans and many had to be buried in the gardens. Each prisoner got a weekly dole of 10 John Players, 10 (unsmokable) "Nosegay" cigarettes and 5/6d pocket money – but they had to buy their own toothpaste and shoe polish. Gleaming boots and scimitar sharp creases were good for morale and mitigated the humiliation of wearing the P.O.W. diamonds between the shoulders and on the knees.

Discipline was not harsh and the C.O. Major Selby was respected. All P.O.W.s were confined to the camp for their first three months. Afterwards they could go out to work at Libby's, on farms, for the River Board, potato picking on Meathop Marsh and bracken clearing on the fells. In charge of the bracken clearers was Frank Casson who was barely five feet high and no match for the youthful representatives of the master race. Once they managed to lure "Little Frank" into a hornet's nest and often not much bracken was cleared.

Many prisoners were repatriated in 1948. Others stayed on at Bela River as "War Ag." Workers, receiving quite good pay of £7 per week with £2 off for their keep. Soon Arnold Tauber blossomed forth in a violently checked double breasted suit, with twenty inch trouser bottoms and, having learnt English from Andrews Sisters song sheets bought at Kendal Woolworths, he was able to woo Sheila in verse. He went back to Germany briefly to discover that his family had lost almost everything; and a cousin had died in a concentration camp. After overcoming various legal difficulties and softening up Mrs. Wheatman with condensed milk and sacks of potatoes, Arnold and Sheila were married in 1949. In the next forty years only one man showed any prejudice against his German origins, though some of the women were "a bit funny at first," he recalled later.

The effect of war on normal attitudes was shown by the enthusiastic support given to Mrs. Churchill's Aid to Soviet Russia Fund. At a Whist Drive for the cause at the Bela Cafe in September 1943 Mrs. Audland, Divisional Superintendant of the St. John's Ambulance, and Mr. R.O. Hodgson, one of the village's most blatant capitalists, expressed gratitude to Russia. "In an impromptu role Mr. R.O. Hodgson auctioned an orange which was sold to Mr. L.G. May for 75s, and on being handed back was resold to Mrs. R.O. Hodgson for 65s and finally to Mr. Dewhurst fo 52s." The previous April Mr. A. Semple had paid £3 for a lemon, the money going to the allied prisoners[129] fund. Citrus fruit was very rare at the time.

Food was a major obsession. To make up for the lack of imported citrus fruits the Heversham and Milnthorpe Women's Institute made, in 1943, 956lbs. of jam and canned 381 tins of fruit.[130] The rationing system was considered to be fair though great inconvenience was experienced by having to go to Kendal for the annual August change of books and for "emergency rations" required when, for example, going on holiday. Moreover, the system involved a household being rationed at a particular shop and dissatisfied customers found it embarrassing and difficult to change and re-register elsewhere. Though many people kept hens in the backyard, eggs were scarce and despite being in the middle of a dairying area, cream disappeared and milk was often in short supply. Several families, however, were able to feed pigs on Libby's Condensed Milk from tins "accidentally damaged" at the Milk Factory.[131] Meagre fare was often supplemented by game; and "poached salmon" was not just a culinary term. Of the few black marketeers caught the best known was Herbert Higham Llewllyn, a J.P. and proprietor of the Inglemere Hotel, Arnside who was fined £450 by Milnthorpe magistrates in 1943, for buying hams at 3s 6d per lb. – one shilling above pre-war prices.

There were, however, concessions at Christmas and grass fed geese were obtainable in 1944 and a Christmas cookery display "featured iced cakes and pastries of all kinds."

Fund raising proliferated. Schemes mentioned in 1943 included: Mr. Miles' war service fund, a rural Pennies campaign, a Red Cross penny week, the Rechabites Comforts Fund for the Merchant Navy (supported by Hull High School – evacuated to Horncop), a car conveyance fund, Mrs. Audland's wool gathers who culled £3 12s worth of wool from hedges and barbed wire, and a war savings week which brought in £35,000 – an average of £10 16s 9d per head, enough to buy 7 Spitfires.[132]

Despite all the cheerful bustle there was constant anxiety at home for far flung armies. In March 1944 came news that Private Patrick J. McVeigh aged 31 had died of wounds in Burma. He had come to Milnthorpe in 1935 and married a Milnthorpe girl, Carrie Wilson. He had served from July 1940 in Northern Ireland and Scotland before embarking to join the 'forgotten army', in Burma. In April Sister Freda Airey from Storth, a member of one of Milnthorpe's oldest families, was lost at sea when her hospital ship was torpedoed while returning from East Africa.

Several local men took part in the D-Day invasions including John Wilkinson, Sid Tugman and Eddie Rushton. During the great break-out from Normandy Lance Corporal John Wilkinson, aged 28, was killed. Having joined up in 1940 he had been released from the army for 18 months so that he could join repair teams in Liverpool after the Blitz, but had returned to arms in time to be one of the first ashore on the 6th June. Another long serving victim was Captain William Kitching Hodgson son of Mr. and Mrs. Parker Hodgson of Highfield. He had joined up in 1939 and having been made a sergeant was commissioned in April 1940. He fought in North Africa in 1943 and took part in the airborne landings in Sicily and Italy. With this experience he was chosen to lead one of the glider landings at Arnhem. Within a few days it was known that he was "wounded and missing" but it took some time before his death was confirmed. His brigadier wrote that he had "done quite splendidly and had fought like a tiger."

Unlike in 1918 the civilian war came to an end gradually, though the Doodle-bug bombings led to a temporary influx of evacuees in the winter of 1944-5. The Home Guard stood down at Christmas 1944 and lighting and other restrictions were gradually eased before hostilities ceased.

As in 1918, the news of the German capitulation reached the Post Office first. The sub-postmaster Dick Carruthers, as dawn broke, sallied into the street in his pyjamas and banged on the windows of lorries waiting at the traffice lights to proclaim the outbreak of peace.

V.E. Day, 8th May 1945, was celebrated in the traditional way: "Every house in Milnthorpe was quickly beflagged and streamers and bunting reaching across some of the streets and particularly Park Road, presented a gay sight. A piano was pulled out of one of the houses and girls from the Land Army hostel took turns in pounding it throughout the day. Peals of bells were sounded in the morning, at noon and in the evening and children's parties were hastily arranged. On Harmony Square the youngsters collected material for a bonfire, on which the effigy of Hitler, well stuffed with sawdust, was burned with evident satisfaction. During the day Hitler was trucked round the village and a collection of £5 raised for Red Cross Funds. A Victory Dance, hastily arranged in the Public Rooms by Sister Cummings brought in a further £26 for the Red Cross."[136] On V.J. Day in August sufficient men had been demobolised for a welcome home dance to be held. "The streets were paraded in darkness of the early hours and there was singing of patriotic and traditional songs, a few fireworks were seen and many houses were beflagged."[137] On the first Monday in September "300 children took part in a Fancy Dress Gala reminiscent of the happy days before the war." The main celebration came with the victory parade in June 1946 which was supported by almost every village organisation. 150 children paraded under a cloudy sky behind the Kirkby Lonsdale brass band. In the evening there was a victory dance attended by prisoners-of-war, who were allowed in free, (to the disgust of the author's Auntie May, a war widow, who was charged entry).

By this time the Public Rooms had been renamed the "Memorial Hall" following a decision made at a meeting held in 1945 to take over the old Public Rooms Company. The principal share-holder, Mr. W.P. Dobson, who had used the hall as a cinema throughout the war years, agreed to sell the hall for £3,100 but donated £1,000 towards the sum.[138] At the same time Mr. R.O. Hodgson (who it was rumoured had supped too well and later regretted the decision) "Coupling himself with the British Legion, whose president he is, stated that he was prepared to give £1,000." Within a short time funds were raised to meet the cost of the purchase price and to cover alterations. Unfortunately, it proved to be a disastrous Memorial. The Hall's once excellent floor had been ruined by the cinema seats, and because the cinema used it for four nights a week, village organisations found it inconvenient and moved elsewhere. When "Milnthorpe pictures" folded up in the early sixties, the Memorial Hall became virtually derelict for ten years. In 1975 it was refurbished as a drinking and entertainment club for the Royal British Legion who took a 21 year lease on the premises.

The end of war meant little amelioration in the standard of living. Even so, at Christmas 1945 village traders were informed that "bananas are expected to be available in February... the Ministry have laid it down in the *Banana (maximum price) Order* that retailers are only allowed to serve bananas against RB2 and RB4 ration cards which must be marked. Sales will only be by weight, the retail price being 1s 1d lb."[139] In the autumn of 1946 J.F. Ramsbottom of Heversham complained to the *Westmorland Gazette* that porridge oats were no longer available and there would be no tobacco for a month. "I am past annoyance, even the promise of an augmented supply of watered beer is no solace and an extra 2oz of sweets in October does not appeal to me."[140]

Sadly, tragedies continued in the War's aftermath. A bizarre road accident occured on the Prince's Way in November 1945 when an American Army Lorry, driven by two drunken G.I. joy riders, crashed at night into Frank Burch's butcher's van, killing instantly his two passengers, Edward Lloyd Wilson, 35, of Whassett Farm and David Stavely, 25, of Ackenthwaite. Dr. P.S. Byrne found the two men, one of whom was sitting on the other's knee, dead but unmarked on the front seat. They were given a double funeral at Milnthorpe Church.[141] The two guilty G.I.'s were arrested at the King's Arms, Hale, the next morning. At the subsequent Court Martial Pt. Andrew G. Anderson, 143rd Army Air Force, was expelled from the army with hard labour; his companion Pt. McGlasky, received a lesser sentence. Although the court had noted that a claim for monetary compensation had been filed and that "the U.S.A. is well able to pay" it took an appeal to Mrs. Roosevelt before the claim was met.

National Service claimed two Milnthorpe men in curiously similar circumstances. Ralph Procter broke his neck and died instantly when thrown from a jeep while serving in British Somaliland in 1948. Four years later Roy Woodhead died as a result of injuries suffered when his jeep crashed in Egypt.

Unlike their parents and grandparents the children who had taken part in the 1946 Victory Parade were able to reach middle age without being summoned to war. Two village men of the next generation, Nigel Robinson and Philip Dobson, took part in the Falklands campaign in 1982 and to the relief of all, came home safely. Curiously this miniscule campaign aroused something of the euphoria of 1914 with the Union Jack being flown by Jack Davidson at Mallow House and from the church tower for two months, bells rung on victory, and coffee mornings and jumble sales being held for the South Atlantic Fund.[143]

Since the Falklands the Remembrance Day ceremonies attracted more support and in the middle 1980's included a procession with band from the Playing Fields to the War Memorial which was itself refurbished at a cost of £2000 in 1985. Thus on the second Sunday in November Brownies and Cubs whose grandparents hardly remembered war joined with the old and very old who in their mind's eye could put a face to the names on the Roll of Honour.

16

Fun and Games

Perhaps no other aspect of local history is so bathed in rose tinted nostalgia as village social life. Yearnings for a jolly rural past bolster the myths of Merry England. Folksy scene setters from Thomas Hardy and Milnthorpe's own Constance Holme, to soap-opera script-writers, have purveyed escapist images of golden olden times to urban masses squirming amidst urban dullness and urban decorum. Fondly they picture a time "just before Grandma was a little girl" when "everyone" lived in the countryside and when young and old, rich and poor together took seasonal delight in May Day revels, in supporting valiant village cricketers and footballers in games of legendary length and hilarity, in following the hunt, in keeping watch at cock-fights, in carousing in taverns and in carolling on snowy garths at Christmas.

Conversely, there is another gloomier story made up of statistics and morose marxian surveys where the softer hues of humanity are hardly glimpsed. Both pictures are false; but being fantasy they have a foundation of truth. Our ancestors were not forever gallivanting on the green but neither were they huddled always in squalid isolation. Man is a social animal and, however nasty, brutish and short his life might seem, his nature impels fun and games.

Of the earthier pastimes cock fighting has a long, if nebulous, tradition in South Westmorland. It has been illegal since the mid-nineteenth century so evidence about this "sport" is dependent on hearsay and a few press reports. At a great "main" held in Kirkby-in-Furness in c.1850 attended by 200 fanciers, four of the best cocks competing for a £10 prize and silver spurs came from "a village near Milnthorpe."[1] Until c.1920 the gates at the Cross Keys yard were closed from time to time on spring evenings where there was dog fighting "for heavy bets" and "the odd 'main' or two."

May Day, 1917.

Milnthorpe fanciers seem to have kept out of trouble though even in the 1950's several cock fighters from Heversham, Beetham and Storth ended up in court. In a notorious raid on a main in the Lyth Valley in June 1931[2] at least one local person evaded arrest by hiding in a rabbit hole! Gaming fowls always figured prominently in the Milnthorpe Fur and Feather show and in 1921 Sir Maurice Bromley-Wilson donated a silver cup for the "best bird in the old English Game Bird Class."[3] Other fanciers were Parker Hodgson and his brother R.O. Hodgson. After the sale of "R.O.'s" house, Harmony Hall, a number of cages for game birds were found in the cellars.[4] In 1959 the present author accidentally stumbled on preparations for a main while walking on the far side of the mosses. A bird had had its body feathers removed, to create a ruff round its neck, and all except two wing feathers had been plucked out. In a nearby Dutch barn was the sanded pit about six feet in diameter surrounded by five feet high poles. However, by the 1980's the cock fighting tradition had degenerated to whispered allegations that so-and so "knew a thing or two about the old sport."

Fox hunting has not been specially popular in Milnthorpe though, unlike much of Cumbria, the surrounding countryside is suited to mounted hunts. Often in the mid-nineteenth century hunts were sponsored by the Inns. Thus in November 1822[5] it was announced that "the annual hunt will be held at the Cross Keys on Wednesday 11th instant. Dinner on the table at 3 o'clock."

"Tom the huntsman" of Dalton came to lead the King's Arms "Bag Hunt" in 1828.[6] Twenty years later the sport was still popular

'Escapist images of golden olden times' - Morris dancing on the green, an annual Easter feature of recent years.

as it was reported that "Mr. T. Bainbridge of the King's Arms has purchased a fine dog fox and intends to bring in Mr. H. Rauthwell's celebrated fox-hounds to hunt it on Monday next (11 March) when it is expected to afford some capital sport."[7] A dozen huntsmen and scores of pedestrians duly set off "but Reynard went to earth" at Rowell and deprived them of their prey. Rauthwell's hounds were more successful in a splendid run over rough country in 1849 when Reynard "though he had employed every stratagem to evade his relentless pursuers" was killed at Waterhouse Mill. "The head and brush were secured by Mr. W. Poole – paper maker – it was a remarkably fine fox."[8] Later George Woodburn of Thurston Villa near Ulverston came regularly to the Cross Keys and the Station Inn with his first rate fox-hounds "and in March 1854 a 3 hour hunt ran

Dallam otter hounds at Underley Hall, c.1900. Sir Henry Bromley in centre foreground (sixth from right). His son, Maurice Bromley-Wilson in the arch (third from left).

as far as Leighton Hall."

[9]Harriers were also sponsored by the inns. When William Robinson was landlord of the White Lion he organised, in January 1862,[10] a hunt when "Miss Puss" led them as far as Rowell. Hare coursing on the marsh also took place during the winter months. In 1854 the Bull's Head hunt was particularly exciting. "Poor Puss was soon found and the hunt set off at a fast rate and was very soon appointed to be dispatched by her relentless pursuers." Not so the next hare which cannily sought refuge in a cottage until "up came Mr. Reamington and three or four other gentlemen on horseback, with dogs and hosts of pedestrians after them, to the cottage door and demanded entrance but the old dame would not suffer them until they had paid her 1s for her prisoner." She eventually settled for 6d when the hare was chased over to Whassett and killed in Purdaston (sic) Lane.

The Cross Keys hunt in March 1875 was a grand affair with many horsemen all well-mounted including "the leading gentry of the neighbourhood amongst whom was a fair sprinkling of the fair sex... about half past eleven the dogs were let loose in a field on the outskirts of the town and a hare was soon found when some excellent sport was had."[13] Three hares were killed before the day concluded with dinner for 160. A less successful hunt was in March 1884 when in the first run the hare was lost on the far side of the Firs where "after encountering the "Black Ditch" there were many empty saddles."[14] Another good run over the hill to St. Anthony's and thence over Parkhill to the marsh, was equally disappointing as the hare got lost and the hounds dropped into the half mile long dyke.

Milnthorpe's most famous blood sport was otter hunting. In the eighteenth century otter hound kennels were situated opposite the Old Bridge,[15] but later they moved to Peat Stack Hill. Until otters became a protected species in the 1980's the large, brown and woolly hounds were a familiar feature of Milnthorpe life and at feeding time their baying could be heard all over the village.

Otters were often trapped as vermin. In February 1851 an otter five feet from nose to tail was caught at Parkhouse and in December 1853 a 17lb otter was caught by the Dallam gamekeeper, John Helme, in a trap by the Old Bridge.[17]

Perhaps the otter hounds greatest period was when E.H. Wilson was squire of Dallam. He was "never in better glee than when heading his hounds along the river banks or during the hot pursuit of the wily plucky otter.[18] Just before his death in 1886 it was decided to present the worthy master with a coat composed entirely of skins of the otter and almost sufficient "fur" had been obtained for the purpose. . . [19]

Occasionally other packs were allowed along the Bela. Captain Thompson's otter hounds had a good run in 1919 chasing from Kidside to Beetham Hall before finding "a good one near Beetham Bridge. . . for an hour and a quarter the hounds chivied the otter amongst the brush wood from one side of the river to another and then back again, then it took to the deep water above the weir and made its way through the cave in the rocks beside the Corn Mill and made its way to the outlet below the waterfall into the lower river taking refuge in the small islets." They then "hunted the varmint from root to root and so made the Belaside wood and finally got into a land drain. It was dug out but made a bolt, but the hounds quickly despatched it." It was a bitch 11½lbs in weight, and was the eleventh kill of the season. From start to finish it had taken 3 hours to kill the "varmint."[20]

Sometimes the Oxenholme stag hounds visited the area, the huntsmen bringing with them their own stag. In March 1888 "thirty fine mounts" chased the stag from the Cross Keys as far as Cow Brow at Lupton where it was captured and "put into a van and returned home none the worse for its long run."[21]

Probably the same reporter believed that otters and foxes also enjoyed being hunted.

A taste of the wild West came to Milnthorpe in January 1889 when the inhabitants "were somewhat surprised on Saturday to witness the novel sight of a red deer running down Main Street hotly pursued by the Oxenholme Harriers. The run was continued to Sandside." It happened to be high tide and when the deer jumped into the estuary "the dogs were called off, boats were manned and horsemen braved the flowing tide. The "lasso" was brought into requisition and after considerable difficulty and combined efforts the animal was secured and taken back to Oxenholme."[22]

Game was strictly guarded by the squires who not only waged war on poachers but, if they sold land, retained sporting rights. Even so, many villagers owned firearms which were used extensively on Bonfire Night, St. Catherine's Day, and at the New Year.[23]

"The Milnthorpians celebrated the anniversary of the Gunpowder treason plot on Saturday evening last (1843) by a large bonfire of tar barrels etc. upon the green. All kinds of firearms were in requisition even Mr. Hinds, the celebrated Blacksmith's, anvil which was fired during the evening and made some excellent reports which were heard all over the neighbourhood."[24] An anvil was 'fired' by hitting gunpowder placed on it.

The most important legitimate use of firearms was for the annual rook shoot before the May fair[25] but pigeon shoots were also arranged. Thus in February 1874 Mr. Faulkner's Station Inn offered a £10 prize for the best pigeon shot. 43 competitors took part but "the best were Thomas Williams (whose name we are informed was Mr. Dixon Bradley of Lancaster) and Mr. George Robinson who killed 9 pigeons each."[26] The entrance money was shared amongst the competitors.

Fishing rights were less jealously guarded though "hard labour" could follow for anyone caught filching a salmon stranded in an estuary pool.

Village anglers were encouraged. The Milnthorpe Angling Association established in 1858[27] obtained rights on the Bela and its tributaries. From the start it had the support of the better off villagers like W. Tattersall of St. Anthony's and T.A. Argles of Eversley. For over 50 years until his death in 1914 Lewis Elburn of Fleet House was secretary of the Association. Fees were not high. In 1875 it was decreed that a member paying an annual subscription of £2 2s could also introduce a friend to the waters. A penny fishing scheme was inaugurated in 1882 for poorer members. "Penny fishers" could, on a daily basis, fish the waters above Hang Bridge. The Association held its first annual dinner in 1862 when 20 members gathered at the Wheat Sheaf, Beetham, to "talk over feats of the past year." To discourage non-members from fishing the water a beck watcher was appointed. From 1879 to 1942 the watcher was Tom Stainton "who never got more than 16/- per week" until 1920 when his wage went up to £2 per week. Over the years Tom was responsible for nobbling many a poacher and in 1887 three men who had used chloride of lime received 6 weeks' hard labour in Lancaster Castle. It was probably as a result of this outrage that the river was stocked with 500, year-old Salmo Levenis at 40/- per 100. £30 worth of Wyredale trout were acquired in 1897, and 2,250 added in 1902 and 2,000 in 1914.

Trout were always the main species and Miss Wilson in 1891 refused to allow a salmon pass on the lower stretch as it would spoil the trout. Nevertheless occasional unwary salmon could be scooped by the crafty from the mill sluices. At the Association's centenary in 1958 members felt that there "are two destructive influences which gravely threaten the full engagement of the sport (pollution from) Libby's Milk Factory, and the Lancashire River Board which with its policy of canalizing the stream, throwing up the beck bottoms onto the land, not only ruins the fishing runs but causes a succession of floods and droughts." Both problems persist into the 1980s but have not stopped the fishing; the Angling Association remains one of the district's oldest societies.

A harmless field sport was hound trailing, introduced in the 1920's. The 1920 trail for 23 hounds went from Haverflatts to Milnthorpe Station, then along Kidside level to Deepthwaite, through Greenside over the shoulder of Heversham Head, down the Slacks, through Eversley and onto the marsh for a straight run along the top of the sea embankment before returning over the drumlins to Milnthorpe. The winning hound "Rodger" belonging to Mr. Browning of Swarthmoor completed the ten mile trail in 24 minutes 30 seconds.[28]

No accounts survive of racing on Milnthorpe Marsh though the course is known to have been on the level stretch between the marsh drain and where the railway embankment was constructed later.[29] Shortly after the railway opened attempts were made to start racing near Milnthorpe Station. A steeple chase was held in 1850 after which two women were unsuccessfully charged with gambling.[30] The next year a selling stakes race was advertised "the winner to be sold by auction immediately after the race, entries to Mr. Richard Atkinson, Milnthorpe Station Inn. The course is within three minutes of the Milnthorpe Station on the Lancaster to Carlisle Railway." Whether this race was successful is not known but nothing else was reported of "Milnthorpe Races."

Henceforward punters had to make do with the "bookie's runner," an ancient office traditionally held in Milnthorpe by the barber, the last old time "runner" being Harold Whitely.

Milnthorpe's luckiest gambler won on his first bet. While

working as a steward on board an ocean liner in 1927 Bertie Kilpatrick bought half a ticket in the Calcutta Sweep and won £60,000. Bertie lost most of his winnings to the demi-monde and died a few years later but not before he had established his mother and sister in a large bungalow on Church Street.[32]

Railways enabled circuses and animal displays to tour the country more widely. From the 1840's such shows as Sergeant Hylton's and Vam Ambergh's beasts and Wombwell's menagerie came regularly to Milnthorpe. Until just after the Second World War a triennial visit was made by a circus to a field on Beetham Road.[33]

A strange "beast" of another sort was reported in July 1844:
"On Tuesday morning last a man named James Dowker of Beetham while drinking with some navvies at the Bull's Head Inn, Milnthorpe, laid a wager for a gallon of ale that he would in less than two hours eat a raw sheep's pluck without using a knife and fork. Upon one being procured which was 9lbs in weight the human brute stripped off his coat and commenced devouring it in a ravenous manner amidst the astonished navvies who declared that they never knew a beast in Wombwell's menagerie so greedy of its prey. Having accomplished his disgusting task he asked for a few slices of back to crown his feat with which he was soon supplied and which he soon demolished."[34]

Literally brutal was prize fighting like the famous "set battle" fought in 1843 between "Thomas Varey, a potter and Evan Davies a Welshman, a miner by trade." A crowd of 200 gathered to witness the event but rather than pay entrance to the field they blocked Beetham Road and so the competitors and officials had to be moved on to another field. An hour and 24 rounds later the Welshman was declared the winner, "the "potter" being very much cut up about the face."[35] Another potter pugilist but of a different sort was a Mr. Lowther, a gypsy, who having bivouacked on the marsh was married at Heversham Church in 1828. During the festivities following the ceremony, the groom gave the bride, a Miss Younger, also "a member of the Sibyl tribe," two black eyes.[36] Milnthorpe was chosen in 1862 as the venue for a boxing match between Lomas and Kelly, but just as the first bout was beginning the fight was stopped by the arrival of a "party of police under Mr. Superintendent Hibbert."[37]

Cumberland and Westmorland Wrestling seems to have been as popular in Milnthorpe as in the Lake District proper. At the Ship Inn in 1840 two Milnthorpe men, Christopher Bellman and James Clark, beat 40 other competitors. The sport could be dangerous and in 1843 Isaac Clemmet, landlord of the Royal Oak, met his death as a result of a wrestling bout with Joseph Birkett of the Bull's Head.[38] This tragedy did not deter other wrestlers. William Barrow

Milnthorpe Wrestling Academy, 1911.

J.H.Jackson, world champion, 1928.

of Milnthorpe beat all comers to win a £2 prize at The Ship Inn Sports in 1848. About 1910 a wrestling "Academy" was founded based on the Public Rooms, with T. Cornthwaite, R. Ormrod and E. Fishwick the leading exponents. After the First World War Milnthorpe lads were outdone by the Blands of Arnside, the Cannons of Holme and the Jackson brothers of Beetham. The Milnthorpe academy's greatest triumph was Jack Jackson's winning the Cumberland and Westmorland Wrestling World Championship in c.1928.

Such feats did not win the approval of the Vicar of Milnthorpe, Christopher Pickering, who in 1923 conceded that "sports may be more edifying than Sundays spent in eating and drinking and idle gossiping" but went on to warn "that if we rush into Sunday games under the excitement of these abnormal times we may deprive many of true rest for which Sunday was ordained."[41]

Much earlier, gymnastics had been encouraged by E.H. Wilson of Dallam Tower, who staged "assaults at arms" with himself as the principal performer. In 1867 he "cut through a solid bar of lead in fine style."[42] At Christmas 1870 the gymnasts displayed vaulting, fencing, boxing, broad sword, "dump bell", sabre and bayonet exercises.

Odd sporting spectacles in nineteenth century Milnthorpe included a gig race in 1844 run between Lancaster and Milnthorpe. The apparently clear winner was foiled on the last lap when the bar and harness broke on Beetham Road.[43] A more sedate event occurred in February 1851 between two pedestrians both aged 76. The favourite was "old Chevy" at 4 to 1, but the victor was "the Doctor" who covered the two and a half miles between the King's Arms at Hale and the Cross Keys in twenty-seven minutes. Betting also accompanied a shorter race on the main road between Milnthorpe and Heversham in October 1871. The prize was £5 and the favourite odds were 6 to 4 against William Wilkinson of Sedgwick. In a 100 yds race however, he was beaten by 8 yards by James Jack of Levens who covered the distance in 22 seconds.[45]

A regular pre-Lenten pastime was Spell and Knur (or Knock) in which a wooden peg hanging from a quintain, about five feet high, was hit by a club resembling a rounder's bat. On Shrove Tuesday 1849 "Mr. E. Garnett of the Coach and Horses Tavern gave a quantity of smoking tobacco to be contended for... a great number contended and John Walton of Milnthorpe won. A Spell Knur stick hit the temples of Thomas Woof aged 5 years (but) Mr. Kitchen sewed it up."

Thanks to a rare run of good summers picnics became popular in the 1860s. Already in June 1860 it was noted that "one might think that all the inhabitants of the locality were wishful to initiate themselves into the art of pic-nicking." The series began with a

An Olde English Fayre held on Market Square in 1934.

"ladies picnic" and a "13 couples picnic" and one for about 20 couples but "the extreme bashfulness and timidity of some of the young ladies (meant that) several young gentlemen had to mourn for want of a mate." Even so "dancing was kept up on the green sod to a late hour." A week or two later 100 children enjoyed "a most excellent cup of tea and currant cake" on Haverbrack. There followed a housewives' picnic, one for mothers and daughters and then "a temperance picnic when the Kendal Workhouse pipe and drum band was in attendance... they had a splendid view, much pleasanter on account of the tide being full on." A temperance concert was held in a neighbouring barn where a glee band's rendition of "Hail Smiling Moon" met with the greatest applause from the audience of 240.

The success of this "picnic" encouraged another but, alas, the weather returned to normal "at three o'clock and all was ready when the rain began... The crowds took shelter in houses until 5 o'clock when a fresh fire was lighted and pans and kettles put on – soon all hands got to work to satisfy the keen appetites which they had got by their ramble upon the fell." This time the entertainment was provided by Mr. Thompson who gave a lecture on "The Temperance League" which "he had spoken the night before in the schoolroom."[48]

For most of the twentieth century village sport has been equated with the Cricket Club and the Milnthorpe Corinthians Football Club. Unfortunately the documentary evidence of their early days is sparse. Matches were mentioned in the press in the 1850s and permanent clubs existed by 1870. In February 1871 "the Milnthorpe Cricketers' Annual Ball was held at Mr. W. Tyson's King's Arms, . . . dancing was kept up with great spirit . . . to a late hour and afterwards 20 took breakfast before departure."[49] In January 1889 a Bowling Green had been "established in conjunction with the Cricket Club." A pavilion (converted into Walker's Bela Cafe in c.1920) was built in 1890 for which a "Bowling Concert" raised funds in January 1891 to pay off the outstanding debt.

The cricket club was not without its critics and an amusing funeral card was printed for one disaster:

"In Affectionate Remembrance
of the
Milnthorpe Cricket Club
who succumbed to a severe attack of Funk
on Sat July 27 1907
After making 5 Runs
Peace to their Ashes

Not as the Light Brigade
But every man dismayed
Each in turn took guard and made
One wild attempt and blundered

Winder to the right of them
Askew to the left of them
Netherfield all round of them
Volleyed and thundered

Flashed every ball so hare
Flashed as they turned in air
Never was a man aware
Till his wickets sundered

When shall their glory fade
O the wild attempts they made
Previous scores were in the shade
And all the field wondered

Would e'er a man survive
And from the crease return alive
Last wicket down – the total five
Thus the match ended"[51]

Football was played in the "Town-Field" behind Church Street and Milnthorpe teams under various names took part in local leagues from c.1870. Soccer violence was not unknown and in 1890 William Hodgshun was fined 5s for running onto the field while

Tom Finney (centre, second row) with Milnthorpe Corinthians after he had switched on the flood lighting. John Garnett, in blazer, left.

calling "Knock the fat headed ... down" and clouting Walter Thompson five or six times.[52] Through the years all the older Milnthorpe families have had playing members and the Ashburners, Garnetts, Dobsons and Shaws have had an almost continuous connection with the game.

In 1900 Maurice Bromley-Wilson made over the Strands Meadow to the village for use as a playing field at a nominal rent. For the next decades the field was administered by a number of trustees including the Dallam Agent, and representatives of the Cricket, Football and Hockey Clubs. A Lawn Tennis Club was quickly started and grass courts were laid out in the south-west corner. In the 1920s a Women's Hockey Team won much local fame and even ventured far afield.

At the Coronation celebrations in 1937 the Vicar, Rev. J.L. Gamble, "announced amidst great cheers that Sir Maurice Bromley-Wilson proposed to let the village have the meadow used as a recreation ground on a long lease at a nominal sum, only stipulating that the management should be placed in the hands of a trust consisting of persons holding permanent office in the parish like the vicar, churchwardens, and agent of Dallam Tower." A 50 year lease to the Parish Council was negotiated by L.G. Powell.

The same solicitor negotiated a renewal of this lease with Dallam in 1983 and ensured that the same generous terms were retained, the rent remaining at a nominal £5 p.a. From 1939 to his death in 1983 the Playing Field's Secretary was John Garnett. For 50 years and more "Dart" dominated and led village sport making the Milnthorpe Corinthians one of the leading soccer teams in the north during the 1940s and 1950s. Dart gave several Professional Footballers a start as amateurs. The most notable was a former prisoner of war Bert Trautman who became the Manchester City goalkeeper and earned permanent fame by completing a Cup Final with what turned out to be a broken neck.

Growing interest in outdoor activities was reflected in the formation of the Girl Guides and Boy Scouts. The Guides came first. A company was formed in March 1917 by St. Thomas's School Headmistress Eva Scott, who with Miss A. Mashiter and Miss H. Tiptaft, "for an hour initiated the girls into making of various kinds of knots, drills, physical exercise, with games in between, and at the close one and all voted it was good fun."[55]

Emulating contemporary militarism, a full dress parade was held in August followed by "a route march to St. John's Cross and Sandside ... some boys followed and 10 year old Fred Mooney climbing a wall, fell off onto rocks and broke his arms." In 1921 the Milnthorpe Guides under Lt. Mashiter and Leaders A. Thompson and Doris Hyde joined Blackburn Grammar School Scouts in a church parade. The Blackburn Scouts camped in Dallam Park on several occasions during the 1920s.

Milnthorpe Scouts only got going when Frederick Comber was Headmaster of the National school, 1923-30. His successor Joe Cookson also became the Scoutmaster, and school and conscripted scouts became almost synonymous. For the next 30 years Joe ensured that his troop was not only the largest in the area but rivalled all comers in the breadth of their outdoor activities.

In earlier times village balls required as much stamina as sport. The main balls were held at the inns by the Friendly Societies, often on the same night, so there was much bantering between the Cross Keys, the King's Arms and the Bull with dancing and music going on until dawn. At an "Auld Wives Hake" held at the Bull's Head in 1848 dancing was to the "far famed fiddler Frank Heaps." At another hake in 1851 "revelling" was to the "thrilling strains of the noted fiddler Mr. James Halliwell."[59] Hakes were arranged by village dames to raise funds for themselves.[60]

A Tradesmen's annual ball started in 1863, with one held to celebrate the wedding of the Prince and Princess of Wales (Albert Edward and Alexandra).[61] By 1866 the Tradesmen were grumbling that the Cross Keys assembly room, holding 60 or 70 dancers, was too small as the "number from year to year increases: it can only be added that it is hoped that this pleasant ball may never go down until dancing ceases to be in fashion and perhaps before then (Milnthorpe) may boast a public hall."[62]

A later venue for balls was the Kitching Memorial Rooms. Soon after their opening in 1881 "a quadrille band played until 5 a.m. to the delight of 120 guests," but a major handicap of the rooms was that everything depended on the donor of the Institute, Mrs. Bindloss, who banned the sale of alcohol on the premises. After "an unsatisfactory reply from the owners of the room" the Tradesmen's Ball for Christmas 1887 was cancelled at the last minute. A letter signed "Pro Bono Publico" was published condemning the fact that "Citizens of the town are to be entirely dependent upon the consent of an individual . . . I hope a company may be formed if private enterprise be not equal to the task."[64]

The Bindloss's ban apparently only applied to the tradesmen, because a week or two later the rooms were decorated with Chinese lanterns, plants and evergreens for a ball organised by the Arnolds of Arnbarrow and the Argles of Eversley. Moreover, Mr. and Mrs. Bindloss sponsored a ball for 60 institute members "providing exotic plants of rare beauty and excellent growth from Flowerden and numerous mirrors which reflected the gay and dazzling scene. King Terphiscore reigned supreme over the gay and happy guests until 4.30 a.m."[65]

None of which mollified the village tradesmen who in March 1889 sent out a letter saying that the "want of a Public Room . . . having been long felt . . . it is proposed to form a Limited Company . . . for the purpose of providing suitable premises. The present Agricultural Hall with the house and shop (built c.1860) and adjoining land at the back thereof can be acquired for £700 . . . It is estimated that the Company will require a capital of £1,200, which it is proposed should be divided into 240 shares of £5 each. A Committee has been appointed . . . and £750 in shares applied for: P. Rheam Secretary pro tem."[66]

The Agricultural Hall (now the top room of the Memorial Hall) above the Market house, had been used regularly for social occasions.

By 1890 a large hall, equipped with "one of the best sprung floors in the North of England," had been built behind the Agricultural Hall, and adjoining the Bull's Head on its west side. The Public Rooms Company continued until 1944 when it was purchased at auction by Mr. W.P. Dobson who in 1945 conveyed it to the War Memorial Committee.[68]

Soon after their opening the Public Rooms were the scene of many fashionable balls. None were more glittering than the Fancy

Dress Dance for 100 guests arranged by Mrs. Tom Argles of Eversley at the New Year of 1894. She was the "belle of the ball" wearing an eighteenth century gown "cut en princesse... made of scarlet and white satin. The skirt had numerous flounces of the two colours each terminating with a silver bell." In contrast Miss Hibbert was "Madame Mort," the Honourable Mrs. Cropper "Autumn" and Mrs. Bagot "in a last century costume very becoming in a broad brimmed hat." Many of the gentlemen wore "Oxenholme Hunt or their Court dress" but "Mr. Hibbert was a Parthian War Chief and Mr. Jacob Wakefield was in Louis XIV dress."[69]

From the turn of the century a "bachelors' ball" was held annually. In 1911 a "spinsters' ball" was judged a great success, "the guests enjoying hunting for a partner in a card dance."[70]

From c.1890 to just before the First World War Mr. S.T. Robinson's dancing classes put on juvenile balls. That of 1893 began at 7 p.m. with "Napoleon's Grand March" for the children and was continued by their elders until 5 a.m.[71]

Before the Public Rooms were opened entertainers both professional and amateurs made do with the inns or the schools. There was a constant variety of lecturers, showmen and fakes. In January 1848 "Chief Pohe-a-Range" gave two lectures on New Zealand at the National School. "Madam Pohe-a-Range performed some beautiful airs upon the musical glasses."[72] During the 1860s Mr. Isaac Whitwell gave regular schoolroom shows of dissolving views on such topics as "India" and "The Old and New Testaments."

A more elaborate show was advertised in 1860 under the Patronage of George Edward Wilson Esq., of Dallam Tower:

Dr. Shaw's MAGICAL, MIMICAL, MUSICAL, and VENTRI-LOQUICAL NEW ENTERTAINMENT, entitled SKETCHES of ANCIENT and MODERN TIMES, with rapid changes of Character, Costumes, Songs, Ballads, and Anecdotes.

In the School Room on Tuesday and Wednesday January 17th and 18th. Reserved seats 2s; Second 1s; Back seats 6d.

After which DR. SHAW will visit BURTON, CARTMEL and ULVERSTON.

See Bills."[73]

Shortly after its opening in 1867 St. Thomas's School began to be used by the Milnthorpe Choral Society. Music must have been a great leveller for "the Chorals" members included "gentry" like the Argles, Arnolds, Raikes and Holmes and village families like the Daffadys, Scots and Mashiters.

Webb's "When the Winds breathe soft" was "the gem of the evening" at the first major concert given in October 1869. It was "repeated on Saturday evening for the benefit of the working classes and others unable to attend the previous evening.''[74]

At first pianofortes (at one concert there were four) accompanied the singing but in 1875 a "large and fashionable audience" listened to music reinforced by four new brass instruments paid for from profits of earlier peformances. By 1883 John Mashiter had formed a pipe and drum section.[76] Youthful musical talent was encouraged by "Tonic sol fa" classes.

Musical activity reached its peak at Christmas and New Year. 1877-78 seems to have been a particularly festive season. A concert organised by Bandmaster Thompson was followed on New Year's Eve by the brass band playing in various parts of the town before assembling in front of the Cross Keys to play the Old Year out and the New Year in. A concert was also given in St. Thomas's School after which the choir had an unusual treat through the kindness and liberality of Mr. Elburn (of Fleet House) who invited them to supper at his house on the evening of the 27th. After supper an adjournment was made to another large room where there was dancing, social games and choral singing.[78]

Things did not always go well on the musical scene. At a concert given in 1891 to mark Miss Derham's fifteen years as Headmistress of St. Thomas's School, "A comic Singer from Kendal performed two songs in the first half with some little ability. But his selection in the second part were of a very low cockney music hall character. The Chairman, the Rev. W.R. Hopper (Curate) made a strong protest at the absence of good taste but did not demand an apology out of respect for the organizers of the concert who were not at all to blame."[80]

Later in the year more sober musical efforts by the Choral Society were not appreciated, as the *Westmorland Gazette* correspondent wrote. "As one of the audience I can say it is a matter of no surprise after listening to such an inefficient performance that this Society, in existence for several years, does not seem to improve with age ... the cantata chosen was beyond their ability ... and the paid soloists did not add any credit to the performance." In a published retaliation the Society commented "that the account must have been written before the performance."[81] Even so the Society altered its regulations so that its repertoire had to be approved by the Committee. By the April concert it was reported that Milnthorpe Choral Society "fully satisfied its existence" with selections from "Handle" (sic) with the Band of the Royal Lancashire Regiment under Mr. Whitehead.

In 1900 Mrs. T.A. Argles, née Agnes Wakefield formed a "Choral Union" comprised of existing societies in Levens, Leasgill, Milnthorpe and Beetham. The Chairman was the Rev. Reade of Milnthorpe, the Secretary W.H. Crewdson of Natland, the Secretary Mrs. Argles and the Conductor Miss Germaine (later Mrs.

Nelson) of Leasgill. An important rule was that members from outlying parts should be given free transport to rehearsals and concerts.[83] Sometime before Agnes Argles' death in 1923 the society had taken the name "Eversley Choral Union," after the Argles' house. This society had great days in the 1920s, and in the 1926 festival won every class. Led by their conductor Eva Scott, the competitors processed from Heversham Station carrying their banners and trophies to receive a great reception in the Square.[84] Leslie Powell took over from Miss Scott and, despite an interruption for war services, for the next 43 years "carried the choral" until his retirement in 1980 when he was succeeded by Roger Cann. Eversley quite regularly won three-quarters of the prizes at the Westmorland Festival and larger works were broadcast. Guest conductors included George Hurst and John Hopkins of the BBC Northern Orchestra, Sir Thomas Armstrong and, a particular favourite, Sir John Barbirolli, who with his wife Evelyn Rothwell, the oboist, was entertained often at Crosby House, the Powell's home.

The length of service of Eversley's members has been extra-ordinary but the most outstanding contribution must be that of Doris Mashiter who celebrated 75 years with the Choral in 1987.[85]

When the Public Rooms were opened the Secretary Joseph Daffady was granted a theatrical license "on condition that the hall had five exits." Soon an amateur group had put on "The Duchess of Bayswater and Co" when "the unbridled hilarity of a large section of the audience prevented not a few from appreciating the great charm of the composition... An orchestra from Kendal under Mr. V.S. Smith played several familiar airs, in a style which shows how invariably wide is the artistic gulf that separates the enthusiastic amateur musician from the enthusiastic actor."

Undeterred by this classic squelch Milnthorpe dramatics were firmly established before 1900, a date later claimed for the society's foundation. A press notice in 1922 stated that "it is now well over thirty years since the village players began under the management of Messrs. W. Scott and G. Dobson." Willie Scott was still a keen member in the the 1950s.

The most popular play was Dion Boucicault's "The Shaughraun" set at the time of the Fenian Rising of the 1860s which, over the years, was repeated four times, At the first performance "owing to the indisposition of the leading lady, Miss E. Hayhurst, and the absence of a capable understudy, the performance could not be considered an unqualified success as the part had to be read from a book." Another Irish play was "Eileen Alannah" in which "Mr. Kennedy was so pathetically aided by Miss Scott that some of the audience were in tears."

Constance Holme regularly supported the dramatics and in

Amateur dramatics in 1911 and 1948. The plays were 'Eileen Alannah' and 'The Gleam'.

1912 and 1913 wrote and produced "Duck Egg Dick" and "Womps," but another dialect piece, "A Martinmas Story" by Constance Holme, produced in 1921, did not go down as well being "grey in tone, its characters not animated."

Lighter notes were struck in the 1920s and 1930s by concert groups like the "Fatuous Frolics" (mainly Hockey Club) and "The Merry Magnets." There were also several semi-professional (and short-lived) bands. The most enduring was "Teddy Davenport's Revelling Band" advertised in 1929 as "the most popular

*Milnthorpe Band, c.1912. The soldier with a cornet (centre) is Chris Scott who was
lost in the Dardanelles.*

combination playing in the County, rhythm and syncopation is
what is wanted and the Revellers have it. Secretaries quickly book
their dates (or as early as possible) as the band are (sic) heavily
booked ahead. For terms, photographs, vacant dates apply E.
Davenport, Rigney Bank House."[91]

Except for Red Cross Concerts and the like the Second World
War put paid to much live entertainment. "The Pictures" at the
Public Rooms drew crowds to the five performances per week
(including two on Saturdays). It was as rudimentary a flea pit as any
in the land. Patrons entered from underneath the screen and many
a close up of a Hollywood clinch was ruined by the silhouette of a
late arrival sometimes chewing fish and chips. The one and
sixpennies on the stage ("the balcony") had real, if second-hand,
tip-up plush seats but being secured to nothing but a portable
plank, they were liable to topple over. Even so "the pictures"
survived the first on-rush of television and "Milnthorpe Cinema"
did not close until the early 1960s.

The amateur dramatics disappeared about the same time though
in the immediate post-war period they had been highly successful.

The Milnthorpe Amateurs were seriously affected in 1948 when a
group led by Nat and Cora Dawson (Headmaster of Heversham
Grammar School and his wife) hived off in 1948 to form the South
Westmorland Stage and Screen Society. They had objected to
Milnthorpe's tradition that there should be a permanent producer
and also wanted a more intellectually demanding programme.

An arch welcoming E.H.Wilson as High Sherriff in 1886. A rare view of the south end of Church Street before the changes to the crossroads. The buildings on the right are now the tyre centre and estate agents.

Throughout the years special occasions periodically gave an excuse for fun and games. Often the village was drawn into the family celebrations of the Wilsons at Dallam. At the "Coming of Age" of George Crowle Wilson in 1869 a dinner for 100 tenants was provided in the dining room, while cottagers, labourers and children were entertained in the National School.

Whenever a Wilson was High Sheriff tenants formed the bodyguard or "javelin men" and all took part in the celebrations. In June 1886 when E.H. Wilson returned from officiating at the Assizes "every house had tried to outstrip its neighbour in display . . . with flags flying from the church and public buildings." Two small arches were erected at the top of Church Street and at the bottom a larger one was emblazoned (in flowers) with "Welcome Home the High Sheriff." On the ancestral porch under a similar banner villagers and gentry drank the toast "Luck to Dallam as long as Bela flows."

Sadly the luck soon ran out. Edward Wilson died the following December of "a chronic chest infection for which he had gone to South America three or four years ago... Few funerals have assumed larger dimensions drawing from Milnthorpe hundreds of sympathetic spectators . . . the mournful tolling of the passing bell at Milnthorpe was borne clearly through the December air." As the mile-long cortege reached Beetham Church the last carriage, containing the game-keeper, was only just leaving Dallam.

Royal events were always well marked and the accounts of the Parish Church at Heversham show that peels were rung at coronations, accessions and royal birthdays.[94] Queen Victoria's Coronation celebrations in 1838 included a tea party for the "deserving poor" provided by Mrs. Thomasin Richardson. Victoria's "bridal day" (10 February 1840) was marked by a procession of the National School children to the Parsonage where the "Rev. Padwick explained the symbols, many made of evergreens, carried by the teachers. One showed the union of hearts, another a cross and crown."[96]

Royal visits have been rare, though Milnthorpe has been as royalist as any place in the land. The first recorded visit was that of the Dowager Queen Adelaide (widow of William IV) on Friday 24 July 1840. "About two o'clock in the afternoon the party passed through the town of Milnthorpe where her Majesty was greeted by loud and repeated cheers by a numerous and highly respectable assemblage who had met for the purpose of paying her Majesty their respects. A congratulatory address from the clergy and other inhabitants of Milnthorpe was handed to Lord Howe for presentation to Her Majesty."

"A Gala Day" marked the marriage of Albert Edward, Prince of Wales to Princess Alexandra of Denmark on March 10th, 1863. Though it was still the tail end of winter 250 children gathered on the green for the first recorded "church steps" service where they were given a special medal. With "a greater number of the inhabitants" they then marched through the town to Dallam Tower where "God Save the Queen" was sung. Returning through the park, each child was presented with an orange and a currant bun, from beneath an arch erected on the Old Bridge.

At noon 200 married couples, widowers and widows were given "a dinner of roast beef and plumb pudding in the school room which was beautifully decorated ... an abundance had been so provided that after the adults had been satisfied there was plenty to give to the greater part of the children." A tea was given later for 300 unmarried people over 15. "In the evening the greater part of the respectable inhabitants illuminated the front of their houses and amongst them were shown several transparent paintings, one of which, 18 feet by 4 feet, the work of Mr. John Whittam, extended over the entrance gateway to the church and displayed the Prince of Wales feathers resting on a rose, shamrock and thistle. Dances were given at the White Lion and the Bull's Head and a concert and ball by the Mechanics' Institute at the Cross Keys."[98]

Queen Victoria, passing twice annually along the main line, was Milnthorpe's most regular royal visitor though she was only seen once, in 1859.[99] She was none-the-less revered and a thanksgiving service was held in March 1882 after she had escaped assassination.

"All classes helped cordially to celebrate the auspicious event" of her Golden Jubilee in 1887. 700 people partook of sports and tea on the show field and dancing was kept up until 9.30 when a jubilee dinner was held at the Bull's Head.[100]

The Prince and Princess of Wales' silver wedding was celebrated with a ball in 1888. For the wedding celebration of the Duke and Duchess of York (George V and Queen Mary) in 1893, 100 boys and 150 girls were presented with a medal before processing behind the Gatebeck Band to the Assembly Rooms where 322 sat down for tea.[101] At the sports, held in Ryley Fields, an exciting 100 yards race was won by George Garnett, Martin Ashburner won "the old man's race" and Polly Atkinson was sent home in disgrace for tearing her best skirt, having refused to change it.[102]

The "Jubilee trees" around the green are permanent reminders of the Diamond Jubilee in 1897. Ephemeral celebrations included a cycle parade and fancy dress procession with 100 in costume and a march past of 42 volunteers under Instructor Carr. The band played until a late hour for dancing and many people "visited Haverbrack bank and other elevated places to witness the bonfires and, indeed, evidenced the desire to prolong the day as long as possible."[103]

Though few inhabitants had ever seen her, Queen Victoria's demise "silenced the streets" in Milnthorpe. The news arrived on the evening of January 22nd 1901, just as choir practice was ending. A short service was held immediately and in the three weeks before the funeral "the passing bell sounded every day for 1 hour . . . flags were at half mast from the church steeple and several private houses. All suffered from the gale and their tattered condition has often caused the remark that they typically express the feeling of people at the present time." Most worshippers wore "some sombre hue" at the service in church where the altar and pulpit were draped in black.

Edward VII was proclaimed a week after the death of his mother on "a day to be remembered by young and old at Milnthorpe." All the local gentry and clergy were on the steps of the Market Cross and "round them gathered a concourse of all classes, many of whom had wended their way from the surrounding district." The High Sheriff first proclaimed the death of Queen Victoria and then Mr. J.G. Gandy, Senior Magistrate, proclaimed the accession of the King. Three cheers were then given for both the King and for Queen Alexandra, "Rule Britannia" was sung followed by the National Anthem "the new and unaccustomed words falling strangely on the ear."[106] – for over sixty years people had sung God save the *Queen*.

Coinciding with victory over the Boers, Edward VII's coronation celebrations were planned in Milnthorpe, as elsewhere, to out-do

Coronation celebrations, Church Street, 1902.

all earlier festivities. Flags were up, bonfires built and ham boiled when news arrived two days before "the" day that the royal appendectomy had prompted an indefinite postponement of the Westminster ceremonies. "The first telegram was discredited, but people gathered in groups in the streets to discuss the situation in hushed tones." As "all was ready" it was decided to give the children their mugs inscribed "Crowned 26 June 1902" and their tea.[107]

Shortly afterwards the Hon. James Dunsmuir, Premier of British Columbia, came to stay at Dallam Tower, having been delayed in returning home owing to the postponement of the Coronation. The visit bore fruit as Lady Bromley's second son Arthur "the Admiral" married Dunsmuir's daughter.

On the actual Coronation Day, August 22, there was a fancy dress and "decorated cycle" parade which included a "ten foot boat on a bike" ridden by Walter Mashiter, the usual sports and, with double luck, tea. The most spectacular event was a gun boat battle on the Bela below the Old Bridge. As estimated crowd of 2,000 watched the rival boats under "Captain" Nanson and "Captain" Semple

Planting trees to commemorate the Queen Mother's 80th Birthday, 1980.

fire from stove pipe guns at each other with the school boys and Mr. Nanson's drill class storming a camp before the Nanson boat was sunk "with all aboard." Fortunately none were lost nor, surprisingly, injured.[109]

At 8 a.m. on Saturday 7th May 1910 the passing bell announced the death of Edward VII, who was succeeded by George V. "Half a gale" was blowing on his Coronation Day, 11 June 1911, and the decorations suffered greatly. On Haverbrack the bonfire was calculated to be 35 feet high, a height only outdone in the area by the beacon on Heversham Head.[111]

George V's Silver Jubilee in 1935 had a full programme with the usual procession but a year later the King was dead and Edward VIII was proclaimed from the Market Cross and a Coronation Committee was set up.[113]

Eleven months later the process was gone through again for the accession of George VI, on his brother's abdication. Fortunately the local committee had not bought Edward VIII Coronation mugs as these were to be supplied by the Local Education Authority!

In contrast to previous occasions the Royal Wedding in 1947 of Princess Elizabeth to Philip of Greece was an austerity affair. There were no sports or tea parties (even bread was rationed), which was perhaps as well as it was a wet November day. The children did have a day off school and they were allowed to keep their "ration" of two fireworks per child over from 5 November in order to salute the happy couple. But by 1953 more sumptuous times had arrived for the Coronation of Elizabeth II, the first such occasion which most

Crowning Milnthorpe Carnival Queen, 1983.

villagers spent mainly round a television set. At the Mental Home "half of Ackenthwaite" was invited to view a "large screen TV installed by the trustees of one of the patients."

There were the usual celebrations and the children received a Coronation beaker bearing a hideous smudged portrait of the sovereign. Despite a thick drizzle the fancy dress parade and sports went on as planned with perhaps rather more of the "we can take it" spirit of Dunkirk than of the bright optimism of the "new Elizabethan Age" said to be dawning. At night the clouds lifted and the crowds round Milnthorpe's splendid fire on Haverbrack could see a full parure of beacons twinkling round the bay and up into Lakeland.

Sir Maurice Bromley-Wilson, harking back to his own Edwardian heyday, had donated several barrels of old cider to the bonfire party and with wicked relish he and his accomplices succeeded in getting the Boy Scouts drunk, a group of whom almost landed in the Bela as they staggered home.

A week or two later, on a sunny June morning, school children and villagers lined the A6 to see the popular Queen Salote of Tonga as she was returning to London following a holiday in the Lake District. She was just the latest of the many Royal visitors who had passed through the village in motor cars – the Prince of Wales in 1927, after opening Prince's Way, Queen Mary in 1937 and the Duke of Gloucester in the same year – he was stuck in a traffic jam!

In August 1956 Queen Elizabeth II came to Milnthorpe at the conclusion of her Westmorland tour and a quarter of a century later Milnthorpe outdid its neighbours in the scope of its Silver Jubilee celebrations. An "Our Village" exhibition of Milnthorpe history attracted great support and donations made by the public went towards the cost of a "Jubilee Seat" placed round one of Queen Victoria's Jubilee trees on the green.

Blatantly royalist Milnthorpe rose to the occasions to celebrate to the full the Queen Mother's 80th birthday and the marriage of Charles, Prince of Wales, to Lady Diana Spencer in 1981. So popular were the sports and processions that villagers decided to hold an annual Milnthorpe Carnival thereafter. In its first years, contrary to all precedent, this latest manifestation of village fun and games never had a wet day.

Notes and Reference to Sources

CHAPTER 1

1. See Below Chapter on Transport.
2. Ibid.
3. Ibid Chapter of Politics and Good Works.
4. Roy Millward and Adrian Robinson: The Lake District Eyre and Spottiswoode, London 1970 Page 152.
5. Ibid.
6. South Lakeland District Council Year Book 1986-1987.
7. History and Topography of Cumberland and Westmorland. William Whellan. Pontefract, William Whellan & Co. 1860.
8. See below Chapter on Markets and Fairs.
9. The Place Names of Cumberland and Westmorland. W.J. Sedgefield, Manchester University Press 1915 P. 164.
10. Westmorland Gazette 1st October 1869.
11. —.
12. The History and Antiquities of the Counties of Westmorland and Cumberland By Joseph Nicolson Esq. and Richard Burn LL.d. London 1777 Vol. II P. 209.
13. Millwood & Robinson 161 et seq.
14. History of Westmorland. Richard S. Ferguson, London. Eilliott Stock, London 1894 P. 17 et seq. also Millward and Robinson.
15. Early History of North West England Vol. 1. M.A. Gordon, Henry Marshall, Kentmere 1963.
16. History, Directory and Gazeteer of Cumberland, Westmorland with Furness and Cartmel. Parson & White, 1829. Michael Moon 1984 P.14.
17. Westmorland Royal Commission on Historical Monuments England. HMSO, 1936 P.104.
18. Ibid.
19. Transactions of the Cumberland and Westmorland Antiquarian & Archaeological Society M.S. XIV P.262 Dr. J.W. Jackson.
20. The Church at Heversham, A History of Westmorland's Oldest Recorded Church. Roger K. Bingham, 1984.
21. Trans. C. & W. M.S. LXIII W00 06 1963 The Dog Hole, Haverbrack By Don Benson and Keith Bland.
22. Millward & Robinson.
23. Ibid.
25. Bingham Chapter 2 P. 10

26. Millward & Robinson P. 136.
28. Ibid P. 129.
29. Gordon P. 13
30. F. Sedgefield P. 134.
31. Nicolson & Burn 217-218.
32. Sedgefield P. 140.
33. Ibid P. 146.
34. Ibid P. 157.
35. Ibid P. 161.
36. Millward & Robinson P. 141.
37. Ibid et seq.
38. Sedgefield P. 160.
40. Ibid P. 167.
41. Ibid.
42. Ibid P. 132.
43. P. 202.
44. Ibid P. 183.
45. Ibid P. 152.
46. Ibid P. 131.
48. P. 151
49. Ibid P. 189.
50. Ibid P. 164.
51. Ibid.
52. Bingham P. 100.
53. Gordon Chapter 5, also Millward & Robinson.
54. Nicholson & Burn Vol. II P. 199.
56. Bingham P. 14.
57. History of Heversham with Milnthorpe. John F. Curwen. Titus Wilson, 1930 P. 1 et seq.
58. Nicolson & Burn P. 200.
59. Ibid et seq.

CHAPTER 2

1. References to topography, geology etc. based partly on information from Mr. L.J. Hobbs B.A., B.Sc., Mr. Colin Patrick M.Sc etc.
2. Heversham Enclosures Award C.R.O./K.
3. Information Mr. J. Frierson.
4. Mashiter/Stones.
5. Ibid.
6. Ibid.
7. W.G. 30 March 1907.
8. Information Mr. W.R. Handley of College Green, 4th generation to the farm the Marsh.
9. W.G. 30 1897.
10. The Salt Marshes, Morecambe Bay. A.S. Gray.
11. Wm. Hutton, Beetham Repository.

12. Antiquity on Horseback. Jane M. Ewbank p.52. Titus Wilson 1963.
13. Ibid.
14. W.G. Oct 1885.
15. W.G. 1 May 1887.
16. W.G. 20 July 1843.
17. W.G. 4 August 1849.
18. W.G. 3 October 1904.
19. W.G. 24 August 1867.
20. W.G. 11 November 1843.
21. W.G. 20 April 1913.
22. W.G. 29 June 1940.
23. W.G. 29 August 1942.
24. 16 September 1905.
25. W.G. 1946 and local memories.
26. Information Mr. D. Johnson.
27. Thomas Gough. The Herons and Heronry at Dallam Tower.
28. Antiquity on Horseback p.53.
29. W.G. 1921.
30. W.G. 4 June 1921.
31. J. Barnes. All Around Arnside.
32. Information Mr. C. Patrick.
33. M.P.C. Sewage Enquiry c.1910.
34. McIntyre. Port of Milnthorpe (1936) p.53.
35. W.G. 1847 also A.A. Gray.
36. McIntyre Port of Milnthorpe.
37. W.G. August 1847.
38. W.G. 12 June 1842.
39. A.J. Gray.
40. Barnes. All Around Arnside.
42. W.G. 1 August 1847.
43. W.G. 24 February 1855.
44. Mashiter/Stones.
45. W.G. 9 September 1905.
46. Information Mr. W.J. Ladell tradition of Inman family also W.G. 16 September 1908.
47. W.G. 6 September 1823.
48. W.G. 15 March 1926.
49. Church at Heversham p.89.
52. W.G. July 1824.
53. W.G. 1 June 1828.
54. W.G. 25 June 1853.
55. Church at Heversham p.49.
56. W.G. 23 June 1855.
57. W.G. June 1852.
58. W.G. 21 August 1852.
59. W.G. 28 May 1853.
60. W.G. 28 May 1853.
61. W.G. 18 August 1855.
62. W.G. 21 August 1858.
63. W.G. 26 June 1914.
64. W.G. 24 June 1939.
65. The Lonely Plough by Constance Holme. Mills & Boon, 1914.
66. W.G. 4 January 1834.
67. W.G. January 1853.
68. W.G. 5 February 1853.
69. W.G. 7 March 1903.

71. Report W.G. 30 March 1907 also Lonely Plough. The author as a child knew many people directly involved in the disaster.
72. Church at Hevesham p.105
73. W.G. 5 November 1927.

CHAPTER 3

1. W.T. McIntyre. The Port of Milnthorpe. Article V in Vol. XXXVI M.S. of Transactions of the Cumberland and Westmorland Archaelogical and Antiquarian Society 1936. He begins the article by writing "it is a matter deeply to be regretted that our early local historians and antiquaries have devoted so small a share of their attention to the old Port of Milnthorpe, Westmorland's sole point of contact with the sea.
2. Curwen p.45, also see below.
3. Mashiter/Stones.
4. There is no documentary evidence of this tradition.
5. See below.
6. Mashiter/Stones.
8. Ibid.
10. Records of Kendale. Vol III p.258.
11. See also Curwen p.72 and chapter on Roads.
13. A member of the Burkett/Birkett family of Leasgill.
14. Mashiter/Stones.
15. Curwen p.73 and below.
16 Mashiter/Stones.
18. W.G. 29 February 1895.
19. McIntyre p.45
21. See below Chapter on Public Rights.
22. Beetham Repository.
23. Author's memories.
24. Sedgefield p.193.
25. Mashiter/Stones.
26. Belle Halliwell – letter to W.G. also C.R.O./K. Box W.D./P.D.
27. Ibid.
28. Church at Heversham p.72.
29. Ibid 102.
30. Will of J. Grigg, Some Westmorland Wills. J. Somervell, Titus Wilson 1928.
31. Belle Halliwell.
32. Nicolson & Burn p.220.
33. W.G. 7 February 1900.
34. Church at Heversham p.11, p.20.
35. See below Chapter on Markets and Fairs.
36. McIntyre p.38 et seq.
38. McIntyre p.38. Curwen p.75.
39. Ibid.
40. Beetham Repository.
41. Church at Heversham p.100/102.
42. C.R.O./K. W.D./C.U. Quote Session

Returns.
43. Author's memories.
44. Some Westmorland Villages by W.I.
46. Quote Session Returns C.R.O./K. M.S./S.O.
47. Barnes. All Around Arnside.
48. Parson & White. Directory & Gazeteer of Cumberland and Westmorland Parson & White p.626.
50. Robinson's Guides to the Lakes.
51. Mashiter/Stones.
52. Day Books. Walter Berry C.R.O./K.
54. Walter Berry.
55. Information Mr. L. Walling.
57. W.G. 16 November 1819.
58. W.G. 25 February 1843.
59. W.G. 7 April 1849.
60. W.G. 28 March 1857.
61. See above Milnthorpe Sands.
62. McIntyre p.43.
63. C.R.O./K. W.D.B/2
64. W.G. 25 October 1856.
65. McIntyre p.56.
66. Navigation of Kent Enquiry. W.G. 26 March 1857.
67. Records Milnthorpe Angling Association.
70. Day Books. Walter Berry.
71. Mashiter/Stones Curwen p.41.
72. Mashiter/ Stones.
73. Ibid.
74. Port of Milnthorpe. Dissertation by C.M.F. Holden, 1974 C.R.O./K.
75. Walter Berry Day Books.
76. W.G. 5 June 1852.
77. W.G. 30 December 1856.
78. W.G. 23 February 1857.
79. W.G. 28 March 1857.
80. Ibid.
81. Ibid.
82. W.G. 22 July 1882.
83. J. Barnes. All Around Arnside.

CHAPTER 4

1. Nicolson & Burn.
2. Trade Directories 1912.
3. Information Mrs M. Dobson.
4. P.C. Minutes C.R.O./K. W.P.R./W.D./88.
5. Millward & Robinson. The Lake District 206 et seq. also N. and B.
6. Ibid and Re – Kendal, see Annals of Kendal. Cornelius Nicholson F.G.S. London, Whitaker & Co., Kendal T. Wilson 1861 p.250.
7. Farrer. Records of Kendale Vol 11 p.146.
8. Mashiter/Stones.
9. Curwen p.51.
10. C.R.O./K. W.P.R./88 also information Mr. F. Rockliffe.
11. Curwen p.49.
12. See Chapter on Politics and Good Works.
13. W.G.'s week falling nearest 12 May.
14. W.G. 18 May 1884.
15. Levens Papers.
16. W.G. 16 May 1890.
17. W.G. 17 May 1891.
18. W.G. 17 May 1902.
19. W.G. 16 May 1903.
20. W.G. 16 May 1910.
21. W.G. 15 May 1915.
22. C.R.O./K/W.P.R./88 P.C. Minutes.
23. Barnes. All Around Arnside.
24. Villagers' recollections.
25. Recollections of Miles family resident at Laburnum House c.1925-1947.
26. W.G. 19 May 1894.
27. W.G. 19 May 1900.
28. W.G. 14 May 1859.
29. W.G. 16 May 1874.
30. W.G. 15 May 1880.
31. The Splendid Fairing. Constance Holme, Mills & Boon 1919.
32. W.G. 17 May 1819.
33. W.G. 21 May 1824.
34. W.G. 18 May 1833.
35. W.G. 17 May 1851.
36. W.G. 19 May 1857.
54. W.G. 21 October 1852.
59. C.R.O./K. W.P.R./88/P.C.
60. W.G. 16 October 1847.
61. W.G. 20 December 1851.
62. W.G. 24 December 1859.
70. W.G. 21 August 1841.
71. See Chapter on the Church.
72. W.G. 23 August 1839.
73. W.G. 28 August 1915.
74. W.G. 9 September 1843.
75. W.G. 28 August 1847.
76. W.G. 10 August 1851.
77. Curwen p.49.
78. Whellan.
79. W.G. 15 December 1837.
81. W.G. 28 October 1842.
82. W.G. 3 January 1847.
83. 15 May 1869.
84. W.G. 17 May 1871.
85. W.G. 18 May 1907.
86. W.G. 19 May 1843.
87. Records of Kendale Vol.11, p.166.
88. W.G. 16 May 1863.
89. W.G. 23 May 1864.
90. W.G. 14 May 1899.
91. W.G. 15 May 1833(?).
92. W.G. 15 May 1856.
93. W.G. 12 October 1807.
94. W.G. 19 May 1855.

95. W.G. 13 May 1837.
96. W.G. 22 May 1869.
97. Curwen p.48-49.
98. W.G. 17 May 1873.
99. 16 May 1875.
100. W.G. 27 May 1873.
101. Ibid.
102. More Odd Corners in English Lakeland. William T. Palmer F.R.G.S. Skeffington & Son, London 1945.
103. W.G. 25 May 1822.
104. W.G. 18 May 1833.
105. Palmer p.67.
108. W.G. 16 May 1852.
109. W.G. 16 May 1896.
110. Information late Mrs. E. Woods.
111. W.G. 19 May 1905.
112. W.G. 16 May 1930.
113. C.R.O./K. W.P.R./88 P.C. Minutes.
114. Ibid.
115. Opinion Mr. J. Balmer and others.
116. W.G. 7 January 1905.
117. W.G. 30 October 1875.
118. C.R.O./K./W.P.R./88 P.C. Minutes.
120. Ibid and W.G. reports.
122. P.C. By-law.
123. The present author regards the new shelter as the only worthy memorial of his time as Chairman of Milnthorpe Parish Council!
124. Minutes of M.P.C.
125. C.R.O./K./W.P.R./88 P.C. Minutes.
126. Ibid.
127. Ibid.
128. Ibid.
129. Despite the fierce nature of the dispute all parties remained on surprisingly amicable terms.

CHAPTER 5

1. See below also Curwen p.6.
2. Ibid.
3. The Illustrated Journey of Celia Fiennes 1682-1712. Macdonald, Webb & Bower p.165.
4. Road Transport in Cumbria in the 19th Century. L.A. Williams, George Allen & Unwin 1975 p.27.
5. Millward & Robinson. The Lake District p.118.
6. Church at Heversham p.13.
7. Roads and Trackways of the Lake District. Brian Paul Hindle, Moorland, 1984 p.49.
8. Ibid p.60-62.
9. Ibid p.65-68.
10. M.S. owner's possession.
11. Church at Heversham p.46-47.
12. Ibid.
13. Author's research in field and Curwen, Stones etc.
14. Records of Kendale, Curwen Vol 111 p.5.
16. Ibid p.224.
17. Hindle p.138.
18. Hindle p.87.
19. C.R.O./K. Audland Papers.
20. Blount map C.R.O./K. and "Our Village".
21. Mashiter/Stones.
22. Ibid.
23. Curwen p.72 also Farrer.
24. Mashiter/Stones.
25. Curwen p.72.
26. Antiquary on Horseback. Jane Ewbank, Titus Wilson.
27. Curwen Records of Kendale Vol. 3. p.275.
28. Ibid.
29. Ibid p.226.
30. Ibid p.277.
31. Turnpike Act 1759.
32. Ibid.
34. W.G. 11 August 1832.
35. W.G. 11 May 1822.
36. W.G. 27 December 1823.
37. Ibid 1823.
38. W.G. 27 March 1824.
39. W.G. 14 August 1834.
40. Newspaper reports etc.
41. W.G.
42. W.G. 27 March 1824.
43. W.G. 26 July 1844.
44. W.G. 12 June 1861.
45. W.G. 9 November 1844.
46. Mashiter/Stones.
47. Ibid also Eva Scott memories.
48. W.G. 22 July 1842.
49. W.G. 1844.
50. Mashiter/Stones.
51. Parsons & White Directory 1829 p.629.
52. Mashiter/Stones.
53. Parsons/White p.629.
54. W.G. 5 April 1844.
55. W.G. 7 June 1844.
56. W.G. 4 September 1847.
57. W.G. 11 December 1847.
58. W.G. 8 May 1852.
59. W.G. 17 November 1849.
60. W.G. 21 May 1852.
61. W.G. 19 May 1855.
62. W.G. 28 February 1874.
63. W.G. 6 June 1874.
64. W.G. 24 April 1880.
65. W.G. 11 January 1890.
66. W.G. 2 June 1894.
67. W.G. report.
68. W.G. 10 November 1855.
69. W.G. 1867.

70. Curwen p.6 31 October 1875.
71. Main Line Over Shap. Dalesman Books.
72. W.G. 1 February 1844.
73. W.G. 10 December 1844.
74. W.G. 3 September 1846.
75. W.G. 30 September 1846.
76. W.G. 10 December 1846.
77. See Chapter on Industry & Trade.
78. W.G. 30 January 1846.
79. W.G. 15 October 1848.
80. Preston Patrick Church Records.
81. W.G. 21 April 1853.
82. Curwen p.67 also W.G. February 1853.
83. W.G.
84. W.G. 13 May 1882.
85. W.G.
88. C.R.O./K.
89. Curwen p.12.
90. W.G. 7 August 1874.
91. W.G. 16 August 1874.
92. W.G. 14 November 1875.
93. W.G. 7 November 1875.
94. W.G. 12 July 1894.
95. W.G. 12 July 1894.
96. Mashiter/Stones.
97. W.G. 17 January 1903.
98. W.G. 2 March 1894.
99. W.G. 23 February 1895.
100. W.G. 22 April 1895.
101. W.G.
102. Ibid.
103. W.G. 5 October 1901.
104. W.G. 7 May 1903.
105. W.G. 1 May 1906.
106. W.G. 29 June 1907.
107. W.G. March 1906.
108. W.G. 28 August 1908.
109. W.G. 4 November 1911.
110. W.G. 13 June 1914.
111. W.G. 29 May 1914.
112. W.G. 18 September 1920.
113. W.G. 16 May 1924.
114. W.G. 20 August 1937.
115. 24 December 1941.
116. W.G. 6 September 1941.
117. W.G. 17 July 1980.
118. W.G. 26 December 1931.
119. -.
121. C.R.O./K. P.C. Records.
122. W.G. 10 June 1911.
123. Memories H. Fawcett.
124. G.D. Abraham, Motor Ways of Lakeland, 1913.
125. P.C. Records.
126. W.G. 9 April 1917.
127. Records of W.C.C. Information Mr. K. Blenkharn.
128. W.G. 21 March 1936.
129. W.G. 20 August 1939.
130. Information H. Fawcett et seq.
131. W.G. 6 December 1980.

132. W.G. 9 January 1932.
133. W.G.
134. W.G. 14 September 1940.
135. Information Mr. K. Blenkharn.
136. Ibid.
137. Curwen, Stones, W.G.
138. W.G. 29 November 1844.
139. Stones, W.G.
142. W.G. 11 February 1824.
143. W.G. 28 March 1828.
144. W.G. 7 August 1847.
148. Ibid.
149. W.G. 15 September 1849.
150. W.G. 11 August 1855.
151. W.G. 14 March 1878.
152. Curwen p.7.
153. Stones.
154. Curwen p.7.
155. W.G.
156. W.G. 11 February 1858.
157. W.G. 27 February 1869.
158. Curwen p.7.
159. Curwen p.35.
160. Mashiter/Stones.
161. Curwen p.46–47.
162. Curwen p.47 also W.G.
163. W.G. 17 September 1842.
164. W.G. 28 December 1842.
165. Curwen p.47.
166. W.G. 11 March 1912.
167. Curwen p.41.
168. W.G. 4 March 1843.
169. W.G. December 1850.
170. See Chapter on Poor Law.
171. W.G. 1869.
172. W.G. 19 January 1907.
173. Curwen p.52.
174. W.G. 12 June 1915.

CHAPTER 6

1. Quoted N. & B. Vol. 111 p.1 et seq.
2. Ibid p.3.
3. Ibid p.7.
4. Ibid et seq.
5. Ibid.
6. Benson & Bland C.W.A. A.C.X.I.U. 1953.
7. Farrer Vol. 11 p.147.
9. Sedgefield p.194
10. Garnett, Westmorland Agriculture 1800–1900, Titus Wilson 1912 p.8.
12. Mashiter/Stones.
13. Farrer p.147.
14. Ibid p.151.
15. C.R.O./K. M.S./50 also C.R.O./K.M/12.
16. J. Somervell, Some Westmorland Wills, 1928 p.XII.
24. Garnett p.21, 57 et seq.

25. Curwen p.10.
26. C.R.O./K./M.S./61.
27. C.R.O./K.W.D./A.G. Box 17.
28. C.R.O./K./M.S./61.
29. C.R.O./K./W.D./A.G. Box 76.
30. Ibid Box 17.
33. C.R.O./K./W.D./A.G. Box 2.
35. C.R.O./K./W.D./A.G. Croft Box 4.
36. W.D./A.G. Box 2.
37. C.R.O./K./M6/64.
38. M. & B. p.9.
39. Curwen p.77.
40. Ibid.
41. C.R.O./K.W.D./A.G. Box 4.
42. Curwen p.11 et seq.
43. Ibid.
44. Curwen p.65.
45. Ibid p.64.
46. Ibid p.65.
47. Kelly's Directories.
48. W.G. March 1864.
49. Curwen p.52, W.G. 13 November 1840.
50. Farrer Vol. 11 p.162.
51. Whellan and Directories.
52. The Act is kept at C.R.O./K. but a contemporary copy of plans is in the Vestry at Heversham Church.
53. See also Church at Heversham p.111–112.
54. Curwen p.59.
55. See "Lonely Plough" and Chapter on Milnthorpe Sands.
56. It was retained by W. Douthwaite until 1962.
57. P.C. Records.
58. Unfortunately no precise map has been retained.
59. Garnett p.128.
60. Information Mr. D. Johnson.
61. Garnett p.8.
62. Ibid p.21.
63. W.G.
64. Day Books. Walter Berry C.R.O./K.
65. W.G. 10 November 1866.
66. Records of Kendal Union C.R.O./K.
67. W.G. 26 May 1849.
68. W.G. 14 July 1855.
69. W.G. 20 September 1873.
70. Garnett p.12, 204, 206.
71. W.G. 6 March 1858.
72. W.G. 16 October 1862.
73. W.G. 24 October 1854.
74. Ibid.
75. W.G. 30 May 1874.
76. W.G. accounts etc.
77. W.G. March 1847.
78. W.G. 14 March 1874.
79. W.G. 27 February 1880.
80. W.G. 11 March 1880.
81. W.G. 12 February 1882.
82. W.G. 17 February 1894.
83. W.G. 18 February 1899.
84. W.G. 27 January 1917.
85. W.G. 21 February 1920.
86. W.G. 10 February 1923.
87. W.G. 17 February 1926.
88. W.G. 10 February 1934.
89. Quoted by Garnett.
90. Ibid.
99. Ibid.
100. W.G. March 1874.
101. W.G. 1 April 1861.
102. Garnett p.169.
103. C.R.O./K. W.P.D. Papers.
104. See Beetham Manorial Court Records and Chapter on Public Right.
105. Garnett p.184.
106. W.G. 22 September 1934.
107. Garnett p.138 et seq.
108. C.R.O./K. Day Book Walter Berry.
110. W.G. 26 December 1891.
111. Garnett Chapter IX.
112. C.R.O./K. Day Book Walter Berry.
113. Author's papers.
114. C.R.O./K. Day Book Walter Berry.
115. W.G. 14 December 1889.
116. W.G. 19 February 1896.
117. W.G. 23 February 1901.
118. C.R.O./K. Day Book Walter Berry.
119. W.G. 5 June 1846.
120. As reports of flood damage shows.
121. W.G. 3 November 1866.
122. W.G. reports etc.
123. Table from W.G.
124. W.G. 23 September 1870.
125. W.G.
128. All W.G. editions nearest to date quoted.
129. W.G. 18 May 1878.
130. W.G. July 1882.
131. W.G. 4 January 1825.
132. W.G. 24 February 1894.
133. W.G. 31 August 1941.

CHAPTER 7

1. See above Chapter, Sedgefield p.164.
2. John Somervell. Water Power Mills of South Westmorland and The Kent, Bela and Gilpin and their Tributaries, Titus Wilson 1930 p.41.
5. Ibid p.74.
6. Church at Heversham p.15.
7. Ibid p.112.
8. Some Westmorland Wills. J. Somervell p.9, 10 et seq.
9. Water Power Mills p.110.
10. Nicolson & Burn p.201–202.
11. e.g. Mounts Map 1826 C.R.O./K.D.
12. Water Power Mills p.14, 16.

13. Information Mrs. A. Hyelman.
14. Quoted, Water Power Mills p.110.
16. C.R.O./K. M.S./50.
19. Heversham Parish Records
    C.R.O./K./W.P.R./8.
20. Mashiter/Stones.
21. C.R.O./K. M.S.50.
22. C.R.O./K. W.D./P.D. Box 3.
23. W.G. 21 January 1854.
24. Mashiter/Stones.
25. Curwen p.51-52.
26. Mashiter/Stones W.G.
27. W.G. 26 June 1912.
28. Mashiter/Stones.
29. Ibid.
30. Parson & White p.628-629.
31. Ibid.
32. W.G. 2 October 1842.
33. 11 October 1851.
34. W.G. 7 October 1854.
35. W.G. October 1869(?).
36. W.G. 3 December 1842.
37. W.G. 12 April 1844.
38. W.G. 7 April 1849.
39. W.G. 2 February 1850.
40. W.G. 17 December 1853.
41. W.G. June 1854.
42. W.G. 24 November 1855.
43. Kelly's Directories 1873 p.936.
44. W.G. May 1861.
45. W.G. 14 December 1878.
47. W.G. 3 November 1888.
48. W.G. July 1894.
49. W.G. 28 February 1860.
50. W.G. 16 March 1861.
51. W.G. March 1895.
52. W.G. 21 October 1916.
53. W.G. 10 January 1925.
54. W.G. 10 November 1926.
55. W.G. 1931.
56. W.G. 21 April 1923.
57. W.G. 12 April 1944.
58. W.G. 8 December 1849.
59. W.G. 26 May 1849.
60. Mashiter/Stones.
61. Ibid.
62. W.G. 30 March 1912.
63. Mashiter/Stones.
67. Mashiter/Stones.
68. Ibid.
69. Curwen p.48.
70. Mashiter/Stones.
71. Curwen p.48.
72. Mashiter/Stones.
73. Our Village. R. Bingham, 1977.
74. Pevsner p.277.
75. W.G. June 1899.
77. Audland Pedigree C.R.O./K. and at
    Ackenthwaite.
78. Church at Heversham p.32.
79. Ibid p.45.

80. Audland pedigree.
81. Church at Heversham p.45.
82. Audland pedigree.
83. W.G. January 1907.
84. W.G. May 1882.
85. W.G. 17 March 1858.
86. Curwen p.64.
87. W.G. 26 March 1915.
88. Always claimed by later generations of
    the family.
89. W.G. 18 December 1909.
90. Information Jack's grandson
    Harold Fawcett.
91. C.R.O./K. W.D./P.D.
92. W.G. 29 August 1885.
93. W.G. 8 October 1891.
94. W.G. 17 September 1898.
95. W.G. September 1905.
96. W.G. 6 June 1908.
97. Curwen p.78 also Mashiter/Stones.
98. Census returns.
99. W.G. 1855.
100. W.G. 10 October 1863.
101. W.G. 20 November 1875.
102. W.G. 19 April 1883.
103. Information Mr. J. Mashiter.
104. W.G. May 1985.
105. W.G. January 1913.
106. W.G. 25 May 1895.
107. W.G. Kelly's Directory.
108. Directory also local memories.
109. W.G. 12 October 1931.
110. W.G. November 1926.
111. W.G. 8 September 1934.

CHAPTER 8

1. Royal Commission on
   Historical Monuments
   Westmorland H.M.S.O. 1936.
2. See below and Curwen p.8.
3. See above Chapter.
4. Ibid.
5. See Vernacular Architecture of the
   Lake Counties, A Field Handbook.
   R.W. Brunskill, Faber 1974, p.50, 56-
   9, 78, 80-81.
6. Curwen p.4.
7. C.R.O./K. M.S./61
   Cragg Papers.
8. See above, Port of
   Milnthorpe.
9. Heversham Parish Accounts.
10. Curwen p.46.
11. Information Miss D. Mashiter.
12. Mashiter Papers - Stones' memories.
13. R.C.H.M. p.175.
14. W.G. 20 May 1870.
15. W.G. 10 October 1874.
16. Brunskill p.44.

17. W.G. 11 May 1834.
18. W.G. 26 September 1832.
19. Ibid 1851.
20. Curwen p.45.
21. W.G. 15 May 1833.
22. R.C.H.M. p.175.
23. Pevsner p.277.
24. Curwen p.57.
25. Fayrer Estate Papers
    C.R.O./K.
26. W.G. 8 September 1814.
27. Curwen p.54.
28. Mashiter Papers/Stones'
    memories.
29. Curwen p.51.
30. Records of Kendale Vol.11 p.144.
31. Ibid p.145.
32. C.R.O./K. M.S./49.
33. W.G. 21 March 1851.
34. W.G. 1 May 1875.
35. Tradition related to author.
36. W.G. 28 April 1823.
37. C.R.O./K. D6/70.
38. Ibid.
39. C.R.O./K. M/4/39.
40. Mashiter Papers/Stones'
    memories.
41. Ibid.
44. C.R.O./K. W.D./A.G.
    Box 13–16.
45. Some Westmorland Wills
    p.9, 10, 11.
49. Mashiter Papers.
51. W.G. 8 February 1873.
52. Ibid 19 May 1894.
53. All W.G.
54. W.G. 11 March 1899.
55. W.G. 5 January 1901.
56. W.G. 22 June 1901.
57. P.C. Records.
58. Our Village. Roger Bingham, 1977.
59. W.G. 26 January 1935.
60. W.G. 31 December 1938.
61. P.L.B.
62. W.G. 29 June 1901.
63. W.G. 10 February 1906.
64. W.G. 24 September 1910.
65. P.C. Records also W.G.
    28 June 1938.
66. Information Mrs. Agnes Pickthall.
67. Information Mrs. Elsie Dix.
68. Information Mrs. B. Harrower.
69. W.G. 5 January 1939.
70. W.G. 1945.

CHAPTER 9.

1. Church at Heversham p.7.
2. C.R.O./K. W.P.R./88.
3. Information late Mrs. M.I. Sheldon
   nee Atkinson.
4. Book of Accounts of Church Wardens
   Heversham Church C.R.O./K.
5. Ibid.
6. Ibid and Church at Heversham p.93.
7. Curwen p.53 and Some Westmorland
   Wills. J. Somervell, Titus Wilson 1927
   p.16.
9. Church at Heversham p.102.
10. Ibid p.36, p.37.
11. Records of Kendale Vol.   p.224.
12. Church at Heversham p.48.
13. W.G. 1 June 1882.
14. Church at Heversham p.49.
15. Pamphlet, Milnthorpe Methodist
    Church 75th Anniversary.
16. Records of Kendale Vol.111 p.230.
17. Curwen p.52.
18. W.G. 7 July 1866.
21. Mashiter papers/Neddy Stones'
    Memories.
22. W.G. 26 May 1835.
23. W.G. 8 December 1835.
24. W.G. 6 June 1835.
25. C.R.O./K. and
26. Mashiter papers.
27. Heversham Enclosure Award
    C.R.O./K.
28. Mashiter Papers.
29. Quoted W.G. 12 October 1837.
30. History of Westmorland & Furness in
    Cartmel. London 1842.
31. W.G. 9 June 1883.
32. Buildings of England: Cumberland &
    Westmorland. Nickolaus Pevsner 1967
    p.277.
33. W.G. 19 August 1836.
34. W.G. 5 December 1835.
35. Ibid 1835.
36. Ibid.
37. Ibid.
38. W.G. 23 September 1837.
39. C.R.O./K. W.P.R./88.
40. Ibid.
41. W.G. 6 October 1837.
42. Curwen p.9.
43. Mashiter Papers/Stones' Memories.
44. W.G. 7 January 1855.
45. W.G. 27 March 1869.
46. W.G. 30 June 1838.
47. W.G. 13 July 1841.
48. W.G. 23 September 1843.
49. W.G. 21 January 1842.
50. W.G. 7 January 1842.
51. W.G. 23 January 1845.
52. W.G. July 1846.
53. W.G. May 1868.
54. W.G. 9 March 1878.
55. W.G. 23 March 1878.
56. Author's memories.
57. P.C.C. Minutes.

58. W.G. 8 February 1845.
59. W.G. August–September 1830.
60. W.G. August–September 1838.
61. W.G. 18 September 1841.
62. W.G. 10 September 1842.
63. W.G. 19 August 1843.
64. W.G. 24 August 1849.
65. Curwen p.45.
66. Mashiter papers/Stones' memories.
67- Information Mr. Eric Walsh.
68. Information Rev. J. Kelly.
69. W.P.R./88.
70. W.G. 9 January 1841.
71. Mashiter papers/Stones' memories.
72. Ibid.
73. Obituary, author's possession also W.G. 6 April 1895, 16 April 1895.
74. -.
75. In Memoriam Documents.
76. W.G. September 1883.
79. Answer to Bishop's queries W.P.R./88.
80. Ibid.
81. W.G. 2 November 1888.
82. W.G. 30 August 1875.
83. W.G. 20 January 1883.
84. Ibid.
85. Ibid.
86. C.R.O./K. + Crockfords.
88. C.R.O./K. W.P.R./88.
89. Church Accounts C.R.O./K.
90. Ibid.
91. Report of Restoration 1883.
92. W.G. 9 May 1869.
93. Village tradition related by H.M. Atkinson.
94. W.G. 20 July 1870.
95. W.G. 16 June 1883.
96. C.R.O./K. W.P.R./88.
97. Ibid.
98. Church at Heversham Ch. VI.
99. W.G. 16 June 1883.
100. W.G. 15 March 1884.
108. W.G. 30 March 1895.
109. W.G. 6 April 1895.
112. Answer to queries W.P.R./88.
113. C.R.O./K. W.P.R./88.
115. W.G. 13 April 1895.
116. W.G. 12 October 1895.
117. W.G. 1 May 1897.
118. P.C.C. Minutes.
120. W.G. 9 July 1898.
121. C.R.O./K W.P.R./88.
122. P.C.C. Minutes.
123. W.G. 6 April 1907.
124. W.G. August 1910.
125. W.G. November 1937.
126. W.G. 1887.
127. W.G. 1912.
128. 1842.
129. W.G. 1906.

130. W.G. September 1903.
132. Ibid.
134. 1911.
135. W.G. 1910.
136. W.G. and C.R.O./K.
137. W.G. 1917.
138. P.C.C.
139. W.G. December 1916.
141. Vestry books.
142. P.C.C. records and press reports.
143. Memories Mrs. M. Atkinson.
144. W.G. 1924.
145. Memories Mrs. B. Harrower.
149. P.C.C. Records.
150. Memories Harold Fawcett (1900–1979).
151. P.C.C Records.
152. Ibid.
153. Ibid.
154. Ibid and W.G.
155. Ibid.
156. Ibid.
157. Ibid.
158. All Ibid.
159. Ibid.
160. Ibid.
164. W.G. 29 March 1947.
165. Ibid.

CHAPTER 10

1. Milnthorpe became a Polling Station on 21st October 1842, Curwen p.2 and Directories.
2. Mashiter/Stones.
3. A. Wainwright, Westmorland Heritage p.271 W.G. 1975.
4. Curwen p.11.
7. Mashiter/Stones.
8. G. Tattersall. Lakes of England.
10. W.G. 1834.
11. Curwen, p.8.
12. W.G. 22 January 1910.
13. W.G. 23 August 1834.
16. W.G. 17 January 1880.
18. W.G. 13 July 1895.
20. W.G. 3 February 1906.
21. W.G. 15 January 1910.
22. W.G. 1 October 1910.
23. W.G. 8 October 1910.
24. W.G. July 1912.
25. W.G. 25 October 1924.
26. Information Mr. W.J. Ladell.
27. W.G. 20 May 1936.
28. W.G. 27 June 1937.
29. C.R.O./K. W.D.B./35.
30. Some Westmorland Wills. J. Somervell, p.16.
31. Whellan p.831.
32. W.G. 11 May 1843.
33. W.G. 10 December 1863.

34. W.G. 15 November 1862.
35. W.G. 18 January 1826.
36. W.G. 11 January 1841.
37. W.G. 15 March 1841.
38. W.G. December 1869.
39. W.G. March 1849.
40. W.G. 18 March 1843.
41. W.G. 17 May 1844.
42. W.G. 11 March 1839.
43. W.G. 29 December 1855.
44. W.G. 11 December 1858.
45. W.G. 6 June 1858.
46. W.G. 6 June 1874.
47. W.G. 30 May 1875.
48. W.G. 11 June 1881.
50. W.G. 30 May 1875.
51. W.G. 10 January 1874.
52. W.G. 1 August 1874.
53. W.G. 3 February 1869.
54. W.G. 30 October 1858.
55. -.
56. W.G. September 1880, 30 May, 22 October 1880.
57. W.G. 13 June 1883.
58. W.G. 15 September 1934.
59. Norman Nicholson. The County Books: Cumberland & Westmorland. Robert Hale Ltd. 1949. p.179.
60. W.G. 13 May 1893.
61. P.C.C. Minutes.
62. W.G. 7 March 1931.
63. Curwen, p.9.
64. W.G. 21 March 1885, 25 April 1885.
65. Trumpet in the Dust. (1921) Constance Holme, Mills & Boon.
66. W.G. 29 November 1862.
67. W.G. 30 December 1865.
68. W.G. March 1911.
69. Opinion Brigadier E.G. Audland, Audland Pedigree.
70. Parson & White Directory.
71. Directories.
73. W.G. 26 April 1885.
74. Curwen, p.8.
75. Author's memories supplemented by information from Mrs. K.M. Byrne and Mrs. P. Hall.
76. See Chapter on Crime & Punishment.
77. W.G. May 1900.
78. W.G. 14 January 1922.
79. W.G. 22 January 1896.
80. Gazette reports.
81. W.G. November 1829.

CHAPTER 11

1. Matt 26:1, Mark 14:7, John 12:8.
2. Oxford History of England: The Reign of Elizabeth. J.D. Black, p.265, 266, 267.
3. Church at Heversham p.93, p.106.
4. Black p.207.
5. The Later Stuarts. George Clark p.52 O.U.P.
6. Black p.207.
7. Church at Heversham p.100.
8. Ibid.
9. Mashiter/Stones.
10. Ibid.
11. C.R.O./K Quarter Session Returns.
12. All Ibid.
13. H.S. Habakuk. English Population in the Eighteenth Century. H.R. 2nd Ser. VI 1953-4 pp.117-133; also O.U.P. The Reign of George III. Seton Watson p.105, and local Census Returns.
16. O.U.P. The Age of Reform. Llewllyn Woodward F.B.A., 1962 p.449-50, 450 et seq.
17. C.R.O./K. W.S.P.U./K./1. Records of Kendal Poor Law Union - Minute books, Agenda etc.
18. Curwen, p.60.
19. Quoted Belle Halliwell.
20. C.R.O./K. W.S.P.U./K.
21. Ibid and Curwen p.60.
22. Curwen p.60 and Whellan.
23. Ibid.
24. W.G. 3 September 1836.
25. Curwen, p.61.
26. W.G. 5 January 1828.
27. C.R.O./K. W.S.P.U./K.
28. Ibid.
29. Ibid.
30. Ibid.
31. W.G. 20 June 1837.
32. W.G. 27 June 1837.
37. C.R.O./K. W.S.P.U./K.
38. W.G. 17 June 1838.
39. C.R.O./K. W.S.P.U./K.
40. W.G. 31 August 1828.
41. C.R.O./K. W.S.P.U./K.
42. Church at Heversham p.77.
43. All C.R.O./K. W.S.P.U./K.
44. W.G. 24 November 1883.
45. W.G. 29 May 1907.
46. I am indebted for this information to Mrs. Ena Hewitt d. of Mr. & Mrs. Charles Mason who confirms C.R.O./K. W.S.P.U./K.1.
47. C.R.O./K. W.S.P.U./K.1.
48. W.G. 13 October 1883.
49. W.G. 12 July 1884.
50. C.R.O./K. W.S.P.U./K.
51. Ibid.
52. Information Mrs. Ena Hewitt.
53. Census Returns.
54. W.G. 4 March 1882.
55. C.R.O./K. W.S.P.U./K.
56. W.G. 4 March 1875.

57. Information Mrs. Ena Hewitt.
58. C.R.O./K. W.S.P.U./K. Poor Law Report.
59. Ibid.
68. C.R.O./K. U.S.P.U./K.
69. W.G. 21 June 1890.
70. W.G. March 1907.
71. W.G. 5 March 1910.
72. W.G. 1909.
73. Information Mrs. B. Harrower nee Douthwaite.
74. W.G. 1914.
75. C.R.O./K. Poor Law Report.
76. W.G. 26 October 1946.
77. Gazette Report.

CHAPTER 12

1. Records of Kendale. W. Farrer, Vol.11 p.45.
2. Curwen. Kirkby Kendale.
3. Curwen: p.50. Farrer, Vol.111 p.225.
4. Farrer, Vol.111 p.225.
5. Ibid p.227.
6. W.G. 15 November 1884.
7. W.G. 20 November 1897.
8. W.G. 23 October 1920.
9. W.G. 19 October 1823.
10. W.G. 1 November 1823.
11. Doc. of M. Association for the Prosecution of Felons - author's possession.
12. W.G. 28 June 1846.
13. W.G. 20 December 1834.
14. W.G. 10 January 1844.
15. W.G. 28 September 1844.
16. W.G. 10 February 1849.
17. W.G. December 1851.
18. W.G. September 1865.
19. W.G. 28 April 1866.
20. W.G. 22 April 1882.
21. W.G. January 1899.
22. W.G. 29 March 1902.
23. W.G. 30 January 1904.
24. W.G. 1908.
25. W.G. 10 February 1906.
26. W.G. 9 September 1845.
27. W.G. 14 December 1846.
28. W.G. 22 December 1847.
29. W.G. 18 May 1870.
30. W.G. 23 May 1873 et seq.
31. W.G. 22 March 1873.
32. W.G. 18 January 1873.
33. W.G. 26 April 1884.
34. W.G. 3 September 1842.
35. W.G. 3 April 1844.
36. W.G. 15 March 1845.
37. W.G. 1 June 1845.
38. W.G. 12 July 1845.
39. Ibid.

40. W.G. 26 July 1845.
41. W.G. 26 July 1845.
42. W.G. June 1866.
43. W.G. 16 June 1900.
44. W.G. 30 May 1904.
45. Ibid.
46. W.G. 23 July 1921.
47. W.G. 11 November 1843 et seq.
48. W.G. 24 October 1846.
49. W.G. 4 August 1849.
50. W.G. 12 October 1850.
51. W.G. 12 December 1851.
52. W.G. October 1865.
53. W.G. 20 August 1865.
54. W.G. 10 August 1854.
55. W.G. 31 December 1898.
56. W.G. 20 April 1900.
57. W.G. 4 March 1910.
58. W.G. 6 January 1917.
59. W.G. 18 April 1908/25 July 1908.
60. W.G. 17 January 1920.
61. W.G. 10 January 1931.
62. W.G. 13 September 1941.
63. - 1945.
64. W.G. 12 May 1951.
65. Daily Mirror 4 March 1961. C.R.O./K. Box 3 W.D./P.D.
66. W.G. 11 July 1954.
67. W.G. 1861.
68. W.G. 29 May 1874.
69. W.G. 10 October 1908.
70. W.G. 17 December 1859.
71. W.G. 15 March 1873.
72. W.G. 27 February 1893.
73. W.G. 12 March 1910.
74. W.G. 12 February 1895.
75. W.G. 4 January 1902.
76. W.G. 30 April 1910.
77. W.G. 2 September 1911.
78. W.G. 11 December 1847.
79. W.G. 14 May 1849.
80. W.G. 12 January 1863.
81. W.G. 28 March 1866.
82. W.G. 28 November 1942.
83. W.G. 28 August 1874.
84. W.G. 27 February 1904.
85. W.G. 6 October 1934.
86. W.G. 30 June 1838.
87. W.G. 4 March 1843.
88. W.G. 28 April 1849.
89. W.G. 20 December 1851.
90. W.G. 3 February 1855.
91. W.G. February 1866.
92. W.G. 16 December 1916.
93. W.G. 19 January 1878.
94. W.G. 1910.
96. Westmorland Advertiser 13 November 1824.
97. W.G. 13 November 1824.
98. Ibid.
99. Memories Mr. H.M. Atkinson.

100. W.G. 6 December 1828.
101. W.G. 16 November 1835.
102. Memories - Mrs. Kathleen M. Byrne & Mr. Jack Thompson.
103. W.G. 11 December 1909.
104. W.G. 17 November 1942.
105. W.G. 23 January 1943.
106. W.G. 11 November 1952.
107. W.G. 10 July 1893.
108. W.G. 10 January 1931.
109. W.G. 1953.
110. Curwen, p.37.
111. C.R.O./K. W.D.4/603.
112. W.G. 19 March 1927 and memories Mrs. Dora Scott.
113. W.G. 12 October 1951.
114. W.G. 30 October 1952.
116. W.G. October 1952.

CHAPTER 13

1. See relevant chapter on Industry & Trade, Roads, Transport and Inns.
2. Mashiter/Stones.
3. W.G. 20 February 1892.
4. Memories Miss D. Mashiter and others.
5. Information Mrs. M.I. Sheldon.
6. C.R.O./K. W.P.R./88 Vestry Books.
7. Memories Mrs. E. Bragg.
9. Mashiter/Stones.
10. W.G. 1 May 1880.
11. W.G. April 1894.
12. Ibid.
13. W.G. 1 March 1890.
14. W.G. 22 April 1893.
15. Mashiter/Stones. See also chapter on Port.
16. W.G. 23 October 1894 et seq.
17. W.G. 14 December 1894.
18. W.G. 21 December 1894.
19. W.G. 4 January 1895.
20. Ibid et seq.
21. It was listening to stories in the 1950's about the "breaking of the ice" that the author first heard of Neddy Stones.
22. W.G. 15 February 1895.
23. W.G. 28 September 1895.
24. W.G. 19 October 1895.
25. W.G. 29 October 1895.
26. Ibid.
27. W.G. 2 November 1895 Manorial Records quoted.
28. W.G. 11 January 1896.
29. W.G. 2 February 1896.
30. W.G. 15 February 1896.
31. Ibid.
32. W.G. 11 April 1896.
33. Ibid.
34. W.G. 15 June 1896.

35. W.G. 18 July 1986.
36. W.G. 4 November 1896.
37. W.P.R./88/11 P.C. Minute books.
38. W.G. 15 July 1899.
39. W.G. 5 May 1901.
40. W.G. 22 July 1898.
41. W.G. 1900.
42. See chapter on Homes.
43. W.G. 10 February 1903.
44. W.G. 4 November 1905.
45. W.G. 4 July 1914.
46. W.G. 22 May 1920.
47. Information Mrs. E. Ladell who recalls also a similar treat when Neddy's sister died.

CHAPTER 14

1. The Worthies of Westmorland. George Atkinson. London, J. Robinson & Son 1844 p.174–176, 185–229.
2. Audland Pedigree, Brigadier E.G. Audland.
3. Mashiter/Stones.
4. -.
5. W.G. advertisements.
6. C.R.O./K. W.P.R./88 P.C. Minutes.
7. Ref in chapter on Industry & Trade and C.R.O./K. M.5/50.
8. C.R.O./K. Paper forwarded by Public Library.
9. Curwen, p.58.
10. W.G. 10 September 1821.
11. W.G. 5 January 1822.
12. Curwen, p.58.
13. W.G. 9 August 1832.
14. Curwen, p.58.
15. W.G. 13 May 1854.
16. Curwen, p.58.
17. Census Returns Local Collection Kendal Public Library.
18. W.G. and Curwen, p.58.
19. W.G. 3 July 1830.
20. Curwen, p.46.
21. Curwen, p.57.
22. W.I. essay c.1930.
23. W.G. 19 June 1851.
24. Curwen, p.57.
25. W.G. 14 December 1844.
26. W.G. 5 July 1844.
27. Curwen, p.55.
28. W.G. c.1865 - see chapter on the Church.
29. Curwen, p.55.
30. W.G. 10 January 1898.
31. W.G. 15 July 1905.
32. Mashiter/Stones.
33. W.G. 28 May 1819.
34. Mashiter/Stones.
35. W.G. 18 February 1844.
36. W.G. 2 January 1830.

37. W.G. 18 December 1841.
38. W.G. 14 September 1844.
39. W.G. 4 May 1844.
40. W.G. 4 December 1841.
42. C.R.O./K. W.P.R./88 Managers' minute book.
43. W.G. 13 March 1856.
44. C.R.O./K. Managers' minute book.
46. All C.R.O./K. W.P.R./88 Minute Books.
47. W.G. 14 May 1887.
48. C.R.O./K. Managers' Minute Books.
49. W.G.
50. Personal memories/information.
51. Ibid.
52. Ibid and Westmorland Gazette.
53. Ibid.
54. W.G. July 1929.
55. C.R.O./K. Managers' Minute Book.
56. Information by J.T. Cookson.
57. Memories F. Rockcliffe, N. Walker.
58. H.M.I. Report Managers' Minutes.
59. Personal information.
61. Managers' Minutes.
62. Information M. McVeigh, K. Blenkharn.
65. C.R.O./K. Managers' Minute Books.
66. Mashiter/Stones.
67. Curwen, p.48.
68. Personal information.
69. W.G. 7 May 1870.
70. H.M.I. Reports.
71. W.G. 2 February 1884, 3 January 1885.
74. Information late Mrs M.I. Sheldon.
75. W.G. 29 June 1907.
77. Curwen, p.48.
78. Information F. Rockcliffe.
79. H.M.I. Report.
80. Cumberland & Westmorland. Norman Nicholson p.178.
81. W.G. January 1951.

CHAPTER 15

1. See above - Setting & Origin.
2. Church of Heversham p.26.
3. Ibid p.38–39.
4. C.R.O./K.J.W.D./A.G. Box 4.
5. e.g. pub in Kendal, former pubs at Farleton and Holme.
6. Church at Heversham p.46–47.
7. C.R.O./K. W.D./S.R.
8. e.g. Church at Heversham p.46.
9. C.R.O./K.
10. W.G. 18 May 1822.
11. W.G. 24 May 1851.
12. W.G. 8 September 1855.
15. W.G. 30 September 1882.
16. W.G. 11 August 1890.
17. All W.G. reports.
18. W.G. 27 June 1896.
19. W.G. 8 June 1897.
20. W.G. 9 December 1899.
21. W.G. 27 January 1900.
22. Ibid.
23. W.G. 26 May 1900.
24. W.G. 13 April 1901.
25. W.G. 7 June 1902.
26. W.G. 21 June 1902.
27. W.G. 7 January 1905.
28. W.G. 14 September 1907.
29. W.G. 19 January 1909.
31. W.G. 17 May 1913.
34. W.G. 8 August 1914.
35. W.G. 15 August 1914.
36. W.G. 22 August 1914.
37. W.G. 19 September 1914.
38. W.G. 14 November 1914.
39. W.G. 5 December 1914.
40. W.G. 12 September 1914.
41. W.G. 21 October 1914.
42. W.G. 21 November 1914.
43. War reports and obituaries February 1926.
49. W.G. 6 February 1915.
50. Information Mr. J. Mashiter - re late brother Major Ernest Mashiter.
51. Information late Henry M. Atkinson.
52. W.G. 15 December 1915.
53. W.G. 13 November 1915.
54. Ibid.
57. W.G. 13 May 1916.
59. W.G. March 1917.
64. W.G. 29 July 1916.
66. W.G. 28 October 1916.
67. Ibid.
68. W.G. 18 November 1916.
70. W.G. 25 November 1916.
72. W.G. 12 February 1916.
73. W.G. 23 December 1916.
82. W.G. 29 December 1917.
83. W.G. 25 May 1918.
84. W.G. 27 April 1918.
85. W.G. 11 August 1918.
86. W.G. 25 May 1918 and information Miss Alice Ashburner.
87. W.G. 12 June 1918.
88. W.G. 19 June 1918.
91. W.G. 10 November 1918.
92. Information late Mrs. M.I. Sheldon and Mr. Jack Black.
93. W.G. 31 January 1920.
94. W.G. 1 March 1919.
95. W.G. 17 September 1919.
96. W.G. 26 July 1919.
98. Information Mr. H.M. Atkinson.
99. W.G. 16 January 1921.
101. W.G. 17 November 1925.
103. W.G. 25 September 1937.
104. W.G. 18 June 1938.

106. W.G. reports.
107. Information Mrs. P. Hall.
108. W.G. 16 September 1939.
109. W.G. report.
113. W.G. 11 November 1939.
114. P.C.C. records.
118. Memories local people.
119. W.G. 22 March 1941.
120. W.G. 7 February 1942.
121. W.G. 26 September 1942, 3 October 1942.
125. Cecil Beaton's Diaries 1939–44: The Years Between. Weidenfeld & Nicholson 1965. p.152.
129. W.G. 3 August 1943.
130. Ibid.
131. Information Mr. K. Blenkharn.
132. W.G. reports.
136. W.G. 13 May 1945.
137. W.G. 23 August 1945.
138. W.G. 6 January 1945.
139. W.G. 15 December 1945.
140. W.G. 20 September 1946.
141. W.G. 29 November 1945.
143. At which the author's hat and coat were sold as a result of a proverbial mistake.

CHAPTER 16

1. W.G.
2. W.G. 20 June 1931.
3. W.G. 3 December 1921.
4. Information Mr. Walter Unsworth.
5. W.G. 2 November 1922.
6. W.G. 10 May 1828.
7. W.G. 9 March 1848.
8. W.G. 7 November 1849.
9. W.G. 9 March 1854.
10. W.G. 20 January 1842.
13. W.G. 10 March 1875.
14. W.G. 12 March 1884.
15. Mashiter/Stones.
17. W.G. 1 December 1853.
18. W.G. 11 December 1886.
19. Ibid.
20. W.G. 27 September 1919.
21. W.G. 3 March 1888.
22. W.G. 19 January 1889.
23. W.G. 9 November 1841.
24. W.G. 14 November 1843.
25. See above chapter on Markets and Fairs.
26. W.G. 28 February 1874.
27. Information Centenary Booklet of Milnthorpe Angling Association C.R.O./K./Dobson Papers e.g. 21 February 1867 and W.G. reports.
28. W.G. 18 November 1920.
29. See chapter on Milnthorpe Sands.
30. W.G. 19 March 1851.

32. W.G. 30 July 1927.
33. W.G.
34. W.G. 26 July 1844.
35. W.G. 20 May 1843.
36. W.G. 10 August 1828.
37. W.G. 10 August 1862.
38. Curwen, p.47.
41. W.G. 23 October 1920.
42. W.G. 11 May 1867.
43. W.G. 7 September 1844.
45. W.G. 20 October 1871.
46. W.G. 26 February 1849.
48. W.G.s June–September 1860.
49. W.G. February 1871.
51. C.R.O./K./Dobson Papers.
52. W.G. 29 March 1890.
55. W.G. 12 March 1917.
59. W.G. 9 February 1851.
60. Curwen, p.47.
61. W.G. 20 March 1863.
62. W.G. December 1866.
64. W.G. 21 December 1887.
65. W.G. 11 February 1888.
66. W.G. 12 March 1889.
68. See chapter on War.
69. W.G. 6 January 1894.
70. W.G. March 1911.
71. W.G. 3 February 1893.
72. W.G. 24 January 1848.
73. W.G. 26 January 1860.
74. W.G. 1 October 1869.
76. W.G. 19 April 1883.
78. W.G. Reports December 1877–January 1878.
80. W.G. 2 May 1891.
81. W.G. 7 May 1891.
82. W.G. April 1893.
83. W.G. 4 August 1900.
84. Information Mrs. Addie Pickthall.
85. Information Mrs. Sylvia Ham.
91. W.G. 4 May 1867.
94. Church at Heversham p.46.
95. W.G. 4 July 1838.
96. W.G. 14 February 1840.
97. W.G. 1 August 1840.
98. W.G. 14 March 1863.
99. See chapter on Transport.
100. W.G. 30 June 1887.
101. W.G. 17 July 1893.
102. Information Mrs. M.I. Sheldon.
103. W.G. 26 June 1897.
105. W.G. 27 January 1901 also information to the author from several contemporaries.
106. W.G. 3 February 1901.
107. W.G. 28 June 1902.
109. W.G. 16 August 1902.
111. W.G. 1 July 1911.
113. W.G. 30 January 1936.
116. Diary, Brigadier E.G. Audland.
117. Author's memories and W.G.

(Readers are advised that not all the references are utilised in the final draft of the book. R.K.B.)

Index

THE SQUARE, MILNTHORPE

Drawn by Peter Fawcett, 1977

SITE OF PADDING CAN

Demolished in c.1946 to make an entrance to Firs Road. The Padding Can was the common lodging house where tramps and poor travellers could get cheap accommodation. It probably got its name from its Irish proprietor, Paddy Connor, who kept the house in the mid 19th C.

GANDY NOOK

According to the Royal Commission on Historical Monuments of 1936, these old cottages contained good 17th C woodwork. This has now disappeared.

THE COOKERY ROOMS

Built in the 1920's as a Domestic Science Centre. The Cookery Rooms are soon (in 1987) awaiting conversion into Milnthorpe's Public Library.

COWARDS COTTAGES

These were built in the 1920's to replace a row of older cottages. Labour Exchange here in 1930's.

THE SUN

One of M dating po The old building crossed its upper Methodi Institute.

MONARCH HOTEL, FLYING DUTCHMAN AND HART'S CABIN

These buildings were occupied by Walter Berry, the carrier for the port of Milnthorpe, in the 19th c. Later the Clark family butchers were based here.
The Flying Dutchman's became a famous (or notorious) haven for teenagers during the coffee bar craze of the 1950's and 60's. Briefly in the 1960's there was a casino here.

These houses were built of Lancaster sandstone, in contrast to the limestone rubble of all other old buildings, in 1903 by Edward Mashiter. One of Milnthorpe's many pumps was situated here.

These attractive properties also date from at least the eighteenth century. From c.1850-1880 Ewan Rawlinson, Chelsea Pensioner and village postman lived here.

MIDLAND BANK THE TALL HOUSE IN THE SQUARE

A good eighteenth century house. During the second world war the Milnthorpe Home Guard platoon was based here.

Th lea typ bet the cel ab he